AMERICAN HISTORY VOLUME II

Reconstruction through the Present

Thirteenth Edition

Editor

Robert James Maddox
Pennsylvania State University
University Park

Robert James Maddox, distinguished historian and professor of American history at Pennsylvania State University, received a B.S. from Fairleigh Dickinson University in 1957, an M.S. from the University of Wisconsin in 1958, and a Ph.D. from Rutgers in 1964. He has written, reviewed, and lectured extensively, and is widely respected for his interpretations of presidential character and policy.

A Library of Information from the Public Press

Cover illustration by Mike Eagle

The Dushkin Publishing Group, Inc.
Sluice Dock, Guilford, Connecticut 06437

The Annual Editions Series

Annual Editions is a series of over 65 volumes designed to provide the reader with convenient, low-cost access to a wide range of current, carefully selected articles from some of the most important magazines, newspapers, and journals published today. Annual Editions are updated on an annual basis through a continuous monitoring of over 300 periodical sources. All Annual Editions have a number of features designed to make them particularly useful, including topic guides, annotated tables of contents, unit overviews, and indexes. For the teacher using Annual Editions in the classroom, an Instructor's Resource Guide with test questions is available for each volume.

VOLUMES AVAILABLE

Africa
Aging
American Foreign Policy
American Government
American History, Pre-Civil War
American History, Post-Civil War
Anthropology
Archaeology
Biology
Biopsychology
Business Ethics
Canadian Politics
Child Growth and Development
China
Comparative Politics
Computers in Education
Computers in Business
Computers in Society
Criminal Justice
Developing World
Drugs, Society, and Behavior
Dying, Death, and Bereavement
Early Childhood Education
Economics
Educating Exceptional Children
Education
Educational Psychology
Environment
Geography
Global Issues
Health
Human Development
Human Resources
Human Sexuality
India and South Asia

International Business
Japan and the Pacific Rim
Latin America
Life Management
Macroeconomics
Management
Marketing
Marriage and Family
Mass Media
Microeconomics
Middle East and the Islamic World
Money and Banking
Multicultural Education
Nutrition
Personal Growth and Behavior
Physical Anthropology
Psychology
Public Administration
Race and Ethnic Relations
Russia, the Eurasian Republics, and
   Central/Eastern Europe
Social Problems
Sociology
State and Local Government
Urban Society
Violence and Terrorism
Western Civilization,
   Pre-Reformation
Western Civilization,
   Post-Reformation
Western Europe
World History, Pre-Modern
World History, Modern
World Politics

Cataloging in Publication Data
Main entry under title: Annual editions: American history, volume two.
   1. United States—History—Periodicals. 2. United States—Historiography—Periodicals.
3. United States—Civilization—Periodicals. I. Title: American history, volume two.
ISBN 1-56134-345-5   973'.05   75-20755

© 1995 by The Dushkin Publishing Group, Inc., Guilford, CT 06437

Copyright law prohibits the reproduction, storage, or transmission in any form by any means of any portion of this publication without the express written permission of The Dushkin Publishing Group, Inc., and of the copyright holder (if different) of the part of the publication to be reproduced. The Guidelines for Classroom Copying endorsed by Congress explicitly state that unauthorized copying may not be used to create, to replace, or to substitute for anthologies, compilations, or collective works.

Annual Editions® is a Registered Trademark of The Dushkin Publishing Group, Inc.

Thirteenth Edition

Printed in the United States of America

Printed on Recycled Paper

Editors/ Advisory Board

EDITOR

Robert James Maddox
Pennsylvania State University
University Park

ADVISORY BOARD

Arthur H. Auten
University of Hartford

Edward H. Beardsley
University of South Carolina

Neal A. Brooks
Essex Community College

Bruce Dudley
Prince George's Community
College

Melvin Holli
University of Illinois

Harry Russell Huebel
Texas A&I University
Kingsville

William Hughes
Essex Community College

Wilma King
Michigan State University

Bryan F. LeBeau
Creighton University

Larry Madaras
Howard Community College

Arthur F. McClure
Central Missouri State University

Ronald McCoy
Emporia State University

Robert Pierce
Foothill College

John Snetsinger
California Polytechnic State
University, San Luis Obispo

Irvin D. Solomon
University of South Florida

James Sweeney
Old Dominion University

Kenneth Werrell
Radford University

Ted Wilkin
University of Southern Colorado

Members of the Advisory Board are instrumental in the final selection of articles for each edition of Annual Editions. Their review of articles for content, level, currentness, and appropriateness provides critical direction to the editor and staff. We think you'll find their careful consideration well reflected in this volume.

STAFF

Ian A. Nielsen, Publisher
Brenda S. Filley, Production Manager
Roberta Monaco, Editor
Addie Raucci, Administrative Editor
Cheryl Greenleaf, Permissions Editor
Deanna Herrschaft, Permissions Assistant
Diane Barker, Proofreader
Lisa Holmes-Doebrick, Administrative Coordinator
Charles Vitelli, Designer
Shawn Callahan, Graphics
Steve Shumaker, Graphics
Lara M. Johnson, Graphics
Laura Levine, Graphics
Libra A. Cusack, Typesetting Supervisor
Juliana Arbo, Typesetter

To the Reader

In publishing ANNUAL EDITIONS we recognize the enormous role played by the magazines, newspapers, and journals of the *public press* in providing current, first-rate educational information in a broad spectrum of interest areas. Within the articles, the best scientists, practitioners, researchers, and commentators draw issues into new perspective as accepted theories and viewpoints are called into account by new events, recent discoveries change old facts, and fresh debate breaks out over important controversies.

Many of the articles resulting from this enormous editorial effort are appropriate for students, researchers, and professionals seeking accurate, current material to help bridge the gap between principles and theories and the real world. These articles, however, become more useful for study when those of lasting value are carefully *collected, organized, indexed,* and *reproduced* in a *low-cost format*, which provides easy and permanent access when the material is needed. That is the role played by *Annual Editions*. Under the direction of each volume's *Editor*, who is an expert in the subject area, and with the guidance of an *Advisory Board*, we seek each year to provide in each ANNUAL EDITION a current, well-balanced, carefully selected collection of the best of the public press for your study and enjoyment. We think you'll find this volume useful, and we hope you'll take a moment to let us know what you think.

Trends in historical writing have changed dramatically in recent years. Scholars are placing much greater emphasis on those who formerly received only passing mention or none at all. These previously slighted individuals and groups include but are not limited to women, African Americans, Asians, Hispanics, and Native Americans. Largely excluded from traditional positions of power in government, industry, and the military, their accomplishments are all the more remarkable because of the obstacles they had to overcome.

Even the more traditional categories of history such as political, economic, and diplomatic are being approached in new ways. Military historians of World War II, for instance, previously focused mostly on strategies, generals, and great battles. Now much is being done on issues such as the lives of ordinary soldiers, the contributions of women, and the deplorable treatment of African Americans who were asked to serve their country while being treated as second-class citizens.

These new approaches augment but do not replace the continuing interest in those who made large differences *as individuals*. That Presidents Franklin D. Roosevelt and Richard M. Nixon in wartime made one decision and not another affected thousands of lives. Henry Ford's approach to the automobile industry helped change the face of America. And a single book by Betty Friedan affected the way millions of women thought about themselves.

This volume attempts to present a selection of articles balanced between the new accent on inclusion of hitherto neglected individuals and groups and the more traditional analyses of well-known leaders such as Franklin Roosevelt, Martin Luther King Jr., and Woodrow Wilson. If the evaluations received of previous editions hold true, some readers will think too much emphasis has been placed on one aspect while other readers will complain there is too little. That is why we encourage teachers and students to let us know what they consider the strengths and weaknesses of this volume.

American History contains a number of features designed to make it "user friendly." These include a *topic guide* to help locate articles on specific subjects; the *table of contents extracts* that summarize each essay with key concepts in boldface; and a comprehensive *index*. Articles are organized into six units. Each unit is preceded by an overview that provides background for informed reading of the articles, briefly introduces each one, and presents *challenge questions*. If you have any suggestions for improving the format, please let us have these too.

There will be a new edition of *American History* in two years, and at least half the existing articles will be replaced. By completing and mailing the postpaid article rating form included in the back of the book, you will help us judge which articles should be retained and which should be dropped. You can also help to improve the next edition by recommending articles (or better yet, sending along a copy of the articles that you think should be included). A number of essays in this edition have come to our attention in this way.

Robert James Maddox

Robert James Maddox
Editor

Contents

Unit

1

Reconstruction and the Gilded Age

Six articles examine the development of the United States after the Civil War. Society was changed enormously by Western expansion and technology.

The concepts in bold italics are developed in the article. For further expansion please refer to the Topic Guide and the Index.

Unit 2

The Emergence of Modern America

Seven articles review the beginnings of modern America. Key issues of this period are examined, including immigration, the dawn of manned flight, racial consciousness, and poverty in the early twentieth century.

The concepts in bold italics are developed in the article. For further expansion please refer to the Topic Guide and the Index.

Unit 3

From Progressivism to the 1920s

Eight articles examine American culture in the early twentieth century. The economy began to reap the benefits of technology, women gained the right to vote, and Henry Ford ushered in mass production.

The concepts in bold italics are developed in the article. For further expansion please refer to the Topic Guide and the Index.

Unit

4

From the Great Depression to World War II

Six selections discuss the severe economic and social trials of the Great Depression of the thirties, the slow recovery process, and the enormous impact of World War II on America's domestic and foreign social consciousness.

The concepts in bold italics are developed in the article. For further expansion please refer to the Topic Guide and the Index.

Unit 5

From the Cold War to the 1990s

Ten articles cover the post-World War II period in the United States. The Truman Doctrine influenced America's foreign policy, equality of education became the law of the land, the Vietnam War changed the way America looked at conflict, and the poor of America increasingly affected society's conscience.

The concepts in bold italics are developed in the article. For further expansion please refer to the Topic Guide and the Index.

The concepts in bold italics are developed in the article. For further expansion please refer to the Topic Guide and the Index.

Unit 6

New Directions for American History

Five articles discuss the current state of American society and the role the United States plays in the world.

The concepts in bold italics are developed in the article. For further expansion please refer to the Topic Guide and the Index.

Topic Guide

This topic guide suggests how the selections in this book relate to topics of traditional concern to American history students and professionals. It is useful for locating articles that relate to each other for reading and research. The guide is arranged alphabetically according to topic. Articles may, of course, treat topics that do not appear in the topic guide. In turn, entries in the topic guide do not necessarily constitute a comprehensive listing of all the contents of each selection.

TOPIC AREA	TREATED IN:	TOPIC AREA	TREATED IN:
African Americans	1. New View of Reconstruction 5. Forgotten Pioneers 8. Afro-Cuban Community 12. George Washington Carver 21. Defending the Home 31. Trumpet of Conscience 38. Disuniting of America/Painful Demise of Eurocentrism	Environment	41. American Environment
		Ford, Henry	19. Citizen Ford
		Government	7. Cycle of Reform 14. Woodrow Wilson, Politician 22. 1933: The Rise of the Common Man 34. Nixon 39. Alms without End?
Asians	24. Racism and Relocation 40. Permanently Unfinished Country		
		Hispanics	8. Afro-Cuban Community 38. Disuniting of America/Painful Demise of Eurocentrism 40. Permanently Unfinished Country
Aviation	10. Wings for Man		
Business	19. Citizen Ford		
Carver, George	12. George Washington Carver	Immigrants	8. Afro-Cuban Community 9. Ellis Island 40. Permanently Unfinished Country
Children	2. First Chapter of Children's Rights		
Cold War	37. Looking Back 42. Revising the Twentieth Century	King, Martin Luther, Jr.	31. Trumpet of Conscience
		Korean War	29. Forgotten War
Culture	13. Learning to Go to the Movies 17. What We Lost in the Great War 28. Buy of the Century 30. Discovering Sex 38. Disuniting of America/Painful Demise of Eurocentrism	Movies	13. Learning to Go to the Movies
		Multiculturalism	8. Afro-Cuban Community 38. Disuniting of America/Painful Demise of Eurocentrism 40. Permanently Unfinished Country
Custer, George	3. Two Faces of George Armstrong Custer	Native Americans	3. Two Faces of George Armstrong Custer 6. Geronimo
Depression, Great	22. 1933: The Rise of the Common Man		
Diplomacy	25. 1943: The Pull of Distant Shores 27. Man of the Century 34. Nixon 37. Looking Back 42. Revising the Twentieth Century	Nixon, Richard	34. Nixon

TOPIC AREA	TREATED IN:	TOPIC AREA	TREATED IN:
Politics	7. Cycle of Reform 14. Woodrow Wilson, Politician 18. Why Suffrage for American Women Was Not Enough 20. 'A Snarling Roughhouse' 32. Chicago '68 34. Nixon	**Society (cont'd)**	28. Buy of the Century 30. Discovering Sex 35. How the Seventies Changed America 36. 1983: Falling Walls, Rising Dreams 38. Disuniting of America/Painful Demise of Eurocentrism
Progressivism	14. Woodrow Wilson, Politician	**Technology**	10. Wings for Man 19. Citizen Ford 41. American Environment
Racism	1. New View of Reconstruction 5. Forgotten Pioneers 8. Afro-Cuban Community 12. George Washington Carver 15. Angel Island 21. Defending the Home 24. Racism and Relocation 31. Trumpet of Conscience 38. Disuniting of America/Painful Demise of Eurocentrism 40. Permanently Unfinished Country	**Urban Problems**	4. *These* Are the Good Old Days 35. How the Seventies Changed America
		Vietnam War	33. Lessons from a Lost War
		West, The	3. Two Faces of George Armstrong Custer 5. Forgotten Pioneers
Reform	2. First Chapter of Children's Rights 7. Cycle of Reform 14. Woodrow Wilson, Politician 18. Why Suffrage for American Women Was Not Enough 22. 1933: The Rise of the Common Man 31. Trumpet of Conscience 39. Alms without End? 40. Permanently Unfinished Country	**Wilson, Woodrow**	14. Woodrow Wilson, Politician
		Women	16. American Women in World War I 18. Why Suffrage for American Women Was Not Enough 26. "What Did You Do in the War, Grandma?" 30. Discovering Sex
Roosevelt, Franklin D.	27. Man of the Century	**World War I**	16. American Women in World War I 17. What We Lost in the Great War
Society	2. First Chapter of Children's Rights 4. *These* Are the Good Old Days 11. Fighting Poverty 13. Learning to Go to the Movies 22. 1933: The Rise of the Common Man 23. The Draft 25. 1943: The Pull of Distant Shores	**World War II**	23. The Draft 24. Racism and Relocation 25. 1943: The Pull of Distant Shores 26. "What Did You Do in the War, Grandma?" 27. Man of the Century

Reconstruction and the Gilded Age

The Civil War ended slavery but left undefined the status of freed peoples. They owned no land, were mostly uneducated by design of their former masters, and few possessed any skills beyond those they had learned on farms and plantations. After a struggle first with Abraham Lincoln, then with his successor Andrew Johnson, "Radical" Republicans sought to reconstruct the South in a way that would attain full equality for freedpeople. Southerners fought back against what they regarded as an intolerable attempt to turn the natural order of things upside down. "The New View of Reconstruction" argues that although it failed to achieve immediate goals, it provided an "animating vision" for the future.

Westward expansion continued after the Civil War, and those Native Americans who stood in its path were shunted off onto "reservations" or hunted down if they resisted. "Geronimo" provides an account of the sorry fate of an Apache leader who reluctantly fought to preserve the Apache way of life. George Armstrong Custer was a man whose legend far overshadowed his real stature. Depicted in countless books and many movies as a golden-haired hero who "died with his boots on" at the battle of Little Big Horn, he was denounced then and later as little more than a blundering "squaw killer." "The Two Faces of George Armstrong Custer" presents a balanced assessment of this controversial figure.

Traditional accounts have presented the westward movement as peopled exclusively by whites. More recent research has revealed the role African Americans played. "The Forgotten Pioneers" tells the story of these previously overlooked individuals, with particular emphasis on the "Exoduster" movement of 1879–1880.

American society changed rapidly from the Civil War to 1900. The growth of industry spawned economic combinations the size of which dwarfed anything that had existed earlier. Urban centers grew crowded as rural Americans arrived from farms in search of work, and immigrants from Europe concentrated in slums from which they could only dream of escaping. "*These* Are the Good Old Days" describes New York City as it was during the latter part of the nineteenth century and finds much that resembles conditions today.

Every year millions of children are referred to protective agencies as victims of abuse. An ongoing dilemma has been to define the point at which society can intervene to shield youngsters from mistreatment at the hands of their parents. "The First Chapter of Children's Rights" tells of the 1874 trial involving little Mary Ellen McCormack that broke new ground in trying to resolve this issue.

Looking Ahead: Challenge Questions

Although their motives were mixed, "Radical" Republicans sought to reconstruct Southern society in a way that would protect the rights of freedpeoples. Did they merely go about it in the wrong way, or were their efforts doomed because of widespread Southern resistance?

Particularly brutal instances of child abuse make headlines and periodically shock public consciousness, but millions of cases go unnoticed. At what point do governmental agencies have the right and duty to intervene?

How could white Americans defend the treatment meted out to Native Americans? Discuss how prejudices help justify mistreatment of people defined as "different."

Unit 1

The New View of Reconstruction

Whatever you were taught or thought you knew about the post–Civil War era is probably wrong in the light of recent study

Eric Foner

Eric Foner is Professor of History at Columbia University and author of Nothing but Freedom: Emancipation and Its Legacy.

IN THE PAST twenty years, no period of American history has been the subject of a more thoroughgoing reevaluation than Reconstruction—the violent, dramatic, and still controversial era following the Civil War. Race relations, politics, social life, and economic change during Reconstruction have all been reinterpreted in the light of changed attitudes toward the place of blacks within American society. If historians have not yet forged a fully satisfying portrait of Reconstruction as a whole, the traditional interpretation that dominated historical writing for much of this century has irrevocably been laid to rest.

Anyone who attended high school before 1960 learned that Reconstruction was an era of unrelieved sordidness in American political and social life. The martyred Lincoln, according to this view, had planned a quick and painless readmission of the Southern states as equal members of the national family. President Andrew Johnson, his successor, attempted to carry out Lincoln's policies but was foiled by the Radical Republicans (also known as Vindictives or Jacobins). Motivated by an irrational hatred of Rebels or by ties with Northern capitalists out to plunder the South, the Radicals swept aside Johnson's lenient program and fastened black supremacy upon the defeated Confed-

eracy. An orgy of corruption followed, presided over by unscrupulous carpetbaggers (Northerners who ventured south to reap the spoils of office), traitorous scalawags (Southern whites who cooperated with the new governments for personal gain), and the ignorant and childlike freedmen, who were incapable of properly exercising the political power that had been thrust upon them. After much needless suffering, the white community of the South banded together to overthrow these "black" governments and restore home rule (their euphemism for white supremacy). All told, Reconstruction was just about the darkest page in the American saga.

Originating in anti-Reconstruction propaganda of Southern Democrats during the 1870s, this traditional interpretation achieved scholarly legitimacy around the turn of the century through the work of William Dunning and his students at Columbia University. It reached the larger public through films like *Birth of a Nation* and *Gone With the Wind* and that best-selling work of myth-making masquerading as history, *The Tragic Era* by Claude G. Bowers. In language as exaggerated as it was colorful, Bowers told how Andrew Johnson "fought the bravest battle for constitutional liberty and for the preservation of our institutions ever waged by an Executive" but was overwhelmed by the "poisonous propaganda" of the Radicals. Southern whites, as a result, "literally were put to the torture" by "emissaries of hate" who manipulated the "simple-minded" freedmen, "in-

flaming the negroes' egotism" and even inspiring "lustful assaults" by blacks upon white womanhood.

In a discipline that sometimes seems to pride itself on the rapid rise and fall of historical interpretations, this traditional portrait of Reconstruction enjoyed remarkable staying power. The long reign of the old interpretation is not difficult to explain. It presented a set of easily identifiable heroes and villains. It enjoyed the imprimatur of the nation's leading scholars. And it accorded with the political and social realities of the first half of this century. This image of Reconstruction helped freeze the mind of the white South in unalterable opposition to any movement for breaching the ascendancy of the Democratic party, eliminating segregation, or readmitting disfranchised blacks to the vote.

NEVERTHELESS, THE demise of the traditional interpretation was inevitable, for it ignored the testimony of the central participant in the drama of Reconstruction—the black freedman. Furthermore, it was grounded in the conviction that blacks were unfit to share in political power. As Dunning's Columbia colleague John W. Burgess put it, "A black skin means membership in a race of men which has never of itself succeeded in subjecting passion to reason, has never, therefore, created any civilization of any kind." Once objective scholarship and modern experience rendered that assumption untenable, the entire edifice was bound to fall.

The work of "revising" the history of

From *American Heritage,* October/November 1983, pp. 10-15. © 1983 by Forbes, Inc. Reprinted by permission of *American Heritage* magazine, a division of Forbes, Inc.

Reconstruction began with the writings of a handful of survivors of the era, such as John R. Lynch, who had served as a black congressman from Mississippi after the Civil War. In the 1930s white scholars like Francis Simkins and Robert Woody carried the task forward. Then, in 1935, the black historian and activist W.E.B. Du Bois produced *Black Reconstruction in America,* a monumental reevaluation that closed with an irrefutable indictment of a historical profession that had sacrificed scholarly objectivity on the altar of racial bias. "One fact and one alone," he wrote, "explains the attitude of most recent writers toward Reconstruction; they cannot conceive of Negroes as men." Du Bois's work, however, was ignored by most historians.

It was not until the 1960s that the full force of the revisionist wave broke over the field. Then, in rapid succession, virtually every assumption of the traditional viewpoint was systematically dismantled. A drastically different portrait emerged to take its place. President Lincoln did not have a coherent "plan" for Reconstruction, but at the time of his assassination he had been cautiously contemplating black suffrage. Andrew Johnson was a stubborn, racist politician who lacked the ability to compromise. By isolating himself from the broad currents of public opnion that had nourished Lincoln's career, Johnson created an impasse with Congress that Lincoln would certainly have avoided, thus throwing away his political power and destroying his own plans for reconstructing the South.

The Radicals in Congress were acquitted of both vindictive motives and the charge of serving as the stalking-horses of Northern capitalism. They emerged instead as idealists in the best nineteenth-century reform tradition. Radical leaders like Charles Sumner and Thaddeus Stevens had worked for the rights of blacks long before any conceivable political advantage flowed from such a commitment. Stevens refused to sign the Pennsylvania Constitution of 1838 because it disfranchised the state's black citizens; Sumner led a fight in the 1850s to integrate Boston's public schools. Their Reconstruction policies were based on principle, not petty political advantage, for the central issue dividing Johnson and these Radical Republicans was the civil rights of freedmen. Studies of congressional policy-making, such as Eric L. McKitrick's *Andrew Johnson and Reconstruction,* also revealed that Reconstruction legislation, ranging from the Civil Rights Act of 1866 to the Fourteenth and Fifteenth Amendments, enjoyed broad support from moderate and conservative Republicans. It was not simply the work of a narrow radical faction.

EVEN MORE STARTLING was the revised portrait of Reconstruction in the South itself. Imbued with the spirit of the civil rights movement and rejecting entirely the racial assumptions that had underpinned the traditional interpretation, these historians evaluated Reconstruction from the black point of view. Works like Joel Williamson's *After Slavery* portrayed the period as a time of extraordinary political, social, and economic progress for blacks. The establishment of public school systems, the granting of equal citizenship to blacks, the effort to restore the devastated Southern economy, the attempt to construct an interracial political democracy from the ashes of slavery, all these were commendable achievements, not the elements of Bowers's "tragic era."

Unlike earlier writers, the revisionists stressed the active role of the freedmen in shaping Reconstruction. Black initiative established as many schools as did Northern religious societies and the Freedmen's Bureau. The right to vote was not simply thrust upon them by meddling outsiders, since blacks began agitating for the suffrage as soon as they were freed. In 1865 black conventions throughout the South issued eloquent, though unheeded, appeals for equal civil and political rights.

With the advent of Radical Reconstruction in 1867, the freedmen did enjoy a real measure of political power. But black supremacy never existed. In most states blacks held only a small fraction of political offices, and even in South Carolina, where they comprised a majority of the state legislature's lower house, effective power remained in white hands. As for corruption, moral standards in both government and private enterprise were at low ebb throughout the nation in the postwar years—the era of Boss Tweed, the Credit Mobilier scandal, and the Whiskey Ring. Southern corruption could hardly be blamed on former slaves.

Other actors in the Reconstruction drama also came in for reevaluation.

Until recently, Thaddeus Stevens had been viewed as motivated by irrational hatred of the Rebels (left). Now he has emerged as an idealist in the best reform tradition.

NEW YORK PUBLIC LIBRARY, PRINT ROOM

LIBRARY OF CONGRESS

Most carpetbaggers were former Union soldiers seeking economic opportunity in the postwar South, not unscrupulous adventurers. Their motives, a typically American amalgam of humanitarianism and the pursuit of profit, were no more insidious than those of Western pioneers. Scalawags, previously seen as traitors to the white race, now emerged as "Old Line" Whig Unionists who had opposed secession in the first place or as poor whites who had long resented planters' domination of Southern life and who saw in Reconstruction a chance to recast Southern society along more democratic lines. Strongholds of Southern white Republicanism like east Tennessee and western North Carolina had been the scene of resistance to Confederate rule throughout the Civil War; now, as one scalawag newspaper put it, the choice was "between salvation at the hand of the Negro or destruction at the hand of the rebels."

At the same time, the Ku Klux Klan and kindred groups, whose campaign of violence against black and white Republicans had been minimized or excused in older writings, were portrayed as they really were. Earlier scholars had conveyed the impression that the Klan intimidated blacks mainly by dressing as ghosts and playing on the freedmen's superstitions. In fact, black fears were all too real: the Klan was a terrorist organization that beat and killed its political opponents to deprive blacks of their newly won rights. The complicity of the Democratic party and the silence of prominent whites in the face of such outrages stood as an indictment of the moral code the South had inherited from the days of slavery.

By the end of the 1960s, then, the old interpretation had been completely reversed. Southern freedmen were the heroes, the "Redeemers" who overthrew Reconstruction were the villains, and if the era was "tragic," it was because change did not go far enough. Reconstruction had been a time of real progress and its failure a lost opportunity for the South and the nation. But the legacy of Reconstruction—the Fourteenth and Fifteenth Amendments—endured to inspire future efforts for civil rights. As Kenneth Stampp wrote in *The Era of Reconstruction*, a superb summary of revisionist findings published in 1965, "If it was worth four years of civil war to save the Union, it was worth a few years of radical reconstruction to give the American Negro the ultimate promise of equal civil and political rights."

As Stampp's statement suggests, the reevaluation of the first Reconstruction was inspired in large measure by the impact of the second—the modern civil rights movement. And with the waning of that movement in recent years, writing on Reconstruction has undergone still another transformation. Instead of seeing the Civil War and its aftermath as a second American Revolution (as Charles Beard had), a regression into barbarism (as Bowers argued), or a golden opportunity squandered (as the revisionists saw it), recent writers argue that Radical Reconstruction was not really very radical. Since land was not distributed to the former slaves, they remained economically dependent upon their former owners. The planter class survived both the war and Reconstruction with its property (apart from slaves) and prestige more or less intact.

Not only changing times but also the changing concerns of historians have contributed to this latest reassessment of Reconstruction. The hallmark of the past decade's historical writing has been an emphasis upon "social history"—the evocation of the past lives of ordinary Americans—and the downplaying of strictly political events. When applied to Reconstruction, this concern with the "social" suggested that black suffrage and officeholding, once seen as the most radical departures of the Reconstruction era, were relatively insignificant.

RECENT HISTORIANS have focused their investigations not upon the politics of Reconstruction but upon the social and economic aspects of the transition from slavery to freedom. Herbert Gutman's influential study of the black family during and after slavery found little change in family structure or relations between men and women resulting from emancipation. Under slavery most blacks had lived in nuclear family units, although they faced the constant threat of separation from loved ones by sale. Reconstruction provided the opportunity for blacks to solidify their preexisting family ties. Conflicts over whether black women should work in the cotton fields (planters said yes, many black families said no) and over white attempts to "apprentice" black children revealed that the autonomy of family life was a major preoccupation of the freedmen. Indeed, whether manifested in their withdrawal from churches controlled by whites, in the blossoming of black fraternal, benevolent, and self-improvement organizations, or in the demise of the slave quarters and their replacement by small tenant farms occupied by individual families, the quest for independence from white authority and control over their own day-to-day lives shaped the black response to emancipation.

In the post–Civil War South the surest guarantee of economic autonomy, blacks believed, was land. To the freedmen the justice of a claim to land based on their years of unrequited labor appeared self-evident. As an Alabama black convention put it, "The property which they [the planters] hold was nearly all earned by the sweat of *our* brows." As Leon Litwack showed in *Been in the Storm So Long*, a Pulitzer Prize–winning account of the black response to emancipation, many freedmen in 1865 and 1866 refused to sign labor contracts, expecting the federal government to give them land. In some localities, as one Alabama overseer reported, they "set up claims to the plantation and all on it."

In the end, of course, the vast majority of Southern blacks remained propertyless and poor. But exactly why the South, and especially its black population, suffered from dire poverty and economic retardation in the decades following the Civil War is a matter of much dispute. In *One Kind of Freedom*, economists Roger Ransom and Richard Sutch indicted country merchants for monopolizing credit and charging usurious interest rates, forcing black tenants into debt and locking the South into a dependence on cotton production that impoverished the entire region. But Jonathan Wiener, in his study of postwar Alabama, argued that planters used their political power to compel blacks to remain on the planta-

EDWARD'S ELLIS, The History of Our Country, VOL. 5, 1900

SCHOMBERG CENTER, NEW YORK PUBLIC LIBRARY

Reconstruction governments were portrayed as disastrous failures (left) because elected blacks were ignorant or corrupt. In fact, postwar corruption cannot be blamed on former slaves.

tions. Planters succeeded in stabilizing the plantation system, but only by blocking the growth of alternative enterprises, like factories, that might draw off black laborers, thus locking the region into a pattern of economic backwardness.

IF THE THRUST OF recent writing has emphasized the social and economic aspects of Reconstruction, politics has not been entirely neglected. But political studies have also reflected the postrevisionist mood summarized by C. Vann Woodward when he observed "how essentially nonrevolutionary and conservative Reconstruction really was." Recent writers, unlike their revisionist predecessors, have found little to praise in federal policy toward the emancipated blacks.

A new sensitivity to the strength of prejudice and laissez-faire ideas in the nineteenth-century North has led many historians to doubt whether the Republican party ever made a genuine commitment to racial justice in the South. The granting of black suffrage was an alternative to a long-term federal responsibility for protecting the rights of the former slaves. Once enfranchised, blacks could be left to fend for themselves. With the exception of a few Radicals like Thaddeus Stevens, nearly all Northern policy-makers and educators are criticized today for assuming that, so long as the unfettered operations of the marketplace afforded blacks the opportunity to advance through diligent labor, federal efforts to assist them in acquiring land were unnecessary.

Probably the most innovative recent writing on Reconstruction politics has centered on a broad reassessment of black Republicanism, largely undertaken by a new generation of black historians. Scholars like Thomas Holt and Nell Painter insist that Reconstruction was not simply a matter of black and white. Conflicts within the black community, no less than divisions among whites, shaped Reconstruction politics. Where revisionist scholars, both black and white, had celebrated the accomplishments of black political leaders, Holt, Painter, and others charge that they failed to address the economic plight of the black masses. Painter criticized "representative colored men," as national black leaders were called, for failing to provide ordinary freedmen with effective political leadership. Holt found that black officeholders in South Carolina mostly emerged from the old free mulatto class of Charleston, which shared many assumptions with prominent whites. "Basically bourgeois in their origins and orientation," he wrote, they "failed to act in the interest of black peasants."

In emphasizing the persistence from slavery of divisions between free blacks and slaves, these writers reflect the increasing concern with continuity and conservatism in Reconstruction. Their work reflects a startling extension of revisionist premises. If, as has been argued for the past twenty years, blacks were active agents rather than mere victims of manipulation, then they could not be absolved of blame for the ultimate failure of Reconstruction.

Despite the excellence of recent writing and the continual expansion of our knowledge of the period, historians of Reconstruction today face a unique dilemma. An old interpretation has been overthrown, but a coherent new synthesis has yet to take its place. The revisionists of the 1960s effectively established a series of negative points: the Reconstruction governments were not as bad as had been portrayed, black supremacy was a myth, the Radicals were not cynical manipulators of the freedmen. Yet no convincing overall portrait of the quality of political and social life emerged from their writings. More recent historians have rightly pointed to elements of continuity that spanned the nineteenth-century Southern experience, especially the survival, in modified form, of the plantation system. Nevertheless, by denying the real changes that did occur, they have failed to provide a convincing portrait of an era characterized above all by drama, turmoil, and social change.

Building upon the findings of the past twenty years of scholarship, a new portrait of Reconstruction ought to begin by viewing it not as a specific time period, bounded by the years 1865 and 1877, but as an episode in a prolonged historical process—American society's adjustment to the consequences of the Civil War and emancipation. The Civil War, of course, raised the decisive questions of America's national existence: the relations between local and national authority, the definition of citizenship, the balance between force and consent in generating obedience to authority. The war and Reconstruction, as Allan Nevins observed over fifty years ago, marked the "emergence of modern America." This was the era of the completion of the national railroad network, the creation of the modern steel industry, the conquest of the West and final subduing of the Indians, and the expansion of the mining frontier. Lincoln's America—the world of the small farm and artisan shop—gave way to a rapidly industrializing economy. The issues that galvanized postwar Northern politics—from the question of the greenback currency to the mode of paying holders of the national debt—arose from the economic changes unleashed by the Civil War.

Above all, the war irrevocably abolished slavery. Since 1619, when "twenty negars" disembarked from a Dutch ship in Virginia, racial injustice had haunted American life, mocking its professed ideals even as tobacco and cotton, the products of slave labor, helped finance the nation's economic development. Now the implications of the black presence could no longer be ignored. The Civil War resolved the problem of slavery but, as the Philadelphia diarist Sydney George Fisher observed in June 1865, it opened an even more intractable problem: "What shall we do with the Negro?" Indeed, he went on, this was a problem *incapable* of any solution that will satisfy both North and South."

As Fisher realized, the focal point of Reconstruction was the social revolution known as emancipation. Plantation slavery was simultaneously a system of labor, a form of racial domination, and the foundation upon which arose a distinctive ruling class within the South. Its demise threw open the most fundamental questions of economy, society, and politics. A new system of labor, social, racial, and political relations had to be created to replace slavery.

The United States was not the only nation to experience emancipation in the nineteenth century. Neither plantation slavery nor abolition were unique to the United States. But Reconstruction was. In a comparative perspective Radical Reconstruction stands as a remarkable experiment, the only effort of a society experiencing abolition to bring the former slaves within the umbrella of equal citizenship. Because the Radicals did not achieve everything they wanted, historians have lately tended to play down the stunning departure represented by black suffrage and officeholding. Former slaves, most fewer than two years removed from bondage, debated the fundamental questions of the polity: What is a republican form of government? Should the state provide equal education for all? How could political equality be reconciled with a society in which property was so unequally distributed? There was something inspiring in the way such men met the challenge of Reconstruction. "I knew nothing more than to obey my master," James K. Greene, an Alabama black politician later recalled. "But the tocsin of freedom sounded and knocked at the door and we walked out like free men and we met the exigencies as they grew up, and shouldered the responsibilities."

YOU NEVER SAW a people more excited on the subject of politics than are the negroes of the south," one planter observed in 1867. And there were more than a few Southern whites as well who in these years shook off the prejudices of the past to embrace the vision of a new South dedicated to the principles of equal citizenship and social justice. One ordinary South Carolinian expressed the new sense of possibility in 1868 to the Republican governor of the state: "I am sorry that I cannot write an elegant stiled letter to your excellency. But I rejoice to think that God almighty has given to the poor of S. C. a Gov. to hear to feel to protect the humble poor without distinction to race or color.... I am a native borned S. C. a poor man never owned a Negro in my life nor my father before me. . . . Remember the true and loyal are the poor of the whites and blacks, outside of these you can find none loyal."

Few modern scholars believe the Reconstruction governments established in the South in 1867 and 1868 fulfilled the aspirations of their humble constituents. While their achievements in such realms as education, civil rights, and the economic rebuilding of the South are now widely appreciated, historians today believe they failed to affect either the economic plight of the emancipated slave or the ongoing transformation of independent white farmers into cotton tenants. Yet their opponents did perceive the Reconstruction governments in precisely this way—as representatives of a revolution that had put the bottom rail, both racial and economic, on top. This perception helps explain the ferocity of the attacks leveled against them and the pervasiveness of violence in the postemancipation South.

The spectacle of black men voting and holding office was anathema to large numbers of Southern whites. Even more disturbing, at least in the view of those who still controlled the plantation regions of the South, was the emergence of local officials, black and white, who sympathized with the plight of the black laborer. Alabama's vagrancy law was a "dead letter' in 1870, "because those who are charged with its enforcement are indebted to the vagrant vote for their offices and emoluments." Political debates over the level and incidence of taxation, the control of crops, and the resolution of contract disputes revealed that a primary issue of Reconstruction was the role of government in a plantation society. During presidential Reconstruction, and after "Redemption," with planters and their allies in control of politics, the law emerged as a means of stabilizing and promoting the plantation system. If Radical Reconstruction failed to redistribute the land of the South, the ouster of the planter class from control of politics at least ensured that the sanctions of the criminal law would not be employed to discipline the black labor force.

AN UNDERSTANDING OF this fundamental conflict over the relation between government and society helps explain the pervasive complaints concerning corruption and "extravagance" during Radical Reconstruction. Corruption there was aplenty; tax rates did rise sharply. More significant than the rate of taxation, however, was the change in its incidence. For the first time, planters and white farmers had to pay a signifi-

COURTESY OF THE ATLANTA *Constitution*

Some scholars exalted the motives of the Ku Klux Klan (left). Actually, its members were part of a terrorist organization that beat and killed its political opponents to deprive blacks of their rights.

RUTHERFORD B. HAYES LIBRARY, FREMONT, OHIO

cant portion of their income to the government, while propertyless blacks often escaped scot-free. Several states, moreover, enacted heavy taxes on uncultivated land to discourage land speculation and force land onto the market, benefiting, it was hoped, the freedmen.

As time passed, complaints about the "extravagance" and corruption of Southern governments found a sympathetic audience among influential Northerners. The Democratic charge that universal suffrage in the South was responsible for high taxes and governmental extravagance coincided with a rising conviction among the urban middle classes of the North that city government had to be taken out of the hands of the immigrant poor and returned to the "best men"—the educated, professional, financially independent citizens unable to exert much political influence at a time of mass parties and machine politics. Increasingly the "respectable" middle classes began to retreat from the very notion of universal suffrage. The poor were no longer perceived as honest producers, the backbone of the social order; now they became the "dangerous classes," the "mob." As the historian Francis Parkman put it, too much power rested with "masses of imported ignorance and hereditary ineptitude." To Parkman the Irish of the Northern cities and the

blacks of the South were equally incapable of utilizing the ballot: "Witness the municipal corruptions of New York, and the monstrosities of negro rule in South Carolina." Such attitudes helped to justify Northern inaction as, one by one, the Reconstruction regimes of the South were overthrown by political violence.

IN THE END, THEN, neither the abolition of slavery nor Reconstruction succeeded in resolving the debate over the meaning of freedom in American life. Twenty years before the American Civil War, writing about the prospect of abolition in France's colonies, Alexis de Tocqueville had written, "If the Negroes have the right to become free, the [planters] have the incontestable right not to be ruined by the Negroes' freedom." And in the United States, as in nearly every plantation society that experienced the end of slavery, a rigid social and political dichotomy between former master and former slave, an ideology of racism, and a dependent labor force with limited economic opportunities all survived abolition. Unless one means by freedom the simple fact of not being a slave, emancipation thrust blacks into a kind of no-man's land, a partial freedom that made a mockery of the American ideal of equal citizenship.

Yet by the same token the ultimate

outcome underscores the uniqueness of Reconstruction itself. Alone among the societies that abolished slavery in the nineteenth century, the United States, for a moment, offered the freedmen a measure of political control over their own destinies. However brief its sway, Reconstruction allowed scope for a remarkable political and social mobilization of the black community. It opened doors of opportunity that could never be completely closed. Reconstruction transformed the lives of Southern blacks in ways unmeasurable by statistics and unreachable by law. It raised their expectations and aspirations, redefined their status in relation to the larger society, and allowed space for the creation of institutions that enabled them to survive the repression that followed. And it established constitutional principles of civil and political equality that, while flagrantly violated after Redemption, planted the seeds of future struggle.

Certainly, in terms of the sense of possibility with which it opened, Reconstruction failed. But as Du Bois observed, it was a "splendid failure." For its animating vision—a society in which social advancement would be open to all on the basis of individual merit, not inherited caste distinctions—is as old as America itself and remains relevant to a nation still grappling with the unresolved legacy of emancipation.

The First Chapter of Children's Rights

*More than a century ago an abused child began a battle
that is still being fought today*

**Peter Stevens
and Marian Eide**

In the quiet New York courtroom, the little girl began to speak. "My name is Mary Ellen McCormack. I don't know how old am. . . . I have never had but one pair of shoes, but can't recollect when that was. I have had no shoes or stockings on this winter. . . . I have never had on a particle of flannel. My bed at night is only a piece of carpet, stretched on the floor underneath a window, and I sleep in my little undergarment, with a quilt over me. I am never allowed to play with any children or have any company whatever. Mamma has been in the habit of whipping and beating me almost every day. She used to whip me with a twisted whip, a raw hide. The whip always left black and blue marks on my body. I have now on my head two black and blue marks which were made by mamma with the whip, and a cut on the left side of my forehead which was made by a pair of scissors in mamma's hand. She struck me with the scissors and cut me. I have no recollection of ever having been kissed, and have never been kissed by mamma. I have never been taken on my mamma's lap, or caressed or petted. I never dared to speak to anybody, because if I did I would get whipped. . . . Whenever mamma went out I was locked up in the bedroom. . . . I have no recollection of ever being in the street in my life."

At the beginning of 1874 there were no legal means in the United States to save a child from abuse. Mary Ellen's eloquent testimony changed that, changed our legal system's view of the rights of the child.

Yet more than a century later the concerns that arose from Mary Ellen's case are still being battled over in the courts. The classic dilemmas of just how deeply into the domestic realm the governmental arm can reach and what the obligations of public government are to the private individual take on particular urgency in considering child abuse.

Early in 1989, in the case of *DeShaney* v. *Winnebago County,* the Supreme Court declared that the government is not obligated to protect its citizens against harm inflicted by private individuals. DeShaney brought the case before the court in a suit against county social service agencies that had failed to intervene when her estranged husband abused their son, Joshua, who, as a result of his father's brutality, suffered permanent brain damage. The father was convicted, but his former wife believes that fault also lies with the agencies, whose failure to intercede violated her son's Fourteenth Amendment right not to be deprived of life or liberty without due process of the law. Chief Justice William H. Rehnquist wrote that intervening officials are often charged with "improperly intruding into the parent-child relationship." Justice William J. Brennan, Jr., dissenting, wrote: "Inaction can be every bit as abusive of power as action, [and] oppression can result when a State undertakes a vital duty and then ignores it."

The difficulty in bringing Mary Ellen McCormack into the New York Supreme Court in 1874 grew from similar controversy over the role of government in family matters, and Mary Ellen's sad history is not so different from Joshua DeShaney's.

When Mary Ellen's mother, Frances Connor, immigrated to the United States from England in 1858, she took a job at the St. Nicholas Hotel in New York City as a laundress. There she met an Irishman named Thomas Wilson who worked in the hotel kitchen shucking oysters. They were married in April 1862, shortly after Wilson had been drafted into the 69th New York, a regiment in the famous Irish Brigade. Early in 1864 she gave birth to their daughter, whom she named Mary after her mother and Ellen after her sister.

The birth of her daughter seems to have heralded the beginning of Frances Wilson's own decline. Her husband was killed that same year in the brutal fighting at Cold Harbor, Virginia, and with a diminished income she found it necessary to look for a job. In May 1864, unable to pay someone to watch the baby while she was at work, she gave Mary Ellen over to the care of a woman named Mary Score for two dollars a week, the whole of her widow's pension. Child farming was a common practice at that time, and many women made a living taking in unwanted children just as others took in laundry. Score lived in a tenement in the infamous warrens of Mulberry Bend, where thousands of immigrants crowded into small, airless rooms, and it is likely that providing foster care was her only means of income.

FINALLY FRANCES WILSON BECAME UNable to pay for the upkeep of her child; three weeks after the payments ceased, Score turned Mary Ellen over to the Department of Charities. The little girl—whose mother was never to see her

From *American Heritage*, July/August 1990, pp. 84-91. © 1990 by Forbes, Inc. Reprinted by permission of *American Heritage* magazine, a division of Forbes, Inc.

again—was sent to Blackwells Island in July 1865. Her third home was certainly no more pleasant than Mulberry Bend. Mary Ellen was among a group of sick and hungry foundlings; fully two-thirds of them would die before reaching maturity.

The same slum-bred diseases that ravaged the children on Blackwells Island had also claimed all three children of a couple named Thomas and Mary McCormack. So when Thomas frequently bragged of the three children he had fathered by another woman, his wife was more receptive to the idea of adopting them than she might otherwise have been. Those children, he told her, were still alive, though their mother had turned them over to the care of the city.

The child belonged to the animal kingdom; perhaps the Society for Prevention of Cruelty to Animals could save her.

On January 2, 1866, the McCormacks went to the Department of Charities to reclaim one of the children Thomas's mistress had abandoned. The child they chose as their own was Mary Ellen Wilson. Because the McCormacks were not asked to provide any proof of relation to the child and gave only the reference of their family doctor, there is no evidence that Thomas was in any way related to the child he brought home that day. More than a month later an indenture was filed for Mary Ellen in which the McCormacks promised to report on her condition each year. There were no other requirements.

Shortly after bringing the child home, Thomas McCormack died, and his widow married a man named Francis Connolly. Little more than that is known of the early childhood of Mary Ellen. She came to her new home in a flannel petticoat, and when her clothing was removed from Connolly's home as evidence six years later, there was barely enough to fill a tiny suitcase. She was beaten, set to work, deprived of daylight, and locked in closets for days at a time; she was rarely bathed, never kissed, and never addressed with a gentle word. During the six years she lived with Connolly, only two reports on her progress

were filed with the Commissioners of Charities and Correction.

Late in 1873 Etta Angell Wheeler, a Methodist caseworker serving in the tenements of New York City, received a disturbing report. It came from Margaret Bingham, a landlord in Hell's Kitchen, and told of a terrible case of child abuse. The child's parents had been tenants of Bingham for about four years, and almost immediately after they moved in, Bingham began to observe how cruelly they treated their child, Mary Ellen. They confined her in close quarters during hot weather, kept her severely underdressed in cold, beat her daily, and left her unattended for hours at a time. On several occasions Bingham tried to intervene; each time the child's mother said she would call upon the fullest resources of the law before she would allow any interference in her home. Finally Bingham resorted to threat: The beatings and ill treatment would have to stop, or the family would be evicted. When her plan backfired and the family left, Bingham, in a last-ditch effort, sent for Etta Wheeler. In order to observe Mary Ellen's predicament, Wheeler went to the Connollys' neighbor, an ailing tubercular woman named Mary Smitt. Enlisting Smitt's aid, she proposed that Mary Ellen be sent over each day to check on the patient. Smitt reluctantly agreed, and on the pretext of inquiring about this sick neighbor, Wheeler knocked on Mary Connolly's door.

Inside she saw a "pale, thin child, bare-foot, in a thin, scanty dress so tattered that I could see she wore but one garment besides.

"It was December and the weather bitterly cold. She was a tiny mite, the size of five years, though, as afterward appeared, she was then nine. From a pan set upon a low stool she stood washing dishes, struggling with a frying pan about as heavy as herself. Across the table lay a brutal whip of twisted leather strands and the child's meager arms and legs bore many marks of its use. But the saddest part of her story was written on her face in its look of suppression and misery, the face of a child unloved, of a child that had seen only the fearsome side of life. . . . I never saw her again until the day of her rescue, three months later. . . ."

Though social workers often witnessed scenes of cruelty, poverty, and grief, Wheeler found Mary Ellen's plight especially horrifying. She went first to

the police; they told her she must be able to furnish proof of assault in order for them to act. Charitable institutions she approached offered to care for the child, but first she must be brought to them through legal means. There were none. Every effort Wheeler made proved fruitless. Though there were laws to protect children—laws, in fact, to prevent assault and battery to any person—there were no means available for intervention in a child's home.

Finally Wheeler's niece had an idea. The child, she said, was a member of the animal kingdom; surely Henry Bergh, the founder of the American Society for the Prevention of Cruelty to Animals, who was famous for his dramatic rescue of mistreated horses in the streets of New York, might be willing to intervene. Within the hour Wheeler had arranged a meeting with Bergh. Despite its apparent strangeness, this sort of appeal was not new to Bergh. Once before he had tried to intervene in a case of child abuse and had failed. This time he was more cautious.

"Very definite testimony is needed to warrant interference between a child and those claiming guardianship," Bergh told Wheeler. "Will you not send me a written statement that, at my leisure, I may judge the weight of the evidence and may also have time to consider if this society should interfere? I promise to consider the case carefully."

WHEELER PROVIDED A STATEMENT IMMEdiately, including in it the observations of neighbors to whom she had spoken. Bergh was convinced. "No time is to be lost," he wrote his lawyer, Elbridge T. Gerry. "Instruct me how to proceed."

The next day Wheeler again visited the sick woman in Hell's Kitchen and found in her room a young man who, on hearing Wheeler's name, said, "I was sent to take the census in this house. I have been in every room." Wheeler then knew him to be a detective for Bergh.

On the basis of the detective's observations and the testimony provided by Etta Wheeler, Bergh's lawyers, Gerry and Ambrose Monell, appeared before Judge Abraham R. Lawrence of the New York Supreme Court to present a petition on behalf of Mary Ellen. They showed that Mary Ellen was held illegally by the Connollys, who were neither her natural parents nor her lawful custodians, and went on to describe the physical abuse

Mary Ellen endured, the marks and bruises on her body, and the general state of deprivation that characterized her existence. They offered a list of witnesses willing to testify on behalf of the child and concluded by stating that there was ample evidence to indicate that she was in clear danger of being maimed or even killed. The lawyers requested that a warrant be issued, the child removed from her home and placed in protective custody, and her parents brought to trial.

Bergh testified that his efforts on behalf of the child were in no way connected to his work with abused animals and that they did not make use of the special legal provisions set up for that purpose. Because of Bergh's association with animal rescue, to this day the case is often described as having originated in his conviction that the child was a member of the animal kingdom. Bergh, however, insisted that his actions were merely those of any humane citizen and that he intended to prevent cruelties inflicted on children through any legal means available.

Judge Lawrence issued a warrant under Section 65 of the Habeas Corpus Act as requested. This provision read in part: "Whenever it shall appear by satisfactory proof that any one is held in illegal confinement or custody, and that there is good reason to believe that he will . . . suffer some irreparable injury, before he can be relieved by the issuing of a *habeas corpus* or *certiorari*, any court or officer authorized to issue such writs, may issue a warrant . . . [and] bring him before such court or officer, to be dealt with according to law."

THE PRESS OF THE DAY HAILED GERRY'S use of Section 65 of the Habeas Corpus Act as brilliant. The act was rarely invoked, and the legal means for removing a child from its home were nonexistent. In using the little-known law, Gerry created a new method for intervention.

That same day, April 9, 1874, Mary Ellen was taken from her home and brought into Judge Lawrence's court. Having no adequate clothing of her own, the child had been wrapped in a carriage blanket by the policemen who held her in custody. A reporter on the scene described her as "a bright little girl, with features indicating unusual mental capacity, but with a care-worn, stunted, and prematurely old look. . . . no change of custody or condition could be much for the worse."

The reporter Jacob Riis was present in the court. "I saw a child brought in . . . at the sight of which men wept aloud, and I heard the story of little Mary Ellen told . . . that stirred the soul of a city and roused the conscience of a world that had forgotten, and as I looked, I knew I was where the first chapter of children's rights was being written." Her body and face were terribly bruised; her hands and feet "showed the plain marks of great exposure." And in what almost instantly seemed to condemn Mrs. Connolly before the court, the child's face bore a fresh gash through her eyebrow and across her left cheek that barely missed the eye itself. Mary Ellen was to carry this scar throughout her life.

Jacob Riis "saw a child brought in at the sight of which men wept aloud, and heard the story that roused the conscience of a world."

Interestingly, there is no further mention in the ample reports surrounding Mary Ellen's case of her foster father, Francis Connolly. He was never brought into court, never spoke publicly concerning the child. All her life Mary Ellen exhibited a frightened timidity around men, yet it was against her foster mother that she testified.

On the evening of her detention, Mary Ellen was turned over to the temporary custody of the matron of police headquarters. The next day, April 10, the grand jury read five indictments against Mary Connolly for assault and battery, felonious assault, assault with intent to do bodily harm, assault with intent to kill, and assault with intent to maim. Once the stepmother had been brought into the legal system, there were ample means to punish her.

Mary Ellen herself was brought in to testify against the woman she had called her mother. On her second appearance in court she seemed almost wholly altered. She was clothed in a new suit, and her pale face reflected the kindness that surrounded her. She carried with her a new picture book, probably the first she had ever owned. She acted open and uninhibited with strangers, and interestingly, seemed to show no great fear of her

mother or any apparent enmity toward her.

The lawyers Gerry and Monell gathered several witnesses against Mary Connolly, among them neighbors, Wheeler, and Mary Ellen herself. Margaret Bingham said she had seen the child locked up in a room and had told other neighbors, but they said there was no point in interfering since the police would do nothing. Bingham had tried to open the window of the child's room to let in some air, but it would not lift more than an inch. As a constant presence and reminder, a cowhide whip was locked in the room with the child. Wheeler recounted her first visit to Mary Ellen, during which the child washed dishes that seemed twice her size and was apparently oblivious of the visitor's presence. The whip lay on the table next to her. The next day, when Wheeler came by again, the child was sewing, and the whip lay on a chair near her.

Then it was the mother's turn to testify. On the witness stand Mary Connolly showed herself to be a woman of some spirit. Despite her treatment of the child, there is something compelling in Connolly's strength and humor. At one point the prosecutor asked if she had an occupation beyond housekeeping. "Well," she said, "I sleep with the boss." As the trial wore on, she became enraged at Gerry's prodding questions; finally she accused him of being "ignorant of the difficulties of bringing up and governing children." Yet she admitted that contrary to regulations, in the six years she had Mary Ellen in her custody, she had reported on her condition to the Commissioners of Charities and Correction only twice.

Two indictments were brought against Connolly, the first for her assault on the child with scissors on April 7, the second for the continual assaults inflicted on the child throughout the years 1873 and 1874. After twenty minutes of deliberation the jury returned a verdict of guilty of assault and battery. Connolly was sentenced to one year of hard labor in the city penitentiary, then known as the Tombs. In handing down this sentence, the judge defined it not only as a punishment to Connolly but also as a statement of precedence in child-abuse cases.

Mary Ellen never returned to the Connollys' home. In the ensuing months the publicity that her case received brought in many claims of relation. But on investigating, her guardian, Judge Lawrence, discovered the stories were fictions, and he finally placed the child in the Sheltering Arms, a home for grown girls; soon after, she was moved to the Woman's Aid Society and Home for Friendless Girls. This mirrors another critical problem in the system's treatment of minors. All juveniles were handled by the Department of Charities and Correction, and whether they were orphaned or delinquent, their treatment was the same. And so it was that the ten-year-old Mary Ellen was placed in a home with mostly delinquent adolescents.

Etta Wheeler knew this was wrong for Mary Ellen, and she expressed her hesitations to Judge Lawrence. He, in turn, consulted with Henry Bergh, and eventually they agreed to turn the girl over to Etta Wheeler herself. Unable to imagine giving up her work in the slums of New York City but believing that Mary Ellen deserved a better environment, Wheeler brought the child to her mother in North Chili, New York. Wheeler's mother became ill shortly afterward, and Mary Ellen was raised mostly by Wheeler's sister.

"HERE BEGAN A NEW LIFE," WHEELER wrote. "The child was an interesting study, so long shut within four walls and now in a new world. Woods, fields, 'green things growing,' were all strange to her, she had not known them. She had to learn, as a baby does, to walk upon the ground,—she had walked only upon floors, and her eye told her nothing of uneven surfaces. . . . But in this home there were other children and they taught her as children alone can teach each other. They taught her to play, to be unafraid, to know her rights and to claim them. She shared their happy, busy life from the making of mud pies up to charming birthday parties and was fast becoming a normal child."

The happiness of her years in the upstate New York countryside lies in stark contrast to her early childhood. And indeed, as Wheeler wrote, she learned by example the ways of normal childhood. She grew up strong and well, learning how to read and playing with friends and pet kittens. In 1875 Wheeler reported to Gerry that Mary Ellen was growing up as a normal child. "She has some faults that are of the graver sort. She tells fibs and sticks to them bravely, steals lumps of sugar & cookies and only confesses when the crumbs are found in

her pocket—in short she is very much like other children, loving—responding to kindness & praise, hating a task unless there be a play, or a reward thereof, and inevitably 'forgetting' what she does not wish to remember—what children do not do some or all of these forbidden things! She is a favorite with nearly all the people who have come to know her."

When she was twenty-four, Mary Ellen married a widower named Louis Schutt and with him had two children, Etta—named after the woman who had rescued her—and Florence. She adopted a third, orphaned child, Eunice. She also raised Louis Schutt's three children from his first wife.

In 1911 Wheeler visited her protégé in her home, "finding her well and happy. . . . The family income is small, but Mary Ellen is a prudent housewife & they are comfortable. The two daughters are promising girls." The eldest daughter, Etta, worked industriously through that summer, finished high school, and became a teacher. Florence followed her sister's path, teaching first grade for thirty-eight years. When she retired, the elementary school in North Chili was renamed in her honor. Eunice earned a business degree, married, and raised two sons.

Florence remembers her mother as a solemn woman who came alive whenever she listened to Irish jigs and especially to "The Irish Washerwoman." She was unfailingly generous with her time and her affection. Her years in North Chili had saved her from the vicious cycle abused children often suffer of becoming abusers themselves. According to Florence her mother was capable of sternness and certainly willing to punish her daughters, but the terrible experiences of her early childhood never spilled into her own child rearing. As Etta Wheeler wrote, "To her children, two bright, dutiful daughters, it has been her joy to give a happy childhood in sharp contrast to her own."

ETTA AND FLORENCE OFTEN ASKED THEIR mother about the Connollys, but Mary Ellen was reluctant to speak of her early years. She did show her daughters the scars on her arms where she had been burned with a hot iron, and of course they could see the scissors scar across her face. Florence distinctly recalls that in the few times they spoke of her mother's years in New York City, she

never mentioned a woman inflicting her injuries; it was always a man.

In October of 1913 Mary Ellen Schutt attended a meeting of the American Humane Society in Rochester. She was accompanied by Etta Wheeler, who was there to present a paper entitled "The Finding of Mary Ellen." The paper concluded: "If the memory of her earliest years is sad, there is this comfort that the cry of her wrongs awoke the world to the need of organized relief for neglected and abused children."

Mary Ellen was survived by three daughters—and by a movement that would help avert tragedies like hers.

Mary Ellen died on October 30, 1956, at the age of ninety-two. She was survived by her two daughters, her adopted daughter, three stepchildren, three grandchildren, and five great-grandchildren. More important, she was survived by the beginning of a movement to prevent the repetition of tragedies like her own. On December 15, 1874, Henry Bergh, Elbridge Gerry, and James Wright founded the New York Society for the Prevention of Cruelty to Children (SPCC) with the ample assistance of Cornelius Vanderbilt. It was the first organization of its kind in America. At the outset of their work the founders signed a statement of purpose: "The undersigned, desirous of rescuing the unprotected children of this city and State from the cruelty and demoralization which neglect and abandonment engender, hereby engage to aid, with their sympathy and support, the organization and working of a Children's Protective Society, having in view the realization of so important a purpose."

The SPCC saw its role essentially as a legal one. As an agent or a friend of the court, the society endeavored to intervene on the behalf of children, enforcing the laws that were in existence to prevent cruelty toward them and at the same time introducing new legislation on their behalf.

At the first meeting of the SPCC on December 16, 1874, Gerry stressed the fact that the most crucial role of the society lay in the rescue of children from abusive situations. From there, he pointed out, there were many excellent groups available to care for and shelter children and many state laws to punish abusive parents. He went on to predict that as soon as abusers learned that the law could reach them, there would be few cases like that of Mary Ellen.

Bergh was less optimistic. At the same meeting, he pointed out that neglected and abused children were to become the mothers and fathers of the country and that unless their interests were defended, the interests of society in general would suffer.

In its first year the SPCC investigated more than three hundred cases of child abuse. Many people felt threatened by the intrusion of the government into their private lives; discipline, they believed, was a family issue, and outside influence was not only unwelcome but perhaps even unconstitutional. When, with the aid of a state senator, James W. Booth, Gerry introduced in the New York legislature a law entitled "An Act to Prevent and Punish Wrongs to Children," the proposal was immediately and vigorously attacked. The New York *World* wrote that Bergh was to be authorized to "break into the garrets of the poor and carry off their children upon the suspicion of spanking." According to the *World,* the law would give Bergh "power to discipline all the naughty children of New York. . . . We sincerely hope that it may not be finally kicked out of the legislature, as it richly deserves to be, until the public mind shall have had time to get itself thoroughly enlightened as to the state of things in which it has become possible for such a person as Mr. Bergh to bring the Legislature to the point of seriously entertaining such an impudently senseless measure. This bill is a bill to supersede the common law in

favor of Mr. Bergh, and the established tribunals of justice in favor of an irresponsible private corporation." The bill was passed in 1876, however, and became the foundation upon which the SPCC performed its work.

From its initial concentration on preventing abuse in the home, the society broadened its franchise to battle neglect, abandonment, and the exploitation of children for economic gain. In 1885, after considerable effort by the SPCC and in the face of yet more opposition, Gerry secured passage of a bill that made labor by children under the age of fourteen illegal.

As THE EXPLOSIVE STORY OF THE DEATH of Lisa Steinberg in the home of her adoptive parents revealed to the nation in 1987, abuse still haunts American society. There are still legal difficulties in removing a child from an abusive situation. In 1987 the House Select Committee on Children, Youth, and Families reported that the incidence of child abuse, particularly sexual abuse and neglect, is rising; in 1985 alone almost two million children were referred to protective agencies. In part, the committee said, this increase was due to a greater awareness of the issue, and there has also been an increased effort to educate children themselves about situations that constitute abuse or molestation and about ways to get help.

Despite a plethora of programs designed to address abuse, the committee concluded that not enough is being done. The most effective programs were found to be those that worked to prevent the occurrence of abuse at the outset through education in parenting techniques, through intervention in high-risk situations, such

as unwanted pregnancies, and through screening for mental and emotional difficulties. However, funding for public welfare programs has fallen far below the demands, and what funding there is must frequently be diverted to intervene in more and more sensational and hopeless cases.

If there is still much hard, sad work ahead, there is also much that has been accomplished. And all of it began when Mary Ellen McCormack spoke and, in speaking, freed herself and thousands of other children from torment.

Peter Stevens, who lives in Quincy, Massachusetts, writes frequently on historical themes. Marian Eide is a graduate student in the Comparative Literature and Critical Theory Program at the University of Pennsylvania. We would like to thank Dr. Stephen Lazoritz for his contributions to the research of this article. Lazoritz, a pediatrician specializing in child-abuse cases, first became interested in Mary Ellen's history when, preparing for a lecture on child abuse, he read "The Great Meddler," Gerald Carson's profile of Henry Bergh in the December 1967 issue of American Heritage. Lazoritz was fascinated by the child and traced her history through a trail of documents and newspaper articles. In the story of Mary Ellen's childhood he found the roots of a movement to prevent child abuse in which he is very much involved today. Lazoritz's youngest daughter was born during his pursuit of the case. Her name is Mary Ellen. Thanks, too, to the New York Society for the Prevention of Cruelty to Children, whose archives contain full documentation of the Mary Ellen case.

The Two Faces of George Armstrong Custer

*Was he a distinguished and honored military hero
or a headstrong, irresponsible egomaniac?*

Gerald F. Kreyche

Dr. Kreyche, American Thought Editor of USA Today, *is emeritus professor of philosophy, DePaul University, Chicago, Ill.*

Heroes are like the phoenix; when they die, they always are resurrected out of their own ashes. Subsequently and inevitably, their lives become legend and, in them, history and myth merge so as to become almost indistinguishable.

A prime example is the case of George Armstrong Custer, who died at the Little Big Horn in southeast Montana, June 25, 1876. About 300 books, 45 movies, and 1,000 paintings have centered on him. Custer has had a city, county, highway, national forest, and school named in his honor.

Controversial in life, he is more so in death. Even his grave marker at West Point was changed at the insistence of his wife, Libby. The original was that of a cavalryman astride a charger; the second, a more simple obelisk. Did his widow, who lived for 55 years after his death, shape the image of both the real-life and mythical Custer?

Custeriana continues to generate controversy. One might say it even thrives on it. Examples are Congress' rescinding Maj. Marcus Reno's court martial verdict a few decades ago. Another is the renaming of The Custer Battlefield that was the site of a national military cemetery and given national monument status by Pres. Harry Truman in 1946. Political correctness, at the urging of Native Americans, won out, and the national monument was renamed the Little Big Horn Battlefield. Apparently, Custer's

Mathew Brady portrait of Custer (c. 1865).

From *USA Today* magazine, May 1994, pp. 89-93. © 1994 by the Society for the Advancement of Education. Reprinted by permission.

Photo courtesy of Ronald H. Nichols

name was anathema. Directorship of the monument also changed. Whites were replaced and the previous and present Monument Director both are of Indian ancestry. To complete the purge of Custer influence, the Custer Battlefield Association, which ran the book store and previously contributed time, material, personnel, and money, was ousted in 1993.

A prominent encyclopedia that, when published in 1975, told of the Indians slaughtering Custer's troops at the Little Big Horn accuses Custer in its new revised edition of effecting a massacre at the western engagement at Washita in the Oklahoma Panhandle. It is instructive that the 1941 Errol Flynn movie, "They Died with Their Boots On," glorified Custer and received rave reviews as a classic. Of course, it served wartime ardor, coming out when the nation was confronting World War II. In the anti-Vietnam War era, Dustin Hoffman's 1970 film, *Little Big Man,* portrayed Custer as a raving maniac.

A major fire on the battlefield in August 1983 (possibly set by disgruntled Indians), exposed the area, and a subsequent two-year archaeological dig with forensic and anthropology experts took place in 1984–85. More than 1,000 additional artifacts were discovered, offering new grist for the interpretation mill, and Custer's Last Stand was fought all over again in a spate of books on topics as diverse as time/motion studies and new archaeological explanations. Opinions as to Custer's blame for the defeat became doubted.

Why is Custer of such perennial and controversial interest? Was Custer a Janus? Were there two George Armstrong Custers—one, the Custer of the East, a distinguished and honored breveted Civil War general; the other, a maniacal regular rank Lt. Col. Custer of the West? Was the first a hero and the second a goat?

George Armstrong Custer was born in 1839 in New Rumely, Ohio. His father was a blacksmith and a staunch Democrat. The family moved to Monroe, Mich., where they joined other relatives. How Democrat Custer got an appointment to West Point from diehard Republican Congressman John Bingham remains a mystery.

After a probationary period, Custer received full cadet status in 1857. Always a prankster and *bon vivant,* he graduated at the bottom of his class and his record

of demerits (mostly for minor infractions) was the highest at the Point. Cadets sympathetic to the South, many who were friends of Custer, already had left the academy. They would be met later on the field of battle. Upon graduation, he married Elizabeth Bacon, known always as Libby, who was well-connected politically and became more so as Custer's career flourished.

He served on the staff of or had contact with famous generals who favored him, including Winfield Scott, George McClellan, Irvin McDowell, Alfred Pleasanton, and the feisty, profanity-spouting Phil Sheridan. It is easy to understand why. Fiercely loyal, Custer was flamboyant, optimistic, brave, impetuous to the point of recklessness—and he was lucky! Nearly a dozen horses were shot from beneath him, but he never was wounded seriously.

A man of incredible energy, needing only a few hours of sleep a night, he led his troops into battle with fearsome saber charges, riding four horse lengths ahead and always on the attack. The press latched onto him, for he was a colorful figure as he led his Michigan troops, their orange-red bandannas flying in the wind, calling, "C'mon, you Michiganders!"

That he was a genuine Civil War hero is disputed by no one. For his leadership and many victories in the conflict, he was praised by the press, generals, and Pres. Abraham Lincoln.

His army career in the East found Custer serving variously as staff officer, spy, balloonist, courier, engineer, and especially as a cavalryman. In the early days of the war, the saying had it that "no one ever saw a dead cavalryman." Custer changed this, and his cavalry charges remind one of the German Panzer units with their blitzkrieg strikes.

He bested the elite of the South's cavalry units headed by J.E.B. Stuart and Jubal Early. Custer actively was involved in such battles as Bull Run, Gettysburg, Antietam, Yellow Tavern, Beverly Ford, The Wilderness, Waynesboro, and Winchester.

Rewarded with rapid promotions, he became the youngest brigadier general (at 23) and, later, major general in the Union Army. During the final six months of the war, Custer's men captured 111 artillery pieces, 65 battle flags, and 10,000 prisoners. It was he who accepted the white-fringed towel as a flag of truce from Maj. William Simms of Gen. James Longstreet's Confederate forces at

Appomattox. Sheridan, who witnessed the formal surrender, brought the table on which the document was signed and asked Custer to give it to Libby. The accompanying note stated: " . . . There is scarcely an individual in our service who has contributed more to bring about this desirable result than your gallant husband."

Custer was accused of being arrogant, a glory hunter, showoff, clothes horse, braggart, risk-taker and one who "cooked the books" on his achievements. All except the latter were true, though his record benefited from occasional exaggeration. Can he be condemned for these characteristics? One might ask about Douglas MacArthur with his 50-mission cap, sunglasses, corncob pipe, penchant for public relations, and eventual insubordination; George Patton with pearl-handled revolvers running his tanks until out of fuel and slapping a soldier he thought was a coward; or Mark Clark's unnecessary decimation of historic Monte Cassino. The fact is, they were all winners, as was the Custer of the East.

With the ending of the Civil War, Custer was reduced to the rank of captain. What could this man of action do during the time of the South's reconstruction? For a while, he drank and gambled in civilian life, despite Libby's efforts to "Christianize" him, and served army administrative roles in Texas, Louisiana, and Kentucky. He was offered a $16,000 position with Mexico's military, but the Army refused to give him leave. However, military opportunity was to come his way once more.

THE INDIAN WARS

West of the Mississippi River, "the Indian problem" became increasingly bothersome to settlers moving to the plains in growing numbers. While liberal-minded Easterners regarded the Indians as children of nature, Westerners knew differently and emphasized the Indians' savagery in pleading for more protection. The official report of Col. Henry Carrington, the post commander at a Bozeman Trail fort, describes the carnage of some 80 soldiers killed: "Eyes torn out and laid on the rocks; noses cut off; ears cut off; chins hewn off; teeth chopped out; joints of fingers; brains taken out and exposed; arms taken out from sockets; private parts severed and indecently placed on the person. . . . All this does not approximate the whole truth."

The 1860s brought what were known as the Indian Wars. Although there were few big battles, there were constant skirmishes, leading up to the massacre at the Little Big Horn.

For instance, in 1862, there was the Minnesota Uprising in which Sioux killed some 600 whites, largely precipitated by corruption in the Indian Agency there. Whites were terrorized and 38 Indians were hanged. The cavalry forces at Ft. Phil Kearney in Wyoming suffered a loss of more than 80 men at the hand of Red Cloud's warriors. In between, settlers were raided, killed, and mutilated; Pony Express and state stations robbed; etc.

Treaty Indians were difficult to distinguish from non-treaty ones. The former were under the jurisdiction of the Interior Department; the latter, under the War Department. A pattern developed whereby Indians fought whites in summer and returned to reservation sanctuary in winter, being fed and armed by the Federal government. Sheridan was furious at this, complaining, "General Hazen feeds them and we fight them."

Custer was called west in 1866 to train and lead the newly created 7th Cavalry Regiment at Ft. Riley, Kans. Appointed to the rank of lieutenant colonel at age 27, he took part in the campaign headed by Gen. Winfield Scott Hancock, which was a dismal failure. A year later, he was accused of "several indiscretions," among which was AWOL to see his wife, who he thought was ill. This brought him a court martial, and he was suspended without pay for one year.

Hancock was replaced by Sheridan, and he and Custer made plans for a winter campaign against the Indians, who were then most vulnerable. About 125 whites had been killed by them in Kansas, and Sheridan was under pressure to do something. The result was the Battle of the Washita in the Oklahoma Panhandle in November, 1868. Sheridan's briefing to Custer was: "I rely upon you in everything, and shall send you on this expedition without giving you any orders, leaving you to act entirely on your judgment."

After surrounding the village, Custer attacked through a foot of snow at the break of dawn. He wrote beforehand that some squaws and children would be killed, as many of them often were combatants. A number were slain, and Custer was villified by the East and dubbed Squaw Killer. Yet, farmers' foodstuff and possessions and Kansas mail were found in the Washita camp. A white prisoner was gutted by a squaw, and the notorious Dog Soldiers, who warred on whites, also were present.

More controversy followed as Maj. Joel Elliot pursued Indians downstream and ran into other encampments. Custer felt he had to return to protect his supplies, and Elliot and 18 troopers were left to fare on their own. All were killed. It was a command decision, but brought considerable criticism. Militarily, the Battle of the Washita was highly successful as, for the first time, the Army demonstrated it could go anywhere at any time to bring the battle to the Indians. Sheridan congratulated Custer, as the latter did what he was ordered to do.

Custer's other assignments included exploration of the Yellowstone and Powder River areas, providing protection for the railroad, leading visiting dignitaries on tours, and making a foray into the Black Hills—an action that was allowed under treaty. In assessing his reputation, it must be realized that the makeup of the Army of the West was different from the East, and Custer felt he had to instill discipline in unmotivated and largely untrained troops. Of the approximately 25,000 soldiers assigned to the West, some were former Union officers waiting out their pension, often reduced to enlisted man rank; others were opportunists who found the army a convenient way to get to the gold fields; and still others foreigners who wanted to learn English and the American way of life. Desertions took a toll of about one-third of the troops and suicide another eight percent.

Custer put spit and polish to the troops, ordered deserters shot, and pushed his men to the extreme to make them become an envied fighting unit that was recognized as elite. This provoked a love/hate relationship. Outsiders and many insiders regarded him as nothing less than a tyrant. His second in command, Maj. Marcus Reno, a distinguished Civil War hero himself, hated Custer, and the two leaked reports to the press criticizing each other. The troops knew of this dissension.

As if not controversial enough, Custer, a talented writer, penned articles exposing the sad plight of the Indians. He also fanned the flames of politics when he testified before Congress about the corruption in Indian Agencies, implicating Ulysses S. Grant's brother, Orvil. Custer always made sure his own name was in the news.

By 1875-76, the Indian Wars were coming to a climax. All Indians were ordered to their reservations, and those who did not return were to be regarded as hostiles. Indian agents lied to the army about the number who presently were on the reservations. A false high count produced surplus supplies for the agents, who thereby profited.

A master plan for a three-prong cleanup of the hostiles was made. General George Crook, Alfred Terry, and John Gibbon were to converge in the Valley of the Little Big Horn, where the Indians supposedly had gathered. Custer was under Terry's command and proceeded from Ft. Abraham Lincoln. He had about 650 in his regiment which was at 60% strength, about one-third new recruits. Their weapons were sidearms and single-shot Springfield carbine rifles that fouled easily. Ejection problems often required one man to repair his weapon while three others continued firing.

The generals believed the number of hostiles to be around 800, largely on the basis of false reports from the Indian Agencies. A scout under Reno's command indicated agreement with this figure. The Army's fatal presupposition was that the Indians would fight a pitched battle, but, as usual when attacked by a major force, would disperse and run away, hence the enclosing pincers movement. Terry's orders were "to preclude the possibility of the escape of the Indians." The fast cavalry would force them to flee, thus confronting the infantry, and a cordoning maneuver would effect their surrender.

Plans go awry, however. On his way to converge with the other columns, Crook ran into a fierce encounter with the Sioux at the Battle of the Rosebud. He retreated after a standoff and never met the other troops. Neither Terry nor Gibbon knew of this situation at the time.

Terry told Custer that "It is impossible to give you any definite instructions in regard to this movement, and, were it not impossible to do so, the Department Commander places too much confidence in your zeal, energy and ability to impose on you precise orders which might hamper your action when nearly in contact with the enemy."

The rest is history. Custer split his regiment into three groups and was killed along with about 230 of his men. His strategy was to have Reno ride through the village creating havoc. Before the Indians had a chance to regroup, Custer and Maj. Frederick Benteen would come to Reno's aid from other directions.

It is true that his scouts told him of a huge encampment ahead, saying the horse herd was so numerous they looked like worms. Custer couldn't see them himself, and so had to make his own judgment. He knew, though, that Indian scouts were superstitious and often unreliable in their reports when encountering omens.

More than a century later, the 1984–85 battlefield excavations revealed how one-sided the fight was. The research showed that the Indians had about 29 different types of weapons, including at least 92 repeating rifles. The minimum number of warriors probably was around 2,000.

In retrospect, Gen. Nelson Miles, a battle-seasoned veteran of East and West, thought Custer acted correctly. Pres. Grant excoriated Custer, and the nation mourned its "Boy General" in the year of its centennial. Out of respect for Libby, many who wanted to speak out against Custer decided to wait until her death to do so. Ironically, she outlived almost all of them, surviving until 1933 and never ceasing to extol her husband's virtues. The Indians told confusing stories, worried about retaliation. Enough is known, however, not to make absolute judgments about the Custer of the West.

Today, George Armstrong Custer, the tragic hero, lies buried under a weeping beech next to his ever-loving wife. Perhaps we can agree with Shakespeare's observations, "The evil that men do lives on long after them, the good is oft interred with their bones."

These Are
the Good Old Days

If You Think the City
Is Dirty and Dangerous Now,
It's Eden Compared With
Life in Old New York

Luc Sante

Today's New York shares much with the city of a century ago. In our time, prostitutes walk where prostitutes walked a hundred years ago; the homeless are camped on the sites of nineteenth-century shantytowns; street peddlers pitch their wares in spots that once saw pushcart lineups or thieves' markets. Around Tompkins Square Park, there are flurries of anarchist factions, just as there were in 1887, when the police were engaged in making preemptive arrests in the wake of Chicago's Haymarket Riot. Itinerant swindlers still, amazingly, operate out of decoy storefronts in the former Hell's Hundred Acres, the present SoHo. While New York has adopted as its nickname the Big Apple, that hopeful tag given it by jazz musicians, the city might more truthfully answer to the twin appellations by which tramps knew it: the Big Smear and the Big Onion.

The adolescence and early adulthood of New York covers roughly 80 years: from about 1840, when the city began to be transformed by railroads, tenements, and other accoutrements of the modern city, until 1919, which was not only the year of the Volstead Act and the Red Scare but a portal into a new technological era that would alter the city yet again.

While upper-class life in this period has been well documented—by the likes of Edith Wharton and Henry James, especially—the views and vices of Manhattan's lower class have not. What noises did common folk hear in the street, what did the posters slapped on fences promise them, what were their fears and lures and temptations? What was New York like as circus and jungle, as the realm of danger and pleasure, the wilderness that it must have been then, as it is now?

SALOON CULTURE

Rat-baiting was the premier betting sport of the nineteenth century. Its prestige can be gauged in economic terms, circa 1875: Admission to a then-illegal prizefight between humans cost 50 cents, to dogfights and cockfights $2, while a fight pitting a dog against rats ran anywhere from $1.50, if the dog faced five rats or fewer, up to $5, in proportion to the number of rats. In the eighteenth century, the biggest draw had been bearbaiting, but that sport gradually dissipated as the number of available bears decreased, although matches continued to be held up to the Civil War, notably in McLaughlin's bear pit at First Avenue and 10th Street. For a while, dog-versus-raccoon contests were popular, but rats were so readily available that they came to dominate the scene; boys were paid to catch them, at a rate of 5 to 12 cents a head. The dogs were always fox terriers, and they were trained for six months before being sent out at a year and a half, retaining the status of novice until they reached two. The pits were unscreened boxes, with zinc-lined wooden walls eight feet long and four and a half feet high. Matches typically drew no fewer than 100 betting spectators, from all walks of life, with purses starting at $125—a substantial sum for the time. A good rat dog could kill 100 rats in half an hour to 45 minutes, although the modern record was set by Jack Underhill, a terrier belonging to one Billy Fagan, who slew his 100 in eleven and a half minutes at Secaucus in 1885. Late in the century, it briefly became popular to pit rats against men wearing heavy boots. The ASPCA finally drove the game out of the city in the early 1890s.

At the intersection of Dover and Water Streets stood the Hole-in-the-Wall, a brawling den run by a well-known crook, One-Armed Charley Monell, and his female adjutants, Gallus Mag and Kate Flannery. On Cherry Street, not far away, were the domiciles of the crimps, operators who specialized in drugging and robbing sailors, sometimes arrang-

From *New York*, August 12, 1991, pp. 26-36. Excerpt from *Low Life: Lures and Snares of Old New York* by Luc Sante. © 1991 by Luc Sante. Reprinted by permission of Farrar, Straus & Giroux, Inc.

ing for them to be shanghaied aboard tramp boats if they survived. At least one place, the Fourth Ward Hotel, had convenient trapdoors through which corpses could be disposed directly into the East River. This hostelry later became famous as the site of the murder of a local woman of uncertain age but dire condition, who was popularly nicknamed Shakespeare because for the price of a drink she could recite all the speeches of the major female roles in *The Merchant of Venice, Hamlet, Macbeth,* and *King Lear.* This talent naturally led to wild speculations about her origins, with most of the locals maintaining that she was of noble birth, and the newspapers capitalized on such rumors. Likewise, her murder, never solved, was exoticized by being attributed to Jack the Ripper, come to New York on vacation.

THE CRIMPS REFINED THE ART OF THE knockout. They used laudanum at first, but this proved inefficient in the long run. A man named Peter Sawyer came from California in the 1850s and became so proficient an artist that for a while all members of his profession were known as "peter players." He is said to have used snuff at first, odd though that may

---

The concert saloon began springing up after the Civil War, mostly along the Bowery, and in cellars along lower Broadway.

---

sound, and employed morphine for a particularly tough or important hit. Then either he or one of his colleagues introduced chloral hydrate around 1866, and it was to remain the drug of choice for many years. Care had to be employed, because the physical action of chloral hydrate (soon permanently dubbed "knockout drops") was to decelerate the heart, and an overdose would paralyze the heart and lungs. The taste was detectable by anyone of sound mind and body, so the victim needed to be thoroughly drunk before he could be thus clobbered. Then he would be robbed, perhaps stripped as well, and dumped in an obscure alley. Some dives maintained an arrangement with the police whereby knocked-out

customers would be brought to a convenient location so that the cops could remove their lifeless bodies to the precinct house, where they would eventually be charged with public intoxication. Sometime during the nineties, technology finally brought a refinement to the art, in the form of the Mickey Finn. This concoction was named after the proprietor of Chicago's Lone Star and Palm Saloons, who supposedly bought the recipe from New Orleans voodoo operators and then went on to sell it to other saloon keepers around the country. The trouble is that no one can seem to agree on exactly what a Mickey Finn was. Some believe it to have been a complex recipe effective only when mixed with alcohol and water; the effect of cigar ashes in beer has also been cited, a dubious possibility.

After the Civil War, vice came into its own, ascending from the gutter to become an institution. Harry Hill's concert saloon, at Houston and Mulberry Streets, lasted almost two decades. A bar stood at one end, and at the other was a stage. On this stage, John L. Sullivan made his first New York appearance, knocking out Steve Taylor in two and a half minutes on March 31, 1881. On most evenings, however, the stage held an orchestra consisting of piano, violin, and bass viol, and patrons were expected either to dance to it with paid female partners or else to leave. This was the major tourist-trap component of Hill's. Actual prostitution was always present but not alluded to publicly; arrangements were to be made in private and the johns taken elsewhere. Hill was flamboyant in his role of protector of peace: He enjoyed intervening in what seemed to be incidents of roughhousing—usually staged for the rubbernecker trade; he often spent all evening dramatically shouting for quiet and order. His rules were posted in rhyme on the wall, forbidding drunkenness, profanity, lack of chivalry toward women, stinting on drinks. Meanwhile, in the basement was a more conventional dive, featuring crooked games, knockout artists, and the like. By the mid-1880s, Hill's profits were estimated at $50,000 a year. By this time, he was a full member of middle-class society, distinguished from mere businessmen only by the adjective *colorful.*

Hill's was known as a concert saloon, but concert saloons were actually a spe-

cific and distinct phenomenon. These establishments began springing up after the Civil War, mostly along the Bowery, and in cellars along the stretch of Broadway between Spring and 4th Streets. Their modus operandi was a prostitution tease, one that has survived into the present day at topless bars and the like. Outside, the concert saloons displayed painted transparencies of 20 or 30 women, who, it was given to understand, were employees of the place, although the pictures were usually bought at random in job lots from photograph dealers, and often included well-known actresses of the day among the assortment. Inside, women were employed as waiter girls— in the parlance of the time—and other women would be sitting around looking vaguely like customers. The sucker would be strongly encouraged to buy numerous drinks for himself and for a minimum of one female companion, whose drinks would be heavily watered or consist simply of colored water; they would cost twice as much as the man's, which were themselves expensive for the time, from 15 to 25 cents. The women did not receive wages but worked on a percentage basis. Sex did not occur on the premises and, in fact, usually did not occur at all; obstreperous customers were treated to knockout drops. The concert saloons derived their name from the fact that some sort of excuse for music, probably three drunks on strings and piano, could be found somewhere on the premises. These houses also usually maintained a sideline in gambling.

VICE—THAT AMORPHOUS CATCHALL OF the time—was also famously on display at the American Mabille, on Bleecker Street, run by "The." Allen, who was popularly known as the "wickedest man in New York," a fortunate bit of publicity encouraged by Allen himself; Allen was also known for having been raided 113 times without a conviction (he was very well connected politically). Nearby, on Bleecker Street, was the Slide, probably the very first—and until recent times virtually the last—open and undisguised gay bar in New York. It is all but impossible to get an idea of what it was like, unfortunately; the loud distaste of contemporary chroniclers made them incapable of turning in an actual description. Frank Stephenson's Black and Tan, also on Bleecker, differed from the average dive in that all the women were white and all the men were something else: African-Americans as well as American Indians, East Indians, Chinese, Malays, Lascars. Reports of the time suggest that non-whites were just as likely to be cold-cocked and fleeced as visiting farmers from upstate.

By popular accord, the very worst dive on the Bowery in the 1890s was John McGurk's Suicide Hall, just above Houston (the building is still standing), and it did not conduct its business in secrecy, since it possessed one of the first electric signs on the avenue. Entertainment consisted of singing waiters and a small band; the customers were, as ever, mostly sailors. "It was said," noted a contemporary, "that his business card reached every seaport in the world." The waiters, led by Short-Change Charley, were equipped with chloral hydrate, and they were reinforced by a formidable bouncer, a mayhem specialist named Eat-'Em-Up Jack McManus. These enforced the house rules, such as that if women were observed stealing from men, they were subjected to spot searches. McGurk's was nearly the lowest rung for prostitutes; hence the suicide craze that gave it its name and, incidentally, its grisly lure as a tourist attraction. Figures are unreliable or uncertain on the total number of suicides that went on there, but in just one year, 1899, there were at least six, as well as more than seven attempts. In October of that year, for example, Blonde Madge Davenport and her partner, Big Mame, decided to end it all, and so they bought carbolic acid, the elixir of choice, at a drugstore a few doors away. Blonde Madge gulped it down, but Big Mame hesitated and succeeded in spilling most of it on her face, and the disfigurement got her permanently barred from the place. Suicide attempts were so common that the waiters, upon getting an indication of same, would form a flying wedge and hustle the party out before she (or occasionally he) succumbed. After a woman named Tina Gordon killed herself, John McGurk gave a speech over her body: "Most of the women who come to my place have been on the down grade too long to think of reforming. I just want to say that I never pushed a girl downhill any more than I ever refused a helping hand to one who wanted to climb." This

rather chilling bit of equivocation overlooks the fact that by then his business depended on the suicides for a good part of its allure. McGurk was shut down in 1902, and he retired to California, supposedly with an estate of $500,000. His last heartbreak came when his daughter was denied admission to convent school after those in charge discovered her father's identity.

PROSTITUTES

In the nineteenth century, a young man born into a poor family, perhaps arrived in New York as an immigrant, might nurse ambitions of wealth and status. If he was sufficiently enterprising, he could practice thrift, save his salary, buy a store, save his earnings, buy another store, keep saving and earning until he had a number of stores or one large store. Or, given that workers' salaries in general were barely enough to live on, let alone save to any appreciable degree, and that acquiring the wherewithal to buy just one store could take decades, he might become a burglar, a footpad, a

---

After the Civil War, the moral complexion of New York City changed, and prostitution spread all over town. The brothels were identified by the red doorway lights.

---

shoulder-hitter, a gambling-house shill, a saloon runner, a swindler of immigrants, a poisoner of horses, a mayhem specialist for hire, a river pirate, a crimp, a dip, a ghoul. Then, with sufficient skill, and luck, and drive, and ferocity, he might come to lead his own gang, and from there, if he managed not to get himself killed, he could be launched into politics, or saloonkeeping, or real-estate management, or the business end of the entertainment industry. A poor young woman who harbored similar ambitions generally had only one route open to her: prostitution.

Prostitution went along with careers on the lower levels of the theater; it was

one of the few means for women of the lower class to meet men of a higher station; it gave the appearance of being a way to avoid the drudgery of housework or sweatshop labor; it fostered the illusion of allowing a woman independent enterprise; it dealt in the outward manifestations of a better life, such as fancy clothes and jewelry; it was associated in the popular mind with the realm of leisure, with the pursuit of pleasure. Or if a young woman was solitary—an orphan, for example—that life might be the only possible one for her. Or she might be lured into it by an older sibling already in the profession, or be procured by a lover or a male acquaintance who sought to establish himself as a pimp, or she might be offered money for favors on the street by a stranger who would probably be aware that he was displaying a sum greater than she might otherwise make in a week, or she might, indeed, be sold into the trade by her own parents. After all, no family below the middle class could afford to support children past the age of twelve; few could support them past the age of eight, and many not past infancy. Girls went to work as early as boys, employed as pieceworkers in "light" manufacturing or as shop assistants. In 1888, shop girls were seldom paid more than a dollar and a half per week, not enough to pay for lodging above the flophouse level.

So a young woman not actually seduced or sold into the profession might start by free-lancing. Opportunities were manifold for comely women in their teens and twenties. There were men on the street, at places of amusement, who could spare a dollar or two for a rapid sexual fix. Any woman by herself was fair game, and two together might be thought a team. Any woman out after dark would be assumed to be a whore. Perhaps the young woman could get away with doing this every so often to supplement her income. Too often, however, hazards would intrude. In the nineteenth century, a poor woman who contracted syphilis or gonorrhea, quite apart from the mortal danger posed by the diseases themselves, would find herself barred from conventional society; she could never marry, and any medical treatment would usually be reported to the police and get her branded. Even without this risk, chances are that, in the smaller and more socially claustrophobic order that then prevailed, someone would spot her with a man not of her class, and word would spread. Then she would be ostracized by such relations and acquaintances as thought themselves respectable, and she would be prey to the threats and manipulations of pimps, and the fresh quality that made her attractive to strange men would be spoiled, and she would need to solicit. A young woman who entered a brothel, where her earnings would be taken by the madam, who would pay her only a meager allowance, and where her movements would be as closely monitored as if she were in a nunnery, could nevertheless count herself fortunate, since the alternatives were so much worse.

Before the Civil War, brothels were restricted largely to the waterfront and the slums, to Cherry and Water Streets, to the Bowery and the Five Points (the slum district centered on the intersection of Baxter, Worth, and Park Streets). Immediately after the war, the moral complexion of the city changed, and prostitution spread all over town. Brothels, now identified by their red doorway lights, sprang up in clusters in the side streets west of Broadway in what was then midtown, and soon all through the Tenderloin, the blocks between 24th and 40th Streets and Fifth and Seventh Avenues. In the Broadway district, there was a literal progression in price and quality as one moved uptown, from the houses near and on Canal Street that catered mostly to sailors to the luxurious establishments around Clinton Place (now called 8th Street). All of them, regardless of tone or price, were essentially the same: redbrick residential houses, with names painted in white above their doors—the Gem, the Forget-Me-Not, Sinbad the Sailor, the Black Crook. The fanciest, called parlor houses, featured an atmosphere of considerable decorum in their parlors, where liquor was sold and imbibed with sophisticated restraint, and where a pianist, always called Professor, provided a cultural note. Flora's and Lizzie's were among the most famous and expensive; Josephine Woods's, on Clinton Place between Broadway and University, sold champagne for the then-outrageous sum of $8 a bottle and was celebrated for its annual blindman's-buff party on New Year's Eve and its open house on New Year's Day. Even fancier was Seven Sis-

ters' Row, on 25th Street near Seventh Avenue, where seven adjacent houses were run by seven women said to be sisters from a small New England village. The sisters ran tidy, expensive houses, with parlors in which their young ladies—as well schooled as if they had been convent-reared, which in a sense they were—played the guitar and practiced the art of refined conversation. They attracted customers by sending engraved invitations to important businessmen staying at Fifth Avenue hotels. On certain nights each week, clients were admitted only if they were attired in evening dress and bore bouquets for the girls. The total proceeds from the Christmas Eve trade were donated to charity, a fact given considerable publicity in the press.

In the Tenderloin—sometimes also called Satan's Circus—there clustered an incredible profusion and variety of manifestations of the sex trade, in and among other institutions of vice (by 1885, it was estimated that half the buildings in the district were entirely given over to some kind of immorality). In this area, where turf was carefully divided up between specialties—where 28th Street, for example, was devoted to high-end gambling houses and 27th Street to poolrooms with bookmaking operations—the streets reserved for whorehouses were 24th, 25th, 31st, 32nd, and 35th, and that was not counting the houses of assignation. The brothels ranged in tone from the Sisters' down to places where sex was incidental and robbery uppermost.

There were the panel houses, for example, where, once a john was safely occupied in bed, a male house employee called a creeper would silently push through a detachable panel in the wainscoting and make for the pockets of the pants hung conveniently on a nearby chair. More sophisticated was the badger game. The gangster Shang Draper, for example, ran a saloon on Sixth Avenue and 29th Street where clients were, by fair means or foul, gotten very drunk. When a customer was sufficiently intoxicated, he would be lured by one of the 40 female employees down to a whorehouse on Prince and Wooster Streets. Very near the climactic moment of his encounter with the woman, an angry man would burst in. He was, he would declare, the woman's husband. Enraged by the evidence of adultery, he would threaten to

beat the customer senseless, to kill him, to take him to court. But perhaps, he would hint, he could be mollified, for a significant financial consideration. Identical scenes would meanwhile be taking place in every other room in the joint. Another of Draper's houses employed girls nine to fourteen years of age. In this variation, the "parents" would burst in, the mother would hit the girl in the face so hard her nose would bleed, and the father would shake down the john. It was estimated that 100 men were taken this way every month. Perhaps the all-time champion of the badger game was a Tenderloin operator named Kate Phillips, who one night landed a visiting coffee-and-tea dealer from St. Louis. In the throes of their clinch, a "policeman" appeared, who "arrested" the merchant and took him to "court," where a "judge" fined him $15,000 for adultery: Kate, according to reports, got the money, and the man was never seen again.

CHILD GANGS

The Reverend Lewis Morris Pease, when he opened his Five Points House of Industry in 1850, was among the first to notice the extent of the youthful underworld. Just as the street gangs had female auxiliaries, they also had farm leagues for children. In the Five Points, there were the Forty Little Thieves, the Little Dead Rabbits, and the Little Plug Uglies, and on the waterfront the Little Daybreak Boys.

Considering that the "adult" gang members were often in their early teens themselves, we may speculate on just how young these trainees might be. Their major value to the gangs was their size. They all worked as lookouts and decoys; among the river gangs, they were important for their ability to crawl through portholes. Pease's efforts to arouse the finer instincts among these waifs did produce one apparent success. He boasted of having converted Wild Maggie Carson, who was the leader of the Forty Little Thieves. He claimed to have overseen her first bath, at the age of nine, and subsequently to have gotten her sewing buttons. Eventually he married her off to the scion of a pious family.

Children as young as five or six were enrolled in Fagin schools to learn pocket picking, purse snatching, and cart robbery, tasks at which they might outdo their seniors. In the 1890s, the major Fagin was Monk Eastman's sidekick Crazy Butch, who had begun his own career very young. He first proved his pedagogic ability by teaching his dog, Rabbi, to snatch purses, and then went on to coach preadolescents. He also formed his charges into the improbably named Squab Wheelmen. They were most noted for one trick: A member would hit a pedestrian, preferably an old woman, with his bicycle, and then dismount and begin screaming at the victim. As an interested crowd gathered, the other members would pick their pockets.

There was very little that adult gangsters practiced or enjoyed that child gangsters did not contrive to reproduce on their own scale. There were boys' saloons, with 3-cent whiskeys and little girls in the back rooms, and there were children's gambling houses, in which tots could bilk other tots at the usual menu of games. If it seems that these children must have very early used up the entire stock of adult pleasures—sex, drink, gambling, extortion, racketeering, fraud, intimidation, terrorism—it should be remembered that the life expectancy for kids under those conditions could not have been very high. The whole adult order of high and low sensations had to be experienced in fifteen or twenty years at best before they succumbed to disease, malnutrition, exposure, stab wounds, or gunfire. In an era during which New York produced three or four adolescent crooks called Billy the Kid, all of whom disappeared in some fashion before they were old enough to vote, and all of whom were reported incorrectly to have gone West and become *that* Billy the Kid, it is remarkable that any young person from the slums survived to adulthood at all. Those who did can be assumed to have been the most pious, the most enterprising, or the most murderous—in any case, the least childlike—of children.

TRAMPS

The phenomenon of tramps—the homeless of yesterday—first appeared in the 1870s. Many of them were probably Civil War veterans who hadn't been able to adjust. They were little noticed in the city at first, for one thing because trampdom was generally rural and was thought of as a menace only in farm and range country; for another, because tramps themselves were generally of rural origin and conducted themselves accordingly, remaining mobile and discreet. In the years when Central Park was new, tramps would hide out there, living in its sylvan recesses. They attracted notice as a public nuisance with their penchant for lying prone on the pavement and draining the lees from empty beer kegs set out in front of saloons. For some years, toward the end of the century, a tramp shelter operated quietly in a former hotel at Prince and Marion (Lafayette) Streets. Vagrants were given bed and board, and in return they chopped logs for the firewood business that financed the institution.

After the turn of the century, tramps and hoboes began showing up in the city in greater numbers: adventurers drifting back eastward from the settled West, stragglers from Coxey's Army, men put out of work from suburban factories as a result of the Panic of 1897. New York was a minor way station for tramps and hoboes, and they were perceived in significant numbers in the city only from about 1901 to 1917. Most of the railroad vagrants shunned the city for its expense, its gangs of hoodlums and lush-rollers, its uncertain police force, and also because of its underground rail platforms, which made it difficult to hop trains from anywhere but the stations of the West Side river line. But in the first decade and a half of the twentieth century, there were so many people without fixed abode in the city that flops of all sorts sprang up; the Western tramps must have heard of New York as a storehouse of cheap beds. When they got to the city, though, they found a great deal of competition. In 1909, it was estimated there were 25,000 people on the bum on the Bowery and Park Row alone, in hotels, lodging houses, flophouses, missions, sleeping on chairs, in barrels, on saloon floors, in doorways, in stairwells, on fire escapes.

Tramps and hoboes provided a good deal more fodder for Sunday-supplement human-interest stories than the more typical city vagrants, however. They were usually native English speakers, for one thing, and they were independent, more or less eccentric and colorful, more or less nonviolent and healthy. Among the tramps and bums were enigmatic sorts and instant legends. There were said to be Oxford graduates and men with dueling scars from German universities. There were remittance men from old families whose month would follow a rigorously determined cycle: Funds would arrive, followed by new clothes and feasting and carousing; then the money would be gone, the clothes would be pawned, and there would follow a week or two of utter destitution, each stage accompanied by a corresponding shift of lodging. One Bowery character, known only as J. Black, would ceremoniously extract a dark suit from hock for a few days each month and disappear to read in the public library. There were the usual legendary rich bums, the authenticity of whose fortunes remains questionable. A man named William Smith, who died in 1913 at the age of 80 after some three decades as a vagrant, was said posthumously to have been playing the stock market all along and to have left some $200,000 in cash and securities. Another man was rumored to have bequeathed $35,000 to two road companions.

The Bowery's term as a magnet for tramps was finally ended by the approach of World War I, especially by the 1917 "Work or Fight" order that conscripted into the armed forces anyone not demonstrably employed, a law that cut a great swath through the area's population and finally killed the street as an entertainment district for anyone but the pathetic derelicts who remained through Prohibition. It provided a handy excuse for the police to make sweeps of the rootless and unprotected in other areas as well, such as Hell's Kitchen and Harlem. The numbers were, of course, to return little more than a decade later, when the Depression struck and shantytowns went up in the parks and Hoovervilles along the waterfront.

CRIMINALS AND LAWYERS

The most famous pirate of the time was a middle-aged crook named Albert E. Hicks, who in 1860 was shanghaied and woke up aboard the sloop *E. A. Johnson,* bound for Virginia to pick up a shipment of oysters. Five days later, the boat was discovered drifting off the coast of New Jersey, empty and with signs of bloodshed. Inquiring policemen found that Hicks had been seen in Manhattan with a great deal of money. He skipped town but was arrested in Providence, Rhode Island, carrying a watch and a daguerreotype that could be traced to the ship's officers. The U.S. Circuit Court found him guilty of murder and piracy on the high seas, and he eventually confessed to having killed all hands with an ax. The case achieved enduring fame when P. T. Barnum acquired a mask of Hicks as well as all his clothes for $25 and two boxes of cigars. Hicks was hanged a mere four months after his deed, to much pomp, on Bedloe's Island (the future site of the Statue of Liberty).

The 1860s and 1870s were the grand era of bank robberies. James L. Ford wrote in his memoirs 50 years later, "Such operations as bank burglary were held in much higher esteem [then] than at present, and the most distinguished members of the craft were known by sight and pointed out to strangers." The district gangs of the time were pikers and barroom brawlers compared with such an outfit as that put together by George Leonidas Leslie, also known as Western George and referred to in the press as King of the Bank Robbers. According to George W. Walling, who was police superintendent from 1874 to 1885, the Leslie gang was responsible for 80 percent of the bank robberies in New York between the Civil War and Leslie's death in 1884; estimates of their total take ranged between $7 million and $12 million. Such statistics must be viewed with suspicion; one set of devious masterminds, after all, does less to damage police prestige than a whole town full of bank robbers.

Fences in the mid-nineteenth century were powerful enough, and perhaps sufficiently liberal with bribes, to operate with a degree of openness. After the Civil War, Frederika Mandelbaum, an impressive, narrow-eyed figure, secure in her 250-pound bulk, had a three-story building on the corner of Clinton and Rivington Streets where she ran a fencing operation with the assistance of her husband, Wolfe, and their son and two daughters, under the guise of a haberdashery. Her first listing in police records dates to 1862, and she is said to have passed between $5 million and $10 million in goods through her mill over the next twenty years. She was also alleged to have operated a Fagin school on Grand Street, but this very popular

allegation was bandied around so carelessly in the decades after the appearance of Dickens's novel that it should be viewed with caution. "Marm" Mandelbaum, whose house was said to be furnished as opulently as any Vanderbilt's—with goods liberated from uptown mansions—was the social leader of the female criminal set. Her friends included such prominent sneak thieves and blackmailers as Big Mary, Ellen Clegg, Queen Liz, Little Annie, Old Mother Hubbard, Kid Glove Rosey, the con woman Sophie Lyons, and Black Lena Kleinschmidt. Black Lena was an uncommonly successful pickpocket and moll-buzzer who was undone by her taste for social climbing. After saving her money for years, she finally moved to the then-fashionable suburb of Hackensack and began entertaining a straight crowd. Legend has it that her end came when, at one of her lunches, a guest recognized a diamond ring Lena was wearing as her own unique piece, stolen years before. Marm Mandelbaum, for her part, was indicted for grand larceny by the district attorney in 1884 but jumped bail and fled to Canada. She had the last laugh, as her bondsmen succeeded in transferring the property pledged for her bail to her possession by means of back-dated documents.

Mandelbaum was represented by the era's paramount criminal lawyers, William Howe and Abraham Hummel, whom she paid a retainer of $5,000 a year. This pair were very nearly a law unto themselves, and were so much a part of the New York scene, both high and low, in the latter half of the nineteenth century that they can hardly be discussed without superlatives. In their 40-odd-year career, they were said to have represented more than 1,000 defendants in murder and manslaughter cases alone, with Howe personally pleading more than 650. The firm was established in 1861 by Howe, a corpulent, flashily dressed practitioner noted for his overwhelmingly theatrical manner, in particular much given to weeping in the courtroom. His partner, the canny, diminutive Hummel, joined as an office boy in 1863 and was elevated by Howe to equal status within a few years. They redefined the word *shyster*. Their offices were in a building on Leonard and Centre Streets, directly across from the Tombs, that was ornamented with a 40-foot sign advertising their practice. Their cable address was LENIENT.

They sometimes obtained the minutes of successful trials, had them reprinted, and distributed them as publicity. They owned reporters at most of the daily papers and kept a regular stable of professional witnesses. Hummel once got 250 of the little more than 300 prisoners on Blackwell's Island (now Roosevelt Island) released all at once on a technicality. Howe and Hummel kept no records.

The mainstay of their practice was the breach-of-promise blackmail suit, which they effectively worked on both sides, representing showgirls who had had affairs with society figures and then been dropped, and at the same time being kept on retainer by many of these playboys as protection against further suits. Their client list virtually defined the newsworthy part of Manhattan society in the last 30 years of the nineteenth century. In the criminal world they represented entire gangs, such as "General" Abe Greenthal's national pickpocket ring, the Sheeny Mob, the forgers of Chester McLaughlin's Valentine Ring, and the foremost downtown gang of their day, the Whyos. They worked for George Leslie (receiving $90,000 from him in the wake of the 1878 Manhattan Savings fiasco, for many years afterward the largest legal fee on record), the counterfeiter Charles O. Brockway, the major bookmaker Peter De Lacey, the procuresses Hattie Adams and the French Madame, the abortionist Madame Restell, the Tammany boss Richard Croker, the dive owners Harry Hill and Billy McGlory, and such once-famous murderers as Dr. Jakob Rosenzweig (the Hackensack Mad Monster), Annie Walden the Man-Killing Race-Track Girl, and Ned Stokes, who shot Jim Fisk. In civil cases of various sorts they represented bridge-jumper Steve Brodie, *Police Gazette* publisher Richard K. Fox, exotic dancer Little Egypt, the anarchist Johann Most, and a slew of theatrical figures that included P. T. Barnum, Edwin Booth, John Drew, John Barrymore, and Lillie Langtry. Their industry did not flag until Howe died in 1902 and Hummel was chased from the country by the reform crusader William Travers Jerome, dying in London in 1926.

Some of the flavor of their ambiguous attitude toward the law can be derived from their sole published work, the 1888 *In Danger*. They describe the temptations in mouth-watering detail: " . . . elegant storehouses, crowded with the choicest and most costly goods, great banks whose vaults and safes contain more bullion than could be transported by the largest ships, colossal establishments teeming with diamonds, jewelry, and precious stones . . . all this countless wealth, in some cases so insecurely guarded." Under the guise of alerting the public to the dangers of big-city crime, they offer explicit directions for making burglars' tools and give formulas for rigging cards. The booklet is, in fact, an advertisement for crime, couched in all the subtlety known to the science of publicity at the time.

PEDDLERS

Virtually every kind of inexpensive article was offered for sale on the streets. This trade went on without benefit of advertising, obviously; instead, cries, costumes, locations, and the age or sex or race of the vendor were an indication of what was for sale. There was the clam seller: "Here's clams, here's clams, here's clams today/ They lately came from Rockaway/ They're good to roast, they're good to fry/ They're good to make a clam-pot pie/ Here they go!" There were chimney sweepers ("Sweep o, sweep o") and ragmen ("Rags, rags, any old rags" or "Old clo', old clo', any old clo' "). Most celebrated were the hot-corn vendors ("Hot corn, hot corn, here's your lily-white hot corn/ Hot corn, all hot, just came out of the boiling pot"), who were almost always young girls and sold their wares from baby carriages and children's wagons. The wares sold by street criers gave a fair indication of the range of fast food of the time: oysters, fish, buns, hot spiced gingerbread, strawberries, ice cream, baked pears—a wholesome-sounding list. Competition with the increasing general noise level of the city is presumably what drove the criers out of business, as little is heard from them after about 1860, with the notable exception of newsboys.

Selling became minutely particularized in the middle nineteenth century, as commercial turf lines were drawn up by various groups. As of the 1880s, for example, Irishwomen (popularly identified as smoking pipes) sold apples, "George Washington pie," St.-John's-

bread, and flat gingerbread cakes called "bolivars"; Chinese men sold candy and cigars. Men in general sold tobacco, socks, suspenders, hose, yarn, and gloves. Women sold most of the food, although, after the era of the hot-corn girl, roasted ears were almost always sold by black men. Boys sold ties, pocketbooks, pocketbook straps, and photographs. Little girls sold matches, toothpicks, songs, and flowers. After the Civil War, lame soldiers held the monopoly on shoestrings, and they also sold ties and a lesser rank of books and magazines. Italians dispensed ice cream; Germans dealt in sausages.

In residential areas, there were itinerant umbrella menders, tinkers, whitewashers, washtub menders, glaziers, paviors, hod carriers, excrement carriers, odd-job men identifiable by their square paper caps. Ballad vendors and encyclopedia salesmen likewise worked the doors. Orange vendors sold their wares in bundles hung from yokes. Street photographers plied the main arteries with samples of their work mounted on boards. Hackmen waited at stands outside train and ferry stations, calling "Keb, keb, keb." Newsboys were everywhere, fighting for territory, hitching rides on horsecars, yelling "Extra!"

In the Bowery, Chatham Square, and the nearby region, another mercantile style prevailed. Many of the shops were run by "cheap Johns" selling shoddy goods, but even the more respectable merchants behaved with frenzied aggressiveness. In contrast with shopkeepers anywhere else in the city, they displayed the bulk of their stock in stalls and boxes on the sidewalk in front, and they were constantly putting on fire sales that had not been occasioned by fire and going-out-of-business sales that might go on for years at a stretch.

Everything on the Bowery was loaded and short-counted. Even the pushcarts sold bad fruit, cutlery made of scrap that broke at first use, used ink bottles filled with water. There were also businesses that could hardly be found anywhere else: tattoo parlors, for instance, which flourished around Chatham Square until the I950s, and black-eye fixers, who were essentially makeup artists and whose ability to maintain sufficient trade to set themselves up in storefronts—while only occasionally keeping a second line in something more workaday

like barbering—is a testament to the continuous violence of the neighborhood.

DIME MUSEUMS

The peculiar institution of the dime museum probably had its origin in the back rooms of eighteenth-century taverns, where curiosities, anatomical anomalies, and the like were exhibited on an irregular basis. The man who made it into an institution was P. T. Barnum, who started in 1835 by exhibiting an ancient black woman named Joice Heth, who, he alleged, was 161 years old and had been George Washington's wet nurse. Barnum showed her in daily sessions in a coffeehouse at Bowery and Division to great popular acclaim, until she died several months after her debut. Barnum next staged diverse attractions at the Vauxhall Saloon, near Astor Place, from 1840 until 1842, when he had accumulated the capital to purchase the old American Museum, a staid exhibition hall of elegant white marble, at Broadway and Ann Street. There he showed wax figures, "human wonders," a menagerie, dioramas, edifying dramas, mechanical contrivances, panoramic views, and sundry frauds, and was legendarily successful at it. He continued throughout the century, even after his museums succumbed to fire—first the one on Ann Street in 1865, then the one on Broadway between Prince and Spring in 1868—after which he left for the theatrical nexus of 14th Street and later became a partner in the grand hall called Gilbert's Garden, eventually renamed Madison Square Garden.

The museum format, which Barnum did not invent but which he broadened in appeal, was widely imitated. In 1867, the moniker was established when, as a result of a price war, admissions were reduced to a dime. The first to reach this mark was Bunnell's Museum on the Bowery, which boasted besides its tattooed man, its "double-brained" child, and the like—a "Dante's Inferno" that featured wax figures of widely despised living figures (Boss Tweed, Henry Ward Beecher, Jay Gould, Victoria Woodhull) writhing in eternal torment. Nevertheless, Bunnell's major attraction for the year 1879 was a grand poultry show. Around the Bowery there were scores of emulators, each with its waxworks, its "moral dramas," its mechanical wonders, its panoramas. Slightly risque tableaux and set pieces began showing up in abundance. Everywhere, the museums whispered of "spicy French sensations," "secrets of artists' models," "secrets of the seraglio," "beautiful minuet dancers from the Jardin Mabille," "bewitching female bathers in real water."

On the Bowery, dense as it was with such diversions as nickel shooting galleries featuring animated, noisemaking figures, such lures hardly stood out, but by the 1880s they were creeping uptown. The Eden Musée, on 23rd Street diagonally across from McCreery's Department Store, featured the usual retinue of freaks, midgets, fire eaters, sword swallowers, waxworks, a Chamber of Horrors, and "Ajeeb, the chess mystery," a pseudo-automaton consisting of a hollow figurine inhabited by a child dwarf. At Huber's Dime Museum on East 14th Street, patrons would be regaled by the spiel of the barker, a formidable gentleman in evening dress, with pomaded hair and waxed mustache, who intoned, "Ladies and gents/ For only 10 cents/ You can see all the sights/ And there on your right/ Is the great fat lady./ She's a healthy baby/ Weighing 300 pounds./ She's six feet around./ Her husband is the living/ Skeleton—see him shivering./ The dog-faced boy/ Will give you all joy/ And the tattooed man/ Does the best he can. The human horse/ Is wonderful of course./ And I'll show to you/ The baby kangaroo," and so on. This worthy is said later to have killed himself "when his muse ceased to be appreciated."

Elsewhere, there were mermaids (usually, dead manatees in a tank), two-headed calves, four-legged chickens, calculating horses, dwarves, giants, bearded ladies, armless wonders, wild men of Borneo, "Circassian princesses" possessing incredibly long hair and usually surrounded by snakes, snake charmers, Indian rubber men, glass eaters, mental marvels, ossified girls, legless ladies, men-fish, "iron-skulled" men, men "who will not smile," men "who cannot stop walking," geeks, living half-men, human pincushions, human claw hammers, human anvils, egg cranks (who could eat something like 120 of them at a sitting), idiot-savant calculators, tattooed marvels ("ninety thousand

stabs and for every stab a tear," at Barnum's Museum). Inarticulate minor celebrities were also displayed, such as Bob and Charlie Ford, after they had killed Jesse James.

Bowery museums were the true underworld of entertainment and could include anything too shoddy, too risqué, too vile, too sad, too marginal, too disgusting, too pointless to be displayed elsewhere. For the inmates, life in the museums was no doubt rather boring and workaday. At Bunnell's, renamed the Globe, George the Turtle Boy played cards between shows with Laloo the East Indian Enigma, who had a small head growing out of his side. An extra nickel would allow one downstairs for the melodrama or variety (Al Jolson, for one, got his start this way). Twelve or 15 shows went on daily, during which the freaks had to stand around and assume typical poses, although when the immortal Jo-Jo the Dog-Faced Boy hit the Bowery, his draw was so great that the schedule was expanded to 23 shows daily.

Mostly the museums were desperately cheap and small-time. A great number lacked even the resources to put on shows or hire human oddities, and so instead displayed any rag end they could get their hands on and elevate in stature through imaginative labeling: old coins, old musical instruments, old furniture, spearheads, Civil War rifles. Worth's Museum claimed to display the pickled head of Guiteau, President Garfield's assassin; three separate Bowery museums insisted they possessed the club with which Captain Cook was killed in the South Pacific. Museums would be plastered with signs warning FOR MEN ONLY; NO MINORS ADMITTED and then turn out to contain a scattering of old newspapers, yellowed envelopes, peepholes with views of ordinary chromolithographs. One such establishment was destroyed in 1899 by a group of soldiers returning from the Spanish-American War, enraged at finding no actual sex or depravity.

Depravity was there to be had, of course, at places like the Grand Museum, which featured tableaux vivants by women clad only in flesh-colored tights. There were joints that promised "nude women" and delivered (after the sucker had paid two or three separate

admissions to sanctums within sanctums within the museum) a single unadorned showroom dummy, or possibly an embryo in a jar. There were "anatomical museums," which displayed wax models of organs and vaguely obscene charts detailing the "secrets of a successful marriage," and where "professors" who claimed to have lately come from Berlin or Paris droned on while showing lantern slides of horrifying venereal deformities in the faces of victims of tertiary syphilis.

CON GAMES

The dazzling variety of short con games in the late nineteenth century ranged from such acting exercises as the Spanish-prisoner swindle (a grieving wife and children would be toured, pleading for funds to release a prisoner of conscience from foreign confinement) to vaudeville routines like the pedigreed-dog swindle.

This con would begin with a man entering a saloon, accompanied by a dog. Over a drink, he would explain to the bartender that the mutt was a prizewinner, an extremely valuable specimen of some mythical breed. Then he would ask the bartender to watch the dog for half an hour while he attended to a crucial matter of business, possibly sweetening the deal by giving the bartender a small tip. While the dog owner was away, another man would come in, spot the dog, exclaim over it, and then ask the bartender if he was willing to sell. When the bartender refused, the man would pretend that the bartender was simply being canny, and he would offer greater and greater sums. Finally, just as the bartender was beginning to weaken, the man would give up and leave, adding as an afterthought that he might come back later in case the bartender had changed his mind.

Soon after that, the dog's owner would return, looking distraught, announcing that he had been ruined. After accepting the bartender's sympathy, he might allow himself to think of selling the dog, and the bartender, not wanting to seem too eager, would name a smallish but still sizable figure. The dog owner would look both stricken and relieved, accept the money, and leave with tears in his eyes. The accomplice, needless to say, would never return.

The Forgotten Pioneers

New scholarship reveals the major role blacks played on the frontier

The U.S. Postal Service tried to update history last spring but instead fell victim to it. The agency used a portrait of African-American rodeo star Bill Pickett in its "Legends of the West" stamp series—only to find that it had printed the wrong picture. The stamp's painter had consulted eight different history books that identified the Cowboy Hall of Famer, but each volume had mistakenly run an image of the cowboy's brother Ben. With the Postal Service's release of a new stamp with the proper portrait this fall, a bit of the historical legacy of African-Americans in the West will be corrected.

Such errors and misunderstandings of the African-American experience in the American West are commonplace—the legacy of both scholarly neglect and racist distortion. But now a burst of new scholarship is correcting the record and bringing to light much of the long-lost history of the true role played by African-Americans in creating the Western frontier. Next year the Smithsonian Institution's National Museum of American History will mount an exhibition that includes a chronicle of the roles blacks played in settling the West as railroad builders, miners and farmers. A new monument celebrating the "Buffalo Soldiers," the all-black Army regiments that helped found the West, was dedicated at Fort Leavenworth, Kan., two years ago. In new books, symposiums and recently launched programs at institutes around the nation, scholars are discovering how, like whites, blacks viewed the West as a land of promise both economically and racially—but also fell prey to the West's mythology.

Rediscovered records show that blacks were part of the West's exploration and conquest from the very beginning. A census of old California shows that by 1790, 18 percent of the population of the territory was African-American. By

MISTAKEN IDENTITY. **For years thought to be a photograph of rodeo star Bill Pickett, this image turned out to be that of Pickett's brother Ben. Inventor of "bull-dogging"—wrestling a bull by its horns—Bill Pickett was later inducted into the Cowboy Hall of Fame.**

1890, 518,986 African-Americans—about 4 percent of the nation's black populace—lived west of the Mississippi. Twenty-six of the original 44 settlers of the pueblo of La Nestra Señora de los Angeles—the well-spring of modern-day Los Angeles—were black, as were many of the explorers at the height of the Western fur trade from the 1820s to the 1840s. As many as 1 in 4 cowboys who participated in the cattle drives through Texas was African-American.

Slave beginnings. Despite the image of the West as luring pioneers with the

From *U.S. News & World Report,* August 8, 1994, pp. 53-55. © 1994 by U.S. News & World Report. Reprinted by permission.

promise of a new freedom, many blacks in fact originally came to the region as slaves. In Harrison County, Texas, for instance, more than half the 15,000 residents were slaves, as were many of the estimated 1,000 blacks present during California's Gold Rush. Several American Indian tribes, including the Cherokee, Choctaw and Chickasaw, also held black slaves. A recent book, *Freedom on the Border*, by historian Kevin Mulroy, reveals that one tribe—the Seminoles—treated blacks almost like feudal vassals. These bondsmen later became military "scouts" who helped fight America's Indian Wars in the West.

But even while in bondage, many blacks saw the West as a Promised Land of freedom. In her new book, *Free Frank, A Black Pioneer on the Antebellum Frontier*, University of Illinois historian Juliet E. K. Walker details the story of a distant relative who named himself Frank Mc-Worter. Born a slave in South Carolina in 1777, McWorter began his trek westward when his owner moved to Kentucky in 1795. By 1817, he had purchased his wife's freedom; two years later he bought his own freedom for $800, and eventually the freedom of 16 members of his family for nearly $14,000. In 1830, he relocated to Illinois to found the town of New Philadelphia.

Many blacks saw the West as an opportunity to start the African-American experience anew in racially separatist settlements. More than 60 all-black towns were founded from Alabama to California. Many were begun by land speculators—black and white—during the 1870s, when persecution brought about by the failure of Reconstruction led to a huge influx of some 40,000 blacks from the South in what was known as the "Exoduster" movement of 1879–80.

Among the most prominent all-black towns was Nicodemus, Kan., established in 1877 by a white land speculator and his black partner. As was often the case during the settling of the West, black pioneers were promised fertile fields, abundant water, shady trees and plenty of game by alluring advertisements. Instead, arriving blacks found that the best farmland surrounding the town was already taken by whites. There were no trees, and game was scarce. One group of black settlers returned home after seeing the place; others were so mad they threatened the speculator's life. Some nearly starved to death.

With the arrival of more settlers to the surrounding region, however, Nicodemus eventually boomed into one of the models of black independence in the West. It boasted a church, a post office, a hotel, a general store and two black-run newspapers. Edward P. McCabe was elected as Kansas's first black auditor general. Similarly, the all-black town of Boley, founded in 1904 in Oklahoma and also lauded as a model of black separatist self-determination, had a black city council and its own waterworks, electric power company, banks and stores.

The pioneer ethos of rugged individualism and self-sufficiency that characterized the West applied to many all-black towns as well. Echoing the principles of self-help popularized by Booker T. Washington, many settlements did not welcome destitute blacks. In the 1890s, one Langston, Okla., newspaper cautioned future settlers with the headline, "Come Prepared Or Not At All."

A key part of the culture and commerce of the black West was the "Buffalo Soldiers," segregated troops of black Army soldiers who fought Indians, intervened in labor disputes and patrolled western borders. In one new study, *Buffalo Soldiers, Braves and the Brass*, Army historian Frank Schubert details how the Buffalo Soldiers' steady wages—coveted in an era when labor markets were still restricted by racism—helped infuse black towns with much needed cash.

In the end, many of these black prairie towns met the same fate as their white counterparts. Nicodemus lost a competition for a railroad station that would have tied it into the larger regional economy, and went into economic decline. Boley fell prey to the demographic shift to big cities. But the legacy of racism also played a role: Jim Crow laws barred blacks from voting and hampered black laborers. Four black men were lynched in a town in Oklahoma in 1910.

Eventually, the memory of African-American achievements and contributions to the founding of the Western frontier faded. Artists like Frederic Remington, who had drawn sketches of the Buffalo Soldiers, wound up eliminating blacks from their later canvases. "History," says Canadian historian Britan Dippie, "was whitened to myth." And with it came a new era in which the real, multicolored frontier was blotted out by the familiar nostalgic West of popular imagination.

Scott Minerbrook in Nicodemus, Kan.
and Boley, Okla.

GERONIMO

Dee Brown

Geronimo had been only a few months in the Sierra Madre when he decided that all the Chiricahuas should be rescued from the semi-starvation and sickness of the reservation and brought to Mexico. Consequently, in April 1882, after careful planning, Geronimo and his warriors stealthily invaded San Carlos, cut the telegraph lines, and sought out all the Chiricahuas they could find for a flight to Mexico. Not all wanted to leave. According to Jason Betzinez, a cousin of Geronimo who was living on the reservation, they were given no time to find their horses and had to flee on foot. "We weren't allowed to snatch up anything but a handful of clothing and other belongings. There was no chance to eat breakfast. Geronimo . . . was out in front guiding us east along the foot of the hills north of the Gila River."

On their way out of the reservation they encountered a patrol of Apache police and killed the white leader, Albert Sterling. With about 100 warriors and 400 women and children, Geronimo now faced the difficult task of avoiding or outrunning several pursuing Army forces. Lieutenant Colonel George A. Forsyth of Beecher Island fame tried to intercept them with cavalry along the recently completed Southern Pacific Railroad, and came close enough for a sharp fight at Horseshoe Canyon on April 23, but he could not stop them.

"After we had crossed into Mexico," Jason Betzinez recalled, "we began to feel safe from attack by U.S. troops, not knowing that the troop commander, hot on our trail, intended to cross the border with or without permission of higher authorities."

Although Forsyth did pursue Geronimo's escaping band across the border, it was not the U.S. cavalry but that of the Mexican Army that was to deal them a

deadly blow. In a dry stream bed within view of the Sierra Madre, the Mexicans struck the flank of the relaxed two-mile-long column of Apaches, shooting down men, women, and children. "As we ran," Betzinez said, "my mother and I heard Geronimo behind us, calling to the men to gather around him and make a stand to protect the women and children."

According to Geronimo's own account, told years afterward, the Mexican commander recognized him and ordered his soldiers to exterminate him and his band at any cost. "From all along the ditches arose the fierce war cry of my people," he said. "The columns wavered an instant and then swept on; they did not retreat until our fire had destroyed the front ranks. . . . That night before the firing had ceased a dozen Indians had crawled out of the ditches and set fire to the long prairie grass behind the Mexican troops. During the confusion that followed we escaped to the mountains." Geronimo failed to mention the severe losses suffered by his people—seventy-eight dead, thirty-three women and children made captive, and many wounded. One-fourth of his fighting force of warriors was gone.

To obtain food supplies and horses, the Chiricahuas made lightning raids upon Mexican villages, taking cattle, horses, and mules, and capturing pack trains of supplies. Because they were unable to obtain ammunition that would fit their American-made rifles, Geronimo risked a foray into Arizona. He succeeded in bringing out large quantities of ammunition as well as saddles, bridles, and blankets. But at the same time his action generated headlines and lurid tales for the voracious American press. From that time until his final surrender, Geronimo would be blamed for almost every major or minor raid by Apaches anywhere in Arizona and New Mexico. This added to his notoriety, gave him a far more blood-

thirsty image than he deserved, and made his capture or destruction the main objective of General George Crook when he returned to Arizona in September 1882.

In preparation for his campaign against Geronimo, Crook put San Carlos under military control and transformed the Apache police into scouts for tracking. He placed Captain Emmet Crawford in charge of the reservation and gave Lieutenant Britton Davis command of the scouts.

To stop the Apache raids Crook devised a plan for striking at Geronimo's base, the location of which he obtained from a Chiricahua who returned to the reservation. In order to avoid violating international law, he had to obtain permission from Mexican authorities to take his soldiers across the border. The slow process of completing these arrangements as well as making preparations for the expedition delayed the start until the spring of 1883.

With a force of 320, which included 76 civilian packers to handle the pack mules, 193 Apache scouts, and a journalist-photographer, Crook crossed into Mexico early in May. When the mountainous country slowed the column's progress, he sent Captain Crawford with 150 scouts ahead of the pack train. On May 15, Crawford surrounded one of Geronimo's *rancherías* and captured the women and children. In a few days several warriors surrendered in order to join their families.

By this time Crook and his pack train had come up, and he learned from the warriors that Geronimo wanted to talk with him. Captain John Bourke, who was with Crook during the meetings that followed, described Geronimo and his warriors as a "fine-looking lot of pirates" all well-armed with breech-loading Winchesters. Geronimo told Crook that he had always wanted to be at peace, but

From *American History Illustrated*, July 1980. © 1980 by Cowles Magazines, Inc. Reprinted through the courtesy of Cowles Magazines, Inc., publisher of *American History Illustrated*.

that he had been ill-treated at San Carlos and driven away. He promised the general that if he would be allowed to go back to the reservation and guaranteed just treatment, he would gladly work for his living and follow the path of peace. Crook kept Geronimo in suspense for a few days, then consented to let him round up his scattered band for the long march back to San Carlos.

THE COLUMN MOVED SLOWLY NORTHward, small groups of Chiricahuas joining it daily until there were more than 300 who had to be fed from the dwindling rations of the pack train. "All the old Chiricahuas were piled on mules, donkeys and ponies," Captain Bourke said. "So were the weak little children and feeble women. The great majority streamed along on foot, nearly all wearing garlands of cottonwood foliage to screen them from the sun." For most of the march Geronimo kept far to the rear, trying to convince reluctant members of his band to join the procession or searching for those who might have been away on hunts or on private raids.

Soon after the column crossed into Arizona on June 10, the territorial newspapers began clamoring for the heads of Geronimo and his warriors, demanding that they be executed and their women and children exiled to Indian Territory. Somehow the Chiricahuas learned of these threats—probably from officers who obtained the newspapers, repeated the stories within hearing of the Apache scouts who then told the Chiricahuas— and Geronimo and his lieutenants vanished again into the mountains.

The main column moved on to San Carlos, however, with the women and children, and months passed before the cautious warriors began coming in to join them. Crook sent Lieutenant Britton Davis with the Apache scouts down to the border to make searches for Geronimo and assure him that he would be safe at San Carlos. Not until late in February 1884 did Geronimo suddenly appear at the border crossing. He was riding on a white pony at the head of a herd of 350 beef cattle that he had stolen from Mexican ranchers for the purpose of starting livestock raising on the reservation.

To avoid difficulties with the Mexican Government, Crook ordered the cattle seized as soon as they reached San Carlos, and authorized payment of compensation to the Mexican ranchers from whom the animals had been stolen. Although Geronimo's anger was aroused by the seizure, in the end his people obtained their share of the beef, which was later issued to them as agency rations. But there was no longer a breeding herd.

As soon as he had settled down again at San Carlos, Geronimo petitioned Crook for a better location for his people, a place where there was plenty of grass and water for ranching and farming. He particularly wanted to move to Eagle Creek, but Crook could not help him. The Eagle Creek lands had been withdrawn from the reservation for settlement by whites. Eventually Geronimo was given an area along Turkey Creek that was suitable for small ranches, but Washington bureaucrats in the Indian Office refused to allow them any livestock, insisting that they adopt methods of farming suited to the East but that were impracticable in the arid Southwest. They were given wagons, plows, and harness that was too large for their wiry ponies. "The ponies, unaccustomed to a slow gait, preferred to trot or gallop," observed Lieutenant Davis, "and the plow-points were oftener above ground than in it."

Yet somehow the Chiricahuas managed to grow small crops of corn. Captain Crawford reported that the grain might make it possible to reduce government food allowances, but the Apaches had other plans. They used a considerable amount of their corn to secretly make tiswin, an alcoholic drink strictly forbidden by General Crook. The brewing process was fairly simple. After being soaked in moistened grass until it sprouted, the corn was then ground and boiled, the resulting liquid resembling beer that, as Geronimo said, "had the power of intoxication, and was very highly prized."

AFTER ONE OF THE CHIRICAHUA LEADERS named Kayatennae was caught making tiswin, he was arrested and sentenced to three years in irons at the federal prison at Alcatraz. Not long after he was taken away rumors began spreading that Kayatennae had been hanged by the Army and that Geronimo was next on the list of victims. This aroused all the old anxieties and fears of betrayal that lingered in Geronimo's mind, and by the late spring of 1885 he was also becoming resentful over the unfairness of reservation rules. He saw the Army officers relieving the tedium of their lives with whiskey and other forms of alcohol, and could not understand why they forbade his people to make and drink their favorite beverage.

On May 15, Geronimo's discontent came to a head when he joined several other tribal leaders in a demonstration outside Lieutenant Davis' tent. The Chiricahuas told Davis that they had agreed on a peace with the Americans, but that nothing had been said about their conduct among themselves. "They were not children to be taught how to live with their women and what they should eat or drink. All their lives they had eaten and drunk what seemed good to them. . . . They had complied with all they had promised to do when they had their talk with the General in Mexico; had kept the peace and harmed no one. Now they were being punished for things they had a right to do as long as they did no harm to others."

Lieutenant Davis told them that tiswin was forbidden because drunken Indians did not know what they were doing. Although Geronimo took little part in the discussion, Davis could see that he was angry and as soon as the Apaches left he sent a warning telegram through channels to Crook. The message was pigeonholed by an inept superior officer, and Crook never received it. Forty-eight hours later Geronimo with 144 followers, including about a hundred women and children, left the reservation. This time Davis could not send a telegram because Geronimo and his warriors had cut the wires in several places, refastening the breaks with thin strips of buckskin so they could not easily be found and repaired.

This last breakaway of Geronimo started one of the longest and most publicized military campaigns of the Indian Wars, involving before it ended thousands of soldiers in pursuit of fewer than fifty warriors, and inspiring a multitude of blood-and-thunder newspaper stories.

"I DID NOT LEAVE OF MY OWN ACCORD," Geronimo was to tell Crook afterward, explaining that he had been informed several times by friends that the Army was planning to arrest and hang him. "I want to know now who it was ordered me to be arrested. I was praying to the light and to the darkness, to God and to the sun, to let me live quietly there with

Geronimo and Natchez at Fort Bowie, Arizona, after surrendering to General Miles in 1886.
Courtesy of the Western History Collections, University of Oklahoma Library.

my family. I don't know what the reason was that people should speak badly of me. . . . Very often there are stories put in the newspapers that I am to be hanged. I don't want that any more. When a man tries to do right, such stories ought not to be put in the newspapers."

With his usual ingenuity, Geronimo eluded pursuit by the cavalry, quickly crossed into Mexico, and reached his old refuge in the Sierra Madre. And once again Crook ordered Captain Crawford to go in pursuit of him. This time Crawford was accompanied by a hardbitten frontiersman, Tom Horn, serving as chief of the Apache scouts. (In an autobiography, which has the veracity of a dime novel, Horn exaggerated his importance in the campaign and added his name to the Geronimo legend.) While Crawford and Horn were tracking into Mexico, an Apache leader named Ulzana conducted bloody raids into New Mexico and Arizona, some of which were credited in the press to Geronimo.

Not until January 9, 1886, did Crawford find Geronimo's *ranchería,* and two days later Geronimo with his characteristic aplomb came in for a conference. After several long discussions he agreed to meet Crook within two moons somewhere near the border. During the inter-

val a large party of Mexican irregular troops in search of bounty scalps attacked the Apache scouts, killing Crawford and slightly wounding Horn. Geronimo nevertheless kept his promise and met with Crook, on March 25.

The meetings just below the Arizona border at El Canon de los Embudos were like scenes from a carefully staged drama. Every word of the rich dialogue of confrontation between Geronimo and Crook was set down by Captain Bourke, and the images of the participants were preserved for history by photographer Camillus S. Fly of Tombstone, Arizona.

In his speeches Geronimo tried to explain his past actions, but Crook responded by calling him a liar. When Geronimo spoke of returning to the reservation, the general bluntly told him that he had only two choices—surrender unconditionally or stay on the warpath, in which case he would be hunted down and killed. By the third day of the meetings, Geronimo knew that Crook meant to make prisoners of him and his warriors, and send them to some distant place. One by one the warriors capitulated, and then Geronimo offered his hand to Crook. "I give myself up to you," he said. "Do with me what you please. Once I moved about like the

wind. . . . That's all I have to say now, except a few words. I should like to have my wife and daughter come to meet me at Fort Bowie."

CROOK PROMISED GERONIMO THAT HIS family would join him in imprisonment, and then left the meeting place to return to Fort Bowie ahead of the column of scouts and the surrendered Chiricahuas. He sent a telegram to the General of the Army, Philip Sheridan, announcing Geronimo's surrender. Three days later he had to send another message informing Sheridan that Geronimo and forty members of his band once again had fled to the Sierra Madre of Mexico. Sheridan was furious, condemning Crook for slackness of command and refusing to accept his explanations. Crook resigned, and on April 2 General Nelson Miles replaced him.

The villain in this last flight of Geronimo was a trader and whiskey runner to the Indians named Bob Tribolett, who had slipped across the border and unknown to the Army officers supplied the Apaches with mescal and other liquors. As soon as the Indians reached a state of intoxication, Tribolett began hinting to them that they would be hanged as soon as the Army got them to Fort Bowie, thus playing upon the suspicions that were always close to the surface in their minds.

"We were not under any guard at this time," Geronimo said afterward. "I feared treachery and decided to remain in Mexico." One of his lieutenants, Natchez, was more direct in his explanation of the flight: "I was afraid I was going to be taken off somewhere I didn't like, to some place I didn't know. I thought all who were taken away would die."

Many Army officers, including General Crook, suspected that Tribolett may have been sent by the "Indian Ring" of Arizona to frighten Geronimo into continuing the fighting. Civilian contractors and traders had profited from the long Apache wars, dealing with both sides, and they had a keen interest in the maintenance of the numerous forts and the continued presence of soldiers in the territories. Whether Tribolett's action was deliberately planned or not, it certainly resulted in a bonanza for the "Indian Ring."

Soon after he took command, the flamboyant and ambitious General Miles quickly put 5,000 soldiers (or about a third of the total combat strength of the U.S. Army) into the field. He also had 500 Apache scouts and many irregular civilian militia. For quick communication he organized an expensive system of heliographs to flash messages back and forth across Arizona and New Mexico. The enemy to be subdued by this powerful force consisted of Geronimo and twenty-four warriors who throughout that summer of 1886 were also under constant pursuit by thousands of Mexican soldiers.

ON AUGUST 23, GERONIMO FINALLY CHOSE to surrender to Lieutenant Charles Gatewood and two Apache scouts who found him in a Sierra Madre canyon. Geronimo laid his rifle down and shook hands with Gatewood, inquiring calmly about his health. He then asked about matters back in the United States. How were the Chiricahuas faring? Gatewood told him that those who had surrendered had already been sent to Florida for imprisonment. If Geronimo would surrender to General Miles, he would be sent to Florida to join them.

Geronimo wanted to know what kind of man General Miles was. Was his voice

harsh or agreeable to the ear? Was he cruel or kind-hearted? Did he look you in the eye or down at the ground when he talked? Would he keep his promises? Then he said to Gatewood: "Consider yourself one of us and not a white man . . . as an Apache, what would you advise me to do?"

"I would trust General Miles and take him at his word," Gatewood replied.

And so, for what was to be the last time in his life, Geronimo surrendered. Many Arizonians as well as President Grover Cleveland wanted to hang the old warrior, but Miles kept his promise to send him to Florida, and on September 8 put him on a railroad train at Bowie Station under heavy guard. Two days later Geronimo's enemies in the War Department in Washington ordered him hauled off the train at San Antonio while they debated whether or not he had surrendered or been captured. If it was the latter, they would hang him. While he awaited his fate in San Antonio a photographer posed him against a wall for a poignant portrait of a defeated 60-year-old Apache halfway into the white man's world, clad in a mixed costume of sack coat, hat, and boots over his native breechcloth.

After a month of bureaucratic haggling, the Army sent him on his way to Florida. For some time he was kept in a separate prison from that of his family and friends; at last in May 1888 they were all brought together at Mt. Vernon Barracks north of Mobile, Alabama. There the dying began in that warm humid land so unlike the high dry country of their birth. More than 100 died of a disease diagnosed as consumption, and when the Government took their children away to the Indian school at Carlisle, Pennsylvania, many more died there. Old friends and old enemies interceded for them. General Crook, Captain Bourke, General Howard, Surgeon Walter Reed, and Lieutenant Hugh Scott all came to offer their help, but the people of Arizona refused to permit Geronimo and his Chiricahuas to return to their homeland.

AT LAST IN 1894 THE KIOWAS AND COmanches, after learning of their plight, offered these ancient Apache enemies a part of their reservation near Fort Sill in Oklahoma. There, nearby the fort, Geronimo and the other survivors built houses and plowed small farms. Ger-

onimo began to enjoy life again with his wife and children, taking pride in his watermelon patch, growing enough melons to sell some at the fort. He adapted quickly to the white man's economic system, and because of his fame found it easy to sell his autograph, or bows and arrows, and even old hats to curious visitors. One visitor in 1905 described him as "a smiling, well-kept, well-dressed Indian about five feet nine inches tall . . . dressed in a well-fitting blue cloth suit of citizen's clothes."

It was at about this time that Stephen M. Barrett, a school superintendent in the nearby town of Lawton, asked Geronimo to dictate the story of his life, a task that he willingly undertook when he was assured that he would be paid for it. The result is a unique account of Indian life told from the viewpoint of a warrior-leader.

Although Geronimo was still technically a prisoner of war, the Army permitted him to attend, under guard, international fairs and expositions at Omaha, Buffalo, and St. Louis. He attracted large crowds and profited from the sale of autographs, buttons, hats, and photographs of himself. One Sunday while in Omaha his guard took him out into the country for a buggy ride and they became lost in the fields of tall corn. Darkness fell before they could find their way back to the fairgrounds, and as they were returning through the city streets they could hear the shouts of newsboys selling an extra edition of a local paper with headlines announcing that Geronimo had escaped and was on his way back to Arizona. He would always be a target for the sensational press, but such stories also helped sell more autographs and photos.

When President Theodore Roosevelt invited him to Washington for the inaugural parade, he was sent a check for $171 to cover his travel expenses. Geronimo took the check to his Lawton bank, deposited all but one dollar, and then boarded the train for Washington. At every stop along the way he sold autographs to crowds at the stations. When he rode down Pennsylvania Avenue with five other Indian "chiefs" he practically stole the show from Teddy Roosevelt, and then went home to Oklahoma with a trunkful of new clothes and his pockets full of money. He was no miser, however; he gave freely of his earnings to less fortunate tribespeople and sent needed goods to relatives and friends in Arizona.

IN HIS LAST YEARS GERONIMO BECAME fond of automobiles, although he never owned one. When he was allowed to attend rodeos and local fairs in Oklahoma, he would often ride in one of these new mobile inventions of the white man, preferring the bright red models with shiny brass trimmings. For a stunt at one Wild West show he shot a buffalo from the seat of a racing car. In one of his last public appearances, he was persuaded by a photographer to pose in a black top hat at the wheel of a resplendent open car— the perfect comic image of the American Indian as he was seen in the popular culture of the nation at the beginning of the 20th century.

It was a fall from a horse that finished the old Chiricahua. On a cold February night in 1909 he was returning home from Lawton, where he had sold some bows and arrows and obtained some whiskey. He fell from his saddle beside the bank of a creek, and lay exposed for several hours. Three days later, February 17, he was dead from pneumonia. His body was scarred with many wounds, but, as he had always boasted, no bullet killed him. At 80, or perhaps a year or two older, he had outlived most of his contemporaries of the Indian wars in the West.

The literature on Geronimo is extensive, but author Dee Brown recommends Geronimo, the Man, His Time, His Place *(1976) by Angie Debo as the best documented and most comprehensive biography.*

The Emergence of Modern America

The last decade of the nineteenth century produced a great deal of social unrest. There always had been rich and poor in the United States, but never had the disparity seemed so great. Business tycoons flaunted their wealth by building ostentatious mansions and throwing lavish parties, while poor families huddled in overcrowded rooms and ate the coarsest foods. Farmers were threatened by low market prices for their products on the one hand, and by having to pay onerous shipping and storage charges to monopolistic railroads on the other.

In 1892 discontented farmers and their allies launched the People's Party, better known as the Populists, because they believed that neither the Republicans nor the Democrats were responsive to their needs. The Populists gained strength the following year when a severe depression struck, resulting in large-scale unemployment, violent strikes, and farm foreclosures. Populist influence peaked in 1896 when the party endorsed William Jennings Bryan for the presidency, but it never succeeded in attracting large numbers of workers because of differences over issues such as inflation. The gradual return of prosperity and the onset of the Spanish-American war in 1898 undermined the movement. "The Cycle of Reform" treats this turbulent decade, and makes some comparisons with more recent years.

During the 1890s and after, many Americans became concerned with what they regarded as the "threat" of immigration. Immigration to the United States previously had come from places such as Ireland and Germany, now the flow was from Eastern and Southern Europe. Italians, Poles, Hungarians, and others, with their cultural, religious, and linguistic differences, seemed more "foreign" than the foreigners who had come before. "Ellis Island and the American Immigration Experience" tells of the estimated 12,000,000 people who passed through this point, and of the efforts made to restrict or halt admittance of those deemed undesirable. "The Afro-Cuban Community in Ybor City and Tampa, 1886–1910" describes another immigrant experience, this one influenced by both race and ethnicity.

Despite a host of social programs designed to help them, the urban poor seem more numerous and worse off than ever before. "Fighting Poverty the Old-Fashioned Way" describes an earlier institution that became popular in a number of cities: the settlement house. Although the author recognizes that various existing agencies already serve some of the purposes settlement houses did, he argues that a similar *approach* might be worth considering.

Two articles in this unit deal with technology. "Wings for Man" describes how Wilbur and Orville Wright achieved one of humanity's oldest dreams. On December 17, 1903, Orville made the first sustained, controlled flight by a powered aircraft. It would change the world forever. "Wings for Man" describes how these two hard-working, inventive men realized their goal, and their subsequent destructive battles to protect their invention through lawsuits.

Motion pictures had been around for a long time, but until the first decade of the twentieth century they were little more than novelties. After about 1905 "nickel theaters" were springing up by the thousands. Most were drab, dirty little places that critics condemned as squalid dens of iniquity. Later, luxurious theaters were built in order to "secure the patronage of a better class of people," as one owner put it. "Learning to Go to the Movies" chronicles the growth of what the author refers to as this "great democratic art form."

"George Washington Carver: Creative Scientist" tells the struggle of a young black man to gain an education appropriate to his intelligence. "He made no great theoretical breakthroughs," the author writes, "and did not develop a single new commercially successful product." What he did do, through his teaching and research, was to make scientific agricultural techniques available to thousands of struggling farmers.

Looking Ahead: Challenge Questions

Is it possible to predict coming events by examining earlier periods in history? How did the "dark period" of 1893 to 1897 lead to an era of reform?

In what ways do complaints about immigration earlier in the century resemble those being made today? Any differences?

How did settlement houses seek to better the lives of the poor? Did they offer anything that would be relevant today?

The Cycle of Reform

William L. O'Neill

William L. O'Neill is professor of history at Rutgers University. He is the author of, among other books, A Better World *and* Feminism in America, *both published by Transaction.*

1890 has a special meaning to historians of the United States, for the census taken that year revealed a momentous fact. The Census Bureau put it as follows: "Up to and including 1890 the country had a frontier of settlement, but at present the unsettled area has been so broken into by isolated bodies of settlement that there can hardly be said to be a frontier line." A young historian, Frederick Jackson Turner, would soon use this sentence to begin one of the most influential articles ever written about our past. "The Significance of the Frontier in American History," a paper first given by Turner in July l0, 1893 during the World's Columbian Exposition in Chicago, has probably inspired the writing of more books and articles than any other piece of scholarship by an American historian. The central idea, advanced by Turner in this and later works, was that "the existence of an area of free land, its continuous recession, and the advance of American settlement westward explain American development."

What became known as "the frontier thesis" stimulated generations of historians, first to spread Turner's gospel, then to demolish it. Almost every key point that Turner made has since been refuted, and few if any accept today that the existence of free land determined the American character. Yet, like the Columbian Exposition itself—perhaps the greatest world's fair and arguably the most exuberant—Turner's thesis remains a monument to the boldness and optimism of his time. His daring is self-evident. Turner was 31, his Ph.D only three years old, and yet at a meeting of the American Historical Association he informed his seniors that they had contrived to miss the point of the entire national experience. His optimism is less manifest since, if American development was produced by a wilderness that had just disappeared, the future might seem gloomy. But Turner's thesis suggested that the frontier had done its work so well that it was no longer needed. Having triumphed over nature, American democracy was now self-renewing. Americans would go on to greater things, using their pioneer virtues to build a great industrial nation.

The Turnerians were right for the wrong reasons. Turner argued that, in addition to democracy, the "composite nationality" of Americans, our blend of ethnic groups, resulted from the frontier experience. But most historians believe that both the integration of people from many different nations and the extension of democratic rights are products of urbanization. No matter, he had identified many of the most important national traits, and by provoking historians to look at America in a fresh way stimulated lines of inquiry that would later prove more fruitful. Historians still admire Turner, for attacking the hard questions, for his originality, for his eloquence, for the breadth of his learning—he drew upon all the contemporary social sciences—for his love of research, and for his democratic values.

We also envy Turner his optimism, which now seems remarkable given the misery around him. Today many consider the fact that at least 15 percent of all Americans live in poverty to be a national disgrace. Yet in 1890 when Jacob Riis wrote his powerful expose of destitution in New York City he called it *How the Other Half Lives,* and understated the case at that since actually three fifths of the nation fell below the poverty line. Others besides Riis were troubled by the great distance between the few who monopolized America's industrial wealth, and the many who toiled to produce it. Edward Bellamy spoke to the worriers in his utopian novel *Looking Backward* (1888). Set in the year 2000, it described a cooperative social order which had replaced the cutthroat capitalism of America's Gilded Age. Although *Looking Backward* sold a million copies to a population one quarter the size of ours, and prompted the formation of many "Nationalist" clubs devoted to Bellamy's gospel, the tangible results were slight. Most educated Americans were unmoved by the suffering of the poor and did nothing about it.

Yet poverty declined all the same. By

 From *Society,* Vol. 27, No. 5, July/August 1990, pp. 63-68. © 1990 by Transaction Publishers. Reprinted by permission.

1920 the earlier figure had been reversed, three-fifths of the population now being above, rather than below, the poverty line. And, irregularly to be sure, poverty would go on declining until the 1970s. In a sense, the optimism of Turner's generation has been justified by events. To us that generation often seems complacent beyond belief, quarreling about tariffs and currency questions while ignoring the distress of millions. But they did not view their era as we do, from the vantage point of a century of further development. In 1890 there were men and women still alive who could remember when nine out of ten Americans scratched a bare living from the soil, when the line of settlement was drawn east of the Mississippi, when travel proceeded no faster than a horse could walk or a ship under canvas sail. To Americans the nineteenth century was an age, not just of steam, but of miracles.

CLASS CONFLICT

Even so the basic confidence of the Gilded Age is all the more extraordinary considering that it was a time of savage industrial warfare, labor-management disputes often being settled by those with the greatest firepower. In the summer of 1877 a wave of railroad strikes, together with sympathetic walkouts by factory workers and miners, brought the nation literally to a halt. In Baltimore after nine strikers were killed by state militiamen, riots broke out that took the lives of another 50 persons. In Chicago 19 perished when police and cavalry attacked an unauthorized demonstration. Twenty-six were killed in Pittsburgh during a night of rioting and looting that saw 2,000 railroad cars destroyed and a wall of fire three miles long engulf the center city. Though the death rate was never so high again, shooting strikers remained a management tool as late as 1937, when guards at a Republic Steel plant killed or wounded almost a hundred unarmed people.

Few issues troubled thoughtful men and women in the 1890s so much as class conflict, which involved not only workers but farmers—who were more numerous than workingmen and more political. In 1892 many of them organized as the People's, or Populist Party, and subsequently gained control of a handful of western states. With a platform calling for nationalization of the railroad and

telegraph companies, extensive government aid to agriculture, and soft money, they threw a fright into the middle classes. Predictions of a bloody apocalypse more often involved workers than farmers, but some alarmists managed to include both. During the presidential campaign of 1896, when William Jennings Bryan inherited the Populists' following—though, except for soft money, not their program—young Theodore Roosevelt compared prominent Democrats and union heads to the leaders of the Paris Commune. They would try to make a revolution, he was sure, and he expected to meet them on the field of battle. Alternatively, or perhaps afterward, he favored "taking ten or a dozen of their leaders out, standing them against a wall, and shooting them dead."

Of course Roosevelt was excitable, others beside Mark Hanna regarding him

---

To Americans, the nineteenth century was an age, not just of steam, but of miracles

---

as a "madman." But fantasies of revolution aside, the 1890s were a remarkably turbulent decade, marred by a series of brutal strikes, notably against Carnegie Steel and the Pullman Sleeping Car Company, the Populist uprising, and a market panic in 1893 followed by the worst depression Americans had yet experienced. The last massacre of the Indian wars took place at a creek known as Wounded Knee in South Dakota, where, on December 28, 1890, almost 200 Sioux, men, women, and children alike, were shot by troopers of the 7th U.S. Cavalry. There were more lynchings by far during the 1890s than in any subsequent decade, 230 during one year alone. The level of collective domestic violence was higher than it ever would be again, including even the riot-plagued 1960s.

GREAT EVENTS HAVE ANTECEDENTS

What does this mean as we look to the end of our own century? One thing it fails to suggest is that rioting will become popular again. The bloody strikes of the 1890s resembled previous ones,

while lynchings and urban mob actions had an even longer tradition. The Populists too were foreshadowed by earlier agrarian movements. Conversely, little has happened in recent years to indicate that the 1990s will be a stormy decade. Anything is possible, and we remember that much of the violence of the 1960s seemed to come out of nowhere. But it remains a rule of thumb that great events have antecedents, which, though easier to recognize after the fact, are usually visible before it. If such exist today they have escaped attention.

On the other hand, the fallow years we have been passing through must end sooner or later. Long ago Arthur M. Schlesinger, Sr. observed that there was a cycle in American political life which produced waves of reform every few decades. Today the pattern seems less regular than he supposed, but that it exists is hard to dispute. In the 1860s Republicans abolished slavery, passed the Homestead Act, and introduced other important measures, before taking the position Andrew Carnegie expressed in 1886: "If asked what important law I should change I must perforce say none; the laws are perfect." The ideology behind his remark was that of laissez-faire, which had created a great body of literature to the effect that government meddling in social and economic affairs always made things worse. In practice advocates of laissez-faire found exceptions to the rule, as when manufacturers secured tariffs to preserve "infant" industries long after they had become giants. Its imperfections notwithstanding, middle class people seemed thoroughly committed to laissez-faire in 1890, and yet, before very long, they would turn their backs upon it.

Knowing this does not help us determine what the prospects are for reforms in the 1990s, but history suggests the kind of indicators we ought to be looking for. Forceful social and political criticism often prepares the way for change, and did so toward the end of the nineteenth century. Edward Bellamy was one such critic, and so also was Henry George, whose great tract *Progress and Poverty* (1879), identified the "unearned increment" owners derived from rising land values as the curse of the laboring classes. Though his proposal for a "single tax" on real estate failed, George, like Bellamy, made people think about the sources of inequality. So too did Henry Demarest Lloyd, whose *Wealth*

Against Commonwealth (1894) brilliantly attacked monopolies as a whole and Standard Oil in particular. It, and Lloyd's personal efforts, led the Populist convention that year to call for public ownership of all monopolies.

The Social Gospel movement was another precursor to the age of reform. Under laissez-faire Protestant clergymen saw inequality as part of the divine order. Henry Ward Beecher, the most famous minister of his day, announced that "God has intended the great to be great and the little to be little." Poverty was thus predestined, and yet at the same time de-

---

Most educated Americans were unmoved by the suffering of the poor and did nothing about it

---

served, for Beecher also said "no man suffers from poverty unless it be more than his fault—unless it also be his sin." This had to change if the leading denominations were not to remain obstacles to reform, and change it did, thanks to Walter Rauschenbusch and other progressive church leaders. Rauschenbusch—then a Baptist preacher in New York, later a theologian—was inspired by Henry George and the English Fabians to believe that it was not the church's role simply to interpret poverty and injustice, but actively to combat them. In 1892 he helped found the Brotherhood of the Kingdom as a means of doing so. Though fundamentalists were beyond reach, Rauschenbusch and his allies would in time win over the mainstream denominations, making them engines of reform instead of barriers to it.

The social settlement movement would also contribute much to the coming struggle, though few could have guessed this in 1890, when there were only a handful of settlements and Hull House was just a year old. Social settlements enabled middle class men and women, usually recent college graduates, to live in slums and mingle with the local population. In time settlements would provide many social services, but the original intent was for residents to be helpful neighbors rather than case workers, to

teach by example and establish rapport between the social classes. For many, including Jane Addams, living with the urban poor was a radicalizing experience. The need was so great, their resources so meager, that residents usually came to believe government alone could provide solutions. Settlements were training camps for young men and women who would become officers in the reform army when it finally mustered.

George, Bellamy, and Lloyd were journalists and best selling authors, but the seeds of reform were being sown by professors, too. The end of the last century was a time of enormous intellectual vitality in a broad range of disciplines. The Ph.D., today often regarded as stultifying, had just been introduced and the first generation of scholars to possess it was notable both for ability and intellectual courage. William James and John Dewey in philosophy, Richard T. Ely, John Commons, Thorstein Veblen, and Simon Patten in economics, Lester Ward, E.A. Ross, and Albion Small in sociology, Turner, Charles Beard and James Harvey Robinson in history, among many others, destroyed the assumptions upon which laissez-faire depended.

Oliver Wendell Holmes, Jr. argued that legal principles were based on history and experience, not logic. The law is made by judges, he insisted, and can be unmade by them as well when circumstances warrant. Veblen struck out against orthodox economics for being static, abstract, and preoccupied with discovering non-existent natural laws. His economics was an evolutionary science that saw man as much more than simply a producer and consumer of wealth. Morality also, Dewey held, was evolutionary and progressive. He denounced contemporary ethics for being archaic survivals that stood in the way of needed social and political improvements.

Together they staged what Morton White called "the revolt against formalism." By formalism White meant traditional logic, classical economics and jurisprudence, deductive reasoning, and all ways of thinking that were not pragmatic, experimental, and inductive. The rebellious scholars were, or tried to be, scientific, not in the sense of establishing new laws in their disciplines to replace old ones, but rather by employing sophisticated methods in their research, and by challenging the received wisdom. Formalists upheld a status quo based, as they saw it, upon immutable truths, un-

like the rebels, who believed that truth was whatever worked for the good of society. Many of their students went on to become a new kind of reformer, a social technician equipped with the latest tools for practical problem solving. Some of these were what we would now call technocrats, but the best were imbued with the humane, rational, tolerant, flexible, and democratic spirit of their teachers.

Though the rebels against formalism did not create progressivism all by themselves, they performed several essential functions in addition to destroying the

---

Under laissez-faire, Protestant clergymen saw inequality as part of the divine order

---

ideology of laissez-faire. Their work supplied a generation of reformers with arguments and ideas. And they fashioned the academic culture as we know it. We too believe that scholarly as well as scientific research ought to be pragmatic, instrumental and deductive, and, many of us still think that ideas should be used to better the human condition. Dewey and Veblen and their colleagues set the standard liberal academicians have measured themselves against ever since.

URBAN REFORM

Besides intellectual excitement, there was another way in which the 1890s were less barren than they seemed at the time. Though frustrated at the national level, reform blossomed in the cities. Eastern urban reformers tended to be businessmen and professionals mobilized against what they saw as corrupt and incompetent political machines. Their ambitions were often confined to making local government honest and business-like. William L. Strong, mayor of New York from 1895 to 1897, was this kind of reformer. Another type, more common in the Midwest, was epitomized by Hazen S. Pingree, mayor of Detroit from 1890 to 1897. Pingree and his colleagues not only wanted good government, but welfare services for the poor, the regulation of utilities and transport companies, and many other changes.

Urban reform was made necessary by the phenomenal growth of cities, especially in the Midwest. In 1880 one out of every five Midwesterners lived in towns over 4,000, a decade later one in three. In only ten years the urban population had doubled, Chicago, for example, growing from 500,000 to a population of about one million. It would have been difficult even for well run urban governments to cope with this breakneck expansion, which put intolerable strains upon even the most basic services. But the cities, far from being efficiently led, were under the control of bosses who, in connivance with dishonest businessmen, ran them for personal profit. The function of urban government, as they saw it, was to generate bribes and graft.

Middle class people resented this system, but, while times were good, not enough to challenge it. Then came the four year business collapse which followed the panic of 1893. Hard times greatly increased demands upon city governments, while their revenue base declined. Public utilities such as trolley systems, telephone companies, and water works, faced with shrinking earnings tended to raise their rates—despite the fact that most of their customers had less money to spend than before. This outrageous behavior, made possible by monopolization and the corrupt public officials who sustained it, aroused widespread anger. Since it affected virtually everyone in their roles as consumers, the arrogance of power had a unifying effect, bringing together small businessmen, professionals, women's organizations, trade union leaders and others who had never joined forces before.

David Thelen has shown in detail how this process worked in Wisconsin. The high levels of unemployment, as much as 50 percent in some cities, and sharp declines in income experienced by the business and professional classes, undermined faith in the status quo. Investigative journalists, discussion clubs, extension lectures by economists and sociologists from the state university, stirred citizens, got them to talking with one another, and helped them define their problems and seek collective solutions. Political organizations were formed to eliminate graft and corruption, place more employees under civil service, and reduce taxes. The discovery that lower taxes meant fewer services at a time when more were needed led to calls for action against wealthy individual and corporate tax evaders. In order to reduce the power of venal or unresponsive officials, reformers fought for instruments of "direct democracy," such as the recall and referendum.

In the nineteenth century, like today, Congress could not lead and the presidents refused to

---

Then came efforts to effectively regulate utilities, and even replace privately owned utilities with cooperative or municipally owned institutions. As many problems could only be solved with the aid or approval of state government, reformers in different communities reached out to one another. Robert M. La Follette was won over to reform in 1897 and elected governor three years later. Under La Follette Wisconsin became the most politically advanced state in the nation, initiating many reforms that were copied elsewhere. In a few more years "progressivism," as the movement came to be called, was a national phenomenon.

Every state had a somewhat different experience, reform did not always prevail, and even when it did the results often fell short of what was expected. Even so, American political life was dramatically altered in the first decade of this century because of what had gone on earlier. The 1890s, and especially the years from 1893 to 1897, which had been a dark period shadowed by economic collapse and abortive farmer and worker uprisings, came in retrospect to assume a larger significance. It turned out to have been the seed time for an age of reform, an overture to greatness. And when the Progressive Era was born its midwife would be none other than Theodore Roosevelt, the onetime conservative having become a liberal in response to changing circumstances.

UNCERTAIN PARALLELS

What this means for us today is uncertain despite some obvious parallels. In 1890, as in 1990, the United States was suffering from decades of feeble government. Then, as now, the major parties were evenly balanced, Republicans winning most presidential elections while Democrats usually controlled the House and sometimes also the Senate. While partisanship was much more intense than today, the parties did not offer strikingly different programs and neither possessed a mandate for change. Unable to cope with poverty or the consequences of growth, politicians fought over the currency question, which, though hardly the nation's most urgent problem, seemed within their power to answer. Like today, Congress could not lead and the presidents refused to.

Our federal system of government requires presidential leadership to solve problems, but in the late nineteenth century chief executives were so retiring that Woodrow Wilson called his study of how the nation conducted its affairs *Congressional Government* (1885). Being locally oriented Congress cannot define the national interest and is always under pressure to service powerful constituents. Congressional government consisted largely of log rolling, pork barreling, and the delivery of favors. In 1890 there had been no strong presidents since Lincoln. We have not had a strong president since Nixon, who was no Lincoln to be sure, yet who made some historic changes.

Ronald Reagan might seem an exception, but though he was politically formidable, he was also the first activist president since Andrew Jackson to weaken the federal government. Reagan destroyed government's ability to solve problems by raising the national debt to paralyzing levels, while at the same time fixing in stone the twin rules that defense spending must not be cut nor new taxes levied. Until the budget is brought under control there can be no new or expanded government programs, but that cannot be accomplished without reducing defense spending or increasing taxes. This fiscal Catch-22 is Reagan's legacy to America and, so long as it lasts, there can only be presidents like Bush—who, weight apart, reminds one of Grover Cleveland.

Yet there remains the hope that a dynamic new leader has arisen who may lead us out of stagnation. That man is, of course, Mikhail Gorbachev. If he brings the cold war to an end, as seems entirely possible, the defense budget will no longer be sacred. And reductions in defense spending can hardly fail to benefit the nation, by reducing the deficit, or funding new programs, or by some combination of both. Most of the traditional harbingers of reform do not now exist. There is no great literature of protest, except against Reaganomics: there are no promising political movements on the state and local level; neither war nor a great depression quickens the pace of change. But if post-cold war America enjoys the kind of affluence this country once knew, that itself might encourage progress. After all, two of the three twentieth-century reform eras came during periods of record abundance. Even now, just off stage, another Roosevelt may be waiting.

READINGS SUGGESTED BY THE AUTHOR:

Billington, R. *Frederick Jackson Turner.* New York: Oxford University Press, 1973.

Davis, A. *Spearheads for Reform: The Social Settlements and the Progressive Movement, 1890–1914.* New York: Oxford University Press, 1967.

Link, A. & R. McCormick. *Progressivism.* Arlington Heights, Ill.: Harlan Davidson, Inc., 1983.

Thelen, D. *The New Citizenship: Origins of Progressivism in Wisconsin, 1885–1900.* Columbia, Mo.: University of Missouri Press, 1972.

White, M. *Social Thought in America: The Revolt Against Formalism.* New York: Viking Press, 1949.

The Afro-Cuban Community in Ybor City and Tampa, 1886–1910

Nancy Raquel Mirabal

Nancy Raquel Mirabal is a doctoral candidate in American history at the University of Michigan. She is working on a dissertation that explores the relationship among race, ethnicity, and identity.

In 1886, the same year that Cuba eliminated slavery, Vincente Martinez Ybor built the first cigar factory in the Tampa area of Florida and established a company town known as Ybor City. Once the cigar factory was constructed, Martinez Ybor had little trouble finding workers. As a result of severe depressions in Cuba during the mid-1880s, the arrival of a million Spanish workers between 1882 and 1894, and the introduction of two hundred former slaves into the Cuban labor force, thousands of Cuban immigrants, both black and white, travelled to the United States in search of employment (1).

When Afro Cubans arrived in Ybor City to work in the cigar factories, local laws and customs defined them as black and assigned them to the same legal category as African Americans, despite the differences in language and heritage (2). At the same time, they maintained an identity with and cultural ties to the larger Cuban community, which was viewed as white (3). Since being both black and Cuban (meaning white) was incompatible with the racial mores of Florida during the Jim Crow era, Afro Cubans created a separate community and a fluid identity which reflected both their cultural heritage and race. The manner in which they negotiated their identity and positioned themselves in

Ybor City, especially during the late nineteenth and early twentieth centuries, complicates the history of race and ethnicity in the United States—especially African American history.

Moreover, the difficulty in defining Cubans solely on the basis of race becomes increasingly clear when one considers that during this period, the Anglo population in Tampa often referred to the Cuban community, regardless of race or background, as "Cuban niggers" (4). By using negative racial references to characterize Cubans, some in the Anglo community in Tampa easily dismissed and devalued the Cuban immigrant community in Ybor City. While those outside the Cuban community failed to differentiate Cubans on the basis of race, within the Cuban community race factored in the participation of Afro Cubans in the Cuban nationalist movement and in the creation of cultural clubs.

To better understand the complex relationship between race and ethnicity it is necessary to briefly explore certain "sites" where contestation and negotiation of identities occurred. In Tampa, these included the cigar factories, nationalist movements and the Afro-Cuban club and mutual aid society *La Union Marti-Maceo*. Afro Cubans who immigrated to Ybor City encountered a community where residents could be heard speaking Spanish, where Spanish newspapers were readily available, and where Cuban immigrants owned grocery stores known as *bodegas* that sold Cuban and Spanish products. Cubans could be found discussing politics over their *cafe con leche* in "hole in the wall cafes," while old Cuban men played dominoes sur-

rounded by the odors of hot Cuban bread and the tang of "bright leaf tobacco mellowing in the dungeons of the cigar factories." The city that Vincente Martinez Ybor founded in 1886 would later be called the "Havana" of America by the Florida Branch of the Federal Writers Project Archives in 1941 (5).

Because immigrants were not expected to "fit in" or to radically alter their lifestyles to accommodate a standing community, Ybor City differed greatly from other cities located in the South. Not only did the city provide Afro Cubans with the space and independence to form a Black immigrant community, but the cigar factories that employed Afro Cubans offered them the needed economic security and social connections to sustain themselves and their community. Although the number of them who immigrated to Tampa was relatively low, ninety percent of the men and fifteen percent of the women worked in the cigar factories (6). More important, the cigar factories were not racially segregated and Afro Cubans sat next to white Cubans rolling cigars and listening to a *lector* read a variety of books and newspapers, including radical presses. This practice, also evident and popular in cigar factories in Cuba, kept cigarworkers informed of political developments in both Cuba and the United States. The *lectura* was taken very seriously by cigarmakers who depended on *el lector* to disseminate news, translate local English language newspapers and entertain them with novels (7).

The cigarworkers transferred a series of Cuban customs and traditions which gave them a degree of control over the

University of South Florida Library, Special Collections

Cigar factories gave immigrants valuable economic and social security within their community. Ninety percent of the men who immigrated to Tampa worked in cigar factories.

workplace. Individual workers arrived and departed freely, drank *el cafecito* throughout the day and smoked an unlimited amount of cigars while in the factory. Although the cigar factories were not racially segregated and Afro Cubans received the same wages as white Cubans for comparable work, labor was divided into several departments and stratified on the basis of sex. The majority of women worked as stemmers while the men rolled the cigars. Initially a boy's occupation, stemming was viewed as a stepping stone to a cigarmaking job. By 1870, however, it was fast becoming a separate occupation and manufacturers usually hired women for this "dirty, dead-end low wage labor" (8).

Many Afro Cubans attempted to transcend racial segregation laws in Ybor City by privileging their ethnicity over their race.

While Afro Cubans moved freely within Ybor City and worked next to white Cubans in the cigar factories, Florida's segregation laws sharpened racial realities for Cuban immigrants elsewhere in the area and state. Schools, hospitals, certain businesses and private clubs all subscribed to Florida's Jim Crow laws (9). Afro Cubans often travelled to the African American section of Tampa to attend school, receive medical attention or go to the only movie theater that was open to blacks. As a result, many Afro Cubans attempted to transcend the seemingly selective applications of racial segregation laws in Ybor City by privileging their ethnicity over their race. Resisting any formal interactions or alliances with African Americans during this period. Afro Cubans viewed themselves as primarily Cuban and participated in clubs and movements that addressed the concerns of Cubans on the island and in the United States (10). While some Afro Cubans responded in this manner because they believed that their stay in the United States was temporary, others, cognizant of the social, economic and political ramifications of being considered black in the United States, chose to alter their status rather than question racial segregation.

Ironically, racial divisions within the Cuban community marred certain pretenses of ethnic solidarity. During the late nineteenth century the emigre community in Ybor City worked to liberate Cuba from Spanish control. Those involved in the nationalist movement were dedicated to a "Cuba Libre" (11). Yet for many of the Afro Cubans who joined white Cubans in providing critical economic, political, and military support, race remained a factor and at times a barrier in organizing efforts for the Cuban War for Independence. Prominent Afro-Cuban leaders, including Bruno Roig, Comelio Brito, and Paulina and Ruperto Pedroso, endured racial animosities within and outside of revolutionary organizations.

When the Cuban patriot and national hero Jose Marti was invited by the Club Ignacio Agramonte in November 1891 to visit Ybor City, he was determined to directly confront the racism within the Cuban community. Marti recognized the importance of incorporating Afro Cubans into the nationalist movement. In his famous "Liceo" speech, Marti demanded that white Cubans alter their racist attitudes in the name of a "Cuba Libre" by reminding Cubans that this would be a "revolution [in which] all Cubans, regardless of color have participated" (12). To maximize his base of support, Marti's words had to be inclusive and yet critical of those who employed racist tactics and practices. He achieved this tenuous balance by requesting that Cubans put aside the racial divisions that stood in the way of a unified nationalist movement. His tactic for diffusing racial divisions was to construct an ethnic identity, a *Cubanidad,* strong enough to overcome racial differences. Moreover, the need to do so underscored the fact that racism was not exclusively a problem of the United States.

Marti recognized the importance of incorporating Afro Cubans into the nationalist movements and made a point of interacting and working closely with prominent Afro Cubans to show his dedication to racial solidarity. His speech in Ybor City indicated the value of Afro Cuban participation and even the very necessity of it if Cuban independence was to be successful. Attempts at unifying a nationalist movement had previously failed, which made Marti fully aware of the destructive consequences of racism to the cause of independence. During the 1890s, Afro Cubans helped found the Cuban Revolutionary Party known as the Partido Revolucionario Cubano (PRC), served as delegates to the PRC, wrote for and assisted in the publication of revolutionary newspapers, collected dues and donations, and raised funds. Nonetheless, despite their dedication to the nationalist cause, few recognized their efforts. Afro Cubans rarely held any positions of power within the nationalist movement and were expected to form separate revolutionary and cultural clubs.

Despite Marti's efforts, however, the Cuban community remained essentially divided and stratified. Revolutionary and cultural clubs formed on the basis of race, ethnicity, gender, and class testify to the degree to which Cubans of all backgrounds sought to separate themselves. ironically, many of these clubs were founded on Marti's nationalist and patriotic principles. Clubs like La Union Marti-Maceo, the Obreras de la Independencia and El Circulo Cubano were active in raising funds, printing revolutionary pamphlets and working with the PRC. Not one of the clubs, however, was racially integrated. By the late nineteenth and early twentieth centuries, La Union Marti Maceo was a male Afro-Cuban club, La Obrera de la Independencia included only white Cuban women, and white Cuban males comprised the membership of El Circulo Cubano.

The experience of Afro-Cuban immigrants in Ybor City during the turn of the century raises important questions concerning race, politics, ethnicity and power. For example, why did Cuban immigrants form separate revolutionary and social clubs if they were all working toward the same goal? Did Florida's Jim Crow laws force Cuban immigrants to adhere to racial segregation or did it simply magnify the racial divisiveness already present in the Cuban community? Why were women expected to organize separate clubs if their participation in the nationalist movement was extensive and invaluable? Why were Afro Cubans able to distance themselves from African Americans while at the same time depending on the resources located in the African-American section of Tampa? These questions help to demonstrate the complex and intricate relationship among race, ethnicity, gender and class.

While these questions provide a skeletal framework for studying the history of Afro Cubans in Ybor City and Tampa during the turn of the century, more research is needed to understand the experiences of Afro-Latino immigrants, a broader and even more diverse group

(13). Rarely included in the history of African Americans and/or Latinos in the United States, the histories of Black Cubans, Puerto Ricans, and Dominicans in the United States often fall through the cracks of historical study. The failure to incorporate the experiences, stories and lives of Afro-Latino immigrants in the United States may render incomplete examinations of racial and ethnic constructions. Perhaps by taking a closer look at the early history of Afro Cubans in Ybor City and Tampa, we can begin to unravel and study the relationship between race and ethnicity in the United States.

ENDNOTES

1. Please refer to Durward Long's "The Historical Beginning of Ybor City and Modern Tampa," *Florida Historical Quarterly* 45 (1966), Susan Greenbaum's "Afro-Cubans in Exile: Tampa, Florida, 1886–1984," *Cuban Studies/Estudios Cubanos* 15 (Winter 1985), and Louis A. Perez's "Cubans in Tampa: From Exiles to Immigrants, 1892–1901," *Florida Historical Quarterly* 576 (October 1978) for more details on the establishment of Ybor City and the development of an immigrant community. For more information concerning Cuban history and how it affected Cuban migration to Tampa please see Louis A. Perez Jr.'s *Cuba Between Empires, 1878–1902* (Pittsburgh: University of Pittsburgh Press, 1983), 22–23 as well as Perez's *Cuba Under the Platt Amendment, 1902–1934* (Pittsburgh: University of Pittsburgh Press, 1986).

2. To better understand how racial segregation laws affected legal definitions of race for African Americans in Florida, please refer to Jerrell H. Shofner, *Nor Is It Over Yet: Florida in the Era of Reconstruction, 1863–1877* (Gainesville: University Presses of Florida, 1974), and Wali Kharif's "Black Reaction to Segregation and Discrimination in Post Reconstruction Florida," *Florida Historical Quarterly* (Fall 1987).

3. Susan Greenbaum characterizes the history of Afro Cubans in Tampa during the turn of the century as a "conceptual relationship between race and ethnicity in American society." Greenbaum, "Tampa's Afro-Cubans," *Cuban Heritage* 1 (Fall 1987), 5.

4. Gary, R. Mormino and George E. Pozzetta, *The Immigrant World of Ybor City: Italians and their Latin neighbors in Tampa, 1885–1985* (Urbana: University of Illinois Press, 1987), 241. This quote was taken from an oral interview of Frank Urso conducted in 1982 by Mormino and Pozzetta. In the interview, Urso stated that "If the crackers (Tampa's Anglo community) really wanted to make us Latins mad they'd call us Cuban niggers."

5. "Ybor City: Tampa's Latin Colony," produced by the Florida Branch of the Federal Writer's Project of the WOA, Special Collections Department, University of South Florida, Tampa, 31 March 1941. While the descriptions were documented by writers visiting the city in 1941, it is clear that from works such as Gary R. Mormino and George E. Pozzetta's *The Immigrant World of Ybor City* and Jose Rivero Muniz's, "Los Cubanos en Tampa," *Revista Bimestre Cubana* 74 (1958), from its inception, Ybor City was an immigrant community where Cubans easily transferred Cuban customs and traditions.

6. Susan Greenbaum, "Afro-Cubans in Ybor City: A Centennial History," Tampa: A publication of the University of South Florida, 1986, 9.

Segregation based on gender was common in many cigar factories. These women are stemming, which was a male precursor to cigar-making before becoming a separate occupation for women.

7. Louis A. Perez Jr., explains the importance of *lectores* to Cuban cigarworkers and the threat *lectores* posed to cigar manufacturers. *Lectores* assisted in the nationalist cause by informing Cuban cigarworkers of political developments in Cuba and requesting funds to aid the nationalist cause. At the same time, *lectores* read newspapers and books that discussed the plight of workers in the United States. In November 1931, as Perez notes, "cigar manufacturers, supported by city and county authorities and vigilante groups, announced the decision to abolish the *lectura.*" Perez, "Reminiscences of A Lector: Cuban Cigar Workers in Tampa," *Florida Historical Quarterly* 53 (April 1975).

8. Patricia A. Cooper, *Once a Cigar Maker: Men, Women and Work Culture in American Cigar Factories, 1900–1919* (Urbana: University of Illinois Press, 1987), 15.

9. During the turn of the century, African Americans in Florida challenged a series of racial segregation laws and were active in changing oppressive and unjust conditions. Both Wali R. Kharif's "Black Reaction to Segregation and Discrimination in Post-Reconstruction Florida," *Florida Historical Quarterly* (Fall 1987) and August Meier and Elliot Rudwick's "Negro Boycotts of Segregated Streetcars in Florida, 1901–1905," *South Atlantic Quarterly* (Autumn 1970) show the strategies African Americans developed and used to affect change in a period of intense racial discrimination and disenfranchisement.

10. While it is difficult to document informal alliances between African Americans and Afro Cubans, the records of La Union Marti-Maceo, an Afro-Cuban club and mutual aid society, dated 17 October 1915, indicate that Afro Cubans finally voted to permit all Black individuals regardless of nationality, as members of La Union Marti-Maceo. However, as the vote count reveals, the Afro-Cuban members were not fully content with the decision. Out of sixty-two members present, only twenty-six members voted in favor, four voted against it and thirty-two abstained.

11. Translated this means a free Cuba. I have used the term "Cuba Libre" throughout the text to show how the notion of a free Cuba, that is a Cuba independent from Spain, fueled nationalist rhetoric and reflected the goals of the exiled Cuban community.

12. Quoted in Joan Marie Steffy, "Cuban Immigration to Tampa, 1886–1898," (Unpublished M.A. Thesis, University of South Florida, 1975), 48.

13. For the purposes of this article I have used the term Afro-Latino to describe Latinos of African ancestry and descent. However, it is an inadequate term, one that in no way considers cultural, political and social ties and experiences. The fact that imprecise terms have to be used to describe these communities shows to what extent a language which speaks to their experiences still needs to be established and developed.

Ellis Island and the American Immigration Experience

The National Immigration Museum pays homage to those who passed through Ellis Island en route to a new life in the land of liberty as well as the unfortunate ones that were turned away.

Robert F. Zeidel

Dr. Zeidel is assistant professor of history, College of St. Thomas, St. Paul, Minn.

On Sept. 9, 1990, the renovated immigration station at Ellis Island, closed since 1954, reopened its doors amidst considerable fanfare as the National Immigration Museum. In the process, descendants of the station's first visitors sought to discover their roots, at perhaps the most tangible remnant of a myriad of journeys from old world to new. A few of the original immigrants also came back, some no doubt hoping to re-experience what must have been a traumatic rite of passage. As these and other invited guests prowled the grounds and toured the renovated Great Hall, America vicariously celebrated its ethnic past.

The site will stand as a monument to the estimated 12,000,000 men, women, and children who passed through on the final leg of their voyage to America, but it also should serve as a reminder of those turned away and to the policy decisions that prompted their exclusion. It is the latter, perhaps the easiest to overlook, which best explains the immigrant's place in American history.

Amid the pomp and circumstance, some commentators have noted that Ellis Island was a place of travail, where immigrants underwent an inspection that determined their admission or rejection. The unlucky went home. In its *Historic Structure Report,* the National Park Service said of the station: "While a 'Portal of Hope and Freedom' for many, it was an 'Island of Tears' for those who were

turned away, when they failed to meet the requirements of the immigration laws and regulations." Even those who met the prerequisites could not escape the indignities of physical examinations and character scrutiny. For example, one former immigrant, who attended the dedication ceremony, recalled being "stripped, poked, prodded, and questioned for what seemed like hours."

Such reminiscences adequately convey the personal traumas experienced by those who passed through the immigrant station, but fail to denote properly either the underlying issue—"the immigration question"—or the years of debate it engendered. Ellis Island owed its existence to a policy of selective immigration restriction, whose authors had concluded that the U.S. must stop taking in every European arrival. (Orientals had been barred previously by the Chinese Exclusion Act of 1882.) Americans came to attribute their social ills to immigration; over time, the restrictionist rationale was that large numbers of otherwise acceptable foreigners could be injurious to the nation's institutions.

Traditional interpretations of the decision to exclude certain new arrivals have focused on the immigrants themselves, but closer examination reveals that the calls for restriction stemmed more from developments within the U.S. The so-called new immigrants—Slavs, Poles, southern Italians, and eastern-European Jews of one generation and the Mexicans, Filipinos, and Vietnamese of another—have aroused enmity because of their different ethnic and cultural characteristics. A number of hard-line restrictionists have expressed the fear that these

peoples somehow would dilute America's theretofore homogeneous population, thereby destroying the nation's unique, positive qualities. At the time of the first calls for restriction, such pundits harped on the non-Teutonic ethnicity of an ever-increasing number and percentage of the new arrivals. Yet, more than either the "new" immigrants' ethnicity or the converse nativists' xenophobia, it has been indigenous American conditions that have fueled the debate over alien exclusion.

BLAMING NEWCOMERS

Throughout the 20th century, restrictionists have focused either on the nation's inability to assimilate properly its large and growing number of immigrants or the vague threats posed by smaller numbers of specifically destructive aliens, and Congress has sought to alleviate the situation by remedial legislation. Ellis Island, and the bureaucracy it served, came into being as a result of this agenda. The station owed its existence not to xenophobia, defined as fear of those who are different, or even to a benign desire to welcome immigrants in an orderly fashion. Ellis Island represented, and continues to do so, the nation's response to changing social conditions, deteriorating in the eyes of many Americans, to which immigrants were accused of contributing.

By the late 19th century, the problems of an increasingly urban and industrial society—urban squalor, labor unrest, and economic uncertainty—heightened citizens' fears that their democratic nation,

From *USA Today* magazine, September 1992, pp. 25, 28-29. © 1992 by the Society for the Advancement of Education. Reprinted by permission.

Until it was closed in 1954, Ellis Island was the first experience faced by millions of immigrants to the United States. For all those that were fortunate enough to enter the United States enormous numbers were turned away due to regulations and a policy of selective immigration.

(U.N. Photo)

with its high standard of living, was on the verge of collapse. It seemed that each shipload of new arrivals exacerbated the situation, making corrective actions that much more difficult. Photo-journalist Jacob Riis' depictions of the urban ghetto, Pullman and Homestead strikes, and depressions combined to give impetus to the initial restrictionist movement of the 1890s. In addition, allegations of anarchism, such as that associated with the violence at Chicago's Haymarket Square in 1886, convinced some Americans that revolution was at hand.

As these social maladies captured national attention, a citizenry that traditionally had sought to solve its problems at the local level increasingly turned to the Federal government for direction and assistance. The Supreme Court left little alternative in the case of immigration, ruling in 1876 that state regulation violated Congress' exclusive right to regulate interstate commerce. This mandate followed a trend toward centralization, as an apprehensive public did little to challenge the concentration of power in Washington. Business leaders supported Congress' move to create a commission to monitor railroads, and property holders approved of Pres. Grover Cleveland's decision to use troops to quell labor unrest. In a similar vein, the Supreme Court acted to define the proper status and behavior of large corporations. It was to be expected, then, that immigration would not escape Federal scrutiny, in this case by Congress.

By 1900, statutes excluded convicts, lunatics, criminals, polygamists, and those suffering from loathsome or contagious diseases. Persons coming to America to fulfill prearranged employment, so-called contract laborers, similarly were barred. Other laws set forth procedures for the steamship lines that transported immigrants, including a provision whereby they had to return excluded persons to their ports of embarkation. To oversee the growing bureaucracy, Congress provided for the appointment of a Superintendent of Immigration, whose duties included preparing an annual report on the workings of the Immigration Service.

The most salient omission from turn-of-the-century immigration policy was a general exclusion law, but its absence was not due to a lack of effort. Starting in 1895, a core group of Congressmen, led by Henry Cabot Lodge (R.-Mass.), had worked assiduously to draft, pass, and secure presidential approval of a literacy test bill, also called the educational qualification, a measure intended to reduce the number of annual arrivals by excluding illiterates. Its proponents admitted that the inability to read and write did not necessarily render an immigrant undesirable, but advocates viewed the measure as a sure and workable means of general exclusion. Those to be prohibited—the illiterates—were described vaguely as qualitatively less welcome because of their difficulty in assimilation, propensity for living in urban slums, and likelihood of falling under venal influences, such as anarchism. Literacy test supporters could not find specific fault with those they wished to exclude, but did agree that a general reduction in the total number of arrivals would help alleviate domestic social problems.

Cleveland's 1897 immigration bill veto temporarily stymied literacy test supporters, but, soon after 1900, they redoubled their efforts. By this time, the educational qualification had become the preferred method of general exclusion, and it remained at the center of immigration policy debate until its enactment in 1917. In the intervening years, Congress did pass several related acts, which tended to follow an established pattern of tailoring legislation to address specific domestic concerns.

The Immigration Act of 1903, for example, barred alien anarchists and extended the time for deporting an already admitted individual found to have such proclivities. The bill passed shortly after the assassination of Pres. William McKinley by native-born anarchist Leon Czolgosz (whose foreign sounding name did not escape notice) in 1901, an event many Americans believed was linked to some nefarious radical conspiracy. Authorities arrested immigrant anarchist Emma Goldman, alleging her complicity in Czolgosz's actions, and tried to find proof that the assassination was part of a larger, clandestine, revolutionary plot. The immense evidence that he acted alone did little to allay public fears and, in 1902–03, at a time when general public concern for immigration restriction had dwindled, Congressmen on both sides of the immigration question readily embraced the prohibition of alien radicals.

Between 1905 and 1910, domestic issues again carried over into immigration policy discussion. The concern centered on white slavery and the paranoid belief among middle-class reformers that well-organized prostitution rings sought to entrap innocent young females and use them for immoral purposes. Newly arrived immigrants, they asserted, were at

particular risk. Therefore, in 1907, Congress acted to prohibit the importation of females for purposes of prostitution, one of a few universally supported sections of an otherwise acrimoniously debated bill. Three years later, the Mann Act gave the Federal government expanded police powers to combat and interdict the interstate movement of immoral women. At the time of its passage, restrictionists hoped the public's call for action on this issue could be converted into demand for general immigration restriction. Exponents sought to attach a literacy test provision to the Mann Act, but their efforts fell short. Still, the transfer of a negative image—that of purveyor of prostitution—to the immigration question follows the pattern of blaming foreign-born arrivals for domestic ills.

In 1917, proponents finally enacted the literacy test. This measure earlier had passed either the House or Senate, and three times had been approved by both chambers. In 1913 and 1915, Presidents William H. Taft and Woodrow Wilson, respectively, had vetoed such bills; Congress failed to override each time. Wilson invoked the veto for a second time in 1917, but this time supporters secured enough votes to override. As they had in the past, arguments centered on the contention that social progress necessitated reducing the number of new arrivals, not on how illiterates undermined America's social or political institutions. As Sen. John F. Kennedy (D.-Mass.) stated in 1958, the literacy test's passage marked "a significant turning point in immigration policy." It signaled a rejection of the notion that America could absorb and assimilate any number of honest, hard-working foreigners. The time had passed when America could (or would) accommodate a limitless number of immigrants. The problem lay not with the immigrants, but with the U.S.

The literacy test's passage paved the way for additional restrictive legislation. During the 1920s, new means of limiting immigration—the use of numerical quotas—were initiated. Ironically, immigration specialists had developed the concept in the 1910s as a more equitable alternative to the literacy test, envisioning a system that would not discriminate against any nationality or ethnic group, including Orientals. The original scheme would have favored recently arriving nationalities by limiting the annual total for each group to a percentage of its number as enumerated in the most recent census.

The proposal received some attention, but preoccupation with the literacy test precluded serious consideration of numerical restrictions for almost a decade.

Congress debated the quota system in a milieu far different from that at the time of its inception. Americans of the 1920s had grown weary of the progressive ethos of the previous decade and, in the words of newly elected Pres. Warren G. Harding, wanted to "return to normalcy." On the immigration question, this meant further repudiation of the belief that the U.S. should attempt to assimilate a host of diverse foreigners or could try to build a heterogeneous and multi-cultural society. As in other areas, Americans' willingness to devote their time, energies, and resources to the cause of reform, often abstract and too often unfulfilled, waned considerably

Concurrently, a wave of conservatism swept the nation. Attorney General A. Mitchell Palmer planned and executed a series of raids against alleged subversive groups. Carried out in November, 1919, and January, 1920, they resulted in the arrest of 6,000 people, some of whom then were deported to Russia. Those deported on the *Buford,* nicknamed the "Red Ark," included Emma Goldman. In this same reactionary vein, Massachusetts tried, convicted, and put to death Nicola Sacco and Bartolomeo Vanzetti, punished as much for their radical political beliefs as for any proof of their connection to a fatal robbery, and the Ku Klux Klan re-emerged, attracting 100,000 members to its campaign of racial violence. Hardly surprising, a new immigration act exhibited little of the reform mentality of its original authors.

In 1921, Congressional opponents embraced the idea of numerical restriction, but wrote the statute so as to discriminate against the newest arrivals. Rather than using the number of each immigrant group as found in the most recent census—in this case, 1920—Congress opted to use the 1910 census. This worked against the so-called new immigrants, who primarily had arrived during the last decade. In 1924, Congress drafted an even more restrictive procedure, using the 1890 census, effectively prohibiting the immigration of those belonging to some recently arrived nationalities or groups. This change, though certainly ethnocentric, nonetheless represented a conservative attempt to militate against domestic unrest or social challenges by taking drastic action against immigration.

THE "RED MENACE"

Cold War conditions of the late 1940s and early 1950s set the stage for yet another immigration controversy. This time, it was not conditions engendered by mass migration that provoked anti-alien reaction; the quota acts effectively had brought such conditions to an end. Instead, Americans returned their attention to an old adversary, imported radicalism, which now had a new name—communism. A small number of subversives, Americans feared, threatened to undermine the U.S.'s democratic government and social values. This concept of "internal security threats" viewed radicalism as being largely of imported origin. Oddly, this occurred at a time when natives, not immigrants, dominated the leadership of the American Communist Party, the most distrusted manifestation of domestic radicalism.

At the height of the Cold War, Congress passed two acts intended to protect America from the imported "red menace." The 1950 McCarran Internal Security Act denied admission to any person who ever had belonged to a communist party or similar "front" organization. The act also called for the deportation of any alien who had belonged to such organizations. The 1952 McCarran-Walter Immigration Act both codified existing legislation and introduced new provisions aimed at interdicting and deporting alien subversives. Like other Cold War policies, the two McCarran acts told more of America's intolerance for political dissent than of the nature of immigration itself.

Pres. Lyndon Johnson's Great Society brought forth a major revision of U.S. immigration laws, and the 1965 Hart-Celler Act ended the use of national origin as the primary determinant of immigrant admission. The total quota was set at 290,000, with the Western Hemisphere having 120,000 places and the Eastern Hemisphere 170,000; the law gave preferential treatment to family members of those living in the U.S. and to refugees. Though long overdue, this revision again represented changing domestic attitudes, as the Johnson Administration took the lead in seeking reform measures in such areas as civil rights and entitlement programs. If not for this liberal spirit, it is doubtful that Congress would have moved to amend the nation's immigration laws.

Autumn, 1990, witnessed another attempt at immigration reform. Though many distinctly immigrant issues warranted action, purely native concerns attracted much of the public attention. In the new measure, Congress intended to facilitate the immigration of the highly skilled, many of whom have been trained at American universities, as well as raise the total annual quota to 700,000. Yet, much of the debate centered not on the bill's provisions, but on the failure of America's educational system to produce individuals capable of filling skill- or knowledge-intensive positions. The entire notion of the U.S. as a refuge has gotten lost in the quagmire of America's inadequate schools, and, once again, immigrants have seen their interests suppressed by a decidedly non-immigrant issue.

On Nov. 11, 1990, Pres. George Bush signed a new immigration act into law, and tourists ferried out to take in the sights of Ellis Island. For those of immigrant ancestry, the National Park Service offered the opportunity to add the names of their forebears to the American Immigrant Wall of Honor for a $100 donation. To complete this historic tableau, another wall should display the names Henry Cabot Lodge, William P. Dillingham, John L. Burnett, Albert Johnson, Pat McCarran, and Alan K. Simpson. Without the work of these men, and the acts that came to bear their names, Ellis Island and the other manifestations of American immigration policy would not have existed. By the same token, this latter wall should contain the words urbanization, industrialization, anarchism, unionism, and communism, without which those men would have had no foundation for their policies.

Wings For Man

The right men at the right time and place in history, Wilbur and Orville Wright applied their natural inventiveness, mechanical skills, extraordinary foresight, and great tenacity to achieve one of mankind's oldest and most nearly impossible dreams—prolonged, controlled human flight. In doing so, they radically changed their world, and ours.

Doug McIntyre

Los Angeles writer Doug McIntyre is author of Ride the Wind, *a screen biography of the Wrights, as well as numerous television comedies, including* Married . . . With Children, WKRP in Cincinnati, *and* Full House.

On the bitter-cold morning of December 17, 1903, Wilbur Wright watched as his nervous brother Orville lay prone on the bottom wing of their first powered airplane. The two men squinted their eyes from the sting of blowing sand and the sharp winter winds that gusted at more than twenty miles an hour across the isolated section of North Carolina's Outer Banks known as the Kill Devil Hills.

The product of three and a half years of research and experimentation, the Wrights' 1903 "Flyer" weighed more than six hundred pounds and measured forty feet from wingtip to wingtip. Above Orv's head was a tank of explosive gasoline; a few inches to his right were the roaring steel engine and whirling chain-drive transmission. Behind him spun the airplane's two eight-foot blades. He was well aware that the steel bracing wires that surrounded him were sharp enough to draw blood on contact. No wonder he was nervous.

John Daniels was also nervous. As a member of the United States Life Saving Corps he was no stranger to physical danger, having often risked death to pluck shipwreck victims from the treacherous waters off the North Carolina coast. Today, however, standing behind Orville's Korona camera, he faced a different challenge. Daniels had been asked by the Wrights to photograph the first moment of human flight. He had never touched a camera in his life.

In a sense, while inventing the airplane, Wilbur and Orville Wright also invented themselves. "The Wright Brothers" became a corporate entity that all but obscured the individuals.

At 10:35 A.M. Orville threw the trip switch that released the Flyer from its tether. The machine gathered speed as it rolled down the "Grand Junction Railroad," the Wright's four-dollar launching system of two-by-fours and bicycle hubs. Wilbur ran beside the machine, holding its right wingtip steady. When Orv judged the speed to be sufficient, he pulled back on the elevator control, and the world's first airplane left the ground.

The five lucky witnesses—Daniels, two other members of the nearby lifesaving station, and two local residents—cheered. They had just seen a miracle!

In his excitement, Daniels was not sure if he had remembered to squeeze the bulb and trip the camera's shutter. It was not until weeks later, back in their darkroom in Dayton, Ohio, that Wilbur and Orville saw the proof they would need to back their claim of "first to fly." The Wright Flyer was captured two feet off the ground, with Orv prone on the lower wing and Wilbur frozen in wonder for all eternity. Daniels' first photograph remains the most famous in the annals of invention and perhaps the most famous in American history.

From the time we were little children, my brother Orville and myself lived together, played together, worked together, in fact, thought together." So wrote Wilbur in 1912. It was an exaggeration.

As a young boy Wilbur was much closer to his older brothers, Reuchlin and Lorin. Orville had many boyhood friends, including the African-American poet Paul Laurence Dunbar. However, Orv's favorite companion—as a child and into adulthood—was his sister Katharine.

Wilbur and Orville *did* grow to be as close as twins, but this happened over many years. In a sense, while inventing the airplane, they also invented themselves. "The Wright brothers" became a corporate entity that has obscured the individuals.

Wilbur was born in Millville, Indiana in 1867, to Milton and Susan Wright. His father, a bishop in the Church of the United Brethren in Christ, named his third son after Wilbur Fisk, a preacher he admired.

In 1871 the Bishop moved his family to Dayton, Ohio, where Orville soon was born in the upstairs bedroom at 7 Hawthorn Street. This simple two-story house would remain the family's primary residence until 1914 when Orville, the Bishop, and Katharine—born three years

From *American History Illustrated*, January/February 1994, 30-42, 66, 69. © 1994 by Cowles Magazines, Inc. Reprinted through the courtesy of Cowles Magazines, Inc., publisher of *American History Illustrated*.

to the day after Orv—moved to a mansion in suburban Oakwood.

As youngsters both Wright boys earned above-average grades, but neither officially graduated from high school. Orv was the born inventor, having inherited mechanical dexterity from his mother. As a child he was fascinated by printing; over time this hobby evolved into the brothers' first career. For many years, "Wright & Wright Job Printers" operated on Dayton's racially integrated west side. The young men edited and published local newspapers on an ingenious printing press they had built from scrap lumber and an old buggy top, with a tombstone serving as the press bed.

The Wrights claimed that their interest in flight began in early childhood when their father, who traveled extensively on church business, returned home with a toy "bat." This rubber-band-powered helicopter-like toy made a tremendous impact upon the boys. They played with it until it fell to pieces; rebuilt it many times; and eventually made larger versions that failed to fly as well as the smaller original. Disenchanted they drifted off to other interests but never forgot their first taste of "flight."

As the Wrights matured, America seemed to go crazy; bicycle madness swept the nation. In the 1880s it was called "wheeling," and Americans couldn't buy bicycles fast enough. The sudden proliferation of "wheels" created a demand for good mechanics. As Wilbur and Orv's reputation for mechanical creativity spread, a second career—bicycle repairing—was virtually thrust upon them.

Orville, the more reckless and impetuous of the two, purchased a brand-new bicycle for the astounding sum of $160. Wilbur bought a used "wheel" for $80. The brothers' personalities were reflected in how they rode. Will preferred long quiet rides in the country, while Orv fancied himself a "scorcher" and won several medals in YMCA races.

Eventually the Wrights built and sold their own line of bicycles. This not only provided a steady, if modest, income; it also gave the Wrights basic engineering skills they would later put to use in building flying machines. That time was rapidly approaching—but first Wilbur and Orville would each have a brush with death.

In 1885, while playing shinny (an early form of ice hockey), Wilbur was struck in the mouth by an opposing player's stick. His teeth were knocked out, and he suffered severe trauma. The family became deeply concerned as Wilbur's recovery dragged on for months, then years. Wilbur withdrew into himself. He no longer went to work and rarely left the house. He complained of heart palpitations and began to speculate that he would not live long. Prior to his accident, Will had expressed an interest in attending Yale University and becoming a teacher. He now dropped his college plans, telling his father that "my health has been such that it might be time and money wasted."

During Will's convalescence, Susan Wright, Wilbur and Orville's mother, was seriously ill with tuberculosis. Wilbur spent what little energy he had caring for his dying mother. When not by her side he was invariably buried in a book, absorbing vast stores of knowledge. He read on a variety of subjects, including the works of Robert Ingersoll, the famous agnostic. Learning was encouraged in the Wright home. The Bishop's religious principles never prohibited the brothers from examining any area of interest. "We were lucky enough," wrote Orville in 1940, "to grow up in an environment where there was always much encouragement to children to pursue intellectual interests; to investigate whatever aroused curiosity. In a different kind of environment, our curiosity might have been nipped long before it could have borne fruit."

The Wilbur Wright who emerged after his hockey accident and the death of his mother was a very different person from the rudderless Wilbur who had followed his younger brother's lead. With his health restored, Wilbur was now confident and self-assured. He had not only studied books during his convalescence; he had evaluated his own strengths and weaknesses. Will concluded that he wasn't cut out for a life in business. Science was his passion—if only he could find the proper venue in which to make his mark.

In Europe, a German engineer named Otto Lilienthal had gained international fame by experimenting with flying machines. Unlike many of the crackpots who earned ridicule and scorn, Lilienthal was a respected man whose public flights drew large crowds and numerous photographers. During his five years of gliding experiments, Lilienthal had accumulated a total of five minutes of actual flight time. As paltry as this might seem, it made him the world's most experienced aviator.

On August 9, 1896, while gliding from his man-made hill near Berlin, Lilienthal's machine was overturned by a sudden gust. His method for controlling the glider required him to shift his body to the left or right to rebalance the craft. "Weight shifting," as it was known, was both slow and dangerous. Lillenthal's glider plunged to the ground, and the crash snapped his neck. Allegedly, his final words were: "Sacrifices must be made."

Back in Dayton, meanwhile, another life-or-death struggle was in progress. Orville had contracted typhoid fever from contaminated well water. For weeks he hovered near death, slipping in and out of a coma. It was during Orv's illness that Wilbur read a newspaper obituary detailing Lilienthal's death. When Orville's fever finally broke, Wilbur, his childhood interest in flight re-awakened, filled his ears with talk of flying machines. Wilbur had found his venue, but the dynamics of the brothers' relationship had changed. From now on Wilbur would lead, not follow.

What happened over the next five years is one of the great American tales, a story so archetypal as to almost define Yankee ingenuity and rugged individualism. It began with a letter.

On May 30, 1899, Wilbur picked up a pen and a sheet of Wright Cycle Company stationary and wrote to Samuel Langley, a well-known flying-machine inventor and secretary of the Smithsonian Institution. He requested copies of the museum's publications on aeronautics as well as a list of other writings on the subject.

Wilbur's letter remains the most important letter the Smithsonian has ever received: "I have been interested in the problem of mechanical and human flight ever since as a boy I constructed a number of bats [helicopters] of various sizes after the style of Cayley's and Pénaud's machines," he wrote. "My observations since have only convinced me more firmly that human flight is possible and practicable. It is only a question of knowledge and skill just as in all acrobatic feats. Birds are the most perfectly trained gymnasts in the world . . . and it may be that man will never equal them . . . [but] I believe that simple flight at least is possible to man. . . . I wish to avail myself of all that is already known and then, if possible, add my mite to help the future worker who will attain final success."

This remarkable letter is significant on three counts. First, it reflects how much research Wilbur had already done. In addition to studying birds, he was familiar with the work of early European experimenters. Secondly, it is clear he did not think that he would invent the airplane; rather some "future worker" would "attain final success." Finally, and most significantly, he made no mention of Orville. This letter, and most of the hundreds of others that Wilbur penned between 1899 and 1902, are written in the first-person singular. Wilbur's famous quotation about how he and Orv "thought together" was apparently not a sentiment he held from the start.

"It is possible to fly without motors, but not without knowledge and skill."

Wilbur Wright

In response to Wilbur's request, the Smithsonian sent him pamphlets on human flight, including some by the late Lilienthal. Also recommended was Octave Chanute's book, *Progress in Flying Machines*. On May 13, 1900, Wilbur wrote to Chanute: "For some years now I have been afflicted with the belief that flight is possible to man. My disease has increased in severity and I feel that it will soon cost me an increased amount of money if not my life. . . . It is possible to fly without motors, but not without knowledge and skill. This I conceive to be fortunate, for man, by reason of his greater intellect, can more reasonably hope to equal birds in knowledge, than to equal nature in the perfection of her machinery."

The language of Wilbur's preamble to Chanute is not only beautiful, it is revealing. It indicates that he had dismissed motors as a detail, not the key to flight. This was a point missed by many of his contemporaries, most notably Dr. Langley, who spent years and thousands of tax dollars developing state-of-the-art engines.

What the letter tells us about Wilbur's state of mind is even more significant. Wilbur Wright was a young man who foresaw early death. When viewed through this prism, perhaps his subsequent condescending treatment of Orville was actually brotherly love, not selfishness. Wilbur would not allow Orv to fly until 1902. Since Wilbur did not believe he had long to live anyway, it made sense for him to risk his neck on their imperfect flying machines, sparing his brother. At the very least, his premonitions of death may have given urgency to his work.

Wilbur concluded that the first major necessity in achieving human flight was the development of a control system. His years in the bicycle business had taught him that it was possible to ride a machine that is inherently unstable. The rider achieves balance by making tiny adjustments as he moves over an ever-changing terrain. So too, thought Wilbur, must an airplane pilot adjust his machine to maintain balance and control in the rapidly changing environment of the sky. What good are powerful engines and wings that lift if you have no control in flight? As obvious as this point seems today, virtually all of the Wright's rivals—including Alexander Graham Bell, Sir Hiram Maxim, John Montgomery, and Albert Santos-Dumont—put their chief efforts into designing wings and/or engines. Most viewed control as a detail rather than as essential for flight.

In 1899 Wilbur built a small kite to test a method of control that he called "wing warping." Modern airplanes still incorporate this breakthrough discovery in the form of ailerons. When the tip of one wing is turned up, the tip of the opposite wing turns down. The resulting change in air pressure over the wing surfaces causes the machine to roll in the opposite direction from the down-turned wingtip.

Wilbur discovered wing warping while fiddling with a bicycle tire inner-tube box. In a spectacular example of creative visualization, he saw the top and bottom surfaces of the box as the upper and lower wings of a biplane. When twisting the box, the corners flared; one up, one down. This is what birds' wings do in flight. He knew that he had discovered something important.

With his kite tests a success and with encouragement from Chanute, Wilbur was now ready to leave the safety of the bike shop: "If you are looking for perfect safety," he later wrote, "you will do well to sit on a fence and watch the birds; but if you really wish to learn, you must mount a machine and become acquainted with its tricks by actual trial."

Why Kitty Hawk? Chanute told Wilbur that the United States Weather Bureau could provide a list of locations offering strong winds and soft sand upon which to land. As chance would have it, a U.S. Life Saving Station located near the lyrically named village of Kitty Hawk doubled as a weather bureau outpost. Wilbur's letter of inquiry was passed along to Kitty Hawk postmaster Bill Tate, who sent Will a friendly reply. According to Tate, the *only* thing Kitty Hawk had was strong winds and soft sand.

On September 6, 1900 Wilbur left Dayton to make the five-hundred-mile journey to the Outer Banks islands of North Carolina. Orville elected to stay behind and run the bike shop—further evidence that flying machines were still primarily Wilbur's passion.

It took Wilbur six days, traveling by train, horse, boat, and on foot to reach Kitty Hawk. Orville, unable to resist sharing in his brother's adventure, arrived two weeks later. His companionship, mechanical skills, and the supplies he brought with him made Orv more than welcome.

The Wrights' arrival made quite an impression on the villagers. Extremely poor, the local inhabitants eked out a living fishing and farming the poor, sandy soil. The Wrights' modest incomes made them wealthy men amongst the Kitty Hawkers. Their ability to pay cash for fresh eggs disrupted the local barter economy.

Will and Orv were the big attractions in town for reasons other than economics; they were spectacular oddballs! In their bowler hats, jackets and ties, they could be seen running up and down the beach, flying their big glider as a kite. The locals were divided: some were fascinated by the brothers; others were convinced the visitors were dabbling with the Devil. The "Bankers' " mindset is best summed up in a popular expression of the day: "If God had meant for man to fly, he would have given us wings."

Wilbur and Orville's first flying season ran from September 13 through October 23, 1900. It could be more accurately described as a "kiting season," since they attempted only one manned flight.

Wilbur, who had used Lilienthal's tables of air pressure when designing his machine, had expected it to be capable of flights of up to 300 meters. However, the glider generated only about half the projected lift—reducing the earthbound

Wrights to flying their glider as a tethered kite, loaded with seventy-five pounds of chain.

In 1901 the Wrights returned to Kitty Hawk, arriving on July 10. They hoped to get in hours of practice, thanks to the additional lift generated by their new and vastly larger machine. The 1901 glider had lifting surfaces totaling 315 square feet—the largest machine anyone had ever attempted to fly. However, it too failed to produce enough lift.

Frustration in the air was only one of the problems the brothers faced that summer. Their tent and shed provided little shelter from the horrendous storms and gale-force winds that rolled in from the ocean. But even the hardships of inclement weather paled alongside the suffering inflicted by swarms of bloodthirsty mosquitoes. Orville, describing their ordeal in a letter to his sister Katharine, complained that "it was the most miserable existence I have ever passed through. The agonies of typhoid fever with its attending starvation are as nothing in comparison. . . . The sand and grass and trees and hills and everything were crawling with [mosquitoes]. They chewed us clean through our underwear and socks. . . . Misery! Misery!"

On August 22 the Wrights packed up their equipment and left for home. On the train to Dayton, a disillusioned Wilbur told Orv that "not within a thousand years would man ever fly."

Back in Dayton, the Wrights threw themselves into their neglected bike business, pushing talk of flying machines to the back burner. Then, Wilbur received a timely invitation. Octave Chanute wanted him to speak to the Western Society of Engineers in Chicago. "Nagged" into accepting by Katharine, Will was forced to re-examine the work that he and Orville had done up to that point. While drafting the speech, Will and Orv became convinced that their lift problem was the result of errors in Lilienthal's air pressure tables and not in their construction techniques. They determined to prove Lilienthal wrong, and resolved to never again rely on data they did not develop themselves. This marked a milestone in the brothers' career: no longer simply engineers, they were becoming theoretical scientists.

Orville described the months of November and December 1901 as the happiest of the brothers' lives. "Wilbur and I" he said, "could hardly wait for the morning to come. To get at something that interested us. *That's happiness!*"

In their bicycle-shop-turned-laboratory, the brothers constructed a small wind tunnel powered by the same gas engine that ran the shop's machinery. Inside the tunnel they placed two ingenious devices called "balances"—one to measure lift; the other, drag.

As crude as they appeared, these balances—cobbled by Orville from bicycle spokes and hacksaw blades—were remarkable instruments; exact mechanical analogues to the mathematical formulas for calculating lift and drag. They worked brilliantly, producing new tables of air pressure whose precision has been confirmed by modern computers. The 1902 Wright glider would be the first flying machine based on accurate data and designed by modern scientific methods.

The Wrights' lab work was important in one more significant respect: it marked Wilbur's acceptance of Orville as a full and equal partner. "My machine" no longer appeared in Wilbur's letters. From this point on it would be "our machine."

The third flying season ran from August 28 through October 28, 1902. With the lift problem behind them, both brothers rolled up flight time. Quickly, Wilbur and Orville became the world's most experienced aeronauts. The new machine functioned perfectly—except for one perplexing and potentially fatal flaw. For no apparent reason, the glider would, sporadically, fall from the sky in a "tail spin."

One night Orville drank a pot of coffee and then found himself unable to sleep. As he tossed in his bunk, it struck him that the tailspin problem could be eliminated by making the tail a movable rudder, rather than a fixed surface. This was the final piece of the puzzle. The Wrights now had a glider with a system that effectively controlled all three axes: the elevator for "pitch," wing warping for "roll," and a movable rudder for "yaw." Three-axis control is the key to flight. The discovery of this principle and the development of a system for achieving it are the Wrights' greatest contributions to aircraft technology. Everything that flies, from a hang glider to the Space Shuttle, still incorporates these epoch-making innovations.

Wilbur and Orville now had a practical glider. During the fall of 1902 they made more than seven hundred flights (375 in one week alone), with their long-est glide covering 622.5 feet in twenty-six seconds. It was time to add an engine and propellers.

Back in Dayton, Wilbur and Orville soon discovered that obtaining an engine powerful enough to lift their machine, yet light enough to be carried aloft, wasn't going to be easy. Most of the big-name engine makers couldn't produce a motor light enough, and those who could refused to sell one to the Wrights for fear of being associated with flying machines.

With significant help from Charlie Taylor, a Dayton machinist the brothers had hired to run the bike shop in their absence, they built their own lightweight internal combustion engine producing twelve horsepower. The crankshaft was turned by hand on their lathe from a nineteen-pound bar of steel; only the aluminum crankcase was made outside the bike shop, cast by a local foundry from a mold provided by the Wrights.

"After running the engine and propellers a few minutes to get them in working order, I got on the machine at 10:35 for the first trial. . . . On slipping the rope the machine lifted from the track just as it was entering on the fourth rail."

Orville Wright's diary entry for December 17, 1903

Having solved one problem the Wrights now ran into a stone wall—propellers. They had envisioned that this would be the easiest part of their work, anticipating a trip to the library to obtain ship propeller data, and then applying that knowledge to design "airscrews." The brothers were astonished to discover that no such data existed on ship propellers; all had been made on a trial-and-error basis. While it is desirable for a ship's propeller to be efficient, it is not essential. An airplane, however, will not leave the ground with an inefficient prop.

The "Great Propeller Debate" has passed down into Wright family lore. During an interview, ninety-seven-year-old Ivonette Wright-Miller, Wilbur and

Orville's niece (and the last person alive who flew with them as a passenger), recalled that her uncles argued "so long and loud they would end up converted to the other's side, only to have the argument start up again, with each brother arguing the other's original position, 'Tis so! 'Tis not!' "

Orville described the complexity of their dilemma: "With the machine moving forward, the air flying backward, the propellers turning sidewise, and nothing standing still, it seemed impossible to trace the various simultaneous reactions."

The Wrights' solution was brilliant. They made a theoretical assumption: a propeller is merely a wing that rotates. If they could predict a wing's performance in a straight path, why couldn't they predict its performance in a spiral? This assumption revolutionized the concept of aircraft propulsion. Wright propellers generated thrust and lift.

There was no argument over the transmission system. Drawing on their bike-building experience, Wilbur and Orville used chains and sprockets to spin their props. They now had everything they needed. It was time to fly.

The Wrights' fourth and most momentous flying season saw them back at Kitty Hawk from September 25 through December 19, 1903. Plagued by a myriad of mechanical and weather delays, the brothers finally had their first powered airplane ready for takeoff on the morning of December 14.

Wilbur won the coin toss for the first shot at human flight. However, a "pilot error" on his part resulted in a crash seconds after liftoff. Although the plane had left the ground, the brothers considered this a "hop," not a "flight."

It took several days to make repairs. During this delay, the weather turned bitter cold, and winter set in. The Wrights feared that they might not get to fly at all in 1903.

On the morning of December 17, the winds were gusting above thirty miles an hour. Despite the grave risks involved in flying an untested machine in air this turbulent, the brothers, for once in their lives, literally threw caution to the wind.

This time, Orville would go first. His first effort produced a twelve-second flight of approximately 120 feet. This is the historic flight immortalized in Daniel's photograph. Wilbur went next, flying 175 feet. Then Orville made his second

attempt, this time reaching the 200-foot mark. The shortness of these flights had nothing to do with machine failure. Wilbur and Orville simply lacked experience controlling the heavy 1903 Flyer. If anything, it responded too well, with the slightest movement of the elevator control causing the machine to dart toward earth.

Wilbur later would write to Chanute, declaring that "those who understand the real significance of the conditions under which we worked will be surprised rather at the length than the shortness of the flights made with an unfamiliar machine after less than one minute's practice."

Orville added in 1913: "With all the knowledge and skill acquired in thousands of flights in the last ten years, I would hardly think today of making my first flight in a strange machine in a twenty-seven mile wind. . . . I look on with amazement upon our audacity in attempting flights with a new and untried machine under such circumstances."

On the fourth flight of the day, Wilbur flew for fifty-nine seconds, spanning a distance of 852 feet. Elated, the brothers made plans to fly the four miles from their camp at Kill Devil Hills to Kitty Hawk village. In an instant their plans were dashed. A huge gust flipped the machine over and cartwheeled it down the beach. The 1903 Flyer was reduced to a jumble of broken spars and ribs. It never flew again. It didn't have to.

The Wrights' famous flight of December 17, 1903 is usually where history drops their story, but it is actually just the second-act curtain in an exciting three-act drama.

Upon arriving home, the Wrights discovered that the newspapers did not believe their story, or misunderstood what they had accomplished. This consequence proved to be both a blessing and a curse for the brothers. The blessing was that it protected their technology while their patents worked their way through the bureaucracy. The curse was that it made it hard for the Wrights to market the machine and for many years deprived them of the glory that should have been theirs.

In 1904 and 1905 the Wrights flew from a cow pasture eight miles north of Dayton. It was at Huffman Prairie, now part of Wright-Patterson Air Force Base, that the brothers perfected their machine and taught themselves how to fly. The first circles and figure eights made by an airplane were flown above Torrance Huffman's field. Word eventually leaked

out of the experiments after the Wrights were seen by passengers on a trolley car. With a record flight of twenty-four miles in thirty-eight minutes under their belts, the Wrights stopped flying for more than two years while they tried to find a buyer for their machine.

The U.S. government had been burned by flying machines in the past (investing $50,000 in Dr. Langley's failure, for example), and the Wrights' offer to provide a practical airplane was rejected out of hand. Insulted by their own country's "snub," Wilbur and Orville then traveled to England, France, and Germany in hopes of making a deal.

Their mission was complicated by unforeseeable obstacles. A sale in France was blocked by a lapse in judgement by their old friend Octave Chanute.

The brothers' relationship with Chanute had soured over time, with Chanute accusing the Wrights of being too secretive. In March 1903, Chanute had traveled to Paris to speak at an Aéro-Club banquet. During his lecture he not only implied that the Wrights were his students; he also let stand the impression that their work had been financed by him. To make matters worse, he showed slides of the Wrights' gliders and told the French about wing warping. The rebirth of European interest in heavier-than-air flight can be traced directly to Chanute.

Fortunately for Wilbur and Orville, Chanute's understanding of wing warping was limited, so his talk didn't give away the store. However, he created the impression that it was just a matter of time before French aviators would have airplanes of their own, so why should France spend money on an American machine?

The brothers knew that nobody else understood the true nature of the flying problem. Still, by 1906 a few brave souls had coaxed machines into the air. These "flights" prompted the Wrights' rivals, and the press, to dismiss Orv and Will as frauds. One Paris newspaper ran this banner headline over a story on the brothers: "Flyers or Liars?"

Why Wilbur and Orville didn't simply make a demonstration flight has never been easy to explain. They had become paranoid that a rival would see their machine and steal its secrets, making it impossible for them to recoup their investment. (Their patent attorney had preached secrecy.) However, the primary reason may have been emotional. The Wrights simply couldn't let go of their "baby." Bishop Wright publicly boasted that his three youngest children never left the "paternal roof."

Wilbur and Orville appear to have inherited their father's possessiveness. Finally, in 1908 everything changed. A consortium of French businessmen agreed to purchase a Wright machine. At almost the same time, the U.S. government accepted a new bid from the brothers to supply the Signal Corps with an airplane. After a quick trip to Kitty Hawk to brush up on their rusty flying skills, the brothers split up to meet the deadlines on their contracts.

In France, in Wilbur's words, "princes and millionaires are as thick as thieves." Huge crowds came out to watch him fly. He astonished the Europeans with the grace of his machine and his skill as its pilot, making flights of more than two hours in length. There was no longer any doubt that the Wrights' claim of "first to fly" was true. The same newspapers that had called them "liars" now hailed them as *Les Premiers Hommes-oiseaux!*—first among the "bird men!"

Orville went to Fort Myer, Virginia, where he flew before large crowds, including President Taft, senators, and congressmen. It was while he was there that Orville suffered the only serious accident of his career. During a flight with Lieutenant Thomas Selfridge as his passenger, a propeller cracked, cutting a bracing wire. The machine crashed, breaking Orv's leg and killing Selfridge. Still, the American public had seen enough to know that the "air age" had arrived.

Back home, the brothers were honored with parades, medals, and trips to the White House. Everywhere they went, huge throngs gathered to see them, speak with them, touch them. Wilbur and Orville were repelled by the hysteria, just as another famous American aviator would be a generation later. The fuss and hoopla was anathema to the pathologically shy Wrights. Orville categorically refused to speak in public, and Wilbur once declined a request for a speech by quipping, "I know of only one bird that talks, the parrot, and they don't fly very high."

Soon after their world triumph, the Wrights found themselves embroiled in messy patent infringement suits—usually initiated by them. The ugliest and most celebrated involved rival aviator Glenn Curtiss. The Wrights won every case but in the process lost the war. To protect their claims of priority in court, the brothers could not make significant changes in their aircraft designs; a big change could be interpreted by the airplane-ignorant courts as an admission by the inventors that their original designs were flawed. So, while they were frozen in 1908 technology, Curtiss and others were free to innovate. Quickly, Wright airplanes became obsolete.

The psychological and physical demands of testifying in court and giving endless depositions destroyed Wilbur's health. In 1912 he contracted typhoid fever, the same illness that Orville had battled in 1896. On May 30, Wilbur died at the family home in Dayton. His premonition of early death had come true. He was only forty-five years old.

When Wilbur died, his place in history was anything but assured. To this day, rumors persist about "flights" made by other aviators prior to December 17, 1903. In Brazil, Santos-Dumont is still hailed as the "father of flight." Books have appeared over the years claiming credit for Connecticut's Gustav Whitehead. Frenchman Gabriel Voisin went to his grave debunking the Wrights. Tourists in California can visit a monument to John Montgomery, a glider pilot of dubious achievement, who died in 1911 in a craft that Wilbur had warned him was a death trap.

Ironically, the greatest threat to the Wrights' place in history turned out to be the Smithsonian Institution. In conjunction with Curtiss, the Smithsonian credited its beloved secretary, the late Dr. Langley, with inventing the airplane. . . . Correcting this gross distortion became Orville's obsession, and ultimately resulted in his sending the 1903 Flyer into exile in England, where it remained until 1948.

Finally, however, Orville's protracted battle with Curtiss and the Smithsonian culminated in a final triumph: the establishment of the Wrights' priority as conquerors of the sky. Whatever doubts serious scholars may have harbored were finally put to rest with publication of *The Papers of Wilbur and Orville Wright* in 1953.

Orv spent the years after Wilbur's death in a laboratory originally intended for both brothers. He tinkered with whatever caught his fancy (spending months on an automatic record changer, for example). He produced no major inventions of his own.

Until his death of a heart attack in 1948, Orville was, literally, a living legend. So quietly had he lived that when his obituary appeared in newspapers most people outside of Dayton were surprised to learn that he had still been alive.

What the Wrights might have accomplished had Wilbur not died so young is one of the great "what ifs?" Wilbur himself shed some light on the vicissitudes of invention in a 1906 letter to Chanute: "If the wheels of time could be turned back . . . it is not at all probable that we would do again what we have done. . . . It was due to a peculiar combination of circumstances which might never occur again."

More so than Thomas Edison, Robert Fulton, or Samuel Morse, the Wrights can claim total credit for the invention that brought them lasting fame. Lifelong diarists, prolific letter writers, and amateur photographers of considerable skill, Wilbur and Orville left a paper trail that documents each step in their systematic program of aeronautical research. They invented more than wings of strength, a lightweight engine, and efficient propellers. They also perfected three-axis control-pitch, yaw, and roll, the three dimensions of flight. They tested their theories in the air, teaching not only themselves how to fly, but the rest of us as well. From humble beginnings, these two bachelor bicycle makers built everything themselves. They paid for their work from their own earnings, risked their lives repeatedly on imperfect gliders, and triumphed with no desire for glory, only a just demand for what was rightfully theirs. It is as much the quality of their character as the brilliance of their work that earns Wilbur and Orville Wright lasting fame in the pantheon of American heroes.

Perhaps the most eloquent testament to their achievement is one simple line from Orville's diary, dated June 7, 1903: "Isn't it astonishing that all these secrets have been preserved for so many years just so that we could discover them!"

Suggested additional reading: The authoritative biography of the Wright brothers is *The Bishop's Boys* by Tom Crouch (W. W. Norton, 1989). An illustrated work fascinating to both young people and adults is *The Wright Brothers: How They Invented the Airplane* by Russell Freedman (Holiday House, 1991). Other pictorial volumes of interest include *Kitty Hawk and Beyond* by Ronald R. Geibert and Patrick B. Nolan (Wright State University Press, 1990), and *How We Invented the Airplane* by Orville Wright (Dover, 1988).

Fighting Poverty the Old-Fashioned Way

Howard Husock

Howard Husock, a former Wilson Center Guest Scholar, is director of Case Studies in Public Policy at Harvard's John F. Kennedy School of Government. Born in Cleveland, Ohio, he received a B.S. from Boston University (1972).

It is difficult to exaggerate the dread sense of crisis that the urban poor inspired in most citizens of the United States a century ago. The phenomenally rapid industrialization that had been underway since the Civil War was attracting millions of eastern and southern Europeans to America's sweatshops, steel mills, and railyards. The influx of these "more foreign foreigners," more alien in language, customs, and religion than the Irish and German immigrants who preceded them, was climbing inexorably toward a one-year peak of 1,285,000 in 1907. Middle-class Protestant America recoiled in fear as entire districts of Chicago, Pittsburgh, New York, and Philadelphia were taken over by what one writer in New York called "the dangerous classes." An early history of this new immigration noted that "districts passed in a few years from the Irish, who were typical of the early influx, to the Russian Jews, who, as they landed represented the extreme of all that was in contrast with the American way of life."

The new masses were not only different but wretchedly poor, and poverty soon began to emerge as a political issue. As early as 1888, President Grover Cleveland warned that "oppressed poverty and toil, exasperated by injustice and discontent, attacks with wild disorder the citadel of rule." Jacob Riis, drawing on his years as a police reporter and photographer on New York's Lower East Side,

lent popular urgency to the problem of urban poverty with the publication in 1890 of *How the Other Half Lives.* Riis attracted national attention with his descriptions of "unventilated and fever-breeding structures," of gangs meeting in "dens" to plan "raids," willing to saw a peddler's head off "just for fun." Nor were such accounts isolated. In Philadelphia, another account, sounding much like a late 20th-century description of the ghetto drug culture, described "boys and girls idling away their time on the street, their characters weakened so that they are liable to the contagion of all kinds of vice."

In his classic 1904 treatise, *Poverty,* reformer Robert Hunter estimated that 10 million of America's 82 million people lived in poverty. In an era without unemployment insurance or workers' compensation, even those with jobs were often but a missed paycheck or an industrial accident away from destitution. "Upon the unskilled masses," wrote Hunter, "want is constantly pressing." He warned, furthermore, of an emerging "pauper" class—an underclass of dangerous and demoralized poor people. On Armour Avenue in Chicago, in Cincinnati's Rat Hollow, in Manhattan's Hell's Kitchen, and in dozens of similar neighborhoods around the country, wrote Hunter, there "lives a class of people who have lost all self-respect and ambition, who rarely if ever work, who are aimless and drifting, who like drink, who have no thought for their children and who live on rubbish and alms."

Today, the astounding upward mobility of this generation of immigrants (or at least of their children) and their assimilation into the American middle class is seen as somehow inevitable—the by-product of an expanding economy, strong demand for unskilled labor, and an immigrant work ethic. By implication, middle-class America today is limited in its

ability to deal with the poor and underclass because both labor conditions and the character of the poor have changed. Yet the upward mobility of the poor hardly appeared inevitable to the contemporary observers of a century ago. Bringing the urban poor into the cultural and economic mainstream was viewed as a challenge requiring extraordinary steps.

OUT OF THE REFORM MAELSTROM OF the turn-of-the-century Progressive era emerged a movement that undertook to bring the poor both hope and the tools of advancement. The settlement-house movement unabashedly promoted bourgeois values and habits—instructing the poor in everything from art appreciation and home economics to the importance of establishing savings accounts. To children in poverty, it offered recreation, books, clubs, as well as a sense of the history of American democratic institutions. It approached thousands of the urban poor, particularly children and teenagers, with a message of inclusion in the larger world beyond the slum. It *expected* them to make it. To make good on that promise, relatively well-to-do Americans, inspired both by religious conscience and fear for the American social fabric, "settled" in poor neighborhoods, there to experience the lives of the poor firsthand, to offer guidance to their neighbors and, in time, to be inspired to suggest policy prescriptions to the nation: child labor laws, industrial safety laws, and old age and unemployment insurance.

Settlements developed in the aftermath of a decades-long debate—in many ways reminiscent of that which has engaged the United States since the early 1960s—over how best to provide financial support to the needy without destroying their incentive to work. Not content with any relief system alone, Jane Addams and other settlement-house

From *The Wilson Quarterly,* Spring 1990, pp. 79-91. © 1990 by the Woodrow Wilson International Center for Scholars. Reprinted by permission.

founders saw a need for a communitarian movement to bring rich and poor together. Their goal was both to broaden the horizons of the poor and to humanize the classes in each other's eyes. The movement, wrote Addams in 1892, rested on three legs. "First, the desire to interpret democracy in social terms; secondly, the impulsive beating at the very source of our lives, urging us to aid in the race progress; and thirdly, the Christian movement toward humanitarianism."

By attending settlement clubs and classes, the poor would be exposed to middle-class values and be given, it was hoped, the tools of self-betterment. The volunteer residents themselves were thought likely to profit as well. Still, the movement indulged neither the personal nor the political whims of youth. Nor did it veer toward wholesale rejection of the American economic system. It sought redistribution not of wealth per se but of "social and educational advantages." Moreover, although it helped put on the public agenda the social insurance programs that were finally passed during the New Deal, it never believed that these could substitute for individual efforts by rich and poor alike.

The American roots of the settlement-house movement date to the practice of "friendly visiting" of the poor, which arose in response to the breakdown of the traditional social-welfare system during the early 19th century. The traditional system, dating to the Elizabethan "poor laws," had provided financial support for community residents (strangers were pointedly excluded) who were sick, widowed, or temporarily down on their luck. By the 1820s, this community-oriented system was growing increasingly unworkable. Cities were becoming too big, workers too transient, and the poor too concentrated in certain urban neighborhoods. Many towns and cities resorted to poorhouses as an economy measure, requiring the poor to live in them in exchange for support.

THESE CHANGED CONDITIONS ALSO INspired new efforts by men such as the Unitarian minister Joseph Tuckerman of Boston. In 1819 he began his ministry to the poor in their own neighborhoods, where, he believed, they were "living as a caste, cut off from those in more favored circumstances." In New York during the 1840s, Robert Hartley, the English-born son of a woolen-mill owner,

Boys at play on a New York street, 1890.

Reproduction from the Library of Congress

founded the New York Association for Improving the Condition of the Poor. He fought for temperance (alcohol was the drug menace of the day) and began a system of friendly visiting in which male volunteers took responsibility for the poor in a given political precinct, bringing such offerings as copies of Benjamin Franklin's *The Way to Wealth*. ("It depends chiefly on two words: industry and frugality," Franklin declared.)

Among Hartley's successors was Charles Loring Brace, a seminarian first drawn to social action through visits to New York City prisons. Convinced that inmates were often beyond help, he founded the Children's Aid Society in 1853 and concentrated his efforts on the 10,000 orphaned or abandoned children then thought to be living on New York's streets. Like the settlement-house workers who came after him, he was persuaded that "formative" efforts were far more effective than "reformative" ones. In language foreshadowing Jane Addams, he wrote: "These boys and girls will soon form the great lower class of our city. They will influence elections . . . they will assuredly, if unreclaimed, poison society all around them. They will help to form the great multitude of robbers, thieves, vagrants and prostitutes who are now such a burden upon the respecting community." Brace offered reading rooms, vocational training, and

"newsboy lodging houses." He also "placed out" thousands of children with farm families in the Midwest and West.*

It was with the settlement-house movement, however, that the uplift impulse peaked. Notwithstanding the example of Hartley and Brace, settlements were most immediately inspired by ideas and events in Britain. With its head start on industrialization, England had been forced during the mid-18th century to confront the need to create a new social welfare system suited to a capitalist economy. In his history of the settlement-house movement, *Spearheads of Reform* (1967), Allen Davis traces the geneaology of settlements to London. There, in 1854, a Utopian clergyman and academic named Frederick Denison Maurice founded the Working Men's College, aiming to use education to erase class distinctions and mitigate the Dickensian social inequities of the era. His faculty included charismatic fine arts professor John Ruskin, England's leading art critic, and a critic as well of

*This effort was violently opposed by the Catholic Church, which suspected Brace's motives in placing Catholic children with Protestant families in the Midwest. But Miriam Langsam concludes in her history of the effort, *Children West: A History of the Placing-Out System of the New York Children's Aid Society, 1853–90* (1962), that most of the children benefited.

19th-century industrialization. Like the settlement residents he would inspire, Ruskin was reform-minded, calling for a social-security system, minimum wage, and higher housing standards.

His disciples included Arnold Toynbee, an economist (and uncle of the famed historian) who moved to London's East End slums to teach and to learn. He died there at age 32 in what a history of the settlement movement would call an atmosphere of "bad whisky, bad tobacco, bad drainage." In 1884, Toynbee Hall was created in the same neighborhood to honor the memory of the reformer. Its founder, a minister named Samuel Barnett, took some of his inspiration from an 1883 church publication entitled *The Bitter Cry of Outcast London*. It described a "gulf daily widening which separates the lowest classes of the community . . . from all decency and civilization." To bridge that gap, Barnett brought college students to his Toynbee Hall, where they mounted art exhibitions, gave lectures, and lobbied local officials for a public library and for park and playground improvements.

Many of the leaders of the American settlement-house movement were directly inspired by visits to Toynbee Hall; Stanton Coit, an Amherst graduate with a doctorate from the University of Berlin, went on to found the nation's first settlement, New York's Neighborhood Guild, in 1886; Jane Addams, the daughter of a small-town Illinois Quaker banker, became co-founder of Chicago's Hull House in 1889; and Robert Woods, a graduate of the Andover Theological Seminary, served as "head resident" at Boston's South End house, founded in 1891. Smith College graduate Vida Scudder studied with John Ruskin in Britain, and along with a group which included Katherine Lee Bates, a Wellesley College professor (and the author of "America the Beautiful"), founded the College Settlement Association in 1889, with houses in Philadelphia, New York, and Boston.

THE BELIEFS OF THE PEOPLE WHO STARTED the settlement movement cut across many of the divides which have since developed in American social-welfare philosophy. They were religious women and men inspired to a secular mission. They were political crusaders who never forgot the importance of maintaining direct contact with the poor and providing them with personal attention ("mentoring," to

What The Social Classes Owe Each Other

In 1889, Hull House was "soberly opened on the theory that the dependence of classes on each other is reciprocal," Jane Addams later recalled. Yet she was anything but confident that Hull House could encourage the spirit of reciprocity. The dire commentary below, which she reprinted in her memoir, was written when Hull House opened its doors.

The social organization has broken down through large districts of our great cities. Many of the people living here are very poor, the majority of them without leisure or energy for anything but the gain of subsistence.

They live for the moment side by side, many of them without knowledge of each other, without fellowship, without local tradition or public spirit, without social organization of any kind. Practically nothing is done to remedy this. The people who might do it, who have the social tact and training, the large houses, and the traditions and customs of hospitality, live in other parts of the city. The clubhouses, libraries, galleries, and semi-public conveniences for social life are also blocks away. We find workingmen organized into armies of producers because men of executive ability and business sagacity have found it to their interests thus to organize them. But these workingmen are not organized socially; although lodging in crowded tenement houses, they are living without a corresponding social contact. The chaos is as great as it would be were they working in huge factories without foreman or superintendent. Their ideas and resources are cramped, and the desire for higher social pleasure becomes extinct. They have no share in the traditions and social energy which make for progress. Too often their only place for meeting is a saloon, their only host a bartender; a local demagogue forms their public opinion. Men of ability and refinement, of social power and university cultivation, stay away from them. Personally, I believe the men who lose most are those who thus stay away from them. But the paradox is here; when cultivated people do stay away from a certain portion of the population, when all social advantages are persis-

Reproduction from the Library of Congress

Jane Addams in 1930.

tently withheld, it may be for years, the result is pointed to as a reason and is used as an argument, for the continued withholding.

It is constantly said that because the masses have never had social advantages, they do not want them, that they are heavy and dull, and that it will take political or philanthropic machinery to change them. This divides a city into rich and poor; into the favored, who express their sense of the social obligation by gifts of money, and into the unfavored, who express it by clamoring for a "share"—both of them actuated by a vague sense of justice. This division of the city would be more justifiable, however, if the people who thus isolate themselves on certain streets and use their social ability for each other, gained enough thereby and added sufficiently to the sum total of social progress to justify the withholding of the pleasures and results of that progress, from so many people who ought to have them. But they cannot accomplish this for the social spirit discharges itself in many forms, and no one form is adequate to its total expression.

—from Twenty Years at Hull-House *(1910).*

use today's term). They were youthful (under 30) cultural radicals who rejected middle-class comforts but saw themselves as mediators between the classes rather than simply as critics of the established order. They were social experimenters who nonetheless championed bourgeois values. They were reformers, not revolutionaries. (This earned them the scorn of writers who were further to the left. Socialist Jack London wrote that settlements "do everything for the poor except get off their backs." Upton Sinclair derisively summed up settlement programs as "lectures delivered gratis by earnest advocates of the single tax, troutfishing, exploring Tibet, pacifism, sea shell collecting, the eating of bran and the geography of Charlemagne's empire.")

THE SETTLEMENT HOUSES FOLLOWED THE wake of the so-called "scientific charity" movement. Scientific charity was designed to achieve some of the same ends as the state and federal welfare initiatives of the past two decades. Its advocates, such as Josephine Shaw Lowell (author of *Public Relief and Private Charity,* 1884), sought to centralize both private and public assistance to guard against fraud and to limit support for the able-bodied, lest the incentive to work be diminished. It is important to note that the settlement movement was not a reaction to scientific charity's callous-sounding agenda. It emerged as an organized supplement to the relief system, designed chiefly for the children of poor families, whether they were receiving relief payments or not. Wrote Jacob Riis: "We have substituted for the old charity coal chute that bred resentment . . . the passenger bridge we call settlements, upon which men go over not down to their duty."

Doing their duty was high on the list of these reformers. They used a vocabulary that seems distant from mainstream social-welfare discussion today. "The impulse to share the lives of the poor, the desire to make social service," wrote Jane Addams in 1892, "to express the spirit of Christ, is as old as Christianity itself. . . . Certain it is that spiritual force is found in the Settlement movement, and it is also true that this force must be evoked and must be called into play before the success of any Settlement is assured." The settlement workers were not missionaries in the literal sense.

If anything, they encouraged the kind of nondenominational religion which has come to typify American life. Theirs was the religion of the social gospel, the belief that social conditions, as well as individual beliefs and practices, come properly under the purview of religion.

The movement believed, too, that there was what Jane Addams called a "subjective necessity" for settlements. "We have in America a fast-growing number of cultivated young people," she wrote, "who . . . hear constantly of the great social maladjustment, but no way is provided for them to change it, and their uselessness hangs about them heavily."*

Movement advocates believed that personal contact between the classes was, as Robert Woods wrote, "not merely a means to some worthy end but, with its implications, as the end above all others. . . . This fresh exchange, continuously growing and deepening, stimulated by the surmounting of barriers of race and religion, was more than anything else to give form and body to the human democracy of the settlement."

The nature of relations between the classes varied. Jane Addams was exhilarated by experiences as mundane as informing a neighborhood woman of the existence of a park several blocks away in a direction the woman had never thought to venture. But Cleveland reformer Frederick Howe found his time in a settlement "anything but fruitful." He felt awkward trying to dance with immigrant women, uncomfortable as a friendly visitor to tenements.

In their early years, the settlements' reach was relatively short, their offerings not that extensive. What activities there were, however, were clearly in the uplift tradition. In the 1892 College Settlement

---

*Most volunteers were children of privilege. Annual reports of the College Settlement Association during the early 1890s, for instance, show that most volunteers were students or graduates of the elite women's colleges: Smith, Wellesley, Vassar, Bryn Mawr, and Mount Holyoke. The 1891–92 report of the College Settlement Association's house on New York's Lower East Side notes that "eighty applications have been received during the year. Many of these it has been necessary to refuse, as the house cannot be crowded beyond a certain point." The length of commitment varied. The New York house had 20 residents between September 1, 1891, and September 1, 1892, each staying an average of four months. Other "visitors" stayed less than one month.

Association's New York house, activities included clubs for boys and girls, establishment of children's savings accounts, a choir for neighborhood men, and home economics classes for neighborhood women. On weekdays, activities did not begin until 3:30 in the afternoon and were over by 9:30 or 10 p.m. A day in the life of the house included a surprising array of activities:

College Settlement Association
New York House, 1892

3 to 5 p.m. Library: Two hundred boys and girls, from ten to 14 years old. Exchange of books and games.

3:30 to 5 p.m. Rainbow Club: Two residents. Twenty girls from ten to fourteen years old. Sewing, singing, gymnastics, and games.

7 to 8 p.m. Penny Provident Bank (Savings account deposits): Two residents. From fifty to one hundred children.

7:30 to 9:30 p.m. Hero Club: One resident, one outside worker. Sixteen boys, fourteen to eighteen years old. Business meeting, talks, music and games. (Discussion of life stories of successful people.)

8 to 9 p.m. The Young Keystones: Ten boys, ten to fourteen years old. Talks on history, music.

Descriptions of even simple programs—carpentry for boys, cooking classes for girls—make it clear that the settlement vision was laden with aspiration for the children of the poor. "The goal of a social programme based on personal interest is to help individuals to the highest level of which each is capable," wrote Lillian Wald of New York's Henry Street Settlement, who was second only to Jane Addams as a voice of the movement. The 1892 report of the College Settlement Association's Philadelphia house stressed what we might now call "empowerment": "Here and there a boy has felt the pleasure, unlike all other pleasures, of creating with the mind and hand that which was not before, and that which was goodly to look upon, even though that something was but a loaf of well-baked bread, a well proportioned step-ladder, or a little clay-modeled apple. When once the boy or girl has felt this pleasure, something of that which inspires our great mechanics or poets has become theirs, and the character transformation begins."

By the turn of the century, the number of settlements had increased (from six in 1891 to 74 in 1897), and their activities had expanded. The activities of houses changed as residents took stock of their environs. Driven by powerful idealism, many settlement workers became political advocates for the poor. Hull House, which had introduced itself to Chicago's Halstead Street in 1889 with an art exhibit, soon opened a kindergarten to make up for the shortage of places in the public schools.* Then the settlement residents took demands for a new school to the Chicago school board. Dismayed by the garbage overflowing in the stables and crowded frame buildings of the 19th ward—with its 50,000 residents of 20 nationalities—Jane Addams and Hull House itself bid on the ward's garbage collection contract. A Hull House resident was eventually appointed garbage inspector.

The settlement impulse also led to efforts beyond the ward. Hull House resident Julia Lathrop organized a campaign to clean up the Cook County poorhouse; Addams and others signed on with a wide variety of reform causes. Hull House resident Florence Kelley was hired by a state commission to investigate child labor conditions. The inquiry (inspired by a Hull House encounter with a 13-year-old Jewish girl who committed suicide rather than admit she had borrowed $3 she could not repay from a coworker at a laundry) led to state legislation banning the employment of children under 14. Settlements even too up the drug abuse issue. Hull House pushed for a 1907 state law banning the sale of cocaine after one of its former kindergarteners fell victim to the drug. "When I last saw him," Addams wrote of the boy, in a line that sounds like countless others being written today, "it was impossible to connect that haggard, shriveled body with what I had known before."

The scope of settlement concerns broadened to the point that by 1904, Robert Hunter, the head resident at New York's University Settlement, wrote his book, *Poverty,* to lay out an ambitious national social welfare program: "Make

*Settlement leaders were strong believers in public education, but the public school systems of the day were limited both in size and what they taught. When the philosopher John Dewey created his famous "laboratory school" in 1896 to test his theories of progressive education, he did so in association with Hull House. In her devastating critique of the progressive education movement, *The Troubled Crusade* (1983), Diane Ravitch nevertheless praises Dewey (and Jane Addams) for seeking to end student "passivity" and "teachers' excessive reliance on rote memorization and drill."

all tenements and factories sanitary; prohibit entirely child labor; compensate labor for enforced seasons of idleness, old age or lack of work beyond the control of the workman." Such demands were not the mere conceits of a political fringe. By the first decade of the 20th century, leading settlement residents had gained the ear of President Theodore Roosevelt. In 1903, Lillian Wald called for the establishment of a federal children's bureau to monitor and investigate such matters as infant mortality, child labor, and education. Invited to Washington to see the president, her efforts led, though slowly, to the 1909 White House Conference on the Care of Dependent Children. That gathering led to a spread of state-supported mothers' pensions—intended to allow widows and the wives of the disabled to stay at home to raise their children—and to the establishment in April 1912 of the federal Children's Bureau. Its first director, appointed by President William Howard Taft, was Julia Lathrop of Hull House.

HISTORIANS HAVE PORTRAYED THIS AS THE movement's zenith. At last, they say, the settlement residents emerged as advocates for reform during the Progressive era and as harbingers of better things to come. But even as settlement leaders became national figures—Jane Addams regularly appeared on lists of the most admired Americans—they remained committed to helping individual poor people get ahead. Settlement leaders did not become directors of interest advocacy groups with offices in Washington, far from the poor. They were representatives of neighborhood organizations who also happened to have an important voice in the national debate over poverty.

Between 1900 and 1920, even after reaching their supposed peak, settlements continued to grow and diversify. No longer did volunteers come strictly from upper-middle-class backgrounds; some settlements even added paid staff in certain specialized areas, such as nursing. In their 1913 *Handbook of Settlements,* Robert Woods and Albert Kennedy of Boston's South End House listed 413 settlement houses, concentrated in New York, Boston, and Chicago, but present in some form in 32 states and the District of Columbia. It was a network of bourgeois outposts in the American Calcuttas, boasting tenements refurbished as community centers, programs of educa-

tion and recreation, and resident volunteers from the nation's best schools, all directed toward poor children and their parents.

Hull House itself grew to encompass eight buildings, including a music school, theater, and gymnasium. It operated a large day nursery for the children of the neighborhood's many working mothers. Major settlements such as Pittsburgh's Kingsley House developed elaborate programs of "manual training," kindergartens for children of slum families, and a summer "country home" where children and their families could gain a brief respite from the tenements. In a single week in January 1904, the house was attended by 1,680 children and teenagers. The 13 Kingsley House residents were assisted by 80 "non-resident volunteers" who came to the house for one month or more. Typical days ran from nine in the morning to 10:30 at night.

The annual reports of the house paint a picture of an institution thoroughly integrated into its neighborhood. "To many boys," said the 1905 annual report, "Kingsley is a place where they may spend their evenings—their club house. They know the people who live here are always glad to see them—that the books, the magazines, the games, the warmth of the fire place is for them as for us." There can be no doubt that settlements such as this were predicated on the belief that the development of ambition and a work ethic in the children of the poor could not be left to chance. Wrote head resident William Mathews: "We cannot begin too early. Life changes quickly from one of instincts to one of habits. The child should be given fair opportunities to master the difficulties that have in many cases already crushed the parents.

"What means the work to the boy hammering, chiseling, planing away on the bookshelf, the table, the sled? It means the calling into eager and enjoyable activity the whole power of his being, and the consequent crowding out of the lower passions that ever find their root in idleness and inactivity."

AFTER THE TURN OF THE CENTURY, settlements became a high-profile cause, attracting generous donations from the well-to-do. In 1906, Kingsley House boasted not only more than 900 individual financial supporters but its own endowment. Unlike the super-rich of today, who often flatter themselves with glittering gifts to museums, fashionable environmental causes, and the like, many of the wealthy during this earlier era felt a duty to provide the poor with means of advancement: libraries, schools, and settlement houses. One of Kingsley's supporters was Andrew Carnegie, who also endowed, among many other institutions, more than 2,800 libraries to help poor people improve themselves.

At its height, the settlement movement was a center not only of uplift efforts but a range of social services, including "milk stations" and vocational education, many of which have been assumed (with varying degrees of effectiveness) by government and those under contract to it. Jane Addams, for one, anticipated and approved this prospect. She thought of settlements as places where experiments could be tried and then adopted by government.

How deeply did settlement efforts penetrate? What were the results? Can settlements truly be credited with having an effect on the poor?

The numbers of those touched by settlement houses sometimes seem impressive. In 1906, Pittsburgh's Kingsley House claimed weekly contact with some 2,000 children from the neighborhood around its 14-room building at Bedford and Fulton Streets. But it is undoubtedly true that, in general, settlements reached a minority of their neighbors. New York's East Side House, in the city's Yorkville section, described itself in 1914 as "a radiant center of spiritual, moral and intellectual light in a thickly settled neighborhood of 150,000." Its clubs enrolled 1,346 children.

Almost inevitably, the settlement workers found themselves focusing on those with the best chance to get ahead. In New York, Vida Scudder found reaching the Italian "peasant" so difficult—despite her own knowledge of Italian—that she frankly admitted that she would concentrate her work on those she identified as intellectuals. "The primary function of the settlement house," observed sociologist William Whyte in *Street Corner Society* (1943), "is to stimulate social mobility, to hold out middle-class standards and middle-class rewards to lower-class people. Since upward mobility almost always involves movement out of the slum district, the settlement is constantly dealing with people on their way out. . . . The social workers want to deal with 'the better element.' "

One can speculate as to whether reaching the right people can change the tone and social fabric of an entire neighborhood. Settlement workers believed it possible. Wrote Robert Woods: "Interaction of residents, volunteers, and supporters with neighbors has its sure effect on local opinion. As working people come to know men and women of culture and organizing power, they understand the responsible and humanizing use of the resources of life and are less moved by irresponsible and railing criticism." Settlement workers were convinced they had succeeded in changing at least the course of lives they touched directly. Reflecting on more than 30 years at the Henry Street Settlement, Lillian Wald wrote: "Frequent on musical and dramatic programs are the names of girls and boys whom we have known in our clubs and classes. Not a few are listed in the ranks of the literary. Some have been elected to public office, others drafted into the public service." Among those who passed through the houses were Frances Perkins, secretary of labor under President Franklin Roosevelt, union leader Sidney Hillman and comedian George Burns. Benny Goodman received his first clarinet lesson at Hull House. A gymnastics lesson at New York's Union Settlement House inspired Burt Lancaster to seek a career in show business—as an acrobat. Even today, decades after the heyday of the settlement-house movement, it is possible to make a long list of prominent people whose lives were touched by a settlement house: Nate Archibald, a former professional basketball player, novelist Mario Puzo, actress Whoopie Goldberg, and Robert P. Rittereiser, who was president and chief executive officer of the old E. F. Hutton brokerage firm (and one of a trio of extremely successful brothers who acknowledge a large debt to Manhattan's East Side House).

By the early 1920s, settlement houses seemed likely to become a permanent fixture of American life. Although their pacifism cost Jane Addams, Lillian Wald, and some other settlement-house leaders public favor during World War I, Robert Woods and Albert Kennedy could still confidently assert in their 1922 survey, *The Settlement Horizon,* that "the strong claims of so thoroughly an established tradition of leadership, and the breadth and momentum of the cause, furnish ample guarantees for the future."

It was not to be. In part, settlement houses fell victim to their own success.

During the boom years of the 1920s, many of the poor headed up and out of the old neighborhoods. "There are many 'empties' [vacant apartments] in our neighborhood," wrote Lillian Wald, "because, as standards of living have been lifted, the uncrushable desire for a bathroom has increased, and the people have moved away." Meanwhile, restrictive federal legislation in 1924 ended mass immigration, thus limiting the number of newcomers in settlement neighborhoods.

Some settlement houses closed down; many merged and became part of the group of charities served by local United Way and Community Chest drives, losing their financial independence and public profile. By 1963, in *Beyond the Melting Pot,* Nathan Glazer and Daniel Moynihan described the settlements' role in elegiac terms: "The Puerto Rican has entered the city in the age of the welfare state. Here and there are to be found the settlement houses of an earlier period, in which a fuller and richer concern for the individual was manifested by devoted people from the prosperous classes."

THERE ARE REMNANTS OF THE MOVEMENT today in the major settlement cities—Boston, New York, and Chicago, where Hull House celebrated its centennial last year. Although aspects of the original impulse are still to be found—New York's Henry Street Settlement operates youth clubs, Boston's United South End settlement runs a fresh-air camp—settlements today are run mostly by paid professionals, social workers whose training has its roots in psychiatric casework. Many settlements are really little more than health and counseling centers, which, like all manner of other institutions today, simply deliver impersonal social services to the poor. Government reimbursement provides the bulk of funding. It turned out, contrary to the expectations of Jane Addams and others, that government was simply incapable of doing what the settlements did—and was not really interested in trying, either.

The settlement idea also suffered as a result of the Depression, which, more than any other event in American life, made clear the limits of private charity. The incontrovertible importance of the 1935 Social Security Act, which established the form of the national social insurance system, has overshadowed a dubious assumption that accompanied it: that as pension programs grew to cover the elderly, the blind, and the families of maimed or disabled workers, poverty, over time, would "wither away." Nobody anticipated the massive influx of unskilled workers from outside the industrial system after World War II, workers who had not been covered by the new social insurance. Poverty did not disappear. Yet the persistence of the withering away fallacy discouraged volunteer activities. Poverty, it had been decided, would and should be taken care of by government.

The affluence of the postwar era and the expansion of government responsibility for management of the economy made government solutions to the poverty problem seem all the more appropriate. The need for federal intervention to break down the legal barriers to the entry of blacks into the mainstream of society reinforced the focus on Washington. The settlement-house philosophy—which embraced the need both for a social insurance safety net below *and* a helping hand from above—was largely forgotten.

Inaugurating the War on Poverty in 1965, President Lyndon Johnson spoke of a "hand, not a handout," but the new federal antipoverty programs were captured by people who sought to mobilize the poor to effect a redistribution of wealth and power through political activism. Although VISTA workers and New Left activists followed the settlement example of taking up residence among the poor, few were driven by the idea of assisting the poor in self-improvement. Indeed, many of them rejected the very notion that the poor needed improvement; "the system" was the problem. To these latter-day settlement workers, the "hero club" and the summer camp seemed pathetically inadequate next to the class action suit and the sit-in at City Hall.

By far the most important response to the new urban poverty was the growth of the Aid to Families with Dependent Children (AFDC) program—a descendant, ironically, of the "widows' pensions" for which settlement residents had lobbied Teddy Roosevelt in 1909. Never meant as a large-scale welfare program when it was created under the Social Security Act, AFDC was pushed along by the growth of single-parent families until it became the nation's most important relief program. From $194 million in 1963, annual outlays for AFDC grew to $2.5 billion in 1972. As welfare payments grew, so did the unease of a society historically loathe simply to provide alms

for the poor. As early as 1962 and as recently as 1988, Congress attempted to build uplift into the AFDC system. Some of these efforts, such as job training programs for welfare recipients in the 1988 Family Support Act, have shown promise. All of these efforts, however, owe more to such antecedents as the scientific charity movement than to the settlement impulse. They are more "reformative" than "formative." They target the "welfare-eligible," those who have a demonstrated difficulty joining the economic mainstream, not those on the margin who might have a better chance of getting ahead with a little help.

IT IS DIFFICULT TO SUGGEST THAT THERE may be ways to go back to a better future for American social-welfare initiatives. Because the United States delayed providing basic social insurance for so long, historians have cast the pre-New Deal era as a Dark Age of Social Darwinism. Surveying this era in his acclaimed book, *In The Shadow of the Poorhouse* (1986), Michael Katz asserted that the 19th-century social-welfare system "reflected the brittle hostility and anger of the respectable classes and their horror at the prospect of a united, militant working class."

Although the American welfare state has never been as generous as such critics might like, times have changed. Having survived the political assault of Ronald Reagan and the intellectual critique of Charles Murray in *Losing Ground* (1984), the American welfare state is in no immediate danger of being rolled back. At the same time, it is clear that there is no political consensus for its expansion. Left and Right seem to agree only that the current social-welfare system is unsatisfactory. A renewed emphasis on the active promotion of upward mobility offers a way out of this paralysis.

The day of the settlement house itself as the major link between the social classes has passed. Too many of its functions have been taken up, however imperfectly, by other institutions, ranging from the public schools to public television. But the need for such a bridge has not been adequately met. Large numbers of Americans cannot find their way into the economic mainstream and are not spurred on to reach "the highest level of which each is capable." Without knowledge of how the world beyond the neighborhood works—that one can become an engineer, that good colleges are eager to

accept black students with potential—the poor will not reach the highest level of their ability. Hard questions must be asked before such bridge building can begin. First, which values are to be taught to the poor? Second, who will teach them? Educators such as Joseph Clark, the controversial black high school principal from Paterson, New Jersey, have come to symbolize a return to an emphasis on bedrock values as part of schooling. People from beyond the neighborhood can help. Potential middle-class volunteers may not feel the tug of religious commitment as strongly as the Jane Addams generation did, but there are still affluent youths whose "uselessness hangs about them heavily."

In poor neighborhoods throughout the nation, thousands of voluntary wars on poverty are already underway. But overall, too few are being won, and most are being waged without much help from middle-class whites. Perhaps the biggest impediment to the growth and success of such efforts is the lingering belief among liberals and others with the means to provide help that they are somehow beside the point, or even dangerous. Today's reformers pay tribute to impulses like those of the settlement workers—as when New York's Governor Mario Cuomo invokes the image of society as family—but only as prelude to calls for expanded social-welfare programs. They dismiss every pre-New Deal response to poverty—and every new proposal reminiscent of such measures—as paltry and mean-spirited. Thus President George Bush's talk of "a thousand points of light" inspires nothing but liberal satire, apparently out of the belief that any private effort to ameliorate poverty is meaningless, intended only to undermine government social-welfare programs. To that, too, the settlement tradition offers an answer.

"The conditions of life forced by our civilization upon the poor in our great cities are undemocratic, unchristian, unrighteous," wrote Vida Scudder of the College Settlement Association in 1900. But efforts to improve them, she said, must be "wholly free from the spirit of social dogmatism and doctrinaire assertion. . . . As we become more practical, we also become better idealists. . . . As we become more useful here and now, we strengthen and deepen all those phases of our common life that vibrate with the demand for a better society to be."

George Washington Carver: Creative Scientist

In the early twentieth century, this prolific and charismatic scientist played a key role in spreading the benefits of scientific agriculture throughout the southern United States.

Vivian E. Hilburn

Vivian E. Hilburn is a guidance counselor and instructor of Spanish at Paul Quinn College in Waco, Texas. She has been the director of the Black Studies Club on campus for many years.

Few scientists—and particularly few specialists in botany or chemistry—have a monument erected in their memory, and still fewer can boast of having a foundation or museum carrying their name. All of these and numerous other honors have come to George Washington Carver, a man of humble birth who, until his death in the middle of this century, etched indelible marks on the history and lives of his people and his nation.

Carver, the son of a female slave in the home of Moses and Susan Carver, was born near Diamond Grove, Missouri, circa 1864. His childhood was tumultuous because of the unstable conditions of the times. Southwest Missouri, a frontier area, was bordered by the slaveholding, secession-oriented Arkansas, "Free Kansas," and the Oklahoma Indian Territory. Moses Carver, a slaveholding Unionist, was caught in the middle of the issues dividing the nation. Linda McMurry writes in *George Washington Carver: Scientist and Symbol,* "Throughout the war, area residents were prey to looting and killing by Confederate bushwackers, Union raiders, and ordinary outlaws taking advantage of the unsettled conditions." Moses Carver's homestead was raided by Confederate bushwackers several times, and on one of those raids,

George and his mother were kidnapped and taken to Arkansas.

The Carvers were fond of Mary and her two sons—their only slaves—and wanted to find them. A neighbor, who was familiar with the guerrilla bands in the area, said he knew their whereabouts and agreed to hunt for them. His search uncovered George, who was returned to the Carvers, but Mary was never found. George and his brother Jim had always lived with their mother in a smaller cabin on the Carver property, but with the disappearance of Mary, the Carvers moved the boys into the main cabin with them and they lived as a family.

George was a frail and sickly child due to an earlier bout with whooping cough. He stuttered because of a speech impediment and had a falsetto voice about which he was often teased. The heavier chores on the farm were allotted to Jim, who was older, healthier, and stronger. George helped Susan around the house, and learned cooking, sewing, laundering, and needle work.

The young George was untiringly inquisitive and could often be seen in the woods, scraping earth, gathering bark from trees, and coddling weeds and flowers. He gathered cans and gourds in which he grew sprouts. He became so adept at cultivating plants that neighbors called him the Plant Doctor. His desire "to know" and "to do" became a lifelong obsession. Until his death Carver enjoyed making things, and his rapport with nature was nurtured by early morning walks in the woods.

From a very early age Carver was recognized as having exceptional intel-

ligence. His desire to learn, however, was thwarted for a while. Although the Missouri Constitution of 1865 made free schooling mandatory for black youngsters from age five, George could not attend school at that time because there were not enough blacks of a qualifying age in his township to warrant a school. There was, however, a school for blacks in the county seat of Neosho, and around age twelve, George left the Carvers to attend school there. In Neosho, only eight miles from Diamond Grove, George lived with his first set of black parents, Mariah and Andrew Watkins. Mariah was a midwife and she, like Susan, cultivated his homemaking skills. He also attended worship services with her at the African Methodist Episcopal Church, where religion became a central focus of his life.

Carver turned down an offer of a permanent position at Iowa State to "be of the greatest good" to his fellow blacks.

Neosho had a large black population and there George felt a sense of belonging. By now, he had learned that he was black, and being so, he could not dream of fame, affluence, or lofty achievements. But his drive "to know" and "to do" spurred him on. What was rain?— the question constantly nagged him. What was creation, order and design?

This article first appeared in *The World & I*, July 1987, pp. 189-197. Reprinted by permission of *The World & I*, a publication of the Washington Times Corporation. © 1987.

What gives soil different colors? These questions echoed through his mind and strengthened his determination to discover truth.

But his excitement about the schooling in Neosho was short-lived. Carver soon learned that the teacher knew little more than he did. Carver's disillusionment with the Neosho school and his desire for knowledge started him on a long trek through several towns in Kansas in search of an education. Eventually, he became an art major at Simpson College in Indianola, Iowa. His cooking and laundering skills provided a livelihood wherever he went.

At Simpson, despite his talent and interest in painting, his art teacher advised him to enroll in the state agricultural college at Ames, where her father was a horticulture professor. She was convinced that his botanical skills offered him more financial security than would a career as a black artist. Despite his desire to cease his wandering, he took her advice and enrolled at Ames.

He quickly overcame the initial reservation of the other students to him as the only black on campus, and he became an active and popular member of the student body. Carver graduated in 1894 with a bachelor of science degree from Iowa State College, and took a position at the Ames Experiment Station as an assistant to Louis Pammell, a noted botanist and mycologist. He also taught freshman biology while pursuing graduate work. By the time he earned a masters degree in 1896, his abilities in mycology and plant hybridization were already remarkable.

EMPLOYMENT AT TUSKEGEE

That same year he was asked by Booker T. Washington, then widely known as an educator, author, lecturer, and reformer, to head the newly established Department of Agriculture at Tuskegee Institute in Alabama. Washington advocated industrial and agricultural education as the key to black advancement. He understood the plight of the farmers, white and black. The one-crop system that had consisted principally of cotton production had drained them of energy and incentive. Most of these farmers were tenants and sharecroppers who eked out a bare existence by borrowing money for planting in the spring and paying it back after harvest in the fall.

Washington sought to free farmers from the burden of debt, and he found an ally in George Washington Carver. Carver turned down an offer of a permanent position at Iowa State to "be of the greatest good" to his fellow blacks. He arrived in Alabama wearing a too-tight gray suit, the top button of his jacket fastened, and a pert pink rose in his lapel. He presented a striking figure with a handlebar moustache, pointed nose, and deep, burning eyes. Thin [and] stooped, he resembled a question mark. While waiting at the Chehaw railroad station for someone to take him to the campus, he immediately began plucking plants and surveying the red clay hills in the distance. "Red! Yellow! Oh! the handiwork of God!" he thought. He saw the undeveloped natural resources that could improve the lives of all Southerners.

As a trained researcher, the first item on Carver's agenda was setting up a proper laboratory. Although Tuskegee was the second best-endowed black school in the nation, it was still poor in comparison to similar white schools. With exceedingly limited funds, Washington sought to elevate an entire people. Thus Carver made his own equipment with retrievals from junk piles. His lamp served as a heater for his hands when they became stiff from the cold, as a Bunsen burner for his scientific experiments, and as a reflector for his microscope. For graders, he punched holes in pieces of tin. He used reeds as pipettes, cut broken bottles clean-edged with string, and pulverized his material using a cracked china bowl as a mortar. And since zinc sulphate was costly, he picked up discarded zinc tops from fruit jars.

It was a far cry from the equipment he had used at Iowa State. One consolation was that soon after he arrived in Tuskegee, the Institute was granted $1,500 annually by the state legislature to establish and run an agricultural experiment station. It became the only all-black-manned station, and not coincidentally the lowest-funded one. Carver's station never received more than $1,500 a year, while a nearby white station got between $60,000 and $100,000 for its annual budget.

Over the years his desire for a better and more adequate laboratory and more time to do research, free from teaching responsibilities, became the main source of a growing rift between him and Booker T. Washington. He clashed with Washington largely because Carver was a gifted teacher and researcher, but not much of an administrator. His assistant, George Bridgeforth, eventually became the head of the Department of Agriculture and Carver was named the director of agricultural research. Although this move freed Carver from the administrative details he hated, it did not sit well with him to have anyone over him. These basic conflicts were never resolved and only ameliorated with Washington's death in 1915.

ROLE AS AN EDUCATOR

In Carver's laboratory, which he called "God's Little Workshop," the students learned the techniques of analyzing soils to determine which elements were lacking. They tested fertilizers and feeds to find out what ingredients increased tissue, fat, or milk. He taught the "trinity of relationship" between the soil, the plants growing on it, and the human beings or animals consuming the plants. He insisted that only by knowing the components of the soil could one determine the proper quantities of minerals needed to nourish each particular crop. He argued that a mastery of the economics of plant life can improve human existence. And above all, Carver preached the unity of the universe and the interrelatedness of all its parts.

Farming was unpopular at the Alabama school because blacks had been the major victims of farming's failures. Carver had to make the vocation attractive. He possessed two essential qualities of a good teacher—a thorough knowledge of his subject and an intuitive sense of how to transmit and instill it while he was able to convey his own motivating compulsion—"I don't know, but I'll find out"—he also knew "you can't teach people anything, you can only draw out what is in them." He was extraordinarily effective. Even when Washington was deeply exasperated with Carver, he admitted that the professor was "a great teacher, a great lecturer, a great inspirer of young men and old men."

Most of his students had only average intelligence, but he brought out the best points in each. He made each of them feel proud of his own ability and fostered a desire to extend it. He moved them to action with scoldings. "Get the drones off you! Remember, the more ignorant we are the less use God has for us." Carver was able to instill the "Tuskegee Ideal"—that the benefits of a student's education were to be shared with his community. Most of his students returned to their homes and spread the gospel of scientific agriculture.

He also promoted a philosophy of thrift and conservation. He thought that saving was not enough; there must be order also. To demonstrate this he showed his students a box of string, saved but snarled and entangled. "This is ignorance," he said. "And this"—he held up another box in which each piece was neatly tied or rolled into balls—"is intelligence."

In 1903 a boy's dormitory, Rockefeller Hall, was erected on the Tuskegee campus and Carver moved into two ground-floor rooms which he was to occupy for 35 years. Initially controversy arose over this special treatment. Many of the other teachers felt it unfair that he be given more space than they and that he was arrogant to expect such treatment. Carver prevailed though, and weathered quite a bit of resentment over a bachelor's occupying so much space on a crowded campus. At the same time, the students loved having him near, and for many of them he played the role of teacher, father, and spiritual adviser.

Carver graduated in 1896 with a master's degree in botany from Iowa State College. Recruited by Booker T. Washington, he then accepted a position at the fledgling Tuskegee Institute. He arrived in Alabama wearing a flower in his lapel, which became an enduring symbol.

DEMONSTRATION AS TEACHING

Carver had come South to help farmers, and the Experiment Station at Tuskegee was the nucleus of this effort. Tuskegee had long engaged in extension activities such as an annual Farmers' Conference. Carver improved and expanded such efforts. He added farmers' institutes, an annual colored fair, and easy-to-read agricultural bulletins.

Throughout the years, he did not limit his scientific demonstrations to the classroom. Believing that demonstration is the purest form of teaching, Carver went into the community to give hands-on illustrations of his theories. He would not rely on publications to relay the results of experiments because many farmers could not read. Since there were no home and farm demonstration agents, he developed the "Jesup Wagon"—a wagon equipped with demonstration materials—to communicate his ideas. Money for the project was donated by Morris K. Jesup. The Jesup Wagon, "a farmers' college on wheels," started its career in May 1906. It was operated by Thomas M. Campbell, a former student of Carver's. In November of that year, the U.S. Department of Agriculture (USDA) employed Campbell as the first "Negro Demonstration Agent." He took the wagon to surrounding communities for regularly scheduled demonstrations of plowing and planting, usually at a house where neighbors had gathered. He returned later at the appropriate time to give instructions on cultivation and harvesting.

Tuskegee was a leader in the development of movable schools. In the United States, Iowa State College was the first to experiment with a "Seed Corn Gospel Train." But the success of Tuskegee's later version was the prime reason for the idea's success. It has since helped to shape educational policies with respect to disadvantaged groups and underdeveloped countries throughout the world. Similar projects were adopted in China, India, Macedonia, and Southern Rhodesia. In regions where road systems could not accommodate motor vehicles, donkeys were used to transport educational materials as "a gift of knowledge" to farmers.

Encouraged by Washington, Carver also published numerous agricultural bulletins. By 1908 he had published fourteen bulletins and devoted many hours to his column, "Professor Carver's Advice." Here he warned farmers of impending dangers such as hog cholera, and he cautioned stockmen against poisonous weeds that their livestock might eat. One bulletin, *Some Cercosporae of Macon County, Alabama,* reflected Carver's favorite field of research, which was largely denied to him by his circumstances. He did not have the equipment or time needed for the proper identification of the many species of fungus. Nevertheless, he continued to collect fungi, and he was the first to identify several species, one of which was named *Taphrina carveri.* In 1935 the USDA made him a "collaborator," and his specimens are still preserved in the USDA herbarium in Beltsville, Maryland.

RESEARCH IN CROPS AND NATURAL RESOURCES

In 1904 the boll weevil invaded American cotton fields. By 1910 it was a full-grown menace. Spraying each plant with

A Man of Faith

I came to know George Washington Carver during the time we were together at Tuskegee Institute, where I was a student and he an instructor. At least three times a day, over a period of eight years, I observed the posture and mood of his daily life. Since both of us were housed on the east end of campus, he at Rockefeller Hall and I at Thrasher Hall, this gave me a splendid opportunity to see him as he went to and from his quarters. We also ate in the same main dining hall—he with the members of the faculty and I with the other students.

Often on long evenings, he would leave the dining room and walk toward the agriculture building. Sometimes, he took a similar route in the early morning, but frequently in the morning hours he could be found examining the roots, plants, shrubbery, and soil around campus. The area of campus where the science building, the Hollis Burke Frissell Library and Logan Hall now stand was then an open field and Dr. Carver spent a lot of time there also. During these excursions, he communed with God and nature.

I believe his intellectual resources profited from his spiritual life. He was able to accomplish so much because he prayed so much. The more difficult the task he confronted, the more time he spent preparing through prayer and meditation. Even though he kept a busy schedule, he took time for reflection and always took stock of his spiritual condition. He labored to be right with God and

he often expressed that he did not want to come to the edge of the grave before manifesting a concern about eternity. He advised that every young person should find a little time to be alone with God each day.

Many mornings I would hear a low-sounding voice under my window, only to look out and observe Dr. Carver examining a lump of dirt or a root or a growth of some kind, asking God to reveal its secrets. He knew the truth of William Cullen Bryant's words: "To him who in the love of Nature holds Communion with her visible forms, she speaks a various language."

He was not only a great scientist, but a great man of faith. Every Sunday, many students and faculty at Tuskegee Institute attended chapel services at 11:00 A.M. Later Dr. Carver would lead a Bible class of about 200 students. He told the same stories I had heard so many times before, but he made the characters in the Bible come alive. Once, while he was discussing a Bible figure, he characterized him in relation to the people with whom he associated. He pointed out his virtues and vices as he walked from one side of the room to the other. Suddenly, he astounded the entire assembly by saying that the character under consideration suffered from hemorrhoids. This is only one example of his uncanny insights into the human character.

The themes of his Bible classes, as well as chance conversations with him on

campus, were pure and uplifting. He was guileless and gentle. For a while, because of his modest and peaceful nature, I had a feeling that he didn't know how to be stern, but that opinion was changed upon several occasions when I heard him strongly scold a student for misbehaving.

His life has had a quiet influence on my own. He was so dedicated to his area of expertise that he had a great deal to do with the deepening and confirming of my own dedication to lifelong goals.

—Rev. Andrew Fowler
Capitol View Baptist, Washington, D.C.

TUSKEGEE UNIVERSITY ARCHIVES

Carver knew the truth of William Cullen Bryant's words: "To him who in the love of Nature holds Communion with her visible forms, she speaks a various language."

calcium arsenate would be financially prohibitive. Only by planting, cultivating, and harvesting early might the damage be minimized. Carver advised farmers to obtain cotton of the greatest vitality—the fastest-growing and the earliest ripening. He developed his own hybrid and distributed its seeds at the Farmers' Conference. At the same time, he urged farmers to plant less cotton and to replace this cash crop with sweet potatoes, cowpeas, and peanuts.

Cowpeas, or black-eyed peas as they were commonly called, had proved to be "the poor man's bank" as a soil health builder and excellent livestock food. At that time few people in the United States had heard of the soybean, another le-

guminous nitrogen fixer. Only much later did the USDA experiment with imported soybeans and adapt them to American soils and climatic conditions. Carver had successfully experimented

He made the results of his and others' research available and understandable to thousands whose lives were thereby enriched.

with them, and they eventually became a major crop in the region.

But Carver's most important studies revolved around the peanut. Farmers already knew about the peanut. Indigenous to South America, it had been relished by conquistadors who carried it to Spain. It found its way to Africa in the seventeenth century, and came back again to the New World with slave traders as their chief bill-of-fare for their human cargo. The African word *goober* for peanut is today an active part of the Southern vocabulary. The peanut is leguminous, and easy to plant, grow, and harvest.

The peanut is equal to sirloin beef in protein content and to potatoes in carbohydrates. Before 1913, Carver published recipes for cooking peanuts in one of his bulletins. By 1916, this bulletin was in its sixth edition, carrying directions for growing peanuts and 105 ways to prepare and eat them. Carver taught a class of senior girls who were studying dietetics the varied usages of the peanut. They served a tasty five-course lunch to Booker T. Washington and nine guests— soup, mock-chicken, vegetable, salad, bread, candy, cookies, ice cream, and coffee—all made from peanuts!

The peanut, soybean and sweet potato had not only helped enrich the soil, but they had provided bumper crops. Yet the market place was still not profitable for farmers due to the lack of viable products from these commodities. Carver's research turned to developing new uses for them in three distinct stages: finding, adapting, and creating. First he used the raw materials nature had provided. Second he rearranged these materials— wood, stones, ores, fibers, skins, metals—targeting their potential industrial use. Third he transformed these materials into new ones for the benefit of people and society.

He knew that a large portion of any farm crop was inedible and was therefore wasted. Carver abhorred waste. His solution was simple and direct: Find uses for a product's waste and thus enlarge its usefulness. He had a vision of farms as not merely food factories but as sources of raw materials for industry. In the meantime, he sought to produce cheap substitutes for the expensive goods whose purchase helped to keep sharecroppers in debt.

From soybeans he had made flour, starch, meal, stains, dyes, ink, breakfast food, oil, milk, and wood fillers. But he knew that soybeans could not be promoted for industrial purposes because of Southern unfamiliarity with them. Instead, Carver concentrated on the peanut. From his research on peanuts emerged such products as beverages, pickles, sauces, meal, coffee, salve, bleach, wood filler, washing powder, metal polish, paper, ink, plastics, shaving cream, rubbing oil, linoleum, shampoo, axle grease, and synthetic rubber.

Carver's interest in the dormant mineral wealth of Alabama became more pressing. In the clay hills near Tuskegee, he discovered marble, limestone, malleable copper, azurite, iron, manganese, sugar quartz, bentonite (a de-inker for newspapers), and heat-resisting and nonconducting micas for the electrical industry. He also discovered and developed various fertilizers and dyes. He was most enthusiastic about the use of native dyes for paints. In one bulletin he told farmers how to make and use such paints for their homes, fences, and barns. Later, he got two patents on processes for paint production and an unsuccessful company was formed to market them.

With World War I the danger of a food shortage came to the United States. Because Carver had always believed that a weed was merely a plant out of place, he began teaching the virtues of eating wild vegetables, both fresh and dehydrated. In January 1918, Carver was summoned to Washington to demonstrate products made from the sweet potato and to exhibit how it could be used to make bread. He demonstrated before Army bakers, chemists, dieticians, technicians, and transportation authorities. This last group was invited because of Carver's work on a method of food dehydration that not only preserved foods indefinitely, but greatly decreased their weight and bulk.

In a press conference at this meeting he said, "I do not like the word *substitute* applied to my products. I prefer to let each stand on its own merits." He defined *synthetic* as a "fourth kingdom of nature," in man's control and in which incompatible elements could unite. He predicted "a new world coming—The Synthetic World."

AWARDS AND LEGACY

George Washington Carver died on January 5, 1943, and was buried on the Tuskegee campus next to Booker T. Washington. His outstanding service to humanity had been recognized in the many awards given to him during his lifetime and has been preserved in his legacy.

International recognition was given Carver as a botanist and chemurgist. He was elected a fellow of the Royal Society of Arts of Great Britain in 1918 and awarded the Spingarn Medal in 1923. Carver received an honorary Doctor of Science degree from Simpson College in 1928 and was appointed collaborator for the USDA Mycology and Plant Disease Survey Bureau of Plant Industry. The George Washington Carver Museum was established on the Tuskegee campus in 1935.

Carver was awarded the Franklin Delano Roosevelt Medal in 1939, and received an honorary doctorate from the University of Rochester in 1941. Carver also received many medals, scrolls, citations, and honorary degrees for his achievements in creative and scientific research and for his contributions to the improvement of health and living conditions of the Southern farmer. The United States honored him with a three-cent postage stamp in 1948, and Congress authorized the establishment of the George Washington Carver National Monument near the site of his birth in 1953.

CARVER AS SYMBOL

Few scientists have become as well known and widely acclaimed as Carver, which raises intriguing questions. He made no great theoretical breakthroughs and did not develop a single new commercially successful product. Many scientists, both white and black, have accomplished more through their research. Why then did Carver become so famous? The answers are found in the nature of his personality and the symbolic value of his work and life story.

Carver's fame was also enhanced by his adoption as a symbol by a myriad of causes.

Carver was both a complex and compelling person with many interests and activities. His prize-winning art, his mastery of the piano and several other musical instruments, and his creativity in such crafts as knitting and weaving bespeak his versatility. Some of his paintings were exhibited at the World's Fair in Chicago in 1893. One of them, *Three Peaches,* done with his fingers and with pigments he developed from the clays of Alabama, was requested by the Luxembourg Gallery.

Considered by many to be an introvert and mystic, Carver was little understood during his lifetime. He was often described by those who knew him as modest, unassuming, yet profound. At the same time, he courted and relished publicity. Deeply religious, he attributed his success in developing new products to divine guidance. He found little pleasure in material goods and frequently refused to accept payment for his services to peanut processors and others. He never asked for an increase in his starting salary of $1,200 during his four decades at Tuskegee Institute. Some of his monthly salary checks were still in his desk drawer when the banks crashed during the Depression. He had just not bothered to deposit them. However, since he rarely spent anything on himself—he continued to wear a suit given to him by his Iowa teachers and fellow students until his death—he did accumulate a sizeable savings.

In 1940, when Carver realized that he would not be able to continue his work much longer, he contributed these savings, more than $60,000 in all, to the establishment of the George Washington Carver Research Foundation, "dedicated to the progress of humanity through the application of science to the problems of agriculture and industry." During his remaining three years, Carver continued to work in the foundation with the aid of his young assistant, Austin W. Curtis.

During the next thirty years the foundation grew from a one-man operation on a meager budget to its current status as a multifaceted research organization with over 100 faculty and staff investigators and an annual operational budget in excess of $5 mlllion. These projects include pure research, training and demonstration, and outreach projects, all proper extensions of such a creative life.

His appeal was and is based on more than his idiosyncrasies or physical legacies, however. After hearing Carver speak, one person wrote, "You are the most seductive person I have ever met." His was not a surface charisma—he had a talent for making people feel special. Most acquaintances became intimate friends, and dozens of people, black and white, believed themselves to be Carver's "closest friend." The force of his personality captivated many, including journalists who wrote scores of articles about him.

Carver's fame was also enhanced by his adoption as a symbol by a myriad of causes. The romance of his rise from slavery to success was used to motivate youth to work hard and to prove the fairness of the economic system. Race relations improvement groups, such as the Commission on Interracial Cooperation, publicized his achievements and sponsored talks by him at white colleges to demonstrate the capabilities of blacks. Ironically, at the same time supporters of segregation used his story and unassuming manner to deny the crippling effects of legalized separation. Because of his publicly proclaimed reliance on divine inspiration, a number of religious groups made him a patron saint in the battle against secularism and materialism. Also, the United Peanut Association and "New South" advocates of crop diversification and industrialism saw obvious value in publicizing his work.

In the end, Carver became famous for inventing hundreds of products and saving the South from cotton dependency. This assessment both exaggerates and distorts the nature of his work. His original goal was not to produce commercially feasible commodities, but to provide impoverished sharecroppers with a way out by the use of available resources to improve their circumstances. What he advocated would later be called "appropriate technology." A lot of what he taught was not original, but he was without equal as a popularizer of scientific agriculture. He made the results of both his and others' research available and understandable to thousands whose lives were thereby enriched.

Learning to Go to the Movies

The great democratic art form got off to a very rocky start. People simply didn't want to crowd into a dark room to look at a flickering light, and it took nearly twenty years for Americans and motion pictures to embrace each other.

David Nasaw

On July 5, 1896, the Los Angeles *Times* greeted the imminent arrival of Thomas Alva Edison's moving-picture projector with enormous enthusiasm: "The vitascope is coming to town. It is safe to predict that when it is set up at the Orpheum and set a-going, it will cause a sensation as the city has not known for many a long day."

Thousands of city residents had already viewed moving pictures by peering into the eyeholes of peep-show machines on display in saloons, railroad terminals, and amusement parlors, but these images were no bigger than a postcard. Never before had anyone seen moving pictures projected big as life on a screen.

The commercial possibilities of such an exhibition seemed boundless, and inventors, electricians, and showmen on two continents had been hard at work on a "screen machine" for several years. That the one about to make its debut at the Orpheum vaudeville theater had not actually been invented by Edison was kept secret by its promoters. The Edison name was much too valuable to compromise by suggesting that there might be others who were the Wizard's equal in imagination and technical skill.

The projector that bore Edison's name had, in fact, been invented by Thomas Armat, a Washington, D.C., bookkeeper, and his partner, C. Francis Jenkins, a government stenographer. After months of tinkering, separately and together, the two men had in the summer of 1895 put together a workable projector, named it the Phantoscope, and arranged to exhibit it at the Cotton States and International Exposition in Atlanta, Georgia, in September of the same year.

John Ripley Collection, Kansas State Historical Society, Topeka

The partners borrowed money from relatives to erect an outdoor tent theater on the fairgrounds, arranged for a series of newspaper articles on their wondrous invention, and printed complimentary tickets. When the expected crowds failed to materialize, in

---

Tally's back room with its three chairs and seven peepholes was arguably the nation's first motion-picture theater.

---

large part because fairgoers were not willing to pay a quarter for an amusement they knew nothing about, Armat and Jenkins hired a barker who invited visitors to enter free and pay at the exit

only if they were satisfied. The offer worked, but the customers it attracted entered the theater with only the vaguest idea of what they were going to see. Never having viewed projected moving pictures before, they did not know that the theater had to be darkened. "The moment the lights turned off for the beginning of the show a panic ensued," wrote the film historian Terry Ramsaye some thirty years later. "The visitors had a notion that expositions were dangerous places where pickpockets might be expected on every side. This was, the movie audience thought, just a new dodge for trapping the unwary in the dark."

Jenkins and Armat never did figure out how to introduce their moving pictures to prospective audiences. They ended up losing the fifteen hundred dollars they had borrowed, and the rights to their projector were eventually sold to the company that licensed and distributed Edison's peep-show machines.

The Los Angeles debut of the Phantoscope, renamed Edison's Vitascope, went off without a hitch. The Orpheum Theater was filled with vaudeville patrons who, though not accustomed to sitting in the dark, had no reason to fear that they would be assaulted by those seated next to them. The Los Angeles *Times* carried a complete description of the exhibition for those who had been unfortunate or unadventurous enough not to buy tickets in advance or to secure standing room at the last minute:

"The theatre was darkened until it was as black as midnight. Suddenly a strange whirling sound was heard. Upon a huge white sheet flashed forth the figure of Anna Belle Sun, [a dancer whose real name was Annabelle Whitford] whirling

From *American Heritage*, November 1993, pp. 78-80, 82, 84-88, 90, 92. Adapted from *Going Out: The Rise and Fall of Public Amusements* by David Nasaw. © 1993 by David Nasaw. Reprinted by permission of BasicBooks, a division of HarperCollins Publishers, Inc.

through the mazes of the serpentine dance. She swayed and nodded and tripped it lightly, the filmy draperies rising and falling and floating this way and that, all reproduced with startling reality, and the whole without a break except that now and then one could see swift electric sparks. . . . Then, without warning, darkness and the roar of applause that shook the theater; and knew no pause till the next picture was flashed on the screen. This was long, lanky Uncle Sam who was defending Venezuela from fat little John Bull, and forcing the bully to his knees. Next came a representation of Herald Square in New York with streetcars and vans moving up and down, then Cissy Fitzgerald's dance and last of all a representation of the way May Irwin and John C. Rice kiss. [*The May Irwin Kiss*, perhaps the most popular of the early films, was a fifteen-second close-up of the embrace in the closing scene of the musical comedy *The Widow Jones*.] Their smiles and glances and expressive gestures and the final joyous, overpowering, luscious osculation was repeated again and again, while the audience fairly shrieked and howled approval. The vitascope is a wonder, a marvel, an outstanding example of human ingenuity and it had an instantaneous success on this, its first exhibition in Los Angeles."

It was through lengthy newspaper descriptions like this one that prospective customers first learned about the magic of moving pictures. Note how the article begins with mention of the darkened theater and refers to the darkness again in mid-paragraph. Note too the reference to "swift electric sparks." Neither audiences nor critics understood how the projectors worked, nor were they convinced that the electricity used to project the pictures was harmless.

After two weeks of sold-out performances, the projector and its operators left the Orpheum for a tour of nearby vaudeville houses. But it turned out that theaters outside Los Angeles could not provide the electrical power needed to run the projector, so the machine was hauled back to Los Angeles and installed in the back of Thomas Tally's amusement parlor.

In the front of his store, Tally had set up automatic phonograph and peep-show machines that provided customers, for a nickel a play, with a few minutes of scratchy recorded sound or a few seconds of flickering moving images. Tally

now partitioned off the back of his parlor for a "vitascope" room. To acquaint the public with what he billed as the "Wizard's latest wonder," he took out ads in the Los Angeles newspapers: "Tonight at Tally's Phonograph Parlor, 311 South Spring St, for the first time in Los Angeles, the great Corbett and Courtney prize fight will be reproduced upon a great screen through the medium of this great and marvelous invention. The men will be seen on the stage, life size, and every movement made by them in this great fight will be reproduced as seen in actual life."

Tally's back room was arguably the nation's first moving-picture theater. But although the technology for projecting moving images was in place, people turned out to be reluctant to enter a dark room to see pictures projected on a sheet. Unable to lure customers into his "theater," Tally did the next best thing. He punched holes in the partition separating the larger storefront from the vitascope room and, according to Terry Ramsaye, invited customers to "peer in at the screen while standing in the comfortable security of the well lighted phonograph parlor. . . . Three peep holes were at chair level for seated spectators, and four somewhat higher for standees—

standing room only after three admissions, total capacity seven. The price per peep hole was fifteen cents."

As Tally and other storefront proprietors quickly discovered, it was not going to be easy to assemble an audience for moving pictures. Projectors were difficult to run and impossible to repair; the electrical current or batteries they ran on seldom worked properly; and the films were expensive, of poor quality, and few.

Harry Davis, a Pittsburgh showman, attached the tony Greek word for theater to the lowly five-cent coin.

But most important, customers balked at entering darkened rooms to see a few minutes of moving pictures. In April 1902 Tally tried again to open an "Electric Theater" but was forced to convert it to vaudeville after six months.

It was the same story everywhere. As a disgusted Oswego, New York, operator reported, at first the vitascope drew

Library of Congress

"crowded houses on account of its novelty. Now everybody has seen it, and, to use the vernacular of the 'foyer,' it does not 'draw flies.' "

Although projected films failed to attract customers to storefront theaters during their first decade of life, they were nonetheless being introduced to millions of vaudeville fans. "Dumb" acts—animals, puppets, pantomimists, magic-lantern slides, and *tableaux vivants*—had traditionally opened and closed the show because, being silent, they would not be disturbed by late arrivals or early departures. The movies were, the managers now discovered, the perfect dumb acts: they were popular, cheaper than most live performers, didn't talk back or complain about the accommodations, and could be replaced weekly.

Most of the early projectors held only fifty feet, or sixteen seconds, of film, which if looped and repeated five or six times could be stretched out to almost two minutes. Seven or eight films, displayed one after another in this fashion, lasted fifteen to twenty minutes, the perfect length for a vaudeville "turn."

The first moving pictures, shot in Edison's Black Maria studio in New Jersey, had been of vaudeville, musical theater, and circus acts. But audiences turned out to prefer pictures that moved across the frame: waves crashing onto a beach, trains barreling down their tracks, soldiers parading, horses racing. At the vitascope's debut performance at Koster & Bial's vaudeville theater in New York City, the crowd cheered loudest on seeing *Rough Sea at Dover,* the one picture shot outside the studio. Still, in the vaudeville halls the "living pictures" constituted one act among many.

Only in the middle of the first decade of the 1900s, after enormous improvements in the quality of the projectors and the production and distribution of films, was a new generation in show business ready to try again to lure customers into a moving-picture theater. What made the moment right was the fact that after 1903 the manufacturers—as the film producers referred to themselves—grew concerned that their customers were weary of the same old "actualities" and began to make pictures that told stories.

Although it was not possible to tell much of a story in a few silent minutes,

audiences were captivated by the new films. As demand increased, the manufacturers developed assembly-line production methods, distributors streamlined the process of getting the films to exhibitors, and businessmen opened storefront theaters to exhibit the increasingly sophisticated product.

The first freestanding moving-picture theater was probably the work of Harry Davis, Pittsburgh's most prosperous showman. In April of 1904 Davis opened an amusement arcade near his Grand Opera House. When a fire burned it down, he rented a larger storefront, but instead of outfitting it as an arcade he filled the room with chairs, gaily decorated the exterior, and, attaching the high-toned Greek word for theater to the lowly five-cent coin, advertised the opening of a "nickelodeon." It was an instant success.

Although Davis was certainly the first exhibitor to use the name *nickelodeon,* similar experiments were taking place in other parts of the country. Marcus Loew on a visit to his Cincinnati arcade in 1905 learned from his manager that a rival across the river in Covington, Kentucky, had come up with a marvelous new "idea in entertainment. . . . I went over with my general manager—it was on Sunday . . . and I never got such a thrill in my life. The show was given in an old-fashioned brownstone house, and the proprietor had the hallways partitioned off with dry goods cases. He used to go to the window and sell the tickets to the children, then he went to the door and took the tickets, and after he did that he locked the door and went up and operated the machine. . . . I said to my companion, 'This is the most remarkable thing I have ever seen.' The place was packed to suffocation." Loew returned

---

Nickelodeon owners realized they had to meld the openness of the saloon with the selectivity of the hotel.

---

to Cincinnati and opened his own screen show the following Sunday. "The first day we played I believe there were seven or eight people short of five thousand and we did not advertise at all. The

people simply poured into the arcade. That showed me the great possibilities of this new form of entertainment." Back in New York City, Loew rented space for similar picture-show theaters alongside each of his arcades.

Across the country arcade owners shut off the backs of their storefronts or rented additional space for picture shows, while vaudeville managers, traveling exhibitors, and show businessmen left their jobs to set up their own nickel picture shows.

There was a great deal of money to be made in the fledgling business, but nickelodeon owners had to work hard to introduce their product. They could not afford to advertise heavily in the papers, but they could and did design their storefront facades to call attention to their shows—with oversized entrances, attraction boards, posters, and as many light bulbs as they had room for. To draw the attention of passersby, they set up phonographs on the street outside and hired live barkers: "It is only five cents! See the moving-picture show, see the wonders of Port Said tonight, and a shrieking comedy from real life, all for five cents. Step in this way and learn to laugh!"

The din became such that local shopkeepers complained it was interfering with business. In Paterson, New Jersey, the Board of Aldermen outlawed "phonographic barkers" after complaints from storekeepers, among them M. L. Rogowski, who claimed that the "rasping music, ground out for hours at a time, annoyed his milliners until they became nervous."

With the aural accompaniment of the barkers the visual displays of glittering light bulbs, and word of mouth, city residents began to throng the new theaters. Contemporary commentators used terms like *madness, frenzy, fever,* and *craze* to describe the rapidity with which nickel theaters went up after about 1905. By November of 1907, a little more than two years after the opening of the first one, there were already, according to Joseph Medill Patterson of *The Saturday Evening Post,* "between four and five thousand [nickel shows] running and solvent, and the number is still increasing rapidly. This is the boom time in the moving-picture business. Everybody is making money . . . as one press-agent said enthusiastically, 'this line is a Klondike.' "

It is, from our vantage point in the 1990s—suffused as we are by television, radio, CD players, and VCRs—difficult to recapture the excitement caused by the appearance of these first nickel theaters. For the bulk of the city's population, until now shut out of its theaters and commercial amusements, the sudden emergence of not one but five or ten nickel shows within walking distance must have been nothing short of extraordinary.

Imagine for a moment what it must have meant to be able to attend a show for a nickel in your neighborhood. City folk who had never been to the theater or, indeed, to any commercial amusement (even the upper balcony at a vaudeville hall cost a quarter) could now, on their way home from work or shopping or on a Saturday evening or Sunday afternoon, enter the darkened auditorium, take a seat, and witness the latest technological wonders, all for five cents.

One understands the passion of the early commentators as they described in the purplest of prose what the moving-picture theater meant to the city's working people. Mary Heaton Vorse concluded a 1911 article in *The Outlook* by referring to the picture-show audiences she had observed on Bleecker Street and the Bowery in New York City, "You see what it means to them; it means Opportunity—a chance to glimpse the beautiful and strange things in the world that you haven't in your life; the gratification of the higher side of your nature; opportunity which, except for the big moving picture book, would be forever closed to you."

The nickelodeon's unprecedented expansion did not go unnoticed by the critics of commercialized popular culture who had for a century complained about and organized against the evils of saloons, bawdy houses, honky-tonks, prizefights, and variety theaters. For the anti-vice crusaders and child savers, the nickel shows presented an unparalleled threat to civic morality, precisely because they were so popular with the city's young and poor.

Although they grossly exaggerated the "immorality" of the pictures and the danger to those who saw them, the anti-vice crusaders and reformers were correct in claiming that never before had so many women, men, and children, most of them strangers to one another, been brought together to sit in the closest physical proximity in the dark for twenty to thirty minutes. The Vice Commission

John Ripley Collection, Kansas State Historical Society, Topeka

of Chicago believed that "many liberties are taken with young girls within the theater during the performance when the place is in total or semi-darkness. Boys and men slyly embrace the girls near them and offer certain indignities." The New York Society for the Prevention of Cruelty to Children presented case after case of such depravities. "This new form of entertainment," it claimed in its 1909 annual report, "has gone far to blast maidenhood. . . . Depraved adults with candies and pennies beguile children with the inevitable result. The Society has prosecuted many for leading girls astray through these picture shows, but GOD alone knows how many are leading dissolute lives begun at the 'moving pictures.' "

While the anti-vice crusaders complained about the moral dangers, other reformers and a number of industry spokesmen worried about the physical conditions inside the "nickel dumps." Not only were the storefront theaters dark, dirty, and congested, but the stench inside was often overpowering. Investigators hired by the Cleveland commission investigating local movie theaters claimed that the "foul air" in the theaters was so bad that even a short stay was bound to result in "sneezing, coughing and the contraction of serious colds."

The Independent reported in early 1910 that the city's "moving picture places" had "become foci for the dissemination of tubercle bacilli," and *Moving Picture World* warned exhibitors to clean up their theaters before it was too late. "Should a malignant epidemic strike New York City, and these conditions prevail, the result might be a wholesale closing down of these germ factories."

Tuberculosis and head colds were not the only, or even the most serious, threats to the safety of movie patrons. In the early years of the storefront theaters, the danger of fire breaking out in the projection booth and sweeping through houses that lacked adequate exits was ever-present, especially since the film stock was highly flammable. There were close to one thousand theater fires in 1907 alone.

While nickelodeon owners and operators were reaping a bonanza, it had become apparent to manufacturers, distributors, and trade-journal editors that the industry had to do something about conditions inside the theaters to forestall government action and broaden the audience base. Homer W. Sibley of *Moving Picture World* warned his colleagues in August of 1911, "the 'dump' is doomed, and the sooner the cheap, ill-smelling, poorly ventilated, badly managed rendezvous for the masher and tough makes way for the better class of popular family theater the better it will be for the business and all concerned."

The enormous success of the nickelodeon was, paradoxically, blocking future growth of the moving-picture business. Potential customers who preferred not to mingle with the lower orders stayed away. In the vaudeville theaters the "refined" could, if they chose, sit safe from the rabble in the more expensive box and orchestra seats. There were no such sanctuaries in the nickel and dime theaters, where customers could sit wherever they pleased.

Nickelodeon owners began to realize that to attract an audience large enough to fill and refill their theaters twenty to thirty times a day, they would have to meld into one institutional space the openness of the saloon and the selectivity of the hotel. They had to welcome all who sought entrance to their amusements, while simultaneously "appearing" to screen their customers and admit only those who were, as Henry James had described the clientele of the American hotel, "presumably 'respectable,' . . . that is, not discoverably anything else."

The trick of remaining open to the street and its passersby while keeping out the riffraff was accomplished by designing an imposing exterior and entrance. The penny arcades had opened their fronts to encourage passersby to "drop in." The nickel theaters re-enclosed them, pulling back their doors about six feet from the sidewalk, in effect extending the distance between the theater and the street. This recessed, sheltered entrance functioned as a buffer or filter between the inside of the theater and the tumult outside. Framing this recessed entrance, massive arches or oversized columns jutted out onto the sidewalk. Thus the nickelodeon owners colonized the sidewalks in front of their establishments, shortening—while emphasizing—the distance between the amusements within and the workaday world outside.

Theater owners did all they could to convince customers that they would be

John Ripley Collection, Kansas State Historical Society, Topeka

By the mid-1910s a huge, heterogeneous urban public had been taught to feel comfortable in movie houses.

safe inside, no matter whom they sat next to in the dark. To guarantee their customers' good behavior, the exhibitors began to hire and parade uniformed ushers through the largest theaters and flashed signs on the screen warning patrons that those who misbehaved would quickly be banished from the house and prosecuted by the law.

The industry also accepted new fire-safety legislation, but perhaps the most important step the exhibitors took to allay the public's anxieties about health hazards was to install new and expensive ventilation systems that, they claimed, removed not only bad odors but germs as well. A. L. Shakman, owner of a Broadway theater, proudly proclaimed that there were "no clothing or body odors noticeable even during the capacity hours of the 81st Street Theater, for the simple reason that the air is changed by dome ventilators every twenty minutes. The air is just as sweet and pure in the balcony as it is downstairs." The Butterfly Theater in Milwaukee advertised that its 'Perfect Ventilation" system provided customers with a "Complete Change of Air Every Three Minutes."

To convince the city's respectable folk that the movie theaters, though cheap, were safe and comfortable, the exhibitors assiduously courted the local gentry, businessmen, and politicians and invited them to their

opening celebrations. The Saxe brothers of Milwaukee launched their Princess Theatre in 1909 with a gala invitation-only theater party, organized, as the owners told the Milwaukee *Sentinel,* "in the effort to secure the patronage of a better class of people." Mayor David S. Rose not only attended but gave the dedicatory address.

Gala openings like this had become routine occurrences by the late 1910s. Just as Barnum propelled Tom Thumb into the rank of first-class attractions by arranging and publicizing the midget's audience with the Queen of England, so did the exhibitors signify that their theaters were first-class entertainment sites by celebrating the patronage of the crowned heads of their communities.

Even though the moving pictures would not reach the pinnacle of their respectability until the early twenties, with the building of the movie palaces, the industry had by the middle 1910s educated a huge and heterogeneous urban public that they could visit movie theaters without danger to their pocketbooks, their reputations, or their health.

When the social researcher George Bevans was writing *How Workingmen Spend Their Spare Time* in late 1912 and early 1913, he discovered that no matter what the men's particular jobs, how many hours a week they worked, whether they were single or married, native-born or immigrant, earned less than ten dollars or more than thirty-five, they unfailingly spent more of their spare time at the picture show than anywhere else. William Fox claimed that the saloons in the vicinity of his theaters "found the business so unprofitable that they closed their doors. . . . If we had never had prohibition," he later told Upton Sinclair, "the

motion pictures would have wiped out the saloon."

More and more what drew these audiences was the emergence of the movie star from the ranks of the wholly anonymous players of a decade earlier. Actors in the early story films had borrowed their gestures, poses, grins, and grimaces from melodrama and pantomime. Villains all dressed, acted, and moved the same way, as did the other stock characters: the heroes, heroines, and aged mothers. Any child in the audience could tell who the villain was (the man in the long black coat), why he acted as he did (he was evil), and what he was going to do next. By 1909 or so critics and audiences alike appeared to be growing weary of these histrionics, and players adopted instead a "more natural" or "slower" acting style. As cameras moved in closer to capture increasingly subtle and personalized expressions, audiences began to distinguish the players from one another. Since the manufacturers never divulged their actors' given names, the fans had to refer to them by their brand names—the Vitagraph Girl, or the Biograph Girl.

It didn't take long for manufacturers to recognize the benefits of exploiting their audience's curiosity. Kalem was the first to identify its actors and actresses by name, in a group photograph published as an advertisement in the January 15, 1910, *Moving Picture World* and made available to exhibitors for posting in their lobbies. In that same year, Carl Laemmle, a distributor who was preparing to manufacture his own films, hired Florence Lawrence to star in them for the then exorbitant salary of fifteen thousand

*The reception accorded **The Birth of a Nation** marked the distance movies had traveled since their disastrous debut.*

dollars a year. To make sure the public knew that the Biograph Girl would now be appearing exclusively in IMP pictures, Laemmle engineered the first publicity coup. In March of 1910 he leaked the rumor that Miss Lawrence had been killed in a St. Louis streetcar accident and then took out a huge ad in *Moving*

Picture World to announce that the story of her demise was the "blackest and at the same time the silliest lie yet circulated by enemies of the 'Imp.' "

It took only a few years for the picture players to ascend from anonymity to omnipresence. The best evidence we have of the stars' newfound importance is the salaries the producers were willing to pay them. On Broadway Mary Pickford had earned $25 a week. In 1910 Carl Laemmle lured her away from Biograph, her first movie home, with an offer of $175 a week. Her starting salary with Adolph Zukor at Famous Players in 1914 was $20,000 a year, soon raised to $1,000 a week and then, in January of 1915, to $2,000 a week and half the profits from her pictures. In June of 1916 another contract raised her compensation to 50 percent of the profits of her films against a guaranteed minimum of $1,040,000 a year, including at least $10,000 every week, a bonus of $300,000 for signing the contract, and an additional $40,000 for the time she had spent reading scripts during contract negotiations. And this was only the beginning.

The stars were worth the money because their appearance in films not only boosted receipts but added a degree of predictability to the business, a predictability that was welcomed by the banks and financiers that in the 1920s would assume a larger role in the picture business. The most reliable, perhaps the only, predictor of success for any given film was the presence of an established star.

The stars were not only bringing new customers into the theaters but incorporating a movie audi-ence scattered over thousands of different sites into a vast unified public. "Stars" were by definition actors or actresses whose appeal transcended every social category, with the possible exception of gender. As the theater and now film critic Walter Prichard Eaton explained in 1915, "The smallest town . . . sees the same motion-picture players as the largest. . . . John Bunny and Mary Pickford 'star' in a hundred towns at once."

John Ripley Collection, Kansas State Historical Society, Topeka

The reception accorded *The Birth of a Nation* that same year marked the distance the movies had traveled since their disastrous debut in Armat and Jenkins's tent just twenty years earlier. While African-Americans and their supporters strenuously protested the film's appalling portrayal of blacks and succeeded in forcing state and municipal censors to cut many scenes, white Americans of every age group, economic status, neighborhood, and ethnicity lined up at the box offices to see D. W. Griffith's Civil War epic.

The Birth of a Nation would eventually make more money than any film of its time and be seen by an audience that extended from prosperous theatergoers who paid two dollars in the first-class legitimate theaters to the women, children, and men who viewed it at regular prices in their neighborhood moving-picture houses. Even the President of the United States, as the promotions for the film asserted, had seen *The Birth of a Nation* and was now a moving-picture fan.

The ultimate confirmation of a picture show's respectability came only a few years later, during World War I, when the federal government, concerned that its propaganda messages might not reach the largest possible audience through the available print media, decided to send its "Four-Minute Men" into the nation's movie theaters. (The speakers were so named to reassure audiences and theater owners that their talks would be brisk.)

As President Wilson proclaimed in an open letter to the nation's moviegoers in April 1918, the picture house had become a "great democratic meeting place of the people, where within twenty-four hours it is possible to reach eight million citizens of all classes." There was nothing wrong with going to the movies while a war was being fought across the Atlantic, the President declared in his letter: "The Government recognizes that a reasonable amount of amusement, *especially* in war time, is not a luxury but a necessity."

From Progressivism to the 1920s

Unlike the Populist movement of the 1890s or the New Deal of the 1930s, what became known as Progressivism arose during a period of relative prosperity. It derived its strength from urban areas, and its leaders were white middle- and upper-middle-class men and women of both political parties. These were people who were disturbed by what they regarded as a coarsening of public life and by the domination big business had come to exert over society. Some wanted to break up the large combines, others to control them in the public interest. Progressives generally believed in opening up government at all levels of democratic participation through means such as referenda and long ballots. To charges that they were radicals, Progressives replied that they merely wanted to use the power of government to create an equitable society.

Woodrow Wilson is most often remembered as the president who failed to achieve his dream of leading the United States into the League of Nations. Some believe this failure crippled the world organization at its birth and undermined its ability to deal with the crisis that led to World War II. During his first term in office, however, Wilson succeeded in having enacted some of the most important Progressive reforms. He was so successful, in fact, that after only 18 months in office he declared his "New Freedom" achieved. "Woodrow Wilson, Politician" examines the way his thinking evolved and the considerable political skills he acquired along the way.

Legislation enacted in 1882 and after greatly reduced immigration from China, but did not halt it entirely. Angel Island, the Pacific counterpart of Ellis Island, officially opened in 1910 and continued to operate until 1940. "Angel Island: The Half-Closed Door" describes the dismal circumstances under which immigrants from China were examined for admittance. Fully 30 percent were rejected for one reason or another and deported. Today, the Angel Island Museum bears testimony to the conditions these people had to endure.

What we call World War I, but which was then referred to as the "Great War," effectively ended chances that Progessivism would lead to greater economic and political reforms, especially after the United States joined the conflict. The war provided new opportunities for American women both in the workplace and in the armed services. "American Women in World War I" shows, however, that women in uniform received generally shabby treatment. "What We Lost in the Great War" concludes that, quite aside from the enormous physical devastation that conflict produced, it also destroyed a way of thinking.

Two articles treat politics. "Why Suffrage for American Women Was Not Enough" argues that, despite having won the right to vote, women continued to accept the notion that they should not compete with men in the political arena. " 'A Snarling Roughhouse,' The Democratic Convention of 1924" tells how sectional strife, racial prejudice, and a host of other issues nearly tore the party apart.

By 1925 Henry Ford's motor company was turning out a Model T every ten seconds. "Citizen Ford" describes how this erratic genius revolutionized the automobile industry. As time wore on, however, his unwillingness to adapt to new ideas caused his company to lose its competitive edge. By the 1930s a business magazine referred to him as "the World's Worst Salesman."

The 1920s were characterized by a great deal of ethnic and racial discrimination. A second Ku Klux Klan emerged during the decade, and it came to wield enormous power in several sections of the country. "Defending the Home: Ossian Sweet and the Struggle against Segregation in 1920s Detroit" tells how a black physician successfully resisted mob efforts to prevent him from living in the house he had purchased. Charged with the murders of several members of the crowd, Ossian Sweet and several friends won their freedom after bitterly emotional trials.

Looking Ahead: Challenge Questions

Evaluate Woodrow Wilson's political career. To what do you attribute his success in getting legislation through Congress? How important was this legislation?

Discuss the article "What We Lost in the Great War." Why did that conflict have such enormous consequences?

Analyze the various conflicts that were fought out during the Democratic Convention of 1924. Why did emotions run so high? What compromises were made?

Woodrow Wilson, Politician

The idealistic architect of a postwar world order that never came into being: such is the popular image of President Woodrow Wilson. What it omits is the savvy, sometimes ruthless politician whose achievements in the domestic sphere were equalled by only two other 20th-century presidents, Franklin Delano Roosevelt and Lyndon Baines Johnson. Robert Dallek here restores the whole man.

Robert Dallek

Robert Dallek is professor of history at the University of California, Los Angeles. He is the author of several books on political and diplomatic history, including Franklin D. Roosevelt and American Foreign Policy, 1932–1945 *(1979), which won a Bancroft Prize, and, most recently,* Lone Star Rising: Lyndon Johnson and His Times, 1908–1960 *(1991).*

Few presidents in American history elicit more mixed feelings than Woodrow Wilson. And why not? His life and career were full of contradictions that have puzzled historians for 70 years. A victim of childhood dyslexia, he became an avid reader, a skilled academic, and a popular writer and lecturer. A deeply religious man, who some described as "a Presbyterian priest" with a dour view of man's imperfectability, he devoted himself to secular designs promising the triumph of reason and harmony in domestic and world affairs. A rigid, self-exacting personality, whose uncompromising adherence to principles barred agreement on some of his most important political goals, he was a brilliant opportunist who won stunning electoral victories and led controversial laws through the New Jersey state legislature and the U.S. Congress. A southern conservative and elitist with a profound distrust of radical ideas and such populists as William Jennings Bryan, he became the Democratic Party's most effective advocate of advanced progressivism. A leading proponent of congressional influence, or what he called "Congressional Government," he ranks

with Theodore Roosevelt, Franklin D. Roosevelt, Harry S. Truman, and Lyndon B. Johnson as the century's most aggressive chief executives. An avowed pacifist who declared himself "too proud to fight" and gained reelection in 1916 partly by reminding voters that he had "kept us out of war," he made military interventions in Latin America and Europe hallmarks of his two presidential terms.

There is no greater paradox in Wilson's life and career, however, than the fact that his worst failure has become the principal source of his historical reputation as a great American president. Administrative and legislative triumphs marked Wilson's service as president of Princeton, governor of New Jersey, and president of the United States. But most Americans who would concede Wilson a place in the front ranks of U.S. chief executives would be hard pressed to name many, if any, of these achievements. To them, he is best remembered as the president who preached self-determination and a new world order. (And not only to Americans: An upcoming Wilson biography by Dutch historian J. W. Schulte Nordholt is subtitled *A Life for World Peace.*) In the 1920s and '30s, when America rejected participation in the League of Nations and a political or military role in a world hellbent on another total war, Wilson's reputation reached a low point. He was a good man whom bankers and munitions makers had duped into entering World War I. He had also led America into the fighting out of the hopelessly naive belief that he could make the world safe for democracy and end all wars.

American involvement in World War II reversed Wilson's historical standing. Now feeling guilty about their isolationism and their rejection of his vision of a world at peace, Americans celebrated him as a spurned prophet whose wisdom and idealism deserved renewed acceptance in the 1940s. A new world league of self-governing nations practicing collective security for the sake of global stability and peace became the great American hope during World War II. When the fighting's outcome proved to be the Soviet–American Cold War, Americans saw it as another setback for Wilson's grand design. Nevertheless, they did not lose faith in his ultimate wisdom, believing that democracy and the international rule of law would eventually have to replace tyranny and lawless aggression if the world were ever to achieve lasting peace.

Now, with America's triumph in the Cold War and the Soviet-American confrontation all but over, the country has renewed faith in a world order akin to what Woodrow Wilson proposed in 1918. The idea took on fresh meaning when President Bush led a coalition of U.N.-backed forces against Iraq's attack upon and absorption of Kuwait. The triumph of coalition arms seemed to vindicate Wilson's belief that collective action through a world body could reduce the likelihood and effectiveness of attacks by strong states against weaker ones and thus make international acts of aggression obsolete.

Yet present hopes for a new world order can plummet overnight—and with them Wilson's standing. If Wilson's rep-

From *The Wilson Quarterly,* Autumn 1991, pp. 106–114. © 1991 by the Woodrow Wilson International Center for Scholars. Reprinted by permission.

utation as a great president rests upon his vision of a new era in world affairs and the fulfillment of some part of that design in our lifetimes, his place in the forefront of U.S. presidents seems less than secure.

Will the ghost of Wilson be plagued forever by the vagaries of world politics? Only if we fail to give scrutiny to his full record. A careful reassessment of Wilson's political career, especially in domestic affairs, would go far to secure his place as a great American president who has much to tell us about the effective workings of democratic political systems everywhere.

FOR ALL HIS IDEALISM AND ELITISM, Wilson's greatest triumphs throughout his career rested on his brilliance as a democratic politician. He was the "great communicator" of his day—a professor who abandoned academic language and spoke in catch phrases that inspired mass support. He was also a master practitioner of the art of the possible, a leader with an impressive talent for reading the public mood and adjusting to it in order to advance his personal ambition and larger public goals. This is not to suggest that his career was an uninterrupted success. He had his share of spectacular failures. But some of these he converted into opportunities for further advance. And even his unmitigated failures had more to do with circumstances beyond his control than with flaws in his political judgment.

Wilson's early life gave little indication of a master politician in the making. Born in 1856 in Staunton, Virginia, the third of four children, he was the offspring of devout Scotch Presbyterian divines. Thomas Woodrow, his maternal grandfather, came from Scotland to the United States, where he ministered to congregations in small Ohio towns. Jesse Woodrow Wilson, Wilson's mother, was an intensely religious, austere Victorian lady with no sense of humor and a long history of psychosomatic ailments. Joseph Ruggles Wilson, Woodrow's father, was a brilliant theologian and leading light in the southern Presbyterian church, holding pulpits in Staunton, Virginia; Augusta, Georgia; Columbia, South Carolina; and Wilmington, North Carolina. Joseph Wilson enjoyed a reputation as an eloquent and powerful speaker whose "arresting rhetoric and cogent thought" made him one of the leading southern preachers and religious teachers of his time. Woodrow Wilson described

his father as the "greatest teacher" he ever knew. Yet theological disputes and clashes with other strong-willed church leaders drove Joseph, who advocated various reforms, from one pulpit to another and left him with a sense of failure that clouded his life. One Wilson biographer notes that "by mid-career, Joseph Wilson was in some ways a broken man, struggling to overcome feelings of inferiority, trying to reconcile a God of love with the frustration of his ambition for success and prominence within the church." To compensate for his sense of defeat, Joseph invested his vaunting ambition in his son Woodrow, whom he hoped would become the "very great man" Joseph himself had wished to be.

Although Joseph imparted a love of literature and politics to his son, Bible readings, daily prayers, and Sunday worship services were centerpieces of Woodrow's early years. His father also taught him the transient character of human affairs and the superiority of religious to secular concerns. Joseph left little doubt in the boy's mind that he foresaw for him a career in the ministry as "one of the Church's rarest scholars . . . one of her most illustrious reformers . . . or one of her grandest orators." But Joseph's defeats in church politics in Woodrow's formative adolescent years soured father and son on Woodrow's entrance into the ministry.

Instead, Woodrow, with his father's blessing, invested his ambitions in a political career. As Richard Hofstadter wrote, "When young Tommy Wilson sat in the pew and heard his father bring the Word to the people, he was watching the model upon which his career was to be fashioned." Before college, he hung a portrait of British Prime Minister William Gladstone above his desk and declared: "That is Gladstone, the greatest statesman that ever lived. I intend to be a statesman, too." During his years as a Princeton undergraduate (1875–79), he rationalized his determination to enter politics by describing it as a divine vocation. A career as a statesman was an expression of Christian service, he believed, a use of power for the sake of principles or moral goals. Wilson saw the "key to success in politics" as "the pursuit of perfection through hard work and the fulfillment of ideals." Politics would allow him to spread spiritual enlightenment to the yearning masses.

Yet Wilson, as one of his later political associates said, was a man of high ideals

and no principles, which was another way of saying that Wilson's ambition for self-serving political ends outran his commitment to any particular philosophy or set of goals. Like every great American politician since the rise of mass democracy in the 19th century, Wilson allowed the ends to justify the means. But Wilson never thought of himself as an opportunist. Rather, he considered himself a democrat responsive to the national mood and the country's most compelling needs. It is possible to scoff at Wilson's rationalization of his willingness to bend to current demands, but we do well to remember that the country's greatest presidents have all been men of high ideals and no principles, self-serving altruists or selfish pragmatists with a talent for evoking the vision of America as the world's last best hope.

Wilson's path to high political office, like so much else in his life, ran an erratic course. Legal studies at the University of Virginia, self-instruction, and a brief law practice in Atlanta were meant to be a prelude to a political career. But being an attorney had little appeal to Wilson, and he decided to become a professor of politics instead. Consequently, in 1883, at the age of 27, he entered the Johns Hopkins University Graduate School, where he earned a Ph.D. for *Congressional Government* (1885). His book was an argument for a Congress more like the British Parliament, a deliberative body in which debate rather than contending interests shaped legislation. For 17 years, from 1885 to 1902, he taught at Bryn Mawr, Wesleyan, and Princeton, beginning at the last in 1890. By 1898 he had grown weary of what he derisively called his "talking profession," and during the next four years he shrewdly positioned himself to become the unanimous, first-ballot choice of Princeton's trustees as the university's president.

WILSON'S EIGHT YEARS AS PRESIDENT OF Princeton (1902–1910) were a prelude to his later political triumphs and defeats. During the first three years of his Princeton term, Wilson carried off a series of dazzling reforms. Offended by the shallowness of much instruction at Princeton and animated by a desire to make it a special university like Oxford and Cambridge, where undergraduate education emphasized critical thinking rather than "the ideal of making a living," Wilson introduced a preceptorial system. It aimed at transforming Princeton "from a place where there are youngsters doing tasks to a place where there are men doing thinking, men who are conversing about the things of thought. . . ." As a prerequisite to the preceptorial system, Wilson persuaded the faculty to reorganize the University's curriculum and its structure, creating 11 departments corresponding to subjects and requiring upperclassmen to concentrate their studies in one of them. Wilson's reforms, biographer Arthur S. Unk asserts, "mark him as an educational statesman of originality and breadth and strength." His achievement was also a demonstration of Wilson's political mastery—a case study in how to lead strong-minded, independent academics to accept a sea change in the life of a conservative university.

The fierce struggles and bitter defeats of Wilson's next five years are a measure of how difficult fundamental changes in higher education can be without the sort of astute political management Wilson initially used. Between 1906 and 1910 Wilson fought unsuccessfully to reorganize the social life of undergraduates and to determine the location and nature of a graduate college. In the first instance, Wilson tried to deemphasize the importance of campus eating clubs, which had become the focus of undergraduate life, and replace them with residential colleges, or quadrangles, where students would live under the supervision of unmarried faculty members residing in the colleges. Wilson viewed the clubs as undemocratic, anti-intellectual, and divisive, and the quadrangle plan as a sensible alternative that would advance the university's educational goals and national standing. Wilson assumed that he could put across his plan without the sort of consultation and preparation he had relied on to win approval for the preceptorial system. But his failure to consult alumni, faculty, and trustees was a major political error that led to his defeat. Likewise, he did not effectively marshal the support he needed to win backing for his graduate-school plan, and again it made his proposal vulnerable to criticism from opponents.

Physical and emotional problems caused by strokes in 1906 and 1907 may partly account for Wilson's defeats in the quadrangle and graduate-school fights. But whatever the explanation for his poor performance in these academic struggles, they were by no means without

political benefit to Wilson. In fact, what seems most striking about these conflicts is the way Wilson converted them to his larger purposes of running first for governor of New Jersey and then for president of the United States.

Colonel George Harvey, a conservative Democrat who owned a publishing empire that included the *New York World* and *Harper's Weekly,* proposed Wilson for the presidency as early as 1906. Although Wilson made appropriate disclaimers of any interest in seeking the White House, the suggestion aroused in him the longing for high political station that he had held for some 30 years. In response to Harvey's efforts, Wilson, who was already known nationally as a speaker on issues of higher education, began speaking out on economic and political questions before non-university audiences. His initial pronouncements were essentially conservative verities calculated to identify him with the anti-Bryan, anti-Populist wing of the Democratic Party. "The nomination of Mr. Wilson," one conservative editor wrote in 1906, "would be a good thing for the country as betokening a return of his party to historic party ideals and first principles, and a sobering up after the radical 'crazes.' " In 1907 Wilson prepared a "Credo" of his views, which, Arthur Unk says, could hardly have failed to please reactionaries, "for it was conservative to the core." It justified the necessity of great trusts and combinations as efficient instruments of modern business and celebrated individualism. In 1908 Wilson refused to support Bryan for president and rejected suggestions that he become his vice-presidential running mate.

During the next two years, however, Wilson shifted decidedly to the left. Mindful of the mounting progressive temper in the country—of the growing affinity of middle-class Americans for reforms that would limit the power of corporations and political machines— Wilson identified himself with what he called the "new morality," the need to eliminate fraud and corruption from, and to restore democracy and equality of opportunity to, the nation's economic and political life. His academic fights over the quadrangles and graduate school became struggles between special privilege and democracy. In a speech to Princeton's Pittsburgh alumni in the spring of 1910, Wilson attacked the nation's universities, churches, and politi-

cal parties as serving the "classes" and neglecting the "masses." He declared his determination to democratize the colleges of the country and called for moral and spiritual regeneration. Incensed at his conservative Princeton opponents, who seemed the embodiment of the privileged interests, and eager to make himself a gubernatorial and then national candidate, Wilson invested idealism in the progressive crusade, leaving no doubt that he was ready to lead a movement that might redeem America.

New Jersey Democratic boss James Smith, Jr., seeing Wilson as a conservative opportunist whose rhetoric would appease progressives and whose actions would favor the corporations and the bosses, arranged Wilson's nomination for governor. Wilson seemed to play his part perfectly during the campaign, quietly accepting Smith's help even as he declared his independence from the party machine and espoused the progressive agenda—the direct primary, a corrupt-practices law, workmen's compensation, and a regulatory commission policing the railroads and public utilities. On election day Wilson swept to victory by a 50,000-vote margin, 233,933 to 184,573, and the Democrats gained control of the normally Republican Assembly. Once in the governor's chair, Wilson made clear that he would be his own man. He defeated Smith's bid for election to the U.S. Senate by the state legislature and skillfully assured the enactment of the four principal progressive measures. As he told a friend, "I kept the pressure of opinion constantly on the legislature, and the programme was carried out to its last detail. This with the senatorial business seems, in the minds of the people looking on, little less than a miracle in the light of what has been the history of reform hitherto in the State." As Wilson himself recognized, it was less a miracle than the product of constant pressure on the legislature at a time when "opinion was ripe on all these matters." Wilson's break with the machine and drive for reform reflected a genuine commitment to improving the lot of New Jersey's citizens. Most of all, they were a demonstration of how an ambitious politician in a democracy bends to the popular will for the sake of personal gain and simultaneously serves legitimate public needs.

WILSON'S NOMINATION FOR PRESIDENT BY a deeply divided Democratic convention in the summer of 1912 was an extraordinary event in the history of the party and the nation. Wilson himself called it "a sort of political miracle." Although Wilson was the frontrunner in 1911 after speaking trips to every part of the nation, by May 1912 aggressive campaigns by Missouri's Champ Clark, speaker of the House of Representatives, and Alabama Representative Oscar W. Underwood made Wilson a decided underdog. When Clark won a majority of the delegates on the 10th ballot, it seemed certain that he would eventually get the two-thirds vote needed for the nomination. In every Democratic convention since 1844, a majority vote for a candidate had translated into the required two-thirds. But 1912 was different. Wilson won the nomination on the 46th ballot after his managers struck a bargain, which kept Underwood's 100-plus delegates from going to Clark. William Jennings Bryan gave Wilson essential progressive support, and the party's most powerful political bosses—the men who, in the words of one historian, had been Wilson's "bitterest antagonists and who represented the forces against which he had been struggling"—decided to back him.

Wilson's campaign for the presidency was another milestone in his evolution as a brilliant democratic politician. He entered the election without a clear-cut campaign theme. The tariff, which he initially focused on, inspired little popular response. In late August, however, after conferring with Louis D. Brandeis, Wilson found a constructive and highly popular campaign theme. Persuading Wilson that political democracy could only follow from economic democracy or diminished control by the country's giant business trusts, Brandeis sold him on the New Freedom—the idea that regulated competition would lead to the liberation of economic enterprise in the United States. This in turn would restore grassroots political power and control. Wilson accurately sensed that the country's mood was overwhelmingly favorable to progressive reform, especially the reduction of the economic power of the trusts. He also saw correctly that Theodore Roosevelt's plea for a New Nationalism—regulated monopoly and an expanded role for federal authority in the economic and social life of the nation—impressed most voters as too paternalistic and more a threat to than an expansion of freedom. As a result, Wilson won a plurality of the popular vote in the four-

way contest of 1912, 42 percent to a combined 58 percent for William Howard Taft, TR, and socialist Eugene V. Debs. Wilson's victory in the electoral column was far more one-sided, 435 to 99 for TR and Taft. His victory was also a demonstration of his talents as a speaker who could satisfy the mass yearning for a new era in national affairs.

Wilson's election represented a triumph of democratic hopes. After nearly five decades of conservative rule by the country's business interests, the nation gave its backing to a reform leader promising an end to special privilege and the economic and political democratization of American life. "Nobody owns me," Wilson declared at the end of his campaign, signaling his readiness to act in behalf of the country's working and middle classes. Despite his own largely conservative background, his political agility and sensitivity to popular demands made it likely that he would not disappoint progressive goals.

HIS FIRST PRESIDENTIAL TERM REPRESENTS one of the three notable periods of domestic reform in 20th-century America. What makes it particularly remarkable, notes historian John Milton Cooper, is that Wilson won his reforms without the national emergencies over the economy and civil rights that respectively confronted the country during the 1930s and the 1960s. Wilson, in other words, lacked "the peculiarly favorable political conditions" aiding Franklin Roosevelt and Lyndon Johnson.

Wilson's successful leadership rested on his effective management of his party and Congress. Following the advice of Texas Representative Albert S. Burleson, a superb politician who became postmaster general, Wilson filled his cabinet with "deserving" Democrats and allowed Burleson to use patronage "ruthlessly to compel adoption of administration measures." Despite Bryan's ignorance of foreign affairs, for example, his prominence persuaded Wilson to make him secretary of state. Wilson's readiness to set a bold legislative agenda found support from both a 73-member Democratic majority in the House and a decisive majority of Democratic and Republican progressives in the Senate. The 28th president quickly proved himself to be an able manipulator of Congress. Eager to create a sense of urgency about his legislative program and to establish a mood of cooperation

Reproduction from the Library of Congress

A NEAR-FUTURIST PAINTING.

Among Wilson's progressive measures was the Underwood Tariff of 1914, the first downward revision of the tariff since the Civil War.

between the two branches of government, Wilson called a special congressional session at the start of his term and then spoke to a joint meeting of both houses. Indeed, he was the first president to appear in person before Congress since John Adams. Presenting himself as a colleague rather than "a mere department of the Government hailing Congress from some isolated island of jealous power," Wilson returned repeatedly to Capitol Hill for conferences to advance his reform program.

In the 18 months between the spring of 1913 and the fall of 1914, Wilson pushed four key laws through the Congress. The Underwood Tariff of October 1914 was the first downward revision of the tariff since the Civil War; it was inspired more by a desire to reduce the cost of living for lower- and middle-class Americans than by any obligation to serve the interests of industrial giants. Wilson drove the bill through the upper house by exposing the lobbyists representing businesses that sought "to overcome the interests of the public for their private profit." Making the tariff law all the more remarkable was the inclusion of the first graduated income tax in U.S. history. Shortly thereafter, Wilson won passage of the most enduring domestic measure of his presidency, the reform of the country's banking and money system. Insisting on public, centralized control of banks and the money supply rather than a private, decentralized system, Wilson once again came before Congress to influence the outcome of this debate. The Federal Reserve Act of December 1913 combined elements of both plans, providing for a mix of private and public control. Although further reforms would occur later to make the Federal Reserve system a more effective instrument for dealing with national economic problems, the Wilson law of 1913 created the basic elements of the banking system that has existed for almost 80 years. During the next nine months, by keeping Congress in continuous session for an unprecedented year and a half, Wilson won passage of the Clayton Antitrust and Federal Trade Commission acts, contributing to the more effective regulation of big business and greater power for organized labor.

In November 1914, Wilson announced that his New Freedom program had been achieved and that the progressive movement was at an end. A man of fundamentally conservative impulses (which he believed reflected those of the nation at large), Wilson did not wish to overreach himself. His announcement bewildered advanced progressives, who had been unsuccessfully advocating a variety of social-justice measures Wilson considered too radical to support. Herbert Croly, the editor of the *New Republic,* charged that "any man of President Wilson's intellectual equipment who seriously asserts that the fundamental wrongs of a modern society can be easily and quickly righted as a consequence of a few laws . . . casts suspicion either upon his own sincerity or upon his grasp of the realities of modern social and industrial life." Similarly, Wilson's refusal to establish a National Race Commission and his active commitment to racial segregation in the federal government incensed African-American leaders who had viewed him as a likely supporter of progressive measures for blacks.

Though he did little to reverse course on helping blacks, Wilson stood ready to return to the progressive position for the sake of reelection in 1916. "I am sorry for any President of the United States who does not recognize every great movement in the Nation," Wilson declared in July 1916. "The minute he stops recognizing it, he has become a back number." The results of the congressional elections in 1914 convinced Wilson that the key to success in two years was a campaign attracting TR's Progressive backers to his standard. Consequently, in 1916, he elevated Louis D. Brandeis to the Supreme Court and signed seven additional reform bills into

law. Among other things, these laws brought relief to farmers and workers and raised income and inheritance taxes on wealthy Americans. The election results in November vindicated his strategy. Wilson gained almost three million popular votes over his 1912 total and bested Charles Evans Hughes, who headed a reunited Republican party, by 23 electoral votes. On this count alone, Wilson's two consecutive victories as the head of a minority party mark him as one of the century's exceptional American politicians.

WHY DID WILSON'S POLITICAL ASTUTENESS desert him during his second term in his handling of the Versailles Treaty and the League of Nations? The answer is not naiveté about world politics, though Wilson himself believed "it would be the irony of fate if my administration had to deal chiefly with foreign affairs." In fact, the same mastery of Congress he displayed in converting so many significant reform bills into law between 1913 and 1916 was reflected in his creation of a national consensus in 1917 for American participation in the Great War.

At the start of the fighting in 1914, Wilson declared America neutral in thought and deed. And though Wilson himself had a decidedly pro-British bias, he understood that the country then was only mildly pro-Allied and wanted no part in the war. His policies initially reflected these feelings. Only as national sentiment changed in response to events in Europe and on the high seas, where German submarine violations of U.S. neutral rights drove Americans more decisively into the Allied camp, did Wilson see fit to prepare the country for and then lead it into the war. His prewar leadership became something of a model for Franklin Roosevelt in 1939–41 as he maneuvered to maintain a national majority behind his responses to World War II.

Wilson's failure in 1919–20, or, more precisely, the collapse of his political influence in dealing with the peacemaking at the end of the war, consisted of a number of things—most of them beyond his control. His Fourteen Points, his formula for making the world safe for democracy and ending all wars, was beyond the capacity of any political leader to achieve, then and now. Yet there is every reason to believe that Wilson enunciated his peace aims assuming that he would have to accept compromise

agreements on many of his goals, as indeed he did in the Versailles negotiations. A number of these compromises on the Fourteen Points went beyond what he hoped to concede, but he recognized that the conclusion of the fighting had stripped him of much of his hold over America's allies and limited his capacity to bend the strong-minded French, British, and Italian leaders to his will or to influence the radical revolutionary regime in Russia. Events were moving too fast in Europe and all over the globe for him to make the world approximate the postwar peace arrangements he had enunciated in 1918.

Faced by such circumstances, Wilson accepted the proposition that a League of Nations, including the United States, would be the world's best hope for a stable peace. Wilson's prime objective after the Versailles conference was to assure American participation in the new world body. But the political cards were stacked against him. After six years of Democratic rule and a growing conviction in Republican Party circles that the Democrats would be vulnerable in 1920, Senate Republicans made approval of the Versailles Treaty and American participation in the League partisan issues which could redound to their benefit. Moreover, between 1918 and 1920, Wilson's deteriorating health, particularly a major stroke in the fall of 1919, intensified a propensity for self-righteousness and made him uncharacteristically rigid in dealing with a political issue that cried out for flexibility and accommodation. As Edwin A. Weinstein has persuasively argued in his medical and psychological biography of Wilson, "the cerebral dysfunction which resulted from Wilson's devastating strokes prevented the ratification of the Treaty. It is almost certain that had Wilson not been so afflicted, his political skills and facility with language would have bridged the gap between [opposing Senate] resolutions, much as he had reconciled opposing views of the Federal Reserve bill . . . or had accepted the modifications of the Treaty suggested in February, 1919."

WILSON'S POLITICAL FAILURE IN 1919–20 was a striking exception in a career marked by a substantial number of political victories. His defeat and its consequences were so stunning that they have eclipsed the record of prior achievements and partly obscured Wilson's contributions to American history.

But it is not only the disaster of 1919–20 that is responsible. Mainstream academia today dismisses political history and particularly the study of powerful leaders as distinctly secondary in importance to impersonal social forces in explaining historical change. What seems lost from view nowadays is just how essential strong and skillful political leadership remains in bringing a democracy to accept major reforms. Wilson is an excellent case in point. For all the public's receptivity to progressivism in the first two decades of the century, it took a leader of exceptional political skill to bring warring reform factions together in a coalition that could enact a liberal agenda. By contrast, Wilson's physical incapacity in 1919 assured the defeat of American participation in a world league for 25 years. This is not to say that an American presence in an international body would have dramatically altered the course of world affairs after 1920, but it might have made a difference, and the collapse of Wilson's leadership was the single most important factor in keeping the United States on the sidelines.

Did social and economic and a host of other factors influence the course of U.S. history during Wilson's time? Without a doubt. But a leader of vision and varied abilities—not all of them purely admirable—was needed to seize the opportunities provided by history and make them realities. To forget the boldness of Wilson's leadership, and the importance of political leaders generally, is to embrace a narrow vision of this nation's past—and of its future.

Angel Island: The Half-Closed Door

Brian McGinty

Brian McGinty is a frequent contributor to American History Illustrated. *His history of earthquakes in California appeared in the March/April 1990 issue.*

From 1910 to 1940, the principal immigration station on the West Coast of the United States occupied a remote site on the northern shore of Angel Island in San Francisco Bay. Facing the blue waters of one of the world's most renowned natural harbors, the Angel Island Immigration Station was the point of entry—or of deportation—for tens of thousands of Chinese and other Asian immigrants. Located only six miles from downtown San Francisco, the processing center was isolated from the mainland by deep water, imposing gray walls, and barbed-wire fences. Immigrants detained there were within easy sight of the "Promised Land," yet still a world away from it—separated from their goal by treacherous straits, discriminatory immigration laws, and bureaucratic obstacles that at times seemed insurmountable.

The history of Asian immigration to the United States is long and painful, fraught with the prejudice of the Western world. During the early years of California settlement, Oriental immigrants (mostly Chinese) were welcomed with civility if not enthusiasm. The Chinese were hard workers, and their labor was badly needed to build the burgeoning frontier's cities, bridges, and railroads. They were good businessmen, too, with rigorously frugal habits and a seemingly natural sense for the give-and-take of commerce.

So successful were the Chinese in the economic life of the West that within a few years demagogic politicians began to blame the newcomers for the economic slowdowns that periodically beset the region. Adopting "The Chinese must go!" as their slogan, these politicians proposed a series of stern laws that would make it difficult for Chinese to live in the United States—and harder yet for new Chinese immigrants to enter the country.

American hostility toward alien cultures ultimately resulted in the Chinese Exclusion Act, passed by Congress in 1882. A series of increasingly restrictive laws that followed were designed to cut the flow of Chinese immigrants to a trickle. The laws worked as planned; in California alone, the number of Chinese declined from almost 9 percent of the total population in 1880 to less than 1 percent in 1940.

But the new legislation did not totally bar Chinese immigration. A small class of "exempts" (officials, merchants, teachers, students, and tourists) were still permitted to enter the country, as were individuals who could prove a claim to U.S. citizenship by birth or by descent from an American citizen.

Beginning in the 1880s, a stream of Chinese claiming the right to enter the country as children of native-born Chinese-Americans arrived in San Francisco. Many of these would-be immigrants were known as "paper sons and daughters," for their claims were frankly based on fraudulent documents. The destruction in the great 1906 earthquake and fire of records that verified citizenship made it easier for many new arrivals in California to fabricate claims to citizenship by right of inheritance. Driven by the poverty and privation that gripped their native land, and desperate to penetrate the legal wall Americans had erected against them, the Chinese were willing to risk their fortunes, their freedom, and even their lives to make new homes in the country they called "The Land of the Flowery Flag."

Before 1910, Chinese arrivals in San Francisco were detained in a dismal wooden shed on the waterfront while their papers were reviewed or, if they had no papers, while witnesses were questioned to prove or disprove their claims. But conditions in the detention shed were so appalling that in 1903, under pressure from Chinatown's community leaders, the Bureau of Immigration announced its intention to build a new immigration station—on the shore of Angel Island.

The largest island in San Francisco Bay, Angel Island covers 740 acres and measures about a mile and a quarter from shore to shore at its widest point. Rising to 781 feet above sea level, the steep and hilly chunk of land lies due north of San Francisco's downtown financial district. Separated from Marin County's Tiburon Peninsula by Raccoon Strait—one of the deepest and most treacherous channels in the bay—the island, first sighted in 1769 by Gaspar de Portolá's overland expedition to Monterey, was named *Isla de Nuestra Señora de Los Angeles* by Spanish explorers under the command of Juan Manuel de Ayala, who anchored there in 1775 while charting San Francisco Bay. When Americans took control of California in the 1840s, they anglicized the name to Angel Island.

During the nineteenth century, the island served many purposes. For nearly twenty-five years, Russian settlers from Fort Ross on the nearby coast used it as a camp from which to hunt sea otters. The

From *American History Illustrated*, September/October 1990, pp. 50-51, 71. © 1990 by Cowles Magazines, Inc. Reprinted through the courtesy of Cowles Magazines, Inc., publisher of *American History Illustrated*.

island was a Mexican cattle ranch during the 1840s, and a decade later a quarry on its rugged eastern shore supplied stone for San Francisco buildings. During the Civil War, the U.S. Army fortified the island against possible Confederate attacks on San Francisco Bay. Over the years, the Army expanded its presence there until the island contained three main camps with officers' quarters, hospitals, parade grounds, and barracks for several thousand troops.

Taking advantage of Angel Island's isolation, the government in 1892 opened the San Francisco Quarantine Station on the northwest shore of the island. There it built housing for surgeons, pharmacists, and attendants, and dormitories and bathhouses for detainees. Passengers arriving in San Francisco were checked for signs of communicable diseases and, if infected, held at the station until they were either certified healthy or returned to their ports of origin. Although the quarantine station's activities slowed after 1915, it continued to operate well into the 1930s.

But it was as Ellis Island's Pacific counterpart that Angel Island became best-known. The new immigration station was designed to alleviate the unsafe and unsanitary conditions that had long prevailed in San Francisco's waterfront detention shed; to prevent newly arriving immigrants from communicating with friends or relatives in the city while they awaited processing; and to establish an escape-proof facility. Although construction was completed in 1908, the processing center did not officially open until January 21, 1910. The following morning, more than four hundred would-be Americans were moved into the two-story barracks serving as the station's main detention center.

Upon arrival at Angel Island, immigrants were ordered to leave their luggage in a warehouse on the wharf while they climbed the hill to the barracks. Separated by race and sex, they were led into drafty dormitories furnished with long rows of steel bunks in tiers of three. As soon as the doctors were ready to receive them, groups of newcomers were led to the hospital and examined for signs of disease. The detainees ate their meager and often scarcely palatable meals in a dining hall in the administration building. Lights went out in the station at about 9:00 P.M., at which time the massive doors to the dormitories were closed and securely locked.

Between two hundred and five hundred immigrants were housed at the Angel Island facility at any one time. Nearly all of the detainees were Asians, and the bulk of these were Chinese.

Immigrants with convincing "papers" were normally detained for only a few days. Others, who had either suspicious documents or no documents at all, had to wait until immigration officers scheduled hearings to examine the newcomers' claims. Witnesses were ferried from San Francisco. To prevent collusion between witnesses and interpreters, the interpreters were rotated on a random basis.

If a young Chinese immigrant claimed to be the son of an American citizen, immigration examiners questioned him closely What was his mother's name? In what village was his father born? How many houses were there in the village? Did he have any brothers or sisters? What were their names? Did they have a dog in the family house? Where was the rice bin kept? The witnesses, always questioned separately, were asked the same questions. Discrepancies in the testimony often resulted in rejection and swift repatriation to China. Reflecting the overwhelmingly hostile American policy toward admitting Chinese, immigration regulations specified that "in every doubtful case the benefit of the doubt shall be given to the United States government." As many as 30 percent of those examined were ultimately rejected and deported.

Depending on the circumstances of the case and the attitudes of the examiner, hearings could end in an hour or drag on as long as a week. Decisions in the applicant's favor were announced immediately; unfavorable decisions were withheld until all testimony had been transcribed and the examiner's report was completed. If an applicant decided to appeal to immigration authorities in Washington, D.C., the case could continue for months—or sometimes even years. All the while, the detainees languished in their barracks, reading the newspapers they managed to obtain from San Francisco, playing Mah-Jongg, and listening to Chinese opera on a scratchy, hand-wound Victrola.

During the long, dreadful wait, some of the detainees inscribed poetry on the walls of the barracks with knives or brushes. Composed in the classical Tan dynasty style, the poems provided a moving record of the immigrants' fears and hopes and served as a link between

succeeding boatloads of detainees. One poet wrote:

This place is called an island of immortals,
When, in fact, this mountain wilderness is
a prison.
Once you see the open net, why throw
yourself in?
It is only because of empty pockets I can
do nothing else.

And another:

Lin, upon arriving in America,
Was arrested, put in a wooden building,
And made a prisoner.
I was here for one autumn.
The Americans did not allow me to land.
I was ordered to be deported.
When the news was told,
I was frightened and troubled about re-
turning to my country.
We Chinese of a weak nation
Can only sigh at the lack of freedom.

Even before the Angel Island Immigration Station was completed, proposals were made to move it back to the mainland where the detainees would be less isolated and witnesses more accessible. The government resisted all of these suggestions until a fire broke out in the administration building on August 12, 1940, reducing the structure to rubble. Less than three months later, the island's last immigrants—about two hundred in all—were transferred to a new station in San Francisco.

During World War II, the former immigrant center housed federal convicts and even some prisoners of war. In 1954—by which time immigrants were screened overseas by American consular officials prior to emigrating—the State of California took over the old quarantine station on the northwest side of the island, creating Angel Island State Park. The park was expanded in 1962 to include the immigration station and other parts of the island, excepting a seven-acre Coast Guard facility.

After a park ranger drew attention to the poems on the walls of the old barracks in 1970, a systematic effort was made to photograph, transcribe, translate, and catalog the inscriptions. In 1976 the State of California appropriated funds for preservation of the barracks building, which was converted into the Angel Island Museum. A thirty-minute walk from the island's visitor center at Ayala Cove, the museum is now one of the best-known sites on the island. There, docents offer tours of the old building. Although the last detainees left fifty years ago, the poem-covered walls still bear silent testimony to their suffering and despair.

Today Angel Island is easily accessible via ferries that regularly ply the waters between Fisherman's Wharf in San Francisco, the town of Tiburon in Marin County, and Ayala Cove. The island boasts picnic grounds, campsites, and miles of well-maintained hiking trails. But the remains of the old immigration station speak most eloquently of the history made there—and of the indelible memories that refuse to be forgotten.

Recommended additional reading: Island: Poetry and History of Chinese Immigrants on Angel Island, 1910-1940 *by Him Mark Lai, Genny Lim, and Judy Yung (Hoc Doi, 1980) contains a representative collection of the poems inscribed by immigration station detainees on their barracks walls, together with interviews and a well-researched history of the station.*

American Women in World War I

Carl J. Schneider and Dorothy Schneider

Carl J. Schneider, Ph.D., and Dorothy Schneider, Ph.D., after careers in higher education as professors and administrators, now write about the condition and history of women. They based their first joint book, Sound Off! American Military Women Speak Out, *on interviews with 300 servicewomen, revising it in 1992 to include participants in Desert Storm. For* Into the Breach: American Women Overseas in World War I, *they uncovered many first-person accounts by these women.*

When the guns of August sounded the beginning of World War I in 1914, a good many Americans could not believe their ears. To their way of thinking, humanity had outgrown war. Even though some other Americans, women as well as men, still thought of war as vital to the health of nations, in 1914 most considered this particular war Europe's business, in which the United States should take no part. But the British and French propagandized skillfully and effectively. Germans stupidly based their diplomacy on the erroneous belief that Americans of German descent would always support Germany, whatever outrages Germany committed, and arrogantly underestimated America's capacity to wage war. And the American president professed peace but refused to intervene among the European powers. By 1917, all of these forces nudged the United States into a deadlocked war.

American women experienced this "Great War" differently than any previous war. For the first time, the Army and Navy nurse corps were activated. It was the first American war in which no woman enlisted as a foot soldier disguised as a man, for it introduced thorough physical examinations. Yet it was the first war in which women officially and openly served in the Navy, the Marine Corps, and the Army Signal Corps. For the first time in the history of the world, 25,000 women, 15,000 of them civilians, crossed a hostile ocean to succor war's victims—many of them long before the United States entered the war. Women struck out on their own like entrepreneurs, finding their own ways to help people and seeking the money and capital to accomplish their goals.

In a period of overt racism, African-American women who tried to participate in these efforts met almost immovable obstacles. After a long struggle, a few black nurses were admitted into the nurse corps, but not until after the war. The military accepted no black women. Although 200,000 black soldiers served overseas, no more than half a dozen black women managed to get there, for with the sole exception of the YMCA all the volunteer organizations excluded them from service abroad. Black women worked nobly in this country in the workplace and as volunteers, but almost always in their own groups, set apart from whites.

BEFORE AMERICA'S ENTRY, 1914–1917

As soon as the shooting started in Europe, American women organized to help its victims, military and civilian. They used their existing women's clubs and lodges and church ladies' aid societies, and they started new groups focused on specific needs. As a need arose, an American women's group sprang up to meet it. The Children of the Frontier collected and shipped money and mounds of clothing to its American-French counterpart overseas to rescue, support, and train refugee and repatriated children. The American Relief Clearing House (ARCH), Le Bienetre du Blesse, and the American Fund for French Wounded furnished and distributed hospital supplies, the French transportation system having broken down. ARCH not only operated the American Ambulance Service but also afforded "5,000 relief organizations, societies, schools, churches, and individuals at the head of small circles . . . its free facilities for transferring material to France." Le Bienetre du Blesse provided special diets for convalescent French soldiers unable to stomach army food. American women established workshops and furnished materials for French seamstresses thrown out of work.

But sending money and goods did not suffice. Beginning in 1914, American women themselves went overseas. Some went for adventure, for the fun of the thing. Some simply refused to be left out of the action, insisting on participating in a great moment in history. Overwhelmingly, they wanted to serve the thousands victimized by the war.

With the United States still officially neutral, from 1914 to 1917 American nurses served in England, France, Serbia, Russia, and even Germany, a handful under the aegis of the American Red Cross, some in foreign military services, some in hospitals supported and staffed by American women. Other American women drove ambulances, ran dormitories or rest houses for European women munitions makers, cared for orphans, fed soldiers on the march, found homes and furniture and tools and seeds for displaced people. Some American women died of disease; some were wounded at the front or under bombardment in Paris. First from the east coast, and then from

From *Social Education*, February 1994, pp. 83-85. © 1994 by the National Council for the Social Studies. Reprinted by permission.

all over the United States, American women sought sponsors or used their life savings to volunteer in Europe.

Meanwhile, women who opposed the war acted with equal verve and enterprise to end it. Members of the Woman's Peace Party in 1915 accepted the invitation of European women to an International Congress of Women at The Hague that included representatives of the warring Allied and Central powers. That remarkable harmonious congress then sent two delegations of its women to present to the heads of state of the belligerents a plan of continuous negotiation conceived by an American women. The women reported its favorable reception to an indifferent Woodrow Wilson—and the deadlocked war ground on.

AFTER AMERICA'S ENTRY

But when in 1917 the United States finally slipped and slid into World War I, American women overwhelmingly supported it—even Jane Addams, who thrust aside her longstanding opposition in order to participate in food conservation drives. Only a courageous radical fringe, led by attorney Christel Eastman, kept up the peace effort.

Many women not only fervently wanted to help in the war effort but knew how, through their years of relief work from 1914 to 1917. They were joined by other activist women who now added war work to their reform work and/or suffrage work and by multitudes of other women willing to do whatever was needed now that the United States was at war. But the establishment clashed with women leaders about just what that was.

Men in government thought they knew exactly what women should do: knit, save food, smile, send their menfolk to war, pass out white feathers to young men not in uniform, cut back on expenses—but not too much (or what would happen to the economy?). Women wanted a more active role and more say-so. The government threw them a bone by establishing a woman's committee of the Council of National Defense, itself only an advisory body, with the redoubtable suffragist Anna Howard Shaw as committee head. She did her excellent best, but without power she could not prevent inefficiency, duplication, and wasted effort.

In this situation women continued to launch out in all directions, in efforts ranging from the essential to the ludicrous (like making plans to evacuate virgins in case the Germans invaded America). Despite absurdities and confusion they accomplished miracles in assuaging the suffering in Europe and making life happier and easier for soldiers and warworkers in the United States and overseas.

Besides these volunteers, women rushed into the workplace to manufacture war materiel and to carry on in jobs vacated by men heading for the trenches. Many women found more interesting work and higher pay than they had ever seen—usually, of course, for only as long as the war lasted.

But what about women actually in the military? Counting is difficult and in some ways meaningless. In thousands of cases, being in or out of the military was a distinction almost without a difference.

Civilian American Red Cross nurses worked side by side with Army Nurse Corps members, doing the same work. They themselves often did not understand the difference in their status. Few Red Cross nurses realized that by not joining the Army Nurse Corps they were rendering themselves ineligible for benefits should they become disabled, and few Army nurses realized that they were committing themselves indefinitely, rather than for the two-year term common in the Red Cross. And, despite their own strenuous efforts for regularization, Army and Navy nurses held only a paramilitary status, since the military refused them the rank and benefits that their responsibilities justified. No wonder chief nurse Carrie Hall wrote: "I feel much like the fly that has accepted the spider's invitation and finds he can't escape."

Women physicians labored under similar difficulties. For the most part the American military refused to accept them, except eventually as civilian contract physicians, without rank. Those overseas reported their own embarrassment vis-à-vis their peers with rank in the British army and the bewilderment of Serbian doctors who inquired why the United States government entrusted women doctors with responsibility and sent them into danger but refused them rank. American medical women responded by organizing, funding, and staffing their own hospitals, some of which served with the French military. They also served impromptu and ad hoc. Third-year medical student Jean Pattison, spending her vacation with an American Women's Hospital, was pressed into service first for the French Army and then in an American military field hospital at Chateau-Thierry. Dr. Rosalie Slaughter Morton, having persuaded the Red Cross to entrust her with taking medical supplies to the Serbian army, seized the chance to volunteer at a French tent hospital for Serbian patients.

The Army Signal Corps' more than 200 telephone operators thought they were in the Army. At the insistence of General John J. Pershing, these American women were recruited to enable communications within the American Expeditionary Force (AEF) and with the allied armies. The American Telephone and Telegraph Company sought out American women who spoke French and trained them to operate switchboards. They were then sworn in and issued uniforms. They were subject to military discipline, and some of them served under fire. But no one else had really given a thought to their military status. The military brass greeted their arrival with cries of relief, sent them gifts, praised their patience and efficiency, treated them like the glamour girls of the AEF, called them "Soldiers of the Switchboard," decorated them, and at war's end forgot about them. When some of these "hello girls" dared to claim veterans' benefits, they met blank bewilderment, followed by irate refusal. Some of the women persisted, for almost sixty years. In 1977, when the youngest of them was nearing eighty, they won recognition as veterans.

The occupational therapists and physical therapists never did. They may well have had an equally valid claim, but none among them chose to pursue it. Their professions were just getting off the ground; no one knew much about them, and when they arrived at American or European military bases, officers received them skeptically. They proved themselves by putting their shoulders to whatever wheels needed turning. Physical therapists acted as nurses and secretaries during the medical emergencies that followed every "push" when soldiers tried to cross No Man's Land to the enemy trenches. At least one group of occupational therapists (OTs), handywomen that they were, won their commanding officer's heart and support by plumbing, making drain pipes from tin cans and lining tubs built by patients for dishwashing. Their carpentry won over the doctors, when the OTs trained patients to fashion desks, bedside tables, chairs, and stools.

No question, of course, about the Yeomen (Female) and the Woman Marines. From the outset they were officially military members. In 1916 Secretary of the Navy Josephus Daniels, contemplating the probable lack of sufficient clerical staff if and when the United States entered the war, asked whether any law prescribed that a yeoman be a man? No, but only because the question of an alternative had been unthinkable. But by that time in civilian life, yeoman's work, clerical work, was identified as woman's work. Daniels's question led to the enlistment of 13,000 women in the Navy and 300 in the Marine Corps. Almost all of them worked in the United States, most in Washington, D.C. Most did clerical work, but some labored in munitions factories and some as radio electricians. Assigned to special duty, Yeomen (F) sold liberty bonds in theater aisles. The whole operation was off the cuff.

Lighthearted youngsters, most of these Navy and Marine women had fun, according to Marie Broglie, who joined up at eighteen. Yes, she took a physical exam—but not much of one, with a sheet between her body and the examining doctor. Once accepted, she loved her work and the friends she made. She and her friends dated officers: no questions raised about fraternization and rank distinctions. Washington-born and -bred, she lived at home, and her mother let her bring other girls who lived at the barracks home on weekends.[1] Saturdays they drilled, and lots of spectators turned

out to watch. Joy Bright Hancock, later a Navy captain, recalled that the Navy began to distinguish its women as Yeomen (Female) only after some of them had been mistakenly called up for duty on shipboard. With the end of the war, the Navy and Marine women departed in peace and without question.

In short, actual membership in the military did not define a woman's usefulness in World War I, her duties, her heroism, the dangers she confronted, or the hardships she endured. Female Salvation Army and YMCA workers, like nurses, encountered hardship and danger: some of them were wounded; some died. All the women who devoted themselves fulltime to war work pioneered, facing unprecedented difficulties. Many found their own means of service.

Although the United States military refused to accredit women journalists, reporter Mary Roberts Rinehart scored a beat with reports from the Belgian front in 1914. Paleobotanist Ruth Holen worked in a maternity hospital for refugee women in Russia as general factotum, negotiating with Russian authorities, chivying workmen, interpreting, traveling around Russia to procure equipment and supplies; she died there. Expatriates Gertrude Stein and Alice B. Toklas delivered hospital supplies in France—Stein driving, though she never learned to back up. Pilot Ruth Law flew over the western front. Elsie Janis entertained the troops. Novelist Edith Wharton developed and ran refugee services and orphan asylums. Quakers and YMCA workers fought overwhelming odds to succor refugees, working women, and American

servicemen in revolutionary Russia. Wealthy young women sailed the submarine-infested Atlantic to drive ambulances during air raids and persuade their fathers to contribute an ambulance or two. Other women mortgaged their houses to finance a trip overseas, ready to offer their services scrubbing floors.

War's end saw disillusion, among women as well as among servicemen. The romance of war that had seduced the American population into the senseless struggle of World War I still blinded their parents; the loyal and sensitive young had no wish to disillusion their elders. But, reported YMCA worker Mary Lee, small boats constantly skirted the ships that were to take servicemen and women workers back to the United States, to prevent their suicide.

NOTE

1. Marie Broglie. Personal interview with authors, March 16, 1985.

REFERENCES

Owings, Chloe. ARCH report of October 21, 1916, quoted in Chloe Owings's unpublished autobiography, "Living through Covered Wagon to Space Ship Age or Life Is a Cooperative," 97, Chloe Owings Papers, Schlesinger Library, Radcliffe College.

Schneider, Dorothy, and Carl J. Schneider. *Into the Breach: American Women Overseas in World War I.* New York: Viking, 1991.

————. *American Women in the Progressive Era, 1900–1920.* New York: Facts on File, 1993.

What We Lost in the Great War

Seventy-five years ago this spring a very different America waded into the seminal catastrophe of the twentieth century. World War I did more than kill millions of people; it destroyed the West's faith in the very institutions that had made it the hope and envy of the world.

John Steele Gordon

John Steele Gordon's article on the origins of the health-care crisis appeared in the May/June 1992 issue of American Heritage.

A few years ago I wrote a book called *The Scarlet Woman of Wall Street* about a place and a people that flourished in the nineteenth century: the New York City of the 1860s and 1870s. We might call it Edith Wharton's New York. Mrs. Wharton herself wrote late in her life, in the 1930s, that the metropolis of her youth had been destined to become "as much a vanished city as Atlantis or the lowest level of Schliemann's Troy." To those of us who know the modern metropolis—what we might call Tom Wolfe's New York—that city of only a century ago seems today as far away and nearly as exotic as Marco Polo's Cathay.

What happened to Edith Wharton's world? Why does the society our grandparents and great-grandparents lived in seem so very much a foreign country to us today?

To be sure, Edith Wharton's New York was a still-provincial city of horses and gas lamps, Knickerbockers and Irishmen, brownstones and church steeples. Its population was characterized by a few people in top hats and a great many people in rags, for in the 1860s grinding poverty was still thought the fate of the majority of the human race.

In contrast, Tom Wolfe's New York— far and away the most cosmopolitan place on earth—is a city of subways and neon, Korean grocers and Pakistani news dealers, apartments and skyscrapers. If poverty has hardly been expunged, the percentage of the city's population living in want has greatly diminished even while society's idea of what constitutes the basic minimums of a decent life has greatly expanded.

It was constant, incremental change that brought about these differences, a phenomenon found in most societies and all industrial ones. Indeed, one of the pleasures of growing old in such a society, perhaps, is that we come to remember personally—just as Edith Wharton did—a world that has slipped out of existence.

But this sort of change comes slowly and is recognized only in retrospect. As the novelist Andrew Holleran explained, "No one grows old in a single day." Rather, something far more profound than incremental change separates us from Edith Wharton's world, and we look at that world now across what a mathematician might call a discontinuity in the stream of time.

ONLY RARELY IN THE COURSE OF HISTORY does such a discontinuity occur and turn a world upside down overnight. When it does happen, it is usually as the result of some unforeseeable cataclysm, such as the volcanic explosion that destroyed Minoan civilization on the island of Crete about 1500 B.C., or the sudden arrival of the conquistadors in the New World three thousand years later.

Edith Wharton's world suffered just such a calamity. The diplomat and his-torian George Kennan called it "the seminal catastrophe of the twentieth century": the First World War.

Certainly that war's influence on subsequent world events could hardly have been more pervasive. Had there been no First World War, there would, of course, have been no Second, and that is not just playing with numbers, for in geopolitical terms the two wars were really one with a twenty-year truce in the middle.

But for the First World War, the sun might still shine brightly on the British Empire. But for the war, there would have been no Bolshevik coup and thus no Soviet state. But for the war, there would have been no Nazis and thus no genocide of the Jews. And, of course, most of us never would have been born.

Far more important, however, than its effect upon the fate of great nations, and on our own individual existence, was the First World War's influence on the way that we heirs of Edith Wharton came to question, and for a while even to dismiss, many of the basic values of the culture she lived in. Because of the war, the word *Victorian* became a term of opprobrium that extended far beyond the ebb and flow of fashion.

The reason for this is simply that the First World War, more than any other in history, was psychologically debilitating, both for the vanquished and for the victors. indeed, there really was no victory. No premeditated policy of conquest or revenge brought the war about—although both those aims had clouded the politics of Europe for years. Therefore,

From *American Heritage*, July/August 1992, pp. 80-91. © 1992 by Forbes, Inc. Reprinted by permission of *American Heritage* magazine, a division of Forbes, Inc.

no aims, beyond national survival, were achieved.

Indeed, relations among the Great Powers of Europe were better in the early summer of 1914 than they had been for some time. The British and Germans had recently agreed about the Berlin to Baghdad railway and a future division between them of Portugal's colonies. Even the French, still bitter over their ignominious defeat at the hands of Prussia in 1871, were moving to improve relations with Germany, a move that Germany welcomed.

Rather, the war came about because a lunatic murdered a man of feathers and uniforms who had no real importance whatsoever. The politicians, seeking to take advantage of circumstances—as politicians are paid to do—had then miscalculated in their blustering and posturing.

The mobilization of an army when railroads were the only means of mass transportation was a very complex undertaking, one that had to be planned in advance down to the smallest detail. Once a mobilization plan was implemented, it could not be stopped without throwing a country's military into chaos, rendering it largely defenseless. Russia, seeking only to threaten Austria and thus prevent its using the assassination of Archduke Ferdinand to stir up trouble in the Balkans, discovered that it could not move just against Austria. It was general mobilization or nothing. Russia chose to mobilize.

At that point the statesmen realized that the war they had threatened so freely—but which no one, in fact, had wanted at all—had now, suddenly, become inescapable. A fearful, inexorable logic had taken decisions out of human hands.

Once it began, the generals found they had no tactical concepts to deal with the new military realities that confronted them. It had been forty-three years since Great Powers had fought each other in Europe. In those four decades the instruments of war had undergone an unparalleled evolution, and their destructive power had increased by several orders of magnitude.

Railroads, machine guns, and barbed wire made an entrenched defense invulnerable. Stalemate—bloody, endless, gloryless stalemate—resulted. For lack of any better ideas, the generals flung greater and greater numbers of men into the mouths of these machine guns and

gained at best mere yards of territory thereby.

In the first day—day!—of the Battle of the Somme in 1916, Great Britain suffered twenty thousand men killed. That was the bloodiest day in the British army's long history. Altogether there were more than a million casualties in this one battle alone. An entire generation was lost in the slaughter of the Somme and other similar battles.

This almost unimaginable destruction of human life, to no purpose whatsoever, struck at the very vitals of Western society. For this reason alone, among the casualties of the First World War were not only the millions of soldiers who had died for nothing, most of the royalty of Europe, and treasure beyond reckoning but nearly all the fundamental philosophical and cultural assumptions of the civilization that had suffered this self-induced catastrophe.

For there was one thing that was immediately clear to all about the Great War—as the generation who fought it called it—and that was that this awful tragedy was a human and wholly local phenomenon. There was no volcano, no wrathful God, no horde of barbarians out of the East. Western culture had done this to itself. Because of the war, it seemed to many a matter of inescapable logic that Western culture must be deeply, inherently flawed.

In four years of blood and smoke and flame, the world of Edith Wharton became the world of W. H. Auden; the Age of Innocence, the Age of Anxiety.

FOR US, WHO CAN SEE THE TRAGEDY THAT was looming up in what was for them the future, and thus, for them, impenetrable, many of the cultural assumptions of Edith Wharton's world smack of the hubris that is the inevitable progenitor of tragedy. But hubris, like the winner in a horse race, can be much more easily discerned in retrospect. And people cannot live—or, for that matter, bet on horses—in retrospect.

Given their vantage point in history, the inhabitants of Edith Wharton's world had every good reason for their attitudes. Their civilization had, after all, entirely remade the world in the preceding two hundred years.

Consider the facts:

In the year 1700 there had been little to distinguish European culture in terms of power, wealth, and creativity from the

other great civilizations on earth. The Ottoman Turks had conquered most of the Muslim world and much of Europe itself in the previous two centuries. The Turkish army had besieged Vienna as recently as 1683.

The Mogul emperor of India, whose father had built the incomparable Taj Mahal, sat on the Peacock Throne, ruling over an empire of a million square miles, and lived in a splendor unmatched even by the Versailles of Louis XIV.

The Chinese Empire was the largest and perhaps the most cultured on earth. It was also the most industrially advanced, running a strong trade surplus with Europe.

But by the year 1700 Europe had already invented a cultural tool of transcendent power called the scientific method. In the eighteenth century this tool was applied to an ever-widening area of inquiry with beneficial results in fields as diverse as agriculture, cloth manufacture, and metalworking. By the close of that century, Europe was clearly the dominant power center of the world and was projecting that power commercially, militarily, and politically over a wider and wider area.

And in 1782 James Watt perfected the rotary steam engine. The Industrial Revolution was under way.

A hundred years later still, at the end of the nineteenth century, any comparison between the West and other cultures bordered on the meaningless, so great had the gap in power and wealth grown. Westerners had projected that power over the entire globe and created the modern world, a world they utterly dominated. The Western people of that world took for granted what seemed to them the manifest superiority of Western technology, governance, and even religion over all others.

TO BETTER UNDERSTAND THE PREDOMInant attitudes of the West before the First World War, consider what it accomplished in the nineteenth century as a result of the Industrial Revolution. Quite simply, the quality of life was miraculously transformed. Indoor plumbing, central heating, brilliant interior lighting, abundant clothing, and myriad inexpensive industrial products from wallpaper to iceboxes gave the middle and upper classes a standard of living undreamed of a century earlier by even the richest members of society.

In 1800 it had required a month to cross the Atlantic in a damp, crowded, and pitching ship. In 1900 vast and luxurious liners made the crossing in a week. Information that once had been limited to the speed of human travel could now circle the entire globe in minutes by telephone, telegraph, and undersea cable.

In the 1830s the lights and shadows of an instant were captured by photography. In the 1870s Edison's phonograph imprisoned sound. To the Victorians it was as though time itself had been tamed.

Newspapers, books, and magazines proliferated by the thousands so that information and entertainment could be quickly and cheaply obtained. Free public libraries spread to nearly every city in the Western world. Andrew Carnegie alone paid for nearly five thousand of them in the United States and Britain.

Physics, chemistry, geology, and biology penetrated farther into the fathomless heart of nature than anyone had thought possible a hundred years earlier. Even the mighty Newton's model of the universe was found to be less than wholly universal when Einstein published his Special Theory of Relativity in 1905.

As the new century began engineers showed the world with the Crystal Palace in London how to enclose vast spaces, with the Brooklyn Bridge in New York how to span great distances, with the Eiffel Tower in Paris how to scale great heights. The automobile, the airplane, the movies, and wireless communication promised still more wonders.

Ever more important than the technological and scientific advances of the age, however, were the economic and political ones.

The nineteenth century is usually perceived as one in which great industrial and commercial fortunes were created in the midst—even because of—the grinding poverty of the masses. This is largely a misperception. To be sure, the absolute number of people living in poverty in the Western world greatly increased in the nineteenth century, but only because the population as a whole greatly increased. Moreover, the movement of workers from agriculture to industry concentrated the poor in highly visible urban areas. But their forebears had been no less poor. The ancestors of those who lived in the unspeakable urban hovels of Dickens's England had inhabited the equally unspeakable rural hovels of Fielding's En-gland. Meanwhile, the percentage of the population living in poverty declined.

In 1800 perhaps 85 percent of the population of Britain—then the richest and most advanced of Western nations—lived in or very near poverty, where 85 percent of the human population had always lived. These people had to work as hard as they could just to get enough to eat and obtain shelter and clothes. They stored up a little in good years, perhaps, in order to survive the bad ones. But luxuries, and even a formal education for their children, were out of the question. For millions, only rum, gin, and other spirits in staggering quantities—often quite literally in staggering quantities—made life endurable.

But by 1900 less than 30 percent of the British population was still at that economic level, and most of the children were receiving at least the rudiments of an education and therefore the hope of a better life. Meanwhile, the per capita consumption of alcohol had fallen sharply. While no one in 1900 thought that 30 percent of the population living in poverty was acceptable, parents and grandparents were there to tell them how far they had come.

In 1800 less than five percent of the British population was allowed to vote for those who represented them in Parliament, and real political power resided in fewer than two thousand families. By 1900 universal male suffrage was taken for granted and women were on the march for equal rights. Democracy, beginning to develop only in the new United States in 1800, was by 1900 the birthright of millions in both the old and new worlds.

IN TWO HUNDRED YEARS WESTERN CIVILI-zation had made itself rich and powerful and learned while the rest of mankind remained poor, and therefore weak and ignorant. Political and economic power in the West had ceased to be the exclusive possession of a narrow upper class and had spread widely to other levels of society, promoting social stability by giving everyone both a stake in society's institutions and the power to affect those institutions.

It was this dispersal of economic and political power that guaranteed that no one person or segment of society could become too powerful and threaten the rights or the prosperity of others. When heavy industry, in pursuit of economies of scale, conglomerated in the late nineteenth century into huge concerns of unprecedented financial and economic power, many Americans believed they threatened a plutocracy. So society moved to check the potential abuse of power with antimonopoly legislation, such as the Sherman Antitrust Act, and to channel that power into productive, not hegemonic, purposes. This may have been a violent and wrenching process; nevertheless, it happened.

Who can blame the people who accomplished all this for feeling good about themselves? Would we, or anyone, have been any wiser or more humble?

Because of this fantastic record of progress, the people of Edith Wharton's world believed in the inevitability of further progress and the certainty that science would triumph. They believed in the ever-widening spread of democracy and the rule of law. They believed in the adequacy of the present and the bright promise of the future. To be sure, they fought ferociously over the details of how to proceed, but they had no doubt whatever that the basic principles that guided their society were correct.

Then, all at once, the shots rang out in Sarajevo, the politicians bungled, the armies marched, the poppies began to blow between the crosses row on row. The faith of the Western world in the soundness of its civilization died in the trenches of the western front.

Seventy-five years later, richer and more learned than ever, the West still struggles to find the self-confidence it had once taken for granted.

Seventy-five years later, richer, more powerful, more learned than ever, the West still struggles to pick up the psychological pieces, to regain its poise, to find again the self-confidence that in the nineteenth century it took entirely for granted.

IF THE GREAT WAR WAS THE RESULT NOT of deliberate policy but of ghastly accident, we now know it was an accident waiting to happen. Still, like most accidents, it resulted from the concatenation of separate chances, each unlikely. Indeed, it can be reasonably argued that the calamity might well never have come to pass at all if only the imperial throne of Germany had been occupied by someone other than that supreme jerk Kaiser Wilhelm II.

Although highly intelligent, he had been burdened from the start with a withered left arm caused by a difficult and medically mishandled birth. Far worse, Wilhelm had been largely raised by pedantic tutors and sycophantic military aides, for his mother was more interested in Prussian politics than in her children's upbringing.

The result was that an undisciplined, impulsive, deeply insecure neurotic inherited the throne of the greatest military power in Europe. Worse, the constitution of the German Empire gave him a very large measure of control over foreign and military policy.

The consequence was disaster for Germany and the world. And in complex societies, just as in simple ones, when disaster strikes, "the king must die." And not just Wilhelm (who spent the last twenty years of his life in exile). The entire pre-war establishment was everywhere blamed for this purposeless, victorless war. The mainstream politicians who had failed to prevent it, the businessmen who had profited from it, the scientists and engineers who had created its lethal technology—all those, in fact who had constituted the nexus of power in Edith Wharton's world suffered a grievous loss of prestige.

Those who had been only on the margins of power and influence in the nineteenth century—the Cassandras who are present in all societies, the philosophers, the artists (in short, the intellectuals)—saw their opportunities and seized them. To use Theodore Roosevelt's famous metaphor, power began to move from the players in the arena to the observers in the seats.

In the relatively peaceful 1880s, Gilbert and Sullivan in *The Mikado* had put on the Lord High Executioner's little list of social expendables "the idiot who praises, with enthusiastic tone,/ All centuries but this, and every country but his own." After the First World War people listened eagerly to just such philosophers, many of whom thought that only a radical restructuring of Western society and its economic system could prevent a recurrence of the calamity. Not sur-

prisingly, the philosophers had no lack of prescriptions for how to accomplish this and no doubt whatever as to just who should be put in charge of the project. Although many of these ideas turned out to be in Winston Churchill's phrase, so stupid that only an intellectual could have conceived" them, people were ready to give them a try.

WE MUST NOW LOOK, BRIEFLY, AT THE philosophical baby that so many intellectuals were ready to toss out with the bath water of war.

At the core of Western thought lies the concept of the importance of the individual human being. It is a uniquely Western idea, with its origins in ancient Israel and Greece (a civilization where the gods themselves were made of all-too-human clay). Later the concept was continued and elaborated on by such Christian philosophers as Augustine, Jerome, and Thomas Aquinas.

In medieval England, safe from foreign invasion behind its watery walls, the emphasis on the importance of the individual resulted in the flowering of the concept of liberty, both political and economic. Individuals, thought the English, were born with rights no one, not even kings, could take away, for the king, like his subjects, was bound by the law. This idea—that the majesty of the law was separate and distinct from the king's own majesty—is today encapsulated in the phrase *the rule of law*. It is one of the most important of Western concepts, for without it the Western achievements of the nineteenth century would not have been possible.

THE AMERICAN REVOLUTION AND THE ECOnomic dominance of Britain in the nineteenth century caused liberty's children—capitalism and democracy—to spread widely through the Western world. The increasing acceptance during the nineteenth century of the individual's right, within an ordered society, to pursue his own concept of happiness—in other words, his self-interest—had, to be sure, many consequences, some of them unpleasant. The Victorians, however, were prepared to accept these consequences. They reasoned that because human beings are social creatures, the betterment of society was, in fact, in almost everyone's self-interest. The people of Edith Wharton's world likewise believed that most of

the attributes of their society resulted from the interaction of history with human nature, and that human nature, with all its faults, was a given.

The Victorians certainly thought that mankind could get ever better and ever wiser, and in support of this idea they pointed to their own century as Exhibit A. But they equally believed that the perfection of mankind could come only with the arrival of what Christians call the Kingdom of Heaven on Earth. Until then, they thought, they would just have to make do with what they had.

But Karl Marx reversed this equation. He maintained that human nature was only a result of the society in which people lived. Change society, thought Marx, and you change human nature. Perfect society, and you perfect mankind. To Marx and the "social engineers" who followed him, the intellectual, not the grace of God, would be the redeemer of the human race.

Marx was the quintessential intellectual, remarkably detached from the real world. Although he dedicated his formidable mind to the betterment of the new industrial working class, he knew of that class only what he read in the library of the British Museum. Not once in his life did Marx ever set foot in a factory. Consequently, at the time of his death, in 1883, his grand vision stood no more chance of adoption by the real world than had Sir Thomas More's Utopia three hundred and fifty years earlier.

Further, Marx, deeply influenced by Thomas Malthus's and David Ricardo's gloomy (and erroneous) ideas, made a classic intellectual mistake. He looked at the social and economic universe around him—the early stages of the Industrial Revolution—and assumed that the conditions he saw were permanent and the trends of that era would continue indefinitely. But, of course, trends hardly ever continue indefinitely.

In fact they were rapidly evolving, as they continue to do today. But the followers of Marx regarded his theories about society and economics as the equal of Newton's theory in physics: the universal explainer of all observed phenomena.

And while Marx was only an intellectual, his greatest intellectual successor, Lenin, was much more. Lenin was a political genius. Thanks to the opportunities arising out of the First World War, he was able to seize control of a great nation and proclaim a Marxist day in which the perfecting of society was the only goal and in which the individual pursuit of happiness, or even the right to hold a contrary opinion, had no place whatever. In the first two years of Lenin's rule, fifty thousand of his political opponents were executed.

In shattered Germany, meanwhile, an already neurotic society slid toward psychosis. United only in 1871, Germany had been a latecomer to the world of Great Power politics and was "born encircled" by the other Great Powers. Lacking a vast colonial empire and a long national history, Germany depended on its economic and military might for its prestige, until its one unquestioned superiority—its incomparable army—was nonetheless defeated.

THE DRACONIAN, SCORE-SETTLING PEACE imposed on Germany at the Versailles Conference worsened matters considerably. So did the hyperinflation of the early 1920s, which wiped out whatever economic security middle-class Germans had managed to hang on to. In their humiliation the German people felt a desperate need for scapegoats, and Hitler stood ready to supply Jews, homosexuals, Gypsies, and others to fill that need—in exchange, of course, for total power. Many other countries, including Spain and Italy, also adopted fascism, as these disparate movements were collectively called. Even countries with firm democratic foundations felt the effects of this intellectual assault upon the nineteenth-century world view. Britain and France elected their first socialist governments in 1924, and both had active fascist movements.

The Second World War destroyed fascism as a political doctrine but greatly strengthened the Soviet Union, which sought to export its system to areas occupied by the Red Army and to countries in the so-called Third World. Meanwhile, the democratic left, especially in Western Europe and Britain, but increasingly in the United States as well, sought to replace the old economic and social order with systems of their devising that they genuinely believed would be fairer and more peaceful and more prosperous. In pursuit of these worthy goals, these systems tended to concentrate power, rather than disperse it as the nineteenth century had done. And democratically elected leaders—just like their totalitarian counterparts—often assumed that

human nature was only clay to be molded in a noble cause.

But human nature has proved recalcitrant. The nineteenth century, it turns out, had it right to start with. The evidence has been piling up through most of the twentieth century, and it is now overwhelming that people act not as Karl Marx and Lenin thought they would but as Adam Smith and John Stuart Mill predicted.

People pursue their self-interests, perceiving those interests to be bound up with themselves, their families—especially their children—and their society as a whole. Class divisions within a society, by which Marxists seek to explain the human universe, are an intellectual construct, with no real-world analogue. Many of the programs advocated by the social engineers, therefore, failed altogether or had vast, wicked, and entirely unanticipated consequences.

Of all the inventions of the nineteenth century, capitalism and representative democracy turned out to be the greatest. To be sure, they are intellectually untidy—often very untidy indeed: just ask Charles Keating, the Reverend Al Sharpton, or the latest congressman under indictment. Nonetheless, they work, for they are consonant with human nature. As Churchill explained, "Democracy is the worst form of government except all those other forms that have been tried from time to time." He could have made the same point about capitalism.

Capitalism made the West rich in the nineteenth century, and that wealth was spread ever more widely through society as the century went on. All the alternatives pursued in the twentieth have led only to poverty.

Democracy increasingly empowered the ordinary people in the nineteenth century as literacy, newspapers, and the franchise spread to every level. All the modern alternatives have resulted only in tyrannies far worse than any known to the world of Edith Wharton.

After decades of experiments brought on by the First World War, it is clear that what maximizes human happiness is ordered liberty—the idea that individuals should be free to pursue their political and economic self-interests under the rule of law and within the limits set by a democratic society. During the last decade, as the promises of systems that concentrated power rather than dispersed it collapsed, country after country has moved toward economic and political

liberty. Today even the citadel of totalitarianism, the Kremlin itself, has fallen to the essential force of these nineteenth-century ideas.

The nineteenth century even knew the reason why these ideas were so forceful, and indeed, one of the century's greatest political philosophers expressed it as dictum. "Power tends to corrupt," Lord Acton wrote in 1887, "and absolute power corrupts absolutely." Perhaps the cruelest legacy of the First World War is that we have required seventy-five years and untold human pain to learn this truth all over again.

All this is not to say that there was nothing to be learned from the First World War and its terrible consequences, that it was all just a ghastly aberration. I think that we heirs of Edith Wharton have learned at least four vital lessons from the catastrophe.

Before the war Westerners believed not only in the superiority of Western culture but in the innate superiority of the white race over what many, twisting Kipling's meaning, referred to as those "lesser breeds without the Law." Today no one but the hopeless bigot believes that those who could inflict the Battle of Verdun upon themselves are a special creation or the sole repository of human genius. The Great War taught us that all human beings are equally human: equally frail and equally sublime.

THE SECOND LESSON OF THE FIRST WORLD War was to hammer home forever the truth first uttered by William Tecumseh Sherman thirty-five years earlier. "I am tired and sick of war," the great general said in 1879. "Its glory is all moonshine. . . . War is hell." At 11:00 A.M., on November 11, 1918, as the guns fell silent after fifty-one months and 8,538,315 military deaths, there was hardly a soul on earth who would have disagreed with him. Nor are there many today. If wars have been fought since, they have been fought by people who suffered few illusions about war's glory.

The third lesson is that in a technological age, war between the Great Powers cannot be won in anything but a Pyrrhic sense. In the stark phraseology of the accountant, war is no longer even remotely cost-effective.

The final lesson is that it is very easy in a technological age for war to become inevitable. The speed with which war is fought has increased many fold since the

Industrial Revolution began. In 1914 the Austrians, the Russians, and the German kaiser rattled one too many sabers, and suddenly, much to their surprise, the lights began to go out all over Europe. This all too vividly demonstrated fact has induced considerable caution in the world's statesmen ever since—if not, alas, in its madmen.

Bearing this in mind, there is one aspect of the First World War for which we might be grateful: If it had to be fought, it was well that it was fought when it was. We learned the lessons of total war in a technological age less than forty years before we developed the capacity to destroy ourselves utterly with

---

There has been joy. There will be joy again.
—Alfred Bester

---

this technology. Had the political situation that led to the Great War coincided with the technological possibilities that produced the hydrogen bomb, it is improbable that there would have been a Tom Wolfe's New York—or even any New Yorkers to look back and wonder what happened to Edith Wharton's.

Rather, the great metropolis, a city humming with human life and human genius, would instead be but one more pile of rubble on a vast and desolate plain, poisoned for centuries. If we have truly learned this final lesson, and we must pray that we have, then those millions who lie today in Flanders fields did not die in vain.

Why Suffrage for American Women Was Not Enough

With Hillary Clinton in the White House as the most political First Lady since Eleanor Roosevelt, the role of women in American politics is in sharp focus. Elisabeth Perry *explains here, via four case-histories, why American women did not break through in politics between the wars, despite having won the vote.*

Elisabeth Perry

Elisabeth Perry directs the graduate programme in Women's History at Sarah Lawrence College, in Bronxville, N.Y. Her most recent publication, The Challenge of Feminist Biography: Writing the Lives of Modern American Women *(Champaign: University of Illinois, 1992) was co-edited with Sara Alpern, Joyce Antler, and Ingrid Winther Scobie.*

As a result of the autumn elections in 1992, a year the American media billed as 'The Year of the Woman', the numbers of women holding elective office in the United States rose to unprecedented heights. The percentage of women office holders at state level climbed to 22.2 per cent for state-wide elected executives and 20.4 per cent for legislators. At the national level, the number of female US Senators tripled (from two to six), while the number in the House of Representatives rose from twenty-eight to forty-seven (there is a forty-eighth, who represents the District of Columbia, but she has no vote). Even with this impressive progress, however, women's share of elective office in the United States remains relatively small.

It is not hard to explain why. Deeply ingrained global traditions have long kept women out of public, authoritative roles. But why have these traditions remained so entrenched in the United States, ostensibly one of the most advanced, modernised countries of the world? A close look at American women's political history in the immediate post-suffrage era might provide a few clues.

American women won the vote in 1920 with the ratification of the Nineteenth Amendment to the federal Constitution. Women had worked for this goal since 1848, when Elizabeth Cady Stanton, a reformer active in the campaigns to abolish slavery and also a temperance advocate, organised a public meeting in Seneca Falls, New York, to discuss women's rights. Many observers ridiculed her demand for the vote. By the turn of the century, this demand had become the focal point of the entire women's movement. Suffrage for women was eventually won in a number of the states, and then nationwide in August, 1920.

By the time this event occurred, women were no longer political novices. For decades they had been organising conventions, giving public speeches, writing editorials, campaigning door-to-door, petitioning and marching. These activities gave them vast political expertise, as well as access to wide networks of other women activists and of male political leaders. This combination of expertise and contacts ought to have placed them at the centre of American political life. It did not.

The winning of female suffrage did not mark the end of prejudice and discrimination against women in public life. Women still lacked equal access with men to those professions, especially the law, which provide the chief routes to political power. Further, when women ran for office—and many did in the immediate post-suffrage era—they often lacked major party backing, hard to come by for any newcomer but for women almost impossible unless she belonged to a prominent political family. Even if successful in winning backing, when women ran for office they usually had to oppose incumbents. When, as was often the case, they lost their first attempts, their reputation as 'losers' made re-endorsement impossible.

American political parties did try to integrate women into their power structures after suffrage. They courted women's votes, especially in the early 1920s, when a 'woman's voting bloc' seemed real. In addition, the parties formed 'women's divisions' or created a committee system of equal numbers of committee women and committee men (with the latter usually choosing the former). But when party leaders sought a candidate for preferment, they tended to look for 'a good man', seldom imagining that a woman might qualify. In short, in the years immediately after suffrage most party leaders confined women to auxiliary, service roles. They expected women to help elect men but not seek office themselves. That party men in the early 1920s held to such an expectation is hardly surprising. That many of the most politically 'savvy' American women went along with them is more difficult to understand.

In the post-suffrage United States, although there were many strong, executive-type women with considerable political expertise, none of them became the vanguard of a new, office-seeking female

This article first appeared in *History Today*, September 1993, pp. 36-41. © 1993 by History Today, Ltd. Reprinted by permission.

Courtesy of Elisabeth Perry

political leadership. Because of women's long exclusion from the vote and political parties, these women had worked for change only in a nonpartisan fashion from within their own gender sphere. After suffrage, in part because men kept them there, they accepted the notion that separate roles for women in politics ought to continue.

The reasons for this acceptance are complex, and probably differ from woman to woman. Some women felt most comfortable operating from within their own sphere. In single-sex groups, they made lifelong friendships with women who shared their interests and problems. In addition, in women's groups they did not have to compete with men for positions of authority. A deep suspicion of electoral politics was yet another important factor. Political women distrusted the world of electoral politics. It was a man's world, a world filled with 'dirty games' that men had been trained to play, and indeed were forced to play, if they wanted to 'get ahead'. For these women, it held few allures. Educated and middle-class, they had not been brought up to be career-orientated or personally ambitious. Rather, they had been taught that their proper role was to serve others and to work for idealistic causes. The winning of the vote did little to change this socialisation.

These were some of the views of women's role in politics held by both men and women in the 1920s. The careers of four suffragists, all politically active in the post-suffrage era and all of

Belle Moskowitz with Eleanor Roosevelt at a 1924 political meeting, and (right) a 1931 portrait of Belle Moskowitz by the celebrated photographer, Lewis Hine.

whom could have held elective office had circumstances differed, serve to illustrate how these views affected individual lives. The four do not comprise a balanced 'sample', for they were all based in New York City and were all active in the Democratic Party. They are exemplars, however, because they thrived in a hotbed of women's activism in the post-suffrage era. If any woman could have risen into electoral political prominence during that era, she would have been a New York City Democrat.

My first example is Belle Lindner Moskowitz (1877–1933). A shopkeeper's daughter born in Harlem, New York, she spent her early career as a social worker on the city's Lower East Side. After her marriage in 1903, while her children were growing up, she did volunteer work until, by the 1910s, she had developed a city-wide reputation as an effective social and industrial reformer. Although considering herself an independent Republican, in 1918, the first year New York State women voted, because of Democrat Alfred E. Smith's reputation as an advocate for labour, she supported him for governor.

After organising the women's vote for him, Moskowitz proposed that Governor-elect Smith establish a 'Reconstruction Commission' to identify and propose solutions for the state's administrative, social, and economic problems. Smith not

only formed the Commission but appointed her its executive director. During the one year of its existence (1919–20), it outlined Smith's legislative programme and launched Moskowitz's career as his closest political advisor. From 1923 on, she ran his state re-election campaigns and guided the legislative enactment of his policies, all the while preparing the ground for his nomination by the Democratic Party as presidential candidate in 1928. In that year, she directed national publicity for the campaign and served as the only woman on the national Democratic Party executive committee.

Al Smith lost that election to Herbert Hoover. But because Belle Moskowitz had played such a central role in his career throughout the 1920s, by the time of his presidential race she was a nationally known political figure. Still, her fame depended on his. Smith had offered her a number of government posts but she had refused them. She believed, and rightly so, that her work from behind the scenes would in the end give her more power than the holding of any bureaucratic, appointive office. Thanks to her, Smith, a man whose formal education had ended at the age of thirteen, was able

Courtesy of Elisabeth Perry

to pursue his legislative programme with enough success to become a viable presidential candidate. But because of her self-effacement, when Smith failed to win the presidency and then lost his party leadership role to Franklin Delano Roosevelt, her career was eclipsed along with his. Future generations of political women would not see her example as an inspiration or model for their own careers.

More famous than Moskowitz, Anna Eleanor Roosevelt (1884–1962) became known worldwide for the role she played as the wife of Franklin Roosevelt, four-term president during the Great Depression and Second World War. Most portraits of Eleanor focus on her activities after 1933, when Franklin became president, until his death in 1945, when she became a United Nations delegate and moral force in world politics. What is less well known is that, before FDR became president, even before he became governor of New York, she had accumulated a vast amount of political experience and influence in her own right.

Unlike Moskowitz, Eleanor Roosevelt was born into wealth and privilege, but endured an unhappy childhood. A measure of fulfillment came to her through her education and volunteer social work. She married Franklin in 1905, bore him several children, and fostered her husband's promising political career. In 1920, this career reached its first culmination when he ran, unsuccessfully, for vice-president. By then their marriage was on shaky ground. Although in 1918 Eleanor had discovered Franklin's affair with Lucy Mercer, the couple had resolved to keep the marriage together. In 1921, Franklin was stricken with polio and withdrew from politics. Franklin's political manager and publicist, Louis Howe, convinced Eleanor to keep her husband's name alive by becoming active herself in women's organisations. Once involved in this work, Eleanor confirmed what she had discovered during her husband's earlier campaigns. She liked politics.

But primarily from within her own sphere. She took up volunteer work for four New York City women's groups: the League of Women Voters and Women's City Club, the Women's Trade Union League, and the Women's Division of the State Democratic Party. For this latter group, from 1925 to 1928 she developed and edited a newspaper that, in bridging the gap between upstate and downstate Democrats, formed a critical base for Al Smith and her husband's future support. Through her other groups she worked for legislation on a variety of important issues: public housing for low-income workers; the dissemination of birth control information, the reorganisation of the state government, and shorter hours and minimum wages for women workers.

To accomplish her goals, she gave talks on the radio and published articles. Journalists interviewed her. She travelled all around the state during and in between campaigns to keep local party leaders connected with one another. She ran the women's campaigns for the Democrats at the state level in 1924 and national level in 1928. As a result, she became a well known figure, almost as well known as her husband, at both state and national level. But when her husband won the governorship in 1928, she gave up all activity. She knew where her duty lay—to become Albany's First Lady, not to hold office herself.

By 1928, in the crucible of New York women's politics, Eleanor Roosevelt had forged for herself acute political skills. These would serve her well as she continued until her husband's death to support his political agendas and afterwards to pursue more directly her own. By 1928, however, she herself had become so prominent that had she wanted she could have run for office and probably won. It did not even occur to her to do so. That was not what women did, especially not women married to ambitious men.

The first woman in the United States to hold cabinet rank was Frances Perkins (1880–1965). Even though she held public office my argument holds true for her as well: her post was appointive, not elective, and she asserted to the end of her life that she had never been interested in a political career. Better educated than either Moskowitz or Roosevelt (she graduated from Mt. Holyoke College), Perkins had a background similar to theirs. After working as a teacher and in a social settlement, she became secretary of the New York Consumers' League, a group seeking labour legislation to improve factory safety and health conditions for all workers. Although always known as 'Miss' Perkins, she was married and bore one child, but her husband suffered from mental illness and was later unable to earn a living. This circumstance gave her a keen interest in finding well paid jobs. Like Moskowitz, she came to admire Al Smith and in 1918 worked for his election as governor. Unlike Moskowitz, when Smith offered her a job as a State Industrial Commissioner, she accepted. This post became the launching pad from which she entered Roosevelt's cabinet in 1933.

Still, when she reflected on her career years later, she denied being a 'career woman' with political ambitions. Doors had opened for her and she had gone through them. She had never dreamed of being Secretary of Labor or Industrial Commissioner, she said. A 'series of circumstances' and her 'own energies' had thrown her into 'situations' where she had assumed responsibility and then was asked to assume more. Before she knew it she 'had a career'.

Here again is an accomplished, talented woman who had matured through social reform and suffrage politics in the 1910s and then moved into appointive office. As she plied her way, although she wanted and needed to work, ideas of personal advancement or career ambition were seldom at the forefront of her thinking. Convinced even at the moment of Roosevelt's elevation of her that she was probably unworthy, she accepted the offer as a 'call to service'. Once she attained office, fearful that men would resist answering to her, she took on the look, dress, and behaviour of a schoolmarm so as to appear less threatening to them. Despite all of her accomplishments, the gender stereotypes and constraints of her time prevailed.

My last example from the period is Mary W. (Molly) Dewson (1874–1962). Like Perkins, Dewson was well educated. After graduating from Wellesley College and holding some research jobs, she became Superintendent of Probation at the nation's first reform school for girls and then executive secretary of the Massachusetts Commission on the Minimum Wage. Never married, she maintained a lifelong partnership with a friend, Polly Porter, with whom she farmed in Massachusetts and did suffrage and war work. Eventually, under the mentorship of Eleanor Roosevelt, Dewson moved into Democratic state and then national politics. Her personal ambitions remained severely limited, however.

When Dewson assessed women's political progress since suffrage, she confessed that their opportunities had barely expanded. usually on the basis of their 'looks, money', or a 'late husband's service to the party', they had received only ceremonial party positions. In these circumstances, Dewson decided that the only way to build women's political strength was through separate women's divisions. As head of the Women's Division of the Democratic National Committee, she organised women workers for FDR's campaigns and co-ordinated support for his programmes between elections. In so doing, she played roles essential to the success of the Democratic Party during the New Deal initiative. Like Perkins, Dewson followed a cautious philosophy in working with men: she took on a maternal or 'aunty'

Courtesy of Elisabeth Perry

A 1917 photograph of Molly Dewson who co-ordinated a separate women's effort in the Democratic Party between the wars, but from a traditionalist standpoint.

pose and disclaimed any relationship to feminism. She also turned down posts when they threatened her partnership with Polly Porter. Only in her old age did she finally enter a political race in her own right. But the race she chose was in a solidly-Republican district where she had no chance of winning.

Among the most politically adept of their generation, all four of these women pursued political goals in the 1920s but none as a man would have done. Moskowitz achieved an important advisory role but lost all her power at the fall of her mentor. Roosevelt sacrificed her own needs to those of her husband. Perkins reached high office but masked her strength and denied personal ambition. Dewson often put domestic happiness before career fulfilment and, like Perkins, downplayed her feminism. Others of their generation who had been leaders in the suffrage struggle acted similarly.

When younger women growing up in the 1920s and 30s looked at their political forbears, Belle Moskowitz, Eleanor Roosevelt, Frances Perkins, and Molly Dewson were among the few successful

ones they saw. But younger women wanted real careers, not roles as an amanuensis to a man or as a behind-the-scenes campaigner. But 'real careers' were denied them. Either men discriminated against them and kept them out of the central circles of power, or when they married they discovered that domestic life and a political career just did not mix.

The door was open to women in politics in the 1920s. But, as Molly Dewson once said, the battle was uphill and most women got quickly discouraged. By accommodating themselves to a reality they could not control, they participated in the perpetuation of a 'separate spheres ideology' long after it had outlived its relevance. Looking back at them from the standpoint of 1993 we might judge these women as 'old fashioned'. But we ought not reject them as important role models. As smart, wily, and skilled political strategists, they have much to teach us. We must reject not them but the constraints that held them back.

Some of those constraints are still with us. Throughout the 1992 campaign, questions about women's appropriate roles in politics continued to surface. They dominated the controversies that swirled around Hillary Clinton, wife of Democratic presidential candidate, Bill Clinton. What role had she played in his years as governor of Arkansas? Why did she keep her maiden name when they were married? What was the quality of their married life together? Had she been a good mother or was she one of those career-orientated, ambitious feminists?

At its national convention in August, the Republican Party exploited popular doubts about Hillary Clinton's ability to operate in the traditional mode of the political wife. In an unprecedented move, convention organisers asked the wives of its candidates, Barbara Bush and Marilyn Quayle, to speak. The shared theme of the women's speeches, 'traditional' family values, sent out a clear message: political wives must adhere strictly to giving priority to their husbands' careers.

The Democratic Party response disturbed many feminists, but it was probably essential to victory. Hillary Clinton got a makeover. She baked cookies and, in response to rumours that she was

childless, trotted out her daughter Chelsea at every possible occasion. Still, when Bill Clinton and his running mate, Albert Gore, Jr., made their victory speeches on election night, women heard some new words on national television. In describing their future government, for the first time in history both president and vice-president-elect included the category of 'gender' as an important test of the diversity they envisioned.

Despite their personal openness to women in government, Hillary Clinton remained vulnerable to further attacks. As a lawyer with a distinguished record of accomplishment concerning the rights of children, she took active part in her husband's transition team discussions. Later, she received an appointment as unpaid head of a task force addressing one of the nation's most pressing problems, the lack of a national health insurance system. In response to a query by the press as to how reporters should refer to her, she asked them to use all three of her names, Hillary Rodham Clinton. The charges flew. Ambitious feminist. Power mad. Who is in charge here? In March 1993, on a flight over Washington DC, an airline pilot joked over the loudspeaker, 'Down below you can see the White House, where the president and her husband live'.

If, on the brink of the twenty-first century, the wife of the President of the United States still cannot perform in an authoritative role without questions being raised about the appropriateness of her behaviour how could the women of the 1920s have stood a chance? Today's 'Hillary factor' shows just how far we have come and how far we have to go before women can at last take up citizenship roles equal to those of men.

FOR FURTHER READING:

Blanche W. Cook, *Eleanor Roosevelt,* volume I (Viking, 1992); J. Stanley Lemons, *The Woman Citizen. Social Feminism in the 1920's* (University of Illinois, 1973); George W. Martin, *Madam Secretary Frances Perkins* (Houghton Mifflin, 1976); Elisabeth Israels Perry, *Belle Moskowitz: Feminine Politics and the Exercise of Power in the Age of Alfred E. Smith* (Routlege, 1992); Susan Ware, *Partner and I: Molly Dewson, Feminism, and New Deal Politics* (Yale University Press, 1987).

Citizen Ford

*He invented modern mass production. He gave the world the first people's car,
and his countrymen loved him for it. But at the moment of his greatest triumph,
he turned on the empire he had built—and on the son who would inherit it.*

David Halberstam

Part One
THE CREATOR

Late in the life of the first Henry Ford, a boy named John Dahlinger, who more than likely was Ford's illegitimate son,* had a discussion with the old man about education and found himself frustrated by Ford's very narrow view of what schooling should be. "But, sir," Dahlinger told Ford, "these are different times, this is the modern age and—" Ford cut him off. "Young man," he said, "I invented the modern age."

The American century had indeed begun in Detroit, created by a man of simple agrarian principles. He had started with scarcely a dollar in his pocket. When he died, in 1947, his worth was placed at $600 million. Of his most famous car, the Model T, he sold 15,456,868. Mass production, he once said, was the "new messiah," and indeed it was almost God to him. When he began producing the Model T, it took twelve and a half hours to make one car. His dream was to make one car every minute. It took him only twelve years to achieve that goal, and five years after that, in 1925, he was making one every ten sec-

---

*Dahlinger, who died in 1984, was baptized in the Ford christening gown and slept as an infant in the crib Henry had used as a baby. His mother was a secretary at the Ford company. —Ed.

onds. His name was attached not just to cars but to a way of life, and it became a verb—to *fordize* meant to standardize a product and manufacture it by mass means at a price so low that the common man could afford to buy it.

When Ford entered the scene, automobiles were for the rich. But he wanted none of that; he was interested in transportation for men like himself, especially for farmers. The secret lay in mass production. "Every time I reduce the charge for our car by one dollar," he said early in the production of the T, "I get a thousand new buyers," and he ruthlessly brought the price down, seeking—as the Japanese would some sixty years later—size of market rather than maximum profit per piece. He also knew in a shrewd, intuitive way what few others did in that era, that as a manufacturer and employer he was part of a critical cycle that expanded the buying power of the common man. One year his advertising people brought him a new slogan that said, "Buy a Ford—save the difference," and he quickly changed it to "Buy a Ford—SPEND the difference," for though he was innately thrifty himself, he believed that the key to prosperity lay not in saving but in spending and turning money over. When one of the children of his friend Harvey Firestone boasted that he had some savings, Ford lectured the child. Money in banks was idle money. What he should do, Ford said, was spend it on tools. "Make

something," he admonished, "create something."

For better or worse Ford's values were absolutely the values of the common man of his day. Yet, though he shared the principles, yearnings, and prejudices of his countrymen, he vastly altered their world. What he wrought reconstituted the nature of work and began a profound change in the relationship of man to his job. Near the end of this century it was clear that he had played a major part in creating a new kind of society in which man thought as much about leisure time as about his work. Ironically, the idea of leisure itself, or even worse, a leisure culture, was anathema to him. He was never entirely comfortable with the fruits of his success, even though he lived in a magnificent fifty-six-room house. "I still like boiled potatoes with the skins on," he said, "and I do not want a man standing back of my chair at table laughing up his sleeve at me while I am taking the potatoes' jackets off." Of pleasure and material things he was wary: "I have never known what to do with money after my expenses were paid," he said, "I can't squander it on myself without hurting myself, and nobody wants to do that."

Only work gave purpose: "Thinking men know that work is the salvation of the race, morally, physically, socially. Work does more than get us our living; it gets us our life."

From *American Heritage,* October/November 1986, pp. 49-64. © 1986 by David Halberstam. Reprinted by permission of William Morrow & Company, Inc.

As a good farm boy should, he hated alcohol and tobacco, and he once said that alcohol was the real cause of World War I—the beer-drinking German taking after the wine-drinking Frenchman. His strength, in his early years—which were also his good years—was in the purity of his technical instincts. "We go forward without facts, and we learn the facts as we go along," he once said. Having helped create an urbanized world where millions of God-fearing young men left the farm and went to the cities, he was profoundly uneasy with his own handiwork, preferring the simpler, slower America he had aided in diminishing. For all his romanticizing of farm life, however, the truth was that he had always been bored by farm work and could not wait to leave the farm and play with machines. They were his real love.

When Ford was born, in 1863, on a farm in Dearborn, Michigan, the Civil War was still on. His mother died at the age of thirty-seven delivering her eighth child. Henry was almost thirteen at the time. He had idolized her, and her death was a bitter blow. "I thought a great wrong had been done to me," he said. Later in his life he not only moved the house in which he grew up to Greenfield Village, and tracked down the Ford family's very own stove, whose serial number he had memorized, he also had a cousin who resembled his mother dress up in an exact imitation of the way she had and wear her hair in just the same style.

His father's people were new Americans. When the great potato blight had struck Ireland in 1846, ruining the nation's most important crop, that country had been devastated. Of a population of eight million, one million had died, and one million had emigrated to America. Among the migrants was William Ford, who had set off to the magic land with two borrowed pounds and his set of tools. He was a skilled carpenter, and when he arrived, he moved quickly to Michigan, where some of his uncles had already settled, and found work laying railroad track. With his savings he bought some land and built a house, in awe of an America that had so readily allowed him to do so. To William Ford, Ireland was a place where a man was a tenant on the land, and America was a place where he owned it.

Henry Ford started school when he was seven. The basic books were the McGuffey Reader; they stressed moral

On the fiftieth anniversary of Ford's first car, in 1946, his adviser Charles Brady King made this sketch of it.

From the Collections of the Henry Ford Museum and Greenfield Village

values but included sections from Dickens, Washington Irving, and other major writers, which enticed many children into a genuine appreciation of literature. Although Ford loved McGuffey, he did not like books or the alien ideas they sometimes transmitted. "We read to escape thinking. Reading can become a dope habit. . . . Book-sickness is a modern ailment." By that he meant reading that was neither technical nor functional, reading as an end in itself, as a pleasure without a practical purpose. But he was wary even of practical volumes. "If it is in a book, it is at least four years old, and I don't have any use for it," he told one of his designers.

What he truly loved was machinery. From the start, he had a gift for looking at a machine and quickly understanding it, not only to repair it but to make it work better. "My toys were all tools," he wrote years later. "They still are!" In his early teens he designed a machine that allowed his father to close the farm gate without leaving his wagon. Watches fascinated him. When he was given a watch at thirteen, he immediately took it

apart and put it back together. He soon started repairing watches for his friends. His father complained that he should get paid for this, but he never listened, for it was a labor of love.

His father wanted him to become a farmer, but it was a vain hope. Henry Ford hated the drudgery of the farm. In 1879 he entered his seventeenth year, which in those days was considered maturity. On the first day of December of that year, he left for Detroit, a most consequential departure. He walked to the city, half a day's journey.

DETROIT WAS A TOWN OF 116,000, A PLACE of foundries and machine shops and carriage makers. There were some nine hundred manufacturing and mechanical businesses, many of them one-room operations but some of them large. It was an industrial city in the making. Ten railroads ran through it. As New York City, in the next century, would be a mecca for young Americans interested in the arts, Detroit was just becoming a city with a pull for young men who wanted to work with machines. The surge in small industries was beginning, and a young man who was good with his hands could always find a job.

Ford went to work at James Flower & Brothers, a machine shop with an exceptional reputation for quality and diversity of product. As an apprentice there, Ford was immersed in the world of machinery, working among men who, like himself, thought only of the future applications of machines. He made $2.50 a week, boarded at a house that charged him $3.50 a week, and walked to work. His salary left him a dollar a week short, and as a good, enterprising young man, he set out to make up the difference. Hearing that the McGill Jewelry Store had just gotten a large supply of clocks from another store, Ford offered to clean and check them. That job added another two dollars to his weekly salary, so he was now a dollar a week ahead.

His fascination with watches led him to what he was sure was a brilliant idea. He would invent a watch so elementary in design that it could be mass-produced. Two thousand of them a day would cost only thirty cents apiece to make. He was absolutely certain he could design and produce the watch; the only problem, he decided, was in marketing 600,000 watches a year. It was not a challenge that appealed to him, so he dropped the

From the Collections of the Henry Ford Museum and Greenfield Village

Ford at Detroit Edison in 1893.

By 1896, at the age of thirty-three, Ford finally had his first car on the street. He couldn't sleep for forty-eight hours before driving it.

project. The basic idea, however, of simplifying the product in order to mass-produce it, stayed with him.

He went from Flower & Brothers to a company called Detroit Dry Dock, which specialized in building steamboats, barges, tugs, and ferries. His job was to work on the engines, and he gloried in it, staying there two years. There was, he later said, nothing to do every day but learn. In 1882, however, at the age of nineteen, he returned to the farm, and his father offered him eighty acres of land to stay there. William Ford did that to rescue his wayward son from the city and his damnable machines; Henry Ford took it because he momentarily needed security—he was about to marry Clara Bryant. Nothing convinced him more of his love of machines than the drudgery of the farm. Again he spent

every spare minute tinkering and trying to invent and reading every technical magazine he could. He experimented with the sawmill on the farm; he tried to invent a steam engine for a plow. Crude stationary gasoline engines had been developed, and Ford was sure a new world of efficient gasoline-powered machines was about to arrive. He wanted to be part of it. In 1891, with all the timber on the farm cut, he asked Clara to go back to Detroit with him. "He just doesn't seem to settle down," his father said to friends. "I don't know what will become of him."

The last thing Henry Ford was interested in was settling down. He intended, he told his wife, to invent a horseless carriage. But first he needed to know a good deal more about electricity. So he took a job with Detroit Edison at forty-five dollars a month. The city had grown dramatically in the few years since he had first arrived; its population was now more than 205,000. The railroads had begun to open up the country, and, except for Chicago, no town in America had grown as quickly. Detroit now had streetlights. There were more machine shops than ever before. In this city the age of coal and steam was about to end.

By 1896, at the age of thirty-two, Ford finally had his first car on the street. He was so excited by the prospect of his inaugural ride that he barely slept for the forty-eight hours before it. He had been so obsessed and preoccupied during the creation of the car that not until it was time for the test drive did he find that the door of the garage was too small for it to exit. So he simply took an ax and knocked down some of the brick wall to let the automobile out. A friend rode ahead on a bike to warn off traffic. A spring in the car broke during the ride, but they fixed it quickly. Then Henry Ford went home so he could sleep for a few hours before going to work. Later he drove the car out to his father's farm, but William Ford refused to ride in it. Why, he asked, should he risk his life for a brief thrill?

Henry Ford sold that first car for $200 and used the money to start work immediately on his next. It was considerably heavier than the first, and he persuaded a lumber merchant named William Murphy to invest in the project by giving him a ride. "Well," said Murphy when he reached home safely, "now we will organize a company." In August 1899 Murphy brought together a consortium

of men who put up $15,000 to finance Ford's Detroit Automobile Company. Ford thereupon left Detroit Edison to work full time on his car.

In February 1900, at the threshold of the twentieth century, Ford was ready to take a reporter from the Detroit *News Tribune* for a ride. The car, he said, would go twenty-five miles an hour. The reporter sensed that he was witness to the dawn of a new era. Steam, he later wrote, had been the "compelling power of civilization," but now the shriek of the steam whistle was about to yield to a new noise, the noise of the auto. "What kind of a noise is it?" the reporter asked. "That is difficult to set down on paper. It is not like any other sound ever heard in this world. It was not like the puff! puff! of the exhaust of gasoline in a river launch; neither is it like the cry! cry! of a working steam engine; but a long, quick, mellow gurgling sound, not harsh, not unmusical, not distressing; a note that falls with pleasure on the ear. It must be heard to be appreciated. And the sooner you hear its newest chuck! chuck! the sooner you will be in touch with civilization's latest lisp, its newest voice." On the trip, Ford and the reporter passed a harness shop. "His trade is doomed," Ford said.

Ford, however, was not satisfied. The cars he was making at the Detroit Automobile Company were not far behind the quality of the cars being made by Duryea or Olds, but they remained too expensive for his vision. Ford desperately wanted to make a cheaper car. His stockholders were unenthusiastic. By November 1900 the company had died. But Ford was as determined as ever to make his basic car, and he decided that the way to call attention to himself and pull ahead of the more than fifty competing auto makers was to go into racing. In 1901 he entered a race to be held in Grosse Pointe. He won and became, in that small, new mechanical world, something of a celebrity. That propelled him ahead of his competitors.

Two years later, in 1903, he set out to start the Ford Motor Company. He was forty years old and had, he felt, been apprenticing long enough. There were 800 cars in the city at that time, and some owners even had what were called motor houses to keep them in. Ford soon worked up his plan for his ideal, inexpensive new car, but he needed money—$3,000, he thought, for the supplies for the prototype (the actual cost was $4,000).

He got the financing from a coal dealer named Alexander Malcomson. Ford and Malcomson capitalized their original company for $150,000, with 15,000 shares. Some of the early investors were not very confident. John Gray, Malcomson's uncle, made a 500 percent return on his early investment but went around saying that he could not really ask his friends to buy into the company. "This business cannot last," he said. James Couzens, Malcomson's assistant, debated at great length with his sister, a schoolteacher, on how much of her savings of $250 she should risk in this fledging operation. They decided on $100. From that she made roughly $355,000. Couzens himself managed to put together $2,400 to invest, and from that, when he finally sold out to Ford in 1919, he made $29 million.

This time Ford was ready. He was experienced, he hired good men, and he knew the car he would build. "The way to make automobiles," he told one of his backers in 1903, "is to make one automobile like another automobile . . . just as one pin is like another pin when it comes from a pin factory, or one match is like another match when it comes from a match factory." He wanted to make many cars at a low price. "Better and cheaper," he would say. "We'll build more of them, and cheaper." That was his complete vision of manufacturing. "Shoemakers," he once said, "ought to settle on one shoe, stove makers on one stove. Me, I like specialists."

But he and Malcomson soon split over the direction of the company: Malcomson, like Ford's prior backers, argued that fancy cars costing $2,275 to $4,775 were what would sell. At the time, nearly half the cars being sold in America fell into this category; a decade later, largely because of Ford, those cars would represent only 2 percent of the market. Malcomson wanted a car for the rich; Ford, one for the multitude. Though the early models were successful—the company sold an amazing total of 1,700 cars in its first 15 months—it was the coming of the Model T in 1908 that sent Ford's career rocketing.

It was the car that Henry Ford had always wanted to build because it was the car that he had always wanted to drive—simple, durable, absolutely without frills, one that the farmer could use and, more important, afford. He was an agrarian populist, and his own people were farmers, simple people; if he could make their lives easier, it would give him pleasure. He planned to have a car whose engine was detachable so the farmer could also use it to saw wood, pump water, and run farm machinery.

THE MODEL T WAS TOUGH, COMPACT, AND light, and in its creation Ford was helped by breakthroughs in steel technology. The first vanadium steel, a lighter, stronger form developed in Britain, had been poured in the United States a year before the planning of the Model T. It had a tensile strength nearly three times that of the steel then available in America, yet it weighed less and could be machined more readily. Ford instantly understood what the new steel signified. He told one of his top men, Charles Sorensen, that it permitted them to have a lighter, cheaper car.

The T was a brilliantly simple machine: when something went wrong, the average owner could get out and fix it. Unimproved dirt tracks built for horses, which made up most of the nation's roads and which defeated fancier cars, posed no problem for it. Its chassis was high, and it could ride right over serious bumps. It was, wrote Keith Sward, a biographer of Ford, all bone and muscle with no fat. Soon the Ford company's biggest difficulty was in keeping up with orders.

Because the Model T was so successful, Ford's attention now turned to manufacturing. The factory and, even more, the process of manufacturing, became his real passions. Even before the T, he had been concerned about the production process. In 1906 he had hired an industrial efficiency expert named Walter Flanders and offered him a whopping bonus of $20,000 if he could make the plant produce 10,000 cars in 12 months. Flanders completely reorganized the factory and beat the deadline by two days. He also helped convince Ford that they needed a larger space. Flanders understood that the increasing mechanization meant that the days of the garage-shop car maker were over. There was a process now, a *line,* and the process was going to demand more and more money and employees. Flanders understood that every small success on the line, each increment that permitted greater speed of production (and cut the cost of the car), mandated as well an inevitable increase in the size of the company. "Henceforth the history of the industry will be the

Ford at the turn of the century.

The way to make cars, Ford said in 1903, is to make one like another, "just as one pin is like another pin, or one match like another match."

From the Collections of the Henry Ford Museum and Greenfield Village

history of the conflict of giants," he told a Detroit reporter.

FORD THEREUPON BOUGHT HIS HIGHLAND Park grounds. Here he intended to employ the most modern ideas about production, particularly those of Frederick Winslow Taylor, the first authority on scientific industrial management. Taylor had promised to bring an absolute rationality to the industrial process. The idea was to break each function down into much smaller units so that each could be mechanized and speeded up and eventually flow into a straight-line production of little pieces becoming steadily larger. Continuity above all. What Ford wanted, and what he soon got, was a mechanized process that, in the words of Keith Sward, was "like a river and its tributaries," with the subassembly tributaries

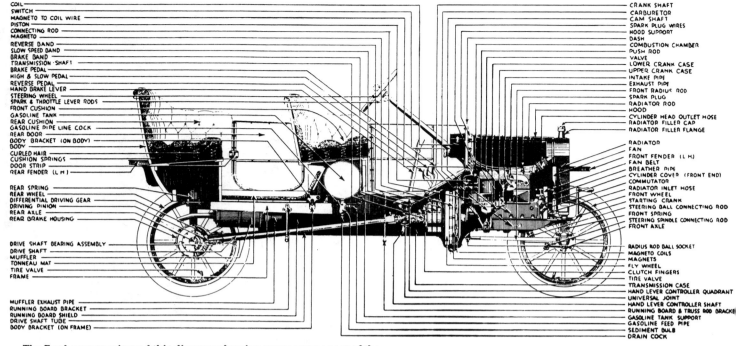

Left side labels:
COIL
SWITCH
MAGNETO TO COIL WIRE
PISTON
CONNECTING ROD
MAGNETO
REVERSE BAND
SLOW SPEED BAND
BRAKE BAND
TRANSMISSION SHAFT
BRAKE PEDAL
HIGH & SLOW PEDAL
REVERSE PEDAL
HAND BRAKE LEVER
STEERING WHEEL
SPARK & THROTTLE LEVER RODS
FRONT CUSHION
GASOLINE TANK
REAR CUSHION
GASOLINE PIPE LINE COCK
REAR DOOR
BODY BRACKET (ON BODY)
BODY
CURLED HAIR
CUSHION SPRINGS
DOOR STRIP
REAR FENDER (L H)
REAR SPRING
REAR WHEEL
DIFFERENTIAL DRIVING GEAR
DRIVING PINION
REAR AXLE
REAR BRAKE HOUSING
DRIVE SHAFT BEARING ASSEMBLY
DRIVE SHAFT
MUFFLER
TONNEAU MAT
TIRE VALVE
FRAME
MUFFLER EXHAUST PIPE
RUNNING BOARD BRACKET
RUNNING BOARD SHIELD
DRIVE SHAFT TUBE
BODY BRACKET (ON FRAME)

Right side labels:
CRANK SHAFT
CARBURETOR
CAM SHAFT
SPARK PLUG WIRES
HOOD SUPPORT
DASH
COMBUSTION CHAMBER
PUSH ROD
VALVE
LOWER CRANK CASE
UPPER CRANK CASE
INTAKE PIPE
EXHAUST PIPE
FRONT RADIUS ROD
SPARK PLUG
RADIATOR ROD
HOOD
CYLINDER HEAD OUTLET HOSE
RADIATOR FILLER CAP
RADIATOR FILLER FLANGE
RADIATOR
FAN
FRONT FENDER (L H)
FAN BELT
BREATHER PIPE
CYLINDER COVER (FRONT END)
COMMUTATOR
RADIATOR INLET HOSE
FRONT WHEEL
STARTING CRANK
STEERING BALL CONNECTING ROD
FRONT SPRING
STEERING SPINDLE CONNECTING ROD
FRONT AXLE
RADIUS ROD BALL SOCKET
MAGNETO COILS
MAGNETS
FLY WHEEL
CLUTCH FINGERS
TIRE VALVE
TRANSMISSION CASE
HAND LEVER CONTROLLER QUADRANT
UNIVERSAL JOINT
HAND LEVER CONTROLLER SHAFT
RUNNING BOARD & TRUSS ROD BRACKET
GASOLINE TANK SUPPORT
GASOLINE FEED PIPE
SEDIMENT BULB
DRAIN COCK

The Ford company issued this diagram showing every component of the Model T in 1913, five years after the car's birth. It was accompanied by the explanation, "The better you know your car the better will you enjoy it."

merging to produce an ever-more-assembled car.

The process began to change in the spring of 1913. The first piece created on the modern assembly line was the magneto coil. In the past a worker—and he had to be skilled—had made a fly-wheel magneto from start to finish. An employee could make 35 or 40 a day. Now, however, there was an assembly line for magnetos. It was divided into 29 different operations performed by 29 different men. In the old system it took twenty minutes to make a magneto; now it took thirteen.

Ford and his men quickly imposed a comparable system on the assembly of engines and transmissions. Then, in the summer of 1913, they took on the final assembly, which, as the rest of the process had speeded up, had become the great bottleneck. Until then the workers had moved quickly around a stationary metal object, the car they were putting together. Now the men were to remain stationary as the semifinished car moved up the line through them.

One day in the summer of 1913, Charles Sorensen, who had become one of Ford's top production people, had a Model T chassis pulled slowly by a windlass across 250 feet of factory floor,

timing the process all the while. Behind him walked six workers, picking up parts from carefully spaced piles on the floor and fitting them to the chassis. It was an experiment, but the possibilities for the future were self-evident. This was the birth of the assembly line, the very essence of what would become America's industrial revolution. Before, it had taken some thirteen hours to make a car chassis; now they had cut the time of

From the Collections of the Henry Ford Museum and Greenfield Village

An oddly wistful 1912 portrait.

assembly in half, to five hours and fifty minutes. Not satisfied, they pushed even harder, lengthening the line and bringing in more specialized workers for the final assembly. Within weeks they could complete a chassis in only two hours and thirty-eight minutes.

Now the breakthroughs came even more rapidly. In January of 1914 Ford installed his first automatic conveyor belt. It was, he said, the first moving line ever used in an industrial plant, and it was inspired by the overhead trolley that the Chicago meat-packers employed to move beef. Within two months of that innovation, Ford could assemble a chassis in an hour and a half. It was a stunning accomplishment, but it merely whetted his zeal. Everything now had to be timed, rationalized, broken down into smaller pieces, and speeded up. Just a few years before, in the days of stationary chassis assembly, the best record for putting a car together had been 728 minutes of one man's work; with the new moving line it required only 93 minutes. Ford's top executives celebrated their victory with a dinner at Detroit's Pontchartrain Hotel. Fittingly, they rigged a simple conveyor belt to a five-horsepower engine with a bicycle chain and used the conveyor to serve the food

When Ford began making the Model T, the company's cash balance was $2 million; when production ceased, it was $673 million.

around the table. It typified the spirit, camaraderie, and confidence of the early days.

Henry Ford could now mass-produce his cars, and as he did so, he cut prices dramatically. In 1909 the average profit on a car had been $220.11; by 1913, with the coming of the new, speeded-up line, it was only $99.34. But the total profits to the company were ascending rapidly because he was selling so many more cars. When the company began making the Model T, its cash balance was slightly greater than $2 million. Nineteen years and more than 15 million cars later, when Ford reluctantly came to the conclusion that he had to stop making the T, the company balance was $673 million. But this was not the kind of success that merely made a company richer; it was the beginning of a social revolution.

Ford himself knew exactly what he had achieved—a breakthrough for the common man. "Mass production," he wrote later, "precedes mass consumption, and makes it possible by reducing costs and thus permitting both greater use-convenience and price-convenience." The price of the Model T touring car continued to come down, from $780 in the fiscal year 1910-11 to $690 the following year, to $600, to $550, to, on the eve of World War 1, $360. At that price he sold 730,041 cars. He was outproducing everyone in the world.

IN 1913 THE FORD MOTOR COMPANY, WITH 13,000 employees, produced 260,720 cars; the other 299 American auto companies, with 66,350 employees, produced only 286,770. Cutting his price as his production soared, he saw his share of the market surge—9.4 percent in 1908, 20.3 in 1911, 39.6 in 1913, and with the full benefits of his mechanization, 48 percent in 1914. By 1915 the

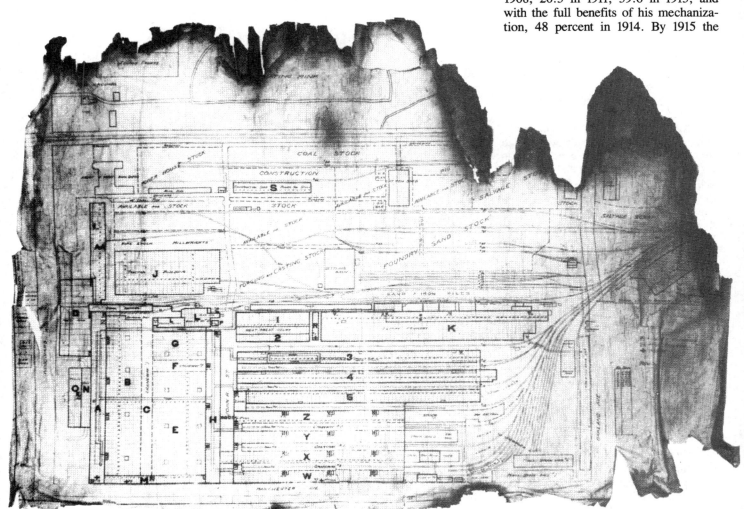

From the Collections of the Henry Ford Museum and Greenfield Village

The only surviving plan of the production line that changed the world and made Ford a billionaire is this badly charred 1918 blueprint of the Highland Park plant.

company was making $100 million in annual sales; by 1920 the average monthly earning after taxes was $6 million. The world had never seen anything remotely like it. The cars simply poured off the line. An early illuminated sign in Cadillac Square said, "Watch the Fords Go By." Ford's dreams, in a startlingly brief time, had all come true. He had lived his own prophecy.

There was a moment, however, in 1909 when Ford almost sold the entire company. William C. Durant, the entrepreneur who put General Motors together from several fledgling companies, felt him out about selling the company. An earlier offer of $3 million had fallen through because Ford wanted cash. This time, his company more successful, Ford demanded $8 million. But again he wanted what he called "gold on the table."

Durant couldn't get the financing.

Ford's timing in holding on to his company, it turned out, had been exquisite. There was no point in designing an Everyman's Car unless the average man could buy fuel cheaply as well. The coming of Ford was almost perfectly synchronized with the discovery in the American Southwest of vast new reserves of oil.

If, as has been said, the American century and the oil century were one and the same thing, then that century began on January 10, 1901, in a field just outside of Beaumont, Texas. The name of the field was Spindletop, so called because of the spindly pines that grew there. For years local children had tossed lighted matches into the field; as the flames hit the strong petroleum vapors seeping up through the soil, there would be a satisfying bang. But anyone who believed that there was real oil beneath the ground was thought an eccentric. Oil was not found in Texas; it was found in places like Pennsylvania, West Virginia, and Ohio. Those states were all Standard Oil territory, and the Rockefeller people had no interest in the Southwest. "I will drink any drop of oil west of the Mississippi," boasted John D. Archbold of Standard.

It was Patillo Higgins, a Beaumont man, who had insisted that there was oil underneath Spindletop, and he had been trying to tap it for several years. It had cost him $30,000 of his own money, and he owed friends an additional $17,000. As each attempt had failed and he had been forced to go to others for financial help in order to continue drilling, his

The Model T and its creator, 1921.

As he became one of the most popular men in America, the forces he had set in motion began to summon the darkness in his character.

From the Collections of the Henry Ford Museum and Greenfield Village

own share of the operation shrank. Higgins's faith had never flagged, but he had become more and more a figure of ridicule in his hometown. "Millionaire," his neighbors nicknamed him. The drilling had gotten harder and harder; just before New Year's Day they had gone through 140 feet of solid rock. That had taken them to a level of 1,020 feet. On January 10 it happened. A geyser of oil roared out of the ground and shot a hundred feet above the derrick. No one had ever seen anything like it before; with it, the word *gusher* came into use.

At first no one could figure out how much oil the field was producing. Some said 30,000 barrels a day, some said

40,000. Capt. Anthony Lucas, who had become a partner of Higgins, said 6,000, because he had never heard of a larger hole in America. In fact, that one gusher was producing 100,000 barrels a day, roughly 60 percent of the total American production. One new well at Spindletop produced as much as the total from all the 37,000 wells back East in the Rockefeller territory. Within a short time there were five more hits. Eventually analysts found that the oil from the first six holes, some 136 million barrels annually, more than twice surpassed what Russia, then the world's leading petroleum producer, could generate.

Spindletop changed the nature of the American economy and, indeed, the American future. Before the strike, oil was used for illumination, not for energy. (Until 1911 the sales of kerosene were greater than the sales of gasoline.) Spindletop inaugurated the liquid-fuel age in America. The energy of the new age was to be oil, and America suddenly was rich in it.

Texas was providing the gas; Henry Ford was providing the cars. The only limits on him were those imposed by production, and he continued to be obsessed by it. He wanted to put as much of his money as he could back into the factory. He hated bankers and financial people anyway, and he did not want to waste the company's money on stockholders. They were, to his mind, parasites, men who lived off other men's labor. In 1917 the Dodge brothers, who had manufactured many of the early components for Ford and who had been rewarded with sizable amounts of stock, sued him for withholding stock dividends. Some $75 million was at stake. During the trial, Ford testified that putting money back into the plant was the real fun he got from being in business. Fun, the opposing attorney retorted, "at Ford Motor Company expense." Retorted Ford, "There wouldn't be any fun if we didn't try things people said we can't do."

That was the trial in which he referred to the profits he was making as "awful," and when questioned about that by attorneys for the other side, he replied, with absolute sincerity, "We don't seem to be able to keep the profits down." Ford lost the suit, and the court ordered him to pay $19 million in dividends, $11 million of which went to him. The decision probably persuaded him to take as complete control of the company's stock as he

The major production problems had been solved, but labor problems lay ahead when this
picture of workers in the Highland Park plant was taken in the 1920s.

From the Collections of the Henry Ford Museum and Greenfield Village

could, so that as little money would be
wasted as possible. Money to stockholders was a waste, money gone idle;
money for the factory was not.

Out of that suit came both the means
and the determination to build the River
Rouge plant, his great industrial masterpiece, a totally independent industrial
city-state. Nothing in the period that followed was too good for the Rouge: it had
the best blast furnaces, the best machine
tools, the best metal labs, the best electrical systems, the most efficient efficiency
experts. Dissatisfied with the supply and
quality of the steel he was getting, Ford
decided to find out how much it would
cost to build a steel plant within the
Rouge. About $35 million, Sorensen told
him. ''What are you waiting for?'' asked
Ford. Equally dissatisfied with both the
availability and the quality of glass, he

built a glass factory at the Rouge as well.
The price of glass had been roughly
thirty cents a square foot early in the life
of the T; soon it had soared to $1.50 a
foot. With the glass plant at the Rouge,
the price came down to twenty cents a
foot.

At the Rouge, barges carrying iron ore
would steam into the inland docks, and
even as they were tying up, huge cranes
would be swinging out to start the un-
loading. Some sixty years later Toyota
would be credited for its just-in-time
theory of manufacturing, in which parts
arrived from suppliers just in time to be
part of the final assembly. But in any real
sense that process had begun at the
Rouge. As Eiji Toyoda, of the Toyota
family said in toasting Philip Caldwell,
the head of Ford, who in 1982 was
visiting Japan: ''There is no secret to

how we learned to do what we do, Mr.
Caldwell. We learned it at the Rouge.''

All of this, the creation of the Rouge
as the ultimate modern plant, speeded up
production even more. Before the opening of the Rouge as an auto plant in 1920
(it had produced submarine chasers for
World War I in 1918), it had taken 21
days from the receipt of raw material to
the production of the finished car. The
Rouge cut that time to 14 days. With the
opening of the Rouge steel plant in 1925,
it took only 4 days.

The Rouge was Henry Ford's greatest
triumph, and with its completion he
stood alone as the dominant figure in
America and the entire developed world.
He had brought the process of manufacture to its ultimate moment; he had given
the world the first people's car and by
dint of his inventive genius had become

America's first billionaire. He was an immensely popular man as well, the man who had lived the American dream. But even then, forces he had helped set in motion would begin to summon forth the darkness in his character.

Part Two
THE DESTROYER

Henry Ford's strengths eventually became his weaknesses. One notorious example was staying with his basic car far too long, ignoring technological change in the cars themselves while obsessively pursuing technological change in their manufacture. From the very start he fought off every attempt to perfect the Model T. In 1912, while he was off on a trip to Europe, his top engineers made some changes intended to improve the car. Their version of the T was lower and some twelve inches longer. It was a better, smoother-riding vehicle, and his associates hoped to surprise and please him. When he returned, they showed it to him. He walked around it several times, finally approaching the left-hand door and ripping it off. Then he ripped off the other door. Then he smashed the windshield and bashed in the roof of the car with his shoe. During all this he said nothing. There was no doubt whose car the T was and no doubt who was the only man permitted to change it. For years anyone wanting to improve a Ford car ran into a stone wall.

What had been another Ford strength, his use of manpower, also turned sour. The early workers at Ford had been skilled artisans, tinkering with designs as they worked. A job at Ford's, as it was known, had been desirable because Henry Ford was at the cutting edge of technology, always trying to do things better, and men who cared about quality wanted to be a part of his operation. In the early days he had his pick of the best men in Detroit. But the mechanized line changed the workplace. These new jobs demanded much less skill and offered much less satisfaction. The pressure to maximize production was relentless. Men who had prided themselves on their skills and had loved working with machines found themselves slaves to those machines, their skills unsummoned. The machines, they discovered to their rage, were more important than they were. The more the plant was mechanized, the more the work force began to unravel.

At the peak of his power, about 1914.

From the Collections of the Henry Ford Museum and Greenfield Village

Every year on his birthday, Ford said, he put on one old shoe to remind himself that he had once been poor and might be poor again.

Men began walking out of the Ford plant.

The turnover in the labor force in 1913, the year of the great mechanization, was 380 percent. It soon became even worse. In order to keep one hundred men working, Ford had to hire nearly a thousand. Ford and his principal business partner, James Couzens, realized they had to stabilize the work force. So they came up with the idea of the five-dollar day—that is, of doubling the existing pay. There were some who thought it was Couzens's idea, though Ford later took credit for it. Perceived by many observers as an act of generosity, it was

also an act of desperation. Ford calculated that a five-dollar day would attract the best workers, diminish labor unrest, and thus bring him even greater profits. Besides, he believed, it was a mistake to spend money on the finest machinery and then put those precious machines into the hands of disgruntled, unreliable, perhaps incompetent men.

Ford's instincts were right. Not only did the decision solidify the work force; it was so successful a public relations gesture that it allowed Ford to cut back sharply on his advertising. He liked to refer to it as one of the finest cost-cutting moves he had ever made and insisted that he had no philanthropic intent. This denial of altruism, a young Detroit theologian named Reinhold Niebuhr said later, was "like the assurance of an old spinster that her reputation as a flirt has been grossly exaggerated." Indeed in 1914, 1915, and 1916, the first three years of the five-dollar wage, the Ford Motor Company's profits after taxes were $30 million, $20 million, and $60 million.

To workingmen, the five-dollar day was electrifying. Ford had also instituted an eight-hour workday and with it a third shift, and the day after his announcement of the new wage, 10,000 men turned up at the gates of the plant looking for work. Ford had wanted the pick of workers; the pick he now had. For days the crowds grew, and policemen were needed to keep them under control. It was probably the first time that the fruits of the oil-fueled industrial age had reached down to the average worker. A worker had a grim and thankless job that rarely let him get ahead. He would end his life as he began it, and his children were doomed to the same existence. Now, however, with cheap oil and mass production, the industrial cycle was different. It was more dynamic; it generated much more profit and many more goods, which required customers with money to buy them. The worker became the consumer in an ever-widening circle of affluence.

Ford became perhaps the greatest celebrity of his time. Reporters hung out at his office, and his every word was quoted. That both helped and hurt him, because although he was a certifiable genius in manufacturing and perhaps a semi-genius for a long time in business, much of what he said was nonsense, albeit highly quotable nonsense. On cigarettes: "Study the history of almost any criminal, and you will find an inveterate cigarette smoker." On Jews: "When there is something wrong in this country, you'll find Jews.'' The Jews, he thought, were particularly unproductive people, and he once vowed to pay a thousand dollars to anyone who would bring him a Jewish farmer, dead or alive. He hated the diet of Americans of his generation—''Most people dig their graves with their teeth,'' he once said. He was prophetic about the nutritional uses of the soybean and intuitive about the value of whole wheat bread, and he wanted his friends to eat no bread but whole wheat. He felt that people who wore glasses were making a serious mistake; they should throw away their glasses and exercise their eyes. For almost all his adult life, he used unadulterated kerosene as a hair cream. He did this because he had observed, he said, that men who worked in the oil fields always had good heads of hair. ''They get their hands filled with the oil, and they are always rubbing their hands through their hair,'' he said, ''and that is the reason they have good hair.'' One of the jobs of E. G. Liebold, his private secretary, was to keep a gallon of No. 10 light kerosene on hand for Ford's hair and constantly to watch that it did not turn rancid.

On one occasion someone noticed that his shoes did not match; he replied that every year on his birthday he put on one old shoe to remind himself that he had once been poor and might be poor again.

He was in some ways a shy man. In the old Ford factory his office had a window through which he used to crawl in order to escape visitors. Nonetheless he was acutely aware that his name was the company name and that his personal publicity generally helped the company. All news from the Ford Motor Company was about him. He was also a hard man, and he became harder as he became older. He distrusted friendship and thought it made him vulnerable: friends might want something from him. He used a company group called the Sociological Department—allegedly started to help workers with personal problems in finances or health—to check up on employees and find out whether they drank at home or had union sympathies. If they were guilty of either, they were fired. For all his populism, he always took a dim view of the average employee. Men worked for two reasons, he said. ''One is for wages, and one is for fear of losing their jobs.'' He thought of labor in the simplest terms—discipline. He once told a journalist named William Richards, ''I

From the Collections of the Henry Ford Museum and Greenfield Village

Edsel and Henry Ford stand with the ten millionth Model T—and the original quadricycle, Ford's first car—shortly after the T made a transcontinental trip in 1924.

have a thousand men who, if I say, 'Be at the northeast corner of the building at 4:00 A.M.,' will be there at 4:00 A.M. That's what we want—obedience.''

Even in the days before he became isolated and eccentric, he liked playing cruel tricks on his top people. He loved pitting them against one another. A favorite ploy was to give the identical title to two men without telling either about the other. He enjoyed watching the ensuing struggle. The weaker man, he said, would always back down. He liked the idea of keeping even his highest aides anxious about their jobs. It was good for them, he said. His idea of harmony, his colleague Charles Sorensen wrote, ''was constant turmoil.'' The same sort of thing was going on in the factories. The foremen, the men who ruled the factory floor, were once chosen for their ability; now, increasingly, they were chosen for physical strength. If a worker seemed to be loitering, a foreman simply knocked him down. The rules against workers talking to each other on the job were strict. Making a worker insecure was of the essence. ''A great business is really too big to be human,'' Ford himself once told the historian Allan Nevins.

Slowly, steadily, in the twenties, Henry Ford began to lose touch. He had played a critical role in breeding new attitudes in both workers and customers. But as they changed, he did not, and he became more and more a caricature of himself. ''The isolation of Henry Ford's mind is about as near perfect as it is

possible to make it,'' said Samuel Marquis, a Detroit minister who had headed the Sociological Department when its purpose had been to help the employees and who later became its harshest critic.

The Ford Motor Company was no longer a creative operation focused on an exciting new idea and headed by an ingenious leader. For its engineers and designers, the company, only a decade earlier the most exciting place to work in America, was professionally a backwater. Sycophants rose, and men of integrity were harassed. Rival companies were pushing ahead with technological developments, and Ford was standing pat with the Tin Lizzie. His own best people became restless under his narrow, frequently arbitrary, even ignorant, policies. He cut off anyone who disagreed with him. Anyone who might be a threat within the company because of superior leadership ability was scorned as often and as publicly as possible.

EVENTUALLY HE DROVE OUT BIG BILL Knudsen, the Danish immigrant who was largely responsible for gearing up the Ford plants during World War I and was widely considered the ablest man in the company. Knudsen was a formidable production man who had been in charge of organizing and outfitting the Model T assembly plants; he had set up fourteen of them in two years. But his prodigious work during World War I made him a target of perverse attacks by Henry Ford. Knudsen was a big, burly man, six foot three and 230 pounds, and he drank, smoked, and cursed, all of which annoyed the puritanical Ford. Worse, Knudsen was clearly becoming something of an independent figure within the company. He was also drawing closer to Ford's son, Edsel, believing him a young man of talent, vision, and, most remarkable of all, sanity. Together they talked of trying to improve the Model T. All of this merely infuriated the senior Ford and convinced him that Knudsen was an intriguer and becoming too big for his place. Ford took his revenge by making a great show of constantly countermanding Knudsen's production decisions. Knudsen became frustrated with these public humiliations and with the company's failure to move ahead technologically. He finally told his wife that he did not think he could work there any longer. He was sure he was going to have a major confrontation with Henry Ford.

"I can't avoid it if I stay," he said, "and I can't stay and keep my self-respect. I just can't stand the jealousy of the place any more."

"Then get out," she said.

"But I'm making $50,000 a year. That's more money than we can make anywhere else."

"We'll get along," she said. "We did before you went to work there."

In 1921 he quit, virtually forced out. "I let him go not because he wasn't good, but because he was too good—for me," Ford later said.

Knudsen went to General Motors for a starting salary of $30,000, but GM soon put him in charge of its sluggish Chevrolet division. It was the perfect time to join GM. Alfred P. Sloan, Jr., was putting together a modern automotive giant, building on Ford's advances in simplifying the means of production and bringing to that manufacturing success the best of modern business practices. Within three years of Knudsen's arrival, GM became a serious challenger to Ford.

By the early twenties the rumblings from Ford's dealers were mounting. They begged him to make changes in the Model T, but he had become so egocentric that criticism of his car struck him as criticism of himself. Ford defiantly stayed with the Model T. Perhaps 1922 can be considered the high-water mark of Ford's domination of the market. The company's sales were never higher, and with an average profit of $50 a car, it netted more than $100 million. From then on it was downhill. As Chevy made

In 1927, last year of the Model T.

After he built his fifteen millionth Model T, Ford's domination over a market that he himself had created came to an end.

its challenge, the traditional Ford response—simply cutting back on the price—no longer worked. The success of that maneuver had been based on volume sales, and the volume was peaking. From 1920 to 1924 Ford cut its price eight times, but the thinner margins were beginning to undermine Ford's success. The signs got worse and worse. For the calendar year ending February 1924, the Ford company's net profit was $82 million; of that only $41 million came from new cars, and $29 million came from the sales of spare parts. If anything reflected the stagnation of the company, it was that figure.

In 1926 Ford's sales dropped from

1.87 million to 1.67. At the same time, Chevy nearly doubled its sales, from 280,000 to 400,000. America's roads were getting better, and people wanted speed and comfort. In the face of GM's continuing challenge, Henry Ford's only response was once again to cut prices—twice in that year. The Model T was beginning to die. Finally, in May of 1927, on the eve of the manufacture of the fifteenth million Model T, Henry Ford announced that his company would build a new car. The T was dead. His domination over a market that he himself had created was over. With that he closed his factories for retooling, laying off his workers (many of them permanently).

The new car was the Model A. It had shock absorbers, a standard gearshift, a gas gauge, and a speedometer, all things that Chevy had been moving ahead on and that Ford himself had resisted installing. In all ways it seemed better than its predecessor, more comfortable, twice as powerful, and faster. When it was finally ready to be revealed, huge crowds thronged every showplace. In Detroit one hundred thousand people turned up at the dealerships to see the unveiling. In order to accommodate the mob in New York City, the manager moved the car to Madison Square Garden. Editorials ranked the arrival of the Model A along with Lindbergh's solo transatlantic flight as the top news story of the decade. The car was an immense success. Even before it was available, there were 727,000 orders on hand. Yet its success was relatively short-lived, for once again Henry Ford froze his technology. Even the brief triumph of the Model A did not halt the downward spiral of the company. Henry Ford remained locked into the past. The twenties and thirties and early forties at Ford were years of ignorance and ruffianism. Henry Ford grew more erratic and finally senile. At the end of his life he believed that World War II did not exist, that it was simply a ploy made up by the newspapers to help the munitions industry. No one could reach the old man any more. His became a performance of spectacular self-destructiveness, one that would never again be matched in a giant American corporation. It was as if the old man, having made the company, felt he had a right to destroy it.

With Knudsen's departure, the burden of trying to deal with Ford fell on his son, Edsel. Gentle and intelligent, Edsel Ford reflected the contradictions in his

From the Collections of the Henry Ford Museum and Greenfield Village

From the Collections of the Henry Ford Museum and Greenfield Village

The trim little Model A appeared in 1927: "Excitement could hardly have been greater,"
said the New York *World* of the crowd shown here, "had Pah-Wah, the sacred white elephant of
Burma, elected to sit for seven days on the flagpole of the Woolworth Building."

father's life. He had been born while the Fords were still poor. (As a little boy, Edsel had written Santa Claus a letter complaining: "I haven't had a Christmas tree in four years and I have broken all my trimmings and I want some more.") By the time he entered manhood, his father was the richest man in the country, unsettled by the material part of his success and ambivalent about the more privileged life to which his son was being introduced. Henry Ford wanted to bestow on his son all possible advantages and to spare him all hardship, but, having done that, he became convinced that Edsel was too soft to deal with the harsh, brutal world of industry, symbolized by nothing better than the Ford Motor Company.

Edsel was not a mechanical tinkerer himself, but he had spent his life in the auto business, and he knew who in the company was good and who was not; he was comfortable with the engineers and the designers. Edsel knew times were changing and that the Ford Motor Company was dying. During his father's worst years, Edsel became a magnet for the most talented men in the company, who came to regard his defeats as their defeats. He was a capable executive, and an exceptionally well-trained one: his apprenticeship was full and thorough—and it lasted thirty years. Absolutely confident in his own judgment about both people and cars, Edsel Ford was beloved by his friends and yet respected in the automobile business for his obvious good judgment. "Henry," John Dodge, Henry Ford's early partner and later his rival, once said, "I don't envy you a damn thing except that boy of yours."

Edsel was the first scion of the automotive world. He married Eleanor Clay, a member of the Hudson family that ran Detroit's most famous department store. They were society, and the marriage was a great event, the two worlds of Detroit merging, the old and the new, a Ford and a Clay. Henry Ford hated the fact that Edsel had married into the Detroit elite and had moved to Grosse Pointe. He knew that Edsel went to parties and on occasion took a drink with his friends, not all of whom were manufacturing people and some of whom were upper class—worse, upper-class citified people—and was sure all this had corrupted him. It was as if Edsel, by marrying Eleanor, had confuted one of Henry Ford's favorite sayings: "A Ford will take you anywhere except into society."

ON TOP OF ALL HIS OTHER BURDENS, IT was Edsel's unfortunate duty to represent the future to a father now absolutely locked in a dying past. Genuinely loyal to his father, Edsel patiently and lovingly tried to talk Henry Ford into modernizing the company, but the old man re-

From the Collections of the Henry Ford Museum and Greenfield Village

Reluctant author of the Model A, 1928.

By the 1930s the business community had begun to turn against Ford: Fortune *called him "the world's worst salesman."*

garded his son's loyalty as weakness and spurned him and his advice.

When everyone else in the company agreed that a particular issue had to be brought before the old man, Edsel became the designated spokesman. With Knudsen now gone, he usually stood alone. He was probably the only person who told the truth to his father. Others, such as Sorensen, were supposed to come to Edsel's defense during meetings with Henry, but they never did. Sorensen, brutal with everyone else in the company but the complete toady with the founder, always turned tail in the face of Henry Ford's opposition.

All the while the competition was getting better faster. Chevy had hydraulic brakes in 1924; Ford added them fourteen years later. Because Chevy had already gone to a six-cylinder car, Edsel pleaded even more passionately with his father to modernize the Ford engine. A six, his father retorted, could never be a balanced car. "I've no use for an engine," he said, "that has more spark plugs than a cow has teats." After all, he had built one back in 1909, and he had not liked it.

The six-cylinder engine, more than any other issue, stood between the two Fords. The quintessential story about Henry Ford and the six-cylinder engine—for it reflects not just his hatred of the new but his contempt for his son as well—concerns a project that Edsel and Laurence Sheldrick, the company's chief engineer, had been working on. It was a new engine, a six, and Edsel believed he had gotten paternal permission to start experimenting with it. He and Sheldrick labored for about six months and they were delighted with the prototype. One day when they were just about ready to test it, Sheldrick got a call from Henry Ford.

"Sheldrick," he said, "I've got a new scrap conveyor that I'm very proud of. It goes right to the cupola at the top of the plant. I'd like you to come and take a look at it. I'm really proud of it."

Sheldrick joined Ford for the demonstration at the top of the cupola, where they could watch the conveyor work. To Sheldrick's surprise, Edsel was there too. Soon the conveyor started. The first thing riding up in it, on its way to becoming junk, was Edsel Ford's and Larry Sheldrick's engine.

"Now," said the old man, "don't you try anything like that again. Don't you ever, do you hear?"

In 1936, his company under mounting pressure, Henry Ford reluctantly built a six-cylinder engine. It went into production a year later. But moves like this were too late. By 1933, *Fortune,* reflecting the growing scorn and indeed the contempt of the business community that Henry Ford had once dazzled, called him "the world's worst salesman."

He became more and more distant from the reality of his own company. As he became more senile and more threatened by growing pressure from a restive labor force, he began to cut back on the power of Charlie Sorensen and grant it instead to Harry Bennett, who was head of the company's security forces. Sorensen had been a savage man, hated by many, capable of great cruelty, eager to settle most disputes with his fists, but at least he knew something about production. Bennett was worse. An ex-seaman who had boxed professionally under the name of Sailor Reese, he had come to power in the post-World War I days, when his assignment was to hire bullies and ex-cons and wrestlers and boxers to help control the plant and keep the union out. Bennett was well suited for that role. His was an empire within an empire, and that inner empire was built on fear. He padded his pockets with Ford money—the finances of the company were in chaos. He built at least four houses with his appropriated wealth. His rise exactly paralleled the decline of the old man, and he played on all the fears the old man had, especially fear of labor and fear of kidnapping. Ford was convinced that Bennett, with his connections in the underworld, could stop any attempt to kidnap his son or grandchildren. Ford loved the fact that Bennett used force to intimidate people. "Harry gets things done in a hurry," he liked to say.

To the distress of Ford's family, Bennett's power over Henry grew almost without check in the 1930s, when the founder was in his seventies. Board meetings were a travesty. Often Ford did not show up. Or he would walk in at the last minute with Bennett and after a few minutes say, "Come on, Harry, let's get the hell out of here. We'll probably change everything they do anyway." Once a magazine writer was in a car with Ford and Bennett, and he asked Ford who was the greatest man he had ever known—after all, in so rich and varied a career he had known quite a few exceptional people. Ford simply pointed at Bennett.

At the very end he used Bennett as his principal weapon against his son. The last years were truly ugly. Sure that he was protected by Ford, Bennett harassed Edsel mercilessly. The old man took obvious pleasure in Edsel's humiliations. Already emotionally beaten down by his father, Edsel had become a sick man. He had remained loyal to his father and endured his humiliations while healthy. Now, battling stomach cancer, he had less and less to fight back with. Edsel's last years were very difficult, as he struggled to expedite the war-production work his father hated while at the same time resisting his illnesses. In 1942 Edsel got undulant fever from drinking milk from his father's dairy; Ford disapproved of pasteurization. The old man blamed it on Edsel's bad habits. In 1943 Edsel died. He was only forty-nine. Almost everyone who knew both Henry and Edsel Ford thought the son had really died of a broken heart.

This was the final, malevolent chapter in Henry Ford's own life. Not only had he destroyed his son, he had all but ruined a once-great industrial empire. By the middle of the war, the Ford Motor Company was in such poor shape that high government officials pondered whether to take it over, for the government had to keep the giant going. Without the stimulus of the war and the work it eventually brought the company, it is possible that Ford might have failed completely. As the government debated, two women stepped forward. Clara Bryant Ford and Eleanor Clay Ford, one Henry Ford's wife and the other Edsel's widow, had watched it all with dismay—the old man's senility, the crushing of Edsel, the rise of Bennett—but with a certain helplessness. "Who is this man Bennett who has such power over my husband and my son?" Clara Ford once asked. She had hated the fact that Bennett and Sorensen had both taken it upon themselves to speak for Henry against Edsel and had participated in and encouraged his destruction. Now both women feared that the same forces might prevent young Henry, Edsel's son, from ascending and assuming power.

Henry Ford II had been serving in the Navy during the war, enjoying a taste of personal freedom. But in August 1943, thanks to intervention by his mother and grandmother, he got orders sending him back to Detroit; the nation's highest officials feared that, after Edsel's death, Harry Bennett might actually take over the company. Young Henry returned reluctantly, but he was the firstborn of Edsel Ford, and familial obligation demanded it. He had no illusions about the challenge ahead. He was well aware that, except for a very few men, the Ford Motor Company was a corrupt and corrupting place.

BENNETT AND SORENSEN IMMEDIATELY began belittling him, Bennett by undoing what Henry was attempting to do each day and Sorensen by demeaning him in front of other people and by always calling him "young man." "He might just as well have called me Sonny," Henry later told friends. Henry Ford II might

have titular power—he was named vice president in December 1943—and the power of blood, but unless his grandfather moved aside and Bennett left the company, he would never be able to take control. Even Sorensen was in the process of being destroyed by Bennett, and young Henry seemed very vulnerable. Again Eleanor Clay Ford put her foot down and forced an issue. Widowhood had stirred in her the kind of indignation her husband had always lacked. He had been too loyal to challenge his father, but now Edsel's company stock was hers to vote. She threatened to sell it unless old Henry moved aside in favor of his grandson. Her son would not be destroyed as her husband had been. Clara Bryant Ford backed her completely. They fought off the old man's excuses and his delaying ploys. With that threat, and a sense that these women were intensely serious, Henry Ford finally, furiously, gave up, and Henry Ford II took control.

The young man—he was just twenty-eight—had not served the long apprenticeship his father had, and he had only the scantest knowledge of the vast and complicated world he inherited. But it soon became clear that he was shrewd and tough. Through the most unsparing work he mastered the business; and he got rid of Harry Bennett. "You're taking over a billion-dollar organization here that you haven't contributed a thing to!" Bennett yelled. But, having no other recourse, he left.

In the end Henry Ford II broke all of Bennett's cronies and put an end to the bad old era. But there was no way to escape the complex legacy of the founder.

Once a popular figure with the average man, Henry Ford had become known as one of the nation's leading labor baiters. He had helped usher in a new age of economic dignity for the common man, but he could not deal with the consequences. His public statements during the Depression were perhaps the most pitiless ever uttered by any capitalist. He repeatedly said that the Depression was good for the country and the only problem was that it might not last long enough, in which case people might not learn enough from it. "If there is unemployment in America," he said, "it is because the unemployed do not want to work." His workers, embittered by his labor policies, marched against him and were put down by Bennett's truncheons and guns. His security people were so vicious that when Ford's workers marched

against the company, the workers wore masks over their faces to hide their identities—something rare in America. Nothing could have spoken more eloquently of tyrannical employment practices.

IN BUSINESS HENRY FORD WAS OVERTAKEN by General Motors, which relentlessly modernized its design, its production, and its marketing. GM fed the appetites Ford had helped create. In addition, GM inaugurated a dynamic that haunted the Ford company for the next fifty years; buyers started out driving Fords when they were young and had little money, but slowly, as their earnings rose, they graduated to more expensive GM cars. As a workingman's hero, Ford was replaced by FDR. What had once been charming about his eccentricity now became contemptible.

Nothing reflected his failures more tellingly than the fate of the River Rouge manufacturing complex. It was an industrial masterpiece, and it should have stood long after his death as a beacon to the genius of its founder. But the treatment of human beings there had been so mean and violent, the reputation of the Rouge so scurrilous, that in the postwar era it stood as an embarrassment to the new men running Ford, a reputation that had to be undone.

The bequeathment had other unfortunate aspects. By fighting the unions so unalterably for so long, Ford and the other Detroit industrialists had ensured that, when the unions finally won power, they would be as strong as the companies themselves, and that there would be a carry-over of distrust and hatred. There were other, more concrete, burdens as well. Because he had been locked in the past and had frozen his technology, the company was on the verge of bankruptcy.

Probably no major industrial company in America's history was ever run so poorly for so long. By the beginning of 1946, it was estimated, Ford was losing $10 million a month. The chaos was remarkable, but some of it, at least, was deliberate. The old Henry Ford hated the government and in particular the federal income tax, and by creating utter clerical confusion he hoped to baffle the IRS. He also hated bookkeepers and accountants; as far as he was concerned, they were parasitical. When Arjay Miller, who later became president of the company, joined Ford in 1946, he was told to get the profit forecast for the next month.

Miller went down to the Rotunda, where the financial operations were centralized, or at least supposed to be. There he found a long table with a lot of older men, who looked to him like stereotypes of the old-fashioned bookkeeper. These men were confronted by bills, thousands of bills, and they were dividing them into categories—A, B, C, D. The piles were immense, some several feet high. To Miller's amazement the bookkeepers were actually estimating how many million dollars there were per foot of paper. That was the system.

Miller asked what the estimates for the following month's profits were. One of the men working there looked at him and asked, "What do you want them to be?"

"What?" asked Miller.

"I can make them anything you want."

He meant it, Miller decided. It was truly a never-never land.

It was not surprising, then, that the young Henry Ford, seeking to bring sense to the madness he found all around him, turned to an entirely new breed of executive—the professional managers, the bright, young financial experts who knew, if not automobiles and manufacturing plants, then systems and bottom lines. To them Henry Ford II gave nearly unlimited power. And they, in turn, would in the years to come visit their own kind of devastation on the company. The legacy of what the old man had done in his last thirty years left a strain of tragic unreason in the inner workings of the company. So, once again did the past influence the future. For the past was always present.

TO FIND OUT MORE There has been a great deal written about Henry Ford— in fact two large new biographies have come out this year—but one older book that David Halberstam found particularly readable was Keith Sward's "irreverent" *The Legend of Henry Ford,* originally published in 1948 and reissued as a paperback by Atheneum in 1968. There is also, he said, a "very good small book" by Anne Jardim, *The First Henry Ford,* published by the MIT Press in 1970. Allan Nevins's trilogy, *Ford,* much praised by scholars, is no longer in print but is still available in libraries. For a vivid sense of the man's life, readers can visit Henry Ford's Greenfield Village in Dearborn, Michigan, which is open year-round. Writing about this "stupendous" museum in the December 1980 issue of American Heritage, Walter Karp said that the collection reflects Ford's mind so intimately that it becomes almost a three-dimensional autobiography.

'A Snarling Roughhouse'
The Democratic Convention of 1924

Edward Ranson describes how an extraordinary 17-day political dogfight in New York, seventy years ago this month, revealed the fault-lines in American society in the Roaring Twenties.

Edward Ranson

Edward Ranson is Lecturer in American History at the University of Aberdeen.

The 1920s in America have attracted a large number of epithets—the Jazz Age, the Era of Wonderful Nonsense, the Age of the Flapper, the Dry Decade, the Lawless Decade, the Golden Age of Sport, the Great Spree, the Automobile Age and most frequently the Roaring Twenties. This was the age of cross-word puzzles, modern dances with strange animal names, radio, the movies and then the talkies, even flag-pole sitting. It was also the decade of new sporting and entertainment stars like 'Red' Grange, 'Big Bill' Tilden, 'Babe' Ruth, Bobby Jones, Jack Dempsey, Rudolph Valentino, Rudy Vallee, Mary Pickford, Theda Bara and Clara Bow. These images and names demonstrate the variety and vitality of a decade noted for its materialism, speculation and self-indulgence.

The First World War was a traumatic experience for the United States, resulting in enormous political, social, economic and psychological stresses and strains that continued to manifest themselves in the twenties. In many ways this is surprising because the nation only entered the war in April 1917, actually benefited economically, suffered few casualties compared to other belligerents and lost more lives in the Great 'Flu' Epidemic of 1918–19. Yet the country quickly became disillusioned with the war, the peace and the post-war scene. Perhaps this was because the nation entered the conflict with crusading zeal but found contact with Europe, the complexities of diplomacy, the threat of Bolshevism, the sordid squabbles over reparations and war debts

disenchanting. Many intellectuals in the US were distressed by post-war America and abhorred the philistinism, xenophobia, organised bigotry and cynicism which led to the 'Red Scare', a series of bitter strikes, a wave of race riots and to calls for immigration restriction.

Immigration was controversial because of the demographic trends confirmed by the 1920 census. The population of the United States rose from 76 million in 1900 to 106 million in 1920, but more alarming to many people, especially old-stock rural Protestants, was the dramatic shift in the urban-rural balance. America had always been predominantly rural, and as late as 1900 country dwellers enjoyed a comfortable three to two advantage over urban residents, with all that implied in terms of political power and cultural norms. However, in 1920 it was revealed that for the first time urban areas outnumbered rural areas by about 2.5 million people. This was a shocking and worrying fact for those who looked upon towns and cities as centres of vice, crime, disease, poverty and corruption, and who feared for America as they knew it. The recent immigrants were perceived to be southern and eastern Europeans, often Catholics and with little experience of democratic processes, who flocked into the expanding cities where they lived in ethnic ghettos.

It is against this background of social, economic and cultural change and tension that the political history of the 1920s must be viewed. Most obviously there was the continuing partisan struggle between the Republicans and the Democrats that dated back to before the Civil War. However, the conflict within the Democratic Party in these years, as the urban and rural factions battled for su-

premacy, was at least as important and a good deal more spectacular, culminating in the head-on confrontation between the two wings of the party in New York in 1924, a meeting one contemporary called 'a snarling, cursing, tedious, tenuous, suicidal, homicidal roughhouse.

It has been well said that for the Republicans politics is a business, which they usually conduct with considerable efficiency, but for the Democrats politics is an emotional experience. In part this is because the Democratic Party is an unlikely coalition of factions that periodically struggle for control, especially in presidential election years and at national conventions. The southern and western wing was predominantly rural, native-born, Protestant and 'dry', supporting prohibition, at least for other people. On the other hand the northern and eastern wing was increasingly urban, and drew strength from recent immigrant groups who were often Catholic and 'wet'. They were drawn together for historical reasons and by shared opposition to the Republicans and the interest groups that supported the Grand Old Party. Otherwise the Democratic factions had so little in common that it was a recurring quadrennial problem to frame a political platform and to nominate a presidential candidate acceptable to the whole party. It has even been contended that the strong infusion of Celtic blood into the party meant they actually derived pleasure from internal fights.

The Democrats' difficulties were compounded by their 'Two-Thirds Rule', dating from the 1830s, which required the presidential nominee to obtain the votes of two out of three delegates at the national convention, unlike the Republican procedure that required only a simple majority. While the 'two-thirds' rule might ensure that the eventual nominee had wide support within the party. it was also a recipe for obstruction. making it possible for a determined minority to block rivals even if they could not nominate their own champion. It had, for example, taken forty-six ballots in 1912 and forty-four in 1920 to select a candidate, and there were distant memories of 1860 when the convention had to adjourn after fifty-seven fruitless ballots without a party standard-bearer, and the rival factions each subsequently nominated its own man.

Given the perennial Democratic problems it might seem that since the Republicans, led by Warren G. Harding, had won the 1920 presidential and congressional elections by handsome margins, Democratic defeat in 1924 was pre-ordained and inevitable. However, by 1922 the Republicans had alienated important sections of the electorate and suffered substantial reverses in the midterm elections. Moreover, by 1923 several embarrassing scandals had surfaced that besmirched the Republicans' reputation, notably the Teapot Dome affair (the scandal that rocked the Harding administration over the illegal lease of naval oil reserves to a private company at Teapot Dome, Wyoming, in 1922) and the activities of Harding's cronies known as the 'Ohio Gang'. Even though the affable but vulnerable Harding died in August 1923, and was replaced by the puritanical, parsimonious and taciturn Calvin Coolidge, 1924 held promise for the Democrats provided they avoided any damaging public split.

In early June 1924 the Republicans met in Cleveland, Ohio. In one of the dullest conventions on record—the humourist Will Rogers suggested the town open up the churches to give a little life to the affair—they overwhelmingly nominated Coolidge, whose transparent honesty and laconic style had endeared him to the public and helped to improve the electoral chances of the Republicans. One of the few noteworthy features was the radio coverage of the proceedings, and the commentator Graham McNamee recalled the convention as 'a rather cut-and-dried affair', which gave the radio stations the false impression that 'convention broadcasting was a cinch'. They would soon be disabused.

Just as Republican prospects brightened, Democratic hopes dimmed. The early Democratic front-runner was Wil-liam Gibbs McAdoo. Born in Georgia in 1863 and trained as a lawyer he moved to New York in 1892 where he became a successful entrepreneur and the driving force behind the construction of the Hudson tunnels. McAdoo supported Woodrow Wilson for governor of New Jersey in 1910 and for the presidential nomination in 1912, and was rewarded with the post of Secretary of the Treasury. His association with Wilson was reinforced in 1914 by his marriage to the president's youngest daughter, Eleanor. McAdoo's own chances of nomination in 1920 were damaged by Wilson's ambiguous attitude and obvious desire for a third term in the White House despite his poor health.

In 1922 McAdoo shifted his residence from New York, where his political prospects had never been good on account of his southern origins and opposition to the New York City Democratic machine, the notorious Tammany Hall, to politically more congenial southern California. He campaigned in the West that year and deserved some credit for Democratic successes. Immediately thereafter he began to build support for a bid for the 1924 presidential nomination, and became an open candidate in December 1923. McAdoo's campaign faltered, however, in February 1924, when his name was linked to that of Edward L. Doheny of the Pan American Petroleum Company during the Teapot Dome investigation because he had accepted legitimate, but unwise, retaining fees from Doheny's company. The revelations, which came as McAdoo was leaving California to travel to Washington where his father-in-law lay critically ill, seemed to herald the end of his political ambitions, and when Wilson died it was commented that McAdoo would arrive in the East in time to attend his own political funeral as well as Wilson's. The *Nation* even ran an article entitled 'Is it McAdieu?'

McAdoo refused to give up, made an appearance before the investigating committee to clear his name, held a conference of supporters in Chicago, and announced he would continue his campaign. But the momentum was lost, and the tarnishing of McAdoo's image in the oil scandal undermined the Democrats' credibility as the party to cleanse the government of corruption.

McAdoo's misfortunes encouraged rivals, notably Senator Oscar W. Underwood of Alabama and Governor Alfred E. Smith of New York. Underwood had a distinguished career in Congress, and had been a candidate for the Democratic nomination in 1912. His strategy was to win primary elections in southern states and to be the second choice of northern delegations. His appeal in the North was based on his generally sympathetic attitude to business and his opposition to both prohibition and the Ku Klux Klan, attitudes which, however, were counter-productive in the South. His verbal assault upon the Klan in October 1923, as an organisation that struck at the foundations of American democracy, was in marked contrast to McAdoo's careful avoidance of the subject. For his temerity the Klan branded Underwood as the 'Jew, jug and Jesuit' candidate. McAdoo's problems might have been expected to help Underwood, but although he won the Alabama primary in March 1924 Underwood lost in every other southern state and had to devise a new plan. Since he had no significant number of delegates his scheme was to hope and work for a stalemate in New York.

Governor Alfred Emanuel Smith of New York, known to all as Al Smith, launched his campaign with the aim of blocking the nomination of McAdoo, who as a southern, rural, Protestant, 'dry' candidate and recipient of Klan support was anathema to northern, urban, Democrats. Unexpectedly, Smith began to show surprising strength, although this was confined to the North-East and parts of the Middle West. Ten years younger than McAdoo, Smith had worked his way up the political ladder within the New York Democratic organisation, but though a loyal member of the Tammany machine he had never been subservient nor corrupt. Smith's intelligence, ability, charm and reform record won him the governorship in 1918, 1922, 1924 and 1926. He was a good speaker and even made figures seem interesting. One of his staff remarked he could make statistics 'sit up, beg, roll over and bark'. The many constructive features of Smith's political career counted less in 1924 than the facts that he was a New Yorker of recent immigrant background, a Catholic and an opponent of prohibition. He was the antithesis of McAdoo, and the symbol of everything the southern and western wing of the party hated and feared.

McAdoo's indiscretion, and the failure of Underwood or Smith to emerge as clear leaders, encouraged other states to support favourite sons. Most of these were not serious candidacies, but marks of courtesy to local leaders and bargaining positions that would allow wheeling and dealing later. Only Senator Samuel Ralston of Indiana and John W. Davis of West Virginia would figure prominently during the convention. Thus McAdoo went to New York with only 270 pledged delegates, Smith with 126, Underwood with 24, and some 200 were committed to favourite sons for the first few ballots at least. The remainder of the 1,098 votes were uncommitted, though since some states allowed votes to be split, 1,436 delegates plus alternates took part in the proceedings. No candidate was remotely near to the 732 votes needed under the two-thirds rule, and the uncertain political outlook was reflected in the betting odds regarding the nomination offered on the eve of the convention. Smith was quoted at 2 to 1, McAdoo at 3 to 1, and Ralston, Underwood and Davis at 4 to 1, but whoever the Democratic candidate might be President Coolidge remained a hot favourite to win in November.

The choice of New York City for the 1924 convention was due to a number of factors. The city had not hosted a major party convention since 1868, local politicians wanted the honour, New Yorkers hoped to prove their city did not deserve its reputation for sin and corruption, local businessmen were willing to finance the city's bid and the decision was made in 1923 before McAdoo's campaign stuttered and Al Smith became a serious candidate. The selection of New York added fresh tension since most southern and western delegates saw it as enemy territory and no better than Sodom or Gomorrah. McAdoo would have preferred San Francisco, but that city had been the scene of the Democratic convention in 1920.

The Democratic National Convention opened on Tuesday June 24th, in the old Madison Square Garden designed by Stanford White and owned and operated by the sports promoter 'Tex' Rickard. Although due to be demolished soon after the convention the Garden was refurbished for the occasion and special facilities installed for the press corps and radio commentators. Whereas the Republican gathering in Cleveland had been marked by austerity and lack of decoration, the Garden was festooned with 3,500 flags, and another 10,000 miniature flags were released from the ceiling at the opening ceremony. Anyone who wondered what was about to happen might well have recalled that the Garden had recently staged a six-day bicycle

race, and the immediately preceding attraction had been the Barnum and Bailey circus.

New York City was determined to make a good impression. Hotels promised not to raise their prices and prepared for an estimated 20,000 visitors. Many restaurants added regional dishes to their menus. Stores, cinemas, theatres, museums and churches welcomed the delegates in their own ways, and numerous receptions and excursions were organised, including visits to West Point, Coney Island and the Stock Exchange. Particular care was taken to provide entertainment and facilities for the 500 female delegates and alternates and for the wives of male delegates. There were naval ships on display on the North River and a pre-convention municipal parade with fifty bands. The police department made every effort to reduce petty crime and assigned hundreds of officers to the convention itself. Twenty-five expectant mothers at the New York Nursery and Child Hospital formed a Mothers' Democratic Club and agreed to name the first boy born after the convention opened in honour of the nominee, whoever he might be.

Unfortunately, these efforts to win over hostile southerners and westerners were unsuccessful. The delegates' preconceptions about New York as a locus of vice, crime, bootlegging, financial chicanery and religious liberalism were quickly confirmed, and New Yorkers beliefs that the rural delegates were hicks and rubes were similarly reinforced.

On June 24th, the convention observed the opening formalities—being called to order, prayers, the national anthem, the keynote address. When one visitor commented on the lack of excitement a reporter replied, 'Just wait, those are Democrats down there'.

On the second day Senator Thomas J. Walsh of Montana was chosen as permanent chairman and made an address attacking the Republicans and all their deeds. Walsh was acceptable to all factions because he was a leader of the oil investigation, and although a westerner and a dry he was also a Catholic and anti-Klan. His handling of the convention with impartiality made him one of the few to emerge from the experience with an enhanced reputation. As the platform committee was not ready to report, the convention moved on to the nomination process which lasted from Wednesday afternoon until late on Friday, June 27th.

By then forty-three speakers had nominated or seconded sixteen candidates. Will Rogers complained he was fifteen minutes late for one session and missed five nominations, and the *New York Times* commented on the list 'It cannot honestly be called an embarrassment of riches'.

The highlights of the nominating process included the speech proposing Underwood, which included a direct condemnation of the Klan that threw the hall into confusion as half the delegates demonstrated against the Klan while the remainder stayed pointedly in their seats. The carefully prepared hour-long demonstration by delegates wearing 'Mc'll Do' hat-bands and chanting 'Mac! Mac! McAdoo!' prompted a counter-demonstration from Smith supporters in the galleries shouting 'Ku, Ku, McAdoo'. Franklin D. Roosevelt's speech nominating Al Smith, whom he referred to as the Happy Warrior of the political battlefield', triggered a seventy-three minute demonstration as Smith's supporters carried out their vow to make a longer and noisier display than McAdoo's delegates. It was clear already that the activities of Smith adherents were antagonising not only McAdoo's forces, but also the uncommitted delegates whose votes they needed.

The platform committee met for four days, June 24th–27th, in an attempt to resolve differences over prohibition, membership of the League of Nations and the particularly difficult Klan issue. The question was whether to include a general condemnation of intolerance and religious bigotry, as the McAdoo men wanted, or specifically to name the Klan, as the Smith men insisted. The committee finally decided not to name the Klan, but the anti-Klan group resolved to challenge this on the floor.

The platform was read to the convention on Saturday afternoon, with 1,200 police present in case of disturbances, and pro-League and anti-Klan amendments were offered which were debated that evening. Former Secretary of War, Newton D. Baker, made an impassioned plea for the United States to join the League, but though moved by Baker's oratory the delegates voted two to one for the official platform that recommended a referendum on the subject. The main event of the evening, however, was the debate on whether to condemn the Klan implicitly or explicitly—an apparently minor difference of enormous symbolic significance. A succession of speakers for and against naming the Klan stirred the emotions of delegates and spectators alike, concluding with an appeal by William Jennings Bryan for party unity and support for the official version. He was greeted with jeers by anti-Klan adherents.

The vote on the Klan began at 11.35pm on Saturday night amidst near pandemonium and took two hours to complete during which time 1,000 extra police were drafted in to keep order while rival delegates exchanged blows and insults. Whichever way the vote went the debate was a catastrophe for the Democrats as it revealed to millions who listened on radio, or read their papers later, the depth and bitterness of the schism. In order to reward loyal party workers with a trip to the national convention some states appointed more delegates than they had votes, and gave each a fraction of a vote to cast. When delegations were divided fractions came into play. When the tally was complete the resolution naming the Klan was rejected 542 $^{3}/_{20}$ to 541 $^{3}/_{20}$ demonstrating how evenly the convention was divided. The result indicated that neither McAdoo nor Smith could win, but that each could, and probably would, thwart the other. Defeating the Republicans was now a secondary consideration.

Sunday, June 29th, was a day of rest, and the convention did not begin balloting for the presidential nomination until Monday when McAdoo led Smith 431 $^{1}/_{2}$ to 241 on the first vote. There was a remarkable correlation between the Klan vote and the support of the leading contenders. This ballot and those that followed, was led off by Governor Brandon announcing, 'Al-a-bam-ah-h-h casts twenty-fo-ah votes for Os-cah Dou-ble-yuh Un-n-n-der-wood!' After the first few ballots the delegates and visitors in the galleries joined in the intonation of what became the best-known phrase in the country and a vaudeville joke. Allegedly, whenever street-car conductors in New York called out 'Alabama' on reaching a street with that name, the passengers replied in unison, 'Casts twenty-four votes for Underwood'.

Thus began the balloting marathon for which the convention is notorious, and eventually fifty-nine names received votes at one time or another. By the end of that week, which included Indepen-

dence Day, seventy-seven votes had been held with no winner in sight. After a second Sunday break balloting resumed on Monday, July 7th, but a result was not achieved until Wednesday, July 9th. McAdoo's strength peaked at 528 $^{1}/_{2}$ on the 70th ballot, and Smith at 368 on the 76th and 83rd, which was enough to give him a veto against McAdoo. Smith received only a single vote from the South throughout, and only a handful from west of the Mississippi. The McAdoo forces accused Smith supporters of deliberately prolonging the convention in the hope that southern and western delegates would be forced to leave due to lack of funds. Numerous plans to end the impasse were proposed but rejected by entrenched and embittered delegates, including complicated schemes gradually to eliminate minor candidates and a proposal to adjourn the whole affair and reconvene later in Kansas City. Occasionally there were shifts to favourite sons like Ralston of Indiana, who did not want the honour due to age and health, but these were usually short lived.

Not until after the 99th ballot, late on July 8th, did McAdoo finally accept that he had no hope of nomination, and even then he only released his delegates rather than withdrawing completely. It was understood that if McAdoo stood aside so would Smith, and this initiated a scramble to see who would benefit from the new situation. One more ballot, the 100th, was taken on July 8th, before the meeting adjourned, and two more on July 9th, with John W. Davis of West Virginia forging ahead of Senators Underwood and Walsh. On the 103rd ballot Davis' total surged past the necessary two-thirds to end the ordeal, though by then the nomination was a poisoned chalice.

Davis was an outstanding lawyer, a former Solicitor-General of the United States, Ambassador to Great Britain and President of the American Bar Association. A man of the highest ability and integrity he was relatively unknown to the general public and had some embarrassing Wall Street connections. He drew votes from both the McAdoo and Smith camps, but his nomination was more a triumph for the urban and industrial North and East than for the rural and agricultural South and West.

Having torn itself apart over religious and related issues, the party tried to persuade Senator Walsh, a dry Catholic,

to accept the vice-presidential nomination, but he declined. In a move many found incredulous the convention then chose Governor Charles W. Bryan of Nebraska, whose comment on being advised of his likely nomination was, 'Quit your kidding'. His elder brother, William Jennings Bryan, added, 'The age of miracles has not passed'. Nevertheless, the choice did add political and geographic balance to the ticket. The convention finally adjourned at 2.30am on Thursday, July 10th, seventeen days after it opened.

Many factors contributed to the imbroglio—prohibition, religion, the Klan, sectional animosities, the urban-rural divide, the choice of New York, accidents of personalities. Together they reproduced inside the cauldron of Madison Square Garden all the conflicts, tensions, passions, fears and prejudices that divided America.

The Democrats wounds were too deep to heal quickly, and, in fact, the struggle for control of the party would go on. The short term consequence was that Davis and Bryan were heavily defeated in November 1924. Indeed, in a dozen western states the Democrats suffered the humiliation of running third behind not only the Republicans but also a third party, the Progressives, led by Senator La Follette of Wisconsin. No party had exposed its internal divisions so publicly before, except possible the Democrats in 1860, and probably no party will ever do so again. The party abandoned the 'two-thirds' rule in 1936, which ought to make another political blood-letting improbable, but it may be dangerous to under-estimate the Democrats.

FOR FURTHER READING:

David Burner, *The Politics Of Provincialism. The Democratic Party In Transition 1918–1932* (New York, 1970); Robert K. Murray, *The 103rd Ballot. Democrats And The Disaster In Madison Square Garden* (New York, 1976); William Allen White, *Politics: The Citizen's Business* (New York, 1924); Lee N. Allen, 'The Underwood Presidential Movement of 1924', *Alabama Review* (vol 15, April 1962); Lee N. Allen, 'The McAdoo Campaign for the Presidential Nomination in 1924', *Journal of Southern History* (vol 29, May 1963); James C. Prude, 'William Gibbs McAdoo and the Democratic National Convention of 1924', *Journal of Southern History* (vol 38, November 1972); David E. Stratton, 'Splattered With Oil: William G. McAdoo and the 1924 Democratic Presidential Nomination', *Southwestern Social Science Quarterly*, 1963.

Defending the Home: Ossian Sweet and the Struggle Against Segregation in 1920s Detroit

Victoria W. Wolcott

Victoria W. Wolcott is writing a dissertation on labor, race, and gender in Detroit during the interwar period. A doctoral student at the University of Michigan, she has presented her work at several professional conferences.

"When I opened the door I saw the mob and I realized I was facing the same mob that had hounded my people throughout our entire history. I was filled with a fear that only one could experience who knows the history and strivings of my race" (1). To understand these words and to know the history of the Sweet case, in which Ossian Sweet and ten other African Americans were acquitted of murder for defending Sweet's home against a white mob, is to know the history of segregation in America. Although much American history has been written as if segregation was not effectively challenged before the 1954 Supreme Court decision of *Brown v. Board of Education,* a more careful examination of African-American racial struggle in the twentieth century reveals a legacy of resistance to segregation in the courts and in the streets. The Sweet case gripped the nation's attention in 1925 and 1926 as race riots became commonplace, the Ku Klux Klan's influence grew, and rapid urbanization and industrialization created an array of new urban problems. Indeed, a close examination of the events surrounding the Sweet case reveals a neglected side of the seemingly upbeat Jazz age—a side of violence, racial intolerance, and segregation. However, it also demonstrates the ongoing growth of African-American self-determination and struggle in a rapidly changing urban America.

> *The Sweet case reveals a neglected side of the seemingly upbeat Jazz age—a side of violence, racial intolerance, and segregation.*

In June of 1925, Sweet purchased a house in the northeast section of Detroit, a largely white immigrant neighborhood. Because the previous owners had been an interracial couple, Sweet harbored few fears of a violent reaction from his neighbors. The residents believed, however, that their light-skinned African American neighbor, Edward Smith, had been white. When they heard the house was sold to an African American family the residents organized the "Waterworks Improvement Association," named for the nearby Waterworks park. Like other neighborhood associations organized in Detroit during this period, this group was formed exclusively for the purpose of maintaining a "whites only" neighborhood. Cognizant of the growing resis-

tance in the area, and hopeful that the tumult over a number of racial incidents in the city that summer would die down, the Sweets decided to delay their move until September.

On 8 September 1925, Sweet and his family moved into their newly purchased house after requesting police protection from the local precinct. Along with Gladys Sweet, his wife, Ossian was joined by his brothers Otis Sweet, a dentist, Henry Sweet, a college student, three friends, a large supply of food, nine guns, and ammunition. Although crowds formed near the house sporadically that first day, the night passed relatively peacefully. The crowd, however, became increasingly belligerent the next day so the Sweets invited four more friends to help protect their property. That evening, as Otis Sweet and a friend arrived from work in a taxi, a white crowd caught sight of them and began to hurl rocks and racial epithets. After Otis and his friend had narrowly escaped injury by racing into their home, the mob began to hurl stones at the house itself, shattering an upstairs window. The Sweets and their friends took position inside and shots rang out both from the house and from the guns of police stationed nearby. A member of the mob, Leo Breiner, was shot in the back and killed, and another man, Erik Halberg, was injured by a bullet to the leg. Police immediately entered the house and arrested all eleven residents for murder.

The Detroit that Ossian Sweet knew in 1925 was a dynamic urban center. The

Archives of Labor and Urban Affairs, Wayne State University

Housing conditions similar to those in this eastside neighborhood of Detroit in the 1930s were not uncommon due to overcrowding which often resulted from segregation.

city had been transformed by the Great Migration and the growth of the industrial sector. The defense industries of World War I and the rapid development of the automobile industry dramatically increased the demand for unskilled labor. The Emergency Immigration Act of 1921, however, had closed off the primary source of unskilled labor in the North—European immigrant workers.

Thus, two major waves of African-American migration hit Detroit, the first in 1916–17 when the war-induced labor shortage was at its most acute, and the second during 1924–25 when the decrease in foreign immigration led Detroit's automakers to open up more jobs to African Americans. As a result, between 1910 and 1930 there was a *twentyfold* increase on Detroit's African-American population, outpacing the growth of any other industrial city.

The city's African-American migrants were usually forced to the eastside where absentee landlords took advantage of the overcrowded conditions by demanding high rents. In 1923, the State Supreme Court of Michigan upheld the constitutionality of restrictive covenants (agreements restricting the use or occupancy of a residence by a person of a particular race) in *Parmallee v. Morris,* a legal precedent that stood until 1948. Thus, neighborhood improvement associations and realtors had the legal right to draft contracts that excluded persons on the basis of race. As a result, African Americans who tried to move into white neighborhoods often faced not only mob violence but legal barriers.

When relatively affluent migrants, like Sweet who was a physician, sought housing outside of the eastside neighborhood, small-scale riots often ensued. In 1925, a series of these disturbances led up to the Sweet riot. In June 1925, Dr. Alex L. Turner bought a house in an all-white northwest Detroit neighborhood. When the Turner family attempted to move into their new home, a mob of five thousand jeering and stone-throwing whites greeted them. They escaped only under police protection. The leader of the Tireman Avenue Improvement Association, who had orchestrated the forced removal of the Turners, helped form the Waterworks Improvement Association, whose members formed the bulk of the September 9 mob. A few weeks after the Turner affair, an African-American undertaker, Vollington A. Bristol, built a home in a white neighborhood and withstood several nights of violent demonstrations before being forced from his house. When it appeared that Bristol might hold out against the mob, a white woman was reported to have stood on a box and shouted, "If you call yourselves men and are afraid to move these niggers out, we women will move them out, you cowards!" (2). In addition to these and other attempts to challenge segregation, in the two years before the Sweet case, fifty-five African Americans were killed by Detroit police with impunity.

On top of unrelenting police brutality and mob violence, there was a series of election campaigns during 1924 and 1925 in which the Ku Klux Klan openly ran a mayoral candidate, Charles S. Bowles. In 1924, Bowles nearly won the mayoral election as a write-in candidate. His opponent, John W. Smith, who was supported by the African American and immigrant communities, was declared the winner only when fifteen thousand ballots were disqualified by the city. On the Saturday prior to this election, the largest meeting of Klansmen and Klanswomen in Detroit's history congregated in a field in nearby Dearborn (3). Thus, the mid-1920s in Detroit was a time of tremendous racism, nativism and violence.

However, there was another side to the racial struggles of the 1920s. African Americans in Detroit and other urban centers were forming strong community institutions that provided an organizational base from which to fight battles such as the Sweet case. Detroit in this period was also a major center for Marcus Garvey's United Negro Improvement Association (UNIA) which preached African-American self-help and self-defense. The National Association for the Advancement of Colored People (NAACP), an extremely important national organization, lent its resources to fight racism at the local level. Its agreement to back the Sweet case with financial and legal support was key to a three-pronged national attack on segregation. In 1917, the NAACP had successfully argued, in *Buchanan v. Warley,* that the state could not pass legislation limiting individuals' right to own or use property because of their race. In 1925, just as the Sweet case began, the NAACP argued *Corrigan v. Buckley* in the U.S. Supreme Court in an attempt to overturn a residential covenant in Washington, D.C. Having addressed housing segregation sanctioned by the state and by private agreement, they hoped to win a third battle against segregation through mob violence by defending the eleven accused in Detroit. Thus, thirty years before *Brown v. Board of Education,* the NAACP was directly challenging both legal and extra-legal attempts to draw a color line in American towns and cities.

In addition to the NAACP leadership, African Americans in many communities outside of Detroit rallied to support the Sweet defendants. Fundraisers were held

Archives of Labor and Urban Affairs, Wayne State University

Henry Sweet, at left, stands with his legal counsel team. The jury in the case found Sweet not guilty and the charges for the remaining ten defendants were later dropped.

in major cities to raise the money necessary to try the case which had captured national attention. After a mass fundraising meeting in New York City, Walter White, assistant secretary of the NAACP, telegrammed Rev. Robert L. Bradby, president of the local chapter, and explained, "It is felt here in New York that in making the fight you are making for Dr. Sweet you are fighting the battle of every one of the eleven million Negroes in the U.S." (4).

The NAACP felt that in order to win the case, the best legal representation should be sought, and although African-American lawyers from Detroit would be allowed to assist in the defense, they recommended a white lawyer be found in order to appeal to an all-white jury. Therefore, James Weldon Johnson, secretary of the NAACP, in early October contacted celebrated lawyer Clarence Darrow who agreed to take the case for a nominal fee of five thousand dollars. Darrow's acceptance of the Sweet case made front-page news in African-American newspapers across the country. By 4 November a jury had been picked in the initial trial of all eleven defendants, and opening arguments were ready to be heard.

Judge Frank Murphy, who later became Mayor of Detroit, Governor of Michigan and a Supreme Court Justice, presided over the trial. Hundreds packed the courtroom each day, and after Darrow complained that African Americans were not being allowed seating, Murphy set aside half of the spectators' section for them. The prosecutor, Robert M. Toms, relied on a conspiracy theory to present his case because he could not prove who had shot the bullet that had killed Breiner, or even if the shot had come from the house. Much of the prosecution's presentation consisted of seventy-five witnesses who testified that they saw no crowds near the Sweet's house on the night of September 9. Apparently the irony of having seventy-five witnesses testify to the absence of a crowd was lost on the prosecution. Darrow's skillful cross-examinations of these witnesses delighted court spectators and reporters. At one point he caught a young boy in a direct lie as his assistant Arthur Garfield Hays remembered: " 'There was a great crowd—no, I won't say a great crowd, a large crowd—well, there were a few people there and the officers were keeping them moving.' Darrow was on his feet. 'Have you talked to any one about the case?' 'Lieutenant Johnson' (the police detective). 'And when you started to answer the question you forgot to say a few people, didn't you?' 'Yes, sir' " (5).

Clarence Darrow transformed the courtroom into a classroom and the jury into students of African-American history.

After discrediting the prosecution's witnesses, Darrow based his defense on sociological evidence describing race relations in America. John C. Dancy, the influential director of the Detroit Urban League, testified about housing conditions in Detroit, and Walter White testified about the history of lynching and racial violence that had pervaded American society since emancipation. However, the most effective witness was Ossian Sweet himself. During his testimony Sweet discussed his childhood in a small town in Florida where the fear of lynching was ever-present. He went on to explain how he witnessed race riots in Washington, D.C., while studying medicine at Howard University and how he had reacted to the series of racial incidents in Detroit that preceded the events that had landed him in jail. Using this strategy, Darrow showed both the defendant's state of mind during the night of the shooting and transformed the courtroom into a classroom and the jury into students of African American history.

"There are persons in the North and South who say a black man is inferior to the white and should be controlled by the whites." Darrow said in his eloquent closing argument which moved many spectators to tears, "There are also those who recognize his rights and say he should enjoy them. To me this case is a cross-section of human history; it involves the future, and the hope of some of us that the future shall be better than the past" (6). The jury deliberated for forty-six hours, arguing so loudly that at times those waiting in the halls could hear them. Finally they announced they were unable to reach a verdict. Expectations had been raised in the African-American community that an acquittal was imminent because of Darrow's skillful defense; therefore, a hung jury was a severe disappointment. However, White concluded that "the case has largely changed public sentiment in Detroit," as evidenced by white newspapers' sympathetic portrayal of the defendants by the close of the trial (7).

The defendants were released on bail after the verdict, but on 20 April 1926, a second trial began. The state had decided to try the defendants separately and began with the prosecution of Henry Sweet, Ossian's younger brother, and the only defendant who admitted firing his gun. This trial proceeded in a similar fashion as the first, with Darrow skillfully uncovering the lies of the prosecution witnesses and providing the sociological background to support his argument of self-defense. Darrow was again passionate in his closing argument:

"Eleven people, knowing what it meant, with the history of the race behind them, with the picture of Detroit in front of them, with the memory of Turner and Bristol . . . with the knowledge of shootings and killings and insult and injury without end, and eleven of them go into a house, gentlemen, and no police protection, in the face of a mob, and in the hatred of a community, and take in guns and ammunition and fight for their rights and for your rights and for mine, and for the rights of every being that lived" (8).

After deliberating four hours on 19 May 1926, the jury found Henry Sweet not guilty, and the charges were eventually dropped for the remaining ten defendants. African Americans across the country had finally gotten the victory they had been seeking.

Race relations in Detroit did improve somewhat after the Sweet trial, but it proved to be a short-lived peace. In 1942, Detroit's Seven-Mile Fenelon Improvement Association attempted to ban African Americans from the desperately needed Sojourner Truth housing project, and one year later, the worst race riot the nation had yet witnessed took place on Detroit's streets. Legal efforts to fight segregation also had a mixed legacy. Although the NAACP's attempt to eradicate residential covenants in 1925 was defeated with the dismissal of the *Corrigan v. Buckley* case by the Supreme Court, in 1948 the Court's ruling in *Shelley v. Kraemer* finally declared implementation of restrictive covenants in private housing unconstitutional. Ironically, Justice Frank Murphy, who twenty-two years earlier had presided over the Sweet case, cast a key vote in this decision.

The Sweet case marked an early victory against housing segregation both by the lawyers and leaders of the Civil Rights movement and by individual African Americans willing to face a white mob with strength and pride. Paradoxically then, the Sweet case foreshadowed both the nonviolent Civil Rights movement and the ideology of self-defense of Malcolm X and the Black Panthers.

BIBLIOGRAPHY

Asher, Cash. Papers. Bentley Historical Library. Ann Arbor, Michigan.

Capeci, Dominic J., Jr. *Race Relations in Wartime Detroit: The Sojourner Truth Housing Controversy of 1942.* Philadelphia: Temple University Press, 1984.

Dancy, John C. *Sand Against the Wind: The Memoirs of John C. Dancy.* Detroit: Wayne State University Press, 1966.

Darrow, Clarence. *The Story of My Life.* New York: Charles Scribner's Sons, 1932.

Fine, Sidney. *Frank Murphy: The Detroit Years.* Ann Arbor: University of Michigan Press, 1975.

Gellein, Hilmer. Papers. Bentley Historical Library. Ann Arbor, Michigan.

Haldeman-Julius, Marcet. *Clarence Darrow's Two Great Trials: Reports of the Scopes Anti-Evolution Case and the Dr. Sweet Negro Trial.* Girard, Kansas: Haldeman-Julius, 1927.

Hays, Arthur Garfield. *Let Freedom Ring.* New York: Horace Liveright, 1928.

Jackson, Kenneth T. *The Ku Klux Klan in the City, 1915–1930.* New York: Oxford University Press, 1967.

Lilienthal, David E. "Has the Negro the Right of Self-Defense?" *Nation* 121 (23 December 1925): 1–3.

Meier, August and John Bracey, eds. *Papers of the N.A.A.C.P.* Microfilm. Frederick, MD: University Publications of America, 1986.

Thomas, Richard W. *Life for Us Is What We Make It: Building Black Community in Detroit, 1915–1945.* Bloomington: Indiana University Press, 1992.

Vose, Clement E. *The Supreme Court, the NAACP, and the Restrictive Covenant Cases.* Berkeley: University of California Press, 1959.

Weinberg, Kenneth G. *A Man's Home, a Man's Castle.* New York: McCall Publishing, 1971.

Widick, B. J. *Detroit: City of Race and Class Violence.* Detroit: Wayne State University Press, 1989.

ENDNOTES

1. Quoted in August Meier and John Bracey, eds. *Papers of the N.A.A.C.P., microfilm* (Frederick, MD: University Publications of America, 1986). Speech by Arthur Garfield Hays at the annual meeting of the N.A.A.C.P., 3 January 1926, pp. 5–6, reel 3.

2. Marcet Haldeman-Julius, *Clarence Darrow's Two Great Trials: Reports of the Scopes Anti-Evolution Case and the Dr. Sweet Negro Trial* (Girard, KS: Haldeman-Julius, 1927), 39.

3. Kenneth T. Jackson, *The Ku Klux Klan in the City, 1915–1930* (New York: Oxford University Press, 1967), 136.

4. *Papers of the N.A.A.C.P.*, telegram from Walter White to Rev. Bradby, 21 September 1925, reel 2.

5. Arthur Garfield Hays, *Let Freedom Ring* (New York: Horace Liveright, 1928), 209.

6. Quoted in Kenneth G. Weinberg, *A Man's Home, A Man's Castle* (New York: McCall Publishing, 1971), 119.

7. Quoted in *Papers of the N.A.A.C.P.*, Press Release, 28 November 1923: "Sweet Jury Disagrees, New Trial in January," reel 3.

8. *Papers of the N.A.A.C.P.*, Transcript of Darrow's closing argument, p. 31, 11 May 1926, reel 3.

From the Great Depression to World War II

The United States enjoyed an unprecedented prosperity during the late 1920s, for which Republicans took full credit. Some groups, such as farmers, did not do as well as others. The middle and upper middle classes, however, received ever larger shares of the wealth. An estimated 9 million individuals, having more disposable income than ever before, began playing the stock market. They were encouraged to do so by various mechanisms that permitted them to purchase stock with what amounted to borrowed money. Stories abounded of speculators who had turned modest amounts of money into fortunes. All this came to an end on "Black Thursday," October 24, 1929, when the stock market crashed. Efforts to shore up prices failed, and the market continued to plummet during the months following.

President Herbert Hoover denied there was any direct connection between the crash and business conditions, which he pronounced as fundamentally sound. Confidence was badly shaken, however, and many firms began retrenching in hopes of riding out the storm. Laying off workers and cutting inventories made the situation worse. The nation headed into the worst depression in its history.

Hoover approved more programs aimed at stimulating recovery than any of his predecessors, yet he was perceived as a do-nothing president who cared little about the common people. He soon became the most reviled man in America: the shacks housing dispossessed people that sprang up on the outskirts of cities became known as "Hoovervilles," and patched trousers became "Hoover" trousers. He was prevented from doing more because of his belief that large scale governmental intervention in the economy would in the long run destroy the system.

The 1932 Democratic candidate for the presidency was Franklin D. Roosevelt. He had served as assistant secretary of the navy under Woodrow Wilson, had been vice presidential candidate in 1920 and, after a battle against polio, had reentered politics. Even though he recently had compiled a credible record as governor of New York, he was not well known nationally. Many regarded him as a lightweight. His campaign against Hoover failed to make clear how he intended to better conditions, but the election was more a referendum *against* the incumbent than *for* anything else. Roosevelt won in a landslide.

"We are at the end of our string," Hoover is supposed to have said, "there is nothing more we can do." Roosevelt could not accept such a notion. "1933: The Rise of the Common Man" describes the grab bag of programs Roosevelt and his advisers put together in an effort to halt and to reverse the slide. Most scholars agree that the New Deal did not cure the Depression, but it bettered the lives of millions of people and launched social programs that still exist, in revised form however.

The Depression had worldwide effects. It helped strengthen the influence of the militarists in Japan, and it contributed to the rise of Adolf Hitler in Germany. Japan committed the first major act of aggression in 1931 when it invaded Manchuria and established a puppet government there. The League of Nations was paralyzed by the unwillingness of the major European countries to do more than censure Japan, and the United States under Hoover merely adopted a policy of refusing to recognize changes brought about by force. This had the effect of insulting the Japanese without deterring them. Failure of the "peace loving" nations to support collective security emboldened Benito Mussolini of Italy as well as Hitler to embark on adventures of their own.

The debilitating effects of the Depression and the growing conviction of many Americans that participation in the Great War had been a mistake precluded any active role by the United States. Beginning in 1935, Congress passed a series of neutrality acts, the sole purpose of which were to keep the United States out of war should one erupt. Roosevelt, uncertain about what, if anything, could be done at first, by the late 1930s had become convinced that the United States had to cooperate with nations threatened by aggression. He had to move slowly because the nation was deeply divided. "The Draft" tells how Roosevelt in 1940 obtained the first peacetime conscription, how it worked, and its effects on Americans.

Historians still debate the course of events that led to Pearl Harbor. Roosevelt's defenders believe that he did what was necessary to help China survive and that Japanese aggressiveness had to be contained. His critics charge that he paid insufficient attention to Japan's legitimate economic and security needs and that he bears large responsibility for what happened. In any event, the attack on Pearl Harbor united the nation behind the war effort.

Anti-Asian sentiment had a long history in the United States, particularly on the West Coast. When war came, a cry arose that all Japanese—citizens or not—were potential traitors. To prevent espionage and sabotage, therefore, they had to be neutralized by isolating them in "reloca-

tion" centers in sparsely inhabited areas. "Racism and Relocation: Telling the Japanese-American Experience" tells the story of one family victimized by this massive violation of civil rights.

The war not only pumped new life into the American economy, it brought about great social change. About 15 million young men and hundreds of thousands of women served in the armed forces. "What Did You Do in the War, Grandma?" uses oral histories to tell the experiences of women during this period. Although most Americans realized that things would never again be the same, they could only wonder what lay in store. "1943: The Pull of Distant Shores" discusses what people were saying and reading during a time when Allied forces were advancing on all fronts but much fighting lay ahead.

Franklin Roosevelt died a few weeks before Germany surrendered and several months before the Pacific War ended. Yet he exerted great influence on the postwar world through agreements he had made at summit confer-

ences with British Prime Minister Winston Churchill and Soviet leader Joseph Stalin. "The Man of the Century" argues that, for all his mistakes, Roosevelt possessed a larger vision than the men with whom he dealt.

Looking Ahead: Challenge Questions

Discuss some of the New Deal programs designed to promote recovery. What were the underlying assumptions about what had to be done?

How did the draft work? Was it a fair system? How did it affect young Americans?

How did those who were responsible for Japanese relocation during World War II defend this violation of civil rights?

The author of "The Man of the Century" argues that President Roosevelt possessed a broader vision than either Winston Churchill or Joseph Stalin. Is the article convincing? Why, or why not?

1933
The Rise of the Common Man

Lewis Lord

It had happened in Russia only 15 years before, and mere days had passed since it occurred in Germany. Now, on March 4, 1933, fears abounded that chaos and totalitarianism soon would strike the United States of America. Herbert Hoover awoke that cold, dreary Saturday, his final morning in the White House, to word that Illinois and New York had joined a long list of states where all the banks had ceased to function. "We are at the end of our string," the president-reject conceded. "There is nothing more we can do."

What, indeed, could anyone do to curb the Great Depression, then in its fourth grim year? Working women could help, several women's magazines suggested, by giving men their jobs. Deport all aliens so more paychecks can go to real Americans, counseled Texas's Rep. Martin Dies. Ship America's 12 million blacks to Africa, proposed Theodore Bilbo, Mississippi's soon-to-be senator. A retired major recommended killing old people "of no use to themselves or anyone else." John Dewey, the educator, favored the death of something less personal. "Capitalism," he said, "must be destroyed."

The hapless Hoover had waited in vain for capitalism to cure itself, with no help from Washington. "Economic wounds," he said, "must be healed by the action of the cells of the economic body—the producers and consumers themselves." But producers quit producing and consumers stopped consuming. Industries operated at less than half their 1929 capacity, and probably a third of the work force was out of work. Despair ruled the land. People slept in sewer pipes in Oakland and hunted food in garbage dumps in Chicago. When a puny child in Appalachia complained of being hungry, her teacher told her to go home and eat. "I can't," the girl replied. "It's my sister's turn to eat."

Hoover's secretary of war, bracing for an Inauguration Day revolt by "reds and possible Communists," massed troops near big cities. East Coast businessmen plotted ways to get out of town in case the jobless cut telephone lines and barricaded highways. The chief of the American Farm Bureau Federation warned of a coming "revolution in the countryside," while Alf Landon, the Republican governor of Kansas, declared "the iron hand of a national dictator" preferable to a paralyzed economy. Franklin D. Roosevelt, the president-elect, sensed what was at stake. A friend told him that if he succeeded, he would go down in history as the greatest president ever and that if he failed, he would be known as the worst. "If I fail," Roosevelt replied, "I shall be the last one."

That Saturday, millions turned on their Philcos and Zeniths to hear Roosevelt's answer to calamity. For months, the 51-year-old New York governor had promised little except a vague "new deal for the American people," especially "the forgotten man at the bottom of the economic pyramid." Now, in his inaugural address, the new president's voice rang out: "This great nation will endure as it has endured, will revive and will prosper. So, first of all, let me assert my firm belief that the only thing we have to fear is fear itself." The crowd stood almost silent in the cold wind. "This nation asks for action, and action now." For the first time since 1929, the capital heard genuine cheers. "We must act, and act quickly." The paraplegic president left the applauding throng like a cocky prizefighter, shaking his hands over his head. Wrote Will Rogers: "If he burned down the Capitol, we would cheer and say, 'Well, we at least got a fire started.' "

Roosevelt did not torch the Capitol, as Adolf Hitler's Nazis had done with Berlin's Reichstag only days earlier. Nor did he seek dictatorial power or set people against people as Hitler was doing. Instead, as 1933 unfolded, this one man who seemed to understand what Americans had in common much better than they themselves had ever known would pull together the nation's degraded down and outs and scared-as-hell upper crust. He would lift up a generation of his countrymen and set back on course a national dream that, though battered and transformed, has endured ever since. "We have had our revolution," *Collier's* magazine would observe that year, "and we like it."

The foundation for saving the middle class was set immediately. FDR chose as his first New Deal patient the banks, most of them reeling from hemorrhages of deposits. Rather than nationalize the system, as Germany did, he closed every bank in the land until examiners ruled them sound. On his eighth day in office, he told a national radio audience why the shutdown was necessary, explaining the crisis so well, Will Rogers said, that even bankers could understand it. Such "fireside chats" would come to represent something new, a bond across the airwaves between the leader and the people, one that in some countries would be a force for evil. In America, for the most part, the tie would reinforce democracy. That week, 3 of every 4 banks reopened. Banks were safe, people concluded, because FDR said so. Cash stashed under mattresses suddenly became bank deposits, and the stock market jumped 15 percent. Raymond Moley, then a top Roosevelt aide, would later become one of his harshest critics, but his assessment

From *U.S. News & World Report*, October 25, 1993, pp. 11-14, 16. © 1993 by U.S. News & World Report. Reprinted by permission.

The Way We Were

Alphabet Soup
The New Deal created 59 new agencies. Growth in federal employees from 1932 to 1936: 46 percent. The agencies included the Federal Theatre Project to produce plays with the help of 3,350 out-of-work actors, and the Federal Writers' Project to compile oral histories and travel guides. Number of commercially published FWP works: 378.

Domestic Demagogues
Populists like Father Charles Coughlin and Louisiana's Huey Long held great sway. In 1933, Coughlin's weekly radio show won a preference poll against the New York Philharmonic broadcast, 187,000 to 12,000. By 1935, Long's Share-Our-Wealth organization, which backed a $2,000-a-year guaranteed income, had 7 million members. Long was assassinated that year.

Opening the Floodgates
The 18th Amendment to the Constitution—enacted in 1920 to outlaw the sale of beverages with more than 0.5 percent alcohol—was repealed in 1933. During the era, a new subculture arose, with women and men drinking together in "speakeasies." In 1930, members of the Women's Organization for National Prohibition Reform: 60,000

Radio Days
The '30s were the "Golden Age of Radio." U.S. homes with radios in 1920: 500,000; in 1930: 14 million. Commercial stations that began in the '30s: 212. Radio advertising revenues in 1930: $40 million; in 1935: $112 million. In October 1938, 6 million heard Orson Welles's broadcast of "War of the Worlds." Many thought the Martian invasion was real, setting off panic in the New York City area.

Big Screens and Small
The Depression arrived almost simultaneously with the "talkies." Weekly U.S. moviegoers, 1930: 115 million; U.S. population: 122 million. U.S. feature films in the '30s: 5,009; in the '80s: 3,774. The most eagerly awaited film of the decade was 1939's *Gone With the Wind.* Meanwhile, by 1938, there were still only 20,000 television sets in service in New York City.

The Long March
In October 1934, Mao Zedong's Red Army began a yearlong, 6,000-mile trek to escape government forces and establish itself throughout China, crossing 24 rivers and 18 mountain ranges, and occupying 62 cities. Troops who began the march: 100,000; who survived: 33,000. After the march, Mao's forces devised communist strategies and, in 1949, took over China.

Re-election Roundup
In the 1936 presidential election, FDR defeated Republican Alf Landon by a landslide, with 61 percent of the popular vote. Still, that same year, Adolf Hitler did somewhat better in a vote of confidence from the German people. Share of votes for Hitler as *führer* in 1936: 99 percent. Other political parties allowed to compete in Germany that year: zero.

Peace in Our Time
On Sept. 30, 1938, British Prime Minister Neville Chamberlain met Hitler in Munich in hopes of averting war and agreed that Germany could annex Czechoslovakia's Sudetenland. Number of days before Hitler broke the Anglo-German nonaggression agreement by invading Poland: 336; number of days after invasion Chamberlain served as prime minister: 219.

---

of what happened that March never changed: "Capitalism was saved in eight days."

It was saved by a distinctively American form of pragmatic planning. All that spring, lights burned late in the White House as Moley and other "Brain Trusters" looked for ways to rescue farmers, revive industries and feed the hungry. "Take a method and try it," Roosevelt urged. "If it fails, try another. But above all, try something." He was asked what he would say when people questioned the ideology behind the Tennessee Valley Authority, a massive public-power scheme some saw as creeping socialism. "I'll tell them it's neither fish nor fowl," he laughed, "but whatever it is, it will taste awfully good to the people of the Tennessee Valley." Some plans fell short, including one aimed at easing hunger in the long run. "People don't eat in the long run," snapped Harry Hopkins, in charge of relief. "They eat every day."

An entirely different way of thinking about American government emerged, with a blizzard of programs known by initials: AAA, CCC, NLRB, HOLC, FERA, FDIC. Everyone seemed to pitch in. For the NRA, or National Recovery Act, the presidents of General Motors and General Electric huddled with labor bosses to create "codes" telling businesses how much to charge customers and pay workers. Sears, Roebuck rescinded a 10 percent pay cut, and dozens of firms raised wages. Pratfalls abounded. "What Is America Up to?" asked a London newspaper after a Jersey City tailor drew 30 days in jail for charging 35 cents to press a suit instead of the 40 cents the NRA's Tailoring Industry Code required. (Two years later, the Supreme Court would kill the NRA, and FDR would try something else.)

The WPA, or Works Progress Administration, put 3½ million of the jobless to work on roads, parks and buildings. Former businessmen who couldn't afford overalls wore business suits to lay sewer pipes. "I hate to think what would have happened if this work hadn't come," a Montana ditch digger said. "I'd sold or hocked everything. And my kids were hungry. I stood in front of the window of the bake shop and wondered just how long it would be before I got desperate enough to pick up a rock and heave it through that window and grab some bread to take home."

During the decade, Roosevelt would become 20th-century America's most loved and most hated public figure. The well-to-do despised him as "that man," the aristocrat who betrayed his class, while Georgia sharecroppers and California pea pickers adorned their shacks with FDR portraits made from news photos glued to cardboard. A reporter quizzed a North Carolina millworker about his enthusiasm for the president: Didn't he realize that FDR's crackpot notions would wreck America? The worker didn't know that, but he did know this: "Roosevelt is the only man we ever

Eyewitness
Down and Out in the Dust Bowl

Cleo Frost, now 77, was 18 years old in 1934 when she and her family left their Sallisaw, Okla., home, bound for California, part of the migration westward by thousands of unrooted people from the dust bowl.

"All you could see was the top of the corn out of the dust. It would drift, so you'd only see the tops of the fence posts. People would cut open old potato sacks, put them over the windows and turn the water on them to try to stop the dust.

"When we decided to come out to California, my dad went to the store that had lent him $35 for that year's crop. 'We're not leaving to beat the bills but to pay them,' he said. And when we came out here, in six weeks we had all of that $35 paid off.

"There were 16 of us, including four young children. My brother bought a Chevrolet truck in Tulsa. We put blankets in the center for the kids to sleep on. Just before Oklahoma City, we stopped in a motel. Before we went to bed, we shook the dust out of the sheets. Mama was scared to death of the dust. So she got some of my dad's handkerchiefs, wet them in water and put them over our faces for us to breathe through. When we got up the next morning, those handkerchiefs looked brown.

"When we stopped in McFarland, Calif., Mr. Lessley was in the store getting groceries when he saw our Oklahoma license plates. He was from Sallisaw, too. And he told us where to go to get work, at the Twin Pines Ranch about a mile out of town.

"I tell you, the Lord did watch over us."

had in the White House who would understand that my boss is a son of a bitch."

The New Deal's reforms would endure, from Social Security and accessible home mortgages to cheap electricity and a supervised stock market. And early on there would come a sure sign that business was picking up: Executives who had begged the government to do something began complaining that it did too much. But the New Deal would not cure America's economic woes—to end the Depression, FDR would swap his "Dr. New Deal" hat for a "Dr. Win the War" cap. Only then, during the massive spending for World War II, would unemployment slip below 15 percent.

The New Deal's start would prove more vital than its finish. Long before political scientists concluded he had created the modern presidency, long before economists decided he had saved capitalism, long before historians ranked him beside Washington and Lincoln as "great," a man who couldn't walk put America on its feet. Nothing summed up 1933's new mood better than a Walt Disney cartoon that hit the movie screens in uplifting color. When the Three Little Pigs sang "Who's Afraid of the Big Bad Wolf?" few missed the symbolism.

The Draft

Draftees formed the heart and sinew of America's fighting forces during World War II. When their "number came up," ten million men answered the call to arms.

Edward Oxford

New York writer Edward Oxford has contributed more than two dozen major articles to American History. *His last contribution—the special D-Day Plus 50 Years issue—appeared in June 1994.*

With the arrival of 1940, Depression-weary Americans dared hope that the new decade would bring better days. But the first months of the year had a bitter taste. As a storm of war swept across Europe and Asia, people on Main Street began to wonder whether even the vast expanses of the Atlantic and Pacific oceans could for long keep the ominous clouds at a safe distance. War and rumors of war filled newspaper headlines and conversations.

There yet lived hundreds of thousands of American men, no longer young, who had done battle in "the war to end all wars." They had been part of the American Expeditionary Forces whose resolute doughboys, back in 1917–18, had trained, fought, and in considerable numbers, died for freedom's cause.

Now the sons of the fathers had come of age. And now again, week after week, American families glimpsed the horror-faces of war in newspaper photographs, magazine layouts, and newsreels. Young American men, seeing those stricken faces, tried not to behold in them their own.

As the threat loomed larger, anxious Americans sought to hold on to some measure of happiness in their lives. *Fantasia, The Philadelphia Story,* and *My Little Chickadee* brightened motion-picture screens. Sports fans cheered Joe DiMaggio, Don Budge, Joe Louis, Sammy Baugh, and Whirlaway. Big-band fans bought the latest recordings by Benny Goodman, Artie Shaw, and Glenn Miller. Couples learned the "Lindy Hop," and a young singer named Frank Sinatra sang "I'll Never Smile Again."

By mid-1940, however, it was no longer possible to pretend that events in Europe and Asia were not America's concern. The time had clearly come for its citizens and their representatives in Washington to ponder the nation's course.

Pulled in one direction by isolationists and in the other by interventionists, Americans were caught in a quandary. Many, especially in small towns and rural areas, had traditionally advocated no U.S. involvement in Europe's affairs. Although news of Axis aggression now brought the wisdom of this stance into question, a considerable isolationist sentiment persisted and was brought to bear on the debates surrounding proposals to aid the struggling British and to strengthen America's defenses.

The "America First" Committee—which attracted such known figures as Eddie Rickenbacker, Alice Roosevelt Longworth, and Lillian Gish—argued forcefully that the United States had more to lose by becoming embroiled in the conflict, especially if Britain were to fall, than it did from coming to a peaceful understanding with a victorious Germany. At the opposite end of the spectrum, playwright Robert Sherwood, whose *There Shall Be No Night* showed audiences how to stand up to totalitarianism, expressed the save-Europe sentiment by running a newspaper advertisement headed "Stop Hitler Now!"

The debate came to focus on the matter of military preparedness. Many Americans held on to the wistful hope that a volunteer army would still be adequate for the troubled times. But Army Chief of Staff George Marshall disagreed, stating forcefully that "paper plans no longer will suffice. The security of our country depends on more trained men. There is no other way to do it."

In Washington, D.C.'s summer heat, the struggle to reach a national consensus began. Senator Edward R. Burke of Nebraska and New York Congressman James W. Wadsworth co-sponsored a bill calling for peacetime military conscription—an action unprecedented in the nation's history. During the third week of June 1940, the bill began its legislative journey through Congress.

A Gallup poll taken at the end of May had indicated that U.S. citizens were divided half-for, half-against conscription. Weeks later, however, France fell before Hitler's onslaught, leaving Britain to stand alone. News accounts told of the Royal Air Force's stirring fight against waves of German bombers. The unforgettable voice of Prime Minister Winston Churchill sounded on radios across America in tribute to the R.A.F. defenders: "Never in the field of human conflict was so much owed by so many to so few."

Listening Americans considered whether they, too, owed something to such brave men; whether, somehow, the Battle of Britain was but prologue to the Battle of America; and whether, will it or not, they soon must take arms against forces that would not otherwise be brought to a halt. By early August, when a new poll was taken, two-thirds of the American people favored some form of draft.

The various individuals and groups who lobbied against conscription "made a weird hash," according to *Time* magazine. Some, like clergyman Harry Emerson Fosdick, could not reconcile war with their religious principles. Labor leader John L. Lewis declared that only a fool would expect that Americans "are gong to send their sons to be butchered in another foreign war." Socialist Norman

Thomas and members of the Communist Party also took an isolationist stance that included opposition to conscription.

The draft bill came before the Senate in late August, and the House debate began early in September. The intemperate words and attention-getting antics of pro- and anti-draft factions frequently sank to distasteful levels that obscured the genuine concerns felt by both sides. A mock petition circulating on the streets of New York lampooned the likes of Nebraska's Senator George Norris, who, while conceding that "dictators would like to conquer the U.S.," would not support peacetime conscription because it was "contrary to the spirit of human freedom." Addressed to Adolf Hitler, Benito Mussolini, and Emperor Hirohito, the petition "most respectfully" requested "that any aggressive intention you might have toward the United States be graciously deferred until the United States has been given ample time to strengthen its Army, Navy, and Air Force by the volunteer system."

Florida's Claude Pepper, speaking in favor of the draft bill on the Senate floor, was hanged in effigy near the Capitol building by a women's group calling itself the Congress of American Mothers. Montana's isolationist Senator Burton Wheeler, clad in a white suit, climaxed his three-hour anti-draft address by admonishing his fellow senators that with the passage of this bill "you slit the throat of the last democracy still living—you accord to Hitler his greatest and cheapest victory to date. On the headstone of American democracy he will inscribe: 'Here lies the foremost victim of the war of nerves.'"

On the steps of the Capitol, "Pauline Revere," a young woman in colonial costume, rode a white horse bearing a sign that read: "Mobilize for Peace and Defeat Conscription." Dressed in widows' garb, six women kept a silent vigil in the Senate and House galleries.

In the House, Congresswomen Clara McMillan of South Carolina and Frances Bolton of Ohio, both of whom had sons of draft age, took the floor to debate the issue. McMillan supported the draft; if men had to go into battle, she maintained, they should be trained. Bolton, however, argued that there was "more danger than defense" in conscription.

Debate on the House floor finally became so intense that a pro-draft Kentucky congressman delivered a hard right-cross to the head of his anti-draft

I WANT YOU for the U.S. ARMY ENLIST NOW

LIBRARY OF CONGRESS.

Ohio counterpart, whom he called "a traitor." The House Doorkeeper rated the fist-fight the liveliest he had witnessed during fifty years of service.

Meanwhile, President Franklin D. Roosevelt, facing a strong challenge from Wendell Willkie as he sought reelection to his third term in office, tried to stay clear of the politically explosive issue.

While the lawmakers went about their deliberations, German bombers stepped up their assault on England. "Every time they bombed London," one pro-draft legislator later observed, "we gained a vote or two in the House or Senate."

In its final form, shaped by thirty-three amendments, the Selective Training and Service Act passed its final hurdle on September 14 by an almost two-to-one margin in both houses of Congress. Two days later President Roosevelt, sitting at his desk in the White House, picked up a pen and signed: "Approved Sept. 16, 1940. Franklin D. Roosevelt. 3:08 P.M. E.S.T."

R oosevelt's pen-strokes marked a dramatic change in the nation's view of itself. The United States would require its citizens to learn the art of self-defense in peacetime. The Selective Service Act expressed America's answer to aggression.

The new conscription law sought men—citizens and resident aliens alike—between the ages of twenty-one and thirty-six. No more than 900,000 could be called up in peacetime. They would be required to serve for only one year, but that would be followed by ten years of reserve duty. Those drafted would not go overseas (except to serve in American possessions), and "sympathetic regard" would be provided for those who claimed dependents. Fines and/or imprisonment awaited anyone failing to comply with the law. Such, at least, was the way the draft started out.

The giant first step—national Registration Day—was set for October 16.* Public officials—from the president to governors to mayors—heralded the day. Radio stations and newspapers announced and re-announced the date. Bars and nightclubs posted "R-Day" reminder-signs. The Selective Service System, from its national headquarters in Washington, urged men in the affected age group: "If in doubt, register. If you are required to register—and fail to do so—you will face the probability of punishment."

The great sign-in began at 7 A.M. on that crisp, cool Wednesday. To 125,000 registration centers across the land—the same locations that served as election polling places—came the young men of America from all walks of life and all ethnic backgrounds.

During the next fourteen hours, Uncle Sam recorded the basic facts concerning some 16,500,000 men—the huge first contingent from which he would call the

new defenders of the nation. More than a million volunteer register-clerks signed the men in at the rate of a million an hour and assigned each a number between 1 and 8,500.

There was, that memorable day, a singular sense of patriotic spirit in the air. Circus midgets and blind men guided by friends appeared for registration. Here and there, a handful of individuals—such as eight Union Theological Seminary students in Manhattan—publicly stated their refusal to register. But, in a remarkable display of like-mindedness, those whose civic duty was to register did so. The massive registration went almost perfectly—a testament to the temper of the times.

O n October 29, Americans witnessed the next step in building the nation's military preparedness: the drawing of draft numbers. The U.S. draft lottery began at noon in the federal government's large Departmental Auditorium, near the Mall in Washington, D.C. Klieg lights shown down on a ten-gallon fishbowl—the same glass container used in the 1917 drawing of World War I draft numbers—that held 9,000 robin's-egg-blue capsules, each containing a registration serial number.*

Looking tired and drawn from campaigning, President Roosevelt made his way to a lectern on the auditorium stage. In his address, broadcast by radio to an anxiously waiting nation, he called the process about to begin a "muster," rather than a draft or a conscription, thus evoking images of America's minutemen at Concord and Lexington. "Ever since the first muster," he stated, "our democratic army has existed for one purpose only: the defense of our freedom. It is for that one purpose and that one purpose only, that you will be asked to answer the call for training."

The auditorium, packed with 1,500 men and women—some of them the parents of draft-registrants—was silent as a blindfolded Secretary of War Henry Stimson reached into the big jar, picked up a capsule, and handed it to the president. With newsreel cameras rolling, Roosevelt opened the capsule and intoned: "The first number is one-five-eight."

LIBRARY OF CONGRESS.

A woman in the auditorium cried out. Mrs. Mildred Bell's twenty-one-year-old son Harry had the registration serial number 158. At that moment he was shopping for furniture in a Washington, D.C. suburb with his bride-to-be and would not learn of his luck for several hours. Harry Bell and other "158s" across the country would be the first in their draft board regions to be considered for induction.*

More than a hundred journalists reported news of the numbers as they continued to be drawn that day. For a while, random volunteers—veterans, onlookers, government clerks—had the chance to draw a capsule from the bowl. Then, after 150 or so capsules had been opened, crews trained by Selective Service headquarters took over. Anyone interested could get an empty blue capsule for a souvenir.

As each number was plucked out of its capsule, an official camera photographed it next to a clock that showed the exact time of its selection. The individual numbers were then attached to large, gummed sheets of cardboard, which would become the master record of the drawing.

By mid-afternoon Selective Service teams were chalking the numbers on a

---

*Five more registrations were held before the process became a continuous one in 1942. From then on American males would register automatically when they turned eighteen.

*Each local draft board was limited to 8,500 registrants. However, just to be safe, the Selective Service System opted for placing 9,000 numbers in the lottery bowl.

*In due time, Bell was inducted into the U.S. Army. He served with distinction in the European Theater, where he was wounded in action. He survived the war and passed away in 1990.

big blackboard at the rate of eight or so a minute. The procedure went on through the night, ending at 5:48 A.M. on October 30. Now 16,500,000 American men knew the order in which they would be considered for the call to colors.

A mood of mingled excitement, pride, and solemnity had taken hold. A *Washington Post* editorial observed that "the men and women and families called upon to sacrifice personal wishes to the national welfare have cause for both the regret and the happiness that comes from unselfish service."

Across America, young men in the "158" number-group learned—to their befuddlement or delight—that Uncle Sam, in his random selecting, was pointing his finger directly at them.

Some holders of "158" were proud, some resentful. Reactions ranged from celebration to consternation. At Victor's Tavern, in Queens, a shout went up as Roosevelt announced that first number, for among the crowd listening was twenty-one-year-old Jim Cody, who held 158. Single, healthy, and jobless, Jim lived with his grandparents. "I'm proud to be called," he later told a reporter. "I'm willing to go. Military training will be good for me."

George Tsatsaronis, a thirty-one-year-old alien who had emigrated from Greece five years earlier, got the news in the coffee shop of which he was part-owner. Through an interpreter, he said: "Good. It's good. I would like to serve America. I could be a cook in the Army. I am a good cook."

Interior decorator Irving Heyman, a married man with two children, was cutting slip covers when he heard his number-group announced over the radio. "I had to drop my shears," he recounted. "I would go in a second if I were single. But they need me—the wife and the kids—at home."

Somehow, in a way few citizens could then comprehend, America had suddenly changed. The people had known a time for peace. Soon enough they would know a time for war.

As the land made its spin beneath the next day's sun, crowds of young American men gathered outside draft boards to peer at the first lists of numbers posted on the wall in sets of hundreds. As the men stared at the columns of figures, each tried to understand, in the larger scheme of things, just where he stood. "If it's gotta be, it's gotta be," Samuel Hookoff told a reporter. A half-smiling

Joe Sloss observed: "At last I'll get away from that hardware store." Theodore Browning related that "I got no job. I got no way to get one. The Army, I don't care for it, I guess. But maybe they'll make a man out of me." Speaking for perhaps tens of thousands of other men, one spotted his number, grimaced, and muttered: "My (blankety-blank-blank) lucky day."

The first of the newly chosen reported early on November 18, 1940 to armories, induction stations, and school buildings. Among those to present themselves for service that wintry morning was John Lawton, of Everett, Massachusetts. A single twenty-one-year-old, Lawton had been out of work for much of the year. Now the government had given him an occupation: he was a soldier. A local newspaper said Lawton had "the distinction of being the very first of the inductees." Though there was no way of accurately saying who was the first man "to go." His picture appeared on the front page as such.

Lawton was one of eleven men lined up shoulder to shoulder in a Boston armory in front of an American flag. "You are the first men in the United States to be inducted under the law," Captain Harold Linderson informed them. "You've got a lot to live up to. We're expecting a lot from you." The men somberly recited the oath of service, then took the required one step forward. The captain told them: "You're in the Army now." Lawton, along with 236 other inductees from New England, would reach Fort Devens that night.

By train, bus, and truck, rookies rolled into training sites from Camp Upton, New York to Fort Ord, California. The newcomers didn't much like the look of their new homes, and the waiting sergeants didn't much like the looks of the new arrivals. Hometown newspapers duly printed names of the newest "boys in uniform."

By the beginning of December 1941, the Selective Service had gathered in the 900,000 men the system had sought. Then came the first Sunday of the month—December 7—and with the Japanese attack on Pearl Harbor, the war's scope became world-wide.

On the morning after the "date which will live in infamy," thousands of young American men, eager to do their patrio-

tic duty, lined up outside recruiting stations. The United States and Great Britain declared war on Japan. By Thursday of that week Germany and Italy had in turn declared war on the United States.

The surprise assault swept away America's last thoughts of isolationism, stirred to action a nation whose will had been held hostage by doubt, and gave grim fulfillment to Roosevelt's prophecy that "this generation has a rendezvous with destiny."

As "Remember Pearl Harbor" became America's battle cry, citizens everywhere volunteered to do whatever they could do to win the war—*their* war, now—against the Axis. Within a week after the Pearl Harbor attack, Congress removed the draft law's restriction against men serving overseas and lowered the minimum age to twenty. Draftees would serve as long as the war lasted—and for six months after it ended. Now a man was in for "duration plus six."

Almost overnight, the Selective Service System took on a powerful, almost intimidating, presence in the minds of millions of American men. General Lewis B. Hershey, its director—previously an abstract figure at a paper-laden desk in Washington—increasingly became the personification of a system whose workings would have a decisive impact upon the nation's fate. A steady, even-handed administrator, Hershey was handed the delicate and enormous task of seeing to it that the armed forces received the full complement of men they needed to wage and to win the war.

A descendant of anti-militarist Mennonites, Hershey nevertheless had specialized in drawing up Army conscription plans since 1926 and brought a unique combination of insights to bear on the problem of drafting men by the tens of thousands. Having learned from history, he saw to it that prospective draftees had no contact with the Army, which had made a muddle of the Union draft in the Civil War. Civilian coordination during World War I had proved a far better model. Throughout World War II, the work of finding and selecting draftees would rest with members of local draft boards across the nation.

As the United States took up arms, Hershey made it clear that the task awaiting those summoned to serve was nothing less than to "save America." And he gave voice to the thoughts crossing the minds of many of his fellow citizens when he stated that everyone "called from a family goes to serve that family and to protect it. All hoped for peace. War has come, actual war, with death and blood its companions." For whatever it might be worth to the men who would be drafted, the General at that desk in Selective Service headquarters in Washington, D.C., sensed and respected their feelings; harbored—much as a father—concern for their well-being; and saluted, soldier to soldier, the service and sacrifice they were being called upon to render.

There were jokes about the draft, at least in the beginning. A comic strip titled "Draftie" appeared; Bob Hope and Dorothy Lamour got laughs in the movie *Caught in the Draft;* and standup comedians rattled off one-liners about reveille, close-order drill, and twenty-mile hikes. But down deep—as they heard about service-life, saw the horror-scenes of battle in each day's newspaper, and pondered the odds of ever coming home safe and sound—draftees-to-be weren't smiling. If the joke was on anyone, it was on them.

Some 6,500 local draft boards from Maine to Oregon carried out the thankless work of actually selecting the men who would go into uniform. These groups of civilians—three to five local citizens on a board who served without pay—were federal officials with letters of appointment from President Roosevelt. Board members were usually white men in their forties or fifties. Some were veterans of World War I; the illustrious Sergeant Alvin York, for example, headed the draft board in Franklin County, Tennessee.

The eight-page questionnaire filled out by draft registrants became the prime document in a draft-board's assessment of each man. Thirteen classifications ranged from "1A" (fit for general military service), and "1B" (fit for limited service), to "4E" (conscientious objector), and "4F" (physically, mentally, or morally unfit for service).

To a telling degree, draft boards determined the makeup of America's World War II Army. Draft board No. 49, in the northwest section of Detroit, for instance, had jurisdiction over about 12,500 registrants, aged eighteen to sixty-five. As of mid-1943, the three-man board, working about twenty hours per week, had placed 2,300 of their registrants into the Army. Draft boards, as General Hershey put it,

had to "do the unpleasant thing." The message from the front line to the rear was: "More bodies."

However great the need for fighting men, the Army chose not put aside its longstanding segregationist policies in order to fill the ranks. Additional black units were planned—the existing six totalled fewer than 4,500 men—but the service needed time to build the segregated facilities that would be required. Since the Army could not accommodate all the black registrants, call-ups were race-specific. Problems arising from this policy, which endangered mobilization, caused Hershey to insist that "the Army must revise its procedure to receive men in such order, without regard to color." The Army accordingly made changes in policy—but slowly and in modest increments.

Soon after being classified 1-A, a potential draftee received his induction notice in the mail. The order read: "Greeting: Having submitted yourself to a local board comprised of your neighbors for the purpose of determining your availability for training and service in the armed forces of the United States in the present emergency, you are hereby notified that you have now been selected for immediate military service." For some ten million American men, this "Greeting" was the most significant single piece of correspondence they would ever receive.

Once notified, the draftee had to report for the "physical." Doctors moved the men through on an almost assembly-line basis, evaluating perhaps twenty-five an hour at a typical induction center. For most self-conscious young men, it was the most comprehensive physical examination they had ever undergone. Selectees who passed were adjudged physically fit for "general service." Those who had minor defects were slotted for "limited service." Roughly one-third failed either of these categories.

The men also underwent a screening session with a psychiatrist who looked for signs of "NP"—neuropsychosis-an inexact term that covered everything from phobias to heavy sweating, which resulted in the rejection of one in every eight men. A psychiatrist who once screened 512 men in a single day remembered the "hectic days when my profiling consisted of four or five rapid-fire questions: 'How do you feel? Have you ever been sick? Are you nervous? How

do you think you will get along in the Army?' " Almost always he would finally ask: "Do you like girls?"

Those who passed both examinations were then fingerprinted and signed their induction papers. Each man received a military serial number and was told to memorize it. "That Army serial number is yours for keeps," an Army sergeant would tell the rookies. "No one else will ever have it." Finally, inductees were assembled before an Army officer who administered the oath. Then the men were instructed to take one step forward.* As of that moment, though they did not yet wear uniforms, they were soldiers in the United States Army.

With this new status, the men found themselves under the provisions of "military law" and had to obey the rules as outlined in the "Articles of War." To underscore the inductees' new legal standing, a sergeant read Articles 58 and 61, dealing with desertion and "being absent without leave" (AWOL). It was the Army's way of saying "You had better show up."

As America's new conscripts began to flood into Army basic training camps at ever-increasing rates, growing numbers of other young men—reluctant to wait and "take their chances" with the draft—found their way to Army Air Corps, Navy, Marine Corps, and Coast Guard recruiting offices to voluntarily enlist.

The Navy's slogan—"Choose While You Can"—worked well. In the first months after Pearl Harbor, thousands of men scheduled to be drafted into the Army signed up with the sea arm. The guiding rule seemed to be: "Whatever you do, stay out of the Infantry."

America's manpower pool was something of a pudding, with everyone fighting for the spoon. Induction and recruiting stations, war plants, and the agricultural industry pushed and pulled against one another—trying to put men into combat boots, behind factory-floor lathes, or atop tractors.

Finally, on January 1, 1943, military policy-makers put an end to the time-honored volunteering. As of that date, a man had to be drafted into the armed forces. Men between the ages of eighteen

---

*In the draft's early stages, men sometimes took the oath on the day they reported to the center for departure to camp.

and thirty-seven all became subject to the Selective Service System.

Even so, the Navy managed to "cream-skim" from the pool by refusing to accept men not meeting certain physical standards or who had been guilty of certain offenses. (To help meet its vast replacement needs, the Army took such men.)

In a radio address on October 12, 1942, less than a year into the war, President Roosevelt sounded the call for eighteen- and nineteen-year-olds. A couple of days later, Secretary Stimson declared that the "Army is getting too old." In draftee-heavy divisions, he pointed out, "the average age was up to twenty-eight years two months. That's too old!" Draft director Hershey stressed that the Army needed *young* men, men who could "jump from planes without breaking ankles, drive tanks in 130-degree temperature, or swim ashore."

They were being realistic. There had been much talk of "modern war"—battles fought with tanks, planes, artillery. But in point of fact, the premium was still on the foot soldiers who led ground actions and served as riflemen, machine-gunners, mortar men. The infantry—in keeping with the Latin root of the word—needed the young. On November 13, 1942, barely a month after FDR had asked that the draft age be lowered to eighteen, the law was amended in accordance with his bidding.

Fatherhood presented the draft-system with a poignant problem. The boards, who well respected marriage and family, were inclined to send bachelors to war first. "Pre-Pearl Harbor" fathers stood the best chance of obtaining deferments. Those whose children had been conceived after December 7, 1941 still figured into the deferment balance, but to a lesser degree.

The American Legion urged that "every eligible single man that can be registered" be removed from government and industry before fathers were taken. But Army and Navy leaders alike argued for the drafting of fathers—contending that their continued exemption would prolong the war. Steadily, draft boards stripped their rolls of single men until, by the last quarter of 1943, the boards started falling short of their quotas.

Finally, across the country, the draft boards had to face up to it; they began drawing upon fathers. In October 1943

fathers accounted for six per cent of that month's draft quota; by April 1944 they made up more than forty per cent.

Colleges—in the persons of their presidents, faculty members, and students—had viewed the draft with particular trepidation. In "Conscription Hits the Campus" in the May 1941 issue of *Harper's* magazine, Professor Gaynor Maddox wrote that certain college students "live in a dream world of escape formulations, self-centered in little greedy and shallow cynicisms. They putter half-heartedly over excuses while all history is in turmoil."

An athlete at a California university asserted that he would help defend America against Hitler—but only in the Army Air Corps. "I Don't intend to go into the infantry," he said. "A foot soldier's just one of a mob, and the whole gang may be slaughtered together." A senior, twenty-two years of age, believed in the draft, but "not for university men studying for careers. Fill up the ranks with Civilian Conservation Corps boys and the unemployed first."

With America in the war, however, the self-serving protestations of some college students faded. The draft proved a remarkably effective equalizer. Board members, themselves volunteers, were unimpressed by power and prestige. "We looked at each man as a man," one draft board member recalled, "no better, no worse, no more important, no less important than the next man."

Surprising numbers of men fit enough to live in peace were initially found unfit to fight in war. A husky young man not capable of detecting "low voice sounds at twenty feet in a quiet room" might be able to play football, yet be rejected by the Army because of poor hearing. A fellow who had half his teeth decayed could be a structural steel worker, but the Army would turn him down.

As manpower needs went up, however, acceptance standards went down. Under later rules, false teeth were no ban to induction as long as they were "well mounted, of good occlusion, and sufficient to sustain a man on the Army ration." Toward war's end, one soldier out of five wore glasses. The services

even took some men who had only one eye.

The American public became increasingly upset as, with more and more men being required to go into uniform, others "less desirable"—individuals with venereal disease or convictions as felons, for example—were barred from service. A Pennsylvania congressman declared that there were "hobos, bums, wife-beaters, drunks, and dissipators of all kinds who should be put into uniform."

The military, in time, concurred. The Army eventually drafted 200,000 men who had venereal disease, treating them with sulfa drugs to make them fit for soldierly duties. And by war's end, more than 100,000 former felons wore the Army uniform—the vast majority of them serving honorably. Some 100,000 men unable to read or write also were accepted, taught the rudiments of English, and assigned to full-duty units.

A file of letters seven feet thick, preserved in the National Archive, attests to the volumes of "fan mail" addressed to Selective Service headquarters. Signed with such names as "Anonymous Citizen" and "True American," they "tattled" on relatives, neighbors, or acquaintances. One woman wrote to tell of her "shiftless" son-in-law, who "could do with" some Army discipline. A wife wrote: "Please locate my husband and put him in the service. He diserted [sic] his family and took another woman with him."

In the course of the war, the Federal Bureau of Investigation picked up thousands of men who had not registered, had not reported for induction, had failed to report for physical examination, or who simply were not carrying their draft cards. Upon confrontation, a culprit usually admitted to the error of his ways and then complied with the law. Some draft boards publicly posted the names of delinquents, shaming them into service. The F.B.I., wielding the threat of legal prosecution, nudged great numbers of reluctant young men into uniform.

Some, however, couldn't be nudged. One Kentuckian devised a most elaborate will-of-the-wisp scheme. By means of telephone calls and letters to his draft board, he impersonated every member of his family in an attempt to prove that he was dead, buried, and bereaved. Later, rather than sooner, the artful dodger was found—alive, well, and rueful. A federal judge sent him to a penitentiary for three years.

One New York City sharpie conducted a "school" where he taught selectees—for sizeable fees—how to fake deafness, mental disorders, or heart ailments in order to avoid being drafted. In Jersey City three men were fined $1,000 apiece for "selling" shipyard jobs (for sums ranging from $300 to $500 apiece) that qualified the holders for deferment from service.

At Orangeville, Pennsylvania, a young registrant and his girlfriend claimed they were married and had a baby. When the draft board asked to see the baby, the couple borrowed one from a relative. It was months before their deception came to light—whereupon the man was given a three-year prison term.

Men had fabricated all sorts of reasons in their attempts to evade the draft, but at least one told the cold truth. His reason for not wanting to be a soldier was one anyone could understand; he was afraid of being killed.

World War II so unified the American people against the Axis onslaught that organized pacifism as such almost vanished from the scene. Of the millions of men called forth to serve, only a minute fraction—fewer than 40,000 men—were classified as "Conscientious Objector." The "C.O." was required to show "sincerity of belief in religious teachings combined with a profound moral aversion to war." Peace sects, such as the Quakers, accounted for most of the conscientious objectors. Yet, when called by their draft boards, seventy-five per cent of the Quakers entered the armed forces unreservedly.

The law required that conscientious objectors assume some noncombat role within the military or perform a civilian service. About 25,000 C.O.s carried out non-fighting military duties. Many served on the battlefront—as ambulance drivers, medical aides, and stretcher-bearers. Said one: "The soldiers were fighting for the same things I believed in—peace in the world and democracy."

Some twelve thousand conscientious objectors served at former Civilian Public Service Corps camps scattered throughout the United States. They cleared underbrush, felled trees, and cut firebreaks in woodlands. Provided with food and clothing by various support groups, the C.O.s lead unexacting, almost indulgent, lives—in sharp contrast to the hard, discipline-ridden regimen that draftees and volunteers were called upon to endure. This state of affairs angered many Americans and disappointed those objectors who had hoped for more meaningful service.

Declared, unyielding resistance to the draft-call was rare. Some thirteen thousand men—among them four thousand Jehovah's Witnesses—went to prison for refusing to serve the nation in any way during the war.* This worked out to a remarkably small four-tenths of one per cent of all registrants, a figure much lower than the World War I rate.

The draft, in World War II, became a rite of passage. "I was just out of high school," recalls Herman Harrington, of Rensselaer, New York. "When my draft notice came, I figured I had to do my duty. Looking back, I was proud to do it."

John Mahoney, who lives in Chicago, remembers: "I registered on my eighteenth birthday. When I got called to the draft board, they had to look high and low for my papers. Did they find them? You betcha they did."

George Thomas, of Phoenix, Arizona, relates: "I was a kid then. I didn't know what to expect when I got drafted. But neither did the others. They were kids, too. We were in it together."

The G.I. Army, by far the largest of the services, had the greatest percentage of draftees in its ranks. It was a cross-section of America's young men, a collection of "the long and the short and the tall." They were the sons, brothers, husbands, and fathers of America. Not per-

*Jehovah's Witnesses had a hard time convincing local draft boards that each of their number was a "minister" and therefore eligible for deferment.

fect men, by any means. Common men, in the main. But men quite good enough, they would prove, to train, to stand fast, to fight, to be wounded and—if need be—to die for their nation's cause. Men able, strong, and brave enough to win World War II.

They would be a long time gone—a lot longer than they wanted to be. But most of them would come back. Older. Wearier. Bearing memories that would be hard to put behind them. Some, when they stepped foot from their troopship, got down and kissed the pier. Newspapers called them "heroes." They counted themselves lucky just to be alive.

Other men would not be back. They would live on in the recollections of those who had come home, but as haunting presences. For men of arms knew what became of the fallen.

More than 403,000 American servicemen were killed on the battlefront or in the line of duty during World War II. Some 670,000 others were wounded. They had gone to their rendezvous with destiny in places many of them had barely heard of, places they had never expected to see—Bizerta, Attu, Anzio, Kwajalein, Normandy, Remagen, the Ardennes, Mindanao, Iwo Jima, and Okinawa.

Dorothy South Alvey, who works in Washington, D.C. as a planner with today's Selective Service System, well remembers her days as an employee in a Leitchfield, Kentucky draft board in 1943. "The people had a patriotic feeling," she recalls. "I remember some young men who *wanted* to be called."

To this day Ms. Alvey keeps a copy of a memorial book titled "Gold Star Boys," containing photographs and brief biographical sketches of men from her home county "who didn't come back from the war." The pictures, some of them simple snapshots, show boyish faces of soldiers, sailors, Marines, and airmen, taken a half-century ago. "For those of us who knew them back home," she says of those who never returned, "all those young men are still with us, in our memories. We think of them as they were."

Racism and Relocation: Telling the Japanese-American Experience

James A. Mackey and William E. Huntzicker

The late James A. Mackey was professor of curriculum and instruction at the University of Minnesota in Minneapolis. William E. Huntzicker is a free-lance writer and lecturer in journalism at the University of Minnesota in Minneapolis.

Gladys Ishida remembers riding with her father in their Chevrolet stake truck filled with fifty-pound lugs (wooden boxes) of apricots and peaches to the cannery at Modesto, California, five miles from their family's orchard. There they sold their dried fruit to the federal government to feed soldiers.

By the standards of the Depression, the Ishida family lived comfortably in the 1930s. They hired Mexican migrant farm workers to help harvest their fruit each year. Gladys's father, Raiji, built his farm with hard work; he came to the United States before World War I. Gladys's mother, Suye, came to the United States in 1922. Like many U.S. farm families, the entire Ishida family worked on the farm along with the hired hands.[1]

Although the Ishidas had built a successful farm, the 1913 Alien Land Law prevented Raiji and Suye from owning their own land. They were *issei,* the first generation of Japanese to emigrate to the United States, and they were not allowed to become U.S. citizens. Since alien land laws kept noncitizens from owning land, a friend of the family, a lawyer, put his name on their property.

As *nisei,* the Japanese-American generation born in the United States, Gladys and her brothers could one day own the

farm, but they were not yet old enough to own land when their father was stricken with colon cancer. He died in November 1940.

A year later, the Japanese attack on Pearl Harbor and the approaching war worried Suye, but 18-year-old Gladys remained optimistic. "At least we have the orchard and we can grow vegetables," she said. But the lawyer, who had dragged his feet on transferring the land to a corporation in Gladys's name, now threatened her mother. He told her not to press the issue or he would burn all records of their transactions. In reality, he said, he owned their farm.

By the spring of 1942, the Ishidas saw notices ordering Japanese Americans to report to an assembly center at Merced, California. From there Gladys and her family were sent to the Amache Relocation Center in southeastern Colorado. "You could only take one suitcase per person," she said. "Everything else was left behind or presumably sold." They would never return to the farm.

Rumors reached them in the internment camp that their well-developed 180-acre orchard sold for $2,500 an acre in 1943. But the lawyer sent the Ishidas only $16,500.

The Ishidas were among 110,000 Japanese Americans forced from their homes, farms, and businesses in the largest deprivation of civil rights in the United States since the abolition of slavery (Weglyn 1976; Thomas and Nishimoto 1969; Irons 1983). Merced was among a dozen California assembly centers. Washington, Oregon, and Arizona each contained one. After processing, Japanese Americans were sent to relocation centers or internment camps in eleven

states. No one was excluded except the critically ill, who could be left in institutions.

The experience of Japanese Americans provides an often overlooked case study of racism in U.S. culture. Its legacy emerges in current attitudes toward Asian Americans who have emigrated since the wars in Indochina.

The symbolic environment in which Californians lived in the 1920s and 1930s carried many stereotypes of Japanese Americans. Of course, Gladys Ishida knew the history of the "yellow peril" in which Californians persecuted Asians because they feared cheap labor would steal jobs from white working people. She also knew that many Asian Americans faced racial discrimination. From a relatively prosperous background, however, she never faced racism herself until the family's lawyer threatened their property and she read evacuation notices.

Californians had been racist toward Japanese long before Pearl Harbor. Although few Japanese had moved to the United States before 1890, westerners drew on a legacy of anti-Chinese sentiment in their attitudes toward Japan. Then in 1900 the annexation of Hawaii freed many Japanese contract laborers on sugar plantations to move to the United States. Japanese immigration increased. Nativist groups warned that the West would be "Japanized" as the South had become "Negroized." Japanese Americans posed an even greater threat, they said, because Japan was rising as a world power and a major Pacific naval power. Like racist southerners, some westerners worried about mixed marriages and the purity of white women (Limerick 1987, 269–273).

From *Social Education,* November/December 1991, pp. 415–418. © 1991 by the National Council for the Social Studies. Reprinted by permission.

Propaganda concerning the Axis powers increased as German aggression spread through Europe and Japanese aggression subdued much of Asia. But a major contrast emerged between attitudes toward the two enemies. German aggression and German enemies were often portrayed in the person of Adolph Hitler. Japanese, on the other hand, were often depicted in ugly caricatures that could be interpreted as any Japanese person. In the case of Germany, the enemy was Hitler; in the case of Japan, the enemy was the Japanese people.

When Japan attacked Pearl Harbor, about 127,000 Americans were of Japanese ancestry and, of them, about 113,000 lived in California, Washington, Oregon, and Arizona. They represented less than 0.01 percent of the U.S. population and less than 2 percent of California's population, where they lived in the heaviest concentration (Thomas and Nishimoto 1969, 1).

Despite their small numbers, the legacy of stereotypes and racism combined with wartime hysteria made the most bizarre charges against Japanese Americans seem plausible. The government declared all Japanese Americans potential spies and subversives; pressure groups, including farm organizations, expressed alarm that Japanese-American farmers threatened the U.S. food supply and that their income could be sent to the enemy in Japan. These claims defied logic, since Japanese Americans constituted a fiercely loyal ethnic group.

Soon after the attack on Pearl Harbor, General J. L. DeWitt, head of the West Defense Command, said that "any proposal for mass evacuation [of Japanese Americans] was 'damned nonsense!'" (Murphy 1972, 233). Restrictions on aliens around military bases were adequate protection, he said. After sensing that the general public disagreed, however, DeWitt advocated the removal of Japanese Americans. "They are a dangerous element," he said. "There is no way to determine their loyalty" (Grodzins 1949, 282). Executive Order No. 9066 issued February 19, 1942, required the evacuation. Two-thirds of evacuees were U.S. citizens and more of them, like Raiji Ishida, would have been if the laws had allowed. Any persons of Japanese ancestry, whether American or not, became inherently suspect. "A Jap's a Jap," DeWitt said (Grodzins 1949, 297).

Eventually, the U.S. Supreme Court held that a national emergency could justify the suspension of civil liberties for a time. Justice Frank Murphy dissented from what he called this "legalization of racism. Racial discrimination in any form and in any degree has no justifiable part whatever in our democratic way of life," he wrote (Murphy 1972, 291). Military discretion should be limited, he said, especially when it lacked substance.

Within the relocation and internment camps, many Japanese Americans faced questions of loyalty. The *issei* were ineligible for U.S. citizenship, but they were asked to "foreswear any form of allegiance or obedience to the Japanese emperor" (Weglyn 1976, 136). This statement forced the *issei* to become stateless. Those who refused the loyalty statement were sent to Tule Lake, which became a high security relocation camp. A few younger *nisei* refused the loyalty pledge on the grounds that it was a civil rights violation. Some *issei,* left penniless by the evacuation, their dreams shattered, returned to Japan with their *nisei* children.

College and military service were the only way out of the camps. Gladys Ishida tried to get out from the moment she arrived at Merced in May 1942. By late August, she and her brother, Calvin, with help from a National Student Relocation Council, attended Washington University in Saint Louis. Financially, their father's insurance money, part-time work, and scholarships enabled the three Ishida children to attend college while their mother remained at the Amache Relocation Center. Julius, the youngest, completed two years of high school in the camp and then attended Wooster College in Ohio.

The National Student Relocation Council helped students get accustomed to their new homes, where few members of their ethnic groups lived. (Gladys recalls being mistaken for an American Indian in Saint Louis.) The government imposed some restrictions, she said. For example, no Japanese-American student could enroll in a university within twenty-five miles of a railroad terminal. "I guess they thought we were all going to bomb or do something with railroad terminals to impede the war effort," she said.

Within a year, she completed her degree at Washington University and enrolled as a graduate student in international relations at the University of Chicago. There she was visited by an FBI agent, who seemed suspicious that a Japanese American would be interested in international relations. The agent was polite, she said, but he showed up on her first day of work and refused to wait until after her working day for the interview. "He insisted that I be available for the interview immediately and he got my boss to provide us a room in which he could interview me," she recalled. "He was polite, but I was embarrassed in my first day on the job. I felt like I was a spy or something." Gladys eventually received a master's degree at Chicago and a doctorate at the University of Michigan.

Other Japanese Americans left the camps for military service. Some served in language training at special camps such as the one at Fort Snelling, Minnesota, where they trained Japanese Americans to speak Japanese so they could either serve in the Pacific War or work to break codes.

Others joined active service, including the segregated 442d Japanese-American combat unit. Dan Inouye, an 18-year-old volunteer, was among the ten thousand Hawaiian *nisei* to join the war. Nine days before the end of the European war, Inouye stood to throw a grenade forty yards into a German machine gun nest in Italy. A rifle grenade severed Inouye's right arm; he picked up a second grenade with his left hand to kill the firing German. He continued directing an assault on the German position, suffering bullet wounds in his abdomen and his right leg. He received a Distinguished Service Cross and a Bronze Star. Although Inouye, now a United States Senator, returned to San Francisco with an empty sleeve, when he walked into a barber shop for a haircut, he was told: "We don't serve Japs here" (Hosokawa 1969, 416–417).

U.S. images of Japan fluctuate. After the war, Japan was seen again as a charming Oriental country represented by silk pillows and James A. Michener's *Sayonara;* and the Japanese were seen as a quaint but benign people. Japanese imports, seen as harmless, cheap toys, began to flood U.S. markets; Japanese cars became the butt of jokes.

In recent years, however, the image has swung back to that of relentless competitor. The tone in the United States continues to be ambivalent: Japan-bashing exists alongside admiration and a flood of imitation and jealousy. The United States demands high tariffs on Japanese goods and equitable trade with Japan, and complains about unfair governmental subsidies of Japanese businesses. At the same time, educators and entrepreneurs in the United States want to imitate Japanese methods. Through it all, Japanese Americans continue to suffer discrimination related to the prevailing view of Japan. White Americans who resent Japanese successes continue to use Japanese Americans as scapegoats, especially in the auto industry where U.S. workers often blame the Japanese for the failures of this country's industry.

The legacy of racism continues against other Asian Americans, even as they become the nation's fastest growing ethnic minority in the wake of the Indochina wars. Asian students excel on student aptitude and college admissions tests while the overall scores of white students have declined. As a result, Asian Americans have been selected to attend the best U.S. universities in larger proportions than their populations. They now find, like Jewish students of the 1940s and 1950s, that major campuses may be limiting their enrollment. A national television report on this issue in 1989 used as its title the old racist assumption about Japanese Americans: They were victims of their own success (ABC News 1989). Racial and ethnic minorities, it seems, are allowed to succeed only within limits. The beat goes on.

Some Japanese Americans have sought governmental review of the decision to evacuate them to relocation camps. In August 1988, the U.S. Congress passed a redress bill to pay $20,000 to each of the Japanese Americans interned in camps during World War II. Suye Ishida never lived to see the money. She died in November 1989 and her heirs received her payment in January 1991. The $20,000 was a pittance compared to the value of the farm she lost. Her children received their own redress payments in October 1991.

Despite progress on redress, Japanese Americans have again become scapegoats. Japan has become increasingly competitive in the automobile, electronics, steel, and other basic industries. At the same time, other Asians have, since the Indochina War, become the fastest growing ethnic groups in the United States. Their immigration has coincided with economic recession. While it is natural, understandable, and realistic to be anxious about relentless competition, it is just as unfair and undemocratic to attribute blame on the basis of race. It is also unjust to blame Japanese Americans for the actions of a nation their families left generations ago.

The three Ishida children, of course, have grown. They have retired from their careers: Calvin Ishida was a mechanical engineer in Northbrook, Illinois; Julius Ishida was an economist and accountant in Chicago; and Gladys Ishida Stone was a professor of sociology at the University of Wisconsin-River Falls. Suye Ishida's ashes are interred in Kitsuki, Japan, with her husband's, which were interred there after World War II when the family was allowed to return with them.

The Ishidas never returned to their family farm. Friends reported that the land became a housing development during the war. All the trees were removed. Gladys Stone returned to the site in September 1991, but development had changed the land so much that she could not even locate where her farm had been.

NOTE

1. Gladys Ishida Stone told her story to the authors in a series of interviews in April and May 1991 in Saint Paul, Minnesota. The authors are grateful for the time and assistance she has given them.

REFERENCES

ABC Television News. "Victims of their Own Success?" "20/20," 5 May 1989.

Grodzins, Morton. *Americans Betrayed: Politics and the Japan Evacuation.* Chicago: University of Chicago Press, 1949.

Hosokawa, Bill. *Nisei: The Quiet Americans.* New York: William Morrow and Co., 1969.

Irons, Peter. *Justice at War: The Story of the Japanese American Internment Cases.* New York: Oxford University Press, 1983.

Limerick, Patricia Nelson. *The Legacy of Conquest.* New York: W. W. Norton, 1987.

Murphy, Paul L. *The Constitution in Crisis Times.* New York: Harper and Row, 1972.

Thomas, Dorothy S., and Richard Nishimoto. *The Spoilage: Japanese-American Evacuation and Resettlement During World War II.* Berkeley: University of California Press, 1969.

Weglyn, Michi. *Years of Infamy: The Untold Story of America's Concentration Camps.* New York: William Morrow and Co., 1976.

1943
The Pull of Distant Shores

Gerald Parshall

On a wintry Saturday in late January 1943, a 25-cent ticket carried Americans to French Morocco, where a man in a white dinner jacket pulled on a cigarette and wrestled with his conscience. "I stick my neck out for nobody," said Rick Blaine. But before "The End" popped up on the silver screen, Rick (Humphrey Bogart) threw himself selflessly into the global struggle—giving up Ingrid Bergman, no less—to help defeat Nazism.

Just one day after *Casablanca* went into general release, another cynical idealist, this one from true life, called a press conference in Casablanca. He sat amid orange trees and purple bougainvillea at a gleaming Moorish villa, waving a long cigarette holder for the newsreel cameras. Franklin Roosevelt, ending 10 days of secret meetings with Winston Churchill and Charles de Gaulle, announced that the Allies would fight until "unconditional surrender" by the Axis. *Casablanca,* the movie, and Casablanca, the conference, bore the same metamessage: Americans wear the white hats in this evil world—and do what they must to keep civilization's lights burning.

Pop culture and presidential pronouncement alike were proclaiming an ethic of global involvement that would resound for the next half century. Japan's attack on Pearl Harbor in December 1941 had triggered a vast mobilization that dominated the national agenda in 1942. The United States had won a stunning naval victory at Midway, had begun pushing back Japan's forces at Guadalcanal and, with the other Allies, had begun driving the Germans from North Africa. By 1943, few Americans doubted that "the greatest country in the world" would win the war. And it was beginning to sink in that even after the war, the world's larger troubles would be America's own. The impulse to stay clear of

power struggles in other hemispheres had pounded in the American breast for 150 years. But America had grown too big and the world too small.

The debate on postwar policies was fired up by a woman famous as a playwright, wit and wife, Clare Boothe Luce. Her husband, Time-Life magnate Henry Luce, had called for an "American century" of democracy and capitalism, only to be corrected by FDR's liberal vice president, Henry Wallace, who invited a "people's revolution" and a "century of the common man." Mrs. Luce, entering Congress as a Republican from silk-stocking Connecticut, used her maiden speech in February to accuse Wallace of showing insufficient regard for U.S. interests. "No matter how you slice it," said the empress of bons mots, Wallace's idealistic patter was "globaloney." The clever coinage brought titters from much of the nation and—a week later—a counterattack. After sarcastically saluting Mrs. Luce's "sparkling beauty and suavity of manner," a fellow freshman, his Arkansas drawl dripping with disdain, mercilessly picked her speech apart, dismissing it as illogical and imperialistic.

From these theatrics sprouted the United Nations. Luce's scold was a 38-year-old J. William Fulbright. He included in his remarks a proposal that the United States pledge itself to help preserve peace in the postwar period, and he soon went to work, with the State Department's encouragement, to secure passage of a congressional resolution. The Allies wanted assurances that America would not again revert to isolationism, repeating its blunder after World War I. In April, the Associated Press found only 24 senators—one fourth of the Senate—willing to endorse U.S. participation in a postwar "international police force." A very different verdict came from the Gallup Poll two weeks later: Seventy-four percent of the public

was in favor. By fall, most lawmakers had caught up with the people they were leading. Resolutions supporting a U.S. role in what would become the U.N. two years later passed the House by 360 to 29 and the Senate by 85 to 5. The *New Yorker* taunted the diehards: "Gentlemen, if you do not know that your country is now entangled beyond recall with the rest of the world, what *do* you know?"

Indeed, the *smallness* of the world was dramatized anew every day. The airplane had shrunk the planet irreversibly. FDR had gone to Casablanca on a Pan American Clipper, speeding 5,000 miles across the war-ravaged Atlantic, becoming the first president to fly in office and the first to leave the United States in wartime. Wendell Willkie's book, *One World,* written after the Wall Street lawyer's own around-the-world trip, became 1943's No. 1 bestseller. "The myriad millions . . . of the Far East are [now] as close to us as Los Angeles is to New York by the fastest trains," the 1940 Republican presidential nominee wrote. "In the future what concerns them must concern us, almost as much as the problems of the people of California concern the people of New York."

In bookstores, nonfiction was rapidly overshadowing fiction (a trend unabated 50 years later). Among other 1943 bestsellers were *Guadalcanal Diary, Suez to Singapore, Head-Hunting in the Solomon Islands* and Walter Lippmann's *U.S. Foreign Policy: Shield of the Republic* (the *Ladies' Home Journal* excerpted Lippmann's book, reducing the distinguished commentator's plea for permanent international peacekeeping to captions for 52 cartoon panels).

At the movies, where 100 million tickets a week were sold in a population of 135 million, Paramount's "eyes and ears of the world" and other newsreels depicted a planet in turmoil. Radio

From *U.S. News & World Report,* October 25, 1993, pp. 20-25. © 1993 by U.S. News & World Report. Reprinted by permission.

The Way We Were

Surprise Attack
At 7:58 a.m., Dec. 7, 1941, became a date that will live in infamy. In less than two hours, the Japanese attack on Pearl Harbor killed 2,397 people. The next day, in a 6½-minute speech, Franklin Roosevelt asked Congress to declare war. Time for Senate approval: 15 minutes; House of Representatives: 40 minutes. Dissenting votes: one, Rep. Jeanette Rankin of Montana.

Communist Father
Joseph Stalin killed 9 million to 25 million people in purges. Then, the former seminarian led the U.S.S.R. through World War II, in which 21.5 million Soviets died. Combined losses suffered by America, Britain and France: 1.2 million. Still, the Soviet Union emerged as a superpower. Years after Stalin's 1953 death before he was denounced by the state: three.

Desegregating Baseball
Jackie Robinson, a grandson of a slave, broke Major League Baseball's color barrier in 1947, and some players threatened a strike. In 1952, 19 blacks were in the major leagues; in 1993, 125. Years that Hall of Famer Satchell Paige played professionally before being admitted to the major leagues in 1948: 22. Years he played in the majors: six.

School for Soldiers
Critics said the GI Bill would encourage sloth among veterans, but fears of mass unemployment after the war got the bill signed into law in June 1944. It gave single veterans $500 a year for tuition and $50 a month for living costs. By 1947, veterans on the bill constituted half of all college enrollment. To date, more than 20 million veterans have been in the program, at a cost of $61.4 billion for education.

The End of Colonialism
Mohandas Gandhi's nonviolent resistance efforts, including fasting for as many as 21 days at a stretch, helped win Indian independence from British rule in 1947. Gandhi's achievement gave momentum to decolonization worldwide. When it was founded in 1945, the United Nations had 51 members; today, the number is up to 184.

Baby Boom
Dr. Benjamin Spock's 1946 *Common Sense Book of Baby and Child Care* became the parents' bible, an alternative to authoritarian child rearing. The book (40 million plus sold) was one mark of the boom's start. Boomers (born 1946–64) alive: 77.1 million; baby busters (born 1965–82): 65.7 million; boomers' parents (born 1928–45): 39.6 million.

Homewardbound
The suburbs took off in 1947 with the construction of 300 houses on a New York potato field by builder William Levitt; by 1951, he had put 17,447 homes there. He would eventually build Levittowns in New Jersey and Pennsylvania, and his developments were models for suburbanization nationwide. Each original home sold for less than $10,000. Different models available: two.

Birth of Israel
After Arabs rejected a 1947 U.N. plan for Palestine, Israel declared itself a state in 1948. More than 600,000 Palestinians became refugees in the ensuing war. By 1951, 684,000 Jews had joined 650,000 others in Israel. Jews killed in the Holocaust: 6 million. German Jews before Nazis took power: 566,000; after the war: 20,000. U.S. aid to Israel since 1948: $52 billion.

---

brought the chaos crackling into the living room. Fully 25 percent of programming was given over to public affairs. The four-star generals of the air—Edward R. Murrow, Lowell Thomas, Gabriel Heatter ("Ah, there's good news tonight!"), Raymond Clapper, William L. Shirer—broadcast pictures that television could not have equaled. An RCA ad caught the excitement: "Radio annihilates distance, sweeps away the barrier of time, penetrates through mountain and sea, stone and steel."

On the home front, the watchword was sacrifice. Volunteers hawked war bonds, planted victory gardens (20 million of them, providing one third of the country's fresh vegetables in 1943) and collected scrap rubber, scrap metal and cooking grease. The government in January 1943 banned pleasure driving on the East Coast and imposed food rationing nationwide. War production gobbled raw materials, creating shortages that ranged from washing machines and bobby pins to lawn mowers and lobster forks.

"Don't you know there's a war on?" was the standard answer to gripes. (Yet, as scarce as luxury goods were, the rich could still find avenues for conspicuous consumption—Stern's of New York advertised mink coats for $1,795.)

The aura of austerity camouflaged an open secret apparent to many but stated by few: The war was a shock cure for a sick economy and a blessing to millions who had languished in the Depression. Nearly twice as many people were working in civilian or military jobs in 1943 than were employed a decade earlier. Farm income was on its way to doubling since 1941 (it did so by 1945). Business profits rose 57 percent in 1943 alone. The great American dream machine was roaring to life, a machine that would provide the United States with a quarter century of improving living standards, rebuild Europe and Japan after the war and guarantee United States leadership in the world.

Bus stations and train depots were choked with servicemen; 10 million were in uniform, 100,000 more each month. Fighting and winning the greatest war in history was a coming-of-age experience that marked an entire generation. The GI generation would give postwar life much of its "can do" tone.

Sociologists theorized during the war that contacts with foreign places and peoples would turn GIs into "citizens of the world" attuned to its diverse cultures. In fact, studies of GI attitudes after the war found just the opposite. The squalor and disorder men saw abroad had merely fortified their home-grown belief in U.S. superiority. American soldiers landing in Italy in mid-1943 were shocked to find actual "two-bit whores"—women so desperate that they sold themselves for 25 cents. Sgt. Ralph Martin reported in the Army's *Yank* magazine: "We are giving the people of Sicily candy, cigarettes and Tom Paine." It was a short step from the candy-bar imperative to the Marshall Plan a few years later. And a series of further steps to the quagmire of Vietnam.

In 1943, most Americans still cherished the illusion that the United States and the Soviet Union would remain allies after the war. The Russians were admired as the heroes of Stalingrad, stoic and brave. Political amnesia had wiped out the crimes of the 1930s. The Warner Brothers film *Mission to Moscow* depicted Joseph Stalin as a twinkly benefactor, whitewashing his murder of millions. *Collier's* magazine revealed that the U.S.S.R. was "a modified capitalist setup" that would soon resemble "our own and Great Britain's democracy."

The tensions that would escalate into the cold war were already surfacing, however. They were seen most clearly in November at the Tehran Conference, where Roosevelt and Churchill tried to resolve conflicts with the Soviets over postwar realignments. FDR poured on the charm, addressing Stalin as "Uncle Joe" and teasing Churchill about his Britishness because he knew it would please Stalin. But the Soviet dictator would give no ground on self-determination for the Baltic republics and refused to recognize the democratic Polish gov-

ernment in exile in London—and the issues had to be deferred. Stalin persuaded FDR to stay in the Soviet compound during the conference, warning that Tehran swarmed with spies. The U.S. Secret Service soon discovered that even the servants in the president's villa were NKVD intelligence agents, each with a pistol hidden up a sleeve or under a skirt. Roosevelt chuckled at such bedchamber espionage. His smile would have faded quickly had he known that, back in the United States, Soviet spies were stealing the secret to the atomic bomb.

Eyewitness
While Six Million Died

Liliane Gaffney, 67, and her mother, Germaine Belline, 85, helped about 30 Jews avoid Nazi authorities as anti-Jewish sentiment grew in their native Belgium during the early 1940s. They provided shelter to many of them, a handful of the few European Jews who were saved from the Holocaust. Both women now live in New Jersey.

"In 1943, one of the women hiding with us was pregnant and had to be delivered. So arrangements were made in the Brussels hospital, about 30 miles north of where we lived, in that hospital there was a nurse we knew could be trusted. And Miryam had a baby boy, Willy.

"And then came the time when we had to go and take them home. But since very often they checked papers, either in the hospital or on the train especially, it was decided that it was not safe for Miryam to come back with the baby. It was better to separate them. So my aunt went to pick up Miryam, and Mother and I went to pick up the little boy. And we took them back on the train and met back at the house.

"I suppose children affect you more than adults for some reason. I remember thinking that if we were to do the legal thing, the thing would be to turn over this lovely boy to the authorities; and it was the Germans, who would have quickly disposed of him. That made a very deep impression on me that sometimes to earn the title of being a human being, you may have to risk a lot. But if you don't, then you don't deserve to be a human being.

"Willy and his parents stayed with us all the way until the end of the war. We had a bris [Jewish circumcision ritual] for Willy after the war, when he was 2 years old. And he was very proud of it."

"What Did You Do in the War, Grandma?" An Oral History of Rhode Island Women During World War II

Linda P. Wood

Linda P. Wood graduated from the University of Michigan with a B.A. and M.A. in English literature, and from the University of Rhode Island with a Masters in library and information science. For seventeen years, she has been a school library media specialist at South Kingstown High School, where she has codirected several oral history projects. She served as president of the New England Association for Oral History in 1986–87.

"What Did You Do in the War, Grandma?" is available for $4.00 plus postage from the Rhode Island Historical Society, 110 Benevolent St., Providence, RI 02906.

Oral history is a unique way to learn about past events and experiences. It is a method that probes memory, evoking feelings that may have long been dormant.

"What Did You Do in the War, Grandma?" was an oral history project which was part of an Honors English class of seventeen ninth grade students. The students interviewed 36 women about their experiences during the Second World War. The teacher and the school librarian, who is also an oral historian, wrote the grant proposal and organized the curriculum as a one semester project. It was funded by the Rhode Island Committee for the Humanities. Two history professors from the University of Rhode Island helped focus the project on historically significant aspects of the women's

stories. After the tape-recorded interviews were transcribed, the students wrote the women's stories from the transcriptions and presented 26 of them in the publication "What Did You Do in the War, Grandma?"

After the publication was released, two public forums were held in which both the students and the interviewees or "narrators" participated. Historians served as moderators and helped set the framework for the discussions to serve as a kind of social commentary on the remembered events. The project was commended by the American Association for State and Local History at their annual conference in 1990.

Students who listen to the voices of the narrators respond emotionally as well as intellectually. Oral history provides a duet of telling and retelling which captures the importance of history through an individual's life. The process of preparing an oral history often creates a special relationship between narrator and interviewer. The interaction can be especially dramatic when the narrator is an older woman, perhaps a grandmother, and the interviewer is a teenage girl whose assignment is to find out about women's experience in a war that began before most teenagers' parents were born.

"What Did You Do in the War, Grandma?" revealed through oral history an aspect of World War II usually ignored in social studies texts. Thirty-six women shared a part of their lives with seventeen young people. The women talked about a time of crisis and hardship that had set a

direction for the rest of their lives—experiences that no one had ever before asked them about in a way that made them realize how significantly those years had affected them.

One of the women was a freshman in college when the war began. She recalled, "I think for girls and women, and perhaps boys and men, of my generation the war forced them to grow up prematurely. It made them far more serious about the bare realities of life: life, death, values. It robbed them, in a sense, of some childhood."

Several weeks after the interview, she told the teacher about another experience, one she said was too sad to tell the young interviewer: a young man she had been dating had been killed in the war. Tears came to her eyes as she said she would always see him just the way he was when she had said goodbye, clear blue eyes, young, handsome, and wearing his navy blue sweater. The woman had received a letter from her mother, and a newspaper clipping fell out: her friend's plane had been shot down several weeks before.

Thousands of young men joined the armed forces, leaving great gaps in industry, in the professions, and at home. There was tremendous demand for labor to build up the war machines necessary to fight. Women answered the call to work. For the first time, women worked in heavy manufacturing jobs, in shipyards, and in airplane hangars. Was it only patriotism and propaganda that made women find war jobs? Or was it

From *Social Education*, February 1994, pp. 92-93. © 1994 by the National Council for the Social Studies. Reprinted by permission.

money, independence, companionship, and pride in learning new skills that motivated them?

There were also gaps at home. Husbands, sons, boyfriends, fathers left home for places far away and dangerous. A grandmother interviewed by her granddaughter told of her personal hardship, "After my husband went into the Seabees, I went to work in a woolen mill. This was considered a service job. In other words, it was important. At the mill the government used to send out all the Purple Heart soldiers to talk to us and tell us that we couldn't take time off, and pushed all this patriotism on us. I had a young baby, and I had to leave him in a nursery. I used to have to take my son on the trolley car, bring him over to the Salvation Army day nursery and leave him there, and go back down the street and get on another trolley and get to work, and the same thing at night. If he was sick I either had to stay home with him or take him up to my sisters or maybe his grandmother. One time he had scarlet fever and the doctor put him in the hospital because I was all by myself and my husband was in the service. It would have been too much to be at home with him. This way I could come and go to work."

Many women had to struggle at home alone. One of the narrators had been a young mother with six small boys and a husband serving his country in the Pacific. "My father was an avid fisherman," she said, "and we ate a lot of fish because meat was rationed. To this day, some of the kids don't like fish. We had difficulty keeping the children in clothes. There was no hand-me-downs. They just wore them out." With no father around, one of her biggest concerns was discipline: "Just keeping track of them, making sure where they were. I took care of that pretty well, but there were times when it should have been a man's job to do these things I had to do. These boys were something else. But it was just that they needed a firm hand to bring them back into line. But I never wrote to him and told him all of these things that went on. I figured he had job enough."

Many women, perhaps out of a sense of duty, perhaps out of a yearning for adventure, joined the armed forces. One woman from a prominent Rhode Island family who had been active in the Junior League joined the WACS. Her brother had signed up and so did she: "I didn't have the gall to stay out. I wasn't married, and practically every single person I knew who was able to walk went in to try to help the country. I felt it was my job to help, too."

She became Commanding Officer of a huge military hospital. "It was a receiving and evaluation hospital for our wounded coming in from Europe," she said. "We were there during the Battle of the Bulge. We would sometimes get a thousand amputation cases on one ship. Most of the kids were 18, 19, 20 years old. It's not easy to see all those thousands of kids so injured. Then we might get a whole shipload of neuro-psychiatric cases."

After the war, what did such a woman do with the rest of her life? "My plans for the future were just to survive. I got married, and we had a baby. We just did what was in front of us. I can tell you, though, women had become much more independent because we had the experience of standing on our own two feet. We had to do it. I suppose that it was a surprise for some of the men."

A young Jewish woman at Brown University joined the WACS for a different reason: "I was the kind of person—I still am—that liked to be involved in things. As more and more news came out of Germany, you just felt you wanted to do something. Hitler's plans were to wipe out the Jews all over the world. It wasn't just wiping out the Jews, it was to take over the world. I think we were all very much worried about what was going to happen to us, and to our way of life."

A young women in nursing school struggled to complete her training when most of the hospital staff left as a unit for the war front: "I was still 18, and I was head nurse on the night ward." She describes the changes that war brought to the hospitals. The length of time a patient stayed was cut by half. To save the nurses' time, mothers were encouraged to nurse their babies instead of give them prepared formula. Penicillin became available. Rare skin diseases began showing up, especially among the young men and women serving in the Pacific.

Convinced by the government to join the WACS after she graduated, the young nurse shipped out to the Philippines: "Our unit was actually going to set up as a front line group that was going into Japan." Instead, she disembarked in the Philippines and took over as head nurse in a psychiatric hospital for several months at the close of the war: "I had ten corpsmen. I was the only nurse. I kind of felt it was worthwhile because if we really could help these people then they might not be sick for the rest of their lives. It was sort of like treating what they called 'shell shock' in World War I, when people had been out [fighting], they got a sort of battle fatigue and they went a little off."

This woman retold her experiences in a kind of reverie, with her eyes closed most of the time. She had scrapbooks filled with clippings and photographs. She concluded, "When we came back to San Francisco there was a rainbow that encircled the bridge. The lights were coming on in the hills. I didn't expect anybody, but there were a lot of people when the ship came in, all cheering and everything. I feel that I was lucky to be involved at that time, and I was glad to participate."

Discrimination and segregation were a fact of life in the United States before and during the war. An African-American woman who graduated top of her class in business was only able to find a job operating an elevator at a department store. "When the war came," she recalls, "women went to work for the first time in factories and driving trucks. I started working in a war plant where they made precision instruments. I did so well that I could take tension in my fingers to know just how a gauge would run."

When her husband came home after the war, somebody else had taken his job. "They would give him a job, but it would have been a menial job. So he had to start all over again. That was very difficult. We had a terrible time buying a house because we were black." The banks said he couldn't get a mortgage even though he had just returned from overseas. "You weren't shown houses in the sections you wanted to buy in," she said. "They would take you over to a place that had all rundown houses."

"Another thing that the war did for us," she said, "it opened up our eyes. . . . [The war] had brought us together. When peace came, people began to separate and then you began to see racial conflicts. Should not have been. Should've been we were with you during the war when things were bad . . . now there's peace, we need to be together goo. That's what we need to learn. To live together in the good times as well as the bad times."

The stories these women told represented stories that could have been told in any community, in any state, by women who had lived through a terrible time, an exciting time, a time that marked their lives forever. Oral history not only brings to life, but keeps alive, personal history. The students learned through the women's first-hand experiences what it was like to have lived at a particular time and place. The students drew from these experiences lessons of war, peace, love, hate, courage, fear, grief, and hope.

Throughout the oral history project, the students often spoke about "penetrating beneath the surface" in their interviews. They wrote about how the women revealed a side of themselves the interviewer would never have guessed was there. "There are two sides to her," wrote one student. "There is the upbeat, enthusiastic side, and the more serious side. [At times] she appeared possessed by a greater force, almost enchanted."

Another spoke of the two personalities revealed in the interview. The students were reflecting the paradox of seeing an elderly woman while listening to her story about a time when she was a young woman. The stories were so vivid that the students would actually "see" the women in uniform, or at home caring for their children, or doing hard labor in a war industry.

A student wrote, "I sigh and look at my watch. I've been interviewing her for over an hour now, and she has just finished her last sentence. Touched, I comment, thank her, and switch off the tape recorder. Sinking into a chair, I drift into thought, digesting what this woman has just shared with me about her experiences."

The Man of the Century

Of all the Allied leaders, argues FDR's biographer, only Roosevelt saw clearly the shape of the new world they were fighting to create

Arthur Schlesinger, Jr.

Arthur Schlesinger, Jr., is currently at work on a memoir.

After half a century it is hard to approach Franklin D. Roosevelt except through a minefield of clichés. Theories of FDR, running the gamut from artlessness to mystification, have long paraded before our eyes. There is his famous response to the newspaperman who asked him for his philosophy: "Philosophy? I am a Christian and a Democrat—that's all"; there is Robert E. Sherwood's equally famous warning about "Roosevelt's heavily forested interior"; and we weakly conclude that both things were probably true.

FDR's Presidency has commanded the attention of eminent historians at home and abroad for fifty years or more. Yet no consensus emerges, especially in the field of foreign affairs. Scholars at one time or another have portrayed him at every point across a broad spectrum: as an isolationist, as an internationalist, as an appeaser, as a warmonger, as an impulsive decision maker, as an incorrigible vacillator, as the savior of capitalism, as a closet socialist, as a Machiavellian intriguer plotting to embroil his country in foreign wars, as a Machiavellian intriguer avoiding war in order to let other nations bear the brunt of the fighting, as a gullible dreamer who thought he could charm Stalin into postwar collaboration and ended by selling Eastern Europe down the river into slavery, as a tightfisted creditor sending Britain down the road toward bankruptcy, as a crafty imperialist serving the interests of American capitalist hegemony, as a high-minded prophet whose vision shaped the world's future. Will the real FDR please stand up?

Two relatively recent books illustrate the chronically unsettled state of FDR historiography—and the continuing vitality of the FDR debate. In *Wind Over Sand* (1988) Frederick W. Marks III finds a presidential record marked by ignorance, superficiality, inconsistency, random prejudice, erratic impulse, a man out of his depth, not waving but drowning, practicing a diplomacy as insubstantial and fleeting as wind blowing over sand. In *The Juggler* (1991), Warren F. Kimball finds a record marked by intelligent understanding of world forces, astute maneuver, and a remarkable consistency of purpose, a farsighted statesman facing dilemmas that defied quick or easy solutions. One-third of each book is given over to endnotes and bibliography, which suggests that each portrait is based on meticulous research. Yet the two historians arrive at diametrically opposite conclusions.

> *If we can't as historians puzzle out what he **was,** we surely must as historians try to make sense of what he **did.***

So the debate goes on. Someone should write a book entitled *FDR: For and Against,* modeled on Pieter Geyl's *Napoleon: For and Against.* "It is impossible," the great Dutch historian observed, "that two historians, especially two historians living in different periods, should see any historical personality in the same light. The greater the political importance of a historical character, the more impossible this is." History, Geyl (rightly) concluded, is an "argument without end."

I suppose we must accept that human beings are in the last analysis beyond analysis. In the case of FDR, no one can be really sure what was going on in that affable, welcoming, reserved, elusive, teasing, spontaneous, calculating, cold, warm, humorous, devious, mendacious, manipulative, petty, magnanimous, superficially casual, ultimately decent, highly camouflaged, finally impenetrable mind. Still, if we can't as historians puzzle out what he *was,* we surely must as historians try to make sense out of what he *did.* If his personality escapes us, his policies must have some sort of pattern.

What Roosevelt wrote (or Sam Rosenman wrote for him) in the introduction to the first volume of his *Public Papers* about his record as governor of New York goes, I believe, for his foreign policy too: "Those who seek inconsistencies will find them. There were inconsistencies of methods, inconsistencies caused by ceaseless efforts to find ways to solve problems for the future as well as for the present. There were inconsistencies born of insufficient knowledge. There were inconsistencies springing from the need of experimentation. But through them all, I trust that there also will be found a consistency and continuity of broad purpose."

Now purpose can be very broad indeed. To say that a statesman is in favor of peace, freedom, and security does not narrow things down very much. Meaning resides in the details, and in FDR's case the details often contradict each other. If I may invoke still another cliché, FDR's foreign policy seems to fit Churchill's description of the Soviet Union: "a riddle wrapped in a mystery inside an enigma." However, we too often forget

From *American Heritage,* May/June 1994, pp. 82-88, 90-93. © 1994 by Forbes, Inc. Reprinted by permission of *American Heritage* magazine, a division of Forbes, Inc.

Franklin D. Roosevelt Library, Hyde Park, N.Y.

The young Assistant Secretary of the Navy stands with Admirals McKean, left, and Sims in 1919.

what Churchill said next: "But perhaps there is a key. That key is Russian national interest." German domination of Eastern Europe, Churchill continued, "would be contrary to the historic life-interests of Russia." Here, I suggest, may be the key to FDR, the figure in his carpet: his sense of the historic life-interests of the United States.

Of course, "national interest" narrows things down only a little. No one, except a utopian or a millennialist, is against the national interest. In a world of nation-states the assumption that governments will pursue their own interests gives order and predictability to international affairs. As George Washington said, "no nation is to be trusted farther than it is bound by [its] interest." The problem is the substance one pours into national interest. In our own time, for example, Lyndon Johnson and Dean Rusk thought our national interest required us to fight in Vietnam; William

Fulbright, Walter Lippmann, Hans Morgenthau thought our national interest required us to pull out of Vietnam. The phrase by itself settles no arguments.

How did FDR conceive the historic life-interests of the United States? His conception emerged from his own long, if scattered, education in world affairs. It should not be forgotten that he arrived in the White House with an unusual amount of international experience. He was born into a cosmopolitan family. His father knew Europe well and as a young man had marched with Garibaldi. His elder half-brother had served in American legations in London and Vienna. His mother's family had been in the China trade; his mother herself had lived in Hong Kong as a little girl. As FDR reminded Henry Morgenthau in 1934, "I have a background of a little over a century in Chinese affairs."

FDR himself made his first trip to Europe at the age of three and went there every summer from his ninth to his fourteenth year. As a child he learned French and German. As a lifelong stamp collector he knew the world's geography and politics. By the time he was elected President, he had made thirteen trips across the Atlantic and had spent almost three years of his life in Europe. "I started . . . with a good deal of interest in foreign affairs," he told a press conference in 1939, "because both branches of my family have been mixed up in foreign affairs for a good many generations, the affairs of Europe and the affairs of the Far East."

Now much of his knowledge was social and superficial. Nor is international experience in any case a guarantee of international wisdom or even of continuing international concern. The other American politician of the time who rivaled FDR in exposure to the great world was, oddly, Herbert Hoover. Hoover was a mining engineer in Australia at twenty-three, a capitalist in the Chinese Empire at twenty-five, a promoter in the City of London at twenty-seven. In the years from his Stanford graduation to the Great War, he spent more time in the British Empire than he did in the United States. During and after the war he supervised relief activities in Belgium and in Eastern Europe. Keynes called him the only man to emerge from the Paris Peace Conference with an enhanced reputation.

Both Hoover and Roosevelt came of age when the United States was becoming a world power. Both saw more of that world than most of their American contemporaries. But international experience led them to opposite conclusions. What Hoover saw abroad soured him on foreigners. He took away from Paris an indignant conviction of an impassable gap between his virtuous homeland and the European snake pit. Nearly twenty years passed before he could bring himself to set foot again on the despised continent. He loathed Europe and its nationalist passions and hatreds. "With a vicious rhythm," he said in 1940, "these malign forces seem to drive [European] nations like the Gadarene swine over the precipice of war." The less America had to do with so degenerate a place, the Quaker Hoover felt, the better.

The patrician Roosevelt was far more at home in the great world. Moreover, his political genealogy instilled in him the conviction that the United States must at last take its rightful place among the powers. In horse breeder's parlance, FDR was by Woodrow Wilson out of Theodore Roosevelt. These two remarkable Presidents taught FDR that the United States was irrevocably a world power and poured substance into his conception of America's historic life-interests.

FDR greatly admired TR, deserted the Democratic party to cast his first presidential vote for him, married his niece, and proudly succeeded in 1913 to the office TR had occupied fifteen years earlier, Assistant Secretary of the Navy. From TR and from that eminent friend of both Roosevelts, Admiral Mahan, young Roosevelt learned the strategic necessities of international relations. He learned how to distinguish between vital and peripheral interests. He learned why the national interest required the mainte-

nance of balances of power in areas that, if controlled by a single power, could threaten the United States. He learned what the defense of vital interests might require in terms of ships and arms and men and production and resources. His experience in Wilson's Navy Department during the First World War consolidated these lessons.

But he also learned new things from Wilson, among them that it was not enough to send young men to die and kill because of the thrill of battle or because of war's morally redemptive qualities or even because of the need to restore the balance of power. The awful sacrifices of modern war demanded nobler objectives. The carnage on the Western Front converted FDR to Wilson's vision of a world beyond war, beyond national interest, beyond balances of power, a world not of secret diplomacy and antagonistic military alliances but of an organized common peace, founded on democracy, self-determination, and the collective restraint of aggression.

Theodore Roosevelt had taught FDR geopolitics. Woodrow Wilson now gave him a larger international purpose in which the principles of power had a strong but secondary role. FDR's two mentors detested each other. But they joined to construct the framework within which FDR, who cherished them both, approached foreign affairs for the rest of his life.

As the Democratic vice presidential candidate in 1920, he roamed the country pleading for the League of Nations. Throughout the twenties he warned against political isolationism and economic protectionism. America would commit a grievous wrong, he said, if it were "to go backwards towards an old Chinese Wall policy of isolationism." Trade wars, he said, were "symptoms of economic insanity." But such sentiments could not overcome the disillusion and disgust with which Americans in the 1920s contemplated world troubles. As President Hoover told the Italian foreign minister in 1931, the deterioration of Europe had led to such "despair . . . on the part of the ordinary American citizen [that] now he just wanted to keep out of the whole business."

Depression intensified the isolationist withdrawal. Against the national mood, the new President brought to the White House in 1933 an international outlook based, I would judge, on four principles.

One was TR's commitment to the preservation of the balance of world power. Another was Wilson's vision of concerted international action to prevent or punish aggression. The third principle argued that lasting peace required the free flow of trade among nations. The fourth was that in a democracy foreign policy must rest on popular consent. In the isolationist climate of the 1930s, this fourth principle compromised and sometimes undermined the first three.

Diplomatic historians are occasionally tempted to overrate the amount of time Presidents spend in thinking about foreign policy. In fact, from Jackson to FDR, domestic affairs have always been, with a few fleeting exceptions—perhaps Polk, McKinley, Wilson—the presidential priority. This was powerfully the case at the start for FDR. Given the collapse of the economy and the anguish of unemployment, given the absence of obvious remedy and the consequent need for social experiment, the surprise is how much time and energy FDR did devote to foreign affairs in these early years.

He gave time to foreign policy because of his acute conviction that Germany and Japan were, or were about to be, on the rampage and that unchecked aggression would ultimately threaten vital interests of the United States. He packed the State Department and embassies abroad with unregenerate Wilsonians. When he appointed Cordell Hull Secretary, he knew what he was getting; his brain trusters, absorbed in problems at hand, had warned him against international folly. But there they were, Wilsonians all: Hull, Norman Davis, Sumner Welles, William Phillips, Francis B. Sayre, Walton Moore, Breckinridge Long, Josephus Daniels, W. E. Dodd, Robert W. Bingham, Claude Bowers, Joseph E. Davies. Isolationists like Raymond Moley did not last long at State.

Roosevelt's early excursions into foreign policy were necessarily intermittent, however, and in his own rather distracting personal style. Economic diplomacy he confided to Hull, except when Hull's free-trade obsessions threatened New Deal recovery programs, as at the London Economic Conference of 1933. He liked, when he found the time, to handle the political side of things himself. He relished meetings with foreign leaders and found himself in advance of most of them in his forebodings about Germany and Japan. He invited his ambassadors, especially his political appointees, to write directly to him, and nearly all took advantage of the invitation.

His diplomatic style had its capricious aspects. FDR understood what admirals and generals were up to, and he understood the voice of prophetic statesmanship. But he never fully appreciated the professional diplomat and looked with some disdain on the career Foreign Service as made up of tea drinkers remote from the realities of American life. His approach to foreign policy, while firmly grounded in geopolitics and soaring easily into the higher idealism, always lacked something at the middle level.

At the heart of Roosevelt's style in foreign affairs was a certain incorrigible amateurism.

At the heart of Roosevelt's style in foreign affairs was a certain incorrigible amateurism. His off-the-cuff improvisations, his airy tendency to throw out half-baked ideas, caused others to underrate his continuity of purpose and used to drive the British especially wild, as minutes scribbled on Foreign Office dispatches make abundantly clear. This amateurism had its good points. It could be a source of boldness and creativity in a field populated by cautious and conventional people. But it also encouraged superficiality and dilettantism.

The national mood, however, remained FDR's greatest problem. Any U.S. contribution to the deterrence of aggression depended on giving the government power to distinguish between aggressors and their victims. He asked Congress for this authority, first in cooperating with League of Nations sanctions in 1933, later in connection with American neutrality statutes. Fearing that aid to one side would eventually involve the nation in war, Congress regularly turned him down. By rejecting policies that would support victims against aggressors, Congress effectively nullified the ability of the United States to throw its weight in the scales against aggressors.

Roosevelt, regarding the New Deal as more vital for the moment than foreign policy and needing the support of isola-tionists for his domestic program, accepted what he could not change in congressional roll calls. But he did hope to change public opinion and began a long labor of popular education with his annual message in January 1936 and its condemnation of "autocratic institutions that beget slavery at home and aggression abroad."

It is evident that I am not persuaded by the school of historians that sees Roosevelt as embarked until 1940 on a mission of appeasement, designed to redress German grievances and lure the Nazi regime into a constructive role in a reordered Europe. The evidence provided by private conversations as well as by public pronouncements is far too consistent and too weighty to permit the theory that Roosevelt had illusions about coexistence with Hitler. Timing and maneuver were essential, and on occasion he tacked back and forth like the small-boat sailor that Gaddis Smith reminds us he was. Thus, before positioning the United States for entry into war, he wanted to make absolutely sure there was no prospect of negotiated peace: hence his interest in 1939–40 in people like James D. Mooney and William Rhodes Davis and hence the Sumner Welles mission. But his basic course seems pretty clear: one way or another to rid the world of Hitler.

Oddly, the revisionists accept geopolitics as an O.K. motive for the Soviet Union but deny it to the United States.

I am even less persuaded by the school that sees Roosevelt as a President who rushed the nation to war because he feared German and Japanese economic competition. America "began to go to war against the Axis in the Western Hemisphere," the revisionist William Appleman Williams tells us, because Germany was invading U.S. markets in Latin America. The Open Door cult recognizes no geopolitical concerns in Washington about German bases in the Western Hemisphere. Oddly, the revisionists accept geopolitics as an O.K. motive for the Soviet Union but deny it to the United States. In their view American foreign policy can never be aimed at strategic security but must forever be driven by the lust of American business for foreign markets.

In the United States, of course, as any student of American history knows, economic growth has been based primarily on the home market, not on foreign markets, and the preferred policy of American capitalists, even after 1920, when the United States became a creditor nation, was protection of the home market, not freedom of trade. Recall Fordney-McCumber and Smoot-Hawley. The preference of American business for high tariffs was equally true in depression. When FDR proposed his reciprocal trade agreements program in 1934, the American business community, instead of welcoming reciprocal trade as a way of penetrating foreign markets, denounced the whole idea. Senator Vandenberg even called the bill "Fascist in its philosophy, Fascist in its objectives." A grand total of two Republicans voted for reciprocal trade in the House, three in the Senate.

The "corporatism" thesis provides a more sophisticated version of the economic interpretation. No doubt we have become a society of large organizations, and no doubt an associational society generates a certain momentum toward coordination. But the idea that exporters, importers, Wall Street, Main Street, trade unionists, and farmers form a consensus on foreign policy and impose that consensus on the national government is hard to sustain.

It is particularly irrelevant to the Roosevelt period. If Roosevelt was the compliant instrument of capitalist expansion, as the Open Door ideologies claim, or of corporate hegemony, as the corporatism thesis implies, why did the leaders of American corporate capitalism oppose him so viciously? Business leaders vied with one another in their hatred of "that man in the White House." The family of J. P. Morgan used to warn visitors against mentioning Roosevelt's name lest fury raise Morgan's blood pressure to the danger point. When Averell Harriman, one of that rare breed, a pro–New Deal businessman, appeared on Wall Street, old friends cut him dead. The theory that Roosevelt pursued a foreign policy dictated by the same corporate crowd that fought him domestically and smeared him personally belongs, it seems to me, in the same library with the historiography of Oliver Stone.

What was at stake, as FDR saw it, was not corporate profits or Latin American markets but the security of the United States and the future of democracy. Basking as we do today in the glow of democratic triumph, we forget how desperate the democratic cause appeared half a century ago. The Great War had apparently proved that democracy could not produce peace; the Great Depression that it could not produce prosperity. By the 1930s contempt for democracy was widespread among elites and masses alike: contempt for parliamentary methods, for government by discussion, for freedoms of expression and opposition, for bourgeois individualism, for pragmatic muddling through. Discipline, order, efficiency, and all-encompassing ideology were the talismans of the day. Communism and fascism had their acute doctrinal differences, but their structural similarities—a single leader, a single party, a single body of infallible dogma, a single mass of obedient followers—meant that each in the end had more in common with the other than with democracy, as Hitler and Stalin acknowledged in August 1939.

The choice in the 1930s seemed bleak: either political democracy with economic chaos or economic planning with political tyranny. Roosevelt's distinctive contribution was to reject this either/or choice. The point of the New Deal was to chart and vindicate a middle way between laissez-faire and totalitarianism. When the biographer Emil Ludwig asked FDR to define his "political motive," Roosevelt replied, "My desire to obviate revolution. . . . I work in a contrary sense to Rome and Moscow."

Accepting renomination in 1936, FDR spoke of people under economic stress in other lands who had sold their heritage of freedom for the illusion of a living. "Only our success," he continued, "can stir their ancient hope. They begin to know that here in America we are waging a great and successful war. It is not alone a war against want and destitution and economic demoralization. It is more than that: it is a war for the survival of democracy. We are fighting to save a great and precious form of government for ourselves and for the world."

Many people around the world thought it a futile fight. Let us not underestimate the readiness by 1940 of Europeans, including leading politicians and intellectuals, to come to terms with a Hitler-dominated Europe. Even some Ameri-

cans thought the downfall of democracy inevitable. As Nazi divisions stormed that spring across Scandinavia, the Low Countries, and France, the fainthearted saw totalitarianism, in the title of a poisonous little book published in the summer by Anne Morrow Lindbergh, a book that by December 1940 had rushed through seven American printings, as "the wave of the future." While her husband, the famous aviator, predicted Nazi victory and opposed American aid to Britain, the gentle Mrs. Lindbergh lamented "the beautiful things . . . lost in the dying of an age," saw totalitarianism as democracy's predestined successor, a "new, and perhaps even ultimately good, conception of humanity trying to come to birth," discounted the evils of Hitlerism and Stalinism as merely "scum on the wave of the future," and concluded that "the wave of the future is coming and there is no fighting it." For a while Mrs. Lindbergh seemed to be right. Fifty years ago there were only twelve democracies left on the planet.

Roosevelt, however, believed in fighting the wave of the future. He still labored under domestic constraints. The American people were predominantly against Hitler. But they were also, and for a while more strongly, against war. I believe that FDR himself, unlike the hawks of 1941—Stimson, Morgenthau, Hopkins, Ickes, Knox—was in no hurry to enter the European conflict. He remembered what Wilson had told him when he himself had been a young hawk a quarter-century before: that a President could commit no greater mistake than to take a divided country into war. He also no doubt wanted to minimize American casualties and to avoid braking political promises. But probably by the autumn of 1941 FDR had finally come to believe that American participation was necessary if Hitler was to be beaten. An increasing number of Americans were reaching the same conclusion. Pearl Harbor in any case united the country, and Hitler then solved another of FDR's problems by declaring war on the United States.

We accepted war in 1941, as we had done in 1917, in part because, as Theodore Roosevelt had written in 1910, if Britain ever failed to preserve the European balance of power, "the United States would be obliged to get in . . . in order to restore the balance." But restoration of the balance of power did not seem in 1941, any more than it had in

1917, sufficient reason to send young men to kill and die. In 1941 FDR provided higher and nobler aims by resurrecting the Wilsonian vision in the Four Freedoms and the Atlantic Charter and by proceeding, while the war was on, to lay the foundations for the postwar reconstruction of the world along Wilsonian lines.

I assume that it will not be necessary to linger with a theory that had brief currency in the immediate postwar years, the theory that Roosevelt's great failing was his subordination of political to military objectives, shoving long-term considerations aside in the narrow interest of victory. FDR was in fact the most political of politicians, political in every reflex and to his fingertips—and just as political in war as he had been in peace. As a virtuoso politician he perfectly understood that there could be no better cloak for the pursuit of political objectives in wartime than the claim of total absorption in winning the war. He had plenty of political objectives all the same.

The war, he believed, would lead to historic transformations around the world. "Roosevelt," Harriman recalled, "enjoyed thinking aloud on the tremendous changes he saw ahead—the end of colonial empires and the rise of newly independent nations across the sweep of Africa and Asia." FDR told Churchill, "A new period has opened in the world's history, and you will have to adjust yourself to it." He tried to persuade the British to leave India and to stop the French from returning to Indochina, and he pressed the idea of UN trusteeships as the means of dismantling empires and preparing colonies for independence.

Soviet Russia, he saw, would emerge as a major power. FDR has suffered much criticism in supposedly thinking he could charm Stalin into postwar collaboration. Perhaps FDR was not so naive after all in concentrating on Stalin. The Soviet dictator was hardly the helpless prisoner of Marxist-Leninist ideology. He saw himself not as a disciple of Marx and Lenin but as their fellow prophet. Only Stalin had the power to rewrite the Soviet approach to world affairs; after all, he had already rewritten Soviet ideology and Soviet history. FDR was surely right in seeing Stalin as the only lever capable of overturning the Leninist doctrine of irrevocable hostility between capitalism and communism. As Walter Lippmann once observed, Roos-

U.S. Army

**The biggest of the three smiles confidently between
his allies at the Teheran Conference, 1943.**

evelt was too cynical to think he could charm Stalin. "He distrusted everybody. What he thought he could do was to outwit Stalin, which is quite a different thing."

Roosevelt failed to save Eastern Europe from communism, but that could not have been achieved by diplomatic methods alone. With the Red Army in control of Eastern Europe and a war still to be won against Japan, there was not much the West could do to prevent Stalin's working his will in countries adjacent to the Soviet Union. But Roosevelt at Yalta persuaded Stalin to sign American-drafted Declarations on Liberated Europe and on Poland—declarations that laid down standards by which the world subsequently measured Stalin's behavior in Eastern Europe and found it wanting. And FDR had prepared a fallback position in case things went wrong: not only tests that, if Stalin failed to meet them,

would justify a change in policy but also a great army, a network of overseas bases, plans for peacetime universal military training, and the Anglo-American monopoly of the atomic bomb.

In the longer run Roosevelt anticipated that time would bring a narrowing of differences between democratic and Communist societies. He once told Sumner Welles that marking American democracy as one hundred and Soviet communism as zero, the American system, as it moved away from laissez-faire, might eventually reach sixty, and the Soviet system, as it moved toward democracy, might eventually reach forty. The theory of convergence provoked much derision in the Cold War years. Perhaps it looks better now.

So perhaps does his idea of making China one of the Four Policemen of the peace. Churchill, with his scorn for "the pigtails," dismissed Roosevelt's insis-

tence on China as the "Great American Illusion." But Roosevelt was not really deluded. As he said at Teheran, he wanted China there "not because he did not realize the weakness of China at present, but he was thinking father into the future." At Malta he told Churchill that it would take "three generations of education and training . . . before China could become a serious factor." Today, two generations later, much rests on involving China in the global web of international institutions.

As for the United States, a great concern in the war years was that the country might revert to isolationism after the war just as it had done a quarter-century before—a vivid memory for FDR's generation. Contemplating Republican gains in the 1942 midterm election, Cordell Hull told Henry Wallace that the country was "going in exactly the same steps it followed in 1918." FDR himself said privately, "Anybody who thinks that isolationism is dead in this country is crazy."

He regarded American membership in a permanent international organization, in Charles Bohlen's words, as "the only device that could keep the United States from slipping back into isolationism." And true to the Wilsonian vision, he saw such an organization even more significantly as the only device that could keep the world from slipping back into war. He proposed the Declaration of the United Nations three weeks after Pearl Harbor, and by 1944 he was grappling with the problem that had defeated Wilson: how to reconcile peace enforcement by an international organization with the American Constitution. For international peace enforcement requires armed force ready to act swiftly on the command of the organization, while the Constitution requires (or, in better days, required) the consent of Congress before American troops can be sent into combat against a sovereign state. Roosevelt probably had confidence that the special agreements provided for in Article 43 of the UN Charter would strike a balance between the UN's need for prompt action and Congress's need to retain its warmaking power and that the great-power veto would further protect American interests.

He moved in other ways to accustom the American people to a larger international role—and at the same time to assure American predominance in the postwar world. By the end of 1944 he had sponsored a series of international conferences designed to plan vital aspects of the future. These conferences, held mostly at American initiative and dominated mostly by American agendas, offered the postwar blueprints for international organization (Dumbarton Oaks), for world finance, trade, and development (Bretton Woods), for food and agriculture (Hot Springs),

for relief and rehabilitation (Washington), for civil aviation (Chicago). In his sweeping and sometimes grandiose asides, FDR envisaged plans for regional development with environmental protection in the Middle East and elsewhere, and his Office of the Coordinator for Inter-American Affairs pioneered economic and technical assistance to developing countries. Upon his death in 1945 FDR left an imaginative and comprehensive framework for American leadership in making a better world—an interesting achievement for a President who was supposed to subordinate political to military goals.

New times bring new perspectives. In the harsh light of the Cold War some of FDR's policies and expectations were condemned as naive or absurd or otherwise misguided. The end of the Cold War may cast those policies and expectations in a somewhat different light.

FDR's purpose was to safeguard the life-interests of the Republic in a world undergoing vast and fundamental transformations.

FDR's purpose, I take it, was to find ways to safeguard the historic life-interests of the Republic—national security at home and a democratic environment abroad—in a world undergoing vast and fundamental transformations. This required policies based on a grasp of the currents of history and directed to the protection of U.S. interests and to the promotion of democracy elsewhere. From the vantage point of 1994, FDR met this challenge fairly well.

Take a look at the Atlantic Charter fifty years after. Is not the world therein outlined by Roosevelt and Churchill at last coming to pass? Consider the goals

of August 1941—"the right of all peoples to choose the form of government under which they will live," equal access "to the trade and to the raw materials of the world," "improved labor standards, economic advancement and social security," assurance that all "may live their lives in freedom from fear and want," relief from "the crushing burden of armaments," establishment of a community of nations. Is this not the agenda on which most nations today are at last agreed?

Does not most of the world now aspire to FDR's Four Freedoms? Has not what used to be the Soviet Union carried its movement toward the West even more rapidly than FDR dared contemplate? Has not China emerged as the "serious factor" FDR predicted? Did not the Yalta accords call for precisely the democratic freedoms to which Eastern Europe aspires today? Has not the UN, at last liberated by the end of the Cold War to pursue the goals of the founders, achieved new salience as the world's best hope for peace and cooperation?

Consider the world of 1994. It is manifestly not Adolf Hitler's world. The thousand-year Reich turned out to have a brief and bloody run of a dozen years. It is manifestly not Joseph Stalin's world. That world disintegrated before our eyes, rather like the Deacon's one-hoss shay. Nor is it Winston Churchill's world. Empire and its glories have long since vanished into the past.

The world we live in today is Franklin Roosevelt's world. Of the figures who, for good or for evil, bestrode the narrow world half a century ago, he would be the least surprised by the shape of things at the end of the century. Far more than the rest, he possessed what William James called a "sense of futurity." For all his manifold foibles, flaws, follies, and there was a sufficiency of all of those, FDR deserves supreme credit as the twentieth-century statesman who saw most deeply into the grand movements of history.

From the Cold War to the 1990s

Throughout World War II one of President Roosevelt's fondest hopes was to convince Soviet dictator Joseph Stalin that the United States and Great Britain could continue the Grand Alliance when the fighting ended. Although he actively promoted the United Nations, Roosevelt believed that in the final analysis only a great power condominium could guarantee lasting peace. His hope was never realized. Even before his death in April 1945 relations became strained and there is good reason to believe that Roosevelt himself would have grown "tougher" toward the Soviet Union had he lived. What would become known as the cold war already was under way.

Many Americans had little interest in foreign affairs when the fighting ended. They had been through a grueling depression, then a global war, and now they wanted to enjoy what they regarded as the good life. A popular dream was to own one's own home, preferably away from crowded city streets. "The Buy of the Century" tells the story of Levittown, where mass production techniques made housing available to those who might otherwise not have been able to realize their dream.

Despite having emerged virtually unscathed from the war as the richest nation in the world, the United States was beset with unrest in the years following. The cold war came to permeate public consciousness, as friction with the Soviet Union seemed to develop everywhere. What had been a wartime ally, then an adversary, now came to be seen as a direct threat to this nation's very existence. Two developments in 1949 were especially frightening: China "fell" to Communism and the Soviet Union exploded its first atomic device.

At war's end Russia had occupied the northern part of Korea and the United States the southern portion. This arrangement was supposed to be temporary, pending establishment of an independent government. The cold war resulted instead in two hostile regimes, each claiming the right to unify Korea under its own auspices. On June 24, 1950, North Korean forces crashed across the border and sent South Korean troops reeling in retreat. President Harry S. Truman committed American forces to the con-

flict, then enlisted the cooperation of the United Nations. Only five years after having slain the dragons of Nazism and Japanese militarism, this nation again found itself at war.

Neither American leaders nor the public perceived the Korean War as a civil war. Instead they believed it to be an operation masterminded by Moscow that, if not defeated, would lead to further aggression elsewhere. Comparisons were made with the failure to stop Hitler during the 1930s. "The Forgotten War" analyzes the Korean conflict and shows its enormous repercussions.

The 1950s have been described as a decade of conformity. What became known as "McCarthyism" was partly responsible, as irresponsible charges of "Communist" were hurled at those who dissented from orthodox views on politics, economics, or foreign policy. But beneath the surface of blandness during the Eisenhower years, a number of individuals were unwilling to accept the status quo. "Discovering Sex" describes how several men and women began questioning conventional beliefs about sex and gender. "Trumpet of Conscience: A Portrait of Martin Luther King Jr." traces the life of Reverend Martin Luther King Jr., a man who burst into public view with his leadership of the Montgomery boycotts of 1955 and who devoted the rest of his short life to eliminating racial injustice.

The 1960s began not much differently from preceding years. For all his dash and charm, President John F. Kennedy held fairly conventional views about most matters, and his administration dealt cautiously with controversial issues. Discontent over continued racial oppression, over what many young people regarded as excessive materialism and, above all, over the destructive Vietnam War spilled beyond the boundaries of conventional politics into protest marches and violent confrontations. "Lessons from a Lost War" analyzes the divisive conflict of the Vietnam War.

By the late 1960s the nation was in turmoil, and some feared it might be torn apart. Many radical groups advocated violence to destroy what they called the "establishment," and law enforcement officials often responded

with violence of their own. Attempts to practice politics as usual were doomed. "Chicago '68: The Democrats' Judgment Days" uses the Democratic Convention that year to illustrate the clash of irreconcilable forces.

The ferment of the 1960s petered out during the next decade. Observers disagreed as to the causes: simple weariness, the worsening of economic conditions, and the aging of a "special" generation of young people, were a few of the answers offered. The presidential election of 1972 marked a watershed. Richard M. Nixon, who advocated all the traditional values, swamped Democratic candidate George McGovern, who was perceived as a radical candidate. "Nixon: An Important but Not a Great President" evaluates this intelligent, driven man. "How the Seventies Changed America" evaluates the decade.

The year 1983 marked the beginning of seven years of low-inflation economic growth. Yet social issues such as soaring crime rates and sagging educational scores perturbed many Americans. "1983: Falling Wall, Rising Dreams" analyzes the widespread sense that something was wrong with the system and getting worse. Almost everyone, however, celebrated one development. Beginning with what some have called the "revolution of '89," the Soviet empire fell apart until finally the Soviet Union itself dissolved. Although new problems would arise to replace the old, an end to the cold war meant an end to the nuclear arms race that had threatened the planet.

Looking Ahead: Challenge Questions

What lessons can be learned from the Korean War? What lessons can be learned from the Vietnam War?

Discuss the influence of those individuals treated in the article "Discovering Sex."

How did the Reverend Martin Luther King Jr. expect to make racial gains through the strategy of nonviolence?

Analyze Richard M. Nixon's strengths and weaknesses. What prevented him from becoming a "great" president?

Discuss the various ramifications of the end of the cold war. Does this mean an end to problems with the regions that were formerly within the Soviet empire?

The Buy of the Century

The generation that fought World War II also won a housing revolution that promised and delivered a home for $7,900

Alexander O. Boulton

Years later, after the fall of his financial empire, William Levitt remembered with some satisfaction the story of a boy in Levittown, Long Island, who finished his prayers with "and God bless Mommy and Daddy and Mr. Levitt." Levitt may well have belonged in this trinity. When he sold his company in 1968, more Americans lived in suburbs than in cities, making this the first suburban nation in history, and his family was largely responsible for that.

Jim and Virginia Tolley met William Levitt in 1949 after waiting in line with three thousand other ex-GIs and their families to buy houses. Bill Levitt pointed to a plot on a map spread out on a long table and advised the Tolleys to buy the house he would build on that spot. Thanks to a large picture window with an eastern exposure, the Tolley's home, Levitt promised, would have sunshine in the coldest months of winter, and its large overhanging eaves would keep them cool in the summer. The Tolleys, who lived in a three-room apartment in Jackson Heights, bought the unbuilt house.

Their story was shared by the more than 3.5 million Americans who had lacked new housing in 1946, housing that had not been built during the Depression and the war. People kept marrying and having babies, but for almost two decades nobody was building new homes.

In providing affordable housing for thousands of Americans after the war, the Levitts were following a basic American success formula; they were at the right place at the right time. Abraham, the patriarch of the family, had been a real estate lawyer in Brooklyn. His two

Alexander O. Boulton

sons, William and Alfred, briefly attended New York University before they began to buy land and design and build houses on a small scale. Alfred was the architect, learning his trade by trial and error, while William was the salesman and became the more public figure. The Second World War transformed their business. Encouraged by wartime contracts for large-scale housing projects, they followed the same mass-production principles that earlier in the century had been developed to build automobiles and that in wartime made ships and airplanes, tanks and guns.

Levittown, Long Island, thirty miles east of New York City, was the first of their postwar projects. Levittown was not the earliest planned community in the country but it was certainly the biggest, and it is still considered the largest housing project ever assembled by a single builder. Between 1947 and 1951 the Levitts built more than seventeen thousand houses, along with seven village greens and shopping centers, fourteen playgrounds, nine swimming pools, two

bowling alleys, and a town hall, on land that had once been potato farms. In addition, the company sold land for schools at cost and donated sites for churches and fire stations.

Following the course of other American industries, the Levitts expanded both horizontally and vertically. They purchased timberland in California and a lumber mill, they built a nail factory, they established their own construction supply company to avoid middlemen, and they acquired a fleet of cement trucks and grading equipment. Instead of the product moving along a production line, however, the Levitt house stood stationary while men, material, and equipment moved around it. At its peak of efficiency the Levitt organization could complete a house every fifteen minutes. Although these were not prefabricated houses, all the materials, including the preassembled plumbing systems and precut lumber, were delivered to the site ready for construction. Twenty-seven steps were required to build a Levittown house, and each work

From *American Heritage*, July/August 1993, pp. 62-69. © 1993 by Forbes, Inc. Reprinted by permission of *American Heritage* magazine, a division of Forbes, Inc.

crew had its specialized task. One man did nothing but move from house to house bolting washing machines to the floor. William Levitt liked to say his business was the General Motors of the housing industry. Indeed, the automobile seems to have inspired many of Levitt's practices. He even produced new house models each year, and a few Levittown families would actually buy updated versions, just as they bought Detroit's latest products.

The first style, a four-and-a-half room bungalow with steeply pitched roof, offered five slight variations in the placement of doors and windows. The result, according to a 1947 *Architectural Forum,* was "completely conventional, highly standardized and aptly described in the public's favorite adjective, 'cute.' " A couple of years later the same publication moderated its tone of easy scorn to pronounce the style "a much better-than-average version of that darling of the depression decade—builder's Cape Cod."

Levittown houses were not what the popular 1960s song called "little boxes made of ticky-tacky." They were exceptionally well built, the product of some of the most innovative methods and materials in the industry. Taking a page from Frank Lloyd Wright's Usonian houses, Levittown homes stood on concrete slab foundations (they had no basements), in which copper coils provided radiant heating. The Tolleys were among the first customers for the 1949 ranch-style houses that replaced the earlier Cape Cod design. The ranches featured Thermopane glass picture windows, fireplaces opening into two rooms, and carports instead of garages. In addition, they had built-in closets and bookcases and swinging shelf units that acted as walls to open up or close the space between kitchen, living room, and entry passage. At twenty-five by thirty-two feet the new houses were two feet longer than the earlier models, and they offered as standard features built-in appliances that were only just coming into general use; many houses contained Bendix washing machines and Admiral television sets. The fixed price of $7,990 allowed the Levitts to advertise "the housing buy of the century." It was probably true. Levitt and his sons seemed to be practically giving homes away. Thousands of families bought into new Levittowns in Pennsylvania, New Jersey,

By the time this 1953 advertisement appeared, the classic Levittown Cape had risen in price, but veterans still needed no down payment.

Levittown Historical Society

Illinois, Michigan, and even Paris and Puerto Rico. The techniques that the Levitts initiated have been copied by home builders throughout the country ever since.

Despite its immediate success, from the earliest days Levittown also stood as a metaphor for all the possible failings of postwar America. The architectural critic Lewis Mumford is said to have declared the tract an "instant slum" when he first saw it, and he certainly was aiming at Levittown when he condemned the postwar American suburb for its "multitude of uniform, unidentifiable houses, lined up inflexibly, at uniform distances, on uniform roads, in a treeless communal waste, inhabited by people of the same class, the same income, the same age group, witnessing the same television

performances, eating the same tasteless pre-fabricated foods, from the same freezers, conforming in every outward and inward respect to the same common mold." Some of the early rules, requiring owners to mow their lawns every week, forbidding fences, or banning the hanging out of laundry on weekends, did indeed speak of the kind of regimentation Mumford snobbishly abhorred.

Today's visitor to the original Long Island Levittown might be surprised by many of those early criticisms. Now almost fifty years old, most of the houses have been so extensively remodeled that it is often difficult to distinguish the basic Cape Cod or ranch inside its Tudor half-timbering or postmodern, classical eclecticism. Greenery and shade trees have enveloped the bare landscape of the 1950s and Japanese sand gardens, Renaissance topiary, and electrically generated brooks and waterfalls decorate many of Levittown's standard sixty-by-one-hundred-foot plots. The place now seems not the model of mass conformity but a monument to American individualism.

Probably Levittown never was the drab and monotonous place its critics imagined. For many early residents it allowed cultural diversity to flourish. Pre-war inner-city neighborhoods often had ethnic divisions unknown in Levittown. Louis and Marylin Cuviello, who bought a one-bathroom house in 1949 and reared eleven children there, found themselves moving in a wider world than the one they had known in the city. She was a German-American married to an Italian-American, and in their Levittown neighborhood most of the householders were Jewish. During their first years there the Cuviellos took classes in Judaism at the local synagogue, and they often celebrated both Passover and Christmas with their neighbors.

But this American idyll was not for everyone. In 1949, after Gene Burnett, like his fellow veteran Jim Tolley, saw advertisements for Levittown in several New York papers, he drove to Long Island with his fiancee. The Levittown salesman he met refused to give him an application form. "It's not me," the agent said. "The builders have not at this time decided to sell to Negroes." This pattern of racial exclusion was set in 1947, when rental contracts prohibited "the premises to be used or occupied by any person other than members of the Caucasian race." In 1992 Gene Burnett, now a retired sergeant in the Suffolk County, Long Island, Police Department, told a reporter, "I'll never forget the ride back to East Harlem."

There were other such episodes. Bill Cotter, a black auto mechanic, and his family sublet a house in Levittown in 1953. When his sublet expired, he was informed that he would not be allowed either to rent or to own a house in Levittown. Despite the protests of friendly neighbors, who launched a petition drive in their behalf, Cotter, his wife, and their five children were forced to vacate. These racial policies persisted. As late as the 1980s real estate agents in the area assured white home buyers that they did not sell to blacks, and in 1990 the census revealed that .03 percent of Levittown's population—127 out of more than 400,000—was African-American.

Levittown has been both celebrated and denounced as the fruit of American laissez-faire capitalism. In fact, it may more accurately be described as the successful result of an alliance between government and private enterprise. Levittown and the rise of American suburbia in general could not have happened without attractive loan packages for home buyers guaranteed by the FHA and the VA. Tax breaks, such as the deductibility of mortgages, encouraged suburbanites, who were also helped by a burst of federally funded highway construction. For almost half a century after World War II, the government has played a major role in helping consumers obtain the products of industry—washing machines, television sets, cars, and, especially, houses. For most of us it's been a great ride.

For Bill Levitt it's been a roller coaster. Things started to go sour for him after the sale of his company to ITT in 1968. He received about fifty million dollars in ITT stock and launched a spending spree that did not stop until the courts finally stepped in. Levitt's agreement with ITT prohibited him from building projects in the United States for ten years, so he turned elsewhere: housing in Nigeria and Venezuela, oil drilling in Israel, and housing and irrigation projects in Iran—just before the fall of the shah. He invested in rotary engines, recording companies, and pharmacies. Most of the projects failed. Meanwhile, the ITT stock that was his major capital asset plummeted from $104 to $12 a share in the first four years.

Levitt re-entered the housing market in the United States in 1978 projects in Orlando and Tampa, Florida. Construction and sales moved quickly at first but soon slowed as contractors began to sue for payment. More than two thousand people, some of them original Levittowners who were now ready to retire, paid deposits for houses in the Florida Levittowns that were never built. Levitt, it was later discovered, had been using the funds from his Florida projects to support his expensive habits. Along the way he had removed more than ten million dollars from a charitable foundation that his family had established. These legal and financial problems have made Bill Levitt a virtual hermit, and today he lives in seclusion not far from the Long Island Levittown that bears his name.

Levittown residents have mixed feeling about their unique heritage. Periodically some of them have attempted to redraw the boundaries of the towns so they could have more elegant addresses. More recently, proud members of the Levittown Historical Society have worked to encourage a new appreciation for their community. They are pushing to establish historic landmark districts while they try to preserve the few houses that have remained relatively unchanged over the years. They are also casting a wide net among their neighbors and former neighbors to gather artifacts and memorabilia for a museum. Recently the Smithsonian Institution announced that it was looking for an original Levittown house to add to its American domestic-life collection. Some African-American groups continue to question the virtue of memorializing a policy of exclusion, but the history-minded residents are pressing ahead, and Eddie Bortell, the Historical Society's vice president, is optimistic. If the work of the historical society has helped bring attention to some of these painful questions, he says, then that in itself is a reward for its efforts.

THE FORGOTTEN WAR

Still unsung after 40 years, the Korean conflict left an enormous legacy that has changed the very course of the world

It was both postscript to the last war and prologue to the next, a brutal struggle that began on a monsoon-drenched morning 40 years ago this week and raged up and down a remote, ravaged Asian peninsula for 37 months. It was the cold war suddenly turned hot, Communism's boldest "war of national liberation" and the United Nations' first—and probably last—"police action." When it finally ended in stalemate, at a bleak "truce village" in a no man's land called Panmunjom, it had involved 22 nations, claimed 5 million lives and set off political and economic tremors that reverberate still.

Yet four decades after it began, the Korean War remains as hazy in America's memory as the mist-shrouded mountains that were its killing fields. Where, for example, is a memorial worthy of those who fell at Pork Chop Hill and Heartbreak Ridge, or during the retreat from the Chosin Reservoir? What colleges tutor the young about "The Korean War: Its Origins and Objectives"? And why is the war's best-known work of art a television sitcom called "M*A*S*H," which was really an allegory about Vietnam?

Slowly, those who have inherited this forgotten war are beginning to realize the size of its lien on posterity. It encouraged seven American Presidents to draw lines against Communist subversion from Vietnam to El Salvador, drew an Atlantic America irreversibly into Asia and helped catapult what had been a declining military establishment to the forefront of American foreign policy. If the Berlin Wall was the symbol of the division of Europe, the border between the two Koreas is its Asian counterpart. When they met two weeks ago in San Francisco, Mikhail Gorbachev and South Korean President Roh Tae Woo may have started a thaw that could someday eliminate the most visible remaining vestige of the cold war: The division of Korea.

Moreover, in this spring of reconciliation in Asia, both Beijing and Moscow are taking new steps toward diplomatic rapprochement with Seoul, a government that Communism's twin giants had tried to destroy in 1950 and in the 40 years since have ignored, denounced and sought to subvert. Even the relentless enmity between the U.S. and Kim Il Sung's Stalinist regime has begun to soften. American diplomats and Pyongyang's representatives have quietly been holding a series of getting-to-know-you meetings that last month resulted in the North Koreans' turning over the remains of five American servicemen who had died in Pyongyang's nightmarish prison camps. "For the first time in four decades," exults South Korea's Lee Hongku, a special assistant to Roh and a former Minister of Unification, "we can look forward with great expectations."

That it has taken almost four decades for such expectations to materialize is a measure of the epic changes wrought by the Korean conflict. The struggle not only saved the southern half of the Korean peninsula from Communist despotism (though not from anti-Communist authoritarianism), but set it on the road toward prosperity and a still precarious democracy. It also helped transform Japan into a technological superpower that is America's most formidable economic competitor. It so chilled relations between the U.S. and the new People's Republic of China that Chinese children born during the war are instantly recognized by such given names as "Resist America" and "Aid Korea."

The war's effects were felt far from its battlefields. Worried that Korea was only a diversion in advance of a Soviet attack on Berlin, the Truman administration sent four U.S. divisions to Europe to bolster the two already on occupation duty and began pressing to transform occupied West Germany into a rearmed anti-Communist bastion.

A model war

At the same time, Korea wrenched a Eurocentric America's attention back to the Pacific, where some of it has remained, uneasily, ever since. After World War II, the U.S. had begun losing interest in the Orient; the Truman administration was even creeping toward a modus vivendi with "Red China." "Asia is outside the reach of the military power, the economic control, and the ideological influence of the Western World," columnist Walter Lippmann wrote.

While there now is evidence that the conflict opened a rift that later became a chasm between China and the Soviet

From *U.S. News & World Report*, June 25, 1990, pp. 30-33, 36. © 1990 by U.S. News & World Report. Reprinted by permission.

Union, at the time it reinforced the image of monolithic Communism on the march, a perception that dogged American policymakers for years. It raised a protective U.S. umbrella over Taiwan, enabling it to survive as an unloved but thriving diplomatic orphan, and it focused America's attention on other likely targets of Communist aggression. One stood out: French Indochina.

More than any other event, the Korean War transformed the cold war from a political and ideological struggle into a military one. In so doing, it was a catalyst not only for the postwar policy of containment, but also for the creation of what Dwight D. Eisenhower dubbed "the military-industrial complex." Defense outlays soared from a planned $14 billion in fiscal 1951 to $54 billion in fiscal 1953.

Even more striking was the militarization of America's foreign-aid program: In fiscal 1950, military aid accounted for only 12 percent of America's aid budget; by 1960, the military's share of foreign aid was 41 percent. In *The Making of America's Soviet Policy*, Ernest R. May put it this way: " ... before mid-1950, containment seemed to involve primarily an effort to create economic, social and political conditions assumed to be inhospitable to Communism, whereas from mid-1950 on, the policy seemed primarily one of preserving military frontiers behind which conditions unsuited to subversion could gradually evolve." With mixed results, later administrations tried to do in South Vietnam, Iran, El Salvador, the Philippines and elsewhere what Truman had done in South Korea—to hold off the Communists and hope democracy could develop.

At the same time, as historian Arthur M. Schlesinger has argued, in dispatching troops to Korea without first asking Congress to declare war, Truman continued to expand the powers of the Presidency and set the White House on a collision course with Congress and with critics of administration policies. An internal White House paper from 1951 eerily presaged Vietnam and later Oliver North's Iran-Contra defense. "The circumstances of the present crisis," the paper said, "make any debate over prerogatives and power essentially sterile, if not dangerous to the success of our foreign policy."

Korea also introduced a fundamental contradiction that was to plague American foreign policy throughout the cold war. On one hand, played out as it was against a backdrop of virulent anti-Communism at home, the war encouraged a succession of American politicians to vow to defeat Communist aggression wherever it appeared. On Sept. 30, 1950, three months after the North Korean attack, Truman enshrined containment as policy by sign-

Washington's missing memorial

Let us now praise forgotten men...

And some there be, which have no memorial; Who are perished, as though they had never been.
—Ecclesiasticus

About 1.5 million Americans served in Korea, 54,000 died there and more than 100,000 were wounded or reported missing. They are the forgotten warriors, neglected by a nation that only eight years before showered their brothers with ticker tape after World War II.

Not until 1986 did Congress decree that the soldiers of Korea should have a monument in Washington. The Korean War Memorial will sit on the Mall just across the Reflecting Pool from the Vietnam Veterans' Memorial. But it will not have the cathartic healing power of the black granite wall across the way. Vietnam's veterans were caught in the cross fire over whether their war was just, and their wall corrects that injustice. Korea's veterans have simply been ignored. Forty years later, the new memorial will honor them. But can it force us to remember them?

Words born in action—a Korean War glossary

Bug-out: Unauthorized retreat.

Chicoms: Chinese Communists.

Chopper: Helicopter.

Gook: Derisive slang for Koreans; a corruption of the Korean *han'guk saram*, which means "Korean."

Hooch: Small house or hut.

MASH: Mobile Army Surgical Hospital.

NAPALM: (Naphthene plus Palmitate) Jellied-gasoline bombs.

R and R: Rest and Recreation. Time away from the front; in-country for GI's, Tokyo for officers.

ROK's: Republic of Korea troops.

KATUSA's: Korean soldiers attached to U.S. Army units.

ing National Security Council paper 68 which, in language foreshadowing John Kennedy's inaugural address a decade later, declared that given the rise of Soviet power, "the nation must be determined, at whatever cost or sacrifice," to defend democracy "at home and abroad." But defending the autocratic Syngman Rhee could hardly be considered serving the cause of democracy.

Fire on the right

On another level, though, the stalemate in Korea was a reminder that in the Atomic Age (the U.S.S.R. announced its first successful nuclear test less than three months before the war began), there were compelling reasons not to let wars escalate. This new concept of "limited war," however, did not suit Gen. Douglas MacArthur, who pushed to end the war by carrying it to China with nuclear weapons. In March, 1951, an increasingly emotional MacArthur openly challenged Truman's concept of limited war in a letter to Representative Joseph Martin, a leading member of the China lobby: "Here in Asia is where the Communist conspirators have elected to make their play for global conquest," he wrote. "If we lose the war to Communism in Asia the fall of Europe is inevitable ... We must win. There is no substitute for victory."

There also was no substitute for obeying orders. Truman finally fired MacAr-

thur for insubordination, but that did not end the debate about how vigorously Communism should be "rolled back." The ouster of the outspoken anti-Communist general encouraged demagogues like Wisconsin's Senator Joseph McCarthy to bluster that Communist sympathizers were at work in the highest ranks of the Truman administration. Thirteen years later, after the fiasco at the Bay of Pigs and with the U.S. heading into another "limited war" in Asia, Senator Barry Goldwater echoed MacArthur, telling the 1964 Republican convention that "extremism in the defense of liberty is no vice." The man who introduced Goldwater, Ronald Reagan, finally carried the conservative torch into the White House.

By demonstrating that it was easier for the U.S. to contain naked aggression than subversion, that wars of national liberation were best fought with stealth, obfuscation and patience, Korea also hastened the onset of a new kind of cold warfare. The frustrating struggle divided Americans and as the foreign policy consensus eroded, a succession of Presidents tried to cloak some of their efforts to contain Communism—in Guatemala, Iran, Cuba and Nicaragua, for example—in secrecy.

Given this far-reaching legacy, what is most surprising about the Korean War is that it has been so completely forgotten. Almost as many Americans fell in Korea (54,000) as would die in Vietnam a generation later (58,000), but the Korean

Key events in the Korean War

1950

Jan. 12 Acheson excludes South Korea from U.S. defense perimeter in Asia
June 25 North Korea attacks
June 28 Seoul is overrun
July 1 U.S. troops arrive in Pusan, move north to engage the enemy
July–August The "bugout": U.S. forces retreat steadily southward
Sept. 10 North Korean offensive is halted at the "Pusan perimeter"
Sept. 15 Inchon landing begins
Sept. 26–29 Seoul recaptured, Syngman Rhee's government returns
Oct. 8 Advancing U.S. forces push across the 38th parallel
Oct. 15 Truman and MacArthur meet at Wake Island
Oct. 19 Chinese troops cross Yalu River into North Korea
Nov. 24–27 Chinese attack Chosin, U.S. forces start retreat to South Korea

1951

Jan. 15 Chinese resistance melts as new S. Korean–U.S. offensive begins
April 11 Truman fires MacArthur
Late May S. Korean–U.S. forces near Pyongyang, Kim Il Sung's capital. Large numbers of Chinese surrender
July 10 Truce talks begin at Kaesong, soon move to Panmunjom

1952

May–October Stalemate, but heavy fighting continues along 38th parallel
Oct. 24 Eisenhower's "I shall go to Korea" speech boosts peace hopes

1953

July 27 Truce signed, fighting stops
Aug. 5 POW exchanges begin

War never gained the same hammerlock on the nation's emotions. To those who had won unconditional surrenders from Germany and Japan, battling to a draw with North Korea and China was anything but memorable. "Korea," says retired U.S. Army Col. David Hackworth, who fought both there and in Vietnam, "was like the 49ers tying Stanford two weeks after winning the Super Bowl."

At first, though, the Americans were fortunate to fight the North Koreans to a tie, finally halting the invasion outside the port city of Pusan. "We sent in troops who'd had almost no training," recalls former Secretary of State Dean Rusk, then assistant secretary for Far Eastern affairs. "Had the North Koreans kept coming," says Rusk, "they could have overrun the entire peninsula."

MacArthur rebounded brilliantly, staging an amphibious landing at Inchon, just west of Seoul, and sending the North Koreans reeling back across the 38th parallel. Triumphant, MacArthur flew off to Wake Island in the mid-Pacific to meet with Truman.

In a hut near the airfield runway, the imperious five-star general assured the homespun former World War I artillery captain that the war would be over by Christmas. If the Chinese were foolish enough to intervene, MacArthur arrogantly predicted, the U.S. Air Force would embark on "the greatest slaughter in military history." Instead, the Chinese routed the United Nations forces so completely that a despairing MacArthur told Washington that unless the U.S. attacked China, it would risk an Asian Dunkirk. "In one cable," Rusk recalls, "he talked about the loss of morale of his troops, when he was talking about his own morale. He was clearly in a state of depression."

Without a word

But led by Lt. Gen. Matthew B. Ridgway, 56, a paratroop hero, the U.S. Eighth Army began moving northward again, inflicting huge casualties on the overextended Chinese. There was little sentiment for crossing the 38th parallel a second time, however. Truce negotiations began on July 10, 1951, but went nowhere fast. On one occasion, both delegations sat staring at each other for 2 hours and 11 minutes without uttering a word. The seesaw war of trenches and numbered hills finally came to a silent, coldly formal conclusion on the morning of July 27, 1953, almost exactly where it had begun three years before.

For all its ups and downs, Korea engaged only a small fraction of the nation. Truman extended the draft, raised taxes and imposed wage-and-price controls, but compared with World War II five years before, the domestic sacrifices were modest. Compared to Vietnam, which was nightly theater in living color, Korea was a map in the morning paper and the black-and-white photographs of David Douglas Duncan and others. As Ohio's Senator John Glenn, who as a Marine combat pilot in Korea shot down three MiG's, explains: "Korea didn't come into every American life the way Vietnam did because you didn't have blood flowing out of your TV set every night."

There is another reason why Korea never had the same mesmerizing effect as Vietnam: It did not set off what in essence was a domestic civil war. Perhaps that is because the generation that fought in Korea, the generation of Levittown and William H. Whyte, Jr.'s *The Organization Man*, had grown up amid a crusade against foreign evils—not, as its rebellious children did, during a civil-rights crusade against evils at home.

Forty years later, as the scars of Vietnam heal and the cold war recedes, there is a discernible connection between the sacrifices at Pork Chop Hill and the birth of fragile democracies in Prague, Warsaw, Budapest and in Seoul itself. Containment worked. America and its allies paid a heavy price to stop Communist aggression in Korea. But given the final outcome, history no doubt will conclude it was a price worth paying.

Discovering Sex

The Story of the Men and Women Who in the 1950s Helped Create the Sexual Landscape We Inhabit Today

David Halberstam

David Halberstam's books include The Best and the Brightest, The Powers That Be, *and* The Reckoning. *This article is excerpted from* The Fifties, *published by Villard Books, a division of Random House.*

When the decade of the fifties began, sex was still something of an illicit subject in America. Nor had there been any serious modernization of the technology of birth control in more than forty years. Never mind that an event as transcending as World War II had profoundly changed people's attitudes on many subjects, including a far greater candor about things sexual among younger adults; these changes were nowhere noticeable in American mass culture. But in the decade ahead ordinary Americans were about to become infinitely more open and sophisticated about their sexual habits and practices. Even as the 1950s progressed, a team of brilliant scientists was speeding forward on its way to discover a simple birth-control device that its developers hoped could be taken orally each day—a kind of pill to control pregnancy. At the same time, by the middle of the decade there were the first signs of new social and political attitudes among American women that would surface in the next decade as the women's movement. In short, a revolution was beginning.

"GOD, WHAT A GAP!"

Alfred Kinsey was both fascinated and troubled by the vast difference between American sexual behavior the society wanted to believe existed and American sexual practices as they actually did ex-

ist. For example, at least 80 percent of successful businessmen, his interviews showed, had had extramarital affairs. "God," he noted, "what a gap between social front and reality!" And he spent the latter part of his career tearing away the facade that Americans used to hide their sexual selves.

Kinsey was no bohemian. He lived in the Midwest, he married the first woman he ever dated, and he stayed married to her for his entire life. Because he was an entomologist and loved to collect bugs, he and his bride went camping on their honeymoon. In his classes at the University of Indiana he always sported a bow tie and a crew cut. He drove the same old Buick for most of his lifetime and was immensely proud of the fact that he had more than a hundred thousand miles on it. On Sundays he and his wife invited faculty and graduate-student friends to their home to listen to records of classical music. They took these evenings very seriously; Kinsey was immensely proud of his record collection. When the wife of one faculty member suggested that they play some boogie-woogie, the couple was never invited back.

Kinsey's house was the only thing he had not paid hard cash for. He bought it with a small down payment and took on a mortgage of thirty-five hundred dollars. He was extremely careful about money and almost everything else. He once told a colleague, Wardell Pomeroy, to drive back from New York at thirty-five miles per hour with some large models showing the reproductive process: "Anything faster than that is not safe for such a heavy load." The mother superior, Pomeroy called him.

Kinsey did not smoke, and he rarely drank. Relatively late in his career he decided to smoke since it would make him more like the men he was interview-

ing and help put them at their ease. Try as he might, he never quite got it right, and his assistants finally suggested that the prop was hurting rather than helping. With drinking it was the same. After his death Pomeroy wrote, "To see him bringing in a tray of sweet liqueurs before dinner was a wry and happy reminder that Alfred Charles Kinsey, the genius, the world figure, was a simple and unsophisticated man in the true sense of the word."

His greatest passion was his work. He approached it with an intensity that was rooted in the Calvinist zeal of his forefathers. He generally worked every day of the year except Christmas Day. He had always been, his biographer Pomeroy shrewdly noted, a *collector.* As a boy he collected stamps, but it was the only collection he ever made that was not designed to be useful. Sickly as a child from rheumatic fever, he had not been able to play; instead he became a student of nature. He wrote his first book in his teens, a small monograph entitled "What Do Birds Do When It Rains?" By the time he was in college at Bowdoin, he had come to love collecting plants and animals.

As a graduate student at Harvard he won a fellowship that allowed him to travel around the country. "No other occupation in the world could give me the pleasure that this job of bug-hunting is giving," he wrote, and he never failed to see the beauty in plants and in animals. Earle March, a San Francisco gynecologist, once spoke of Kinsey's rare ability to "look through the ugliness to something lovely beyond." March added, "I often thought about him as an athlete of the spirit." During the early forties he published *Edible Wild Plants of North America,* which was voted the most important book of the year by the trustees

From *American Heritage,* May/June 1993, pp. 39-45, 48-52, 54, 56-58. Excerpt from *The Fifties* by David Halberstam. © 1993 by David Halberstam. Reprinted by permission of Villard Books, a division of Random House, Inc.

of the Massachusetts Horticultural Society.

He seemed by this time to be the least likely candidate to become one of the most controversial figures of his generation. He was a highly respected professor of zoology in a good department at Indiana University. Esteemed by his colleagues for his collection of gall wasps, he was also popular with his students, a kind and humane teacher who was generous with his time.

Mrs. Kinsey said, "I hardly see him at night any more since he took up sex."

Then, in 1938, a group of his students came to him and asked questions about marriage. He was touched by their innocence. At first he refrained from answering, fearing he knew too little. Then he went out and read everything he could on the subject and was appalled by the available material—in both quantity and quality. Some of the students petitioned the university to start a course on sexuality and marriage. From the start it was Kinsey's course. He was one of eight faculty members who taught it, and he gave three of the basic lectures. The course was a huge success. It soon became an obsession with him. Clara Kinsey was known on occasion to tell friends. "I hardly see him at night any more since he took up sex."

When he began his studies of human sexuality, one of his oldest friends, Edward Anderson, by then the director of the Missouri Botanical Garden in St. Louis, wrote him: "It was heartwarming to see you settling down into what I suppose will be your real life work. One would never have believed that all sides of you could have found a project big enough to need them all. I was amused to see how the Scotch Presbyterian reformer in you had finally got together with the scientific fanatic with his zeal for masses of neat data in orderly boxes and drawers. The monographer Kinsey, the naturalist Kinsey, and the camp counsellor Kinsey all rolling into one at last and going full steam ahead. Well, I am glad to have a seat for the performance. It's great to have it done, and great to know that you are doing it."

He began by taking the sexual histories of his students. He conducted the interviews in his tiny office, where he locked the door and sent his assistant elsewhere. The enrollment for the class grew every year; before long four hundred students were signing up for it. But his heart was in the research. Soon he was not only taking the sexual histories of his students but traveling out of town on weekends to find additional subjects. As the project took an increasing amount of his time, there was an inevitable conservative reaction against him in Indiana.

In 1940 Herman Wells, the president of Indiana University, who was largely sympathetic to Kinsey and his work, called him in and, citing complaints from local ministers, told him that he would have to make a choice: He could either teach the course or take his histories, but he could not do both. Wells assumed that Kinsey would give up the case histories. Kinsey resigned from the course. Those who thought he would do otherwise, he noted, "do not know me." From then on he devoted himself exclusively to his research.

The study of American sexual habits was a delicate business. Kinsey wanted a certain bland neutrality to his researchers. Though he was a generous, abidingly tolerant man, he did not hire Jews or blacks or those with names that were not distinctly Anglo-Saxon. He knew the prejudices of the time and wanted no distractions from the already sensitive job that his interviewers faced.

During the forties, while much of the rest of the country was going off to war, Alfred Kinsey and a handful of assistants set off to interview as many men and women as they could on their sexual habits. At first they had limited resources; Kinsey used part of his own small salary to hire others.

In 1941 he got his first grant from a foundation, for sixteen hundred dollars; in 1943 he received his first grant from the Medical Sciences Division of the Rockefeller Foundation, a gift of twenty-three thousand dollars; by 1947 that figure was forty thousand dollars. The foundation thereby became the principal financial backer of his studies. By 1947 he was preparing to publish the first book of his results—a simple report on the human animal studied in one of its highest-priority biologic acts. His conclusions do not seem particularly startling today: that healthy sex led to a healthy marriage; that there was more extramarital sex on the part of both men and women than they wanted to admit; that petting and premarital sex tended to produce better marriages; that masturbation did not cause mental problems, as superstition held; that there was more homosexuality than people wanted to admit.

President Wells had made a few minor requests of him: He asked Kinsey not to publish during the sixty-one days that the Indiana legislature was in session, and he asked him to use a medical publisher in order to minimize sensationalism. Kinsey chose W. B. Saunders, an old-line firm in Philadelphia. The original printing was slated for ten thousand but as prepublication interest grew, Saunders increased it to twenty-five thousand. The book cost $6.50, had 804 pages, and weighed three pounds. Kinsey had received no advance against royalties, and whatever money he made, he turned back to his own think tank, which by then was known as the Institute for Sex Research of Indiana University.

Though he continued to sign himself on letters "Alfred Kinsey, professor of zoology," his days as a mere professor were behind him. His name from then on was a household word; everyone knew of him as the sex doctor. Within ten days of the book's release the publisher had to order a sixth printing, making 185,000 copies in print, a remarkable number for so scholarly a piece of work. To the astonishment of everyone, particularly Kinsey, the book roared up the bestseller lists, a fact somewhat embarrassing to *The New York Times,* which at first neither accepted advertising for Kinsey's book nor reviewed it. The early critical response was good. The first reviews saw his samples adequate, his scientific judgments modest, his tone serious. Polls taken of ordinary Americans showed that not only did they agree with his evidence but they believed such studies were helpful.

Then his critics weighed in. They furiously disagreed with almost everything: his figures on premarital sex, his figures on extramarital sex, his figures on homosexuality, and above all, his failure to condemn what he had found. Not only had he angered the traditional conservative bastions of social mores—the Protestant churches on the right, and the Catholic Church—but to his surprise he had enraged the most powerful voices in the liberal Protestant clergy as well. Henry Pitney Van Dusen, the head of Union Theological Seminary, and Reinhold Niebuhr attacked. Harry Emerson Fosdick, the head of Riverside Church and the brother of the head of the Rockefeller Foundation, complained that the advertising for the book was not sufficiently sedate. Harold Dodds, president of Princeton, said, "Perhaps the undergraduate newspaper that likened the report to the work of small boys writing dirty words on fences touched a more profound scientific truth than is revealed in the surfeit of rather trivial graphs with which the reports are loaded." By trying to study our sexual patterns, Kinsey was accused of trying to lower our moral standards.

Kinsey was at first stunned, then angered, but never embittered. He was appalled by the failure of other scientists and doctors to come to his defense, but what surprised him most was the absence of scientific standards in most of the assaults. His critics were, he noted, merely "exposing their emotional (not their scientific) selves in their attacks."

The attacks wounded Kinsey, yet he refused to show it in public. Besides, there was a second book to finish. His biggest fear was that he might lose his key source of support, the Rockefeller Foundation. Unfortunately Henry Pitney Van Dusen was not just the head of Union Theological; he was also a member of the Rockefeller Foundation board.

Kinsey well knew that his second book was even more explosive than the first.

At first the foundation stood firm. Alan Gregg, who was in effect Kinsey's man at the foundation, congratulated Kinsey for handling himself so well in the face of such venomous criticism. But soon Gregg's tone began to change. He started suggesting that Kinsey show more statistical evidence in the next volume, and before long he was warning that it might be harder than he had expected to sustain the funding.

The trouble, Kinsey learned, was the new head of the Rockefeller Foundation, Dean Rusk. Rusk had come over after serving as the assistant secretary of state for Far Eastern affairs. Cautious to a fault, wary of the power of conservatives in Congress, he was not eager to take serious political risks on behalf of something that must have seemed as periph-

eral to him as sex research. B. Carroll Reece, a conservative Republican from Tennessee, was threatening to investigate the foundation, and one of the reasons was the Kinsey report. Kinsey sensed that Rusk was distancing himself from the institute.

The second book, *Sexual Behavior in the Human Female,* was published in the fall of 1953. Kinsey was well aware that it was even more explosive than the first; he was, after all, discussing wives, mothers, and daughters. As a precaution Kinsey invited journalists to come to Bloomington for several days so that he could explain the data to them and thereby help them interpret it.

Like the first book, it was a sensation. Within ten days the publishers were in their sixth printing; it would eventually sell some 250,000 copies. Again the initial reception was essentially positive; some of the magazine reporting was thoughtful. Then the fire storm began. "It is impossible to estimate the damage this book will do to the already deteriorating morals of America," Billy Graham pronounced. The worst thing about the report, Van Dusen said, was not Kinsey's facts, if they were indeed trustworthy, but that they revealed "a prevailing degradation in American morality approximating the worst decadence of the Roman Empire. The most disturbing thing is the absence of spontaneous ethical revulsion from the premises of the study and the inability on the part of the readers to put their fingers on the falsity of its premises. For the presuppositions of the Kinsey Report are strictly animalistic. Again Kinsey was disheartened: "I am still uncertain what the basic reason for the bitter attack on us may be. The attack is evidently much more intense with this publication of the Female. Their arguments become absurd when they attempt to find specific flaws in the book and basically I think they are attacking on general principles."

The new book was the final straw for the Rockefeller Foundation. In November 1953 Kinsey's supporters there made passionate presentations on his behalf and put in a request for eighty thousand dollars. Rusk rejected it. It was a shattering moment. Kinsey wrote a note to Rusk pleading with him to come out to Bloomington to see what they were doing and telling of how well things looked for the future. Later, in another letter to Rusk, he noted, "To have fifteen years of accumulated data in this area fail to

reach publication would constitute an indictment of the Institute, its sponsors, and all others who have contributed time and material resources to the work."

Kinsey redoubled his efforts. If he had been driven before, now there was a manic quality to his work. His friends began to worry about his health. He suffered from insomnia, began to take sleeping pills, and started showing up groggy at work in the morning. Problems with his heart grew more serious. On several occasions he was hospitalized, and by the middle of 1956 he was forced to stay home and rest. In the summer of 1956 he conducted sex interviews number 7984 and 7985. On August 25, 1956, he died at the age of sixty-two.

"THIS IS THE MAGIC AND MYSTERY OF OUR TIME"

There had never been any doubt among those who knew him that Goody Pincus was a genius. Born in 1903, in Woodbine, New Jersey, Pincus was the son of Russian Jewish immigrants who lived in a Jewish farm colony founded by the Baron de Hirsch Fund, a German Jewish philanthropy. Joseph Pincus, Goody's father, ran the local farm, lectured to Jewish farmers all over the East, and for a time was editor of the Yiddish-language newspaper *The Jewish Farmer.* As a boy Goody was fascinated by animals and told his father he wanted to be a farmer when he grew up; his father told him there was no money in farming. The oldest of six children, Goody was always studying or reading and usually seemed pleasantly preoccupied. The Pincus home was filled with intellectual energy and curiosity, and Goody always seemed to be at its center. Evelyn Isaacson, a cousin, remembered a typical evening. John, the youngest of the children, then about six, turned to Goody, then about sixteen, and said, "Goody, I have three questions for you." "What are they, John?" asked the obliging older brother. "One, why are we here? Two, why were we born? And three, there is no God." The family believed Goody a genius; his IQ was said to be 210. He remained fond of animals and eventually majored in biology. He continued his studies at Harvard Graduate School under William Castle, the leader of the first generation of American geneticists. Genetics seemed a perfect vocation for someone with

Pincus's immense talents. The field was just beginning to explode as scientists forged breakthrough after breakthrough.

Goody Pincus's early work involved parthenogenic—that is, fatherless—rabbits. In 1934 he announced that he had achieved in vitro (that is, inside a test tube) fertilization of rabbit eggs. Pincus took great joy in his work and was uncommonly candid about it. That candor might have served him well in other fields, but in genetics it got him into trouble. His work, some contemporaries felt, scared people, creating visions of Frankenstein—*Brave New World* nightmares. The *New York Times* headline ran: RABBITS BORN IN GLASS: HALDANE-HUXLEY FANTASY MADE REAL BY HARVARD BIOLOGISTS. The *Times,* as one writer observed, "pictured Pincus as a sinister character bent on hatching humans in bottles."

But that was nothing compared with an article in *Collier's* entitled "No Father to Guide Them." The article managed, as the writer James Reed noted, to combine antifeminism, anti-Semitism, and a phobia of science. Pincus was depicted as a kind of Rasputin of the science lab, bent on evil deeds. In Pincus's world, the *Collier's* author J. D. Ratcliff wrote, "man's value would shrink. It is conceivable that the process would not even produce males. The mythical land of the Amazons would then come to life. A world where women would be self-sufficient; man's value precisely zero."

In reality, Pincus was the gentlest and most orthodox of men, a devoted husband and father, who left little poems behind on the pillow for his wife when he went to the lab in the morning. Still, the publicity did not sit well at Harvard. Pincus was already something of a controversial figure: he was Jewish in an age when American academia was still largely anti-Semitic, and his critics claimed he was too ambitious for his own good (and probably theirs).

In 1936 Harvard, celebrating its tercentenary, cited Pincus's work as one of the university's outstanding scientific achievements in its entire history. The next year, when Pincus was thirty-two, it denied him tenure. He was devastated. Fortunately, his old colleague Hudson Hoagland had just gone to Clark University in Worcester as the chairman of its biology department. Clark was a small school with a long tradition of excellent

science departments. Enraged by Harvard's cowardice and pettiness, Hoagland invited Pincus to come as a visiting professor.

From the start Hoagland had a vision that went far beyond Clark's tiny three-man biology department. He began to build a research center with talented young scientists who were drawn by his and Pincus's reputations. Min-Chueh Chang, for example, was delighted to come to Worcester. A young Chinese scientist who had received a Ph.D. from Cambridge in 1941, he had read Pincus's book "The Eggs of Mammals" in 1936. "A path-finding book, done when he was only thirty-three years old," Chang said years later. "*Everyone* in our field knew about him. You must remember that until then no one knew mammals had eggs." Soon Clark's research team numbered fifteen scientists, all of them considered brilliant by their peers and many of them nationally renowned. Their salaries were underwritten by dint of Hoagland's vigorous fund-raising in the Worcester community. Their lab was a converted barn. Hoagland's people did not, however, have faculty status and could not eat in the faculty dining room. Wallace Atwood, Clark's relatively conservative president, hated Hoagland's end runs, but he could harass him only by denying such small privileges.

Atwood represented the kind of academic bureaucracy that Hoagland and Pincus wanted to leave behind. Since Clark's only contribution to their work was Hoagland's rather small salary and a limited amount of space, they became independent of the university in 1944 and founded the Worcester Foundation for Experimental Biology. As its co-directors they estimated an annual budget of about a hundred thousand dollars and declared its purpose to connect new biology to practical medicine.

The two men complemented each other. Hoagland's son noted years later that his father never seemed as happy as when he was working directly with Goody Pincus. Hoagland was immensely skillful in tapping into the Worcester establishment for money. He persuaded businessmen to contribute twenty-five thousand dollars for an old mansion that became their headquarters. The staff was young and confident, full of the excitement that comes with having no institutional limits placed on it.

At first their funds were so limited that Pincus cleaned the animal labs, Mrs.

Hoagland was the bookkeeper, Hoagland cut the lawn, and Chang was the night watchman. When a local businessman saw Hoagland, stripped to the waist, pushing a lawn mower, he added a grounds keeper's salary to the budget. In 1950 Chang won an award of one thousand dollars for a paper on fertilization of rabbit eggs from the American Sterility Society; it allowed him to buy his first car. That same year Oscar Hechter, another research associate, won an award from the Endocrinological Society. "We don't have to worry about money and salaries anymore," an enthusiastic Pincus told Hoagland. "Our staff members can live on their awards."

They were among the early leaders in this country in steroid research. In the late forties Hechter had won the CIBA award for a paper on producing adrenal hormones, but in the race to produce cortisone, the Worcester group was beaten by the scientists at Upjohn—at least partly because Worcester's major benefactor, the Searle Pharmaceutical Company, was not particularly supportive of their effort. When the next great challenge came, the intensely competitive Pincus swore they would not be beaten again.

Pincus already had a sense that hormones could be used to control reproduction from his work in mammalian reproduction. As a young lab assistant he had been intrigued by what happened when too many rats were placed in the same cage: They attacked one another. His own ideas about the problems of human overcrowding stemmed from those experiments. He asked the people at Searle to finance research in the development of a drug for contraception, but again the answer was not encouraging. In fact, Albert Raymond, Searle's director of research, came down hard on him: "You haven't given us a thing to justify the half-million that we have invested in you . . . yet you have the nerve to ask for more research. You will get more only if a lucky chance gives us something originating from your group which will make us a profit."

If the attitude at Searle reflected the wariness of a large corporation to be involved in something as sensitive as contraceptive research, then nonetheless the Worcester Foundation was remarkably isolated from the prejudices of the era. Its funding sources were varied, the contributors in the local community generally liberal, and there was no board to answer to. That did not mean that they were not wary. One night in the early fifties a woman knocked on the door of Pincus's house. She was desperate, almost out of control. She was pregnant, she said, and needed help. Could he help her? Pincus was very gentle with her, his son John noted, but kept his distance. It was, he was sure, a setup; he knew of no other such incidents.

Then, in the winter of 1950, Pincus met Margaret Sanger. For nearly forty years she had been fighting hard to spread the gospel of birth control. She asked the scientist if some sort of drug was possible to stop conception. Pincus said yes, and out of that conversation came the first grant from Planned Parenthood. Not long after, Sanger introduced Pincus to Katharine McCormick, heir to the International Harvester fortune and deeply committed to the issue of birth control. She would become an early and crucial financial supporter of Pincus's work. It was after an early meeting with the two women that Pincus first envisioned the device as a pill and one that would probably use progesterone in some manner to block ovulation. When he arrived home, he was so excited that he told his wife that he had discovered a new device for contraception.

Pincus was the driving figure of the team that made the assault, the leader who kept everyone aligned, whose vision guided the search from the start. Personal politics did not matter to him; only science did. To that end he could be quite cold-blooded. He was capable of secretly undermining the attempts of a valued assistant to get a better position elsewhere. He could cut loose a staffer whom he particularly liked and promote another whom he loathed if he thought it would benefit the project.

He had the ability to remain focused on the central issue, no matter how complicated the problem. He envisioned a pill that would prevent conception by mimicking the hormonal condition of pregnancy, when the body blocked ovulation of its own natural instincts. If you could suppress ovulation, he believed, you could suppress fertilization. Significant earlier studies had suggested that progesterone might be an effective inhibitor of ovulation and that it might be taken orally.

Progesterone was then available in large part because of the work of an eccentric, maverick scientist named Russell Marker, who in 1940 discovered a cheap and plentiful source in the root of a wild yam that grew in the Mexican desert. Previously progesterone had been obtained only in minute amounts from animal sources and, as a result, was fabulously expensive—too expensive, in fact, to be wasted on humans; it was used exclusively to improve fertility in world-class racehorses. But with virtually no support or encouragement from others, Marker set up a primitive lab, and by 1943 he was able to walk into a small wholesale pharmaceutical company in Mexico City carrying two pickle jars filled with powder worth about $150,000 on the open market. Did the owners want some progesterone? he asked.

Personal politics didn't matter to Pincus; only science did.

The first tests on the effect of progesterone on rabbit ovulation were started on April 21, 1951. The actual lab work was carried out by Chang, who was still so poorly paid that he lived in the laboratory, giving rise to persistent rumors among the neighbors that a Chinaman was kept chained in the basement.

Both Sanger and McCormick kept pushing Pincus for quick results; science, he tried to explain, does not necessarily work that way. Even so, the work went surprisingly well. Because of McCormick there was always enough money. Chang was a brilliant lab man, the perfect counterpart to Pincus. He had the patience to endure the seemingly endless laboratory work required in the effort.

From the start Pincus was optimistic. Chang was, he said, equally pessimistic, and he remained so even when test after test succeeded.

By 1952 there was an article in *Look* that predicted that Pincus would soon discover an oral contraceptive. Searle then passed on to the lab a progesterone steroid called norethynodrel, which, Chang reported back to Pincus, was more powerful than natural progesterone by a factor of at least ten to one. That meant it was time to go on to the next stage.

One thing that Pincus wanted from the start was a medical doctor as a collaborator; eventually the pill would have to be tried out on humans. For a time he considered Alan Guttmacher and Abraham Stone, both doctors and leaders in the birth-control movement. But Pincus worried that this affiliation might diminish their legitimacy for the project; moreover, both were Jewish, which might prove to be a liability, for opposition to birth control came primarily from Catholics and fundamentalist Christians. (For all its freedom from administrative control, the Worcester people maintained caution in publicly discussing what they were doing. The 1955 annual report was more than a little disingenuous; it spoke of unspecified work with animals to control ovulation. The 1956 report detailed the use of steroids to help control painful menstruation.)

Finally Pincus turned to an old colleague and friend, Dr. John Rock. Rock was a distinguished physician, the chief of gynecology and obstetrics at Harvard Medical School. He was also a devout Catholic. Rock and Pincus had known each other since the thirties by dint of their common interest in hormones, although for diametrically different reasons: Rock was trying to use them to cure infertility in women. He believed progesterone and estrogen might stimulate the womb, and he sent one of his assistants to work with Pincus to learn from his experience in retrieving mammalian eggs. Gradually their work brought Rock and Pincus closer together.

In 1953 Pincus suggested to Planned Parenthood that they get Rock to do a study on the use of progesterone as a contraceptive device. Rock, whose attitudes toward contraception had been slowly changing, was finally ready to participate. In 1954 he tried the new synthetic hormone from Searle on three women.

Rock was in many ways a very conservative man. He had argued against the admission of women to Harvard Medical School and often told his own daughters that he did not think women were capable of being doctors. But his views on birth control evolved steadily. In 1943, when he was fifty-three years old, he had come out for the repeal of legal restrictions on physicians to give advice on medical birth control. In the mid-forties, although scrupulous about not offering contraceptives to his own patients, he began to teach his young students at

Harvard Medical School how to prescribe them. Years later he would pinpoint the late forties as the time when he became aware of what he called "the alarming danger of the population explosion." He began to fit some of his patients with diaphragms, which so enraged some of his Catholic colleagues that they tried to have him excommunicated from his church. In 1949 he wrote a book with David Loth called *Voluntary Parenthood,* which was a comprehensive survey of birth-control methods available for the general public. Still, Rock's primary motivation in joining with Pincus was to benefit couples who, despite all physiological evidence to the contrary, were unable to have children. In the past he had had some success injecting the women with natural progesterone.

He gave the progestin steroids to a group of fifty childless women at his clinic, starting in December 1954. The dosage was ten to forty milligrams for twenty successive days for each menstrual cycle. When the women came off the progestin, seven of the fifty, or 14 percent, were able to get pregnant. That was wonderful news for Rock. In addition, there was among the fifty a virtual 100 percent postponement of ovulation. That was wonderful news for Pincus and Chang. Pincus became so confident that he had begun to refer to "the Pill."

By the fall of 1955, when the International Planned Parenthood meeting took place in Tokyo, Pincus had decided to go public with his research. He asked Rock to join him, but Rock was uneasy; the research, while positive, was not yet conclusive, and he was also sensitive about making the announcement at a meeting of birth-control advocates. It was the closest the two men came to a break.

In Tokyo Pincus gave the most optimistic report yet on the coming of an inexpensive oral contraceptive agent. What he needed now were more patients and a broader selection of them; it was one thing to succeed with middle-class, college-educated women, but what about poor and illiterate women? Puerto Rico and Haiti were chosen as locales for mass testing. These were the perfect places for their needs—poor and overcrowded. Public officials there were more than ready for a serious study of birth control. In April 1956 the tests began on 100 women in a poor suburb of San Juan. It had been exceptionally easy to get volunteers; the problem was keeping other women out. The pill used was

Enovid, made by Searle, whose officials were still nervous about being associated with Pincus in the program and whose top public relations people warned that this activity might destroy the company's good name. The early returns from Puerto Rico were very good: In the first eight months 221 patients took the Pill, without a single pregnancy. There were some side effects, primarily nausea, but Pincus was able to reduce them by adding an antacid.

The FDA approved the Pill in 1960; by 1963 over 529 million women were on it.

Pincus's daughter, Laura, took some time off from her studies at Radcliffe to help with the tests in Puerto Rico. Upon her return to Boston she was sent to brief McCormick, who lived in a grand mansion in Back Bay, a forbidding house that seemed to have neither lights nor life to it. Laura Pincus was, in her own words, rather naive about sex, and she got a little flustered talking to this old woman about the experiments. But Kate McCormick did not become unsettled; she talked openly and frankly. The sex drive was so strong, she kept insisting, that it was critical that it be separated from reproductive functions. Then there was a brief discussion of the pleasures of sex followed by a casual remark to the effect that sex between women might be more meaningful. This was spoken dispassionately, not suggestively. Nonetheless, young Ms. Pincus was stunned. Here she was in this nineteenth-century setting hearing words that seemed to come from the twenty-first century. Then, knowing that her visitor had to take the subway back to college, McCormick summoned her butler, who brought her a silver tray with coins. She reached down and picked out two dimes and handed them to her visitor. Later, after she had left, Laura Pincus looked down at the coins and noticed they had been minted in 1929.

The test in Puerto Rico proved to be an extraordinary triumph for Pincus. He began to travel around the world, talking with great enthusiasm of the coming breakthrough in contraception. He would tell his audiences "how a few precious facts obscurely come to in the laboratory may resonate into the lives of men everywhere, bring order to disorder, hope to

the hopeless, life to the dying. That this is the magic and mystery of our time is sometimes grasped and often missed, but to expound it is inevitable."

The people in Planned Parenthood thought Pincus was too optimistic and precipitous in his judgments, but this optimism was now shared by the more conservative Rock. They both were now pushing for acceptances of the Pill, and they were getting results: in 1957 the U.S. Food and Drug Administration authorized the marketing of the Pill for treatment of miscarriages and some menstrual disorders. By 1959 both Pincus and Rock were convinced that Enovid was safe for long-term use by women. In 1959 Pincus completed a paper on the uses of Enovid for oral contraception and sent it to Margaret Sanger. "To Margaret Sanger," he wrote, "with affectionate greetings—this product of her pioneering resoluteness."

In May 1960 the FDA approved Enovid as a contraceptive device. By the end of 1961 some 408,000 American women were taking the Pill, by the end of 1962 the figure was 1,187,000, and by the end of 1963 it was 2,300,000 and still rising. Of it Clare Boothe Luce said, "Modern woman is at last free as a man is free, to dispose of her own body, to earn her living, to pursue the improvement of her mind, to try a successful career."

The discovery made Searle a very rich company. To Chang's great regret the Worcester Foundation never took any royalty. Nor in the eyes of the Worcester people was Searle generous in later years. Despite several representations on behalf of his family and of the Worcester people, Searle paid only three hundred dollars a month in benefits to Pincus's widow after his death in 1967. When the Worcester people suggested repeatedly to Searle that the company might like to endow a chair at the Worcester Foundation in Pincus's honor, Searle not only declined but soon after donated five hundred thousand dollars to Harvard to endow a chair in reproductive studies. It was the supreme indignity: rewarding the institution that had once denied Pincus tenure with a chair in his own specialty.

"A QUIET DISCUSSION ON PICASSO, NIETZSCHE, JAZZ, SEX"

Marilyn Monroe was the stuff of which male fantasies were made. She was at once both lush and childlike. She knew the power of her own sexuality, knew how to turn it on and turn it off. In a way she was a photographer's dream. "The first day a photographer took a picture of her, she was a genius," said the director Billy Wilder, who understood her talent better than anyone in Hollywood. In 1949, very much down and out on her luck and still trying to crash Hollywood as a starlet, she agreed to do a nude shot for a photographer friend named Tom Kelley. He paid only fifty dollars, but she was living hand to mouth and she owed him a favor—he had lent her five dollars on an earlier occasion for cab fare. Besides, fifty dollars was precisely the amount of money she needed for the monthly payment on her secondhand car. She was not nervous about the nudity, only its potential effect on her career, and she signed the model release with the name Mona Monroe. In fact, Kelley noted that once she took her clothes off, she seemed more comfortable than before, in his words, "graceful as an otter, turning sinuously with utter naturalness. All her constraints vanished as soon as her clothes were off."

The picture Tom Kelley shot was soon hanging on the walls of thousands of barbershops, bars, and gas stations. It also helped launch a sexual empire. For in the fall of 1953 a young man named Hugh Hefner, anxious to start his own magazine, read in an advertising trade journal that a local Midwestern company had the rights to the photo. Hefner drove out to suburban Chicago and bought the rights for five hundred dollars.

At the time Hefner felt himself a failure. He had been born in Chicago in 1926. His father worked as an accountant for a large company, and even in the worst of the Depression theirs was a comfortable home financially. However, there was little emotional warmth. His grandparents were pious Nebraska farmers, and theirs remained a God-fearing home: no drinking, no swearing, no smoking. Sunday was for church. Hefner's first wife later noted that she never saw any sign of affection or anger displayed by either parent.

Hugh Hefner was a bright, somewhat dreamy child; in terms of social skills and popularity he was always on the outside looking in. He graduated from high school in 1944, went into the Army, caught the last months of the war, although he saw no combat. When he came home, he drifted for a time, unsure

of his future. Then he entered the University of Illinois to be with his high school girl friend Millie Williams. He had been dating Millie for several years, but they still had not consummated their affair. After they were married in 1949, Hefner continued to drift, supported by Millie, who was teaching school.

The one thing he loved was cartooning, at which he was, regrettably, not particularly talented; for the next two or three years, he went back and forth between jobs, usually in the promotion departments of magazines. For much of the time he and Millie lived with his parents in order to save money. At one point in his drive to become a cartoonist, he quit work and stayed at home to draw. The results tended to be pornographic reworkings of popular comic strips. Millie Hefner was convinced this erotic sketching was a rebellion of sorts against his family's Calvinist roots and the emotional and sexual aridity of that household.

As a convert to the cause of more open sexuality, he became a crusader, taking up that cause with the passion his puritan grandparents had espoused in their religion. For all his subsequent success in terms of personal sexual freedom, there was, according to some who knew him well, a certain grimness to his pursuit of pleasure.

Hefner was only twenty-seven when he started his magazine. All of his small savings and some of his friends' were tied up in it; if it failed, he would owe several thousand dollars. *Playboy* was not Hefner's original choice for a name. He had wanted to give it the cruder title of *Stag Party,* but a letter from the lawyers of a girly magazine in New York called *Stag* threatened legal action if he did not change it. *Playboy* it became, as an afterthought.

Hefner printed seventy thousand copies of the first issue, hoping that it would sell at least thirty thousand of them at fifty cents each. Instead, bolstered in no small part by word of mouth on the Monroe photos, it sold fifty-three thousand—a huge success. He was in business. Within a year, by December 1954, circulation had reached one hundred thousand. By early 1955 *Playboy* had $250,000 in the bank, and Hefner had turned down an offer of $1,000,000 for the magazine from a group in Chicago. Hefner demanded ever more glossy photos and used what he considered sophisticated writing; he was trying to make *Playboy*

legitimate and stated his purpose of bringing sex out into the open.

The Calvinists, Hefner believed, thought sex was dark and furtive, and the other girly magazines of the period were so cheap and crude they seemed to confirm that judgment. It was Hefner's particular genius to know that it was now going to be permissible to have an upscale, far more sophisticated magazine of male sexual fantasies that customers might not be embarrassed to be seen buying—or even leaving out on their coffee tables.

Alfred Kinsey was his hero, and he had understood from reading the Kinsey report that he was not alone, that his sexual attitudes and fantasies were mirrored by millions of other young men. In his first issue Hefner wrote: "We like our apartment. We enjoy mixing up cocktails and an hors d'oeuvre or two, putting a little mood music on the phonograph, and inviting in a female for a quiet discussion on Picasso, Nietzsche, jazz, sex." There it was: the *Playboy* ethic, sex not only as legitimate but as a sophisticated life-style. By the end of 1956, still operating with a skeleton staff, *Playboy* was a phenomenon. Circulation was six hundred thousand. "A lot of it," said Ray Russell, a writer and editor who was one of Hefner's first hires, "was good luck, random choice, being carried on the tides of the times rather than the leader of the times. It was a matter of being the right magazine able to take advantage of a rising economy, more than any degree of conscious planning."

Hugh Hefner's great strength was his lack of sophistication.

Hefner was pretty much living in his offices in those early days. Then as he became more successful he converted a Chicago mansion into his home; even so he remained distant and remote, a kind of latter-day Gatsby who opened this plush residence to an endless stream of people whom he did not know, and who did not know him. In some ways he was still an outsider looking in. "Hefner," said Don Gold, an editor at *Playboy* in the fifties, "is not a very complicated man. He thinks Poe is the best writer in the world. When he buys a pipe, he buys two dozen of the same pipe. He likes his mashed potatoes to have a dimple of gravy on them. He is mid-America personified. The Marquis de Sade would have told him to wait in a corner, though he is, in a healthy way, by sex possessed."

Despite the magazine's intellectual pretensions, Hefner's great strength was his lack of sophistication. He was square but longed to share in the wider, hipper world that television and movies were bringing so tantalizingly close. In that, he mirrored the longings of millions of other young men from similar backgrounds, fantasizing a faster and freer life.

His success—for he soon became the most successful magazine publisher of the decade, a millionaire who styled himself an authority on the fast-lane life for the young, monied, and restless—echoed powerful new chords in American life. The first was a more candid view of sex and sexuality. Hefner sought to abolish America's puritan past, so evident in his own background. In the broader sense *Playboy* represented the transition to the better, more affluent life that more and more Americans were enjoying as they lived decidedly better than their parents in material terms. The magazine explained how to buy a sports car and a hi-fi, how to order in a restaurant, what kind of wine to drink. It provided an elementary tutorial on the new American affluence for newcomers to the middle class, midwifing young men who were often the first members of their families to graduate from college into a world of increasing plenty.

Ordinary Americans now wanted (and could often afford) things that in the past had been the domain only of the very wealthy, and they wanted the personal freedoms those people had enjoyed too. In the onslaught, old restraints were loosened. If religion existed only as a negative force, Hefner seemed to be saying, if it spoke only of denial of pleasure and made people feel furtive about what was natural, then it was in trouble.

Hefner's colleague Frank Gibney believed he had worked for two of the most important magazine publishers of the era, first Henry Luce and then Hugh Hefner, and he thought there was an interesting comparison to be made between the two. Luce was idiosyncratic, on occasion authoritarian, and overbearing, but he was driven by a curiosity that made him a man of breadth almost in spite of himself; Hefner, thought Gibney, had very little curiosity

at all. He was essentially a narrow man, but he knew what he liked and he trusted it. "That magazine," said Jack Kessie, an early editor, "was written and edited for Hugh M. Hefner." Hefner was the square who wanted to be cool and as such he had a perfect sense of what other squares wanted to know and how they wanted to feel.

"IF I DON'T GET OUT, I'LL DIE"

"Indian summer is like a woman. Ripe, hotly passionate but fickle, she comes and goes as she pleases so one is never sure whether she will come at all, nor how long she will stay." The prose caused neither John Cheever nor John O'Hara to look over their shoulders as the pre-eminent chroniclers of American social mores. But the story struck a nerve among the great mass of American readers. "One year, early in October, Indian summer came to a town called Peyton Place. Like a laughing lovely Indian woman, Indian summer came and spread herself over the countryside and made everything hurtfully beautiful to the eye . . ."

In 1956 the most surprising book on the best-seller list was *Peyton Place* by Grace Metalious, a young woman who had never published a word before. It was brought out in hardcover by a small publisher and went on to become the third best-selling novel of the year. Allan Barnard, an editor at the paperback house Dell, read the manuscript just before it was published and told his boss, Frank Taylor, "I have something I want to buy, but I don't want you to read it." Taylor gave Barnard permission to make the successful bid of eleven thousand dollars in the auction for paperback rights. It turned out to be one of the great bargains of all time. A few years later Taylor asked Barnard why he had asked him not to read it. "Because you wouldn't have let me buy it," Barnard said.

Peyton Place was considered in the lexicon of the day a sexy book, although Metalious was far less explicit than Henry Miller and Allen Ginsberg—more serious writers who were struggling with the oppressive censorship laws of the era. But *Peyton Place* was such a phenomenon that the title entered the language as a generic term for all the small towns that appeared placid on the surface but that underneath were filled with dark secrets.

In her book Metalious tore away the staid facade of Peyton Place (or Gilmanton, New Hampshire, where she lived) to reveal a hotbed of lust and sexual intrigue. "To a tourist these towns look as peaceful as a postcard," Metalious told Hal Boyle of the Associated Press in an early interview. "But if you go beneath that picture, it's like turning over a rock with your foot—all kinds of strange things crawl out. Everybody who lives in town knows what's going on—there are no secrets—but they don't want outsiders to know."

Indeed, the principal occupation of Peyton Place was not so much farming or the town's textile factory but gossip; people there not only led secret lives, they devoted most of their waking hours to sitting around and talking about them—at least about everyone else's.

It was a small town of some thirty-seven hundred people, still largely cut off from the rest of the society. Class lines ran right through the center of it; a handful of powerful men—the factory owner, the lawyer, the editor of the newspaper, and the doctor—play poker once a week and decide what is going to happen in Peyton Place. When Betty Anderson, a local girl from the wrong side of the tracks whose father works for Leslie Harrington (the mill owner), becomes pregnant after a fling with Harrington's son, the senior Harrington hands his employee a check for $500. A furious Betty charges in to see Harrington in his office and announces that she plans to marry his son. Harrington tells her that it will take only six men to say that they also had relations with her to make her legally a prostitute. Then he tears up the $500 check and gives her one for $250, promising that it will be $125 if she comes to see him again.

Mostly the town's secrets stay secret with much less fuss. Constance MacKenzie, the prim, attractive young widow who runs the town's dress shop, dreads that people will learn that in her brief time in New York she had an affair with a married man, who is the father of her daughter; another local girl is sexually assaulted and impregnated by her sinister stepfather, and the kindly local doctor must decide to save the young girl's reputation by disguising an abortion as an emergency appendectomy.

The paperback, published in the fall of 1957, sold six million copies in the first two years. At the time, the novel was perceived as being successful because of its "hot passages." Gradually, however, a revisionist view took hold that Metalious had powerfully and viscerally captured the problems faced by women in the modern world. If the author did not exactly become a role model to the generation of young feminists who emerged in the sixties and seventies, they nonetheless could find in her pages independent women who dissented from the proscribed and limited roles assigned them. Feminists suspected—for there was little evidence of this in the initial reviews of the book—that Metalious had achieved this almost without anyone's knowing it. As Kenneth Davis noted in his book on the paperback revolution, *Two Bit Culture,* the women in *Peyton Place* "were on the cutting edge of a movement that had not yet arrived and still had no voice. They wanted more than to simply find the right man, settle down and begin breeding and keeping house."

Rather, as Davis pointed out, Metalious's characters might have come right out of the Kinsey report on women. They had sexual feelings and appetites that contrasted starkly with the attitudes women were supposed to have, as set down in endless books written by men. Nor were Metalious's women nearly as admiring of men as in their mothers' books. In fact, they often considered men unreliable and childish.

Emily Toth points out in her book *Inside Peyton Place,* a serious, feminist reappraisal of Metalious and her work, that the novel brought very different attitudes to sexual politics. It presented rape not as an act of sexual pleasure but as violence; the doctor who performs an abortion is described as saving a life. In Peyton Place, Toth notes, the women who depend too greatly on men lose out, while the women who are independent are winners.

Metalious would have been surprised to find herself a feminist hero.

Metalious had written as she did—roughly, simply, but powerfully—because it was her own story. She was angrier and more rebellious than she herself realized, although she had always shown little ambition to be a traditional housekeeper; Grace Metalious's home was littered with garbage, dirty dishes,

and beer cans. Women were supposed to be good mothers, putting their children above their own ambitions; Grace Metalious loved her three children in her own erratic way, but she let them do pretty much as they wished, and any real supervision tended to come from neighbors. Women were supposed to be dutiful handmaidens to their husbands' careers; Metalious made no such efforts. She dressed in a way that jarred small-town sensibilities—in blue jeans, checked shirts, and sneakers. She never fully articulated her own feminist vision and probably would have been surprised had someone told her that one day she would be a heroine of the women's movement. With a few exceptions she was not close to other women.

She was a lower-middle-class French-Canadian girl who grew up in small towns in New Hampshire, living always involuntarily in a matriarchy. The men in her family were bit players; her own father deserted them when she was young, and she was raised by her grandmother. Her mother fantasized a better life but slipped into alcoholism at a relatively early age. Grace loved to read and fancied that she could be a writer one day; at thirteen she had already begun a historical novel.

In high school Grace was bright and unusual, and teachers noticed her. Nonetheless, a literary future seemed out of reach. It seemed dimmer still when in February 1943, at the age of eighteen, she married George Metalious, a high school friend, because she was pregnant. When George soon went off to war, Grace was stunned by his decision to enlist; she was not caught up in the patriotic cause, and remembering her father, she saw her husband's desire to serve as an escape from family responsibility. She worked at different jobs and raised her daughter, Marsha. When George Metalious came back, sure that his Army salary had been salted away for the down payment on a dream house, he was astounded to find that she had saved none of it. Rather, she had been supporting an extended family with his allotment checks. "How could you be so stupid!" he shouted at her.

They were like many couples trying to make their way after the war. George had come back to a child and a wife he barely knew. They struggled for a time, had a second child, both of them held jobs, yet they could save very little. Finally it was decided that the only way

to succeed was for George to go to the University of New Hampshire on the GI Bill. His family would follow, so common an arrangement in those days that there was even a phrase for it: PHTS, Putting Hubbies Through School. But if other young couples were caught up in the excitement of those years, always sure that their current sacrifices would be rewarded one day in the future, Grace Metalious was having none of it. "I am trapped, I screamed silently," she said later of those years. I am trapped in a cage of poverty and mediocrity, and if I don't get out, I'll die."

By 1950 a third child had arrived. When George graduated, they were so poor that they had to borrow three hundred dollars to pay his debts so that the university would release his degree. His first job as a teacher at a tiny school in Belmont paid twenty-five hundred dollars.

Through it all she wrote every day, and in 1953 she began searching for a literary agent. She perused various writers' magazines and finally came up with a name, Jacques Chambrun, an agent with a good deal of charm and a most unfortunate reputation for siphoning off the earnings of his writers. By early 1955 she had sent him her first novel, *The Quiet Place,* a routine story about a young couple struggling through GI Bill life at a New England college. It was rejected everywhere. Around the same time she sent off her second novel, entitled *The Tree and the Blossom.* She had read *King's Row,* an extremely popular novel of the forties, which dealt with an incestuous relationship of an adolescent girl and her father. By chance a similar situation had occurred where Metalious lived, in which a young girl shot her father to protect herself and the rest of her family. In it Metalious had seen a sensational incident that would give her novel a special darkness. The manuscript, renamed *Peyton Place,* was mailed to publishers in May 1955.

Several houses turned it down, but a young woman named Leona Nevler, who had a good eye, read it while she was working as a freelance editor for Lippincott. It was impressive, Nevler thought; there was something poignant, vital, and real about the book. But it was not right for Lippincott, an unusually staid house. A few days later Nevler was interviewed for a job as a full-time editor by Kitty Messner, the head of Julian Messner. She had founded the small firm with her husband, Julian Messner, had divorced him, but had continued to work with him. When he died, she took over the company, so when Nevler mentioned the book, Kitty Messner was especially receptive to the theme, which dealt with a young woman's desire for a better life. Messner, one of the first women to head a publishing house, made a note of it, called Chambrun, got a copy, and stayed up all night reading it. She understood immediately the force of the book and made Chambrun an offer. "I know this is a big book," she told him. "I have to have it." Chambrun cabled Metalious, who was so excited that she forgot to ask how much her advance was; the answer was fifteen hundred dollars. He told her to come immediately to New York to sign the contracts, which she did. She was awed by the elegant Kitty Messner. It was mid-August, and Metalious felt wilted by New York's steamy heat; by contrast, Messner "looked as if she had never had a hot uncomfortable moment in her life. As for me, my armpits itched, I stuck to my chair, and my hair had gone all limp."

Messner thought the book might sell three thousand copies, but Howard Goodkind, who handled the publicity, believed it could be promoted into a best seller; he suggested spending an additional five thousand dollars to get a publicist to create a special promotion campaign. The sum was a considerable risk in those days, but Messner agreed. The ads for the book employed a series of headlines reflecting its controversial nature. When it was published in late September, it shot up some best-seller lists, and a number of studios were bidding for the film rights. It sold sixty thousand copies in the first ten days. The reviews were generally respectful.

Fame and success were sweet for Grace Metalious at first. All her dreams seemed to be coming true. She sold the book to the movies for $250,000. But if she had been well prepared to overcome the adversities of her life, she proved significantly less able to deal with the pressures of success. "This book business," she wrote in November 1956, "is some evil form of insanity." Everyone suddenly seemed to want something from her and demanded she play the role of a sexy writer. She was uneasy about press and television appearances, and she partic-

ularly disliked being asked whether or not *Peyton Place* was autobiographical.

Even before the book's publication her marriage had started falling apart. Liberated by her success and her changed financial position, she took up with a disc jockey. She began to spend money freely; at the same time, she stopped writing. Driven mostly by a Hollywood producer, she eventually wrote a listless sequel that she was not proud of, called *Return to Peyton Place*. (At the last minute a writer named Warren Miller was brought in to doctor it into a readable book.) Nonetheless, *Return* too sold well, though not as well as its predecessor.

For all the fame and the attention, Metalious's emotional needs did not abate. "Our mother had to be told with the consistency of a flowing brook that echoes, 'I love you, love you,' " her daughter Marsha remembered. "We did love her strongly, but after a while 'I love you' became a ludicrous expression—worn to its nap like a rug travelled on day after day, night after night." Her work habits continued to deteriorate. A glass of Canadian Club and 7-Up never left her hand.

By 1960 George Metalious had come back. In 1960 she published *The Tight White Collar*, which became her favorite book. It sold well, but shrewd editors saw that her audience was beginning to slip away. Soon she had serious financial problems and was said to owe the government more than $150,000 in back taxes. *No Adam in Eden*, a book about her French-Canadian family, was published in September 1963, but her emotional state continued to deteriorate. George Metalious left her again in the fall of 1963, and a few months later, in February 1964, she died of chronic liver disease.

"IT WAS A STRANGE STIRRING"

Throughout the fifties Madison Avenue often depicted the American woman as a new kind of modern princess, freed from the drudgery that burdened her mother's generation by wondrous new appliances and gadgets that promised to make odious housework obsolete. But was this new woman indeed happier? That was one of the more interesting questions of the era, for the great migration to the suburbs and the parallel great ascent into the new middle class reflected a number

of profound changes taking place in American society, not the least of which was the changing role of women.

Women had come a long way in America during the twentieth century. In the 1930s twenty-six states still had laws prohibiting the employment of married women. A poll of both men and women at the time asked, "Do you approve of a married woman earning money in business or industry if she has a husband capable of supporting her?" Eighty-two percent did not. Nevertheless, during the Depression large numbers of women worked because their families needed every cent they could get.

With the coming of World War II, a profound change occurred overnight. That which had been perceived as distinctly unfeminine became a patriotic necessity. A study by the War Manpower Commission in July 1943 showed that some four million additional workers were needed in the armed forces and munitions industries and that a great many of them would have to be women. Suddenly eight million women were entering the work force.

That trend came to a stunning halt almost as quickly as it began. Within two months after the end of the war, some eight hundred thousand women had been eliminated from well-paying jobs in the aircraft industry, and the same thing was happening elsewhere. In the two years that followed, two million women lost their jobs. Part of the reason for the change was the ever increasing affluence of the country; families could now live easily with only one income.

As the fifties progressed, there was little encouragement for women to seek professional careers; in fact, it was often deliberately discouraged. In middle-class homes boys were from the start put on a very different track; they were inculcated with the requisite skills critical to supporting a family. A daughter, on the other hand, was educated to be genteel and get married.

In cases where equally well-educated men and women arrived at the same company, the men from the start were taken more seriously. The women were relegated to the job of being support troops, often working harder and longer for less pay with lesser titles. It was an unspoken assumption that whatever their skills and talents they would soon get married, become pregnant, and duly leave. Only some one more than a little eccentric or destined to be an old maid would stay the course. Short stories in women's magazines tended to show career women as unhappy and emotionally empty, while glorifying the modern wife who devoted her life to raising her children and doing all that she could to help her husband's career.

"The more educated a woman is, the greater chance there is of sexual disorder."

An influential book of pop sociology by Ferdinand Lundberg and his psychoanalyst collaborator Marynia Farnham, entitled *Modern Woman: The Lost Sex,* attacked the very idea of career women. "The independent woman is a contradiction in terms," they wrote. Feminism "was a deep illness . . . the psychosocial rule that takes form, then is this: the more educated a woman is, the greater chance there is of sexual disorder, more or less severe. The greater the disordered sexuality in a given group of women, the fewer children they have."

The ideal that women were to strive for was pinpointed by *McCall's* magazine in 1954: togetherness. A family was as one, its husband the captain, the wife his first mate. It was a single universe, and the hopes, ambitions, and fortunes of its members were entwined.

"The two big steps that women must take are to help their husbands decide where they are going and use their pretty heads to help them get there," Mrs. Dale Carnegie, wife of one of the nation's leading experts on how to be likable, wrote in the April 1955 *Better Homes and Gardens.* "Let's face it, girls. That wonderful guy in your house—and in mine—is building your house, your happiness and the opportunities that will come to your children." Split-level houses, Mrs. Carnegie added, were fine, "but there is simply no room for split-level thinking—or doing—when Mr. and Mrs. set their sights on a happy home, a host of friends, and a bright future through success in HIS job."

What all these magazines were portraying were women's lives of the most conventional type; the wife was to be the new all-purpose support troop of the suburbs, taking care of the children, helping her husband, and, it seemed,

never having any thoughts—and, equally important, any identity—of her own. But not every woman of that era accepted those rules so readily.

Like a lot of her contemporaries, Betty Goldstein graduated from college determined to lead a life that was unconventional and as much in contrast to her mother's as she could. When she had entered Smith College in 1939, she had found everything that she had longed for as a smalltown girl in Peoria, Illinois: at Smith women were rewarded instead of being punished for being smart and different. She graduated in 1942, summa cum laude, full of optimism about the future even though the war was going on. She was offered several scholarships. Ambitious, admired by her classmates, Betty Goldstein was certain that she would lead a life dramatically different from that of her mother, a writer for the Peoria newspaper who gave up her career after marrying a local store owner. But at graduation time Betty Goldstein turned down the scholarships because she was interested in a young man; he had not been offered a comparable scholarship, and she was afraid it would tear their relationship apart if she accepted hers. That single decision, she later wrote, turned her into a cliché. Looking back on her life, Betty Goldstein Friedan, one of the first voices of the feminist movement, noted her young man's face was more quickly forgotten than the terms of the scholarship.

Instead of getting married, she moved to the exciting intellectual world of Greenwich Village and became part of a group of liberal young people involved in labor issues and civil rights before it was fashionable. The women all seemed to be graduates of Smith, Vassar, and Radcliffe; they were bright and optimistic. Betty Goldstein worked as a reporter for a labor newspaper, and after the war she met a young veteran named Carl Friedan who was funny and charming. In 1947 they were married; in 1949 they had their first child. When she was pregnant with her second child, she was fired from the labor paper, whose radicalism, it appeared, did not extend to women's rights. She took her grievance to the Newspaper Guild and was told that it was her own fault.

Friedan soon found herself part of the great suburban migration, swept away from the Village, where her friends were and where ideas seemed so important. As Carl Friedan made more money, they

moved from a Queens apartment to a rented house in fashionable Sneden's Landing and finally bought an old house worthy of Charles Addams in Rockland County. There Friedan spent her time scraping eight layers of paint off a fireplace ("I quite liked it"), chauffeuring children to and from school, and helping run the PTA.

In some ways her life was full, she would later decide, but in some ways it was quite empty. She liked being a mother, and she liked her friends, but she was not sure she was living up to her potential. She began to freelance for women's magazines. Her early articles, "Millionaire's Wife" (*Cosmopolitan,* September 1956), "Now They're Proud of Peoria" (*Reader's Digest,* August 1955), "Two Are an Island" (*Parents* magazine, May 1957), were not exactly the kinds of intellectual achievements she had had in mind when she left Smith.

She was also quickly discovering the limits of what women's magazines would publish. She read in a newspaper about Julie Harris, the actress, who had had a natural childbirth. That was something Betty Friedan, who had undergone two cesareans, admired and even envied, so she got permission from the magazine to do a piece on Harris. She had a glorious time with the actress; was completely captivated by her, and wrote what she thought was one of her best articles. It was turned down because it was too graphic. That was hardly her only defeat. When she suggested an article about Beverly Pepper, just beginning to experience considerable success as a painter and sculptor, the editors of another magazine were scornful. American women, they told her, were not interested in someone like this and would not identify with her. Their market research showed that women wanted to read exclusively articles that examined their roles vis-à-vis their husbands and children.

Then on the occasion of her fifteenth Smith reunion, in 1957, she and two friends were asked to do a report on what had happened to the members of the class of '42. She made up a questionnaire and got an assignment from *McCall's* to pay for her time. The piece was supposed to be called "The Togetherness Woman." The questions were: What difficulties have you found in working out your role as a woman?" "What are the chief satisfactions and frustrations of your life today?" "How do you feel about getting older?" "How have you changed inside?" "What do you wish you had done differently?" The answers stunned her. She had tapped into a great reservoir of doubt, frustration, anxiety, and resentment. The women felt unfulfilled and isolated with their children; they often viewed their husbands as visitors from a far more exciting world.

"Look, only the most neurotic housewife would identify with this."

The project also emphasized Friedan's own frustrations. All those years trying to be a good wife and mother suddenly seemed wasted; it had been wrong to suppress her feelings rather than to deal with them. The surprise for her was that there were thousands of women just like her out there. As she later wrote, "It was like a strange stirring, a sense of dissatisfaction, a yearning that women suffered in the middle of the twentieth century in the United States. Each suburban wife struggled with it alone. As she made the beds, shopped for groceries, matched slip cover materials, ate peanut butter sandwiches with her children, chauffeured Cub Scouts and Brownies, lay beside her husband at night, she was afraid to ask of herself the silent question—'Is this all?' "

As she had walked around the Smith campus during her reunion, she was struck by the passivity of the young women of the class of 1957. Her generation had been filled with excitement about the issues of the day; when Friedan asked these young women about their futures, they regarded her with blank looks. They were going to get engaged, be married, and have children, of course. She thought, This is happening at Smith, a place where I found nothing but intellectual excitement when I was their age. Something had gotten deep in the bloodstream of this generation.

She left and started to write the piece for *McCall's,* but it turned out to be very different from the one that she had intended to write. It reflected the despair and depression she had found among her contemporaries, and it reflected, she was sure, the feelings of a great many women who lived through their husbands and children. Not surprisingly, *McCall's,* the inventor of togetherness, turned it down. She heard that all the women editors at the magazine there wanted to run it but had been overruled by their male superiors. So she sent it to the *Ladies' Home Journal,* where it was accepted—and rewritten so completely that it seemed to make the opposite points. She pulled it. That left *Redbook,* where Bob Stein, an old friend, worked. He turned it down and called her agent. "Look," he said over the phone, "only the most neurotic housewife would identify with this." She was, she realized later, challenging the magazines themselves. She was saying that it was wrong to mislead women to think they should feel one way when in fact they often felt quite differently. She had discovered a crisis of considerable proportions, and these magazines would only deny it.

It was nothing less than censorship, she believed. Women's magazines had a single purpose, she decided—to sell a vast array of new products to American housewives—and anything that worked against that, that cast doubt on the happiness of the millions of women using such products, was not going to be printed.

At about that time she went into New York to hear a speech by Vance Packard, the writer. He had just finished his book *The Hidden Persuaders,* about subliminal tactics in advertising. His own efforts to write about this phenomenon in magazines had been completely unsuccessful, he said, so he turned it into a book, which had become a major best seller. The parallels between his problems and hers were obvious. Suddenly she envisioned "The Togetherness Woman" as a book.

After all, she reasoned, books were not dependent upon ads, they were dependent upon ideas, and the more provocative the idea, the more attention and often the better the sales. She called

George Brockway, an editor at W. W. Norton & Company who had liked her magazine work. He knew there had already been a number of attacks on conformity in American society, particularly as it affected men. Here was an attack that would talk about its effect on women, who were, of course, the principal buyers of books. He was impressed by Friedan. She was focused and, to his mind, wildly ambitious.

She told Brockway that she would finish it in a year; instead it took five years. Her research was prodigious. Three days a week she went to the New York Public Library for research. The chief villains, she decided, were the women's magazines. What startled her was the fact that this had not always been true. In the same magazines in the late thirties and forties there had been a sense of women moving steadily into the male professional world; they celebrated the career woman who knew how to take care of herself and who could make it on her own. But starting around 1949, these same magazines had changed dramatically. It was as if someone had thrown a giant switch. The new woman did not exist on her own. She was seen only in the light of supporting her husband and his career and taking care of the children.

Some psychiatrists, she found, had noticed a certain emotional malaise, bordering on depression, among many women of the era. One called it "the housewife's syndrome"; another referred to it as "the housewife's blight." No one wrote about it in popular magazines.

So, gathering material over several years, she began to write a book that was to come out in 1963 not as *The Togetherness Woman* but as *The Feminine Mystique.* She was approaching forty as she began, but she was regenerated by the project; it seemed to give her her own life back. The result was a seminal book on what had happened to women in America. It started selling slowly, but word of it grew and grew, and eventually, with three million copies in print, it became a handbook for the new feminist movement that was coming together.

Trumpet of Conscience
A Portrait of Martin Luther King, Jr.

A noted biographer examines the life and legacy of the civil rights leader who may have been the most-loved and most-hated man in America during the turbulent 1960s.

Stephen B. Oates

Biographer and historian Stephen B. Oates is Paul Murray Kendall Professor of Biography and Professor of History at the University of Massachusetts, Amherst. He is the author of twelve books, including award-winning biographies of John Brown, Nat Turner, Abraham Lincoln, and Martin Luther King, Jr. His newest biography, William Faulkner: The Man and the Artist, *was published by Harper & Row in 1987. "This article on Martin Luther King," writes Oates, "is dedicated to the memory of James Baldwin, who had a powerful influence on me in the 1960s, when I was a young writer trying to understand the complexities of American race relations."*

He was M.L. to his parents, Martin to his wife and friends, Doc to his aides, Reverend to his male parishioners, Little Lord Jesus to adoring churchwomen, De Lawd to his young critics in the Student Nonviolent Coordinating Committee, and Martin Luther King, Jr., to the world. At his pulpit or a public rostrum, he seemed too small for his incomparable oratory and international fame as a civil rights leader and spokesman for world peace. He stood only five feet seven, and had round cheeks, a trim mustache, and sad, glistening eyes—eyes that revealed both his inner strength and his vulnerability.

He was born in Atlanta on January 15, 1929, and grew up in the relative comfort of the black middle class. Thus he never suffered the want and privation that plagued the majority of American blacks of his time. His father, a gruff, self-made man, was pastor of Ebenezer Baptist Church and an outspoken member of Atlanta's black leadership. M.L. joined his father's church when he was five and came to regard it as his second home. The church defined his world, gave it order and balance, taught him how to "get along with people." Here M.L. knew who he was—"Reverend King's boy," somebody special.

At home, his parents and maternal grandmother reinforced his self-esteem, praising him for his precocious ways, telling him repeatedly that he was *somebody*. By age five, he spoke like an adult and had such a prodigious memory that he could recite whole Biblical passages and entire hymns without a mistake. He was acutely sensitive, too, so much so that he worried about all the blacks he saw in Atlanta's breadlines during the Depression, fearful that their children did not have enough to eat. When his maternal grandmother died, twelve-year-old M.L. thought it was his fault. Without telling anyone, he had slipped away from home to watch a parade, only to find out when he returned that she had died. He was terrified that God had taken her away as punishment for his "sin." Guilt-stricken, he tried to kill himself by leaping out of his second-story window.

He had a great deal of anger in him. Growing up a black in segregated Atlanta, he felt the full range of southern racial discrimination. He discovered that he had to attend separate, inferior schools, which he sailed through with a modicum of effort, skipping grades as he went. He found out that he—a preacher's boy—could not sit at lunch counters in Atlanta's downtown stores. He had to drink from a "colored" water fountain, relieve himself in a rancid "colored" restroom, and ride a rickety "colored" elevator. If he rode a city bus, he had to sit in the back as though he were contaminated. If he wanted to see a movie in a downtown theater, he had to enter through a side door and sit in the "colored" section in the balcony. He discovered that whites referred to blacks as "boys" and "girls" regardless of age. He saw "WHITES ONLY" signs staring back at him in the windows of barber shops and all the good restaurants and hotels, at the YMCA, the city parks, golf courses, swimming pools, and in the waiting rooms of the train and bus stations. He learned that there were even white and black sections of the city and that he resided in "nigger town."

Segregation caused a tension in the boy, a tension between his parents' injunction ("Remember, you are *somebody*") and a system that constantly demeaned and insulted him. He struggled with the pain and rage he felt when a white woman in a downtown store slapped him and called him "a little nigger" . . . when a bus driver called him "a black son-of-a-bitch" and made him surrender his seat to a white . . . when he stood on the very spot in Atlanta where whites had lynched a black man . . . when he witnessed nightriding Klansmen beating blacks in the streets. How, he asked defiantly, could he heed the Christian injunction and love a race of people who hated him? In retaliation, he determined "to hate every white person."

Yes, he was angry. In sandlot games, he competed so fiercely that friends could not tell whether he was playing or fighting. He had his share of playground combat, too, and could outwrestle any of his peers. He even rebelled against his father, vowing never to become a preacher like him. Yet he liked the way Daddy King stood up to whites: he told them never to call him a boy and vowed to fight this system until he died.

From *American History Illustrated*, April 1988, pp. 19-27, 52. © 1988 by Cowles Magazines, Inc. Reprinted through the courtesy of Cowles Magazines, Inc., publisher of *American History Illustrated*.

Still, there was another side to M.L., a calmer, sensuous side. He played the violin, enjoyed opera, and relished soul food—fried chicken, cornbread, and collard greens with ham hocks and bacon drippings. By his mid-teens, his voice was the most memorable thing about him. It had changed into a rich and resonant baritone that commanded attention whenever he held forth. A natty dresser, nicknamed "Tweed" because of his fondness for tweed suits, he became a connoisseur of lovely young women. His little brother A.D. remembered how Martin "kept flitting from chick to chick" and was "just about the best jitterbug in town."

AT AGE FIFTEEN, HE ENTERED MOREHOUSE College in Atlanta, wanting somehow to help his people. He thought about becoming a lawyer and even practiced giving trial speeches before a mirror in his room. But thanks largely to Morehouse President Benjamin Mays, who showed him that the ministry could be a respectable forum for ideas, even for social protest, King decided to become a Baptist preacher after all. By the time he was ordained in 1947, his resentment toward whites had softened some, thanks to positive contact with white students on an intercollegiate council. But he hated his segregated world more than ever.

Once he had his bachelor's degree, he went north to study at Crozer Seminary near Philadelphia. In this mostly white school, with its polished corridors and quiet solemnity, King continued to ponder the plight of blacks in America. How, by what method and means, were blacks to improve their lot in a white-dominated country? His study of history, especially of Nat Turner's slave insurrection, convinced him that it was suicidal for a minority to strike back against a heavily armed majority. For him, voluntary segregation was equally unacceptable, as was accommodation to the status quo. King shuddered at such negative approaches to the race problem. How indeed were blacks to combat discrimination in a country ruled by the white majority?

As some other blacks had done, he found his answer in the teachings of Mohandas Gandhi—for young King, the discovery had the force of a conversion experience. Nonviolent resistance, Gandhi taught, meant noncooperation with evil, an idea he got from Henry David Thoreau's essay "On Civil Disobedience." In India, Gandhi gave Thoreau's theory practical application in the form of strikes, boycotts, and protest marches, all conducted nonviolently and all predicated on love for the oppressor and a belief in divine justice. In gaining Indian independence, Gandhi sought not to defeat the British, but to redeem them through love, so as to avoid a legacy of bitterness. Gandhi's term for this—Satyagraha—reconciled love and force in a single, powerful concept.

As King discovered from his studies, Gandhi had embraced nonviolence in part to subdue his own violent nature. This was a profound revelation for King, who had felt much hatred in his life, especially toward whites. Now Gandhi showed him a means of harnessing his anger and channeling it into a positive and creative force for social change.

AT THIS JUNCTURE, KING FOUND MOSTLY theoretical satisfaction in Gandhian nonviolence; he had no plans to become a radical activist in the segregated South. Indeed, he seemed destined to a life of the mind, not of social protest. In 1951, he graduated from Crozer and went on to earn a Ph.D. in theology from Boston University, where his adviser pronounced him "a scholar's scholar" of great intellectual potential. By 1955, a year after the school desegregation decision, King had married comely Coretta Scott and assumed the pastorship of Dexter Avenue Baptist Church in Montgomery, Alabama. Immensely happy in the world of ideas, he hoped eventually to teach theology at a major university or seminary.

But, as King liked to say, the Zeitgeist, or spirit of the age, had other plans for him. In December 1955, Montgomery blacks launched a boycott of the city's segregated buses and chose the articulate twenty-six-year-old minister as their spokesman.* As it turned out, he was unusually well prepared to assume the kind of leadership thrust on him. Drawing on Gandhi's teachings and example, plus the tenets of his own Christian faith, King directed a nonviolent boycott designed both to end an injustice and redeem his white adversaries through love. When he exhorted blacks to love their enemies, King did not mean to love them

*See "The Father His Children Forgot" in the December 1985 issue of American History Illustrated.

as friends or intimates. No, he said, he meant a disinterested love in all humankind, a love that saw the neighbor in everyone it met, a love that sought to restore the beloved community. Such love not only avoided the internal violence of the spirit, but severed the external chain of hatred that only produced more hatred in an endless spiral. If American blacks could break the chain of hatred, King said, true brotherhood could begin. Then posterity would have to say that there had lived a race of people, of black people, who "injected a new meaning into the veins of history and civilization."

During the boycott King imparted his philosophy at twice-weekly mass meetings in the black churches, where overflow crowds clapped and cried as his mellifluous voice swept over them. In these mass meetings King discovered his extraordinary power as an orator. His rich religious imagery reached deep into the black psyche, for religion had been the black people's main source of strength and survival since slavery days. His delivery was "like a narrative poem," said a woman journalist who heard him. His voice had such depths of sincerity and empathy that it could "charm your heart right out of your body." Because he appealed to the best in his people, articulating their deepest hurts and aspirations, black folk began to idolize him; he was their Gandhi.

Under his leadership, they stood up to white Montgomery in a remarkable display of solidarity. Pitted against an obdurate city government that blamed the boycott on Communist agitation and resorted to psychological and legal warfare to break it, the blacks stayed off the buses month after month, and walked or rode in a black-operated carpool. When an elderly woman refused the offer of a ride, King asked her, "But don't your feet hurt?" "Yes," she replied, "my feet is tired but my soul is rested." For King, her irrepressible spirit was proof that "a new Negro" was emerging in the South, a Negro with "a new sense of dignity and destiny."

That "new Negro" menaced white supremacists, especially the Ku Klux Klan, and they persecuted King with a vengeance. They made obscene phone calls to his home, sent him abusive, sickening letters, and once even dynamited the front of his house. Nobody was hurt, but King, fearing a race war, had to dissuade angry blacks from violent retaliation. Finally, on November 13, 1956, the U.S. Supreme Court nullified the Alabama laws that enforced segregated buses, and handed King and his boycotters a resounding moral victory. Their protest had captured the imagination of progressive people all over the world and marked the beginning of a southern black movement that would shake the segregated South to its foundations. At the forefront of that movement was a new organization, the Southern Christian Leadership Conference (SCLC), which King and other black ministers formed in 1957, with King serving as its president and guiding spirit. Operating through the southern black church, SCLC sought to enlist the black masses in the freedom struggle by expanding "the Montgomery way" across the South.

The "Miracle of Montgomery" changed King's life, catapulting him into international prominence as an inspiring new moral voice for civil rights. Across the country, blacks and whites alike wrote him letters of encouragement; *Time* magazine pictured him on its cover; the National Association for the Advancement of Colored People (NAACP) and scores of church and civic organizations vied for his services as a speaker. "I am really disturbed how fast all this has happened to me," King told his wife. "People will expect me to perform miracles for the rest of my life."

But fame had its evil side, too. When King visited New York in 1958, a deranged black woman stabbed him in the chest with a letter opener. The weapon was lodged so close to King's aorta, the main artery from the heart, that he would have died had he sneezed. To extract the blade, an interracial surgical team had to remove a rib and part of his breastbone; in a burst of inspiration, the lead surgeon made the incision over King's heart in the shape of a cross.

THAT HE HAD NOT DIED CONVINCED KING that God was preparing him for some larger work in the segregated South. To gain perspective on what was happening there, he made a pilgrimage to India to visit Gandhi's shrine and the sites of his "War for Independence." He returned home with an even deeper commitment to nonviolence and a vow to be more humble and ascetic like Gandhi. Yet he was a man of manifold contradictions, this American Gandhi. While renouncing material things and giving nearly all

of his extensive honorariums to SCLC, he liked posh hotels and zesty meals with wine, and he was always immaculately dressed in a gray or black suit, white shirt, and tie. While caring passionately for the poor, the downtrodden, and the disinherited, he had a fascination with men of affluence and enjoyed the company of wealthy SCLC benefactors. While trumpeting the glories of nonviolence and redemptive love, he could feel the most terrible anger when whites murdered a black or bombed a black church; he could contemplate giving up, turning America over to the haters of both races, only to dedicate himself anew to his nonviolent faith and his determination to redeem his country.

In 1960, he moved his family to Atlanta so that he could devote himself fulltime to SCLC, which was trying to register black voters for the upcoming federal elections. That same year, southern black students launched the sit-in movement against segregated lunch counters, and King not only helped them form the Student Nonviolent Coordinating Committee (SNCC) but raised money on their behalf. In October he even joined a sit-in protest at an Atlanta department store and went to jail with several students on a trespassing charge. Like Thoreau, King considered jail "a badge of honor." To redeem the nation and arouse the conscience of the opponent, King explained, you go to jail and stay there. "You have broken a law which is out of line with the moral law and you are willing to suffer the consequences by serving the time."

He did not reckon, however, on the tyranny of racist officials, who clamped him in a malevolent state penitentiary, in a cell for hardened criminals. But state authorities released him when Democratic presidential nominee John F. Kennedy and his brother Robert interceded on King's behalf. According to many analysts, the episode won critical black votes for Kennedy and gave him the election in November. For King, the election demonstrated what he had long said: that one of the most significant steps a black could take was the short walk to the voting booth.

The trouble was that most blacks in Dixie, especially in the Deep South, could not vote even if they so desired. For decades, state and local authorities had kept the mass of black folk off the voting rolls by a welter of devious obstacles and outright intimidation. Through

1961 and 1962, King exhorted President Kennedy to sponsor tough new civil rights legislation that would enfranchise southern blacks and end segregated public accommodations as well. When Kennedy shied away from a strong civil rights commitment, King and his lieutenants took matters into their own hands, orchestrating a series of southern demonstrations to show the world the brutality of segregation. At the same time, King stumped the country, drawing on all his powers of oratory to enlist the black masses and win white opinion to his cause.

Everywhere he went his message was the same. The *civil rights issue*, he said, *is an eternal moral issue that will determine the destiny of our nation and our world. As we seek our full rights, we hope to redeem the soul of our country. For it is our country, too, and we will win our freedom because the sacred heritage of America and the eternal will of God are embodied in our echoing demands. We do not intend to humiliate the white man, but to win him over through the strength of our love. Ultimately, we are trying to free all of us in America— Negroes from the bonds of segregation and shame, whites from the bonds of bigotry and fear.*

We stand today between two worlds— the dying old order and the emerging new. With men of ill-will greeting this change with cries of violence, of interposition and nullification, some of us may get beaten. Some of us may even get killed. But if you are cut down in a movement designed to save the soul of a nation, no other death could be more redemptive. We must realize that change does not roll in "on the wheels of inevitability," but comes through struggle. So "let us be those creative dissenters who will call our beloved nation to a higher destiny, to a new plateau of compassion, to a more noble expression of humaneness."

That message worked like magic among America's long-suffering blacks. Across the South, across America, they rose in unprecedented numbers to march and demonstrate with Martin Luther King. His singular achievement was that he brought the black masses into the freedom struggle for the first time. He rallied the strength of broken men and women, helping them overcome a lifetime of fear and feelings of inferiority. After segregation had taught them all their lives that they were *nobody*, King taught them that they were *somebody*. Because he made them believe in themselves and in the beauty of chosen suffering, he taught them how to straighten their backs (''a man can't ride you unless your back is bent'') and confront those who oppressed them. Through the technique of nonviolent resistance, he furnished them something no previous black leader had been able to provide. He showed them a way of controlling their pent-up anger, as he had controlled his own, and using it to bring about constructive change.

THE MASS DEMONSTRATIONS KING AND SCLC choreographed in the South produced the strongest civil rights legislation in American history. This was the goal of King's major southern campaigns from 1963 to 1965. He would single out some notoriously segregated city with white officials prone to violence, mobilize the local blacks with songs, scripture readings, and rousing oratory in black churches, and then lead them on protest marches conspicuous for their grace and moral purpose. Then he and his aides would escalate the marches, increase their demands, even fill up the jails, until they brought about a moment of ''creative tension,'' when whites would either agree to negotiate or resort to violence. If they did the latter, King would thus expose the brutality inherent in segregation and so stab the national conscience so that the federal government would be forced to intervene with corrective measures.

The technique succeeded brilliantly in Birmingham, Alabama, in 1963. Here Police Commissioner Eugene ''Bull'' Connor, in full view of reporters and television cameras, turned firehoses and police dogs on the marching protestors. Revolted by such ghastly scenes, stricken by King's own searching eloquence and the bravery of his unarmed followers, Washington eventually produced the 1964 Civil Rights Act, which desegregated public facilities—the thing King had demanded all along from Birmingham. Across the South, the ''WHITES ONLY'' signs that had hurt and enraged him since boyhood now came down.

Although SNCC and others complained that King had a Messiah complex and was trying to monopolize the civil rights movement, his technique worked with equal success in Selma, Alabama, in 1965. Building on a local movement

there, King and his staff launched a drive to gain southern blacks the unobstructed right to vote. The violence he exposed in Selma—the beating of black marchers by state troopers and deputized possemen, the killing of a young black deacon and a white Unitarian minister—horrified the country. When King called for support, thousands of ministers, rabbis, priests, nuns, students, lay leaders, and ordinary people—black and white alike—rushed to Selma from all over the country and stood with King in the name of human liberty. Never in the history of the movement had so many people of all faiths and classes come to the southern battleground. The Selma campaign culminated in a dramatic march over the Jefferson Davis Highway to the state capital of Montgomery. Along the way, impoverished local blacks stared incredulously at the marching, singing, flag-waving spectacle moving by. When the column reached one dusty crossroads, an elderly black woman ran out from a group of old folk, kissed King breathlessly, and ran back crying, ''I done kissed him! The Martin Luther King! I done kissed the Martin Luther King!''

In Montgomery, first capital and much-heralded ''cradle'' of the Confederacy, King led an interracial throng of 25,000—the largest civil rights demonstration the South had ever witnessed—up Dexter Avenue with banners waving overhead. The pageant was as ironic as it was extraordinary, for it was up Dexter Avenue that Jefferson Davis's first inaugural parade had marched, and in the portico of the capitol Davis had taken his oath of office as president of the slave-based Confederacy. Now, in the spring of 1965, Alabama blacks—most of them descendants of slaves—stood massed at the same statehouse, singing a new rendition of ''We Shall Overcome,'' the anthem of the civil rights movement. They sang, ''Deep in my heart, I do believe, We have overcome—*today*.''

Then, within view of the statue of Jefferson Davis, and watched by cordons of state troopers and television cameras, King mounted a trailer. His vast audience listened, transfixed, as his words rolled and thundered over the loudspeaker: ''My people, my people listen. The battle is in our hands. . . . We must come to see that the end we seek is a society at peace with itself, a society that can live with its conscience. That day will be a day not of the white man, not of the black man. That will be the day of

man as man.'' And that day was not long in coming, King said, whereupon he launched into the immortal refrains of ''The Battle Hymn of the Republic,'' crying out, ''Our God is marching on! Glory, glory hallelujah!''

Aroused by the events in Alabama, Washington produced the 1965 Voting Rights Act, which outlawed impediments to black voting and empowered the attorney general to supervise federal elections in seven southern states where blacks were kept off the rolls. At the time, political analysts almost unanimously attributed the act to King's Selma campaign. Once federal examiners were supervising voter registration in all troublesome southern areas, blacks were able to get on the rolls and vote by the hundreds of thousands, permanently altering the pattern of southern and national politics.

In the end, the powerful civil rights legislation generated by King and his tramping legions wiped out statutory racism in America and realized at least the social and political promise of emancipation a century before. But King was under no illusion that legislation alone could bring on the brave new America he so ardently championed. Yes, he said, laws and their vigorous enforcement were necessary to regulate destructive habits and actions, and to protect blacks and their rights. But laws could not eliminate the ''fears, prejudice, pride, and irrationality'' that were barriers to a truly integrated society, to peaceful intergroup and interpersonal living. Such a society could be achieved only when people accepted that inner, invisible law that etched on their hearts the conviction ''that all men are brothers and that love is mankind's most potent weapon for personal and social transformation. True integration will be achieved by true neighbors who are willingly obedient to unenforceable obligations.''

Even so, the Selma campaign was the movement's finest hour, and the Voting Rights Act the high point of a broad civil rights coalition that included the federal government, various white groups, and all the other civil rights organizations in addition to SCLC. King himself had best expressed the spirit and aspirations of that coalition when, on August 28, 1963, standing before the Lincoln Memorial, he electrified an interracial crowd of 250,000 with perhaps his greatest speech, ''I Have A Dream,'' in which he described in rhythmic, hypnotic cadences his vision of an integrated America. Because of his achievements and moral vision, he won the 1964 Nobel Peace Prize, at thirty-four the youngest recipient in Nobel history.

STILL, KING PAID A HIGH PRICE FOR HIS fame and his cause. He suffered from stomachaches and insomnia, and even felt guilty about all the tributes he received, all the popularity he enjoyed. Born in relative material comfort and given a superior education, he did not think he had earned the right to lead the impoverished black masses. He complained, too, that he no longer had a personal self and that sometimes he did not recognize the Martin Luther King people talked about. Lonely, away from home for protracted periods, beset with temptation, he slept with other women, for some of whom he had real feeling. His sexual transgressions only added to his guilt, for he knew he was imperiling his cause and hurting himself and those he loved.

Alas for King, FBI Director J. Edgar Hoover found out about the black leader's infidelities. The director already abhorred King, certain that Communist spies influenced him and masterminded his demonstrations. Hoover did not think blacks capable of organizing such things, so Communists had to be behind them and King as well. As it turned out, a lawyer in King's inner circle and a man in SCLC's New York office did have Communist backgrounds, a fact that only reinforced Hoover's suspicions about King. Under Hoover's orders, FBI agents conducted a ruthless crusade to destroy King's reputation and drive him broken and humiliated from public life. Hoover's men tapped King's phones and bugged his hotel rooms; they compiled a prurient monograph about his private life and showed it to various editors, public officials, and religious and civic leaders; they spread the word, Hoover's word, that King was not only a reprobate but a dangerous subversive with Communist associations.

King was scandalized and frightened by the FBI's revelations of his extramarital affairs. Luckily for him, no editor, not even a racist one in the South, would touch the FBI's salacious materials. Public officials such as Robert Kennedy were shocked, but argued that King's personal life did not affect his probity as a civil rights leader. Many blacks, too, declared that what he did in private was

his own business. Even so, King vowed to refrain from further affairs—only to succumb again to his own human frailties.

As for the Communist charge, King retorted that he did not need any Russians to tell him when someone was standing on his neck; he could figure that out by himself. To mollify his political friends, however, King did banish from SCLC the two men with Communist backgrounds (later he resumed his ties with the lawyer, a loyal friend, and let Hoover be damned). He also denounced Communism in no uncertain terms. It was, he believed, profoundly and fundamentally evil, an atheistic doctrine no true Christian could ever embrace. He hated the dictatorial Soviet state, too, whose "crippling totalitarianism" subordinated everything—religion, art, music, science, and the individual—to its terrible yoke. True, Communism started with men like Karl Marx who were "aflame with a passion for social justice." Yet King faulted Marx for rejecting God and the spiritual in human life. "The great weakness in Karl Marx is right here," King once told his staff, and he went on to describe his ideal Christian commonwealth in Hegelian terms: "Capitalism fails to realize that life is social. Marxism fails to realize that life is individual. Truth is found neither in the rugged individualism of capitalism nor in the impersonal collectivism of Communism. The kingdom of God is found in a synthesis that combines the truths of these two opposites. Now there is where I leave brother Marx and move on toward the kingdom."

BUT HOW TO MOVE ON AFTER SELMA WAS a perplexing question King never successfully answered. After the devastating Watts riot in August 1965, he took his movement into the racially troubled urban North, seeking to help the suffering black poor in the ghettos. In 1966, over the fierce opposition of some of his own staff, he launched a campaign to end the black slums in Chicago and forestall rioting there. But the campaign foundered because King seemed unable to devise a coherent anti-slum strategy, because Mayor Richard Daley and his black acolytes opposed him bitterly, and because white America did not seem to care. King did lead open-housing marches into segregated neighborhoods in Chicago, only to encounter furious mobs who waved Nazi banners, threw bottles

and bricks, and screamed, "We hate niggers!" "Kill the niggers!" "We want Martin Luther Coon!" King was shocked. "I've been in many demonstrations all across the South," he told reporters, "but I can say that I have never seen—even in Mississippi and Alabama—mobs as hostile and as hate-filled as I've seen in Chicago." Although King prevented a major riot there and wrung important concessions from City Hall, the slums remained, as wretched and seemingly unsolvable as ever.

That same year, angry young militants in SNCC and the Congress of Racial Equality (CORE) renounced King's teachings—they were sick and tired of "De Lawd" telling them to love white people and work for integration. Now they advocated "Black Power," black separatism, even violent resistance to liberate blacks in America. SNCC even banished whites from its ranks and went on to drop "nonviolent" from its name and to lobby against civil rights legislation.

Black Power repelled the older, more conservative black organizations such as the NAACP and the Urban League, and fragmented the civil rights movement beyond repair. King, too, argued that black separatism was chimerical, even suicidal, and that nonviolence remained the only workable way for black people. "Darkness cannot drive out darkness," he reasoned: "only light can do that. Hate cannot drive out hate: only love can do that." If every other black in America turned to violence, King warned, then he would still remain the lone voice preaching that it was wrong. Nor was SCLC going to reject whites as SNCC had done. "There have been too many hymns of hope," King said, "too many anthems of expectation, too many deaths, too many dark days of standing over graves of those who fought for integration for us to turn back now. We must still sing 'Black and White Together, We Shall Overcome.' "

In 1967, King himself broke with the older black organizations over the ever-widening war in Vietnam. He had first objected to American escalation in the summer of 1965, arguing that the Nobel Peace Prize and his role as a Christian minister compelled him to speak out for peace. Two years later, with almost a half-million Americans—a disproportionate number of them poor blacks—fighting in Vietnam, King devoted whole speeches to America's "immoral" war against a tiny country on the other side of the globe. His stance provoked a fusillade of criticism from all directions—from the NAACP, the Urban League, white and black political leaders, *Newsweek, Life, Time,* and the *New York Times,* all telling him to stick to civil rights. Such criticism hurt him deeply. When he read the *Times*'s editorial against him, he broke down and cried. But he did not back down. "I've fought too long and too hard now against segregated accommodations to end up segregating my moral concerns," he told his critics. "Injustice anywhere is a threat to justice everywhere."

That summer, with the ghettos ablaze with riots, King warned that American cities would explode if funds used for war purposes were not diverted to emergency antipoverty programs. By then, the Johnson administration, determined to gain a military victory in Vietnam, had written King off as an antiwar agitator, and was now cooperating with the FBI in its efforts to defame him.

The fall of 1967 was a terrible time for King, the lowest ebb in his civil rights career. Everybody seemed to be attacking him—young black militants for his stubborn adherence to nonviolence, moderate and conservative blacks, labor leaders, liberal white politicians, the White House, and the FBI for his stand on Vietnam. Two years had passed since King had produced a nonviolent victory, and contributions to SCLC had fallen off sharply. Black spokesman Adam Clayton Powell, who had once called King the greatest Negro in America, now derided him as Martin Loser King. The incessant attacks began to irritate him, creating such anxiety and depression that his friends worried about his emotional health.

Worse still, the country seemed dangerously polarized. On one side, backlashing whites argued that the ghetto explosions had "cremated" nonviolence and that white people had better arm themselves against black rioters. On the other side, angry blacks urged their peo-

ple to "kill the Honkies" and burn the cities down. All around King, the country was coming apart in a cacophony of hate and reaction. Had America lost the will and moral power to save itself? he wondered. There was such rage in the ghetto and such bigotry among whites that he feared a race war was about to break out. He felt he had to do something to pull America back from the brink. He and his staff had to mount a new campaign that would halt the drift to violence in the black world and combat stiffening white resistance, a nonviolent action that would "transmute the deep rage of the ghetto into a constructive and creative force."

OUT OF HIS DELIBERATIONS SPRANG A BOLD and daring project called the poor people's campaign. The master plan, worked out by February 1968, called for SCLC to bring an interracial army of poor people to Washington, D.C., to dramatize poverty before the federal government. For King, just turned thirty-nine, the time had come to employ civil disobedience against the national government itself. Ultimately, he was projecting a genuine class movement that he hoped would bring about meaningful changes in American society—changes that would redistribute economic and political power and end poverty, racism, "the madness of militarism," and war.

In the midst of his preparations, King went to Memphis, Tennessee, to help black sanitation workers there who were striking for the right to unionize. On the night of April 3, with a storm thundering outside, he told a black audience that he had been to the mountaintop and had seen what lay ahead. "I may not get there with you. But I want you to know tonight that we as a people *will* get to the promised land."

The next afternoon, when King stepped out on the balcony of the Lorraine Motel, an escaped white convict named James

Earl Ray, stationed in a nearby building, took aim with a high-powered rifle and blasted King into eternity. Subsequent evidence linked Ray to white men in the St. Louis area who had offered "hit" money for King's life.

For weeks after the shooting, King's stricken country convulsed in grief, contrition, and rage. While there were those who cheered his death, the *New York Times* called it a disaster to the nation, the *London Times* an enormous loss to the world. In Tanzania, Reverend Trevor Huddleston, expelled from South Africa for standing against apartheid, declared King's death the greatest single tragedy since the assassination of Gandhi in 1948, and said it challenged the complacency of the Christian Church all over the globe.

On April 9, with 120 million Americans watching on television, thousands of mourners—black and white alike—gathered in Atlanta for the funeral of a man who had never given up his dream of creating a symphony of brotherhood on these shores. As a black man born and raised in segregation, he had had every reason to hate America and to grow up preaching cynicism and retaliation. Instead, he had loved the country passionately and had sung of her promise and glory more eloquently than anyone of his generation.

They buried him in Atlanta's South View Cemetery, then blooming with dogwood and fresh green boughs of spring. On his crypt, hewn into the marble, were the words of an old Negro spiritual he had often quoted: "Free at Last, Free at Last, Thank God Almighty I'm Free at Last."

Recommended additional reading: Let the Trumpet Sound: The Life of Martin Luther King, Jr. *by Stephen B. Oates (Harper & Row, 1982), and* A Testament of Hope: The Essential Writings of Martin Luther King, Jr. *edited by James M. Washington (Harper & Row, 1986).*

Chicago '68: The Democrats' Judgment Days

Summary: In the heat of August in 1968, the whole world was watching as student protesters descended on Chicago, site of the Democratic National Convention. The ensuing violence had repercussions for the Democratic Party and liberalism that many believe are still being felt. Views vary as to what those effects have been, but there is little doubt that Chicago changed the face of politics in America.

Michael Rust

"The Death of Liberalism" was the blaring headline on the cover of *Ramparts* magazine's October 1968 issue. It was printed over a poster of a smiling Hubert Humphrey—deposited in a trash can.

That was how *Ramparts,* a now-defunct voice of late 1960s radicalism, interpreted the 1968 Democratic National Convention. Twenty-five years later, a former co-editor of the magazine says the headline has proved accurate. "Liberalism was killed" when the Democrats met in Chicago that year, says David Horowitz, who in the intervening years has become a convert to.Reaganism. "It was a disaster for the Democratic Party and for the country."

Not all veterans of the political and cultural wars share Horowitz's view. But few contest the idea that when the Democrats convened in 1968—one of the most troubled years in modern American history—the upheaval was of such magnitude that tremors are still felt today.

President Clinton's current difficulties with Congress show that controlling both Congress and the White House doesn't guarantee a return to what Humphrey called "the politics of joy." Democrats united to win the White House last year, but that doesn't mean they share a common vision or even the same policy goals. Just as physical trauma can leave psychological scars, the roots of the current Democratic dysfunction can be seen in the unrestful sojourn in Chicago long ago.

In the hot August of 1968, the state of political debate was represented by tear-gas-filled streets rather than smoke-filled rooms. By the time the four-day convention closed, 28,000 police, Army troops, Illinois National Guardsmen and federal agents had been deployed in the streets of Chicago. The evening before the convention opened, the stage was set for violence when police forcibly cleared protesters from Lincoln Park. The night Humphrey was nominated, the TV networks cut away from delegates voting at the convention hall to focus on violence at Grant Park. As tear gas filled the air, police there attacked protesters who—in one of the more memorable media moments of the era—began to chant, "The whole world is watching! The whole world is watching!"

Meanwhile, at the International Amphitheater, Democrats tore their party apart as veterans of the insurgent candidacies of Eugene McCarthy and the recently assassinated Robert Kennedy attempted to block passage of a platform plank endorsing the Vietnam War policies of President Lyndon Johnson. Tensions over the war ran so high that no Democrat could guarantee the incumbent president a friendly reception, so Johnson—a landslide winner four years before—watched the convention on television from his ranch in Texas.

"It was probably the rawest division and the most damaging political division the Democratic Party has suffered," says former South Dakota Sen. George McGovern, the party's 1972 presidential nominee who mounted a last-minute bid for the nomination at Chicago in 1968. McGovern is no stranger to the policy rifts and personal feuds that have enlivened Democratic politics over the years, but he maintains that there was "a harsher tone to that Chicago convention than to most of the other issues that have separated Democrats."

Certainly, the short-term consequences were disastrous. The implosion of the party at Chicago placed nominee Humphrey in a political hole from which he was unable to extricate himself. The vice president would narrowly lose in November to Richard Nixon—the first GOP presidential candidate in 40 years (with the exception of war hero Dwight Eisenhower) to grab the White House prize. Nixon's razor-thin win would be followed by Republican victories in four of the next five presidential contests.

The impact of the Chicago upheaval went far beyond a ruptured presidential campaign. For sociologist Todd Gitlin, a founder of the radical Students for a Democratic Society, or SDS, the violence in Chicago was the culmination of a decade of pressure—student activists had been growing more reckless, authorities more vengeful, and mainstream liberals more exhausted. The voices of youthful protest emerged from Chicago "committed to an impossible revolution," writes Gitlin in his book *The Sixties.* "The Right emerged armed for power and a more possible counter-revolution; liberals barely emerged at all. Chicago confirmed that no centers were

Reprinted with permission from *Insight,* September 13, 1993, pp. 7-13. © 1993 by the Washington Times Corporation. All rights reserved.

going to hold, no wisdom was going to prevail." Gitlin maintains that "the polarizations etched into the common consciousness that week are still working their way through American politics."

And for apostate radical Horowitz, Chicago marks the point where the media legitimized leftism. "The poison of the left was contained in the 1950s," he says. "It was quarantined in a left-wing ghetto." Media coverage of the convention helped radicalism emerge from that ghetto to gain cultural acceptance, he says, adding that it will take "many generations to recover from this disaster."

For political analyst Jeffrey Bell—who in 1968 was moving from a stint as an enlisted man in Vietnam to a staff position with Nixon's campaign—the convention marked a split between populist and elite opinion that signaled the end of the old Democratic coalition, which had united blue-collar workers with upper-middle-class liberals since the time of Franklin D. Roosevelt. "It was indicative of this whole thing that governs our politics," he says. "At Chicago, it became starkly evident there was a split between populists, who sided with the police, and elite opinion, which sympathized clearly with the students."

"At Chicago, it became starkly evident there was a split between populists, who sided with the police, and elite opinion, which sympathized clearly with the students," says political analyst Jeffrey Bell.

It wasn't just liberal elites, either. Bell argues that those who sympathized with the protesters were wealthier and better educated. Polls showed that the vast majority of voters in "Middle America" (a term that itself is a late 1960s artifact, coined by columnist Joseph Kraft) sided with the police rather than the demonstrators, even if they had doubts about the war and the Johnson administration in general.

For McCarthy, who had galvanized antiwar Democrats with his New Hampshire primary challenge to Johnson, the

turmoil in Chicago was the result of the Democrats refusing to accept responsibility for the Vietnam War, which had become, along with racial issues, a flash point for political upheaval. "As far as the party was concerned, I don't think it ever recovered from it."

1968 was a banner year for political trauma. The Viet Cong's Tet offensive in January had increased American skepticism about the government's ability or willingness to prosecute an effective war in Southeast Asia. McCarthy's antiwar challenge and the belated entrance of New York Sen. Robert Kennedy into the race were followed by the withdrawal of Johnson. Student revolt in Paris and a strike in New York's Columbia University seemed to indicate that the youth culture was capable of flexing political muscle.

The political tumult assumed a nightmarish aspect with the assassinations of Martin Luther King Jr. in April and of Kennedy after the California primary in June. In Chicago, King's assassination had been followed by rioting in the West Side ghetto, inspiring Mayor Richard J. Daley to instruct police to "shoot to kill arsonists and shoot to maim looters." In the weeks prior to the convention, Daley, doyen of one of the country's last old-fashioned urban political machines, refused to issue permits for rallies or to suspend the nightly curfew so young protesters could camp out in Lincoln Park.

Daley's hard-line position was bolstered by the tendency of city officials to believe just about any rumor they heard, says *Chicago Tribune* columnist Mike Royko. Wild reports about potential disruptions were spread by "Yippies"—specialists in guerrilla theater led by Jerry Rubin and Abbie Hoffman and who combined left-wing politics with counter-culture put-on, claiming to be promoting the presidential candidacy of a hog named Pigasus.

Virtually all accounts of the convention week agree that some protest organizers—such as SDS veterans Tom Hayden and Rennie Davis—were looking forward to a violent confrontation. James Miller, in his history of SDS, *Democracy Is in the Streets,* says that by the time the convention opened, some protest leaders were "in a mood of near-euphoria" after watching an NBC News correspondent conclude that barbed wire around the convention site was "the most chilling sight of the decade."

However, the response of the Democratic old guard, as personified by Daley, played directly into the hands of the extremists. The mayor could have avoided the violence, says Royko. "There's no question Hayden and Abbie and that whole crowd wanted to be on television. It didn't have to be that way and wouldn't have been" if the response had been more restrained. By midnight before the opening of the convention, participants in the Yippies' "Festival of Life" were stymied in Lincoln Park. To the east was Lake Shore Drive and to the west was the park border, "Where there were enough cops to fight a small war," Royko says. "Unless they rented limos, they would have had to get by the police, march through Mayor Daley's neighborhood, and then go through an unfriendly black neighborhood before they would reach the convention hall—which was seven miles away."

Royko says police officers told him after the riot that they should not have responded to taunts by the Yippies. Instead, they could have kept the protesters in the park hemmed in and awake all night by notifying them via bullhorn every half-hour that they weren't supposed to be there. The next morning, commuter traffic on Lake Shore Drive—which pauses for nothing, even social upheaval—would have isolated them further.

"There's no question Hayden and Abbie and that crowd wanted to be on television. It didn't have to be that way. The protesters would have had to get by the police, through Daley's neighborhood, and then through an unfriendly black neighborhood before they would reach the convention hall—seven miles away."

Chicago's mayor was simply too enraged by the idea of half-naked hippies defiling his city to think strategically, says Royko. "Daley thought of the city of Chicago as his family business."

Horowitz says that's exactly why Chicago was picked by organizers such as Hayden and Davis. "They knew that Daley could be provoked. The object was to produce a riot that would discredit the Hubert Humphrey wing of the Democratic Party, and it was successful."

It was an "institutionalized" response, says *New York Post* columnist Jack Newfield, who covered the convention for the *Village Voice*. "I know some of the demonstrators were coming to provoke that kind of violence, and I think the Chicago police are very tough and aggressive." Newfield believes it is possible that conservative Democrats wanted a show of force to lure back blue-collar voters who were drifting to the third-party campaign of Alabama Gov. George Wallace. "I think the whole thing may have been a setup."

Certainly, among Chicago's blue-collar wards, few tears were shed for the demonstrators, who never numbered more than 10,000, although organizers had hoped for 100,000. Heavily Democratic Chicago is "basically a conservative-minded city where most of the people were supportive of Daley's approach to the convention," says Royko. "The white reformers were appalled. The blacks were indifferent." The mayor "knew his constituency," he adds, although Daley's actions had an ironic result.

"Daley was always described as the kingmaker. The only guy he ever elected president was Nixon," says Royko, who agrees that the Democratic Party never really recovered from Chicago. Without the convention turmoil, "Humphrey would certainly have been elected."

When McCarthy and McGovern look back at Chicago, they don't see a party under assault from the left. Rather, they still see a party establishment that refused to see the Vietnam War as a moral issue.

Both of the 1968 candidates believe that overanxious police and incendiary radicals were "incidental," in McGovern's words. "The larger question was what caused the eruption at Chicago," he says. "That was the Vietnam War." Six months after the convention, McGovern was chairman of a commission to develop changes in the Democrats' delegate selection process. Daley was the leadoff witness at the commission's hearing in Chicago, and, McGovern says, "in an exchange with me, he made that statement—the prob-

lem in Chicago was the war in Vietnam. I think that's absolutely true."

McCarthy says the Democratic Party has faced two great moral tests in his lifetime—the 1948 convention, at which Humphrey led the successful fight for a strong civil rights plank, and 20 years later when the party "faced a similar moral problem—the fact that the Democrats were primarily responsible for the deeper and deeper involvement of the United States in Vietnam."

The party's response is why the turmoil could have been expected, says McCarthy. "The people who had to accept it and say, 'This is our war,' resented having to do so. I guess the classical response was to blame the people who made them face that decision."

McCarthy believes that as result, "what you have now is a different kind of Democratic Party." Not better, he adds—different. The Clinton administration "doesn't really have a line of connection" to the Democratic Party of 25 years ago, because the party set about to make itself over in the wake of the debacle at Chicago.

In the wake of Chicago—where Humphrey won the nomination with 1,567 votes despite the fact that 80 percent of the primary voters had voted for antiwar candidates—McGovern's commission began the process of remaking the Democratic nominating procedure. The reforms were an attempt to ensure that certain groups of party constituents, such as women, blacks, Hispanics and American Indians, would be represented in Democratic delegations in proportion to their share of the state's Democratic population.

Bell explains that many party organizations adapted to these reforms by switching from nominating conventions to primaries. In *Populism and Elitism*, Bell writes that the result was twofold. First, state parties sympathetic to the reforms were likely to conform to liberal interest groups by picking delegations that were both "balanced" and more left of center than mainstream voters. Second, it made primaries the dominant force in picking presidential nominees, thus weakening the influence of party elders.

McGovern feels this has led to a happier, healthier party. Reforms "helped to the extent [that] they made the disaffected feel they had a voice in the process—that there was a place for women, there was a place for blacks and

Hispanics and young people and the anti-war crowd. They at least felt they would have their day in court."

Now, McGovern says, the ruptures of the time "have been pretty much smoothed over," although he points out that the Democratic Leadership Council, which supplied Clinton with much of his intellectual firepower during last year's campaign, was set up by "New Democrats" to oppose what they saw as overly liberal Democratic positions on issues such as defense and racial quotas.

While party moderates are concerned that too much emphasis is being placed on getting the right racial, ethnic and gender numbers at nominating conventions, McGovern maintains that the 1968 troubles derived not just from a bewildering and costly war—that delaying action on minority concerns also played a role. "We went through a youth revolution and a black revolution and a sexual revolution in America," he says. "All of those came into focus in the momentum that created the McGovern reforms in the early seventies."

Joshua Muravchik, a resident scholar at Washington's American Enterprise Institute, laughs at the idea that the McGovern reforms saved the party. Democrats won seven of 10 presidential elections before the commission and lost four of six afterward, he points out. "We went from a 70 percent winning record to a 33 percent winning record. So if that's being saved, let's see who else lines up for such salvation."

What the McGovern reforms did was "take the Democratic Party out of the hands of the rank and file, blue-collar, working-class Democratic voter who had been the party's main base and deliver it into the hands of the college-educated, liberal activists."

McGovern says the violence at the convention made his reforms palatable to old-style pols "who saw it as a matter of survival for the party." He understands why some Democrats feel that the party went off the tracks during this era. "But that's always the view when you undertake painful and difficult reform. It's not easy to swallow, but I think it was essential for the Democratic Party to survive."

Critics of the reforms also believe that in the wake of Chicago, the party faced a fork in the road—but instead of reaching out to the wing of the middle class that had been horrified by the rioting, the Democratic elites chose to reach out to the demonstrators.

Now a neoconservative Democrat, Muravchik in 1968 chaired the Young People's Socialist League, the youth wing of the old Socialist Party. At the time, he was appalled by events in Chicago. He was "a kind of traditional Marxist in the sense that I believed that the working class were the good guys," he says. It was obvious, however, that the New Left which took to the streets was "very much the product of the college scene and the college-educated world."

There was "a spirit of class conflict" in the demonstrations, with the young radicals opposed to the working-class police, he says. "There was a hostility between them. The students, of course, were much more clever at manipulating it." Muravchik is another who believes the Democrats never recovered. "The party was transformed and it became the party of the 1960s left—a watered-down version."

Bell believes this party was able to win in 1992 because "Clinton was smart enough—as was Carter—to know the elites they had to win over were not representative of most rank and file Democrats." In 1968, he points out, many voters wondered why Humphrey hadn't taken a firmer stand against the protesters. "To many voters, he appeared to be an emblem of the governing Democrats themselves," Bell writes in *Populism and Elitism,* "unable to take sides, and thus no more able to end the rioting in their own convention city than the earlier rioting in black communities and college campuses." Chicago placed Humphrey in a vise hold. The electorate regarded him as indecisive, while the elite scorned him as a representative of an establishment that had been all too decisive in crushing dissent at the convention.

Bell points out that while Humphrey foundered in this morass, an interesting phenomenon was taking place. "Hardly any *articulate* voice in August 1968 assigned more blame to the students" than to the police and mayor, he writes. Yet, while elite observers on both the left and the right regarded the disruption as a "police riot"—as the Walker Report, an investigation conducted for the National Commission on the Causes and Prevention of Violence, would refer to it—polls showed that an overwhelming majority of the American people sided with the police. Bell says it was as if everyone in America felt forced to make a choice between the police and the students. The choice they made proved predictive of their later political choices for years, he says.

Sociologist Alan Wolfe believes that both political parties need to appeal to the divided middle class if they hope to win elections, and both, as a result, have tried to rationalize away the contradictions that inevitably occur.

This was apparent in the fall of 1968 in downstate Illinois, says Royko—who like most Chicagoans defines downstate as anywhere outside the metro area. "Before, any candidate who wanted to win downstate denounced the Daley machine. All of a sudden, Daley was a hero."

For the following quarter-century, there has been a basic contradiction in Democratic politics. In order to win the presidency, a Democrat must avoid the kind of party rupture that culminated in Chicago. At the same time, he must simultaneously please both party activists—who tend to the left—and middle- and working-class voters, whose defections in the wake of Chicago kept the Democrats out of the White House.

The Vietnam War and the counterculture split the middle class as a political force, suggests Alan Wolfe, a sociologist at the New School for Social Research. Both parties need to appeal to this divided bloc if they hope to win elections, and both, as a result, have tried to rationalize away the contradictions that inevitably occur.

The Democrats do this through an "ideology of modernization," and the GOP through a form of populism, he says. In this summer's issue of the *Wilson Quarterly,* Wolfe writes that the Democratic view holds that history moves toward greater "enlightenment" associated with material prosperity. The schools and the courts should be used to teach a more elevated morality, according to this view. The trouble with this approach, Wolfe points out, is evident in what has happened to the Democrats since 1968: "It can convey an unrelenting smugness and elitism."

The Republicans counter the Democratic approach, he argues, by claiming to have "a gritty, reality-based morality" that sees the world as it really is. This populist conservatism maintains that tapping public anger isn't demagoguery, but true democratic politics.

The result is that both Democrats and Republicans are uneasily attempting to balance cultural liberalism with more conservative economics. "I think it's an unstable set of ideas," says Wolfe. Liberals have created a mirror image of the "great schism in the conservative movement—between people who are free marketeers and people who are cultural conservatives."

If Chicago and 1968 didn't end a war, they did help change a party. Not only did that year usher the Democrats, for better or worse, into a new era—one in which the voices of protest would play a greater role—it also became part of the collective memory of a new generation of Democrats. In fact, some onetime revolutionaries have become a new party establishment. Hayden is a California state senator, while former Black Panther Bobby Rush is a congressman from Chicago.

McCarthy laughs when asked if he sees any irony in this. "It was a funny time," he says. "To expect people as young as the ones involved not to change is to expect too much."

Lessons from a Lost War

What has Viet Nam taught about when to use power—and when not to?

The customary reward of defeat, if one can survive it, is in the lessons thereby learned, which may yield victory in the next war. But the circumstances of our defeat in Vietnam were sufficiently ambiguous to deny the nation [that] benefit.
—Edward N. Luttwak
The Pentagon and the Art of War

Ten years after the fall of Saigon, the debacle in Southeast Asia remains a subject many Americans would rather not discuss. So the nation has been spared a searing, divisive inquest—"Who lost Viet Nam?"—but at a heavy price. The old divisions have been buried rather than resolved. They seem ready to break open again whenever anyone asks what lessons the U.S. should draw from its longest war, and the only one to end in an undisguisable defeat.

Was that loss inevitable, or could the war have been won with different strategy and tactics? Was the war fought for the right reasons? Did its aftermath prove or explode the domino theory? The questions are not in the least academic. They bear on the all-important problem of whether, when and how the U.S. should again send its troops to fight abroad.

Pondering these questions, Secretary of Defense Caspar Weinberger argues, citing Viet Nam, that "before the U.S. commits combat forces abroad, there must be some reasonable assurance that we will have the support of the American people and . . . Congress." Secretary of State George Shultz replies that "there is no such thing as guaranteed public support in advance." The lesson Shultz draws from Viet Nam is that "public support can be frittered away if we do not act wisely and effectively." And this open dispute between two senior members of the Reagan Cabinet is mild compared with the arguments among policy

"I want to rail against wind and tide, kill the whales in the ocean, sweep the whole country to save people from slavery."
—TRIEU AU, VIET NAM'S "JOAN OF ARC" A.D. 248

"France has had the country for nearly 100 years, and the people are worse off than at the beginning."
—FRANKLIN D. ROOSEVELT 1944

"Kill ten of our men and we will kill one of yours. In the end, it is you who will tire."
—HO CHI MINH 1946

analysts, Viet Nam veterans and the public about what kinds of wars can be won or even deserve public support in the first place.

A number of experts doubt that the U.S. can evolve any common view of Viet Nam and its lessons for many years to come. Says Graham Martin, the last U.S. Ambassador to South Viet Nam: "I estimated at the end of the war that it probably would be at least two decades before any rational, objective discussion of the war and its causes and effects could be undertaken by scholars who were not so deeply, emotionally engaged at the time that their later perceptions were colored by biases and prejudices." William Hyland, editor of *Foreign Affairs* magazine, thinks an even longer perspective may be required: "We always want to make historical judgments two days after the fact. Historians need 100 years."

But the U.S. is unlikely to have anywhere near that much time to decide what lessons to draw from Viet Nam and how to apply them. The initial impulse after the American withdrawal was to avoid any foreign involvement that might conceivably lead to a commitment of U.S. troops. Scholars differ on how seriously this so-called Viet Nam syndrome inhibited an activist U.S. foreign policy, but in any case it is fading—witness the enthusiastic approval of the Grenada invasion in late 1983 (to be sure, that was a rare case in which the U.S. was able to apply such overwhelming force that it could not have failed to win quickly). Says Maine's Republican Senator William Cohen: "The legacy of Viet Nam does not mean that we will not send our sons anywhere. It does mean that we will not send them everywhere." Even some fervent doves agree that memories of Viet Nam should not keep the U.S. from ever fighting anywhere. Sam Brown, onetime antiwar leader who now de-

From *Time*, April 15, 1985, pp. 40-42, 45. © 1985 by Time, Inc. Magazine Company. Reprinted by permission.

U.S. AIR FORCE

POWER

B-52 dropping bombs on guerrillas, 1966: Was it a matter of too much force, or not enough?

velops low-cost housing in Colorado, remains convinced that if it were not for the protests against U.S. involvement in Viet Nam that he helped organize, "we would have three or four other wars now." Even so, concedes Brown, some "wrong lessons" might be drawn, among them "the risk that we won't be prepared if our national interest is genuinely threatened."

But if the specter of Viet Nam no longer inhibits all thought of projecting U.S. military power overseas, it still haunts every specific decision. In the Middle East, Weinberger's fears of entrapment in a drawn-out conflict fought without public support caused him at first to oppose sending Marines to Lebanon and then to insist on their withdrawal after terrorist attacks left 266 U.S. servicemen dead. Shultz objected that the pullout would undercut U.S. diplomacy in the area, and still regards it as a mistake. But Ronald Reagan ordered the withdrawal anyway and won the approval of voters, even though critics portrayed the pullout as a national humiliation. The reason, suggests Democratic Political Analyst William Schneider, is that the President sensed the persistence of a popular attitude toward foreign military commitments that is summarized by the Viet Nam-era slogan "Win or Get Out." Says Schneider: "In Grenada we won. In Lebanon we got out. So much for the Viet Nam syndrome."

The Viet Nam experience colors al-

"Master fear and pain, overcome obstacles, unite your efforts, fight to the very end, annihilate the enemy."
—GENERAL GIAP
1954

"I could conceive of no greater tragedy than for the U.S. to [fight] an all-out war in Indochina."
—DWIGHT D. EISENHOWER
1954

"You have a row of dominoes set up, you knock over the first one and [the last one] will go over very quickly."
—EISENHOWER
1954

"We do commit the U.S. to preventing the fall of South Viet Nam to Communism."
—ROBERT MCNAMARA
1961

most every discussion of Central American policy. Nebraska Governor Bob Kerrey, who won a Congressional Medal of Honor and lost part of a leg fighting with the Navy SEAL commandos in Viet Nam, maintains that if memories of the ordeal in Southeast Asia were not still so strong, "we'd be in Nicaragua now." In Congress, Kerrey's fellow Democrats fret that the Administration's commitment to resist the spread of Marxist revolution throughout the isthmus could eventually bog down American troops in another endless jungle guerrilla war.

Reaganites retort, correctly, that while Viet Nam is halfway around the world and of debatable strategic importance to Washington, Central America is virtually next door, an area where U.S. interests are obvious. Moreover, the amounts Washington is spending to help the government of El Salvador defeat leftist guerrillas and to assist the contra rebels fighting the Marxist Sandinista government of Nicaragua are pittances compared with the sums lavished on South Viet Nam even before the direct U.S. military intervention there. Still, the Administration every now and then feels obliged to deny that it has any plan or desire to send U.S. troops to fight in Central America. Weinberger last November coupled his remarks about the necessity of popular support for any foreign military commitment with a pledge that "the President will not allow our military forces to creep—or be drawn gradually—into a combat role in Central America."

One of the few propositions about Viet Nam that commands near unanimous assent from Americans is the obvious one that the U.S. lost—and a growing number would qualify even that. Richard Nixon, in his new book, *No More Vietnams,* argues that "we won the war" but then abandoned South Viet Nam after the Communist North began violating the 1973 Paris accords that supposedly ended the fighting. Though the former President's self-interest is obvious, parts of his analysis are supported even by the enemy. U.S. Army Colonel Harry Summers Jr., who considers Viet Nam "a tactical success and a strategic failure," was in Hanoi on a negotiating mission a few days before Saigon fell. Summers recalls telling a North Vietnamese colonel, "You know, you never defeated us on the battlefield." The foe's reply: "That may be so, but it is also irrelevant." In essence, the U.S. was outlasted by an enemy that proved able and willing to fight longer than America and its South Vietnamese allies.

Given the weakness of South Viet Nam, the determination of the North and the extent of the aid it could count on from the Soviet Union and neighboring China, even some hawks concede that Hanoi's victory might have been inevitable. Says Military Analyst Luttwak: "Some wars simply cannot be won, and Viet Nam may have been one of them." Nonetheless, the main lesson they would draw from the war is that the U.S. threw away whatever chance for victory it may have had through blunders that must not be repeated.

The most detailed exposition of this view comes from Colonel Summers, whose book, *On Strategy: A Critical Analysis of the Vietnam War,* has become must reading for young officers. Summers argues that the U.S. should have sealed off South Viet Nam with a barrier of American troops to prevent North Viet Nam from sending troops and materiel through Laos and Cambodia to wage war in the South. Instead, he says, the U.S. "wasted its strength" fighting the guerrillas in the South, a hopeless task so long as they were continually reinforced from the North and one that American troops had no business trying to carry out in the first place. The U.S., he contends, should have confined itself to protecting South Viet Nam against "external aggression" from the North and left "pacification," the job of rooting out the guerrillas, to the South Vietnamese. By in effect taking over the war, the U.S. sapped the initiative and ultimately the will of its Southern allies to carry out a job only they could do in the end.

Luttwak carries this analysis a step further by pouring scorn on the tactics used in the South: "The jet fighter bombing raids against flimsy huts that might contain a handful of guerrillas or perhaps none; the fair-sized artillery barrages that silenced lone snipers; the ceaseless firing of helicopter door gunners whereby a million dollars' worth of ammunition might be expended to sweep a patch of high grass." This "grossly disproportionate use of firepower," says Luttwak, was not just ineffective; it alienated South Vietnamese villagers whose cooperation against the guerrillas was vital. At least equally important, "Its imagery on television was by far the most powerful stimulus of antiwar sentiment" back in the U.S. Former CIA Director William

Y.R. OKAMOTO—LBJ LIBRARY

POLITICS
Defense Secretary McNamara brooding after troop call-up, 1965: Would Americans have backed a bigger war?

"But it will be just like Berlin. The troops will march in; the bands will play; the crowds will cheer; and in four days everyone will have forgotten. Then we will be told we have to send in more troops."
–JOHN F. KENNEDY 1961

"There just isn't any simple answer. We're fighting a kind of war here that I never read about at Command and Staff College. Conventional weapons just don't work here. Neither do conventional tactics."
—FROM GRAHAM GREENE'S *THE UGLY AMERICAN*

"You let a bully come into your front yard, the next day he'll be on your porch."
—LYNDON B. JOHNSON ON SEVERAL OCCASIONS

Colby agrees that the U.S. got nowhere as long as it tried to defeat guerrillas with massed firepower and only began to make progress when it shifted to a "people's war" in which the South Vietnamese carried the main burden of the fighting. By then it was too late; American public sentiment had turned irreversibly in favor of a fast pullout.

According to Hyland, "The biggest lesson of Viet Nam is that we need to have a much better notion of what is at stake, what our interests are, before we go into a major military undertaking." Weinberger voiced essentially the same thought last fall in laying down several conditions, beyond a reasonable assurance of public support, that must be met if U.S. troops are again to be sent into battle overseas: "We should have clearly defined political and military objectives, and we should know precisely how our forces can accomplish those." Other criteria: "The commitment of U.S. forces to combat should be a last resort," undertaken only if it "is deemed vital to our national interest or that of our allies," and then "with the clear intention of winning" by using as much force as necessary.

Weinberger's speech, delivered after he had talked it over with President Reagan, is the closest thing to an official Administration reading of the lessons of Viet Nam. But some rude jeers greeted the Weinberger doctrine. Luttwak, for example, called Weinberger's views "the equivalent of a doctor saying he will treat patients only if he is assured they will recover. Columnist William Safire headlined a scathing critique ONLY THE 'FUN' WARS, and New York Democrat Stephen Solarz, who heads the House Subcommittee on Asian and Pacific Affairs, pointed out, "It is a formula for national paralysis if, before we ever use force, we need a Gallup poll showing that two-thirds of the American people are in favor of it."

More important, what is a "vital interest"? To some Americans, the only one that would justify another war is the defense of the U.S. against a threat of direct attack. Decrying "this whole practice of contracting our military out just for the survival of some other government and country," Georgia Secretary of State Max Cleland, who lost an arm and both legs in Viet Nam, insists, "There is only one thing worth dying for, and that is this country, not somebody else's."

Diplomats argue persuasively that a policy based on this view would leave the U.S. to confront Soviet expansionism all alone. No country would enter or maintain an alliance with a U.S. that specifically refused to fight in its defense. But in the real world, an outright Soviet attack against a country that the U.S. is committed by treaty to defend is quite unlikely. The decision whether or not to fight most probably would be posed by a Communist threat to a friendly nation that is not formally an ally. And then the threat might well be raised not by open aggression but by a combination of military, political and economic tactics that Moscow is often adept at orchestrating and Washington usually inept at countering: the front groups, the street demonstrations, the infiltrated unions, the guerrilla units. One reason the U.S. sent troops to Viet Nam is that it lacked other alternatives to help its allies prevail against this sort of subversion. In fact, developing a capacity to engage in such political action and shadowy paramilitary activities might help the U.S. to avert future Viet Nams.

Merely defining U.S. interests, in any event, can prove endlessly complicated. Geography alone is no guide in an age of ocean-spanning missiles. Economics may be vital in some areas like the Persian Gulf, where the flow of oil must be maintained, unimportant in others like Israel, where political and moral considerations are paramount. There may be

"In the final analysis it is their war . . . We can help them . . . but they have to win it, the people of Viet Nam."
—KENNEDY 1963

"We are not about to send American boys 10,000 miles away to do what Asian boys ought to be doing for themselves."
—JOHNSON 1964

"Hell no, we won't go!"
—ANTIWAR CHANT 1965

"I'm not going to be the first President who loses a war."
—RICHARD NIXON 1969

"Peace is at hand."
—HENRY KISSINGER 1972

times too when U.S. intervention, even if it seems justified, would be ineffective. Not much is heard these days of the once fashionable argument that in Viet Nam the U.S. was on the wrong side of history because it was fighting a nationalistic social revolution being waged by a regime that was, deep down, benign; Hanoi's brutality within Viet Nam and its swift move to establish hegemony over all of Indochina removed all doubt that the foe was and is not only totalitarian but imperialistic besides. Today, with the focus on Central America, the argument is often heard that economic and social misery have made leftist revolution inevitable. To those who maintain that revolution is the only way to progress, the counterargument is that whatever social and economic gains may be achieved by Communist takeovers usually carry an extremely high price tag: the establishment of tyranny.

About the only general rule that foreign-policy experts can suggest is not to have any general rule, at least in the sense of drawing up an advance list of where the U.S. might or might not fight. They still shudder at the memory of a 1950 definition of the U.S. "defense perimeter" in Asia that omitted South Korea—which promptly suffered an outright Communist invasion that took three years and 54,000 American lives to repel. Walt Rostow, who was Lyndon Johnson's National Security Adviser, recalls how the late Soviet Foreign Minister Andrei Vishinsky "told a group of Americans that we deceived them on Korea." Says Rostow: "I believe that's correct."

The decision on where American military intervention might be both necessary and effective can only be made case by case, based on a variety of factors that may be no easier to judge in the future than they were in Viet Nam: the nature and circumstances of war, the will and ability of the nation under attack to defend itself, the consequences of its loss. Any such debate is sure to revive another long buried but still unresolved controversy of the Viet Nam era: whether a Communist takeover of one country would cause others to topple like a row of dominoes. Hawks insist that this theory was vindicated by Communist triumphs in Laos and Cambodia after the fall of Saigon. Opponents point out that the Asian "dominoes" that most concerned the U.S.—Thailand, Burma, Malaysia, Singapore, Indonesia, the Philippines—

have all survived as non-Communist (in several cases, strongly anti-Communist) societies. Rostow, now a professor of political economy at the University of Texas, offers a counterrebuttal. Those countries might have gone under if Saigon had fallen in 1965, he contends. The U.S. intervention in Viet Nam bought them ten years to strengthen their economies and governments and, says Rostow, "bought time that was used extremely well by Asians, especially Southeast Asians."

Be that as it may, the evidence would seem to argue against any mechanical application of the domino theory. It originated in the 1950s, when world Communism was seen as a monolithic force headquartered in Moscow, with Peking a kind of branch office. Today China, never really comfortable with its Hanoi "allies," has resumed its ancient enmity toward Viet Nam; both Washington and Peking are aiding guerrillas battling against the Soviet-backed Vietnamese in Kampuchea. That does not mean that the domino theory has lost all validity everywhere, but its applicability is also subject to case-by-case application.

The most bedeviling of all the dilemmas raised by Viet Nam concerns the issue of public support. On the surface it might seem to be no issue at all: just about everybody agrees that Viet Nam proved the futility of trying to fight a war without a strong base of popular support. But just how strong exactly? Rostow argues that the only U.S. war fought with tremendous public backing was World War II. He points out that World War I "brought riots and splits," the War of 1812 was "vastly divisive" and even during the War of Independence one-third of the population was pro-revolution, one-third pro-British and one-third "out to lunch." Rostow proposes a 60-25-15 split as about the best that can be expected now in support of a controversial policy: a bipartisan 60% in favor, 25% against and 15% out to lunch.

A strong current of opinion holds that Lyndon Johnson guaranteed a disastrously low level of support by getting into a long, bloody war without ever admitting (perhaps even to himself) the extent of the commitment he was making. Colonel Summers, who considers Viet Nam a just war that the U.S. could and should have won, insists that any similar conflict in the future ought to be "legitimized" by a formal, congressional declaration of war. Says Summers: "All of America's previous wars were fought in the heat of passion. Viet Nam was fought in cold blood, and that was intolerable to the American people. In an immediate crisis the tendency of the American people is to rally around the flag. But God help you if it goes beyond that and you haven't built a base of support."

At the other extreme, former Secretary of State Dean Rusk defends to this day the Johnson Administration's effort "to do in cold blood at home what we were asking men to do in hot blood out in the field." Rusk points out that the war began with impressive public and congressional support. It was only in early 1968, says Rusk, that "many at the grassroots level came to the opinion that if we didn't give them some idea when this war would come to an end, we might as well chuck it." The decisive factor probably was the defection of middle-class youths and their parents, a highly articulate segment that saw an endless war as a personal threat—though in fact the burden of the draft fell most heavily on low-income youths.

Paradoxically, though, Johnson might well have been able to win public support for a bigger war than he was willing to fight. As late as February 1968, at the height of the Tet offensive, one poll found 53% favoring stronger U.S. military action, even at the risk of a clash with the Soviet Union or China, vs. only 24% opting to wind down the war. Rusk insists that the Administration was right not to capitalize on this sentiment. Says he: "We made a deliberate decision not to whip up war fever in this country. We did not have parades and movie stars selling war bonds, as we did in World War II. We thought that in a nuclear world it is dangerous for a country to become too angry too quickly. That is something people will have to think about in the future."

It certainly is. Viet Nam veterans argue passionately that Americans must never again be sent out to die in a war that "the politicians will not let them win." And by win they clearly mean something like a World War II-style triumph ending with unconditional surrender. One lesson of Viet Nam, observes George Christian, who was L.B.J.'s press secretary, is that "it is very tough for Americans to stick in long situations. We are always looking for a quick fix." But nuclear missiles make the unconditional-surrender kind of war an anachronism. Viet Nam raised, and left unsolved for the next conflict, the question posed by Lincoln Bloomfield, an M.I.T. professor of political science who once served on Jimmy Carter's National Security Council: "How is it that you can 'win' so that when you leave two years later you do not lose the country to those forces who have committed themselves to victory at any cost?"

It is a question that cannot be suppressed much longer. Americans have a deep ambiguity toward military power: they like to feel strong, but often shy away from actually using that strength. There is a growing recognition, however, that shunning all battles less easily winnable than Grenada would mean abandoning America's role as a world power, and that, in turn, is no way to assure the nation's survival as a free society. Americans, observes Secretary of State Shultz, "will always be reluctant to use force. It is the mark of our decency." But, he adds, "a great power cannot free itself so easily from the burden of choice. It must bear responsibility for the consequences of its inaction as well as for the consequences of its action."

—By George J. Church.
Reported by David S. Jackson/Austin and Ross H. Munro/Washington, with other bureaus.

Nixon: An Important but Not a Great President

Stephen E. Ambrose

Stephen E. Ambrose is the author of a three-volume biography of Richard Nixon.

Richard Milhous Nixon's place in history is not what he sought. He wanted to be known as a great president, even the Lincoln of the twentieth century, but he left no such legacy. Two hundred years from now, when he will get only a paragraph or two in a high school American history text, the first sentence will read, "Richard Nixon, thirty-seventh president, resigned his office because of the Watergate scandal."

Watergate is the spot that will not out. The paragraph will then go on to note his opening to China, his pioneering efforts at establishing détente, his role in ending the American involvement in Vietnam, and his saving of Israel in October 1973.

If there is a second paragraph, it will note that on the domestic side Nixon had no major accomplishment to compare with Teddy Roosevelt and conservation, Woodrow Wilson and the Federal Reserve system, Franklin Roosevelt and Social Security, Dwight Eisenhower and the interstate highway system, or Lyndon Johnson and civil rights.

Richard Nixon was born on January 11, 1913, in a modest home in Yorba Linda, California. His parents, Frank and Hannah, were hard-working Quakers living on the edge of poverty, because of crashing medical bills for their oldest son, but who never accepted a handout.

Nixon was a bright but not very likable boy; a cousin remarked that "he wasn't the kind of boy you wanted to pick up and hug." His awkwardness and shyness led him to strive harder. He won a scholarship to Whittier College, where he excelled in campus politics and in the classroom.

Another scholarship made it possible for him to attend Duke Law School. After graduation in 1937, he returned to Whittier to set up a law practice. He married a local schoolteacher, Patricia Ryan, in 1940. The marriage was a solid one. It lasted until her death in 1993 and produced two daughters, Tricia and Julie.

Nixon volunteered for the Navy in World War II and served as a supply officer in the South Pacific. In 1946 he began his political career by challenging Rep. Jerry Voorhis. He was slashing in his attacks on Voorhis, accusing him of accepting communist support in an early version of what came to be called McCarthyism.

Nixon won and, in his freshman term, had the good luck to get on the House Committee on Un-American Activities. In that capacity, he exposed Alger Hiss, a communist spy for the Soviet Union who had been a high-ranking official in the Roosevelt administration. The case made Nixon into a national and highly controversial figure. New Dealers hated him; conservatives admired him without stint.

At home, Nixon was so popular that he was unopposed for reelection in 1948. In 1950 he challenged Helen Gahagan Douglas for her Senate seat. He accused her of following the communist line and called her "the pink lady." It worked again; he won big. So popular was he nationally that in 1952 Dwight Eisenhower selected him as his running mate.

NATIONAL PROMINENCE

Nixon ran another aggressive campaign, charging that Democratic presidential candidate Adlai Stevenson was a graduate of "Dean Acheson's 'cowardly college of communist containment,'" that Harry Truman was "a traitor to the principles of the Democratic Party," and that the Truman administration was shot through with scandal and corruption. His holier-than-thou attitude backfired on him when it was revealed that he had a "secret fund" contributed by California millionaires.

Richard Nixon wanted to be known as the Lincoln of the twentieth century, but he left no such legacy.

Most Democrats and many Republicans said he should resign. Instead he went on national television to defend himself in the famous Checkers speech, now a part of American political folklore and the first use of television in politics on a national basis. Nixon was effective; he stayed on the ticket; the Republicans won in a landslide.

As vice president, Nixon's job was to attack the Democrats while Eisenhower stayed above the battle. Nixon did it with relish, becoming even more hated—and admired—in the process of becoming America's most polarizing politician.

His eight years as vice president had many highlights, including Eisenhower's 1955 heart attack, when Nixon won praise from all quarters for his calm, skillful conduct in the crisis; a 1958 trip to South America, where communist demonstrators threatened to kill him, but he stood up to them, to his own great political advantage back in the States; and a 1959 trip to Russia, where he engaged in a heated debate with the Soviet dictator and was so successful that he was called "the man who stood up to Khrushchev."

This article first appeared in *The World & I*, July 1994, pp. 88-93. Reprinted by permission of *The World & I*, a publication of the Washington Times Corporation. © 1994.

In 1960, Nixon ran against Sen. John F. Kennedy in one of the hardest-fought presidential campaigns ever, matching the two youngest candidates ever. The campaign was noted for four nationally televised debates that drew the largest audiences ever to that time, thus marking another Nixon innovation in TV and politics. Kennedy was declared winner in a still-disputed election.

Nixon returned to California, where he ran in 1962 for governor against incumbent Pat Brown. He lost, badly. The morning after the election, in a press conference, he accused reporters of biased coverage and blamed them for his defeat. He told them to "think how much you are going to be missing. You won't have Nixon to kick around anymore, because, gentlemen, this is my last press conference."

He never meant it. He made a bid for the Republican nomination for president in 1964, supported Barry Goldwater as a good team player, and won the nomination in 1968. In a three-way race between Nixon, Hubert Humphrey, and George Wallace, with Vietnam and law and order as the main issues, Nixon won a narrow victory with 43 percent of the vote.

A Brief Biography

❖ Born January 11, 1913, in Yorba Linda, California.

❖ Married schoolteacher Patricia Ryan in 1940.

❖ Volunteered for the Navy in World War II and served as a supply officer in the South Pacific.

❖ Elected to the House of Representatives in 1946.

❖ Elected to the Senate in 1950.

❖ Elected as Eisenhower's vice president in 1952 and 1956.

❖ Lost close presidential race to John Kennedy in 1960.

❖ Lost California gubernatorial race to Pat Brown in 1962.

❖ Won presidential election in 1968 and 1972.

❖ Visited communist China in 1972.

❖ Resigned the presidency due to the Watergate scandal in 1974.

❖ Died April 22, 1994, in New York. Buried at his boyhood home.

HIGH AND LOW POINT

Vietnam dominated Nixon's first term. He had said during the campaign that he had a plan to end the war, which he finally announced in June 1969. It was Vietnamization, and it wasn't a plan to end the war but one to continue the war with the South Vietnamese replacing the Americans as the fighting force and the United States supplying the weapons and material. It allowed Nixon to announce the beginning of withdrawal from Vietnam and to begin bringing troops home.

On November 3, 1969, in one of his most famous speeches, he concluded: "To you, the great silent majority of my fellow Americans, I ask for your support. Let us understand: North Vietnam cannot defeat or humiliate the United States. Only Americans can do that." The speech bought him time. By early 1972, there were no U.S. combat troops in Vietnam, and by January 1973 an armistice had been reached, based on complete American withdrawal and the return of American POWs.

Nixon claimed he had won peace with honor. Many in the military and on the Right said he had presided over an ill-disguised surrender; many on the Left said he could have had the same agreement in 1969 that he finally signed in 1973.

There were always at least two ways to look at Nixon's accomplishments. In February 1972, he went to China, astonishing everyone and laying the base for a new foreign policy, called triangular diplomacy—playing China off against Russia, and vice versa.

He boasted that he was the only man who could have opened the door to China. His critics on the Right said he never should have done it, while those on the Left pointed out that for 20 years he had been the man more than any other who had kept the door closed.

For those 20 years, Nixon had been the world's No. 1 anticommunist. He had always called for more arms and insisted that the West could never trust the Soviets. But in 1972, after going to China, he went to Moscow, where he established a policy of détente with Soviet dictator Leonid Brezhnev. It included the first arms control agreement in the Cold War.

Critics charged that Nixon's dramatic turnarounds on basic policy questions showed what a cynic he was; his reply was that times change and the pragmatic politician changes with them. Whatever his motives, his activist, realpolitik foreign policy surely brought great changes to the world.

At home, he was not so successful. In his first term he got little significant legislation passed. Most of the time and energy he put in on domestic politics centered on the antiwar movement. The Nixon White House developed a besieged, bunker mentality. To fight back, the president ordered wiretaps on reporters and political activists, IRS audits of his perceived enemies, and other actions described collectively by Attorney General John Mitchell as "the White House horrors."

In the 1972 reelection campaign against challenger George McGovern, burglars working for the Committee to Re-Elect the President got caught breaking into the Watergate offices of the Democratic National Committee to place a telephone tap. Although the story had no effect on the election, in which Nixon carried 49 states in the second-biggest landslide in American history, it became the political scandal of the century.

Nixon had no prior knowledge of the break-in, but, as soon as he heard of it, he plunged into an effort to cover up. But the Democrats controlled Congress, and in February 1973 they began hearings in the Senate into the Watergate affair. From then until August 1974, the country was consumed with Watergate.

In 1972, after going to China, Nixon went to Moscow, where he established a policy of détent with Leonid Brezhnev.

One shock followed another. The president's counsel, John Dean, turned on his boss and charged that Nixon was in on the cover-up from day one. Nixon denied it. In July 1973, when Alexander Butterfield revealed that there was a secret, voice-activated taping system in the Oval Office, it was suddenly possible to find out who was telling the truth simply by listening to the tapes.

Dean was delighted; Nixon, downcast. For the next year, Nixon struggled to retain control of the tapes. He eventually lost on a unanimous Supreme Court vote in *U.S. v. Nixon* that ordered him to give up certain tapes. When he complied, he was finished, as they showed Dean had told the truth.

On August 9, 1974, facing certain impeachment, Nixon resigned. He is the only president ever to do so. He returned to California. One month after his resignation, President Gerald Ford granted him a full and free pardon for any crimes he may have committed.

REGAINING RESPECTABILITY

Soon thereafter, a life-threatening illness spared him from having to testify in the trials of his aides John Ehrlichman, Bob Haldeman, and John Mitchell (all of whom went to jail), so Nixon never had to answer questions about Watergate in a court of law.

He did answer questions from British reporter David Frost on national television, in return for a substantial fee. He refused to apologize to the American people, because he insisted he had done nothing wrong. Next came his memoirs, which he completed in 1977. The book was a huge success. With regard to Watergate, the most he would admit to was being too loyal to his subordinates.

He was well into his last campaign, this one for elder statesman. He wanted the respect given to other former presidents. Through the 1980s, he won it. His old standby, foreign trips, served him well: Nixon in Europe, Nixon in China, Nixon in Israel. *Nixon in China* was always a headline item.

He never spoke out on divisive domestic issues, but he did speak out on foreign affairs, boldly but in generalizations that could not offend. He was shrewd enough and self-confident enough to go before his former tormentors—the reporters, the publishers, the editors—for speeches and questions and answers. They loved it; he gave them great copy.

He published eight books, all well received. He sent advice, privately, to each of his successors—advice that was usually welcome, whether on foreign policy or campaign strategy. In March 1994, when he was 81 years old, he made a trip to Moscow, where he had a meeting with another out-of-power politician and caused an international incident that made headlines around the world.

Who else but Dick Nixon could have done that?

He died on April 22, 1994, and is buried beside his wife, Pat, at his birthplace, the home of the Nixon Library.

He will be regarded, in short, as an important president, perhaps the most fascinating of all our presidents, a precedent-setting president, but not a great president.

ADDITIONAL READING

Stephen E. Ambrose, *Nixon: The Education of a Politician, 1923–1962,* Simon & Schuster, New York, 1988.

————, *Triumph of a Politician,* Simon & Schuster, New York, 1990.

————, *Nixon: Ruin and Recovery, 1973–1990,* Simon & Schuster, New York, 1991.

How the Seventies Changed America

The "loser decade" that at first seemed nothing more than a breathing space between the high drama of the 1960s and whatever was coming next is beginning to reveal itself as a bigger time than we thought

Nicholas Lemann

Nicholas Lemann, a national correspondent for The Atlantic, *is the author of* The Promised Land: The Great Black Migration and How It Changed America, *published by Alfred A. Knopf [1991].*

"That's it," Daniel Patrick Moynihan, then U.S. ambassador to India, wrote to a colleague on the White House staff in 1973 on the subject of some issue of the moment. "Nothing will happen. But then nothing much is going to happen in the 1970s anyway."

Moynihan is a politician famous for his predictions, and this one seemed for a long time to be dead-on. The seventies, even while they were in progress, looked like an unimportant decade, a period of cooling down from the white-hot sixties. You had to go back to the teens to find another decade so lacking in crisp, epigrammatic definition. It only made matters worse for the seventies that the succeeding decade started with a bang. In 1980 the country elected the most conservative President in its history, and it was immediately clear that a new era had dawned. (In general the eighties, unlike the seventies, had a perfect dramatic arc. They peaked in the summer of 1984, with the Los Angeles Olympics and the Republican National Convention in Dallas, and began to peter out with the Iran-contra scandal in 1986 and the stock market crash in 1987.) It is nearly impossible to engage in magazine-writerly games like discovering "the day the seventies died" or "the spirit of the seventies"; and the style of the seventies—wide ties, sideburns, synthetic fabrics, white shoes, disco—is so far interesting largely as something to make fun of.

But somehow the seventies seem to be creeping out of the loser-decade category. Their claim to importance is in the realm of sweeping historical trends, rather than memorable events, though there were some of those too. In the United States today a few basic propositions shape everything: The presidential electorate is conservative and Republican. Geopolitics revolves around a commodity (oil) and a religion (Islam) more than around an ideology (Marxism-Leninism). The national economy is no longer one in which practically every class, region, and industry is upwardly mobile. American culture is essentially individualistic, rather than communitarian, which means that notions like deferred gratification, sacrifice, and sustained national effort are a very tough sell. Anyone seeking to understand the roots of this situation has to go back to the seventies.

The underestimation of the seventies' importance, especially during the early years of the decade, is easy to forgive because the character of the seventies was substantially shaped at first by spill-over from the sixties. Such sixties events as the killings of student protesters at Kent State and Orangeburg, the original Earth Day, the invasion of Cambodia, and a large portion of the war in Vietnam took place in the seventies. Although sixties radicals (cultural and political) spent the early seventies loudly bemoaning the end of the revolution, what was in fact going on was the working of the phenomena of the sixties into the mainstream of American life. Thus the first Nixon administration, which was decried by liberals at the time for being nightmarishly right-wing, was actually more liberal than the Johnson adminis-tration in many ways—less hawkish in Vietnam, more free-spending on social programs. The reason wasn't that Richard Nixon was a liberal but that the country as a whole had continued to move steadily to the left throughout the late sixties and early seventies; the political climate of institutions like the U.S. Congress and the boards of directors of big corporations was probably more liberal in 1972 than in any year before or since, and the Democratic party nominated its most liberal presidential candidate ever. Nixon had to go along with the tide.

In New Orleans, my hometown, the hippie movement peaked in 1972 or 1973. Long hair, crash pads, head shops, psychedelic posters, underground newspapers, and other Summer of Love-inspired institutions had been unknown there during the real Summer of Love, which was in 1967. It took even longer, until the middle or late seventies, for those aspects of hippie life that have endured to catch on with the general public. All over the country the likelihood that an average citizen would wear longish hair, smoke marijuana, and openly live with a lover before marriage was probably greater in 1980 than it was in 1970. The sixties' preoccupation with self-discovery became a mass phenomenon only in the seventies, through home-brew psychological therapies like est. In politics the impact of the black enfranchisement that took place in the 1960s barely began to be felt until the mid- to late 1970s. The tremendously influential feminist and gay-liberation movements were, at the dawn of the 1970s, barely under way in Manhattan, their headquarters, and certainly hadn't begun their

From *American Heritage*, July/August 1991, pp. 39-49. © 1991 by Forbes, Inc. Reprinted by permission of *American Heritage* magazine, a division of Forbes, Inc.

spread across the whole country. The sixties took a long time for America to digest; the process went on throughout the seventies and even into the eighties.

The epochal event of the seventies as an era in its own right was the Organization of Petroleum Exporting Countries' oil embargo, which lasted for six months in the fall of 1973 and the spring of 1974. Everything that happened in the sixties was predicated on the assumption of economic prosperity and growth; concerns like personal fulfillment and social justice tend to emerge in the middle class only at times when people take it for granted that they'll be able to make a living. For thirty years—ever since the effects of World War II on the economy had begun to kick in—the average American's standard of living had been rising, to a remarkable extent. As the economy grew, indices like home ownership, automobile ownership, and access to higher education got up to levels unknown anywhere else in the world, and the United States could plausibly claim to have provided a better life materially for its working class than any society ever had. That ended with the OPEC embargo.

While it was going on, the embargo didn't fully register in the national consciousness. The country was absorbed by a different story, the Watergate scandal, which was really another sixties spillover, the final series of battles in the long war between the antiwar liberals and the rough-playing anti-Communists. Richard Nixon, having engaged in dirty tricks against leftish politicians for his whole career, didn't stop doing so as President; he only found new targets, like Daniel Ellsberg and Lawrence O'Brien. This time, however, he lost the Establishment, which was now far more kindly disposed to Nixon's enemies than it had been back in the 1950s. Therefore, the big-time press, the courts, and the Congress undertook the enthralling process of cranking up the deliberate, inexorable machinery of justice, and everybody was glued to the television for a year and a half. The embargo, on the other hand, was a nonvideo-friendly economic story and hence difficult to get hooked on. It pertained to two subcultures that were completely mysterious to most Americans—the oil industry and the Arab world—and it seemed at first to be merely an episode in the ongoing hostilities between Israel and its neighbors. But in retrospect it changed everything, much more than Watergate did.

By causing the price of oil to double, the embargo enriched—and therefore increased the wealth, power, and confidence of—oil-producing areas like Texas, while helping speed the decline of the automobile-producing upper Midwest; the rise of OPEC and the rise of the Sunbelt as a center of population and political influence went together. The embargo ushered in a long period of inflation, the reaction to which dominated the economics and politics of the rest of the decade. It demonstrated that America could now be "pushed around" by countries most us had thought of as minor powers.

MOST IMPORTANT OF ALL, THE EMBARGO now appears to have been the pivotal moment at which the mass upward economic mobility of American society ended, perhaps forever. Average weekly earnings, adjusted for inflation, peaked in 1973. Productivity—that is, economic output per man-hour—abruptly stopped growing. The nearly universal assumption in the post–World War II United States was that children would do better than their parents. Upward mobility wasn't just a characteristic of the national culture; it was the defining characteristic. As it slowly began to sink in that everybody wasn't going to be moving forward together anymore, the country became more fragmented, more internally rivalrous, and less sure of its mythology.

Richard Nixon resigned as President in August 1974, and the country settled into what appeared to be a quiet, folksy drama of national recuperation. In the White House good old Gerald Ford was succeeded by rural, sincere Jimmy Carter, who was the only President elevated to the office by the voters during the 1970s and so was the decade's emblematic political figure. In hindsight, though, it's impossible to miss a gathering conservative stridency in the politics of the late seventies. In 1976 Ronald Reagan, the retired governor of California, challenged Ford for the Republican presidential nomination. Reagan lost the opening primaries and seemed to be about to drop out of the race when, apparently to the surprise even of his own staff, he won the North Carolina primary in late March.

IT IS QUITE CLEAR WHAT CAUSED THE Reagan campaign to catch on: He had begun to attack Ford from the right on foreign policy matters. The night before the primary he bought a half-hour of statewide television time to press his case. Reagan's main substantive criticism was of the policy of détente with the Soviet Union, but his two most crowd-pleasing points were his promise, if elected, to fire Henry Kissinger as Secretary of State and his lusty denunciation of the elaborately negotiated treaty to turn nominal control of the Panama Canal over to the Panamanians. Less than a year earlier Communist forces had finally captured the South Vietnamese capital city of Saigon, as the staff of the American Embassy escaped in a wild scramble into helicopters. The oil embargo had ended, but the price of gasoline had not retreated. The United States appeared to have descended from the pinnacle of power and respect it had occupied at the close of World War II to a small, hounded position, and Reagan had hit on a symbolic way of expressing rage over that change. Most journalistic and academic opinion at the time was fairly cheerful about the course of American foreign policy—we were finally out of Vietnam, and we were getting over our silly Cold War phobia about dealing with China and the Soviet Union—but in the general public obviously the rage Reagan expressed was widely shared.

A couple of years later a conservative political cause even more out of the blue than opposition to the Panama Canal Treaty appeared: the tax revolt. Howard Jarvis, a seventy-five-year-old retired businessman who had been attacking taxation in California pretty much continuously since 1962, got onto the state ballot in 1978 an initiative, Proposition 13, that would substantially cut property taxes. Despite bad press and the strong opposition of most politicians, it passed by a two to one margin.

PROPOSITION 13 WAS TO SOME EXTENT another aftershock of the OPEC embargo. Inflation causes the value of hard assets to rise. The only substantial hard asset owned by most Americans is their home. As the prices of houses soared in the mid-seventies (causing people to dig deeper to buy housing, which sent the national savings rate plummeting and made real estate prices the great conversation starter in the social life of the middle class), so did property taxes, since they are based on the values of the houses. Hence, resentment over taxation became an issue in waiting.

The influence of Proposition 13 has been so great that it is now difficult to recall that taxes weren't a major concern in national politics before it. Conservative opposition to government focused on its activities, not on its revenue base, and this put conservatism at a disadvantage, because most government programs are popular. Even before Proposition 13, conservative economic writers like Jude Wanniski and Arthur Laffer were inventing supply-side economics based on the idea that reducing taxes would bring prosperity. With Proposition 13 it was proved—as it has been proved over and over since—that tax cutting was one of the rare voguish policy ideas that turn out to be huge political winners. In switching from arguing against programs to arguing against taxes, conservatism had found another key element of its ascension to power

The tax revolt wouldn't have worked if the middle class hadn't been receptive to the notion that it was oppressed. This was remarkable in itself, since it had been assumed for decades that the American middle class was, in a world-historical sense, almost uniquely lucky. The emergence of a self-pitying strain in the middle class was in a sense yet another sixties spillover. At the dawn of the sixties, the idea that *anybody* in the United States was oppressed might have seemed absurd. Then blacks, who really were oppressed, were able to make the country see the truth about their situation. But that opened Pandora's box. The eloquent language of group rights that the civil rights movement had invented proved to be quite adaptable, and eventually it was used by college students, feminists, Native Americans, Chicanos, urban blue-collar "white ethnics," and, finally, suburban homeowners.

Meanwhile, the social programs started by Lyndon Johnson gave rise to another new, or long-quiescent, idea, which was that the government was wasting vast sums of money on harebrained schemes. In some ways the Great Society accomplished its goal of binding the country together, by making the federal government a nationwide provider of such favors as medical care and access to higher education; but in others it contributed to the seventies trend of each group's looking to government to provide it with benefits and being unconcerned with the general good. Especially after the economy turned sour, the middle class began to define its interests in terms of a rollback of government programs aimed at helping other groups.

As the country was becoming more fragmented, so was its essential social

unit, the family. In 1965 only 14.9 percent of the population was single; by 1979 the figure had risen to 20 percent. The divorce rate went from 2.5 per thousand in 1965 to 5.3 per thousand in 1979. The percentage of births that were out of wedlock was 5.3 in 1960 and 16.3 in 1978. The likelihood that married women with young children would work doubled between the mid-sixties and the late seventies. These changes took place for a variety of reasons—feminism, improved birth control, the legalization of abortion, the spread across the country of the sixties youth culture's rejection of traditional mores—but what they added up to was that the nuclear family, consisting of a working husband and a nonworking wife, both in their first marriage, and their children, ceased to be so dominant a type of American household during the seventies. Also, people became more likely to organize themselves into communities based on their family status, so that the unmarried often lived in singles apartment complexes and retirees in senior citizens' developments. The overall effect was one of much greater personal freedom, which meant, as it always does, less social cohesion. Tom Wolfe's moniker for the seventies, the Me Decade, caught on because it was probably true that the country had placed relatively more emphasis on individual happiness and relatively less on loyalty to family and nation.

LIKE A SYMPHONY, THE SEVENTIES FINALLY built up in a crescendo that pulled together all its main themes. This occurred during the second half of 1979. First OPEC engineered the "second oil shock," in which, by holding down production, it got the price for its crude oil (and the price of gasoline at American service stations) to rise by more than 50 percent during the first six months of that year. With the onset of the summer vacation season, the automotive equivalent of the Depression's bank runs began. Everybody considered the possibility of not being able to get gas, panicked, and went off to fill the tank; the result was hourslong lines at gas stations all over the country.

It was a small inconvenience compared with what people in the Communist world and Latin America live through all the time, but the psychological effect was enormous. The summer of 1979 was the only time I can remember when, at the level of ordinary life as

opposed to public affairs, things seemed to be out of control. Inflation was well above 10 percent and rising, and suddenly what seemed like a quarter of every day was spent on getting gasoline or thinking about getting gasoline—a task that previously had been completely routine, as it is again now. Black markets sprang up; rumors flew about well-connected people who had secret sources. One day that summer, after an hour's desperate and fruitless search, I ran out of gas on the Central Expressway in Dallas. I left my car sitting primly in the right lane and walked away in the hundred-degree heat; the people driving by looked at me without surprise, no doubt thinking, "Poor bastard, it could have happened to me just as easily."

In July President Carter scheduled a speech on the gas lines, then abruptly canceled it and repaired to Camp David to think deeply for ten days, which seemed like a pale substitute for somehow setting things aright. Aides, cabinet secretaries, intellectuals, religious leaders, tycoons, and other leading citizens were summoned to Carter's aerie to discuss with him what was wrong with the country's soul. On July 15 he made a television address to the nation, which has been enshrined in memory as the "malaise speech," although it didn't use that word. (Carter did, however, talk about "a crisis of confidence . . . that strikes at the very heart and soul and spirit of our national will.")

TO REREAD THE SPEECH TODAY IS TO BE struck by its spectacular political ineptitude. Didn't Carter realize that Presidents are not supposed to express doubts publicly or to lecture the American people about their shortcomings? Why couldn't he have just temporarily imposed gas rationing, which would have ended the lines overnight, instead of outlining a vague and immediately forgotten six-point program to promote energy conservation?

His describing the country's loss of confidence did not cause the country to gain confidence, needless to say. And it didn't help matters that upon his return to Washington he demanded letters of resignation from all members of his cabinet and accepted five of them. Carter seemed to be anything but an FDR-like reassuring, ebullient presence; he communicated a sense of wild flailing about as he tried (unsuccessfully) to get the situation under control.

I REMEMBER BEING ENORMOUSLY IM-pressed by Carter's speech at the time because it was a painfully honest and much thought-over attempt to grapple with the main problem of the decade. The American economy had ceased being an expand-ing pie, and by unfortunate coincidence this had happened just when an ethic of individual freedom as the highest good was spreading throughout the society, which meant people would respond to the changing economic conditions by looking out for themselves. Like most other members of the word-manipulating class whose leading figures had advised Carter at Camp David, I thought there *was* a malaise. What I didn't realize, and Carter obviously didn't either, was that there was a smarter way to play the situation politically. A President could maintain there was nothing wrong with America at all—that it hadn't become less powerful in the world, hadn't reached some kind of hard economic limit, and wasn't in crisis—and, instead of trying to reverse the powerful tide of individualism, ride along with it. At the same time, he could act more forcefully than Carter, especially against inflation, so that he didn't seem weak and ineffec-tual. All this is exactly what Carter's successor, Ronald Reagan, did.

Actually, Carter himself set in motion the process by which inflation was con-quered a few months later, when he gave the chairmanship of the Federal Reserve Board to Paul Volcker, a man willing to put the economy into a severe recession to bring back price stability. But in No-vember fate delivered the *coup de grâce* Carter in the form of the taking hostage of the staff of the American Embassy in Teheran, as a protest against the United States' harboring of Iran's former shah.

As with the malaise speech, what is most difficult to convey today about the hostage crisis is why Carter made what now looks like a huge, obvious error: playing up the crisis so much that it became a national obsession for more than a year. The fundamental problem with hostage taking is that the one sure remedy—refusing to negotiate and thus allowing the hostages to be killed—is politically unacceptable in the demo-cratic media society we live in, at least when the hostages are middle-class sym-pathetic figures, as they were in Iran.

There isn't any good solution to this problem, but Carter's two successors in the White House demonstrated that it is possible at least to negotiate for the re-

lease of hostages in a low-profile way that will cause the press to lose interest and prevent the course of the hostage negotiations from completely defining the Presidency. During the last year of the Carter administration, by contrast, the hostage story absolutely dominated the television news (recall that the ABC show *Nightline* began as a half-hour five-times-a-week update on the hostage situ-ation), and several of the hostages and their families became temporary celeb-rities. In Carter's defense, even among the many voices criticizing him for ap-pearing weak and vacillating, there was none that I remember willing to say, "Just cut off negotiations and walk away." It was a situation that everyone regarded as terrible but in which there was a strong national consensus support-ing the course Carter had chosen.

So ended the seventies. There was still enough of the sixties spillover phenome-non going on so that Carter, who is now regarded (with some affection) as having been too much the good-hearted liberal to maintain a hold on the presidential electorate, could be challenged for re-nomination by Ted Kennedy on the grounds that he was too conservative. Inflation was raging on; the consumer price index rose by 14.4 percent between May 1979 and May 1980. We were being humiliated by fanatically bitter, pre-modern Muslims whom we had expected to regard us with gratitude because we had helped ease out their dictator even though he was reliably pro-United States. The Soviet empire appeared (probably for the last time ever) to be on the march, having invaded Afghanistan to Carter's evident surprise and disillusionment. We had lost our most recent war. We couldn't pull together as a people. The puissant, unified, prospering America of the late 1940s seemed to be just a fading memory.

I WAS A REPORTER FOR THE *WASHINGTON Post* during the 1980 presidential cam-paign, and even on the *Post's* national desk, that legendary nerve center of poli-tics, the idea that the campaign might end with Reagan's being elected President seemed fantastic, right up to the weekend before the election. At first Kennedy looked like a real threat to Carter; re-member that up to that point no Kennedy had ever lost a campaign. While the Carter people were disposing of Ken-nedy, they were rooting for Reagan to

win the Republican nomination because he would be such an easy mark.

He was too old, too unserious, and, most of all, too conservative. Look what had happened to Barry Goldwater (a sitting officeholder, at least) only sixteen years earlier, and Reagan was so divisive that a moderate from his own party, John Anderson, was running for President as a third-party candidate. It was not at all clear how much the related issues of inflation and national helplessness were dominating the public's mind. Kennedy, Carter, and Anderson were all, in their own way, selling national healing, that great postsixties obsession; Reagan, and only Reagan, was selling pure strength.

IN A SENSE REAGAN'S ELECTION REPRE-sents the country's rejection of the idea of a sixties-style solution to the great problems of the seventies—economic stag-nation, social fragmentation, and the need for a new world order revolving around relations between the oil-produc-ing Arab world and the West. The idea of a scaled-back America—husbanding its re-sources, living more modestly, renounc-ing its restless mobility, withdrawing from full engagement with the politics of every spot on the globe, focusing on issues of internal comity—evidently didn't appeal. Reagan, and the country, had in effect found a satisfying pose to strike in response to the problems of the seven-ties, but that's different from finding a solution.

Today some of the issues that domi-nated the seventies have faded away. Reagan and Volcker did beat inflation. The "crisis of confidence" now seems a long-ago memory. But it is striking how early we still seem to be in the process of working out the implications of the oil embargo. We have just fought and won a war against the twin evils of Middle East despotism and interruptions in the oil supply, which began to trouble us in the seventies. We still have not really even begun to figure out how to deal with the cessation of across-the-board income gains, and as a result our domestic poli-tics are still dominated by squabbling over the proper distribution of govern-ment's benefits and burdens. During the seventies themselves the new issues that were arising seemed nowhere near as important as those sixties legacies, mi-nority rights and Vietnam and Watergate. But the runt of decades has wound up casting a much longer shadow than any-one imagined.

1983
Falling Walls, Rising Dreams

Michael Barone

It was not a milestone widely expected: the day in early 1983 when AST Research's sales reached $1 million a month. This was a company that didn't exist when the decade began, a company started in a one-stall garage in Orange County, Calif., by three immigrant engineers—two of them from Hong Kong, the other side of the Pacific Rim. It was a company whose first great success as an add-on to a product that didn't exist before 1981 and that most experts predicted would flop: a 256-kilobyte memory expansion board to increase the power of IBM's personal computer.

Here is the story of the 1980s writ small—or, rather, on a computer screen. AST's success was not predicted, nor was it always smooth. Likewise, the economic growth in the 1980s was unpredicted; it came from small firms, often started by unknown entrepreneurs, and was concentrated in the Sun Belt and other high-tech centers (half of U.S. population growth in the 1980s was in California, Texas and Florida).

AST's greatest growth would come later, after serious convulsions, much as the economic success of the 1980s would have its unexpected costs. Americans worked harder and made more money, but their jobs were less secure and they had less time for their families. Despite the unprecedented affluence, real wealth seemed tantalizingly out of reach. Americans watched as high technology produced an efflorescence of information outlets. But they were also left wondering whether something was missing in a society with high rates of crime and low rates of student learning. Around the world, people were voting for democracy. But Americans had a nagging sense that their own system had growing flaws.

Many observers had expected only the downside of all this, warning (as in Lester Thurow's *Zero-Sum Economy*) that America could not achieve low-inflation growth. But on Jan. 1, 1983, when Ronald Reagan's tax cuts went into full effect, America began seven years of such growth, the longest period in history. In 1983, there were 99 million jobs, no more than in the preceding four years. By 1984, there were 105 million jobs—and 118 million by 1990. Many low-skill, high-wage union jobs did disappear. But if 20 million jobs evaporated, 38 million—more than all those in Germany—were created.

The year 1983 was the start of a five-year period when most new jobs went to women. If not the norm, the two-earner family was the ideal: Affluent America was made up largely of two-paycheck families. By 1983, almost half of women ages 16 and over and more than two thirds of those 20 to 55 were working—the highest figures ever. Moreover, women's earnings were rising as a share of men's; although the drive for the constitutional equal rights amendment sputtered noisily in 1983, feminists' economic goals were quietly progressing.

Of course, advances meant more children came home to empty houses. Children, in fact, were in many ways missing from the 1980s boom. By 1983, it was becoming clear that many were in classrooms empty of learning: In April, the Carnegie Foundation's "Nation at Risk" report warned that schools were producing "a tide of mediocrity." Life outside the classroom was changing, too. By 1983, 20 percent of babies were born to single mothers. And children tended to get less respect from the popular culture. A rawness emerged—especially in media sex and violence—that threatened innocence. In 1983, preteen girls were avid wannabes, imitating a vamp named Madonna whose first album won raves and who had anything but innocence in mind.

Actually, it was growing rare for an entertainment figure to hold the whole nation's attention; neighbors and coworkers of different races or religions were going their own way. The electronic revolution underway in 1983—8 million Americans had VCRs, twice as many as in 1980—inspired media segmentation. Cable television was becoming the norm, as the three main broadcast networks—once dominant sources of mass culture—saw their evening audience share fall from 84 percent in 1980 to 64 percent in 1990. TV, America's postwar town square, had become a magic carpet carrying viewers to varied destinations.

Even as more Americans watched what they wanted, their sensitivity deepened about whether society respected their values. On the right, religious parents felt assaulted by a hostile culture; on the left, people felt attacked by zealots. Both fears had some grounding, and both found expression in political issues on which moral beliefs led to irreconcilable differences. The most prominent of these was abortion rights: In 1983, supporters celebrated *Roe v. Wade's* 10th anniversary, while opponents decried 10 million legal abortions in that decade. Single-issue politics was on its way to the political-correctness fights of the '90s.

Despite the fragmentation, American ideals were making a comeback, in sharp contrast to the Post-Vietnam demoralization. As 1983 began, thousands of protesters abroad were urging President Reagan not to put Pershing 2 missiles in Europe. (One hundred million viewers had their nightmares reinforced in November 1983 with the TV broadcast of *The Day After,* a nuclear war docudrama.) But Reagan and Europeans held firm; the missiles were installed, with none of the predicted response from the

From *U.S. News & World Report,* October 25, 1993, pp. 58-61, 64-65. © 1993 by U.S. News & World Report. Reprinted by permission.

The Way We Were

Just Like Starting Over
Former Beatle John Lennon was shot to death at age 40 on Dec. 8, 1980, in New York City. By the time of his death, some 22 percent of baby boomers had reached 30—the age beyond which one was never to be trusted in the '60s. In 1987, people who said earning a good living was more important to them than five years before: 51 percent; less important: 6 percent.

Computer Revolution
Americans bought 40 million personal computers in the '80s; 1 in 5 households had a PC by 1990, and 70 percent are expected to have one by 2000. Nearly 60 percent of U.S. households had VCRs by the end of the '80s. But the microwave oven may have been the appliance of the decade; American homes that had one in 1980: fewer than 15 percent; in 1989: 8 in 10.

We Were the World
International crises prompted a new charity: the all-star intercontinental rock extravaganza. Live Aid raised $70 million for African famine relief. Still, by 1990, one fourth of Ethiopians died before the age of 5. Three Farm Aids raised $9 million for U.S. farmers. Meanwhile, activists said the number of homeless in America had tripled to 3 million; U.S. government tally: 350,000.

Reach Out and Buy
In 1985, America became a debtor nation for the first time since 1914. By 1990, the savings rate was half its 1980 level. A new marketing category, the yuppie (young urban professional), and other well-off Americans stockpiled power ties, brie and BMWs to the tune of $100 billion by 1987. Another import rich and poor Americans took to was cocaine; the Drug Enforcement Administration seized 280 tons in the '80s—roughly a third in 1989 alone. Seized in 1979: 1 ton.

Dreams Die Hard
The space shuttle Challenger exploded 73 seconds after its launch on Jan. 28, 1986, killing all seven crew members, including schoolteacher Christa McAuliffe. It was the worst disaster in the history of America's space effort; before the Challenger explosion, three other astronauts had died on the launch pad. Time it took NASA to make a comeback with its successful launch of the space shuttle Discovery: 32 months.

The Iran-Contra Scandal
President Reagan denied that he had approved selling weapons to Iran and financing Nicaragua's Contras with the profits. White House national security aide Oliver North was convicted of three felonies, including obstruction of Congress. (He was later acquitted of all three.) Favorable opinion of North during congressional investigation: 67 percent; after conviction: 59 percent.

Standoff in China
After Chinese troops rolled into Tiananmen Square to crush the June 1989 prodemocracy movement, President Bush suspended U.S. arms sales to China; yet calls for breaking diplomatic ties were rejected. Civilians killed: more than 1,000; Chinese government estimate: about 200.

Beyond the Cold War
Operation Desert Storm, the international effort to force Iraq out of Kuwait in 1991, lasted only 43 days, the ground war segment took just 100 hours. U.S. servicemen and women who died: 146. Americans with confidence in the military after the war: 85 percent; with confidence in big business: 26 percent.

Contributors to the features in this special section: Thom Geier, Amy Bernstein, David Bowermaster, Katherine T. Beddingfield, Greg Ferguson and John Simons

Soviet Union's aging leadership. In March 1983, Reagan surprised Americans with his Strategic Defense Initiative. Ridiculed as "Star Wars," the proposed antimissile shield knocked Soviet leaders on their heels. In 1983, the man who above all others would symbolize the dismantling of the Soviet state was still the agriculture commissar, a protégé of Yuri Andropov who hoped to head a system that almost everyone thought was permanent. But Mikhail Gorbachev knew the Soviets could not keep up with a resurgent America. In Reykjavik, Iceland, in 1986, and afterward, he made arms concessions hoping to halt SDI.

Among the few who believed communism's days were numbered in 1983 were two Poles. Lech Walesa emerged from prison to regain a job in a Gdansk shipyard, as his Solidarity union survived a Communist ban; Pope John Paul II spoke to millions of fellow Poles in Warsaw and Krakow, showing that the nation was behind its spiritual leader, not the Communists or the Army. Walesa, the pope

and Reagan—who called the Soviet empire a "focus of evil"—helped delegitimize Soviet rule, even as new communications breakthroughs made clear its profound economic weakness. Thus, when Gorbachev was unwilling to use force, the Soviet empire collapsed almost immediately, first in Eastern Europe in 1989 and then in the Soviet republics after a failed coup in August 1991.

But in 1983, America was just beginning to end its era of defensiveness. The dispatch of U.S. Marines on an ill-defined mission to Lebanon ended in tragedy in October, when a bomb at a Beirut barracks killed 241 servicemen. Hours later, however, Reagan, in his pajamas, ordered troops to Grenada to oust Communist rebels who had overthrown the government. Democrats feared another Vietnam. It wasn't: Caribbean leaders and the Grenadians welcomed the action, and U.S. students, liberated by U.S. troops, walked off a plane and kissed their home soil.

Even as they did, White House aide Michael Deaver was planning a trip to

Normandy, where, in 1984, Reagan would stand atop the heights of Pointe du Hoc and recall the Americans who liberated France's beaches 40 years earlier—celebrating a past triumph. And a onetime fraternity brother of Deaver's named Peter Ueberroth was planning a celebration of America's present, the 1984 Olympics in Los Angeles. Part of the triumph of the games was that they were held in the city that was becoming the world's No. 1 immigrant destination.

Despite fears to the contrary, immigrants were becoming one of the U.S. economy's great strengths. Nearly 7 million came to America in the 1980s, more than in any decade since 1900–10, 2.4 million from Latin America and the Caribbean and 2.5 million from Asia. Some people worried that the newcomers would cling to old ways. But much like earlier immigrants, they learned English, sought jobs far more than welfare and typically moved rapidly up the economic ladder.

The debate about the 1980s would go on well into the 1990s. Capitalism, which two generations of intellectuals had consigned to the junk heap of history, showed new vitality, while socialism was fading; but the social fabric was fraying in many important patches. After years of debunking old mores, many adopted a certain restraint: Americans led the world in smoking less tobacco, drinking less alcohol and becoming less sexually promiscuous. Still, there were reminders of the terrible costs of unrestrained behavior: high rates of violent crime and drug use, rampant homelessness and the spread of AIDS. Those problems went unattended nationally, as many sought to avoid the cost of fixing what was going awry; at the same time, charitable contributions rose from $48 million to $122 million in the '80s. and there was a new yearning for something deeper, although that, too, had unexpected twists: Church membership rose, from 135 million to 148 million; but there were sharp increases in the membership of fundamentalist denominations and declines in mainline faiths.

Neither progress nor decline proceeded in a straight line—not unlike one California company. In Orange County, AST grew mightily after 1983: It went public in 1984, but its stock fell in 1986; to survive, AST had to shift from mem-

---

Eyewitness
THE WALL CAME TUMBLING DOWN

Barbara Henniger, a political cartoonist living in a town just outside the former East Berlin, was celebrating her birthday the night the Berlin Wall began its fall.

"I never was really at ease with my birthday. See, Nov. 9, 1938, was Reichskristallnacht, when Nazi mobs rushed through almost every major German city smashing Jewish stores and burning synagogues.

"But then came my 51st birthday, Nov. 9, 1989. My daughter invited my husband and me to the opera in Berlin. We went there from our hometown east of Berlin. Nothing was going on in the streets, although the days before had been quite exciting with so many huge antigovernment demonstrations and thousands of East Germans fleeing via Hungary. Even at 10 p.m., when we drove back to my daughter's apartment, we didn't notice anything special. We turned on the television. Suddenly, we saw a West German reporter standing right next to one of the inner-city checkpoints along the wall. "I just learned an Eastern Berlin couple all in tears crossed the open border near Brandenburg Gate," he said.

"We were stupefied, almost paralyzed. But within a second, we grabbed champagne, glasses and my birthday flowers and were on our way to Bornholmer Strasse, the closest checkpoint.

"The streets were already crowded with people cheering, crying and practically dancing. I just couldn't help it—I told everybody that it was my birthday. We were delirious. At Bornholmer Strasse, still before midnight, the border police first tried to channel the crowd through a small gate, but it was impossible and they had to open the main gate. And then, everybody just danced into the West."

---

ory boards to PCs, which brought in most of a whopping $534 million in 1990. Like AST's success, life in the '80s required nothing so much as a willingness to adapt to unpredicted, indeed unpredictable, change.

Looking Back

The Cold War in Retrospect

Raymond L. Garthoff

Raymond L. Garthoff, senior fellow in the Brookings Foreign Policy Studies program, is the author of The Great Transition: American-Soviet Relations and the End of the Cold War *(Brookings, 1994), from which this article is drawn. An earlier version of the article also appeared in the spring 1992 issue of* Diplomatic History.

The Soviet Union and the United States waged the Cold War in the belief that confrontation was unavoidable, that it was imposed by history. Soviet leaders were convinced that communism would ultimately triumph in the world and that the Soviet Union was the vanguard socialist-communist state. They were also convinced that the Western "imperialist" powers were historically bound to pursue a hostile course against them. For their part, American and other Western leaders assumed that the Soviet Union was determined to enhance its power and to pursue expansionist policies by all expedient means to achieve a Soviet-led communist world. Each side thought that it was compelled by the very existence of the other to engage in zero-sum competition, and each saw the unfolding history of the Cold War as confirming its views.

The prevailing Western view was wrong in attributing a master plan to the Kremlin, in believing that communist ideology impelled Soviet leaders to expand their power, in exaggerating communist abilities to subvert a Free World, and in thinking that Soviet officials viewed military power as an ultimate recourse. But the West was not wrong in believing that Soviet leaders were committed to a historically driven struggle between two worlds until, in the end, theirs would triumph. To be sure, other motivations and interests, including national aims, institutional interests, and even personal psychological considerations, played a part. These influences, however, tended to enhance the ideological framework rather than weaken it. Moreover, the actions of each side were sufficiently consistent with the ideological expectations of the other side to sustain their respective worldviews for many years.

IDEOLOGY AND GEOPOLITICS

Within that ideological framework, the Americans and the Soviets carried on the Cold War as a geopolitical struggle, based more realistically on traditional balance-of-power politics than on world class struggle or global containment and deterrence theory. If ideology alone had driven the superpowers, the Cold War would be seen as arising from the October Revolution of 1917 rather than from the ashes of World War II. But in 1917 and during the next 25 years the Soviet Union was relatively weak and only one of several great powers in a multipolar world. By the end of World War II, however, Germany and Japan had been crushed, Britain, France, and China were weakened, and the Soviet Union, even though much weaker than the United States, seemed to pose an unprecedented threat by virtue of its massive armies and their presence deep in Central Europe. Under these circumstances, Josef Stalin's reassertion in 1946 and 1947 of the division of the world into two contending camps seemed more valid and more threatening than ever before.

Thus charged by geopolitical circumstances, a Manichean communist worldview spawned a Manichean anticommunist worldview. Each side imputed unlimited objectives, ultimately world domination, to the other. Each side looked to realize its ambitions (or its historical destiny) over the long term and thus posited an indefinite period of conflict. But even though both sides envisioned a conflict of indefinite duration, and even though policy decisions were pragmatic and based on calculation of risk, cost, and gain, the hazard of a miscalculation always existed. And that could be fatally dangerous, given the historical coincidence of the Cold War and the first half-century of the nuclear age. Nuclear weapons, by threatening the existence of world civilization, added significantly to the tension of the epoch; the stakes were utterly without precedent and beyond full comprehension.

Nuclear weapons also helped to keep the Cold War cold, to prevent a third world war in the 20th century. Nonetheless, in the final analysis and despite their awesome power, nuclear weapons did not cause, prevent, or end the Cold War, which would have been waged even had such weapons never existed. The arms race and other aspects of the superpower rivalry were, however, driven in part by ideological assumptions. As a result, while the Cold War and the nuclear arms race could be attenuated when opportunities or constraints led both sides to favor relaxing tensions, neither could be ended until the ideological underpinnings of the confrontation had fallen. And fall they did—under the leadership of Mikhail Gorbachev, who set in motion a fundamental reevaluation of the processes at work in the real world, a basic reassessment of threats, and finally a deep revision of Moscow's aims and political objectives. The United States and the West in general were cautious but eventually recognized this fundamental change and reciprocated.

DETERRENCE: REDUNDANT BUT REASSURING

The West did not, as is widely believed, win the Cold War through geopolitical containment and military deterrence.

From *The Brookings Review*, Summer 1994, pp. 10-13. © 1994 by the Brookings Institution. Reprinted by permission.

Still less was the Cold War won by the Reagan military buildup and the Reagan Doctrine, as some have suggested. Instead, "victory" came when a new generation of Soviet leaders realized how badly their system at home and their policies abroad had failed. What containment did do was to preclude any temptations on the part of Moscow to advance Soviet hegemony by military means. It is doubtful that any postwar Soviet leadership would have deliberately resorted to war. That was not, however, so clear to many at the time. Deterrence may have been redundant, but at the least it was highly successful in providing reassurance to the peoples of Western Europe. For four decades it performed the historic function of holding Soviet power in check, or being prepared to do so, until the internal seeds of destruction in the Soviet Union and its empire could mature. At that point, however, Gorbachev transformed Soviet policy and brought the Cold War to an end.

Despite important differences among them, all Soviet leaders before Gorbachev had shared a belief in an ineluctable conflict between socialism and capitalism. Although Gorbachev remained a socialist, and in his own terms even a communist, he renounced the Marxist-Leninist-Stalinist idea of inevitable world conflict. His avowed acceptance of the interdependence of the world, of the priority of human values over class values, and of the indivisibility of common security marked a revolutionary ideological change. That change, which Gorbachev publicly declared as early as February 1986 (though it was then insufficiently noted), manifested itself in many ways during the next five years, in deeds as well as words, including policies reflecting a drastically reduced Soviet perception of the Western threat and actions to reduce the Western perception of a Soviet threat.

In 1986, for example, Gorbachev made clear his readiness to ban all nuclear weapons. In 1987 he signed the Intermediate-range Nuclear Forces Treaty, eliminating not only the Soviet and U.S. missiles deployed since the late 1970s but also the whole of the Soviet strategic theater missile forces that had faced Europe and Asia for three decades. What is more, the treaty instituted an intrusive and extensive verification system. In 1988 Gorbachev proposed conventional arms reductions in Europe under a plan that would abandon the Soviet Union's

numerical superiority, and he launched a substantial unilateral force reduction. In 1988–89 he withdrew all Soviet forces from Afghanistan. At about the same time, he encouraged the ouster of the old communist leadership in Eastern Europe and accepted the transition of the former Soviet-allied states into noncommunist neutral states. By 1990 he had signed the Conventional Forces in Europe Treaty accepting Soviet conventional arms levels much lower than NATO's. By that time he had not only accepted Germany's reunification but also the membership of a united Germany in NATO. Within another year he had jettisoned the Warsaw Pact and the socialist bloc and agreed, in the Strategic Arms Reduction Treaty, to verified deep cuts in strategic nuclear forces.

A NEW CONCEPT OF SECURITY

Although Gorbachev had not expected the complete collapse of communism (and Soviet influence) in Eastern Europe that took place in 1989 and 1990, he had made clear to the 27th Congress of the Soviet Communist Party as early as February 1986 that a new conception of security had to replace the previous one, and that the confrontation of the Cold War had to end. No longer speaking in Leninist terms of contending socialist and capitalist worlds, Gorbachev spoke instead of one world, an "interdependent and in many ways integral world." He denied that any country could find security in military power, either for defense or deterrence. Security, he said, could be found only through political means and only on a mutual basis. The goal, he asserted, should be the "creation of a comprehensive system of international security" that embraced economic, ecological, and humanitarian, as well as political and military, elements. Hence, the Soviet decision to give new support to the United Nations, including collective peacekeeping, and to join the world economic system. Hence, the cooperative Soviet efforts to resolve regional conflicts in Central America, Southern Africa, the Horn of Africa, Cambodia, Afghanistan, and the Middle East, not to mention the Soviet Union's support for the collective UN-endorsed action against Iraq in 1991. And hence Moscow's willingness to countenance the dissolution of the Eastern European alliance and socialist commonwealth, which had been

fashioned to meet security requirements and ideological imperatives that had now been abandoned.

Although Gorbachev remained a socialist, and in his own terms even a communist he renounced the Marxist-Leninist-Stalinist idea of inevitable world conflict.

In the final analysis, because the Cold War rested on Marxist-Leninist assumptions of inevitable world conflict, only a Soviet leader could have ended it. And Gorbachev set out deliberately to do just that. Although earlier Soviet leaders had understood the impermissibility of war in the nuclear age, Gorbachev was the first to recognize that reciprocal political accommodation, rather than military power for deterrence or "counterdeterrence," was the defining core of the Soviet Union's relationship with the rest of the world. He accepted the idea of building relations on the basis of a "balance of interests" among nations, rather than trying to maximize the power of one state or bloc on the basis of a "correlation of forces," a balance of power. The conclusions that Gorbachev drew from this recognition, and consequent Soviet actions, finally permitted the Iron Curtain to be dismantled and the global confrontation of the Cold War to end.

Gorbachev, to be sure, seriously underestimated the task of changing the Soviet Union, and his miscalculation led to policy errors that contributed to the failure of his program for transforming Soviet society and polity. His vision of a resurrected socialism built on the foundation of successful *perestroika* and *demokratizatsiya* was never a realistic possibility. He knew deep economic reform was necessary, and he tried; he did not find the solution. A revitalized Soviet political union was perhaps beyond realization as well. The reasons for Gorbachev's failure were primarily objective, not subjective; that is, they were real obstacles he was unable to overcome—internal opposition, powerful inertia, intractable problems of economic transformation, and the politically charged problem of redefining a democratic relationship between a traditional imperial center and the rest of the country—*not* unwillingness or inability to give up or modify his ideological presuppositions and predispositions.

In the external political arena, however, Gorbachev both understood and successfully charted the course that led to the end of the Cold War, even though in this area, too, at first he had an exaggerated expectation of the capacity for reform on the part of the communist governments in Eastern Europe.

AMERICAN IMPERIALISM?

The American role in ending the Cold War was necessary but, naturally, not primary. How could it be when the American worldview was derivative of the communist worldview? Containment was hollow without an expansionist power to contain. In this sense, it was the Soviet threat, partly real and partly imagined, that generated the American dedication to waging the Cold War, regardless of what revisionist American historians have to say. These historians point to Washington's atomic diplomacy and to its various overt and covert political, economic, paramilitary, and military campaigns. Supposedly designed to counter a Soviet threat, they argue, these initiatives actually entailed an expansion of American influence and dominion.

The revisionist interpretation errs in attributing imperial initiative and design to American diplomacy, but it is not entirely wrong. American policymakers were guilty of accepting far too much of the communist worldview in constructing an anticommunist antipode, and of being too ready to fight fire with fire. Indeed, once the Cold War became the dominant factor in global politics (and above all in American and Soviet perceptions), each side viewed every development around the world in terms of its relationship to that great struggle, and each was inclined to act according to a self-fulfilling prophecy. The Americans, for example, often viewed local and regional conflicts of indigenous origins as Cold War battles and acted on that assumption. Like the Soviets, they distrusted the neutral and nonaligned nations and were always more comfortable when countries were either their allies or the satellites and surrogates of the other side.

Thus, many traditional diplomatic relationships not essentially attendant on the superpower rivalry were swept into the vortex of the Cold War, at least in the eyes of the protagonists—and partly in fact as a result of their actions.

True, the Cold War led in some instances to constructive American involvements. The Marshall Plan is a prime example, not to mention American support for some democratic political movements and for the Congress for Cultural Freedom and the liberal journal *Encounter.* But overt and covert involvements were more frequently less constructive, and often subversive, of real liberalism and democracy. Apart from the loss of American lives and treasure in such misplaced ventures as the Vietnam War and in the massive overinvestment in weaponry, one of the worst effects of forcing all world developments onto the procrustean bed of the Cold War was the distortion of America's understanding and values. By dividing the globe into a communist Evil Empire controlled by Moscow and a Free World led by Washington, American policymakers promoted numerous antidemocratic regimes into membership in the Free World as long as they were anticommunist (or even rhetorically so). Washington also used the exigencies of the Cold War to justify assassination plots, to negotiate deals with war lords, drug lords, and terrorists, and to transform anticommunist insurgents, however corrupt or antidemocratic, into "freedom fighters." Alliance ties, military basing rights, and support for insurgencies were routinely given priority over such other American objectives as promoting nuclear nonproliferation, economic development, human rights, and democracy.

Parallel Soviet sins were at least as great. While Soviet foreign assistance to socialist and "progressive" countries was sometimes constructive (building the Aswan Dam, for example, or providing economic assistance to India), it was also skewed by the ideological expectation of moving the world toward communism and by expectations of Soviet geopolitical advantage in the Cold War. Often dictatorial regimes, "Marxist" or "socialist" only according to the cynical claims of their leaders, provided the basis for Soviet support, as with Siad Barre in Somalia, for example, or Mengistu in Ethiopia. The Soviet Union also

engaged in many covert political operations and lent support to national liberation movements (some authentic, others less so) that sometimes included elements engaged in terrorism. On both sides, then, ideological beliefs combined with geopolitical considerations to fuel a Cold War struggle that left many victims in its wake.

REALITY CHECK

Although the decisive factor in the end of the Cold War was a change in these beliefs, it is worth repeating that the Soviet leaders could discard a long-encrusted and familiar ideology only because of a powerful transformation in the way Gorbachev and some colleagues perceived reality, and because they were ready to adapt domestic and foreign policies to the new perception. Over time, the extent and depth of these changes became inescapable and their validity compelling, bringing the Cold War to an end. The critical culminating event was the Revolution of '89.

The year between the destruction of the Berlin Wall in November 1989 and the European conference in Paris in November 1990 saw the removal of the most important manifestation of the Cold War: the division of Germany and Europe. The division of Europe had symbolized the global battle between the two ideological and geopolitical camps in the years immediately after World War II. When that division came to an end, the consequences for the international balance of power were so substantial that even the most hardened cold warriors in the West were forced to acknowledge that the Cold War had ended—even before the collapse of communist rule in the Soviet Union or of the Soviet Union itself. Moreover, the Revolution of '89 in Eastern Europe was decisive not only in demonstrating that the ideological underpinnings of the Cold War had been removed but also in shifting the actual balance of power. The removal of Soviet military power from Eastern Europe dissolved the threat to Western Europe and also restored a reunified Europe to the center of the world political stage. Russia and even the United States have now become less central. American-Russian relations nonetheless remain of great importance in the post-Cold War world.

New Directions for American History

For decades concentration on the cold war provided a unifying theme for American diplomacy, however much disagreement there was over particular policies. Military and scientific procurement for this conflict also deeply affected the economic system. The "peace dividend" that some predicted has been only partially realized, as conflicts in various parts of the world have been used to justify the need for substantial military spending. American intervention in the Middle East against Iraq in 1991, the ongoing turmoil in the Balkan countries, and the landings in Haiti in 1994 have made a mockery of former president George Bush's prediction that a "new world order" lay at hand.

The two-part essay "The Disuniting of America" and "The Painful Demise of Eurocentrism," as well as "The Permanently Unfinished Country" deal with related subjects. The first part of the two-part essay argues that while attention and respect should be accorded to all racial and ethnic groups, the new emphasis on what has become known as "multiculturalism" has been on those factors that divide Americans, not on what unites them. This emphasis, the author believes, can only result in the "Balkanization" of racial and ethnic communities. The second part of the essay "The Painful Demise of Eurocentrism," protests that what has passed as "unity" within the United States actually has been the domination of society by white males of European origins, who have structured the system to benefit themselves at the expense of others. Whatever view one takes, "The Permanently Unfinished Country" makes clear that the immigration to the United States of people from all over the world will make this nation more diverse than ever before.

People of all political persuasions largely can agree that the existing welfare system is a mess. Some want to enlarge it, some to reform it, others want to dismantle it almost entirely. "Alms without End? A History of Welfare in America" surveys past efforts to balance off helping the poor without providing them with permanent vacations. The author concludes that history has shown that the problem is inherently difficult to solve and warns against thinking there are any "quick fixes."

When the first European settlers came to what is now the United States, they found vast lands of abundant resources peopled only lightly (in European terms) by those whom they chose to call "Indians." Over the course of centuries, westward expansion and the subsequent growth of cities radically changed the environment. Forests were cut, land misused, rivers and the very air itself polluted. Some protested early on against this degradation, but only in recent years have major commitments been made to reverse the damages. "The American Environment: The Big Picture Is More Heartening than All the Little Ones" concludes that while there is a long way to go, a start has been made and the effort must be sustained.

One's view of the past helps shape one's ideas as to what should be done in the future. "Revising the Twentieth Century" points out that after both world wars and during the lengthy cold war, individuals who became known as "revisionists" came forward to denounce American conduct as wrong and against the public interests. With few exceptions, most of this criticism came from the left of the political spectrum. The author of this essay discusses examples of "revisionism" from the right in Great Britain and Western Europe, and he thinks it may soon appear in the United States.

Looking Ahead: Challenge Questions

Few would argue against showing respect for all cultures, from wherever they might come. But will "multiculturalism" lead to disunity in the United States, or will it help liberate the society from what has been the dominant elite? Might it do both? What impact will continued immigration from various parts of the world have on the situation?

Americans traditionally have believed that they must be free to develop the resources they own without interference. Such an attitude has resulted in massive degradation of the environment. To what extent should society attempt to regulate enterprise for the benefit of the present and future generations?

The Disuniting of America

Arthur M. Schlesinger, Jr.

The fading away of the cold war has brought an era of ideological conflict to an end. But it has not, as forecast, brought an end to history. One set of hatreds gives way to the next. Lifting the lid of ideological repression in eastern Europe releases ethnic antagonisms deeply rooted in experience and in memory. The disappearance of ideological competition in the third world removes superpower restraints on national and tribal confrontations. As the era of ideological conflict subsides, humanity enters—or, more precisely, re-enters—a possibly more dangerous era of ethnic and racial animosity.

For the mutual antipathy of tribes is one of the oldest things in the world. The history of our planet has been in great part the history of the mixing of peoples. Mass migrations produce mass antagonisms. The fear of the Other is among the most instinctive human reactions. Today, as the twentieth century draws to an end, a number of factors—not just the evaporation of the cold war but, more profoundly, the development of swifter modes of communication and transport, the acceleration of population growth, the breakdown of traditional social structures, the persistence of desperate poverty and want—converge to stimulate mass migrations across national frontiers and thereby to make the mixing of peo-

ples a major problem for the century that lies darkly ahead.

What happens when people of different ethnic origins, speaking different languages and professing different religions, settle in the same geographical locality and live under the same political sovereignty? Unless a common purpose binds them together, tribal hostilities will drive them apart. Ethnic and racial conflict, it seems evident, will now replace the conflict of ideologies as the explosive issue of our times.

On every side today ethnicity is the cause of the breaking of nations. The Soviet Union, Yugoslavia, India, South Africa are all in crisis. Ethnic tensions disturb and divide Sri Lanka, Burma, Ethiopia, Indonesia, Iraq, Lebanon, Israel, Cyprus, Somalia, Nigeria, Liberia, Angola, Sudan, Zaire, Guyana, Trinidad—you name it. Even nations as stable and civilized as Britain and France, Belgium and Spain and Czechoslovakia, face growing ethnic and racial troubles. "The virus of tribalism," says the Economist, "risks becoming the AIDS of international politics—lying dormant for years, then flaring up to destroy countries."

Take the case of our neighbor to the north. Canada has long been considered the most sensible and placid of nations. "Rich, peaceful and, by the standards of

almost anywhere else, enviably successful," the Economist observes: yet today "on the brink of bust-up." Michael Ignatieff (the English-resident son of a Russian-born Canadian diplomat and thus an example of the modern mixing of peoples) writes of Canada, "Here we have one of the five richest nations on earth, a country so uniquely blessed with space and opportunity that the world's poor are beating at the door to get in, and it is tearing itself apart. . . . If one of the top five developed nations on earth can't make a federal, multiethnic state work, who else can?"

The answer to that increasingly vital question has been, at least until recently, the United States.

Now how have Americans succeeded in pulling off this almost unprecedented trick? Other countries break up because they fail to give ethnically diverse peoples compelling reasons to see themselves as part of the same nation. The United States has worked, thus far, because it has offered such reasons. What is it then that, in the absence of a common ethnic origin, has held Americans together over two turbulent centuries? For America was a multiethnic country from the start. Hector St. John de Crèvecoeur emigrated from France to the American colonies in 1759, married an American

From *The World & I,* April 1992, pp. 279-295. Excerpt from *The Disuniting of America* by Arthur M. Schlesinger, Jr. © 1992 by Arthur M. Schlesinger, Jr. This book was first published by Whittle Books as part of *The Larger Agenda Series.* Reprinted by arrangement with Whittle Communications, L.P.

woman, settled on a farm in Orange County, New York, and published his *Letters from an American Farmer* during the American Revolution. This eighteenth-century French American marveled at the astonishing diversity of the other settlers—"a mixture of English, Scotch, Irish, French, Dutch, Germans, and Swedes," a "strange mixture of blood" that you could find in no other country.

Ethnic and racial conflict will now replace the conflict of ideologies as the explosive issue of our times.

He recalled one family whose grandfather was English, whose wife was Dutch, whose son married a Frenchwoman, and whose present four sons had married women of different nationalities. "From this promiscuous breed," he wrote, "that race now called Americans have arisen." (The word *race* as used in the eighteenth and nineteenth centuries meant what we mean by nationality today; thus people spoke of "the English race," "the German race," and so on.) What, Crèvecoeur mused, were the characteristics of this suddenly emergent American race? *Letters from an American Farmer* propounded a famous question: "What then is the American, this new man?" (Twentieth-century readers must overlook eighteenth-century male obliviousness to the existence of women.)

Crèvecoeur gave his own question its classic answer: *"He* is an American, who leaving behind him all his ancient prejudices and manners, receives new ones from the new mode of life he has embraced, the new government he obeys, and the new rank he holds. The American is a new man, who acts upon new principles. . . . *Here individuals of all* nations *are melted into a new race of men."*

E pluribus unum. The United States had a brilliant solution for the inherent divisibility of a multiethnic society: the creation of a brand-new national identity, carried forward by individuals who, in forsaking old loyalties and joining to make new lives, melted away ethnic differences. Those intrepid Europeans who had torn up their roots to brave the wild Atlantic *wanted* to forget a horrid past

and to embrace a hopeful future. They *expected* to become Americans. Their goals were escape, deliverance, assimilation. They saw America as a transforming nation, banishing dismal yesterdays and developing a unique national character based on common political ideals and shared experiences. The point of America was not to preserve old cultures, but to forge a new *American* culture.

One reason why Canada, despite all its advantages, is so vulnerable to schism is that, as Canadians freely admit, their country lacks such a unique national identity. Attracted variously to Britain, France, and the United States, inclined for generous reasons to respect diverse ethnic inheritances, Canadians have never developed a strong sense of what it is to be a Canadian. As Sir John Macdonald, their first prime minister, put it, Canada has "too much geography and too little history."

The United States has had plenty of history. From the Revolution on, Americans have had a powerful national creed. The vigorous sense of national identity accounts for our relative success in converting Crèvecoeur's "promiscuous breed" into one people and thereby making a multiethnic society work.

This is not to say that the United States has ever fulfilled Crèvecoeur's ideal. New waves of immigration brought in people who fitted awkwardly into a society that was inescapably English in language, ideals, and institutions. For a long time the Anglo-Americans dominated American culture and politics. The pot did not melt everybody, not even all the white immigrants.

As for the nonwhite peoples—those long in America whom the European newcomers overran and massacred, or those others brought against their will from Africa and Asia—deeply bred racism put them all—red Americans, black Americans, yellow Americans, brown Americans—well outside the pale. The curse of racism was the great failure of the American experiment, the glaring contradiction of American ideals and the still crippling disease of American life.

Yet even nonwhite Americans, miserably treated as they were, contributed to the formation of the national identity. They became members, if third-class members, of American society and helped give the common culture new form and flavor. The infusion of non-Anglo stocks and the experience of the New World steadily reconfigured the British legacy

and made the United States, as we all know, a very different country today from Britain.

Crèvecoeur's vision of America prevailed through most of the two centuries of the history of the United States. But the twentieth century has brought forth a new and opposing vision. One world war destroyed the old order of things and launched Woodrow Wilson's doctrine of the self-determination of peoples. Twenty years after, a second world war dissolved the western colonial empires and intensified ethnic and racial militancy around the planet. In the United States itself new laws eased entry for immigrants from South America, Asia, and Africa and altered the composition of the American people.

In a nation marked by an even stranger mixture of blood than Crèvecoeur had known, his celebrated question is asked once more, with a new passion—and a new answer. Today many Americans turn away from the historic goal of "a new race of man." The escape from origins has given way to the search for roots. The "ancient prejudices and manners" disowned by Crèvecoeur have made a surprising comeback. A cult of ethnicity has arisen both among non-Anglo whites and among nonwhite minorities.

The eruption of ethnicity had many good consequences. The American culture began at last to give shamefully overdue recognition to the achievements of minorities subordinated and spurned during the high noon of Anglo dominance. American education began at last to acknowledge the existence and significance of the great swirling world beyond Europe. All this was to the good. Of course history should be taught from a variety of perspectives. Let our children try to imagine the arrival of Columbus from the viewpoint of those who met him as well as from those who sent him. Living on a shrinking planet, aspiring to global leadership, Americans must learn much more about other races, other cultures, other continents. As they do, they acquire a more complex and invigorating sense of the world—and of themselves.

But, pressed too far, the cult of ethnicity has had bad consequences too. The new ethnic gospel rejects Crèvecoeur's vision of individuals from all nations melted into a new race. Its underlying philosophy is that America is not a nation of individuals at all but a nation of groups, that ethnicity is the defining experience for most Americans, that ethnic

The curse of racism was the great failure of the American experiment, the glaring contradiction of American ideals and the still crippling disease of American life.

ties are permanent and indelible, and that division into ethnic groups establishes the basic structure of American society and the basic meaning of American history.

Implicit in this philosophy is the classification of all Americans according to ethnic and racial criteria. But while the ethnic interpretation of American history like the economic interpretation, is valid and illuminating up to a point, it is fatally misleading and wrong when presented as the whole picture. The ethnic interpretation, moreover, reverses the historic theory of America—the theory that has thus far managed to keep American society whole.

Instead of a transformative nation with an identity all its own, America increasingly sees itself in this new light as preservative of diverse alien identities. Instead of a nation composed of individuals making their own unhampered choices, America increasingly sees itself as composed of groups more or less ineradicable in their ethnic character. The multiethnic dogma abandons historic purposes, replacing assimilation by fragmentation, integration by separatism. It belittles *unum* and glorifies *pluribus*.

The historic idea of a transcendent and unifying American identity is now in peril in many arenas—in our politics, our voluntary organizations, our churches, our language. And in no arena is the erosion of faith in an overriding national identity more crucial than in our system of education.

The schools and colleges of the republic train the citizens of the future. Our public schools in particular have been the historic mechanisms for the transmission of the ideal of "one people." What students are taught in schools affects the way they will thereafter see and treat other Americans, the way they will thereafter conceive the purposes of the republic. The debate about the curricu-

lum is a debate about what it means to be an American.

The militants of ethnicity now contend that a main objective of public education should be the protection, strengthening, celebration, and perpetuation of ethnic origins and identities. Separatism, however, magnifies differences and stirs antagonisms. The consequent increase in ethnic and racial conflict lies behind the hullabaloo over "multiculturalism" and "political correctness," over the iniquities of the "Eurocentric" curriculum, and over the notion that history and literature should be taught not as intellectual disciplines but as therapies whose function is to raise minority self-esteem.

One wonders. Do not the ethnic militants see any dangers in a society divided into distinct and immutable ethnic and racial groups, each taught to cherish its own apartness from the rest? What is ultimately at stake is the shape of the American future. Will the center hold? or will the melting pot give way to the Tower of Babel?

I don't want to sound apocalyptic about these developments. Education is always in ferment, and a good thing too. Schools and colleges have always been battlegrounds for debates over beliefs, philosophies, values. The situation in our universities, I am confident, will soon right itself once the great silent majority of professors cry "enough" and challenge what they know to be voguish nonsense.

The impact of ethnic and racial pressures on our public schools is more troubling. The bonds of national cohesion are sufficiently fragile already. Public education should aim to strengthen those bonds, not to weaken them. If separatist tendencies go on unchecked, the result can only be the fragmentation, resegregation, and tribalization of American life.

I remain optimistic. My impression is that the historic forces driving toward "one people" have not lost their power. For most Americans this is still what the republic is all about. They resist extremes in the argument between "unity first" and "ethnicity first." "Most Americans," Governor Mario Cuomo has well said, "can understand both the need to recognize and encourage an enriched diversity as well as the need to ensure that such a broadened multicultural perspective leads to unity and an enriched sense of what being an American is, and not to a destructive factionalism that would tear us apart."

Whatever their self-appointed spokesmen may claim, most American-born members of minority groups, white or nonwhite, while they may cherish particular heritages, still see themselves primarily as Americans and not primarily as Irish or Hungarians or Jews or Africans or Asians. A telling indicator is the rising rate of intermarriage across ethnic, religious, even (increasingly) racial lines. The belief in a unique American identity is far from dead.

But the burden to unify the country does not fall exclusively on the minorities. Assimilation and integration constitute a two-way street. Those who want to join America must be received and welcomed by those who already think they own America. Racism, as I have noted, has been the great national tragedy. In recent times white America has at last begun to confront the racism so deeply and shamefully inbred in our history. But the triumph over racism is incomplete. When old-line Americans, for example, treat people of other nationalities and races as if they were indigestible elements to be shunned and barred, they must not be surprised if minorities gather bitterly unto themselves and damn everybody else. Not only must *they* want assimilation and integration; *we* must want assimilation and integration too. The burden to make this a unified country lies as much with the complacent majority as with the sullen and resentful minorities.

The American population has unquestionably grown more heterogeneous than ever in recent times. But this very heterogeneity makes the quest for unifying ideals and common culture all the more urgent. And in a world savagely rent by ethnic and racial antagonisms, it is all the more essential that the United States continue as an example of how a highly differentiated society holds itself together.

Low self-esteem is too deep a malady to be cured by hearing nice things about one's own ethnic past. Institutionalized separatism only crystallizes racial differences and magnifies racial tensions.

THE DECOMPOSITION OF AMERICA

Low self-esteem is too deep a malady to be cured by hearing nice things about one's own ethnic past. History is not likely to succeed where psychiatry fails. Afrocentrism in particular is an escape from the hard and expensive challenges of our society—the need for safer schools, better teachers, better teaching materials, greater investment in education; the need for stable families that can nourish self-discipline and aspiration; the need for jobs and income that can nourish stable families; the need to stop the ravages of drugs and crime; the need to overcome the racism still lurking in the interstices of American society. "The need," William Raspberry observes of his own people, "is not to reach back for some culture we never knew but to lay full claim to the culture in which we exist."

I

The ethnicity rage in general and Afrocentricity in particular not only divert attention from the real needs but exacerbate the problems. The recent apotheosis of ethnicity, black, brown, red, yellow, white, has revived the dismal prospect that in happy melting-pot days Americans thought the republic was moving safely beyond—that is, a society fragmented into ethnic groups. The cult of ethnicity exaggerates differences, intensifies resentments and antagonisms, drives ever deeper the awful wedges between races and nationalities. The end game is self-pity and self-ghettoization.

Now there is a reasonable argument in the black case for a measure of regrouping and self-reliance as part of the preparation for entry into an integrated society on an equal basis. Integration on any other basis, it is contended, would mean total capitulation to white standards. Affirmation of racial and cultural pride is thus essential to true integration. One can see this as a psychological point, but as a cultural point?

For generations blacks have grown up in an American culture, on which they have had significant influence and to which they have made significant contributions. Self-Africanization after 300 years in America is playacting. Afrocentricity as expounded by ethnic ideologues implies Europhobia, separatism, emotions of alienation, victimization, paranoia. Most curious and unexpected

of all is a black demand for the return of black-white segregation.

"To separate [black children] from others of similar age and qualifications solely because of their race," Chief Justice Warren wrote in the school-integration case, "generates a feeling of inferiority as to their status in the community that may affect their hearts and minds in a way unlikely ever to be undone." In 40 years doctrine has come full circle. Now integration is held to bring feelings of inferiority, and segregation to bring the cure.

This revival of separatism will begin, if the black educator Felix Boateng has his way, in the earliest grades. "The use of standard English as the only language of instruction," Boateng argues, "aggravates the process of deculturalization." A "culturally relevant curriculum" for minority children would recognize "the home and community dialect they bring to school." (Not all black educators, it

---

The militants of ethnicity now contend that a main objective of public education should be the protection, strengthening, celebration, and perpetuation of ethnic origins and identities.

---

should be said, share this desire to handicap black children from infancy.) "One fact is clear," notes Janice Hale-Benson of Cleveland State University "Speaking standard English is a skill needed by Black children for upward mobility in American society and it should be taught in early childhood.")

If any educational institution should bring people together as individuals in friendly and civil association, it should be the university. But the fragmentation of campuses in recent years into a multitude of ethnic organizations is spectacular—and disconcerting.

One finds black dormitories, black student unions, black fraternities and sororities, black business and law societies, black homosexual and lesbian groups, black tables in dining halls. Stanford, Dinesh D'Souza reports, has "ethnic theme houses." The University of Pennsylvania gives blacks—6 percent of the

enrollment—their own yearbook. Campuses today, according to one University of Pennsylvania professor, have "the cultural diversity of Beirut. There are separate armed camps. The black kids don't mix with the white kids. The Asians are off by themselves. Oppression is the great status symbol."

Oberlin was for a century and half the model of a racially integrated college. "Increasingly," Jacob Weisberg, an editor at *The New Republic,* reports, "Oberlin students think, act, study, and live apart." Asians live in Asia House, Jews in "J" House, Latinos in Spanish House, blacks in African-Heritage House, foreign students in Third World House. Even the Lesbian, Gay, and Bisexual Union has broken up into racial and gender factions. "The result is separate worlds."

Huddling is an understandable reaction for any minority group faced with new and scary challenges. But institutionalized separatism only crystallizes racial differences and magnifies racial tensions. "Certain activities are labeled white and black," says a black student at Central Michigan University. "If you don't just participate in black activities, you are shunned." A recent study by the black anthropologist Signithia Fordham of Rutgers concludes that a big reason for black underachievement is the fear that academic success will be taken as a sellout to the white world. "What appears to have emerged in some segments of the black community," Fordham says, "is a kind of cultural orientation which defines academic learning in school as 'acting white.'"

Militants further argue that because only blacks can comprehend the black experience, only blacks should teach black history and literature, as, in the view of some feminists, only women should teach women's history and literature. "True diversity," according to the faculty's Budget Committee at the University of California at Berkeley, requires that courses match the ethnic and gender identities of the professors.

The doctrine that *only* blacks can teach and write black history leads inexorably to the doctrine that blacks can teach and write *only* black history as well as to inescapable corollaries: Chinese must be restricted to Chinese history, women to women's history, and so on. Henry Louis Gates criticizes "ghettoized programs where students and members of the faculty sit around and argue about whether a white person can think a black thought." As for the notion that there is a "mystique" about black studies that requires a person to have black skin in order to pursue them—that, John Hope Franklin observes succinctly, is "voodoo."

The voodoo principle is extended from scholarship to the arts. Thus the fine black playwright August Wilson insists on a black director for the film if his play *Fences.* "We have a different way of responding to the world," Wilson explains. "We have different ideas about religion, different manners of social intercourse. We have different ideas about style, about language. We have different esthetics [*sic*]. . . . The job requires someone who shares the specifics of the culture of black Americans. . . . Let's make a rule. Blacks don't direct Italian films. Italians don't direct Jewish films. Jews don't direct black American films." What a terrible rule that would be!

In the same restrictive spirit, Actors' Equity tried to prevent the British actor Jonathan Pryce from playing in New York the role he created in London in *Miss Saigon,* announcing that it could not condone "the casting of a Caucasian actor in the role of a Eurasian." (Pryce responded that, if this doctrine prevails, "I'd be stuck playing Welshmen for the rest of my life.") Equity did not, however, apply the same principle to the black actors Morgan Freeman and Denzel Washington who were both acting in Shakespeare at that time in New York. *The Wall Street Journal* acidly suggested that, according to the principle invoked, not only whites but the disabled should protest the casting of Denzel Washington as Richard III because Washington lacked a hunchback.

The distinguished black social psychologist Kenneth B. Clark, whose findings influenced the Supreme Court's decision in the school-integration case, rejects the argument that blacks and whites must be separated "because they represent different cultures and that cultures, like oil and water, cannot mix." This, Clark says, is what white segregationists have argued for generations. He adds, "There is absolutely no evidence to support the contention that the inherent damage to human beings of primitive exclusion on the basis of race is any less damaging when demanded or enforced by the previous victims than when imposed by the dominant group."

II

The separatist impulse is by no means confined to the black community. Another salient expression is the bilingualism movement, ostensibly conducted in the interests of all non-English speakers but particularly a Hispanic-American project.

Bilingualism is hardly a new issue in American history. Seven years after the adoption of the Constitution, a proposal to print 3,000 sets of federal laws in German as well as English was narrowly defeated in the House of Representatives. (This incident gave rise to the myth, later cherished by Nazi propagandists like Colin Ross, that German had nearly displaced English as America's official language.) In the nineteenth century, newly arrived immigrants stayed for a season with their old language, used it in their homes, churches, newspapers, and not seldom in bilingual public schools, until acculturation reduced and the First World War discouraged the use of languages other than English.

The separatist impulse is by no means confined to the black community. Another salient expression is the bilingualism movement.

In recent years the combination of the ethnicity cult with a flood of immigration from Spanish-speaking countries has given bilingualism new impetus. The presumed purpose is transitional: to move non-English-speaking children as quickly as possible from bilingual into all-English classes. The Bilingual Education Act of 1968 supplies guidelines and funding; the 1974 Supreme Court decision in *Lau v. Nichols* (a Chinese-speaking case) requires school districts to provide special programs for children who do not know English.

Alas, bilingualism has not worked out as planned: rather the contrary. Testimony is mixed, but indications are that bilingual education retards rather than expedites the movement of Hispanic children into the English-speaking world and that it promotes segregation more than it does integration. Bilingualism shuts doors. It nourishes self-ghettoization, and ghettoization nourishes racial antagonism. Bilingualism "encourages concentrations of Hispanics to stay together and not be integrated," says Alfredo

Mathew, Jr., a Hispanic civic leader, and it may well foster "a type of apartheid that will generate animosities with others, such as Blacks, in the competition for scarce resources, and further alienate the Hispanic from the larger society."

Using some language other than English dooms people to second-class citizenship in American society. "Those who have the most to lose in a bilingual America," says the Mexican-American writer Richard Rodriguez, "are the foreign-speaking poor." Rodriguez recalls his own boyhood: "It would have pleased me to hear my teachers address me in Spanish. . . . But I would have delayed . . . having to learn the language of public society. . . . Only when I was able to think of myself as an American, no longer an alien in *gringo* society, could I seek the rights and opportunities necessary for full public individuality."

Monolingual education opens doors to the larger world. "I didn't speak English until I was about 8 years of age," Governor Mario Cuomo recently recalled, "and there was a kind of traumatic entry into public school. It made an immense impression on me." Traumatic or not, public school taught Cuomo the most effective English among politicos of his generation.

Yet a professor at the University of Massachusetts told Rosalie Pedalino Porter, whose long experience in bilingual education led to her excellent book *Forked Tongue,* that teaching English to children reared in another language is a form of political oppression. Her rejoinder seems admirable: "When we succeed in helping our students use the majority language fluently . . . we are empowering our students rather than depriving them."

Panicky conservatives, fearful that the republic is over the hill, call for a constitutional amendment to make English the official language of the United States. Seventeen states already have such statutes. This is a poor idea. The English language does not need statutory reinforcement and the drive for an amendment will only increase racial discrimination and resentment.

Nonetheless, a common language is a necessary bond of national cohesion in so heterogeneous a nation as America. The bilingual campaign has created both an educational establishment with a vested interest in extending the bilingual empire and a political lobby with a vested interest in retaining a Hispanic constituency. Like Afrocentricity and the ethnicity cult, bilingualism is an elitist, not a popular, movement—"romantic ethnicity," as Myrdal called it; political ethnicity too. Still, institutionalized bilingualism remains another source of the fragmentation of America, another threat to the dream of "one people."

III

Most ominous about the separatist impulse is the meanness generated when one group is set against another. What Harold Isaacs, that acute student of racial sensitivities and resentments, called the "built-in we-they syndrome" has caused more dominating, fearing, hating, killing than any other single cause since time began.

Blacks, having suffered most grievously (at least in America) from persecution, have perhaps the greatest susceptibility to paranoia—remembering always that even paranoids may have real enemies. After all, considering what we now know about the plots against black Americans concocted by J. Edgar Hoover and executed by his FBI, who can blame blacks for being forever suspicious of white intentions?

Still, the *New York Times*—WCBS-TV poll of New Yorkers in 1990 is startling. Sixty percent of black respondents thought it true or possibly true that the government was making drugs available in black neighborhoods in order to harm black people. Twenty-nine percent thought it true or possibly true that the AIDS virus was invented by racist conspirators to kill blacks.

When Mayor Edward Koch invited the irrepressible Leonard Jeffries of CCNY to breakfast to discuss the "ice people-sun people" theory, Jeffries agreed to come "but said he would not eat because white people were trying to poison him. When he arrived," Koch reports, "I offered him coffee and danish, but he refused it. I then offered to be his food taster, but he still declined."

On another occasion, Jeffries observed that "AIDS coming out of a laboratory and finding itself localized in certain populations certainly has to be looked at as part of a conspiratorial process." After a Jeffries class, 10 black students told the *Times* reporter that AIDS and drugs were indeed part of a white conspiracy. "During the Carter administration," one said, "There was a document put out that said by the year

2000, one hundred million Africans had to be destroyed." "Because of who's being devastated the most, and growing up in the U.S. and knowing the history of slavery and racism in this country," an older black man said, "you can't be black and not feel that AIDS is some kind of experiment, some kind of plot to hit undesirable minority populations."

Nor is such speculation confined to the feverish sidewalks of New York. "Let me make a speech before a black audience," testifies William Raspberry, "and sometime during the Q & A someone is

---

A common language is a necessary bond of national cohesion in so heterogeneous a nation as America.

---

certain to ask if I believe there is a conspiracy against black Americans. It doesn't matter whether the subject is drugs or joblessness, school failure or teen pregnancy, politics or immigration. I can count on hearing some version of the conspiracy question."

The black case is only a more extreme version of the persecution complex—the feeling that someone is out to get them—to which nearly all minorities on occasion succumb. Mutual suspicion and hostility are bound to emerge in a society bent on defining itself in terms of jostling and competing groups.

IV

"The era that began with the dream of integration," Richard Rodriguez has observed, "ended up with scorn for assimilation." Instead of casting off the foreign skin, as John Quincy Adams had stipulated, never to resume it, the fashion is to resume the foreign skin as conspicuously as can be. The cult of ethnicity has reversed the movement of American history, producing a nation of minorities or at least of minority spokesmen—less interested in joining with the majority in common endeavor than in declaring their alienation from an oppressive, white, patriarchal, racist, sexist, classist society. The ethnic ideology inculcates the illusion that membership in one or another ethnic group is the basic American experience.

Most Americans, it is true, continue to see themselves primarily as individuals and only secondarily and trivially as adherents of a group. Nor is harm done when ethnic groups display pride in their historic past or in their contributions to the American present. But the division of society into fixed ethnicities nourishes a culture of victimization and a contagion of inflammable sensitivities. And when a vocal and visible minority pledges primary allegiance to their groups, whether ethnic, sexual, religious, or, in rare cases (communist, fascist), political, it presents a threat to the brittle bonds of national identity that hold this diverse and fractious society together.

A peculiarly ugly mood seems to have settled over the one arena where freedom of inquiry and expression should be most unconstrained and civility most respected—our colleges and universities. It is no fun running a university these days. Undergraduates can be wanton and cruel in their exclusion, their harassment, their heavy pranks, their wounding invective. Minority students, for the most understandable reasons, are often vulnerable and frightened. Racial cracks, slurs, insults, vilification pose difficult problems. Thus posters appear around the campus at the University of Michigan parodying the slogan of the United Negro College Fund: A MIND IS A TERRIBLE THING TO WASTE—ESPECIALLY ON A NIGGER. Decent white students join the protest against white bullies and thugs.

Presidents and deans begin to ask themselves, which is more important—protecting free speech or preventing racial persecution? The Constitution, Justice Holmes said, embodies "the principle of free thought—not free thought for those who agree with us but freedom for the thought that we hate." But suppose the thought we hate undercuts the Constitution's ideal of equal justice under law? Does not the First Amendment protect equality as well as liberty? How to draw a bright line between speech and behavior?

One has a certain sympathy for besieged administrators who, trying to do their best to help minority students, adopt regulations to restrict racist and sexist speech. More than a hundred institutions, according to the American Civil Liberties Union, had done so by February 1991. My own decided preference is to stand by the First Amendment and to fight speech by speech, not by censorship. But then, I am not there on the firing line.

The black case is only a more extreme version of the persecution complex to which nearly all minorities on occasion succumb.

One can even understand why administrators, not sure what best to do for minorities and eager to keep things quiet, accept—even subsidize—separatist remedies urged by student militants. They might, however, ponder Kenneth Clark's comment: "The white liberal . . . who concedes black separatism so hastily and benevolently must look to his own reasons, not the least of them perhaps an exquisite relief." And it is sad, though instructive, that the administrations especially disposed to encourage racial and ethnic enclaves—like Berkeley, Michigan, Oberlin, the University of Massachusetts at Amherst—are, Dinesh D'Souza (himself an Indian from India) points out, the ones experiencing the most racial tension. Troy Duster, a Berkeley sociologist, finds a correlation between group separatism and racial hostility among students.

Moderates who would prefer fending for themselves as individuals are bullied into going along with their group. Groups get committed to platforms and to we-they syndromes. Faculty members appease. A code of ideological orthodoxy emerges. The code's guiding principle is that nothing should be said that might give offense to members of minority groups (and, apparently, that anything can be said that gives offense to white males of European origin).

The Office of Student Affairs at Smith College has put out a bulletin listing types of oppression for people belatedly "realizing that they are oppressed." Some samples of the Smith litany of sins:

ABLEISM: Oppression of the differently abled by the temporarily able.

HETEROSEXISM: Oppression of those of sexual orientation other than heterosexual, such as gays, lesbians, and bisexuals; this can take place by not acknowledging their existence.

LOOKISM: The belief that appearance is an indicator of a person's value; the construction of a standard for beauty/attractiveness; and oppression through stereotypes and generalizations of both those who do not fit that standard and those who do.

Can they be kidding up there in North-ampton? The code imposes standards of what is called, now rather derisively, "political correctness." What began as a means of controlling student incivility threatens to become, formally or informally, a means of controlling curricula and faculty too. Clark University asks professors proposing courses to explain how "pluralistic (minority, women, etc.) views and concerns are explored and integrated in this course." A philosopher declined to sign, doubting that the university would ask professors to explain how "patriotic and pro-family values are explored and integrated."

Two distinguished American historians at Harvard, Bernard Bailyn and Stephan Thernstrom, offered a course in population history called "The Peopling of America." Articles appeared in the *Harvard Crimson* criticizing the professors for "racial insensitivity," and black students eventually presented them with a bill of particulars. Thernstrom, an advocate of ethnic history, the editor of the *Harvard Encyclopedia* of *American Ethnic Groups,* was accused of racism. He had, it developed, used the term "Indians" instead of "Native Americans." He had also referred to "Oriental" religion—the adjective was deemed "colonial and imperialistic." Bailyn had recommended diaries of Southern planters without recommending slave narratives. And so on, for six single-spaced pages.

The episode reminds one of the right-wing students who in Joe McCarthy days used to haunt the classrooms of liberal Harvard professors (like me) hoping to catch whiffs of Marxism emanating from the podium. Thernstrom decided to hell with it and gave up the course. A signal triumph for political correctness.

Those who stand up for what they believe invite smear campaigns. A favorite target these days is Diane Ravitch of Columbia's Teachers College, a first-class historian of American education, an enlightened advocate of school reform, and a steadfast champion of cultural pluralism. She is dedicated to reasoned and temperate argument and is perseveringly conciliatory rather than polemical in her approach. Perhaps the fact that she is a woman persuades ethnic chauvinists that they can bully her. Despite nasty efforts at intimidation, she continues to expose the perils of ethnocentrism with calm lucidity.

Ravitch's unpardonable offense seems to be her concern about *unum* as well as about *pluribus*—her belief that history should help us understand how bonds of cohesion make us a nation rather than an irascible collection of unaffiliated groups. For in the end, the cult of ethnicity defines the republic not as a polity of individuals but as a congeries of distinct and inviolable cultures. When a student sent a memorandum to the "diversity education committee" at the University of Pennsylvania mentioning her "deep regard for the individual," a college administrator returned the paper with the word *individual* underlined: "This is a *red flag* phrase today, which is considered by many to be *racist*. Arguments that champion the individual over the group ultimately privileges [sic] the 'individuals' belonging to the largest or dominant group."

The contemporary sanctification of the group puts the old idea of a coherent society at stake. Multicultural zealots reject as hegemonic the notion of a shared commitment to common ideals. How far the discourse has come from Crèvecoeur's "new race" from Tocqueville's civic participation, from Emerson's "smelting pot," from Bryce's "amazing solvent," from Myrdal's "American Creed"!

Yet what has held the American people together in the absence of a common ethnic origin has been precisely a common adherence to ideals of democracy and human rights that, too often transgressed in practice, forever goad us to narrow the gap between practice and principle.

The American synthesis has an inevitable Anglo-Saxon coloration, but it is no longer an exercise in Anglo-Saxon domination. The republic embodies ideals that transcend ethnic, religious, and political lines. It is an experiment, reasonably successful for a while, in creating a common identity for people of diverse races, religions, languages, cultures. But

What has held the American people together has been precisely a common adherence to ideals of democracy and human rights that forever goad us to narrow the gap between practice and principle.

the experiment can continue to succeed only so long as Americans continue to believe in the goal. If the republic now turns away from Washington's old goal of "one people," what is its future?—disintegration of the national community, apartheid, Balkanization, tribalization?

"The one absolutely certain way of bringing this nation to ruin, of preventing all possibility of its continuing to be a nation at all," said Theodore Roosevelt, "would be to permit it to become a tangle of squabbling nationalities, an intricate knot of German-Americans, Irish-

Americans, English-Americans, French-Americans, Scandinavian-Americans, or Italian-Americans, each preserving its separate nationality." Three-quarters of a century later we must add a few more nationalities to T.R.'s brew. This only strengthens his point.

The Painful Demise of Eurocentrism

Arthur Schlesinger cannot see his own Anglo-Saxon bias nor multiculturalism's nourishing contribution to America's core identity.

Molefi Kete Asante

Molefi Kete Asante is professor and chair of the Department of African American Studies at Temple University. He is the author of thirty-two books including three seminal works on the Afrocentric philosophy Afrocentricity, The Afrocentric Idea, *and* Kemet, Afrocentricity, and Knowledge.

Arthur Schlesinger, Jr., won Pulitzer prizes for his books *The Age of Jackson* (1945) and *A Thousand Days* (1965). These works and the *Age of Roosevelt, The Imperial Presidency,* and *Robert Kennedy and His Times* established him as a leading American historian. Yet Schlesinger's latest book, *The Disuniting of America,* serves to call into question his understanding of American history and his appreciation of diversity. As a designated great American historian, he is supposed to know something about what he writes. However, one of the most obvious manifestations of hegemonic thinking in cultural matters is pontification. Measuring the amount of pontification in *The Disuniting of America,* one comes away with a certain distrust of Schlesinger's writing as well as his perspective on American society. This is doubly so if one is an African American.

Schlesinger envisions an America rooted in the past, where whites, actually Anglo-Saxon whites, defined the protocols of American society, and white culture itself represented the example to which others were forced to aspire. He loves this vision because it provides a psycho-

logical justification for the dominance of European culture in America over others. In his vision, there is little history of enslavement, oppression, dispossession, racism, or exploitation. In effect, there is no disunion in the Union; adjustments need to be made, for sure, but they are minor ripples in the perfect society. Fortunately, many whites as well as African Americans see this vision as corrupted by the arrogance of political, academic, and cultural dominance. How, they ask, can one have such a vision of America with what we know of our history? Yet this is Schlesinger's perspective on American society.

Alas, the vision is clouded by Afrocentrists, the bad guys in Schlesinger's book, who bring disunity to this perfect world. Trapped in his own cultural prison, Schlesinger is unable to see the present American cultural reality, and I believe he has missed the point of the past as well. The evidence suggests that he holds a nearly static view of America. Perhaps the America of his youth—its academic life, social life, business environment, and political institutions—was framed for him in some version of the white American dream.

There is, of course, a nightmarish side to Schlesinger's vision or fantasy. He peoples his vision with negations, colored by axioms that support no truth but that are ultimately structured to uphold the status quo of white male privilege and domination. Had Schlesinger admitted this as a goal of his book, it would have allowed a more honest footing for

discussion and debate. Nevertheless, this mixture of fact and fiction presents itself for analytical deinvention, not national disunity.

DISUNION AND DISBELIEF
Schlesinger might have cited any number of issues as disuniting America: unequal protection under the law, taxation without representation, gender strife, economic class antagonisms, corrupt politicians, rampant anti-Africanism, growing anti-Semitism, or pollution of the environment. Instead, he focuses on the African-American challenge to the educational system, calling it a disuniting element; indeed, he believes it is a frightening development. Why should an Afrocentric position—that is, a position where Africans describe themselves as subjects rather than objects—create such an uproar?[1]

Are we to conclude that Schlesinger does not see the hegemonic imposition of the Eurocentric idea? Or do we conclude that he sees it and understands it and supports it? If he does not see it, then he will not understand the substance of what I am saying in this essay. Hegemonic thinking is like a person standing on the lid of a manhole. The fact that another person will rise out of that manhole means that the person standing on the lid will have to change positions.

---

1. See Molefi Kete Assante, *The Afrocentric Idea* (Philadelphia: Temple University press, 1987).

This article first appeared in *The World & I,* April 1992, pp. 305-317. Reprinted by permission of *The World & I,* a publication of the Washington Times Corporation. © 1992.

Will the Afrocentric perspective affect the Eurocentric hegemony on information and in education? Absolutely, because our perceptions are altered by new information whether we admit it or not. A lifetime of delusion that denies Africans and Africa a place in human history creates a basic disbelief in facts that are presented in an Afrocentric framework. Indeed, *The Age of Jackson* did not indicate any real appreciation of the nature of Jackson's racism and anti-Indian sentiments. Schlesinger's glorification of Andrew Jackson, whom even Davy Crockett considered a scoundrel, is demonstrative of Schlesinger's disregard for the multiethnic, multicultural, pluralistic reality of American society.

Schlesinger envisions an America rooted in the past, where whites, actually Anglo-Saxon whites, represented the example to which others were forced to aspire.

One must be factual, and in trying to be factual I have always believed primary description is better than secondary interpretation. Thus, when Afrocentrists say that George Washington and Thomas Jefferson were slaveowners, *inter alia,* who did not believe in the equality of Africans, that is a fact descriptive of those two individuals. One can excuse the fact on the grounds of interpretation, one can claim ignorance, one can argue that their good points outweighed their bad points, and so on; but the fact is that they believed in the inferiority of Africans. Students must be introduced to this factual information in order to make proper assessments and judgments. Schlesinger would insist that we not mention the racist heritage of the "founding fathers" because that would create disunity. If that be creating disunity, I am guilty, as he claims in his book, and I will create more disunity. Nothing is more valuable than the truth in bringing about national integration.

Eurocentric control of space and time in publishing and the media has meant that legitimate intellectual and scholarly voices of African Americans are seldom heard by whites who refuse to read Afri-

can-American scholarly journals. The *Journal of Black Studies,* the *Journal of Negro Education,* the *Journal of African Civilizations, Western Journal of Black Studies,* and *Imhotep* are a few of the prominent journals that are accessible to scholars. They remain relatively unread by writers such as Schlesinger, who apparently believes that there is little outside of the "white" journals worth reading. That is a serious mistake in scholarship, because reading the African-American journals would greatly increase appreciation for new findings and new ideas.

Can Schlesinger really believe that only whites or blacks who believe they are white have reasonable ideas? Afrocentrists, who got their degrees from the same institutions as white scholars, tend to have a far broader reading program that allows for more critical leverage to analysis. The fact that cyclopean stone tombs dating from 5700 B.C., among the earliest in the world, have been found in the heart of the Central African Republic may not be a part of one's knowledge base, but if it were known, it would add to any discussion of historical time lines. Yet without reading any of my books or those of other Afrocentrists in depth, as far as I can discern, Schlesinger attempts to paint Afrocentrists as some kind of wild bunch out to create disunity in American society.

What this celebrated white American historian seeks is a dismissal of historical facts related to Africans as insignificant in the American nation. He seems to operate within a closed system of thought, and such systems are prodigious in producing closed minds. Education within such a system is found to produce those who speak a certain restrictive language, use a handed-down political vocabulary, and believe in elves.

The danger, quite frankly, is that Schlesinger's attitude toward difference creates insiders and outsiders, those who are free to define themselves and others and those who are the defined. There is no question in his mind about who will do the defining. Afrocentrists flatly reject this kind of thinking and insist on defining their own reality within the context of society.

To be Afrocentric is not to deny American citizenship. Just as to be a Chinese American, live in Chinatown, employ Chinese motifs in artistic expression, and worship Buddha is not anti-American, the person who believes that the African

American must be recentered, relocated in terms of historical referent, is not anti-American. This is neither a destructive nor a disuniting behavior. It suggests the strengths of this country compared to other countries. The conviction that we will defend the rights of all cultural expressions, not just Greco-Roman-Hebraic-Germanic-Viking cultures, must be strongly embedded in our political psyches if the nation is to survive.

In this way we avoid what I call the Soviet problem, that is, the Russification of the empire. Respect for each other's culture must be the guiding principle for a truly remarkable society. Since the American idea is not a static but a dynamic one, we must constantly reinvent ourselves in the light of our diverse experiences. One reason this nation works the way it does is our diversity. Try to make Africans and Asians copies of Europeans and women copies of men and you will force the disunity Schlesinger fears. This does not mean, as some dishonest writers have said, that black children will be taught black information and white children will be taught white information and so forth. No Afrocentrist has articulated such a view, though it has been widely reported in the news.

UNITY IN AMERICA

The unity of America is based upon shared goals, a collective sense of mission, a common purpose, and mutual respect. It should be clear to the reader, upon reflection, that Schlesinger's view of America is too provincial; it is as if he has not outgrown the way of thinking he expressed in *The Age of Jackson*. I believe his view is planted in the narrow confines of a particular ethnic or racial identity. Thus, it cannot produce a harvest of unity. The unity of the American nation is not a unity of historical experiences or cultural backgrounds. Because each of us could give a different version of the same story, there must be an acceptance of pluralism without ethnic or cultural hegemony. Only in this manner can we build a common culture. For the present we have many cultures, occasionally interacting with each other, but we have only one society. This means that it is no longer viable for white cultures to parade as the only American culture.

I find it curious that Schlesinger, who has spent a lifetime championing an elitist educational program, is now interested in a multicultural one. This may be a result of his professorship at City University of New York, or of the controversy surrounding a number of his colleagues at the City University. I should not be mistaken. I like the idea that Schlesinger sees multiculturalism as important; it is just that he would be the last person I would consider knowledgeable of this field.[2]

There is no particularist multiculturalism or pluralist multiculturalism; there is, quite simply, multiculturalism. I pointed out in response to Diane Ravitch (a deputy assistant secretary of education) who came up with the notions of particularist and pluralist multiculturalisms, that the first is an oxymoron and the second a redundancy. Multiculturalism is not a complicated proposition; it is clear and simple. In a multicultural society, there must be a multicultural curriculum, a multicultural approach to institution building, and so forth.

Afrocentrists say that one should not be able to declare competency in music in America without having been introduced to the spirituals, Duke Ellington, or the blues. Yet every year this happens in major American universities.

AN AFROCENTRIC ORIENTATION

What Schlesinger dislikes in the Afrocentric position is the emphasis on recentering of African Americans in a subject position vis-à-vis history, culture, and science. However, 374 years of white domination have disoriented, dislocated, and displaced many African Americans. This is the legacy of stealing us from Africa, of dehumanizing and enslaving us. So fearful of Africans were the slave masters that they sought to rob us of our heritage, memory, languages, religion, customs, traditions, and history. In the end, it is true, some of us did

---

2. There are a great number of intercultural communicationists who have written intelligently on this subject. Schlesinger might have looked at two of my works in this field, *Transracial Communication* and *Handbook of Intercultural Communication*. Others such as Andrea Rich, William Gudykunst, Erika Vora, Tulsi Saral, and Thomas Kochman, have written extensively on the question of culture and cultural interactions.

lose our way and *our* minds, and decentered, disoriented, and often alienated— would claim that we came to America on the *Mayflower.*

Afrocentricity seeks to understand this phenomenon by beginning all analysis from the African person as human agent. In classes, it means that the African-American child must be connected, grounded to information presented in the same way that white children are grounded, when we discuss literature, history, mathematics, and science. Teachers who do not know this information when it comes to Africans must seek it out from those who do. Afrocentrists do not take anything away from white history except its aggressive urge to pose as universal.

The meaning of this school of thought is critical for all Americans. I make a claim that we must see ourselves within American society, with points of reference in our culture and history. Our children as well as other children must know about us in the context of our own history. The Afrocentric school of thought becomes useful for the expansion of dialogue and the widening of discourse—the proper function of education. The white self-esteem curriculum now present in most school systems is imposed as universal.

We know this curriculum is not universal, of course, but rather specific social studies and humanities information centered on a particular culture. There is nothing fundamentally wrong about a Eurocentric curriculum so long as other cultures are not denied. The real question is whether Eurocentrism can exist without denial of the Other. To speak arrogantly of this model as a conquest model is to assert a claim of right by force, not on the basis of facts nor on the ground of what is useful for this society. We ought to be able to develop a curriculum of instruction that affirms all people in their cultural heritages.

A FINISHED PARADIGM

It is bizarre to find that Schlesinger attacks my vision of a multicultural nation without having read any of my works. At the end of the twentieth century, the United States must be spared the intellectual intolerance, xenophobia, ethnic hatred, racist thinking, and hegemonic attitudes that now seem to be running rampant in Europe.

Schlesinger makes judicious use of the

critical remarks of African-American scholars such as John Hope Franklin, Henry Louis Gates, and Frank Snow in order to divide African-American intellectuals into two camps. There are also women who accept the male view of history. There were Jews who accepted the German version of culture. There will always be members of the dominated group who will accept certain ideas from those dominating. We all experience our particular dislocations. But as for me, an American citizen of African descent, I shall never abandon my ancestors' history. Neither would I expect Schlesinger to abandon his, though that is his right. Whatever he does about it, I will not say he is sowing disunity.

Dividing African scholars in order to set off conflict is an old game, but it avoids raising the issue discussed by the Afrocentrists. Why should a monocultural experience and history dominate a multicultural and multiethnic nation? There is no good answer to this question, so Schlesinger believes in shoring up the old, "perfect" order as the best procedure. But it will not wash. His description is of a paradigm that is finished. It is not enough for Schlesinger to cite majority support, since popular belief and mass acceptance are not adequate for validating ideas. Description and demonstration are the principal calling cards of proof, not authoritative pronouncements, even if they come from a well-known historian. Neither hegemony nor power can determine truth.

NATIONALITY AND CULTURE

Schlesinger's book is unfortunate at this stage in national integration and development. He confuses American nationality with American culture. Whether by choice or circumstances, we are American in nationality. So one can say that my nationality and citizenship are American, but my historical and cultural origins are African. My ancestors did not arrive in this country from Europe. They did not see a mountain of possibility but a valley of despair.

It is this distinction, this historical cleavage, that cannot be resolved by some mythical idea that we all came here on the *Mayflower.* The preferred resolution of such dual experiences is a true multiculturalism, where Europeans are seen working for national purpose alongside other people, not in a hegemonic position. This takes a measure of humility that is not evident in Schlesinger's book. Without a reorientation from conquest, from dominance, from superiority, the whites in this country can never understand the discourse of unity expressed by Africans, Latinos, Asians, and Native Americans.

I agree with Franklin Roosevelt's observation that "Americanism is not a matter of race and ancestry but of adherence to the creed of liberty and democracy." This means that the litmus test for Americanism must not be how Eurocentric a person becomes but whether the person adheres to the idea of mutual individual and cultural respect. One cannot equate a Chinese American's love of Chinese motifs, food, decorations, and myths with a rejection of Americanism: It *is* Americanism. Of course, we all are free to reject our ethnic or cultural past, but that does not mean we do not possess culture.

Schlesinger writes in a very condescending manner: "Nor is there anything more natural than for generous-hearted people, black and white, to go along with Afrocentrism out of a decent sympathy for the insulted and injured of American society and of a decent concern to bind up the wounds." But Afrocentrism is not about sympathy or insult; it is about the proper presentation of factual information in a multicultural society. To frame an argument in the context of the generous hearted doing something for Africans is to miss the point. What we do by making America safe for diversity is to ensure the unity of the nation.

Schlesinger's continuation suggests that his condescension is unabated, "Still, doctrinaire ethnicity in general and the dogmatic black version in particular raise questions that deserve careful and dispassionate examination." This representation seeks to diminish the Afrocentric movement's rational arguments through hyperbole. Doctrinaire ethnicity, if it exists in America is not to be found in the African-American community. He is especially exercised by "the dogmatic black version," which he does not describe in any detail. Yet he says that the Afrocentric campaign most worries him. His problem with Afrocentric scholarship is that he cannot dismiss it. For example, he wants to question the African origin of civilization and counterposes Mesopotamia as the cradle of civilization. But this does not work, either in theory or in reality.

THE AFRICAN ORIGIN OF CIVILIZATION

Cheikh Anta Diop wrote in *The African Origin of Civilization* that Africa is the cradle of human civilization. He expanded his argument in his massive work *Civilization and Barbarism,* assembling evidence from disparate sources such as linguistics, botany, osteology, history, and molecular biology. Numerous scholars have supported the arguments Diop made in those books. In fact, Theophile Obenga has shown the origin of medicine, theology, queenship, astronomy, mathematics, ethics, and philosophy in Africa. There is no comparable evidence of antiquity in any other continent.[3]

Mesopotamia does not figure in ancient civilization, either concretely *or* philosophically, at the same level as ancient Egypt. Even were one to take evidence from the ancient Egyptian, Hebrew, Greek, and Ethiopian peoples, one would find that the Nile Valley of Africa rather than the Tigris Euphrates Valley was considered the most ancient cradle of human civilization.

Plato's corpus includes twenty-eight extant dialogues; in twelve of those dialogues, he discusses Egypt, not Mesopotamia, Sumer, or Babylon. Of course, Plato himself was taught in Africa by Seknoufis and Kounoufis. He did not think of Mesopotamia as a high civilization on the level of Egypt. The Hebrew Bible mentions Egypt nearly one thousand times but refers to Mesopotamia no more than twenty times. The Ethiopians refer to Egypt, not to Mesopotamia, in their ancient sacred books, the *Kebra Nagast* and *The Book of Henok*. While I believe Mesopotamia is a significant civilization, I also believe that it is advanced as a sort of contemporary anti-African project, a kind of counterpoint to the African origin of civilization. This is why some writers claim that Mesopotamian civilization can be dated one hundred years prior to the First Egyptian Dynasty. However, dynastic Egypt was not the beginning of civilization in the Nile Valley. There had been at least sixteen kings of Upper (Southern) Egypt before Narmer (Menes), who is normally given as the first dynastic king. My point is that the ancients did not consider Mesopotamia more important than Egypt; this is preeminently a contemporary project.

Let us examine Schlesinger's assault on the Egyptian scholarship of African scholars. He admits that he is no expert on ancient Egypt and, in a broad stroke for justification, claims, "neither are the educators and psychologists who push Afrocentrism." I do not know what special criteria Schlesinger is using for expertise, but Cheikh Anta Diop, Theophile Obenga, Wade Nobles, Jacob Carruthers, Maulana Karenga, Asa Hilliard, and others have spent more than one hundred collective years in the study of ancient Africa. Their research and publications are accessible and well known to those of us who consider ourselves Afrocentrists. All of these scholars are students of ancient languages: Mdu Netr, the language of the ancient Egyptians, Ge'ez, Greek, and Latin. Although my knowledge of ancient languages is not nearly at the level of the scholars I have mentioned, my familiarity with the ancient literatures is indicated in many of the books that I have written. My book *Kemet, Afrocentricity and Knowledge* explores various aspects of the historiography of ancient Africa.

Schlesinger's attack seeks to undermine the Africanness of the ancient Egyptian. Indeed, he brings three witnesses to his case: Frank Snowden, Frank Yurco, and Miriam Lichtheim. All three of these people have deeply invested interests in the Eurocentric paradigm of history (that is, the projection of Eurocentric concepts in African people). Snowden, a retired Howard University professor, has written on the African image in Greece and Rome. He does not read Mdu Netr and certainly is no scholar of ancient Africa. Yurco, a librarian at the University of Chicago, has produced nothing of the caliber of any of the Afrocentrists. From his Regenstein Library desk at the University of Chicago, Yurco has made a career of responding to Diop, Carruthers, Bernl, Hilliard, and, lately, my book *Kemet, Afrocentricity, and Knowledge*. His ideological perspective appears to fog his analysis. His essay, cited by Schlesinger, in *Biblical Archaeology Review is* a nasty

---

3. Theophile Obenga, *African Philosophy in the Time of the Pharaohs* (Paris: Presence Africaine, 1991). Furthermore, the works of Maulana Karenga and Jacob Carruthers are useful documents. See *The Husia,* edited by Maulana Karenga (Los Angeles: University of San Kore Press) and Carruthers, *Essays in Ancient Kemetic Studies* (Los Angeles: University of San Kore Press, 1985).

little piece written against Martin Bernal.

Lichtheim is by far the best-known ancient Egyptian scholar, but the comment Schlesinger chooses to use from Lichtheim is rather strange.

I do not wish to waste any of my time refuting the errant nonsense which is being propagated in the American black community about the Egyptians being Nubians and the Nubians being black. The Egyptians were not Nubians, and the original Nubians were not black. Nubia gradually became black because black peoples migrated northward out of Central Africa. The "Nile Valley School" is obviously an attempt by American blacks to provide themselves with an ancient history linked to that of the high civilization of ancient Egypt.

Neither Schlesinger nor Lichtheim names or quotes any African or African-American scholar as saying anything "about the Egyptians being Nubians." However, it is possible to say that the difference between Nubians and Egyptians was much like that of Sicilians and Italians, Icelanders and Danes, or Germans and Austrians. Lichtheim's comment and Schlesinger's use of it is meant to suggest that the ancient Egyptians and ancient Nubians were of different races. Nubians and Egyptians looked alike and came from the same general culture. In addition, both were black-skinned peoples.

Lichtheim's denial of the blackness (that is, the black-skinnedness) of the ancient Nubians borders on intellectual incompetence because it disregards the available concrete evidence in texts, sculptures, paintings, and linguistics. Lichtheim's statement that the "Egyptians were not Nubians" is correct but misleading. One can say that the French are not Spanish or the Swedes are not Norwegians, but that is not a statement about the color of skin. I can say that the Yoruba are not Ibo, but that tells me something about ethnicity and perhaps national identity, not about their complexions. So to say that the Egyptians were not Nubians is to say no more than that the two people who lived along the Nile occupied different geographical areas.

The fact is that the Egyptians saw themselves and Nubians as looking exactly alike in physical appearance as well as dress. One only needs to know the first ethnology in the world, the Biban el-Moluk bas-relief from the tomb of Sesostris I, to see that Egyptians painted themselves and Nubians as coal black and whites and Asians as lighter in com-

plexion. There are four people on the bas-relief, representing four different cultures: Egyptian, Nehasi (Nubian), Namou (Asian), and Tamhou (Aryan). The Egyptian and the Nehasi are exactly alike, even to their clothes. They are visibly different from the Namou and the Tamhou.

But the greater nonsense is Lichtheim's statement that the "original Nubians were not black." Does Lichtheim mean to imply that they were what we would call white today? Does she mean they were lighter complexioned blacks? Or does Lichtheim mean to suggest, as some white Egyptologists suggested in the past, that the people were black-skinned whites? The problem here is racialist thinking. Since the discourse under which white academics have often operated is Eurocentric, it is difficult for them to admit that civilization started in Africa and that it was black people who started it.

As far as we know, human beings originated on the African continent and migrated outward. No scientist suggests that the people who migrated outward and who peopled the continent of Africa were white.[4] Indeed, the monogenesis thesis argues that hominids, the Grimaldi, migrated to Europe and emerged after the Ice Age as white in complexion because of environmental and climatic factors.

The Nubians were not only black physically but shared with the Egyptians and others of the Nile Valley the same African cultural and philosophical modalities. Present-day Egypt, like present-day America, is not a reflection of its ancient past. Arabs came from Arabia with the jihads of the seventh century A.D. Therefore, Arabic is not indigenous to Africa, as English is not indigenous to the United States.

The aim of Schlesinger's remarks and Lichtheim's quote is not the Nubian issue but the question of the complexion of the ancient Egyptians. Afrocentrists claim that Eurocentric scholars have attempted to take Egypt out of Africa and to take Africans out of ancient Egypt in a whitening process of the earliest civilizations. Children's books still exist with Egyptians looking like Scandinavians.

The evidence of the blackness of the ancient Egyptians is overwhelming. The

early Greeks said that the Egyptians were black. They never wrote that the Egyptians were white. In fact, Aristotle wrote in *Physiognomonica* that both the Egyptians and the Ethiopians (Nubians) were black. Herodotus writes in *Histories* that the people of Colchis must be Egyptians because "they are black-skinned and have woolly hair."[5] One could cite Sfrabo, Pindar, and Apollonius of Rhodes as making similar attestations about how the Egyptians looked.

Thus, Lichtheim's statement is not only errant but pure nonsense. It flies in the face of all available evidence and, beyond that, it defies logic. Perhaps this style of written pontification by white scholars is the source of confusion in the minds of the American public. Lichtheim proposes what Bernal has aptly called the Aryan Model of Ancient History, which suggests, among other things, that civilization could not have started in Africa, and, if civilization is found in Africa, it had to be the results of an external movement into Africa.

E PLURIBUS UNUM

Schlesinger likes to quote Diane Ravitch. But both Schlesinger and Ravitch are wrong when they suggest that *e pluribus unum* meant out of many cultures, one. Actually, this expression was initially applied to the fact that several colonies could produce one federal government. Thus, out of many colonies, one central government. To apply this term of political structure to the American cultural reality is to miss the point of both politics and culture. A nation of more than 130 cultural groups cannot hope to have all of them Anglo-Saxonized. Such a vision is disastrous and myopic. What we can wish for and realize is a society of mutual respect, dynamism, and decency. Rather than labeling or setting cultural groups against each other, we should empower a vision that sees the American kaleidoscope of cultures as uniquely fortunate. Schlesinger sees multiculturalism as a danger. I see it as a further indication that the shift to a new, more operable paradigm in this mighty nation is well on its way.

---

4. Martin Bernal, *Black Athena*, vols. 1 and 2 (New Brunswick: Rutgers University Press, 1987).

5. *The Works of Aristotle*, W. D. Ross, vol. VI, *Physiognomica* (Oxford: Clarendon Press, 1913), 812.

Alms Without End?

A History of Welfare in America

History shows that the welfare problem will neither go away nor be simply solved.

Hugh Heclo

Hugh Heclo is Robinson Professor of Public Affairs at George Mason University

For anyone seeking to reform the welfare system, the history should be sobering. For at least six hundred years reformers in Western societies have been trying to rationalize public assistance so as to help the truly needy while denying a free ride to work-shy scroungers. And always the latest new idea to distinguish the deserving from the undeserving has failed to live up to expectations. Some critics claim the prevailing welfare system is too punitive, hurting people who are poor through no fault of their own. Others respond that welfare is too permissive, creating dependency among those it seeks to help. The cycle of reform, argument, and counterargument seems to repeat itself from one generation to the next.

Until roughly the fifteenth century, "welfare" was scarcely considered a social problem as we understand the term today. Idealized views of Christian poverty and the religious duty to give alms coexisted with fear of rebellious paupers and distrust of troublesome beggars. In either case, almsgiving and other charitable acts were routine customs justified mainly by the good they did for the giver, not the recipient or society at large.

By the 1400s traditional religious charity was increasingly being supplemented by civil authorities' efforts to cope with the surges of pauperism and wandering beggars brought about by urban growth and economic changes in the countryside. As the Reformation accelerated the secularization of poor relief, the now familiar arguments began to be heard. Reformers criticized individual almsgiv-ing as an encouragement to begging and ineffective in dealing with the needs of the poor. The fundamental question, they recognized, was how to keep the genuinely needy from starving (or rioting) without breeding a class of paupers who chose to live off public charity. Civil authorities evolved a variety of techniques to distinguish the "true pauper" from the "unworthy beggar," and these became known collectively as the old poor law.

After 1800, reformers argued with good reason that the traditional poor law was hopelessly out of date.

EARLY AMERICA

Early settlers to America brought with them this bundle of traditions, laws, and social regulations. In general, each township or county (parish in the South) was legally responsible for organizing relief for any destitute inhabitant who did not have kin to care for him or her. Rough classifications were applied such that the aged or infirm without relatives might be offered alms or a place in an almshouse, orphaned children apprenticed out to farmers or artisans, and the able-bodied set to work or threatened with punishment. As a typical saying of the time had it, "work for those that will labor, punishment for those that will not, and bread for those who cannot."

In practice, provisions varied greatly and distinctions between deserving and undeserving poor were never clear-cut. Four techniques were typically combined and in widespread use at the end of the eighteenth century: (1) Settlement laws emphasized the local basis of relief policy, as poor persons were shunted from one township to the next in an often cumbersome legal process of trying to find the home jurisdiction with responsibility for support. (2) Auctions were held by local officials to find the lowest bidder who would contract to support one or more poor persons for a given period of time. (3) Almshouses, or poor houses, could often be found in the larger cities, usually with the sick, elderly, insane, orphaned, and otherwise homeless indigents jumbled together. (4) Finally, "outdoor relief" (so-named for being given outside an institutional setting) was commonly given by locally chosen overseers of the poor. Such relief usually took the form of winter fuel, clothing, food, and small amounts of cash.

AFTER 1800

As the pace of social and economic change accelerated after 1800, reformers argued with good reason that the traditional poor law was hopelessly out of date. By midnineteenth century numerous efforts had been made to replace the old customs with a new, more deliberately and systematically organized poor law that was claimed to be both more humane and more efficient. Specialized institutions such as asylums, penitentiaries, orphanages, and reform schools proliferated. But the centerpiece of social reform was the poorhouse, which eventually became a well-known presence in nearly every county in the country. Poorhouse advocates pointed to

This article first appeared in *The World & I*, September 1992, pp. 60-75. Reprinted by permission of *The World & I*, a publication of the Washington Times Corporation. © 1992.

the cruelty of the auctioning system, the ineffectiveness and costs of resettlement, and above all to the growing welfare rolls that were said to be created by the indiscriminate giving of relief. As the Report of the Massachusetts Committee on the Pauper Laws put it in 1821, all of the "evils" of the current poor law system could be traced to the same root: "the difficulty of discriminating between the able poor and the impotent poor [i.e., incapable of work] and of apportioning the degree of public provision to the degree of actual impotency." Advocates claimed that properly run poorhouses would not only deter the unworthy and shiftless poor. They would rehabilitate people through good work habits and prohibition of alcohol, educate pauper children, and save money by having inmates perform useful work. Poorhouses (or poor farms) spread.

As it turned out, poorhouses usually failed to live up to reformers' expectations. Administration of poorhouses did not attract particularly competent people and desensitized those who entered the work with good intentions. Expectations of productive work from impoverished, wretched people proved unrealistic. Above all, hopes for humane treatment and appropriate rehabilitating services were flatly contradicted by the pervasive desire to hold down costs and avoid attracting people who should support themselves. Poorhouse keepers who did not minimize costs could expect to run afoul of locally elected overseers of the poor as well as taxpayers, who were generally billed separately for the "poor rate" (i.e., earmarked taxes for public poor relief).

'SCIENTIFIC CHARITY'

Although they failed in their original more positive purposes, poorhouses continued throughout the nineteenth century and into this century as custodial institutions deterring potential paupers. Outdoor relief also expanded as industrialization, immigration, and sharper, nationwide swings in the business cycle strained local relief budgets. By 1870, New York State, with a population of 4.4 million, had 64,000 residents in poorhouses and 106,000 on outdoor relief. By then a new round of reforms was beginning, as socially concerned middle-class men and women took up the cause of "scientific charity." Mobilized across the country in Charity

Organization Societies, the reformers sought to systematically apply scientific principles learned through the giving of relief. In this view, public outdoor relief should be replaced by private charity, which would be given by persons whose personal knowledge of cases would tailor the aid to avoid doing moral harm to the recipients. All public aid should be given in institutions (poorhouses, asylums, etc.) where proper care, moral discipline, and education could be assured. As one of the founders of the movement, Josephine Shaw Lowell, put it in 1883: "To cure paupers and make them self-supporting, however costly the process, must always be economical as compared with a smaller but constantly increasing and continual outlay for their maintenance."

The scientific charity movement achieved only modest and temporary success. Of the forty American cities with populations over 100,000, about one-quarter had abolished outdoor relief by 1899. For one thing, many poor resented the often condescending visits by middle-class charity workers, who were trying to be both case investigators and morally uplifting friends. Then too, urban political machines, merchants, and overseers of the poor resisted efforts to abolish outdoor relief and the benefits they derived from its distribution. Above all, periodic economic crashes simply overwhelmed Charity Organization Societies' efforts to deal with the floods of needy people.

MOTHERS' PENSIONS

The next major attempt to change assistance under the poor law occurred early this century with Mothers' Pensions. Such pensions were begun in 1910 on the initiative of a few reformist juvenile court judges in the Midwest. In these pre-Social Security days, mothers who lost the family's male breadwinner typically faced two financial alternatives if they did not have relatives to support them. Either they and/or their children had to go to work or else they had to throw themselves on poor law relief and possibly see their children sent to an orphanage. The aim of Mothers' Pensions was to provide state funds to localities that could be used to help mainly widowed mothers stay in the home and have their children in school rather than the work force. The cause was taken up by federations of women's clubs across

the country and a few key reformers in married women's magazines. Campaigners for Mothers' pensions spoke of "an honorable salary to remove the stigma of pauperism . . . allowing mothers to build a good homelife, the highest product of civilization . . . providing the State the best possible type of citizen."

Against the opposition of private charity organizations, which repeated their familiar argument that such use of public money for outdoor relief was morally corrupting, women's groups had succeeded in enacting Mothers' Pensions in forty states by 1920. In practice, Mothers' Pensions were quite restrictive. Most states and localities were reluctant to support deserted or divorced women, and by 1931, only three states allowed such pensions to go to unmarried mothers. As the New York State Commission on Relief for Widowed Mothers put it, "to pension desertion or illegitimacy would, undoubtedly, have the effect of putting a premium on these crimes against society." Widows themselves had to demonstrate they were personally worthy, which is to say living soberly, in a clean home, without male partners and without work outside the home. They had to do so both in applying for aid and in monthly "proper-home" visits by many of the same charity workers who had originally opposed Mothers' Pensions.

Even so, state funding was never adequate to cover all those eligible or to allow recipients more than the barest physical necessities without at least some part-time work. The discretionary nature of the program also produced huge local variations in the presence and level of Mothers' Pensions. By 1931, forty-six thousand families with one-quarter million children were receiving pensions. Of these, 80 percent were widows, 3 percent were black, and only 55 recipients in the entire nation were unmarried mothers.

THE 1935 SOCIAL SECURITY ACT

With no political fanfare, a process of transformation began with the 1935 Social Security Act. In that year, the Federal Children's Bureau in effect slipped Mothers' Pensions into an obscure portion of the Social Security bill. This section provided federal matching grants for state welfare assistance to two other categories of needy persons deemed deserving: the aged and blind. With Mothers' Pensions renamed Aid to Dependent Children (ADC), children of what were assumed to be mainly widows took their place alongside impoverished aged and blind persons as one of the three categories of nonable-bodied people presumed deserving of federally supported cash relief.

Immediately there began a sustained skirmishing between liberal national officials hostile to the racist and paternalistic administration of welfare in many jurisdictions, on the one hand, and local forces together with their representatives in Congress, on the other. The latter were intent on keeping control of a system that still carried many echoes of the poor law while taking advantage of the new federal funds. In the 1935 act liberal New Dealers managed to win elimination of local residency requirements and a maximum five-year limit on state residency requirements for these welfare programs, thus all but abolishing the settlement provisions of the centuries-old poor law. They also obtained a provision in the law requiring operation of federally supported welfare programs in all state subdivisions, thereby reducing the patchy coverage that had bedeviled Mothers' Pensions. This did much to raise the number of children aided under Mothers' Pensions/ADC from three hundred thousand in 1935 to seven hundred thousand in 1939. But in all other important respects—such as eligibility conditions and benefit levels—fiscal conservatives and southern Democrats in Congress succeeded in keeping administrative control of federally supported welfare localized.

The Depression years saw little effort to change the prevailing welfare system, much less engage in social engineering.

Thus the New Deal created federal aid for the three categories of deserving poor on "welfare" and a Social Security system that eventually would raise more people, mainly the elderly, above the poverty line than all means-tested "welfare" programs combined. Beyond this, the Depression years saw little effort to change the prevailing welfare system,

much less engage in social engineering to educate and train poor people for self-support. First, emergency cash relief (the dole) for the unemployed and then work relief (so-called make-work projects under the WPA and other federal agencies) were used to provide temporary help and tide over employable people in the 1930s. But Franklin Roosevelt in traditional fashion warned that to dole out relief was "to administer a narcotic—a subtle destroyer of the human spirit," and the president declared that the federal government "must and shall quit this business of relief." As work relief programs faded away with the onset of World War II's full employment, all responsibility for general relief assistance for those poor persons who were presumably unemployable was left where it had always been, with state and local governments. Supporting more than four million families annually between 1936 and 1940, state-run general assistance programs aided more Americans than any other social program, federal or state.

In 1950, officials in Washington succeeded in adding a caretaker grant for mothers to ADC benefits.

COVERING MORE AND MORE PEOPLE

In 1939, liberalizations in Social Security began the process of covering an ever-greater percentage of widows under the survivors' benefits of the nation's social insurance program. The result was that after the end of World War II, ADC caseloads increasingly became composed of divorced, deserted, and unmarried mothers' children. National welfare officials kept adding to the federal rules and regulations of ADC in an effort to bring about more equal treatment. Conservative politicians and local officials responded with "suitable home" and other requirements that typically served to withhold benefits from illegitimate children and nonwhites in general. White southern leaders in particular worried about the effect of federal ADC benefits on the supply of cheap black labor. As

Georgia Gov. Eugene Talmadge put it: "The Federal [Social Security] Board in Washington is going to make them add on nearly every Negro of a certain age in the country to this pauper's list. What will become of your farm labor—your washwomen, your cooks, your plowhands?"

In 1950, officials in Washington succeeded in adding a caretaker grant for mothers to ADC benefits, something that had been present in Mothers' Pensions but had been dropped out as an oversight in hurriedly drafting the 1935 act. Thus, mothers were formally added to the federal "welfare" rolls, and the program's name was changed to the now-familiar AFDC (Aid to Families with Dependent Children). At the same time, Congress added an amendment to the welfare program requiring local welfare agencies to notify law enforcement officers whenever aid was granted to children whose father had deserted the family. Aware or not of this provision in national law, many state and local welfare officers made "midnight raids" to catch fathers or other employable males visiting overnight with mothers on welfare.

CRITICISM OF AFDC

As the incidence of broken families increased in the postwar years, criticisms of the AFDC welfare system rose apace. In point of fact the societal changes under way far overweighed anything that might be attributed to federal welfare policy. The number of ADC/AFDC recipients rose from 701,000 in 1945 to 3.1 million in 1960. But the number of mothers and children in female-headed families climbed from 3.4 million in 1940 to approximately 6 million in 1960. With the numbers on welfare rising, states redoubled their efforts to cut welfare dependency. In 1960, for example, Louisiana used its suitable home rules to cut off aid to families in which the mother had given birth to another child since receiving AFDC benefits. In 1961 the city of Newburgh, New York, added to a furious public debate by adopting policies that, among other things, cut benefits to unwed mothers who had another child, limited welfare for able-bodied persons to three months, and required forced labor from able-bodied adult males.

THE 1960s

The 1960s were a watershed in the struggle over welfare policy. But what happened is more complex than any current references to the "failure of Great Society programs." It was as if a number of previously disparate forces came crashing together at the same intersection of time. Today we are still living with the repercussions. The 3.1 million AFDC recipients of 1960 rose to 4.3 million in 1965, 6.1 million by 1969, and topped out in the late Nixon administration (1972–74) at about 10.8 million. From then until 1990 caseloads held generally steady, fluctuating between 10.1 and 10.9 million.

One thing that happened in the 1960s was a dawning realization that what had evolved—largely inadvertently—as the federal government's centerpiece "welfare" policy was a system of income support for unmarried, working-age mothers outside the work force. Each of the major and growing criticisms of AFDC was directed at program features that had simply continued, as if by inertial force, the logic of Mothers' Pensions. Thus, AFDC was said to encourage family dissolution, since benefits were lost if a father or any other employable male was around the home. But that provision existed because mothers were supposed to maintain a suitable home after the loss of the father. Thus too, AFDC was said to discourage work and self-support by taking away a dollar of AFDC benefit for every dollar earned. True enough, but that provision simply reflected the original idea that mothers were supposed to devote themselves to making a home and raising their children, not toiling outside the home all day in Dickensian circumstances.

Gradually modifications began to be made to try and take account of the mismatch between early twentieth-century assumptions and later twentieth-century social realities. In the name of discouraging family breakup, AFDC amendments in 1961 gave states the option of granting benefits to two-parent families with unemployed fathers. Half the states refused the option. (It would later be made mandatory on states in the 1988 Family Support Act.) In 1962 the Public Welfare Amendments Act provided funds for intensive social services that advocates claimed would reverse the trend toward cash handouts by rehabilitating those on welfare and preventing others from falling into welfare dependency. But almost none of this traditional social work had anything to do with providing job training and employment services for working-aged women.

This time, unlike the last major period of liberal reform in the New Deal, ambitious goals of social engineering took center place in the presidential agenda.

In 1967 Congress enacted welfare amendments imposing the first modest work- and job-training requirement on recipients. This Work Incentive program (WIN) allowed AFDC recipients to add the first $30 per month from work to their welfare check as well as keep one-third of earnings above that $30. What became known as "workfare" provisions of the law allowed states to drop from AFDC rolls those parents and children over sixteen who declined without good cause to participate in work or training programs. But welfare officials interpreted "good cause" loosely, and as the provisions were implemented only unemployed AFDC fathers, school dropouts over sixteen, and a few mothers of school-age children with access to free day care ever had to register for work. Moreover, funds and administrative capacities were wholly inadequate for any serious job-training or day-care services to help the usually poorly educated mothers enter the work force. The tiny fraction of AFDC recipients in the WIN program who got training and jobs (about fifty-two thousand persons in 1972 after four years of operation) did little more than enter the insecure ranks of the working poor. What the work incentive amendments mainly did was to serve notice that with the growing tendency of nonwelfare mothers to enter the work force, expectations for welfare mothers—though not their realistic job prospects—were changing as well. What was once seen as the "honorable" Mothers' Pension and then as aid to "deserving" dependent children had now become a popularly despised image of "welfare mothers."

THE GREAT SOCIETY

Meanwhile, another force crashing into the 1960s was long pent-up demands for social reform. On a variety of policy fronts these demands crystalized with the Kennedy administration and gained almost irresistible impulse after Kennedy's assassination and President Johnson's exploitation of his overwhelming 1964 election victory. This time, unlike the last major period of liberal reform in the New Deal, ambitious goals of social engineering took center place in the presidential agenda. In one sense this impulse reaffirmed a long-standing American desire to attack poverty through prevention and rehabilitation. In another sense, the Great Society programs were a wholly unique venture in using the national government to address poverty problems that had always been cast off into state and local welfare offices.

Neither Great Society programs as a whole nor the War on Poverty in particular advocated permissive, income-maintenance approaches for the poor. Apart from Medicare and other programs for the elderly, the emphasis was on creating economic opportunities and enhancing individuals' capacities to take advantage of those opportunities. None of the programs—from Head Start, education grants, Job Corps, and child nutrition to community action agencies, Foster Grandparents, rural development, and Model Cities projects—aimed merely at providing income support to poor people. In this sense the Great Society's war on poverty stood four-square with traditional norms of advancing individual opportunity and self-help, or what new thinking in the 1990s would term "empowerment."

Putting this aim into practice was another thing. In the first place, using education, job training, and other services to change people's lives proved a slow and uncertain process. When quick fixes were not forthcoming many politicians, group advocates, and policy experts lost patience with the programs.

In the second place, implementing the new programs was far more difficult in a sheer administrative sense than anyone had foreseen. In one area after another (urban planning, community economic development, job training, and so on) Washington policymakers embarked on activities where there were few strong administrative capacities to do the work in a knowledgeable, effective way. Moreover, as a price of passage in Congress, new domestic legislation invariably required accommodations to congressmen's alliances with local power centers interested in claiming a share of the new federal programs. Thus the Model Cities program, the only Great Society effort to launch a concerted attack on poverty in urban ghettos, was quickly broadened by Congress to include most congressional districts. In this and other ways the net result was to erect barriers to priority setting and effective management into the very structure of new social programs. Then too, the unforeseen consequences of America's foreign entanglement in anticommunist crusades came home to domestic policy. Vietnam contaminated domestic social programs identified with Johnson and presidential unpopularity grew. Perhaps the most powerful force to come crashing onto the scene in the 1960s was the growing turmoil over civil rights and race relations. Never before had welfare policies been developed in a context that openly confronted and legitimized demands for racial equality. In fact for almost two hundred years concerns about the poor hardly even made a pretense of considering conditions of racial inequality. In the 1960s all that changed. America's poverty agenda became inseparably and no doubt permanently bound up with the debate on race relations.

BURNOUT OF THE GREAT SOCIETY

The political results of trying to deal simultaneously with the problems of poverty and racial injustice were profoundly disruptive. Great Society programs originally justified in terms of individual advancement soon were perceived, and in part became, means of group advancement for blacks. Before any Great Society programs were fully in place (much less had time to adversely affect the ghetto poor as would be claimed after the Los Angeles riots of 1992), the Watts riot of August 1965 had begun the process of alienating white support from antipoverty efforts.

Not only did the potential for white backlash grow within and without the Democratic Party, along the way making AFDC welfare mothers even more unpopular. Perhaps equally important, heightened racial sensitivities also made it extremely difficult to even talk about traditional concerns in welfare policy without opening oneself to charges of racism. In the public conversation about welfare and fighting poverty, problems of illegitimacy, family stability, and work expectations became virtually forbidden

territory. Hence the racist abuses of the past in welfare programs came to haunt any present thinking about antipoverty policy.

Antipoverty efforts of the 1960s lost support because politicians taught the people to expect quick fixes and because they became part of a racial imbroglio.

History needs to be recalled honestly. Antipoverty efforts of the 1960s did not lose public support because they contradicted basic American values. They lost support because politicians taught the people to expect quick fixes, because they were often ineffectively administered, because they became part of a racial imbroglio, and because their chief political sponsor lied to the people in fighting a fruitless foreign war.

In the midst of this political quagmire, AFDC moved toward an income-maintenance approach by default, not design. This occurred in several ways.

Increasingly confident of their professional stature, economists played a newly prominent role in the public debate on welfare policy in the 1960s. In 1964 the president's economists for the first time defined an officially measured poverty line. Once this was done, much thinking about poverty policy became dominated by what could be measured. This facilitated evaluations of policy and proposals by considering how far they managed to close the rather arbitrary income gap of those below the poverty line. Effectiveness in poverty policy could be seen in terms of how many people, after government transfer payments, had their incomes brought up to the poverty line. This orientation was reflected in the failed plans of the Nixon and Carter administrations to reform welfare with something resembling an income guarantee for closing the poverty income gap.

Advocates of a more liberal income-maintenance approach had greater success in the courts than they did in Congress during the 1960s and 1970s. In these years a complex series of decisions struck down many state eligibility restrictions, such as residency requirements and suitable home rules. The net

effect was to move cash welfare assistance somewhat (but by no means all the way) in the direction of a solely need-based entitlement.

The drift toward welfare entitlements based purely on low income certainly did not proceed unopposed. Under the leadership of Russell Long (D-Louisiana), the Senate Finance Committee produced a steady stream of counterproposals to roll back the work of welfare rights advocacy groups in the courts. In 1972 the Talmadge amendment tightened work requirements for AFDC parents with children over six years (the 1967 WIN requirements applied to parents with children over sixteen), and in 1973–74 the first significant federal measures to enforce support payments from absent fathers were passed by Congress. Around the same time, California Gov. Ronald Reagan battled in the courts to maintain his more traditional, work-oriented welfare reform program in that state.

THE ANTIGOVERNMENT '80s

These, however, were only skirmishes. In the 1980s, with a growing antigovernment mood and the arrival of the Reagan administration in Washington, a sustained attack on permissive "Great Society" approaches was under way. AFDC bills attached to budget legislation did not produce large savings, nor were they intended to. But they did reverse much of the previous court-sanctioned momentum toward needs-based income entitlements. Many state eligibility requirements overturned by the courts were statutorily reintroduced by Congress. The "work incentive" exclusion of earned income from calculations of claimants' available income was dropped, removing some four hundred thousand cases of mainly working poor persons from the AFDC rolls. Support obligations for men living with the family as spouses and "lodgers" were reinstated. But, perhaps as a sign of changing social mores, there was no congressional interest in reviving the old custom in some states (overturned by the Supreme Court in 1968) of treating any sexual partner as a substitute parent disqualifying the children in the family from AFDC payments.

The 1980s also witnessed a reassertion of the pre-1960s tradition of state variation in welfare assistance. The Nixon and Carter welfare reform proposals, as well as most court decisions in the 1960s and

1970s, carried a presumption favoring greater national uniformity in AFDC benefits and administration. In those years it was conservatives who argued in favor of giving states more discretionary control over the programs. With the advent of the Reagan administration the stances were reversed, and in 1981 it was Democrats who fought conservatives' efforts to impose mandatory federal work and other requirements on state-administered welfare programs. The result was a victory for the Democrats that allowed increased state experimentation in combining AFDC with work, training, and employment services.

These state experiences and a growing body of social science research studies of their results produced what some saw as a new consensus in the fairly small circle of politicians and poverty experts who paid serious attention to welfare policy. As one of the leaders in this network, Sen. Daniel Patrick Moynihan (D-New York), put it, "Conservatives have persuaded liberals that there is nothing wrong with obligating able-bodied adults to work. Liberals have persuaded conservatives that most adults want to work and need some help to do so." As usual, the theme throughout the debate on welfare reform in the 1980s was prevention, rehabilitation, and work, as well as criticism of the current system for its indiscriminate cash handouts. In the words of the final Family Support Act of 1988, public welfare recipients would be "encouraged, assisted, and required to fulfill their responsibilities to support their children by preparing for, accepting, and retaining such employment as they are capable of performing." Provisions were made for education and job training for AFDC recipients who needed it to work. Medical and child-care services would be continued for a year after a recipient left the welfare rolls and entered the work force. Republicans insisted on mandatory federal standards requiring states to achieve given levels of participation in work and training programs for employable AFDC clients. The final compromise, passed by congressional Democratic leaders and the Reagan White House over the heads of more liberal Democratic congressmen, required states to have one-fifth of employable recipients in work or training programs by fiscal 1995. How states do that is largely their business.

THE DEMISE OF THE 1988 CONSENSUS

Translated into practice and the play of partisan politics at both state and national levels, it turned out there was less to the policy consensus of 1988 than met the eye. That the Family Support Act had to be implemented in the midst of a sustained economic downturn certainly did not help. The result, together with years of cuts in federal spending to aid states and cities, was a powerful squeeze on state budgets. Thus, new state spending to match federal funds for the act's various activities was often hard to obtain.

Budget pains were only part of the story. The Family Support Act had been crafted within a fairly self-contained fraternity of policymakers specializing in the subject. The mundane work of carrying through the various education, training, and employment programs aroused scarcely any political or public interest. Meanwhile, outside this circle, the "welfare problem" proved an irresistible target to other politicians in the early 1990s, especially at a time when many Americans were feeling their own economic hardship. Soon in statehouses and in Congress new "tough love" proposals for straightening out the welfare mess could be heard. These included cutting back the level of AFDC benefits, strengthening mandatory work requirements, and limiting the period of welfare receipt, tying welfare benefits to stay-in-school rules for teen parents and cutting adult parents' welfare benefits should their children fail to attend school, paying monetary bonuses to encourage marriage, and cutting benefits for additional children born while the mother was on welfare. Many of these, of course, have a familiar ring to anyone familiar with the history of welfare policy.

Holding hearings to find out what had gone awry with the intended direction and spirit of the Family Support Act, Senator Moynihan concluded, "I'm afraid all this originates with David Duke. He started talking about the 'threat' of people on welfare, and it struck a nerve." Meanwhile, the research findings on welfare reform programs continued to pile up, telling people what they did not want to hear: namely, that overcoming the employment and other problems of people on welfare for long periods is a costly and slow process that yields only modest results in terms of increased earnings and welfare savings.

Everyone wishes the "welfare" problem would be solved and simply go away. But it won't.

Those familiar with America's welfare legacy will find little of this surprising. Serious reforms are often costly, slow, undramatic, and modest in effect. More alluring in the political arena are promises that are cheap, splashy, and short term, for politicians generally derive political rewards for proposing, not implementing changes in the welfare system. Looking from the long perspective of the poor law and welfare policy, one can also understand that there has always been a combination of positive and punitive impulses and measures, of insisting that poor people behave in certain ways and of trying to change the conditions that inhibit their ability to behave in those ways. Everyone wishes the "welfare" problem would be solved and simply go away. But it won't. That is the other lesson of history.

The Permanently Unfinished Country

The United States, on the eve of the twenty-first century, is a cumulative fusion of immigrant nations, a synthesis that has come to embody a "world" of international culture.

Reed Ueda

Reed Ueda teaches history at Tufts University and has been a visiting professor at Harvard and Brandeis universities. He is writing a book on immigration and nationality in twentieth-century America.

The twentieth century has been called the "American century" because of the rise of the United States to world leadership. It has also been the era when the country became a world immigrant nation. The historical role of the United States as the quintessential magnetic society built from immigration has expanded to accommodate greater ethnic diversity. By the 1990s, the flow of newcomers included people from every region and culture of the globe.

However, this "new diversity" is merely a child of old historic patterns. Unless this is grasped, we are likely to mistake this new diversity as a new threat or new utopia, when it is in reality an outgrowth of roots imbedded in our national past. Thus the question "How new is diversity?" should actually be, "How old is diversity?"

The historical record shows that ethnic diversity is as old as the United States. The first U.S. census in 1790 revealed that the majority of Americans then were not of English origin. California had a higher proportion of Asians in 1880 than it did in 1980. In 1900, the majority of inhabitants in the largest cities were immigrants or the children of immigrants. In 1910, more than 50 languages were spoken by immigrants in the United States. Government and census records of the past amply prove the longstanding reality of American diversity.

This phenomenal ethnic diversity is largely due to certain unique characteristics of American immigration. The first key feature is the sheer magnitude of immigration: By 1990, 57 million people had migrated to the United States, the largest international movement of population in history. More immigrants came to the United States than to all other major immigrant-receiving countries combined. From 1820 to 1930, 38 million people moved to the United States, while 24 million migrated to Canada, Argentina, Brazil, Australia, New Zealand, and South Africa combined. The United States attracted three-fifths of the population flocking to major immigration countries. From the mid-nineteenth century to the Great Depression, the United States received more than 30 million newcomers, while Argentina received 6.4 million, Canada 5.2 million, Brazil 4.4 million, and Australia 2.9 million.

The second defining feature of American immigration is that it encompasses the greatest variety of nationalities among all the modern international population movements. Fifteen percent of American immigrants came from Germany, 11 percent from Italy, 10 percent from Ireland, 9 percent from Austria-Hungary, 8 percent from Canada, and only 7 percent from England. More Latin American, Caribbean, and Asian immigrants have journeyed to America than to any other nation. By contrast, other English-speaking immigrant countries have drawn new settlers almost wholly from other English-speaking nations. Eighty percent of immigrants to Australia came from Great Britain, while in Canada 37 percent arrived from Great Britain and another 37 percent from the United States. Immigration into Latin America is limited chiefly to those of Iberian or Italian origin. In Argentina, 47 percent of the immigrants came from Italy and 32 percent from Spain; in Brazil, 34 percent came from Italy, 29 percent from Portugal, and 14 percent from Spain.

Every immigrant, from the Mexican farm laborer to the Polish steelworker, has been a bold adventurer on a voyage of discovery. Emma Lazarus was wrong in describing immigrants as "wretched refuse" in her poem "The New Colossus" that adorns the Statue of Liberty. In reality, the immigrants are brave, resourceful, and vigorous, with the immigrant resiliency to cope with tremendous social change and social loss.

The early immigrants made enormous sacrifices, and persevered to realize a new vision of man and society. They found that the novel American conditions of tolerance toward pluralism and variety made the forging of new identities and cultural ties inescapable. The immigrant American is a person who absorbs new ways from neighboring people who are different. The children of Japanese immigrants in Hawaii learn new games, new words, new values, new tastes in food, new dress and hairstyles, new friendships and relationships from their neighbors, who are Hawaiian, Filipino, German, Chinese, and Portuguese. Americans are not bound to tradition but are

This article first appeared in *The World & I*, October 1992, pp. 42-49. Reprinted by permission of *The World & I*, a publication of the Washington Times Corporation. © 1992.

open to change and choices that come from outsiders. They learn from people unlike themselves about different foods, music, skills, arts and values. The American language is an immigrant language, a blending of many ethnic vocabularies.

A NEW SOCIETY

American immigrants have created a new society completely different from old societies like Sweden, Scotland, or Japan. These societies had taken strength from homogeneity. Solidarity came from all people being the same. American immigrants have built a society that substitutes a radical new self-definition for the nation. In the United States, the strength of the nation comes from the immense multiplicity of ethnic groups. Moreover, it hinges upon the existence of conditions that permit dissimilar groups to act and live together. The resultant mutual fusion and interdependency help integrate the nation. The large majority of nations in the world have little historical experience or political interest in operating as an immigrant-receiving nation. The German political leader Volker Ruhe expressed this viewpoint in 1991 by announcing "We [in Germany] are not an immigration country and we will not become one." But other societies—such as Japan, Norway, Scotland, Sweden, or Korea—also have no tradition of immigration and little interest in developing one.

By contrast, immigration has been the shaping force of the American nation and its role in world history. It has contributed an endless flux to American social history, making the nation, in the words of sociologist Nathan Glazer, "the permanently unfinished country." Immigration to America has adjusted the balance of human and material resources between nations, creating new international economic and cultural ties. Otto von Bismarck, the "Iron Chancellor" who unified Germany, called American immigration the "decisive fact" of the modern world.

Thus, at the heart of American history lies the cycle of national creation and re-creation through immigration. The social foundation of the political nation has been a historical immigrant nation that has been ever-changing. Historically, three immigrant nations arose successively and fused into each other in the two centuries after the American Revolu-

tion, producing immense changes in social organization, cultural life, and nationality. The new republic built by Protestant colonials from the British Isles had to accommodate, by the Civil War, an immigrant nation of Irish Catholics and newcomers from Germany and Scandinavia. After the turn of the century, a new immigrant nation formed principally from migrations from southern and eastern Europe, with input also from east Asia, Mexico, and the Caribbean. In the late twentieth century, a multicultural immigrant nation coalesced out of the expansion of immigration onto a global stage. The United States, on the eve of the twenty-first century, is a cumulative fusion of these immigrant nations, a synthesis that has come to embody a "world" or international culture.

The contemporary multicultural focus on the differences and separate experiences of diverse groups often starts from a myopia toward the enormous magnitude of ethnic assimilation that is part of American history. When David Dinkins, the first black mayor of New York City, delivered his inaugural address, he paid homage to his city as a "beautiful mosaic." The discrete and static parts of the mosaic form an image employed to legitimize a model of ethnic relations that favors cultural preservationism. This image, however, only pictures one part of American social history, the unmelted elements found among all groups. The other part of the picture has been the chemistry of change in status, culture, and identity. This process has not been as far-reaching or uniform as the earlier image for ethnic relations, the melting pot, once described and predicted. But it would be unrealistic to ignore the dimensions of social mobility and acculturation experienced over the span of generations by every group since the arrival of immigrant ancestors.

It is a cliché to disparage the melting-pot model of ethnic relations as a path toward homogenization or even "Anglo-conformity." It is true that Anglo-Saxon nativists of the early twentieth century prescribed this method of dealing with ethnic pluralism. But, recently, this stereotypical view of the melting-pot culture has been resuscitated by journalists and advocates seeking to use it as a target for the movement to promote multicultural difference.

The melting pot as a social and cultural reality in history was never Anglo-conformist or homogeneous. It was the

shared national culture, a fusion of elements taken from a multitude of group cultures. Assimilation has been a multidirectional process, undertaken with mutual concern among local groups. Groups changed and merged like the images of a kaleidoscope, with astounding and unpredictable patterns of diversity that yet cohered into a unity. Moreover, many features of group life were left unmelted and unfused. Melting has been incomplete, not always linear, and it proceeded at a variety of paces for different groups. Northern European groups that were two or more generations removed from the Old World had the most attenuated sense of ethnic identity. Some examples of European groups that no longer stressed specific loyalties have been the Scotch-Irish, the Welsh, and the Dutch. Although they retained a stronger sense of special identity, the Norwegians, Danes, Swedes, and Germans have also grown distant from an ethnic identity based on the homeland. Americans descended from forebears who came from southern and eastern Europe, Asia, the Caribbean, and Latin America exhibited a stronger tendency to retain distinctive ethnic features.

One of the most sensitive signs of mutual assimilation or multidirectional fusion of American society has been intermarriage. The Japanese Americans and Jews who most stressed marriage within the ethnic group early in the twentieth century now marry out at the highest rates, about one out of two marrying spouses of other ethnic backgrounds. The dramatic story of the rise of intermarriage is recorded in the multiple ancestry table of the 1980 federal census.

Prejudice and discrimination based on ethnic identity have affected all groups at one time or other, but the immigrants found niches on the social pyramid that would provide a foothold for further ascent. The new immigrants—such as the Greeks, Jews, Italians, Slavs, Armenians, Chinese, Japanese, and Mexicans—faced severe exclusion from jobs, schools, and neighborhoods. Most workers advanced little and lived a life of transiency and grinding poverty. But equality of opportunity increased for their children and grandchildren, upon which they capitalized to chart a course of multigenerational advancement. The descendants of even the most impoverished and powerless immigrants have obtained better jobs, more education, and higher status than their immigrant forebears. In the

■ *Chinatown in New York:* The dynamic conditions of American society that detached people from their origins and reabsorbed them into new communities created novel combinations of ethnic identity.

media culture and political culture of mass parties they have achieved more representation and greater voice than their ancestors. Recent immigrants from Latin America, Asia, the Caribbean, and the Middle East appear to be starting their own multigenerational cycle of social mobility. Any verdict on America's identity as a land of opportunity must rest on the broader view of the promise of American life as directed to the children and grandchildren of immigrants.

The groups that were involuntarily incorporated into the nation through conquest and slavery, American Indians and African blacks, encountered greater difficulty in achieving social mobility. Treated as separate quasi-nations, Indians were quarantined in the reservation system; blacks had to struggle against slavery and its residual barriers. The elimination of poverty within the Indian and black populations remains a crucial challenge.

The immigrant's need to deal with outsiders who were different in order to survive made ethnic boundary crossing practical and opportunistic. An individual's opportunities increased according to the ability to diversify social contacts. To tap the full range of opportunity, it was necessary to overlook ethnic differences and loyalties. Ethnic group members were willing to ignore the religion or ancestry of the person with whom they developed instrumental and mutually beneficial social relations and economic ties. Immigrants could only gain political power and office by forming alliances with outsiders. No ethnic group constituted a secure majority except at the most localized level. In order to become a force, groups had to form coalitions that leapfrogged ethnic divisions. Ethnic groups in America lacked the size and power to isolate their members. Their members forged and dissolved linkages with people from other groups as made necessary by self-interest and permitted by the limits of discriminatory boundaries. The dynamic conditions of American society that detached people from families and groups of origin and reabsorbed them into new families and new communities created novel combinations of ethnic identity.

The kaleidoscopic complexity of American identity also reveals that the dynamics of social history have made ethnicity only a part of human identity. The nature of ethnic identity changed as it was outflanked and decentered by the forming of multiple identities and competing loyalties. Members of ethnic minorities forged overlapping bonds with other types of communities that increased as one generation succeeded the next. Even the youngest new Americans are shaped by the heterogeneous world of classmates and playmates.

In fact, many Americans have come not to identify with a particular ethnic group; their identity derives primarily from their occupation, consumer habits, generation, geographic location, and mass culture. In a special census survey in 1970, nearly half of the sample group of European origins chose not to identify with a specific ethnic heritage. If the sample had included Hawaiian persons of mixed ancestry, a similar pattern probably would have emerged. These populations represent a transnational group that has grown in size and importance, inclusive of the increasing numbers of people of mixed ethnic and racial parentage.

California: Wave of the Future?

Phillip Martin

California is often a bellwether for events that later appear throughout industrial nations. In California, the arrival of three million immigrants and refugees during the 1980s gave the state a population growth rate of 2.4 percent, comparable to that of Morocco. If California continues to get one-third of all U.S. immigrants, then the state's population of 30 million today is projected to be 38 million in 2000.

Most immigrants to California are unskilled Hispanics and Asians, and their availability during the 1980s showed what is possible with a First-World infrastructure and a Third-World labor force. Los Angeles, for example, emerged as the nation's largest manufacturing center despite rising housing costs and declining manufacturing wages. One reason for this growth was defense, computer, and other high-tech expansion, but rapid job growth also occurred in the low-wage garment, shoes and furniture industries.

California and the United States have diamond-shaped work forces. About one-fourth of the work force is comprised of college-educated professionals and managers; one-half are semiskilled and skilled operatives, craftsmen, and clerks; and one-fourth are the less-than-high-school graduates who are often laborers, maids, and janitors. Immigrants tend to have more or less education than American workers: 30 percent are highly skilled, 20 percent are in the middle, and 50 percent are unskilled.

Large-scale immigration reinforces the other factors promoting inequality by adding workers to the top and bottom of the labor force. At the top, immigrant scientists and engineers play important roles in American education and industry. At the bottom, immigrant farm workers and laborers help to hold down wages and to slow down the search for labor-saving technologies. Unskilled immigrants did not cause the underclass problems that led to social tensions such as erupted in May 1992 in Los Angeles, but there is no denying that large-scale immigration has made it harder for disadvantaged American workers to find promising jobs.

Europeans seem surprised that the United States and Canada, despite their centuries of experience with immigration, could not better predict the consequences of immigration policy changes. The discussion of this issue suggests that even in these countries, we are in a new era. Bringing unskilled minorities into societies that are economically uncertain and politically unsure how to deal with the disadvantaged and multiculturalism is different from the past large-scale immigration of slightly different Europeans into societies that had strong convictions about and institutions to assimilate them. Housing segregation today limits interaction in schools, which in any event are less sure how they should deal with newcomer languages and culture, and the absence of horizontal mixing institutions, such as conscription for the military, increases the potential for isolated immigrants.

Some argue that industrial nations need immigrants to maintain their aging and declining populations. However, this argument can be misleading for four reasons. First, demographic projections are frequently wrong: Few demographers projected the baby boom or bust, and thus history would put little confidence in current projections of continued low fertility in the industrial countries. Second, importing even large numbers of youthful immigrants does not have much effect on the age structure because the number of births exceeds the number of immigrants, and babies begin at a 0 age, while immigrants are scattered across the age spectrum. A small increase in fertility has a much bigger effect on "youthening" the population than even large-scale immigration: In the United States, there are almost four million births annually, but one million immigrants.

Third, admitting young immigrants to maintain pension plans is a Ponzi scheme, because ever-more young immigrants must be admitted to pay ever-more pensions. If pension plans favor lower-wage earners, then admitting unskilled immigrants to maintain them can quickly turn a short-run benefit into a long-run cost. Fourth, immigration is usually more controversial when population growth is slow because the effects of "different immigrants" show up quicker in schools and other institutions. With fewer native children beginning school each year, immigrant children are more visible and, if their presence is perceived negatively, native parents feel compelled to shelter their children from "too many" immigrants in the schools.

Managing immigration and the tensions that surround it is likely to be a major challenge for the world community. The lacunae in the research and policy discussions are the in-between policy responses—between changing a law or definition at one end of the response spectrum, and slowing world population growth at the other. During the 1990s, industrial countries are likely to explore much more what they can really do about demand-pull, supply-push, and network immigration.

Phillip Martin is professor of agricultural economics at the University of California at Davis.

The conditions that promoted intergroup and intercultural fusion nevertheless retained the capacity to support the preservation of cultural heritages. American conditions have allowed the melted and the unmelted to coexist in equilibrium. The Jews, Koreans, Irish, and Armenians and others who were persecuted in their homelands saw melting-pot America as the land where they were at greatest liberty to maintain their way of life. This was the advantage of democracy that made the difficult journey worth it. Here, government left them alone to pursue their religion, build their neighborhood institutions, start their own schools. The tendency today is to see the historic United States as callously assimilationist. But let us not forget that immigrants throughout history voted with their feet that the United States was the most tolerant nation in the world. Today's sophisticates give in too readily to skepticism or cynicism about the historic nation as a haven of multicultural pluralism. The unsophisticated immigrants of 1910 found in America a place of refuge to protect their group life and culture. The Irish, Italians, Greeks, Japanese, Chinese, and Mexicans did not have activist government programs to protect their cultures, yet the historical record shows that their cultural identities were systematically and enduringly preserved. Irish parochial schools, Jewish religious schools, and German and Japanese language schools reached a flourishing pinnacle in the late nineteenth and early twentieth centuries, when public institutions did not give them support.

Americans have long seen their country as the land of opportunity and individual freedom. However, fears that the United States would disintegrate through the social disorders wrought by immigration have surfaced time and again. American authorities, such as the great economist Francis Walker and anthropologist Madison Grant, have sounded the alarm that immigration is a force corroding the nation.

Ultimately, their views gave way to the ascendant idea that immigration played a positive role in the nation's development.

The intellectual turning points in this ideological change were marked by the work of historians Marcus Lee Hansen and Oscar Handlin. They viewed immigration as a source of the national ethos of liberty and individualism. Handlin's historical writings on immigration formed the intellectual and ethical capstone of the view of immigration as a liberating and nationalizing force. In his work, immigration was transfigured into a myth-history of the creation of modern identity. The immigrant American became the archetype of the individual freed from the shackles of prescribed roles by moving into an alien world to discover a new empowering identity. Immigration facilitated the fulfillment of the national and global destiny of the United States as the prototypical modern nation unified by the joint effort of dissimilar groups.

The vision of Hansen and Handlin can help refocus the public mind on the historic liberal conditions conducive to forging a national community. It is needed in our time to allay destructive anxiety over the new diversity. It also is needed to counteract the artificial division of society into separate ethnic classes under government social policies. The historically rooted forces that made American identity heterogeneous and transcendent of differences were ineluctable and are still vital. The mutual assimilation of immigrants, their need to establish interdependency with surrounding groups, and their vision of American democracy as the best haven for cultural pluralism probably ensure that voluntary and fluid identities will continue to make immigration a nationalizing experience.

Fifty-seven million people had migrated to the United States by 1990, the largest international movement of population in history.

The American Environment

The Big Picture Is More Heartening than All the Little Ones

John Steele Gordon

John Steele Gordon writes the "Business of America" column for American Heritage.

The Cuyahoga River died for our sins. In 1796 The Cuyahoga, which promised easy transportation into the wilderness of the Ohio country from Lake Erie, prompted the city of Cleveland into existence. Over the next 170 years a primitive frontier town grew into a mighty industrial city, one that stretched for miles along the banks of its seminal river.

By the mid-twentieth century, however, the river no longer served as a major artery of transportation, having been superseded by railroads and highways. Now, instead of carrying the products of civilization into the vast interior, it carried the effluent of a far more technically advanced civilization out into the lake. The once crystalline waters of the river had become turbid and rank with its new cargo of chemicals and sewage. Its once abundant wildlife had long since fled, leaving only a few carps and suckers to eke out a living in the foul sullage on its bottom, testifying thereby to the very tenacity of life itself.

Finally, late in the morning of June 22, 1969, the Cuyahoga could no longer bear the burden humankind had placed upon it. In a sort of fluvial *cri de coeur,* the river burst into flames.

The fire was no will-o'-the-wisp flickering over a transient oil slick. Rather, it roared five stories into the sky, reduced wooden railroad trestles to ruins, and demonstrated to the people of Cleveland and the nation as no scientific study or news report ever could that the burden being placed on the environment was reaching limits that could be crossed only at the peril of the future.

Less than a year later, on April 22, 1970, Earth Day was held, one of the most remarkable happenings in the his-

tory of democracy. Fully 10 percent of the population of the country, twenty million people, demonstrated their support for redeeming the American environment. They attended events in every state and nearly every city and county. American politics and public policy would never be the same again.

Today, nearly a quarter-century after the fire, sunlight once more sparkles off the surface of the Cuyahoga. Boaters cruise its waters for pleasure, and diners eat at riverside restaurants. Mayflies—so characteristic of a Great Lakes spring—once more dance in the air above it in their millions while their larvae provide food for at least twenty-seven species of fish that have returned to its waters.

The Cuyahoga is not pristine, and barring an alteration in human priorities and circumstances beyond anything now imagined, it will not become so. But it has changed greatly for the better and continues to improve. It is once more a living river.

The Cuyahoga and its history is a microcosm of the American environment. For the history of that environment is the story of the interaction between a constantly changing, ever-more-powerful technology and an only slowly shifting paradigm of humankind's proper relationship with the natural world.

"DOMINION . . . OVER EVERY LIVING THING"

Human beings evolved in the Old World, a fact that more than once would have sudden and drastic consequences for the New.

The beginning of the Upper Paleolithic period was marked by a dramatic technological development as humans acquired tools and weapons that were far more sophisticated than any known before and became the most formidable

hunters the world has ever known. In the Old World both our prey and our competitors, evolving alongside, quickly learned to treat the emerging biological superpower with the greatest respect, and most were able to adapt successfully. But the New World lay in innocence while human hunters perfected their newfound skills in the Old.

The first settlers saw the wilderness not as beautiful but as barren and threatening.

When the land bridge that was a temporary consequence of the last ice age allowed humans to migrate into it, the results were swift and devastating: much of the North American Pleistocene fauna went extinct. Horses, camels, mastodons, mammoths, true elephants, several species of deer, bison, and antelope, ground sloths, glyptodonts, and giant beavers vanished, as did their associated predators, such as saber-toothed cats, giant lions, and cheetahs.

It cannot be known for sure to what extent the arrival of human hunters affected this great extinction, but there is little doubt that it was an important, perhaps fundamental, factor. But the evolutionary equilibrium that had been shattered by the arrival of the super-hunters eventually returned, for the human population of the New World, limited by numerous other factors besides food supply, remained low. And the surviving among the species they had encountered quickly adapted to the new conditions.

Thus the next human culture that appeared in the New World, the Euro-

From *American Heritage,* October 1993, pp. 30-51. © 1993 by Forbes, Inc. Reprinted by permission of *American Heritage* magazine, a division of Forbes, Inc.

COURTESY OF DeGOLYER LIBRARY, SOUTHERN METHODIST UNIVERSITY, DALLAS, TEX.

The Kansas-Pacific Railway touts its bison-hunting parties with a show of the animals' heads, 1870.

peans, found it to possess a biological abundance and diversity of, to them, astounding proportions. But these newcomers failed almost entirely to appreciate this aspect of the New World, for hunting in their culture had been reduced to, at most, a secondary source of food.

They were heirs to the agricultural revolution that began in the Old World at the end of the last ice age. It, too, was marked by a profound leap in technology. In turn the more settled conditions of agricultural communities allowed the development of still more elaborate technologies as well as social and political organizations of unprecedented complexity. The result was what we call civilization.

But the early civilizations were acutely aware that they were small islands surrounded by vast seas of wilderness from which savage beasts, and savage men, might come at any time and wipe them out. Thus their inhabitants came to look on the wilderness as an alien place, separate and apart. Not surprisingly under these circumstances, the religions that developed in the Near East in the wake of the agricultural revolution reflected this worldview, sanctioned it, and cod-

ified it. Because it became, quite literally, Holy Writ, it persisted unquestioned for centuries.

The Book of Genesis, in fact, could hardly be more direct on the subject. "God said unto [man], Be fruitful, and multiply, and replenish [i.e., fill up] the earth, and subdue it: and have dominion over the fish of the sea, and over the fowl of the air, and over every living thing that moveth upon the earth."

Over the next more than two thousand years, humans operating with this worldview in mind transformed the continent of Europe, and by the time they began to expand overseas, wilderness had disappeared from all but the margins of that continent.

Thus the world they encountered in North America was unlike anything they had ever seen. The greatest temperate forest in the world, teeming with life, stretched almost unbroken from the Atlantic seaboard to well west of the Mississippi. The grasslands that filled the Great Plains in the rain shadow of the Rocky Mountains also abounded with animal life as millions of bison, pronghorn antelope, elk, white-tailed and mule deer roamed it, as did their associated

predators, the wolf, the mountain lion, the bear, and the jaguar.

Farther west still, the forests of the Northwest and the deserts of the Southwest reached to the Pacific.

A "HOWLING DESART"

When the new settlers arrived, they did not see the beauty or abundance of the wilderness that greeted them. Far from it; they regarded it as barren and threatening because the ancient paradigm that dated to the dawn of civilization still molded their thinking. Thus they regarded their first task in the New World to be a re-creation of what they had known in the Old, an environment shaped by the hand of man, for man's benefit.

But while they sought, as nearly as possible, to re-create the Europe they had left behind, converting the "remote, rocky, barren, bushy, wild-woody wilderness" into a "second England for fertilness," there was one way in which the New World was utterly unlike the Old: it possessed an abundance of land so great that it seemed to the early settlers, and to their descendants for many generations, to verge upon the infinite. "The great happiness of my country," wrote the Swiss-born Albert Gallatin, Jefferson's Secretary of the Treasury, "arises from the great plenty of land."

Because the supply seemed without end, the value placed on each unit was small. It is only common sense to husband the scarce and let the plentiful take care of itself. Caring for the land, an inescapable necessity in Europe, was simply not cost-effective here. After all, the settlers could always move on to new, rich land farther west. For three hundred years they did exactly that, with ever-increasing speed.

Americans also developed other habits in the early days that stemmed directly from the wealth of land and scarcity of the population. Today, when American archaeologists investigate a site, they know that the place to look for the garbage dump is on the far side of the fence or stone wall that was nearest to the dwelling. In Europe that was likely to belong to a neighbor; in America it was often wilderness and thus beyond the human universe. This out-of-sight-out-of-mind attitude would have no small consequences when technology increased the waste stream by orders of magnitude.

The early settlers, while they greatly altered the landscape of the Eastern seaboard, clearing whole stretches of the primeval forest and converting the land to fields, pastures, and meadows, did not greatly diminish the biological diversity. They opened up the best land for farming but left untouched the steep or rocky areas as well as, to a great extent, the wetlands and mountains. Indeed in some ways the early settlers increased the diversity by expanding habitat for such grassland species as bluebirds, ground hogs, and meadowlarks. The ecosystem as a whole remained intact.

North America was transformed within a century. There was a vast price to pay.

Only in the South, where plantation agriculture became the rule in areas to which it was suited, did monocultural husbandry greatly diminish the fertility and texture of the soil. Virginia, the largest and, thanks to its tobacco exports, most powerful of the colonies, found its yields declining sharply toward the end of the eighteenth century as the best land was exploited and exhausted. Erosion became an increasing problem. As early as the 1780s Patrick Henry thought that "the greatest patriot is he who fills the most gullies."

"A THOUSAND YEARS"

Meanwhile, as a new civilization was being built out of the wilderness of North America, new attitudes toward wilderness itself were emerging in Europe. The ancient paradigm that had gripped Western thinking since Genesis was beginning, partially, to shift at last.

In the seventeenth century, wilderness had been universally regarded as at best a waste, if not an evil. In the eighteenth, however, it began to be seen for the first time as a thing of beauty. Mountains came to be viewed as majestic, not just as an impediment to travel or a barrier against invasion.

In Britain the aristocracy began to lay out gardens, such as those by Capability Brown, that were highly stylized versions of nature itself, rather than the direct refutation of it that seventeenth-century gardens, like those at Versailles, had been.

Biology became a systematic science (although the word itself would enter the language only in the early nineteenth century). Linnaeus studied the relationships of plants and animals. Georges Cuvier, William Smith, and others began to examine fossils and to sense, for the first time, a history of the earth that was at variance with the account given in Genesis.

The new attitude toward wilderness soon came to this country and contributed to the growing American sense of uniqueness. James Fenimore Cooper's novels and Thoreau's essays displayed a love of wilderness that would have been inconceivable a century earlier.

Of course, in Europe wilderness was largely an abstraction. In America it was just down the road. At the end of the Revolution, it nowhere lay more than a few days on horseback from the Atlantic shore, and Thomas Jefferson, no mean observer, thought it would be "a thousand years" before settlement reached the Pacific.

Jefferson was wrong. He did not realize—no one could have—that a third technological revolution was just getting under way, one that would give humankind the power to transform the world far beyond anything provided by the first two. It had taken millennia to reshape the face of Europe to human ends. North America would be transformed in less than a century. But there would be a vast price to pay for this miracle.

The steam engine and its technological successors allowed energy in almost unlimited quantity to be brought to bear on any task. So forests could be cut, fields cleared, dams built, mines worked with unprecedented speed. As a result, in less than a single human lifetime an area of eastern North America larger than all Europe was deforested. Virtually uninhabited by Europeans as late as 1820, the state of Michigan by 1897 had shipped 160 billion board feet of white pine lumber, leaving less than 6 billion still standing.

As early as the 1850s it was clear that something irreplaceable was disappearing.

But the new engines needed fuel. At first waste wood supplied much of it, and later coal and then oil. The byproducts of this combustion were dumped into the atmosphere as they had always been, but now their quantity was increasing geometrically. In 1850 Americans were utilizing more than eight million horsepower, animal and mechanical. By 1900 nearly sixty-four million, almost all mechanical, was being used by what economists call prime movers.

The factory system and mechanization brought many commodities within the financial reach of millions, while new transportation systems created national markets and made economies of scale both possible and necessary. This, in turn, caused the demand for raw materials to soar. The great mineral wealth that was being discovered under the American landscape was exploited with ever-increasing speed. Again the waste products were dumped at the lowest possible cost, which meant, in effect, on the far side of the nearest stone wall.

Increasing wealth and the new technologies allowed cities to bring in fresh, clean water for their rapidly increasing populations. This water was used to flush away the dirt and sewage of human existence, but only into the nearest body of water. The quality of life in the human environment was immeasurably improved by this, as the squalor that had characterized the urban landscape since Roman times disappeared. But the quality of the nation's waterways sharply deteriorated.

The new technology allowed us to turn more and more of the landscape to human use. The old-fashioned moldboard plow, in use since medieval times, could not deal easily with the rich, heavy soils and deep sod of the American Midwest. The steel plow invented by John Deere in 1837 quickly opened up what would become the breadbasket of the world. Wetlands could now be drained economically and made productive. Millions of acres vanished, and their vast and wholly unappreciated biological productivity vanished too.

So rapid an alteration of the landscape could only have a severe impact on the ecosystem as a whole. The loss of so much forest caused runoff to increase sharply, eroding the land and burdening the waters with silt, destroying more wetlands. Many animals' habitats disappeared. And because the ancient biblical notion that humans had dominion over the earth still held, others vanished entirely.

The beautiful Carolina parakeet, North America's only native parrot, proved a major agricultural pest. Because it lived in large, cohesive flocks, it made an easy target for farmers with the shotguns that the Industrial Revolution made cheap. It was extinct in the wild by the turn of the century; the last known specimen died in the Cincinnati Zoo in 1914.

Another avian casualty was the passenger pigeon, one of the great natural wonders of America, as amazing as Niagara Falls or the Grand Canyon. The passenger pigeon almost certainly existed in larger numbers than any other bird in the world. Moreover, it was concentrated in flocks of unbelievable immensity. Audubon reported one flock that took a total of three days to pass overhead and estimated that, at times, the birds flew by at the rate of three hundred million an hour.

The passenger pigeon nested in heavily forested areas in colonies that were often several miles wide and up to forty miles long, containing billions of birds. Trees within the colony each had hundreds of nests, and limbs often broke under the weight. The squabs, too heavy to fly when abandoned by their parents at the end of the nesting season, were easy prey. With railroads able to ship the fresh-killed birds to the great Eastern cities quickly, hunters slaughtered them in the millions to meet the demand.

Unfortunately it turned out that passenger pigeons needed the company of huge numbers of their fellows to stimulate breeding behavior. Once the size of the flocks fell below a certain very large minimum, the birds stopped reproducing, and the population crashed. Just as with the Carolina parakeet, the last passenger pigeon died in the Cincinnati Zoo in 1914.

The herds of the Great Plains also fell to hunters. It is estimated that upward of thirty million bison roamed the grasslands of North America in the middle of the nineteenth century. By the dawn of the twentieth, less than a thousand remained alive.

"FOREVER WILD"

As early as the 1850s it was clear to the more thoughtful that something precious and irreplaceable was rapidly disappearing. The wilderness that had helped define the country seemed ever more remote. It was now recognized the natural world could provide refreshment whose need was becoming more and more keenly felt.

Urban parks, such as New York City's incomparable Central and Prospect parks, were intended to provide the population with a taste of nature that many could now obtain no other way. But these parks were, like the aristocratic gardens created in eighteenth-century Britain, wholly manmade and no more truly natural than a sculpture is a rock outcropping.

Movements began to take hold to preserve portions of the fast-vanishing wilderness itself. As early as the 1830s the painter George Catlin put forward the idea of a wild prairie reservation, a suggestion that, alas, was not implemented before nearly all of the country's prairie ecosystem was destroyed. But the movement took root, and in 1864 the first act of preservation was undertaken when

ownership of the Yosemite Valley and a stand of sequoias was transferred from the public lands of the United States to the state of California.

In 1872 the first national park in the world was created when reports of the splendors of Yellowstone were delivered to Congress. James Bryce, British ambassador to the United States, called the national parks the best idea America ever had. Certainly they have been widely copied around the world. Today American national parks protect 47,783,680 acres, an area considerably larger than the state of Missouri.

States, too, began to set aside land to protect what was left of the wilderness. New York turned five million acres—15 percent of the state's land area—into the Adirondack Park and Forest Preserve, to remain "forever wild."

In the 1870s Carl Schurz, Secretary of the Interior, began moving for the preservation of federally owned forests. Born in Europe, where forests had long since become scarce and thus precious, and where forest-management techniques were far more advanced than those in this country, Schurz and many others helped create a new concern for America's fast-dwindling woodlands. By the end of Theodore Roosevelt's Presidency, almost sixty million acres were in the forest reserve system.

Today hundreds of millions of acres in this country enjoy various levels of protection from development, and more are added every year. But while the parks and reserves created by this movement are national treasures that have greatly enriched the quality of life, their creation was predicated on the part of the ancient paradigm that still survived. That part held that the natural world and the human one were two separate and distinct places. And it was still thought that each had little effect on the other.

"THE HARMONIES OF NATURE"

It was George Perkins Marsh, lawyer, businessman, newspaper editor, member of Congress, diplomat, Vermont fish commissioner, and lover and keen observer of nature, who first recognized the folly of this unexamined assumption. Growing up in Vermont, he had seen how the clear-cutting of the forests and poor farming practices had degraded the state's environment.

In 1864 he published *Man and Nature,* which he expanded ten years later and published as *The Earth as Modified by Human Action.* Individual instances of human effect on the natural world had been noted earlier, but Marsh, like Darwin with evolution, gathered innumerable examples together and argued the general case. He decisively demonstrated that the impress of humankind on the whole world was deep, abiding, and because it was largely unnoticed, overwhelmingly adverse. "Man is everywhere a disturbing agent," he wrote. "Wherever he plants his foot, the harmonies of nature are turned to discords."

Recognizing that technology, energy use, population, food production, resource exploitation, and human waste all were increasing on curves that were hyperbolic when plotted against time, he feared for the future. "It is certain," he wrote, "that a desolation, like that which overwhelmed many once beautiful and fertile regions of Europe, awaits an important part of the territory of the United States . . . unless prompt measures are taken."

Marsh observed in 1864, "Man is everywhere a disturbing agent." Nobody listened.

Darwin's book *On the Origin of Species* provoked a fire storm of controversy in the intellectual world of his time when it was published in 1859. It changed humankind's perception of the world profoundly and immediately. But *Man and Nature* changed nothing. Published only five years later, it met with profound indifference, and its author sank into the undeserved oblivion of those who are out of sync with their times. As late as 1966, when the science of ecology he was instrumental in founding was already well developed, so commodious a reference work as the *Encyclopaedia Britannica* made no mention of him whatever.

Perhaps the difference was that Darwin's ideas had only philosophical, religious, and scientific implication. Marsh's ideas, on the other hand, had profound economic consequences. An America rapidly becoming the world's

foremost industrial power did not want to hear them, even though as early as 1881 the mayor of Cleveland could describe the Cuyahoga River as "an open sewer through the center of the city."

"A DIFFERENT WORLD"

In fact, the seeds of the country's first great man-made ecological disaster were being planted even as Marsh wrote.

In the 1860s railroads pushed across the Great Plains and opened them up to settlement by connecting them to Eastern markets. On the high plains toward the Rockies, as hunters slaughtered bison and pronghorns by the millions, ranchers replaced them with cattle, which overgrazed the land. Then farmers began moving in.

World War I greatly increased the demand for wheat, while the tractor made plowing the tough, deep sod of the high plains a more practical proposition. The number of farms in the area east of the Rocky Mountains burgeoned in the 1920s, taking over more and more of the ranchland.

The mean annual rainfall in this area varied between ten and twenty inches, not enough for crop farming except in the best of years. But the early decades of the century happened to see many such

years. Then, in the late twenties, the rains slacked off, and drought swept the plains.

This had happened hundreds of times in the past, and the plants and animals that had evolved there were adapted to it. Wheat and cattle were not. Worse, over the last few years, the sod, the deep net of grass roots that had bound the soil together, had been broken over millions of acres by the farmers with their plows. The topsoil, without which no plant can grow nor animal live, now lay exposed to the ceaseless, drying winds.

In 1933 no rain fell for months in western Kansas, and little elsewhere. The crops withered, the livestock died of thirst or starvation, and the dust, bound by neither sod nor moisture, began to blow. On November 11 a howling, rainless storm sprang up. "By midmorning," a reporter wrote of a farm in South Dakota, "a gale was blowing cold and black. By noon it was blacker than night, because one can see through the night and this was an opaque black. It was a wall of dirt one's eyes could not penetrate, but it could penetrate the eyes and ears and nose. It could penetrate to the lungs until one coughed up black. . . .

"When the wind died and the sun shone forth again, it was on a different world. There were no fields, only sand drifting into mounds and eddies that

George Perkins Marsh around 1880, two decades after his *Man and Nature* showed how humans unbalance nature.

UNIVERSITY OF VERMONT LIBRARY, BURLINGTON

swirled in what was now but an autumn breeze. There was no longer a section-line road fifty feet from the front door. It was obliterated. In the farmyard, fences, machinery, and trees were gone, buried. The roofs of sheds stuck out through drifts deeper than a man is tall."

The dust of this storm, uncountable millions of tons of topsoil, darkened the skies of Chicago the following day and those of Albany, New York, the day after that. Terrible as it was, the storm proved but the first of many that ravaged the high plains in the next several years, as the drought tightened its grip and the unforgiving winds blew and blew. In the middle years of the 1930s, they laid waste thousands of square miles of what had been, just a few years earlier, a vibrant ecosystem. It was now the Dust Bowl. Upward of two hundred thousand people were forced to abandon their farms and trek westward in desperate search of the necessities of life itself.

The rains finally came again, and in the 1940s the discovery of the Oglala aquifer, a vast reservoir of water that underlies much of the Midwest, rescued the farmers who remained. Tapped by ever-deeper wells, the aquifer is now seriously depleted. And economics is slowly rescuing the land as the price of water increases every year.

It was always marginal for farming, and so it remains. Even with many, though mostly ill-conceived, federal programs, the farmers on the high plains are finding it ever harder to compete in world markets. Every year more and more farms are abandoned, and the land reverts to what in a perfect world it would never have ceased to be—short-grass prairie.

"A PHRASE CONCEIVED IN ARROGANCE"

The technological leap that had begun in Jefferson's day only accelerated in the twentieth century. The burdens that had been placed on the environment in the nineteenth century by such things as fuel use and sewage disposal increased sharply as the population expanded and new technologies spread across the land.

The limits of the ability of the environment to cope with the load were being reached more and more often. In October 1947 a thermal inversion settled over Donora, Pennsylvania. The town is set in a natural basin and was home to much heavy industry. The layer of cold air trapped the effluent of that industry and of the cars and furnaces of the population. By the time the inversion ended, four days later, twenty people were dead and six thousand ill enough to require treatment.

To an astonishing extent—at least as viewed from today's perspective—the people of the time accepted such happenings as the price of the Industrial Revolution that had brought them so much wealth and material comfort. A *New Yorker* cartoon of the day showed a woman sitting at a table set for lunch in the garden of a New York brownstone. "Hurry, darling," she calls to her unseen husband, "your soup is getting dirty."

New burdens were also added. The chemical industry grew quickly in this century, fueled by an explosion in knowledge. The disposition of chemicals was, as always, over the nearest stone wall: into a landfill or convenient body of water.

Agriculture became more businesslike as farms grew in size, became much more mechanized, and increasingly specialized in one or two crops. Of course, even Patrick Henry had known, two centuries earlier, that monocultural farming depletes the soil and is vulnerable to insects and other pests. But now the chemical industry could overcome this, thanks to synthetic fertilizers and pesticides.

Such chemicals as DDT were greeted as miracles of modern science when they first became available, and their use spread rapidly. In 1947 the United States produced 124,259,000 pounds of chemical pesticides. Only thirteen years later, in 1960, production was up to 637,666,000 pounds of often far more potent pesticides.

Diseases such as malaria and agricultural pests such as the boll weevil were declared on the verge of eradication. And the "control of nature," the final realization of the dominion enjoined by Genesis, was said to be at hand. DDT and other pesticides sprayed from airplanes blanketed vast areas, to kill gypsy moths, budworms, and mosquitoes.

But there were troubling signs for the few who looked. The pesticides were nondiscriminatory; they killed all the insects they touched. Honeybees, essential for the pollination of many crops and innumerable natural plants, were often wiped out by spraying programs aimed at other insects. Beekeepers began to fight back with lawsuits. "It is a very distressful thing," one beekeeper wrote, "to walk into a yard in May and not hear a bee buzz."

More than two hundred new pesticides were introduced in the years following World War II. The reason was that the older ones became increasingly ineffective. Many species of insects go through numerous generations a year and can evolve very rapidly, especially when a severe pressure such as a new pesticide is applied. In a monument to the vigor with which life clings to existence, they did exactly that.

And birdwatchers noticed a troubling decline in the numbers of some species, especially the large raptors that lived at the top of the food chains. Charles Broley, a retired banker, banded bald eagles in Florida beginning in 1939 as a hobby. He usually banded about a hundred and fifty young birds a year on the stretch of coast he patrolled. Beginning in 1947, more and more nests were empty or held eggs that had failed to hatch. In 1957 he found only eight eaglets, the following year only one.

But these troubling events were scattered, knowledge of them dispersed over a huge country and many scientific disciplines. They were no match for the chemical companies. But these, it turned out, were no match for a frail middle-aged woman named Rachel Carson.

Within a few years of Silent Spring, *the demand for action became irresistible.*

Rachel Carson was trained as a marine biologist, but she was a born writer. In 1952 her book *The Sea Around Us* was published with a very modest first printing. To everyone's astonishment—most of all hers—it became a titanic bestseller that made its author famous across America. Ten years later she published *Silent Spring*. It changed the world.

Again a huge bestseller, *Silent Spring* detailed in lucid, often poetic, and always accessible prose how pesticides were playing havoc with the air, land, and water of the country and how their uncontrolled use was doing far more harm than good. Further, it introduced millions of Americans to the concept that the natural world was an intimately interconnected web. This web, Carson made clear, included humans quite as much as every other living thing that shared planet Earth. What killed insects would, if not handled carefully, one day kill us too. George Perkins Marsh had said much the same thing a hundred years earlier. This time the people read and believed.

The ancient paradigm from the dawn of civilization, when man was frail and nature omnipotent, was dead at last. Dead with it was what had been in theory a dream and in fact a nightmare—the control of nature. It had been, Rachel Carson wrote on the last page of *Silent Spring,* "a phrase conceived in arrogance."

"THE SKY IS FALLING"

Within a few years the public demand for action in behalf of the environment became irresistible, and it caught a complacent government by surprise. John C. Whitaker, Nixon's cabinet secretary, later recalled that "we were totally unprepared for the tidal wave of public opinion in favor of cleaning up the environment."

Earth Day cleared up any lingering doubts about the public's opinion on the matter. Federal government agencies uch as the Environmental Protection Agency were created, and goals and timetables for air and water quality were established. We Americans set out on a crusade to rescue the land from ourselves. In many ways we shared the fervor with which the medieval world had set out to rescue the holy Land from the infidel.

Today, nearly a quarter-century after the crusade to the new Jerusalem of a clean environment began, there is vast progress to report. In 1959, 24.9 million tons of particulate matter—soot—were emitted into the air in the United States. By 1985, 7.2 million were, and less every year. In 1970, 28.4 million tons of sulfur oxides, a prime contributor to smog, were released by power plants and automobiles. In 1990, 21.2 million tons were, a drop of nearly 25 percent. Carbon monoxide emission has fallen by 40 percent since 1970, and lead has been eliminated as an additive to gasoline.

Cars being manufactured in the 1990s emit only a fifth as much pollution as those made before 1975. Thus 80 percent of all automobile pollution today is generated by just 10 percent of the cars on the road. In the next few years, as these clunkers end up on the scrap heap, automobile pollution will decrease sharply.

Already the number of days per year when the air quality is below standards in most of the country's cities has fallen significantly, by 38 percent in the 1980s alone. Even Los Angeles, the smog capital of the country thanks to its geography and automobile-oriented infrastructure, has enjoyed a 25 percent decline in smog-alert days.

In 1960 only about 50 million Americans were served by municipal sewage plants that provided secondary or tertiary treatment. Today more than half the population is. As a result, many urban waterways are now cleaner than they have been since the early 1800s. New York used to dump the sewage of eight million people into the Hudson, Harlem, and East rivers. Today, in a development that would have stunned turn-of-the-century New Yorkers, there is an annual swimming race around Manhattan Island.

Rural rivers too have greatly benefited. Most of the Connecticut River's four-hundred-mile length was declared "suitable only for transportation of sewage and industrial wastes" in the 1960s. Today 125 new or upgraded water treatment plants, costing $900 million, have transformed it. Fishing and swimming are now allowed almost everywhere, and wildlife such as ospreys, bald eagles, blue crabs, and salmon has returned in numbers.

The sludge that is the end product of sewage treatment was until very recently dumped in the ocean or into landfills. Now it is increasingly being sought by farmers as cheap fertilizer and soil conditioner. New York City produces 385 tons a day, all of it once dumped beyond the continental shelf. One hundred tons of that is being used by farmers in Colorado and Arizona. Initially skeptical, fifty of those farmers recently sent New York's mayor a letter asking for more. He's likely to oblige. Boston sludge now fertilizes Florida citrus groves. And because sewage sludge not only fertilizes but improves soil quality, it is displacing chemical fertilizers.

As old factories reach the end of their productive lives and are replaced by new ones built under stringent controls, the non-sewage pollution of the waterways is also steadily declining. The violation rate (the percentage of tests where the amount of pollutants was found to be above standards) for lead and cadmium fell to less than one percent. Dissolved oxygen is an important measure of a water body's biological viability. The

percentage of times it was found to be below standard fell 60 percent in the 1980s.

Many bodies of water, such as Lake Erie, declared dead in the 1970s, have bounded back with the improved situation and with the help of life's ferocious determination to go on living. The amounts of pesticides being used every year fell by more than a quarter in the 1980s, and those in use today are far less persistent and far less toxic than most of those in widespread use in the 1960s. The level of DDT present in human fatty tissue, a fair measure of its presence in the environment, was 7.95 parts per million in 1970. By 1983 it had fallen to 1.67 parts per million. Today, ten years latter, no one even bothers to gather the statistic.

The land, too, has improved. In the eastern part of the United States, the area of forest land has been increasing for more than a century, as clear-cut areas have been allowed to regenerate. It will be another hundred years, at least, before they reach the climax stage, but they are on their way. And today 28 percent of all farmland is no longer plowed at all, and the percentage is growing quickly. Conservation tillage is used instead; the method sharply reduces erosion and improves soil quality while slashing costs, producing crops for as much as 30 percent less.

Programs to reduce the use of chemical fertilizers are being tried in more and more areas as farmers learn new techniques. In Iowa in 1989 and 1990 a joint EPA-state program helped farmers cut their use of nitrogen fertilizer by four hundred million pounds without sacrificing crop yields. Because agricultural fertilizers and pesticides now account for more than 65 percent of all water pollution (factories account for only 7 percent), this trend has no small implication for the future.

Wildlife is on the mend in many ways. To be sure, the number of species on the endangered list has grown sharply in the last two decades, but that is much more an artifact of increased knowledge than of a still-deteriorating situation.

Many species have rebounded sharply, thanks in some cases to protection and in others to the explosion of biological and ecological knowledge that has so marked the last twenty-five years. To give just two examples, alligators, once hunted mercilessly for their skins, are no longer on the list at all. And peregrine falcons, almost extirpated in the Eastern United

One Town's Environment
The ebb and flow of tooth and claw, fifty miles from Times Square

One winter Sunday morning a few years ago, I happened to look out my bedroom window as I was getting dressed. There on the lawn below was the carcass of a deer, its hindquarters half-eaten by whatever had brought it down. Tufts of its fur were scattered across the grass. Its eyes, glassy in death, stared back at me sightless. A coyote, slat-thin and mangy, was taking furtive bites, looking up every few seconds as if expecting to be attacked. A few feet away three turkey vultures were walking about in that peculiar loping gait unique to vultures, waiting their turn at the carcass.

This nature-red-in-tooth-and-claw scene was so reminiscent of the "Nature" series on PBS that I half-expected George Page to come around the corner at any moment, camera crew in tow. But what is most astonishing of all, perhaps, is that I do not live in some remote part of the country. Far from it. I live in North Salem, New York, less than fifty miles from Times Square. That so vibrant a habitat could exist so close to the center of the nation's largest city is powerful evidence that life is far more resourceful and tenacious than many environmental activists would like to admit.

North Salem is a small place. The town occupies twenty-two square miles (about the size of Manhattan Island), but only forty-eight hundred people call it home. Economically they range from getting by to *Forbes*-four-hundred rich. There is only one traffic light, a recent and much-resented addition. The hamlet of Purdys has a First Street but no longer has a Second Street. In the hamlet of Croton Falls, a local bank occupies a corner of the fishing-supplies store.

Although there is a town historian and an active historical society, precious little history beyond the purely local has ever taken place here. Ogden Mills, a major figure in California history, was born in North Salem, and his house still stands, now a small herb farm. General Rochambeau and his troops marched through in 1781 on the way to the siege of Yorktown. The expedition that resulted in the capture of the British spy Major André was supposedly planned at the Yerkes Tavern, whose foundation—all that remains of it—is on my property, and whose front door is now the front door of my house. But that's about it, and even the Yerkes Tavern plot, alas, is almost certainly a myth.

Altogether it's the sort of place where most people feel no need to lock their doors, where neighbors leave excess zucchini on your front porch unasked, knowing you don't have a garden, where everyone calls the town officials by their first names, even when bawling the hell out of them at town board meetings. I suspect Thornton Wilder would have liked North Salem.

The crest of Keeler Hill includes the highest point in Westchester County, and from it one can see, across rolling hills and fields, clear to the Hudson River, twenty miles away, and even Bear Mountain on the far side. The landscape is peaceful, gentle, and apparently timeless.

It is not. The beautiful lake that you can see from Keeler Hill dates only to 1893, when New York City dammed the town's major waterway, the Titicus River, and created a new reservoir for its ever-growing thirst. Even the spruce forest that runs up one side of Turkey Hill, a mile or so away, is only about sixty years old, planted by Tom Purdy when he wanted to cut down on the number of fields that had to be mowed during the Great Depression.

In the last hundred years wave after wave of ecological change has swept over North Salem. Even in the not quite half a century of my existence, the changes have been many, and I have marked them. For it has been my pleasant fate to spend much of my life here, first as a constant visitor to the farm my grandparents used as a summer place and for the last thirteen years as a resident on a piece of that farm, living in a small eighteenth-century house that my grandmother lovingly restored sixty years ago, her own mini-Williamsburg project.

Like most of the rest of the northeast part of the country, North Salem before the arrival of Europeans was heavily forested with deciduous trees, oaks and hickories predominating on the higher, drier slopes, maples, sycamores, and tulip trees marking the wetter areas. The local Indians practiced agriculture using slash-and-burn techniques that created open areas and a good deal of edge, the part of woodlands most attractive to game such as deer and wild turkeys.

North Salem was first established by Europeans in 1731, but the effect of Europeans on its environment began a century earlier.

The Dutch came to this area to trade for furs. By the time farming began in North Salem, beavers, martens, minks, and many other fur-bearing animals had long since been extirpated or greatly reduced. The major carnivores too, such as bears, mountain lions, wolves, and coyotes, soon vanished.

The farmers moving in girdled the trees to kill them and created pastures for their livestock and fields for their crops. By 1800 much of the original forest had vanished, replaced by open fields, meadows, and pastures. Only the wetlands and steeper slopes remained covered by trees. With the loss of most of the edge, game declined in numbers, and human hunters added to the pressure. Wild turkeys were gone by the middle of the nineteenth century, and deer became vanishingly rare.

But North Salem was never rich farming country. Its soil is thin in most parts of the town, for there is little bottomland and much hillside. The glacier that retreated about ten thousand years ago scoured the bedrock clean and left an infinity of stones behind as it melted. One boulder left by the glacier and weighing about sixty tons rests on five smaller stones. The Balanced Rock, as it is called, is the town's distinctly modest—but only—tourist attraction.

While the glacier provided North Salem with what one local calls "our answer to the Grand Canyon," it also gave the early farmers a big problem. Before fields could be plowed, they had to be cleared of the stones the glacier had left. At a cost in human and animal labor that staggers the imagination, the early farmers built hundreds of miles of stone walls on the edges of their fields, walls made so well that most remain to this day and provide the modern landscape with its most abiding characteristic.

Because the land was relatively poor, dairy farming and orchards were always the dominant forms of agriculture, and most field crops that were grown—principally hay—were for local consumption.

Like all towns before the Industrial Revolution, North Salem had to provide for virtually all its own needs. Individual households made most items. But blacksmith shops, slaughterhouses, flour mills, nail factories, and others supplied the rest. This local industry was powered mostly by the

States by DDT, have been with infinite care and effort put on the road to recovery. Today there is a pair nesting on the Verrazano Bridge at the entrance to New York's Upper Bay, and there is even a pair nesting on the top of the Met Life (formerly Pan Am) building in midtown, exploiting the distinctly unendangered local pigeon population.

Nor has public interest in rescuing the environment slackened. *The New York Times Index* for 1960 needed less than 19

Titicus River, which runs east to west through the center of the town, and the Croton River, which forms the town's western border. Both those waterways also, of course, served as giant disposal systems and were foul and smelly for most of the nineteenth century. The part of town where many of these small factories were concentrated, along what is now called Titicus Road, was known then as Bedbug Hollow. Today it is the center of the town's most affluent area.

In the 1840s the railroad reached North Salem. New York City had been, at best, a long day's journey away; it was now a two-hour ride. The railroads also soon connected the Middle Western grainlands and upstate dairy areas to the Eastern seaboard. Marginal agricultural areas close to the city, which had prospered by their proximity, prospered no more. North Salem's population, which had doubled since the Revolution, peaked in the 1840s and then began a long, slow decline that lasted until 1950, when the town's population was back to what it had been when Rochambeau marched through.

The railroads also spelled the slow death of the local industries. As manufacturing enterprises of national scope evolved in the late nineteenth century, the local factories shut down one by one. The Titicus and Croton rivers soon cleansed themselves and sparkled once more in the sunlight.

By 1900, 90 percent of the land was still open fields, but around that time agriculture began, slowly, field by field, to disappear from the town. The poorest pastures were let go and were soon tangles of brush, briars, and saplings, difficult to walk through but a paradise for many birds, such as song and field sparrows, whose numbers increased.

Soon the abandoned fields were second-growth forests, on their way back to the climax deciduous forest that had once covered the town. As this process, called succession, began, the habitat diversified, and more and more species of birds returned or increased their numbers. Just in the last ten years, as second-growth forests grew old enough to produce a substantial number of dead trees, the magnificent pileated woodpecker reappeared. Its strident cry and air-hammer-like drilling now resound through North Salem's woods.

Today perhaps 70 percent of the town is forest, nearly a reversal of the situation at the beginning of the century, and agriculture is nearly gone. There is a vineyard, producing a variety of wines (memo to Mouton Rothschild: Don't worry), and Outhouse Orchards, which produces vegetables as well as fruits and cider.But the last dairy farm closed down ten years ago, and today the farms are only horse farms, really boarding stables.

Still the horse farms and the open fields maintained by wealthy, mostly horse-loving landowners preserve much open space. This open land allows the continuation of a major fox hunt in North Salem, adding vast color and cheerful noise to the landscape and, because years go by between kills, doing little harm.

The patchwork of open fields and small woods that now characterizes the town provides much edge, and with the decline of hunting (only bow and arrow can be used), it has sparked a major revival of game species. Wild turkey are once again present (just the other day a hen strolled across my back lawn as though she owned the place, as, in a sense, I suppose she does).

Deer, seldom seen when I was a child in North Salem, are now a thoroughgoing pest to gardeners and a serious threat to the habitat as a whole. For while North Salem's ecosystem is a vibrant one, it is not a complete one. Coyotes have returned in numbers, and bobcats are to be found, but they are merely hunters of opportunity when it comes to deer. The major carnivores are gone forever. With human hunting light, nothing checks the population of deer, and they tend to breed up to the limit of the food supply, doing much damage to diversity as they extirpate favored species of plants and destroy the forest understory. It is not at all uncommon to see herds of twenty or more browsing in open fields.

Control of the deer population is largely a political problem. Hunters' license fees fund the state's Department of Environmental Conservation, and hunters' interests—because there's a rich supply of animals to shoot at—get first attention as a result. Many animal lovers, who apparently studied ecology only at Walt Disney University, fiercely resist any control measures at all. As a result, Westchester County has one of the densest deer populations in the country.

But except for the deer, North Salem's environment is in better shape and more diversified and richly populated than it has been since before the coming of the Europeans. In my lifetime the improvement has been noticeable. Although I've been walking the town's fields and woods with binoculars since I was old enough to focus them, I was thirty-four before I ever saw a bluebird. Today the bird that wears the sky on its back (as Thoreau described it) is once again common, thanks to hundreds, perhaps thousands, of birdhouses that dot the town. Last year even a bald eagle was spotted.

Has anything gotten worse? Yes, two things. One, the night sky has seriously deteriorated. The glow of lights to the south, where the population has increased much more rapidly than it has in North Salem, blots out most stars in that direction. And today the Danbury Mall, although more than ten miles away, gives the northeast sky a pink glow as unnecessary as it is obnoxious. Towns with major astronomical observatories, such as Flagstaff, Arizona, have developed ordinances to protect the observatories while maintaining safety and convenience. The adoption of these ordinances nationwide would give us back the night sky and save very significant amounts of energy as well, a win-win situation if ever there was one.

The other deterioration is the noise. When I was a child, I loved to wander off into the fields of my grandparents' farm. There, sitting on a stone wall or lying in the grass, I would listen, just listen. All I would hear were the sounds of the earth that Oscar Hammerstein II thought were music itself: the lowing of cattle, a distant dog, the rustle of the wind through the hay, the song of meadowlarks, the caw of crows.

Today human-generated noise always intrudes, like someone jingling coins at a concert. There is always the hum of traffic from the interstate, although it is three and a half miles from my house. Small planes buzz around the sky in astonishing numbers. Somewhere there is always a chain saw working, or a weed whacker running, or a police siren racing to the scene of an accident.

If there is a solution to this problem (beyond my increasing deafness), I do not know it. I do know I miss the silence that was so full of music.

—J.S.G.

inches to list all the references to air pollution that year, and only 15 for water pollution. In 1991 the two subjects required 87 and 107 inches respectively.

Local organizations monitoring local situations have multiplied across the country. Many hire professionals, such as the Hudson River Fisherman's Association,

whose "river-keeper" patrols the Eastern seaboard's most beautiful waterway.

And public opinion has become a powerful force. In the fall of 1992 the governor of Alaska proposed culling the number of wolves in the state in order to increase the number of moose and caribou for human hunters. It was not long before he wished he hadn't. The state, heavily dependent on tourist dollars, was soon backpedaling furiously before the onslaught of intensely negative public reaction.

So is the American environment once more pristine? Of course not. Many pollutants have proved unexpectedly stubborn and persistent. Many businesses have resisted changing their ways. In most cities the storm and waste sewers are still one and the same, and sewage overflows in bad weather. It will take many years and billions of dollars to correct that. An unknowable number of species are still threatened by human activity.

But the nation's water, air, land, and wildlife are all better, in many respects, than they have been in a century, and they continue to improve. To put it another way, if the task of cleaning up the American environment were a journey from Boston to Los Angles, we would be well past the Appalachians and might even have the Mississippi in sight.

Then why is the impression so widespread that we are, at best, entering Worcester, if not actually marching backward somewhere in Maine? There are many reasons, and as so often happens, human nature lies at the root of all of them.

A first reason is that environmental bureaucrats, like all bureaucrats, want to maximize the personnel and budgets of their departments. So from their point of view, it simply makes good sense to highlight new problems and to minimize news about the old ones that have been successfully addressed. Similarly, environmental organizations live and die by fundraising. The-sky-is-falling stories are simply more effective in getting someone to reach for a checkbook than are things-are-looking-up stories. And environmental bureaucrats and lobbyists alike know that they must struggle hard to maintain their constituencies and budgets to fight the serious problems that do persist. They fear, not without reason, that if they don't play up the troubles that endure, they may lose the ability to address them at all—and we might lose much of what we've won.

A second reason is that the media have often failed to evaluate environmental stories with scientific competence and sometimes even honesty. As fundraising, bad news sells better than good news.

As a result, tentative data have often been presented as irrefutable fact, and short-term or local trends have been extrapolated into global catastrophes. In the 1970s there were many stories about the coming ice age. Ten years later global warming was destined to extinguish civilization.

A third reason that things often seem to be getting worse here at home is extremists. Extremists are always present in great reform movements, and the goal of environmental extremists is not a clean environment but a perfect one. They are few in number, compared with the legions now dedicated to cleaning the American environment, but like many extremists, they are often gifted propagandists and they are willing to use ignoble means to further noble ends.

Consider the support given by some environmental organizations to the Delaney Clause. This law, passed in 1958, requires that even the slightest residue of pesticides that have been shown to cause cancer in laboratory animals may not be present in processed foods. The Delaney Clause made some sense in the 1950s, when our ability to detect chemicals was limited to about one part in a million and our knowledge of carcinogenesis rudimentary at best. Today it is nothing short of ludicrous, for we can now detect chemicals in amounts of one part in a quintillion. To get some idea of what that means, here is the recipe for making a martini in the ratio of 1:1,000,000,000,000,000,000: Fill up the Great lakes—all five of them—with gin. Add one tablespoon of vermouth, stir will, and serve.

As a result, to give just one example, propargite, a nonpersistent pesticide that controls mites on raisins, can't be used because it has been shown to cause cancer when fed to rats in massive doses. But a human being would have to eat eleven tons of raisins a day to ingest the amount of propargite needed to induce cancer in laboratory rats. Had it been available in the 1950s, propargite's use would have been perfectly legal because the infinitesimal residue would have been completely undetectable.

Every first-year medical student knows it is the dosage that makes the poison. Yet many environmental organizations are adamantly against any revision of the Delaney Clause for reasons that amount to nothing less than scientific know-nothingism. They are wasting time, money, and, most important, credibility on the chimera of perfection.

But time, money, and most of all credibility are precious commodities. For even if we are at the Mississippi on the journey to clean up the American environment, we still have two-thirds of the journey to go. And it will be the most difficult part.

For as we proceed, the problems will become more and more intractable, and thus more and more expensive to deal with. For instance, it was easy to get a lot of lead out of the atmosphere. We simply stopped adding it to gasoline as an anti-knock agent, virtually the sole source of atmospheric lead. But getting the fertilizers and pesticides out of agricultural runoff—now far and away the greatest source of water pollution in the country—will be another matter altogether, especially if we are to keep the price of food from rising sharply.

Part of the problem is the iron law of diminishing returns. Getting, say, 90 percent of a pollutant out of the environment may be easy and relatively cheap. But the next 9 percent might cost as much as the first 90, and so might the next .9 percent, and so on. At some point we have to say, "That's clean enough." Where that point will be, in case after case, is going to have to be decided politically, and democratic politics requires give and take on all sides to work.

Another part of the problem is that, increasingly, environmental regulations have been impinging on private-property rights. In the early days, the environmental movement was largely about cleaning up the commons—the air and water that belong to us all. The rule of thumb was easy: He who pollutes—whether the factory owner or the commuter in his automobile—should bear the cost of cleaning up now and of preventing that pollution in the future. Today, however, new regulations are more likely to affect the ways in which someone can use his or her own property and thus gravely affect its economic value.

There is a genuine clash of basic rights here. One is the individual right to hold, enjoy, and profit from private property. The other is the general right to pass on to our children a healthy and self-sustaining environment.

To give just one specific example of how these rights can clash, a man in South Carolina bought beachfront property in the 1980s for $600,000. The property was worth that much because it consisted of two buildable lots. He intended to build two houses, one for himself and one to sell. But the state then changed the regulations, to protect the delicate shoreline ecosystem, and his property became unbuildable. Its value plummeted from $600,000 to perhaps $30,000.

Not surprisingly, the owner sued for the economic loss he had suffered. But the state ruled that it was merely regulating in the public interest and that no compensation was due as it was not a "taking": the property still belonged to the owner. The property owner argued that the regulations, however valuable a public purpose they served, had indeed effected a taking, because the state had sucked the economic value out of his property, leaving him the dried husk of legal title.

This case is still in the courts, and cases like it are multiplying. A general acknowledgment of the validity of both sides' rights and motives is necessary if difficult matters such as these are to be resolved successfully.

Still a third problem is that, increasingly, environmental issues are global issues, beyond the reach of individual sovereign states. Worse, scientists have been studying the earth as a single, interlocking ecosystem for only the last few decades. Global weather and ocean temperature data nowhere stretch back more than a hundred and fifty years and usually much less. The amount of data we possess, therefore, is often insufficient to allow for the drawing of significant conclusions. Has the recent increase in atmospheric carbon dioxide caused an increase in average temperatures, or has a normal cyclical increase in temperature caused an increase in carbon dioxide? We just don't know the answer to that question. But billions, perhaps trillions of dollars in spending may depend on the answer.

Another issue is growth versus the environment. Many feel that economic growth and increased pollution are two sides of the same coin, that it is impossible to have the one without the other. Others feel that economic growth is the very key to cleaning up the environment because it alone can provide the wealth to do so.

Obviously, in some absolute sense, the more production of goods and services, the more waste products that must be dealt with. But if the wealth produced greatly exceeds the pollution produced, the pollution can be dealt with while standards of living continue to rise. Certainly among the world's densely populated countries, the correlation between wealth and environmental quality is striking. People cannot worry about the problem of tomorrow's environment if the problem of tonight's supper looms large. It is landless peasants, more than timber barons, who are cutting down the Amazon rain forest.

So far there has been no flagging of the pace or weakening of the spirit on the crusade to a clean American environment. The commitment of the American people is firm. Doubtless it will remain firm, too, if, in the midst of the ferocious political debates sure to come, we all keep in mind the fact that honorable people can disagree about means without disagreeing about ends; that there is more than one road to the New Jerusalem; and, especially, that cleaning up the American environment is far too important to be left to bureaucrats, activists, journalists, and fanatics. This is our crusade.

Revising the Twentieth Century

The Great struggles of our century have all been followed by tides of revulsion: Americans decided we were mad to have entered World War I; Russia should have been our enemy in World War II; the United States started the Cold War. Now another such tide has risen in Europe, and it may be on its way here.

John Lukacs

History is revisionism. It is the frequent—nay, the ceaseless—reviewing and revising and rethinking of the past. The notion that the study and the writing of history consist of the filling of gaps or the adding of new small bricks to the building of the cathedral of historical knowledge was a nineteenth-century illusion ("We have now histories of the Federalists in every New England State, except for Connecticut. You must do Connecticut"), allied with the fantasy that once the scientific method has been followed precisely, with all extant documents exhausted, the result will be definite and final ("the definitive account of Waterloo, approved by British as well as by French and German and Dutch historians"). There are important differences between historical and legal evidence, one of them being that the historian deals in multiple jeopardy that the law eschews; the former is retrying and retrying again. There is nothing very profound in this observation, since that is what all thinking is about. Not the future, and not the present, but our past is the only thing we know. All human thinking involves the rethinking of the past.

There may be five hundred biographies of Lincoln, but there is no certainty that the 501st may not furnish our minds with something new and valid—and not necessarily because its author has found a new cache of Lincoln documents. What matters more than the accumulated *quantity* of the research (note the word: "re-search") is the crystallizing *quality* of the revision. What is its purpose? Is it exposé, scandal, sensation, or the more or less honest wish to demolish untruths? Is it the author's desire for academic or financial success, to further his advancement in front of his colleagues or in the greater world of affairs? Or (as is, alas, often the case) is it to further the cause of a political ideology? This is where the subject of this article comes in.

The term *revisionism* is of German origin. It was first applied to those German socialists who, around 1875, chose to mitigate the doctrine of the inevitability of the proletarian revolution. This Marxist usage does not concern us. But the other, and still present, use of historical "revisionism" has a German origin too. It arose after 1919, reacting to the punitive and condemnatory treaty imposed on Germany and on its World War I allies. The wish to revise their terms, to change the then drawn frontiers of Europe was a powerful impulse, eventually leading to Hitler and to World War II. However, the aim of this historical revisionism was not directed at injustices of geography; it was directed at injustices of the record—that is, at the unjust condemnation of Germany as responsible for the war, stated in the Treaty of Versailles. The Germans had every reason to combat that. As early as 1919 the new republican and democratic German government began to publish documents to prove that the guilt for the coming of the war in 1914 was not Germany's alone. A much more extensive and scholarly documentation was published in a series of volumes a few years later. The Germans felt so strongly about this that in 1923 a German amateur historian, Alfred von Wegerer, began issuing a scholarly journal, *Die Kriegsschuldfrage* (The War Guilt Question).

By that time the first wave of revisionism among American historians had begun to form. Of the four waves of revisionism in the twentieth century this was the longest and the strongest one. It began as an intellectual and academic (and sometimes also a political and an ethnic) reaction against the extreme condemnation of Germany in 1917 and 1918 that had been broadcast from many sources, including the Creel Committee, Wilson's own propaganda machine, with many exaggerations and falsehoods. It was a reaction by liberals and radicals against superpatriotism, not very different from (and often allied with) their opposition to American conformism, to the post-war Red Scare, to the Ku Klux Klan, to the American Legion of the twenties. As early as 1920, for example, *The Nation* started to attack the dangers of French, not of German, militarism. In September 1921 the magazine raised the question: "Who has contributed more to the myth of a guilty nation plotting the war against a peaceful Europe than the so-called historians who occupy distinguished chairs in our universities?" They were "willing tools" of "professional propaganda." The young and later

From *American Heritage*, September 1994, pp. 83–89. © 1994 by Forbes, Inc. Reprinted by permission of *American Heritage* magazine, a division of Forbes, Inc.

distinguished Sidney Bradshaw Fay, then of Smith College (*not* a typical revisionist, I must add), had already published three successive articles in *The American Historical Review* ("New Light on the Origins of the World War"), a result of his reading of the recently published German, Austrian, and Russian documents. Within five years this first wave of revisionism swelled into a tide. From a scattered group of mavericks, revisionists now included respected members of the historical profession and reputable intellectuals: the prominent Charles A. Beard, the University of Chicago historian Ferdinand Schevill (who wrote in 1926 that "there are today among reputable historians only revisionists"), the sociologist turned historian Harry Elmer Barnes, whose *Genesis of the World War* was published by the reputable house of Knopf in 1926. Their cause was supported by amateurs such as the German-American judge Frederick Bausman (*Let France Explain*), by literary figures such as Albert J. Nock and H. L. Mencken, and by the editors of *The Nation* and of *The New Republic,* while the lumbering *Atlantic Monthly* was tacking over gradually to that side too.

By the time Hitler was rising in power, 70 percent of Americans thought us wrong to have entered World War I.

By the late twenties the revisionist tide was further swelled by the predictable confluence of another historical argument, about 1917 and not 1914. The time had come to revise not only the thesis of German war guilt but the story of American involvement in the war. Much of that argument had already been suggested by the above-mentioned historians, especially by Barnes; but the first substantial book denouncing Wilson and American intervention, *Why We Fought,* was published in 1929 by C. Hartley Grattan, a onetime student of Barnes. By the early thirties article after article, book after book, was attacking American intervention in World War I. The most serious work was Walter Millis's *The Road to War* in 1935. The most

determined book by a professional historian was Charles Callan Tansill's *America Goes to War* in 1938. By that time their arguments had filtered down from the margins of academia and from intellectuals' periodicals through the reading public to the broad lowlands of popular sentiment. *The Road to War* was a best seller, with as many as sixty thousand copies in print by 1936. A few months later Dr. Gallup reported that 70 percent of Americans thought it had been wrong to enter World War I. Meanwhile Hitler, Mussolini, and the Japanese were rising in power.

In 1938 and 1939 another current in the revisionist tide came to the surface. Many revisionists were now worried over what they saw as an ominous change in Franklin Roosevelt's foreign policy. (In 1932 Roosevelt ran as an isolationist, and as late as 1935 he went so far as to suggest his acceptance of the revisionist thesis.) Foremost among them were Barnes, Tansill, and the big gun among American historians, Charles Beard. In September 1939 Beard published a powerful blast against American intervention in Europe, *Giddy Minds and Foreign Quarrels* (the Republican senator D. Worth Clark, of Idaho, used his franking privilege to distribute ten thousand copies of this little book). Yet by 1940 the revisionist camp was badly split. Many of the liberals were coming around to support Britain against Hitler. Others were not. In 1940 Beard came out with another book, *A Foreign Policy for America.* Eleven years later Sen. Robert A. Taft published a book with a virtually identical title, but already in 1940 it was evident that the formerly radical and Jeffersonian Democrat Beard and the rigid Republican Taft were seeing eye to eye. But before the next year was out, the news of Pearl Harbor roared over them both.

Revisionism was submerged but not sunk. After 1945 came the second wave of American revisionism, attacking Roosevelt for having maneuvered the country into war, indeed, for having contributed surreptitiously and willfully to the catastrophe at Pearl Harbor. Many of the historian figures were the same ones as before, the two principal professionals among them Beard (*American Foreign Policy in the Making, 1932–1940* and *President Roosevelt and the Coming of the War*) and Tansill (*Back Door to War*).

There were many others; but this second wave of revisionism received relatively little attention; many of the revisionist books were now printed by minor publishers. Yet the effect of this kind of revisionism was wider than what the publishing record might indicate. The majority of the so-called conservative movement that began to coalesce in the early 1950s was composed of former isolationists and revisionists. The principal element of the Republican surge after 1948 was a reaction against Roosevelt's foreign policy, including such different figures as Joseph R. McCarthy, John Foster Dulles, and the young William F. Buckley, Jr. It was part of the emergence of the New Right in American politics. Still, Hitler and Tojo had few public defenders, and this second wave of revisionism failed to swell into an oceanic current.

During the fretful sixties, historians of the New Left attempted to rewrite the origins of the Cold War.

The third, and much larger, wave of revisionism came not from the New Right but from the New Left. These were the historians who during the fretful sixties attempted to rewrite the origins of the Cold War with Russia, arguing and claiming that American foreign policy and aggressiveness were at least as responsible for the coming of the Cold War as was the Soviet Union. The principal ones (again, there were many others) of those New Left historians were D. F. Fleming (*The Cold War and Its Origins*), William Appleman Williams (*The Tragedy of American Diplomacy*), Gar Alperovitz (*Atomic Diplomacy*), David Horowitz (*The Free World Colossus*), Gabriel Kolko (*The Politics of War*), Diane Shaver Clemens (*Yalta*), and Lloyd C. Gardner (*Architects of Illusion*), all their books issued between 1959 and 1970 by the most reputable university presses and trade houses.

Unlike the revisionists of the 1920s and 1940s, these authors had little opposition from most of their historian colleagues, for such was the, generally Leftist, intellectual tendency of the American sixties. These authors were praised, and portions of their works anthologized in college readers and textbooks. Whereas the revisionists of the 1920s and 1930s had their greatest effect among general readers, most of the consumers of this third wave of revisionist prose were college students. When Robert Maddox, in his calm and serious *The New Left and the Origins of the Cold War* (1973), pointed out some of the dishonesties of the documentation and the inadequacies of scholarship in these books, he was treated with tut-tutting and fence-sitting by most academic reviewers, so many vicars of Bray. However, as with so many fads and fashions of the sixties, the tide of Cold War revisionism, though temporarily overwhelming, did not endure for long.

Twenty or more years later we may detect the rise of a fourth wave of revisionism, coming again from the so-called Right rather than from the Left. Again this began in Germany, in the mid-1980s, developing there in *Historikerstreit* (historians' quarrel), whose main figures have been German professional historians who, while unwilling to whitewash Hitler and his regime (that has remained the work of self-appointed extreme pamphleteers for decades now, as well as of fanatical amateur historians such as the English David Irving), attempted to make their case against the uniqueness of the crimes committed by the Germans during the Third Reich. This tendency to revise some of the lately accepted and hitherto hardly questioned histories of the Second World War had recently appeared in Britain, with historians such as Maurice Cowling (in *The Impact of Hitler* and elsewhere: "the belief that Churchill had understood Hitler . . . was not true"), the younger Andrew Roberts (*The Holy Fox—A Biography of Lord Halifax:* "Churchill as Micawber," simply waiting for something to turn up; "Britain finally won, but at appalling cost, and ruin for her standing in the world"). John Charmley in his recently published *Churchill: The End of Glory* goes much farther: he questions not only Churchill's personal character but his policy to resist and fight Hitler's Germany at any cost; Charmley goes so far as to suggest that not to acquiesce in Hitler's domination of Europe was a mistake.

These books are more scholarly in their equipment than are the productions of pamphleteers who, among another things, deny the existence of the Holocaust. Excessive attention directed to such fanatics may be as useless as the criticism aimed at the new revisionists' theses without a detailed analysis of their sources and a careful refutation of their methods. Three years ago in my *The Duel: May 10–31 July 1940: The Eighty-Day Struggle Between Churchill and Hitler* I could write that "we are at (or, more precisely, already beyond) a watershed in the political and intellectual history of the world because of the evident collapse of the reputation, and consequently, of the influence of Marxism as well as of 'Leftist' liberalism; and this is bound to lead to all kinds of novel, though not necessarily salutary, tendencies of historical interpretation." This is a symptom of the rise of a New Right, not only in Germany and Britain but throughout Europe and Japan, when people, disillusioned with the malfunctioning liberal and socialist policies of their governments, project their disappointments backward, to the Second World War; when, for example, the condemnation of Churchill's statesmanship, at least indirectly, suggests some kind of a rehabilitation of Hitler's. During the Reagan years in this country we saw, here and there, a tendency to question not only the evident problems of the American welfare state but the establishment of its tenets by Roosevelt and the New Deal, and there is reason to believe that new indictments (and I fear not always well-warranted or judicious ones) of Roosevelt's foreign policy before and during the Second World War are also due to appear—in sum, that this newest wave of revisionism about the war will spill over to this side of the Atlantic too.

What revisionist historians claim, or at least emphatically suggest, is that their scholarship is better and their intellectual independence stronger than that of the majority of their opponents. Yet this has seldom been true. To the contrary, few of the revisionists have been immune to the ideological tendencies of their times. In the preface to *The American Revisionists,* Warren I. Cohen, the careful historian of what I have called the first wave, wrote in 1967: "I am equally convinced that if I had

graduated from Columbia College in 1925 instead of 1955, the revisionist cause would have had one more adherent. It is not a question of the logic of the revisionist argument but . . . largely a matter of the prevailing climate of opinion. . . ." Or as W. J. Ghent (cited by Cohen) wrote in his 1927 attack on the revisionists in an article called "Menckenized History": "Vociferous and sweeping denunciation of existing beliefs, customs, standards, and institutions is the current mode, and 'revisionism' is merely one of its phases." After the First World War there was a growing revulsion to war and an embracing of new ideas, including pacifism. After the Second World War there was another reaction, against Roosevelt and the sometimes unspoken questions of whether America should have entered the war against Germany, and on the side of Russia, at that. During the sixties there was the reaction against the Vietnam War and against the ideology of the Cold War. During the nineties nationalism is on the rise, and we shall see . . .

In 1917 Beard was an extreme interventionist: The United States "should help eliminate Prussianism from the earth . . ." Germany represents "the black night of military barbarism . . . the most merciless military despotism the world has ever seen." By 1926 he was a Germanophile, influenced not only by the revelations of the German diplomatic documents but by German philosophies of history. Beard was not an opportunist, and even in the 1930s he insisted that he was not really an isolationist; rather, he was struggling with that seemingly concrete but, alas, often malleable concept of national interest. (In 1932 Beard received a twenty-five-thousand-dollar grant—a very large sum then—from the Social Science Research Council for the precise definition of "national interest." The result was one of his few unreadable books.) At that time he was a fervent supporter of Franklin Roosevelt, but soon he turned even more fervently against him. The case of Barnes is more telling. His first revisionist articles appeared in 1924, arguing for a division in the responsibilities for the outbreak of the war. By 1926 he was going farther: France and Russia were responsible. Thereafter he became more and more extreme and violent. He was invited to lecture in Hitler's Germany, as was Tansill. In 1940 Barnes volunteered to promote the circulation of German propaganda volumes. After the war he became an admirer of Hitler: "a man whose only fault was that he was too soft, generous and honorable." The Allies had inflicted worse brutality on the Germans "than the alleged exterminations in the gas-chambers." This, of course, was the extreme case of a once talented but embittered man, driven to such statements by what he called *The Historical Blackout,* one of his later pamphlets. Everything was grist to his mill, including the most dubious of "sources" and "evidences." The same was true of Tansill, who in 1938 wrote in his introduction to *America Goes to War:* "Crusading zeal is hardly the proper spirit for an impartial historian." Yet Tansill was the prototype of a zealous crusader, in both of his big revisionist works about the two world wars. Eventually he became a member of the John Birch Society.

Revisionists such as Barnes were often obsessed with the idea of a conspiracy against them. He called the anti-revisionists the "Smear-bund." When the Chicago historian Bernadotte Schmitt first criticized his *Genesis of the World War,* Barnes wrote" "There is the very important fact [fact?] that Mr. Schmitt seems to live in daily dread of being mistaken for a member of the detestable Teutonic breed." Barnes even thought that there was a conspiracy among booksellers not to reorder his *Genesis.* Mencken's relationship to Barnes (they corresponded for decades) is also telling. In May 1940, when the German armies lurched forward into Holland, Belgium, and France, Mencken wrote Barnes that the American press "would be hollering for war within two months"; in June he wrote that "Roosevelt will be in the war in two weeks, and . . . his first act will be to forbid every form of free speech." Mencken, like Barnes and other revisionists, was bitterly against a war with Hitler's Reich, but after the war he thought that the United States should go to war against "the Russian barbarians." That inconsistency—if that was what it was—was typical of the inclinations of almost all the post-World War II revisionists. The opposite was true of the Cold War revisionists of the 1960s, who accused the United States of having provoked the Cold War with Russia, while almost all of them approved the American involvement in the war against Ger-

many. They, too, did little else but project backward their then widespread and fashionable dislike of the Vietnam War to events that had happened twenty or more years earlier, manipulating that record for their own purposes. In the 1970s most of them turned to other topics, and at least one of them (Horowitz) became a neoconservative publicist.

There is, however, more involved here than a few historians adjusting their ideas to a prevalent climate of opinion. In some instances their writings affected American history, through a momentum that was slowly gaining ground. In the 1920s the writings of the revisionists had an influence on those members of Congress, mostly Western populists—George W. Norris, Gerald P. Nye, William E. Borah, for example—who had opposed the war and the Versailles Treaty. By 1934 the isolationist and revisionist tide ran so strong that a congressional committee, presided over by Nye, found it politic to investigate the doings of bankers and munition makers and other villainous promoters of the American entrance into the war seventeen years before. (One of the Nye Committee's counsels was an ambitious young lawyer, Alger Hiss.) In 1935 Congress passed the first Neutrality Act, a definite reaction against the memories of World War I. It was extended in 1937. By that time Sen. Homer Bone of Washington could report "a fact known even to school children in this country: Everyone has come to recognize that the Great War was utter social insanity, and was a crazy war, and we had no business in it at all."

The slowness with which ideas move gives the lie to the famous saw about Ideas Whose Time Has Come.

This illustrates a significant phenomenon to which few, if any, historians have yet devoted attention. It is the time lag in the movement of ideas, the slowness of the momentum with which ideas move and then appear on the surface at the wrong time, giving the lie to victor Hugo's famous saw about

Ideas Whose Time Has Come. The high tide of revisionism occurred from 1935 to 1938, when the German danger was rising anew—not, say, in 1919 and 1920, when there had been cogent reasons to mitigate a mistreatment of Germany. The high tide of Second World War revisionism occurred in 1954 and 1955, when the reputations of Franklin Roosevelt and of Yalta were at a low ebb. The high tide of the revisionism about the origins of the Cold War came around 1965, when American-Russian relations were actually improving.

Of course, it takes time for historians to complete their researches and produce their books, but there is an agitated tone in many revisionist works that stands in odd contrast with the slow momentum of their eventual effects. One reason for this is the often weak and tergiversating reaction of the revisionists' historian opponents. At the beginning the seemingly radical performance of the former is often ignored, but then, gradually, the revisionists' ideas may be adopted by respectable historians when it seems politic for them to do so or when they feel safely convinced by their judiciousness. Thus, for example, Tansill's radical and Germanophile *America Goes to War* was praised in *The Atlantic* and the *Yale Review* and by such eminent historians as Allan Nevins and Henry Steele Commager: Tansill traced, "in magisterial style, the missteps which carried the United States along the road to war. It is an impressive performance, conducted with skill, learning, and wit, *illuminating the present as well as the past.*" The italics are Cohen's as well as mine, for this was written by Commager as late as 1938, the most ominous and successful year in Hitler's career along the road to another war. The title of Beard's trenchant 1939 *Giddy Minds and Foreign Quarrels* is not really appropriate. So many of his colleagues' minds were not at all giddy; they were alarmingly slow. Even more disheartening was the reaction of many historians to the New Left revisionists of the 1960s, when the scholarship of those books was wanting. As Maddox wrote, "Reviewers who have been known to pounce with scarcely disguised glee on some poor wretch who incorrectly transcribed a middle initial or date of birth have shown a most extraordinary reluctance to expose even the most obvious New Left fiction," including false statements to which tens of thousands of students were subsequently exposed in our colleges and universities. Finally, when it comes to the newest wave of revisionism, lamentably few historians have taken the trouble to track down and point out the selective methodology and frequently sloppy scholarship of Charmley's denigration of Churchill. Spending, instead, long paragraphs and pages debating his thesis, they pursue the obvious, as Wilde once said, with the enthusiasm of shortsighted detectives.

In science, it is the rule that counts; in history, often the exceptions. And there have been exceptions to the shortcomings of scholars involved with revisionism. Millis, who, as we saw earlier, was the author of the most successful revisionist book in 1935, a few years later

found himself appalled by the use people were making of his work, which, after all, had dealt with 1917, with the past and not with the then present. By 1938 Millis stood for resistance against Hitler and other dictators. "1939 is not 1914" was the title of his article in *Life* in November 1939, when Roosevelt had to struggle against a senseless Neutrality Act. Maddox, whose study of the New Left revisionists was ignored or criticized by other historians, refused to make common cause with the New Right; he remained unimpressed by the selective argumentation of Leftist and Rightist, of Marxist and anti-Communist, of neoliberal and neoconservative historians alike, because of his personal integrity, the essence of human integrity being its

resistance to temptations, perhaps especially to intellectual ones.

Such temptations are the bane of historians, and not only of those who are in pursuit of attractive intellectual novelty. This does not mean a defense of "orthodox" history, because there is no such thing. Historians should be aware of the inevitably revisionist nature of their thinking and work. But the revision of history must not be an ephemeral monopoly of ideologues or opportunists who are ever ready to twist or even falsify evidences of the past in order to exemplify current ideas—and their own adjustments to them.

Credits/ Acknowledgments

Cover design by Charles Vitelli

1. Reconstruction and the Gilded Age

Facing overview—Photo courtesy of the Solomon D. Butcher Collection, Nebraska State Historical Society.

2. The Emergence of Modern America

Facing overview—Public Health Service photo, the National Archives.

3. From Progressivism to the 1920s

Facing overview—Photo reproduced from the collections of the Library of Congress.

4. From the Great Depression to World War II

Facing overview—U.S. Navy photo.

5. From the Cold War to the 1990s

Facing overview—Photo by Fred J. Maroon.

6. New Directions for American History

Facing overview—Photo courtesy of the New York State Department of Commerce, Albany.

PHOTOCOPY THIS PAGE!!!*

ANNUAL EDITIONS ARTICLE REVIEW FORM

■ NAME: _____ DATE: _____

■ TITLE AND NUMBER OF ARTICLE: _____

■ BRIEFLY STATE THE MAIN IDEA OF THIS ARTICLE: _____

_____

_____

_____

_____

■ LIST THREE IMPORTANT FACTS THAT THE AUTHOR USES TO SUPPORT THE MAIN IDEA:

_____

_____

_____

_____

_____

_____

_____

■ WHAT INFORMATION OR IDEAS DISCUSSED IN THIS ARTICLE ARE ALSO DISCUSSED IN YOUR
TEXTBOOK OR OTHER READING YOU HAVE DONE? LIST THE TEXTBOOK CHAPTERS AND PAGE
NUMBERS:

_____

_____

_____

_____

_____

_____

_____

_____

■ LIST ANY EXAMPLES OF BIAS OR FAULTY REASONING THAT YOU FOUND IN THE ARTICLE:

_____

_____

_____

_____

_____

■ LIST ANY NEW TERMS/CONCEPTS THAT WERE DISCUSSED IN THE ARTICLE AND WRITE A
SHORT DEFINITION:

_____

_____

_____

_____

_____

_____

*Your instructor may require you to use this Annual Editions Article Review Form in any number of ways:
for articles that are assigned, for extra credit, as a tool to assist in developing assigned papers, or simply
for your own reference. Even if it is not required, we encourage you to photocopy and use this page;
you'll find that reflecting on the articles will greatly enhance the information from your text.

ANNUAL EDITIONS:
AMERICAN HISTORY, Vol. II
Reconstruction through the Present
Article Rating Form

Here is an opportunity for you to have direct input into the next revision of this volume. We would like you to rate each of the 42 articles listed below, using the following scale:

1. Excellent: should definitely be retained
2. Above average: should probably be retained
3. Below average: should probably be deleted
4. Poor: should definitely be deleted

Your ratings will play a vital part in the next revision. So please mail this prepaid form to us just as soon as you complete it.
Thanks for your help!

Annual Editions revisions depend on two major opinion sources: one is our Advisory Board, listed in the front of this volume, which works with us in scanning the thousands of articles published in the public press each year; the other is you—the person actually using the book. Please help us and the users of the next edition by completing the prepaid article rating form on this page and returning it to us. Thank you.

Rating	Article	Rating	Article
	1. The New View of Reconstruction		24. Racism and Relocation: Telling the Japanese-American Experience
	2. The First Chapter of Children's Rights		25. 1943: The Pull of Distant Shores
	3. The Two Faces of George Armstrong Custer		26. "What Did You Do in the War, Grandma?" An Oral History of Rhode Island Women during World War II
	4. *These* Are the Good Old Days		
	5. The Forgotten Pioneers		27. The Man of the Century
	6. Geronimo		28. The Buy of the Century
	7. The Cycle of Reform		29. The Forgotten War
	8. The Afro-Cuban Community in Ybor City and Tampa, 1886–1910		30. Discovering Sex
			31. Trumpet of Conscience: A Portrait of Martin Luther King Jr.
	9. Ellis Island and the American Immigration Experience		32. Chicago '68: The Democrats' Judgment Days
	10. Wings for Man		
	11. Fighting Poverty the Old-Fashioned Way		33. Lessons from a Lost War
	12. George Washington Carver: Creative Scientist		34. Nixon: An Important but Not a Great President
	13. Learning to Go to the Movies		35. How the Seventies Changed America
	14. Woodrow Wilson, Politician		36. 1983: Falling Walls, Rising Dreams
	15. Angel Island: The Half-Closed Door		37. Looking Back: The Cold War in Retrospect
	16. American Women in World War I		
	17. What We Lost in the Great War		38. The Disuniting of America The Painful Demise of Eurocentrism
	18. Why Suffrage for American Women Was Not Enough		39. Alms without End? A History of Welfare in America
	19. Citizen Ford		
	20. 'A Snarling Roughhouse,' The Democratic Convention of 1924		40. The Permanently Unfinished Country
			41. The American Environment: The Big Picture Is More Heartening than All the Little Ones
	21. Defending the Home: Ossian Sweet and the Struggle against Segregation in 1920s Detroit		
	22. 1933: The Rise of the Common Man		42. Revising the Twentieth Century
	23. The Draft		

ABOUT YOU

Name_____ Date_____

Are you a teacher? ☐   Or student? ☐

Your School Name _____

Department _____

Address _____

City _____ State _____ Zip _____

School Telephone # _____

YOUR COMMENTS ARE IMPORTANT TO US!

Please fill in the following information:

For which course did you use this book? _____

Did you use a text with this Annual Edition?   ☐ yes   ☐ no

The title of the text? _____

What are your general reactions to the Annual Editions concept?

Have you read any particular articles recently that you think should be included in the next edition?

Are there any articles you feel should be replaced in the next edition? Why?

Are there other areas that you feel would utilize an Annual Edition?

May we contact you for editorial input?

May we quote you from above?

AMERICAN HISTORY, Vol. II, Thirteenth Edition
Reconstruction through the Present

BUSINESS REPLY MAIL

First Class   Permit No. 84   Guilford, CT

Postage will be paid by addressee

The Dushkin Publishing Group, Inc.
Sluice Dock
DPG **Guilford, Connecticut 06437**

No Postage
Necessary
if Mailed
in the
United States